People, Politics & Public Power

By Ken Billington

People, Politics & Public Power

People, Politics & Public Power

by

Ken Billington

Washington Public Utility Districts' Association
Seattle, Washington

Library of Congress Catalog Card No.: 87-51001

ISBN: 0-9619682-0-6 (Cloth)

ISBN: 0-9619682-1-4 (Paper)

Library of Congress Cataloging-in-Publication Data
Billington, Ken, 1916–
    People, politics & public power

    Includes index.
    1. Electric utilities—Government ownership—
Washington (State)—History. 2. Electric utilities—
Government ownership—Oregon—History. 3. Public utility
districts—Washington (State)—History. 4. Public utility
districts—Oregon—History. I. Washington Public Utility
Districts' Association. II. Title, III. Title: People,
politics, and public power.
HD9685.U6W19   1988   363.6'2'09797   87-51001
ISBN 0-9619682-0-6
ISBN 0-9619682-1-4 (trade pbk.)

First edition.

Printed in the U.S.A.

Contents

Illustrations

Preface

THE LOCAL public power program in the Pacific Northwest states of Washington and Oregon—as embodied in the public utility districts—is unique in our nation.

It was one of the greatest social improvement programs ever to occur in this country, and it was truly a "grassroots," or local effort, movement. It did not come easily and was secured only by hard work and determination.

The primary purpose of the program was to stop the consumer abuses practiced by the private monopoly power companies. These included charging exorbitant rates to provide special holding company profits; failure or refusal to provide electric service in rural areas; proposing single-purpose underdevelopment of the region's vast falling water resources; and political domination in the state legislatures to thwart attempts to eliminate such abuses.

The PUD public power movement started in many of the rural Grange halls and local labor union meetings. It gained strength as the federal government, responding to the Great Depression of the early 1930s, commenced constructing the huge multiple-purpose dams on the great Columbia River, which produced large amounts of low-cost public power. Getting this power to people without paying a profit to the intervening private monopoly power companies became important.

This book includes basic background information about why and how the program evolved; the difference between electric service by a public power utility and a private power utility; firsthand accounts of legislative activities in Olympia and Washington, D.C.; and profiles of some of the public power pioneers and personalities.

Many dedicated men and women volunteered time and money to the start, growth, and success of this program. Its success can be measured first by the way the widespread use of the "electric servant"—in homes, offices, factories, and farms—made everyone's life easier and better, and second by the fact that every dollar saved on an electric bill meant an extra one to spend in other pursuits. The millions of dollars saved through lower electric bills were used to enrich personal lives, and low-cost public power was used to promote economic development on farms and in factories.

Without this local public power program, many of the low-cost public power dams constructed by the federal government and the public utility districts would not have been built. Private power officials opposed the program on principle, but supported it when it provided them with low-cost power from which they could make a profit.

Today, the people of the Pacific Northwest have a built-in reservoir of integrated low-cost public power systems which help to keep electric rates the lowest in the nation. This reservoir would not be here without the broad local public power program.

Ever since my retirement on July 1, 1981, from the active ranks of public power, friends, acquaintances, and even some "friendly enemies" have been saying I should write a book on my experiences of nearly forty-five years of participation in public power development in the Pacific Northwest. These people have shown particular interest in the thirty-plus years I was a lobbyist at the State Legislature in Olympia and on the congressional scene in Washington, D.C. Conflict between public and private power centered in political arenas and elections. It involved gubernatorial, congressional, and national elections, statewide initiative fights, and local public power district formation and election of officials—erupting in total conflict in the State of Washington Legislature. This book describes the legislative fights between these two powerful forces in the State of Washington and Washington, D.C., from 1951 to 1981.

The most active and interesting period of electric power development in the Pacific Northwest stretches from the days when the public utility districts (local public power districts) were being formed by local voters in Washington and Oregon, to the present time, when we are implementing the first regional power plan under the new Regional Power Act, and suffering conflict and confusion over the "Whoops" (Washington Public

Power Supply System) lawsuits. The period covers the federal public power development of large dams on the Columbia River system, and the building of Bonneville Power Administration's huge federal transmission power grid. I was where the action was from 1935 until my retirement in 1981.

One thing which prompts me to write is to give recognition to those men and women who serve in the legislative branch of our democracy. Being a lobbyist gave me a chance to observe these people directly at work. As a lobbyist, I have personally shared some of the criticism and sarcasm leveled at politicians and political types.

The legislators who serve their fellow citizens are, in the main, above average, and many of them are outstanding. It is through electing them and making sure that they represent our views if they want to stay in office that we Americans get, keep, and enjoy the greatest freedom of any people on this earth. Much of the low-cost public power in the Pacific Northwest is a result of their keeping the faith with their constituents. Persons such as U.S. Senators Warren G. Magnuson and Henry M. Jackson, Legislator and then Congresswoman Julia Butler Hansen, Congressman Walt Horan; on the State legislative level, Speakers of the House Charles Hodde and John O'Brien, State Senator Nat Washington, and Lieutenant Governor John Cherberg; and many, many more legislative officials deserve tribute and thanks. Even those who stood opposed to public power in the legislative arena served a purpose, because a democracy gains strength by discussion, debate, and overcoming opposition democratically.

Special thanks go to those persons who have helped and encouraged me, because this writing has been an effort to be accurate about dates, names, and events. First I want to thank my wife Virginia, who kept up the pressure on me to "Finish your book!" Second I want to thank my former assistant, Vera Edinger Claussen, for saying, "Billington, you owe it to the many dedicated men and women who put this local public power program in place, and you owe it to the future students who will want to know why and how a lot of it happened." Third I want to thank Kirby Billingsley who was involved with local public power from the beginning of the fight for Grand Coulee to my retirement, and who wouldn't let me rest until I wrote this book.

Halfway through the book I hit a road block. I found that after spending a life with efficient secretaries and assistants to whom I could dictate what I wanted to say and get clean clear drafts, my personal typing was not doing the job.

When a good friend, Herb Westfall of R. W. Beck and Associates, inquired about my progress, I vented my frustration on him. He said, "Ken, I have a very efficient secretary, Jeanne Murakami, who I know would enjoy helping you. She's been with us since 1957. And then there is Anita Hodges, who also has been with the firm a long time. I'm out of town a lot. Use their abilities and services." About three months later, Herb called to ask why I hadn't used the assistance. I said it did not seem right for me to load my work on his staff, but I thanked him for his offer.

The next thing I knew there was a call from both gals saying they wanted to help. They, too, had spent a lot of time in public power activity and they are entitled to credit and my special thanks for helping me put this local public power story down in writing.

Finally, I want to remember and honor those other men and women who volunteered their time and money to fight the entrenched private monopoly power trust to bring electricity to rural areas, as well as urban areas, without the extra cost of private monopoly profit. It could not have happened without all of them.

KEN BILLINGTON

Seattle
November 1987

People, Politics & Public Power

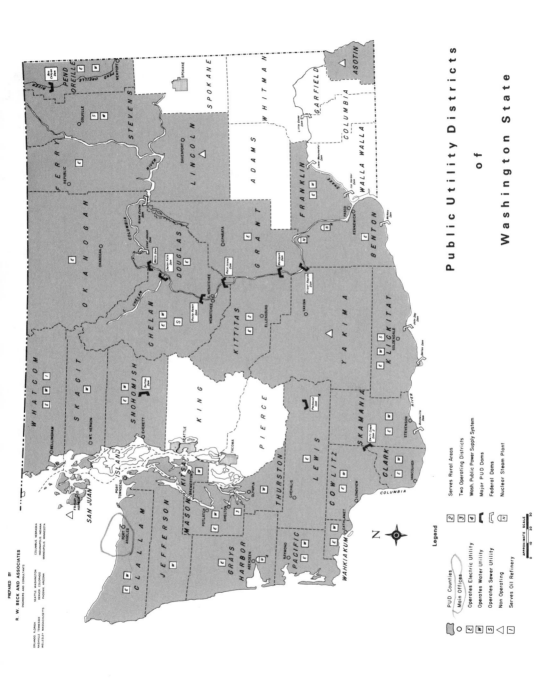

Public Utility Districts

of

Washington State

PREPARED BY

R. W. BECK AND ASSOCIATES

ENGINEERS AND CONSULTANTS

ORLANDO, FLORIDA   SEATTLE, WASHINGTON   COLUMBIA, NEBRASKA
NASHVILLE, TENNESSEE   DENVER, COLORADO   INDIANAPOLIS, INDIANA
WELLESLEY, MASSACHUSETTS PHOENIX, ARIZONA   MINNEAPOLIS, MINNESOTA

Legend

Serves Rural Areas

Two Operating Districts

Wash. Public Power Supply System

Major PUD Dams

Federal Dams

Nuclear Steam Plant

PUD Counties

Main Offices

Operates Electric Utility

Operates Water Utility

Operates Sewer Utility

Non Operating

Serves Oil Refinery

APPROXIMATE SCALE

N

1

1924–1951
Background and Personal Involvement

The Public Utility District (PUD) Movement

JULY 30, 1938, was not just another Saturday. It was my twenty-second birthday and the day of my marriage to a lovely young lady, Virginia Gaither. Just a few months before, another "involvement" nearly as serious had begun, one that would materially affect our lives in future years. Neither of us recognized it then, but now, looking back at the many, many days — yes, months — I was absent from Virginia and our two children, it is clear that the other involvement demanded a lot of sacrifice on their part as well as mine. This was my introduction to local public power and the fight against the entrenched private power monopoly trust. It was the beginning of a life which, by the end of the 1970s, had earned me the label "Mr. Public Power" by some of the news media, while others were calling me a "public power zealot." I feel that neither title was entirely merited.

The involvement with public power started when I met U.S. Senator Homer T. Bone, who was running for re-election to his second term. It took place at the home of D. Elwood Caples, Democratic State Chairman, in Vancouver, Washington. Caples, or "Doug" as his friends called him, had asked if I would like to meet a U.S. Senator and I told him I most certainly would.

After dinner, we spent a late night talking about the local public power program in which Bone had played, and still was playing, a very effective role. The voters of Clark County, headed by their local Grange leadership, were circulating petitions to get approval of the Clark County PUD on the coming fall election ballot. Bone, in his own campaigning, was giving them a boost. He urged me to get involved as a "young political activist." The next morning, I looked up the Grange leaders and joined their ranks by circulating some of the petitions to get signatures. I later joined the Hazel Dell Grange in 1946.

Formation of the Clark County PUD in 1938 occurred just ten years after the Washington State Grange, using its local Granges, had obtained 60,000 voter signatures on petitions to send Initiative 1 to the Legislature, which I will discuss in detail later. This was the first time this kind of initiative was successfully started by the people in our State. When the 1929 Session refused to pass it, the initiative went to a statewide vote in the 1930 General Election. Upon voter approval, it became Chapter 1, Laws of 1931 – the basic public utility district (public power) law of our State.

National issues were also being debated in Congress at that time centering on who was going to control and develop the public water resources. In the 1920s, arguments focused on production of fertilizers for farms at Muscle Shoals on the Tennessee River. Thus, as a farm organization, the National Grange became involved, favoring public not-for-profit development instead of private power development. The 1920s were indeed turbulent.

I have often stated that "public power only grew in our State because of the abuses and failures of private power." Those abuses and failures were (1) charging exorbitant and unfair rates; (2) denying electric service to certain groups, especially to persons living in rural areas; (3) proposing to underdevelop the public hydroelectric resources; and (4) dominating the State Legislature for the benefit of special interests.

At the time Initiative 1 was approved, the private power companies serving in the Pacific Northwest were wholly owned subsidiaries of large Eastern utility holding companies. In Clark County, where I got involved, electric service was mainly provided by the Northwestern Electric Company, which did not own the electric utility properties but leased its lines and transformers from Pacific Power and Light Company. American Power and Light Company (a Chicago-based holding company) owned all the common stock of Northwestern Electric and Pacific Power and Light. In turn, AP&L's common stock was wholly owned by EBASCO (Electric

Bond and Share) of New York. EBASCO also enjoyed many profitable service contracts with AP&L and its subsidiaries. Thus, the ratepayer served by Northwestern Electric paid not only an exorbitant rate to cover "sweetheart" leasing costs to its fellow company, Pacific Power and Light, but also paid a high rate so that Northwestern Electric could "earn a profit" on its common stock in order to earn a profit on the AP&L stock in order to earn a profit on the EBASCO stock. "A profit on a profit for a profit" was the order of the high rate days under the holding company stock and service contracts hierarchy. Even though this electric service was to the Pacific Northwest, which had over 40 percent of the nation's potential low-cost hydroelectric power, private power monopoly profits did not allow low electric rates.

A greater abuse than overcharging ratepayers was refusing to serve the rural areas. If a farmer were to get electric service, private power's policy was "make them pay twice." Many a farm family, to get electric service, had to purchase the poles, set the poles, string the lines, and then deed the lines they paid for and the rights of way on their private property to the power company. The company would then add these improvements into its rate base and charge the farmer higher rates to "make a return on the company's investment." It was no wonder that the farmers got angry.

Proposals to underdevelop the water resources affected not only the national issue of private monopoly power companies being granted perpetual hydro development licenses, but also local site development controversies. Congress established the Federal Power Commission to govern issuance of hydroelectric licenses under a 50-year limitation, subject to renewal. But this focused public attention on moves such as that of The Washington Water Power Company to kill the construction of Grand Coulee Dam so that they could build the Kettle Falls Dam in the reservoir area of the proposed great dam, thus blocking the large dam's construction.

Political special interest domination of the Legislature was administered by the presidents of Washington Water Power and Puget Sound Power and Light Company. It has been told to me firsthand that a "triumvirate" of Mark Reed (long-time head of the Simpson Logging Company, who was a House member from 1915 through 1929, and Speaker of the House in 1923), President Frank Post of Washington Water Power, and President A. B. Leonard of Puget Power were not only in control of electric power issues at Olympia, but also had a great effect on most all local legislators on other matters. Money for a new county road or bridge would not materialize too readily if local legislators, especially those outside of Seattle or Tacoma, bucked the system.

Seattle and Tacoma had long-standing local public power systems. A total of eighteen other cities and towns in the State had exercised their municipal powers of "home rule" and had established this type of electric service. But most of them were dependent on the private power companies for a power supply, so the political influence of these companies reached into most city light systems. (Richland became the twenty-first city-owned electric utility in our State when it acquired properties in 1959 from the General Electric Company serving the federally owned Hanford area as a defense contractor.) A brief explanation of the differences between private power and public power may help the reader to better understand what was then happening in our State and Oregon.

The first glimpse here of electric lights occurred in Elliott Bay off the shores of Seattle in 1881 when the steamer *Willamette*, outfitted with electric arc lights, docked. This followed Thomas Edison's light bulb invention in 1879 and barely preceded his progress to "central station service" in 1882. In 1882, the Tacoma Mill Company installed electric lights at its mill. Electric service came to Seattle in 1886 with completion of a central station by the Seattle Electric Lighting Company. The first local public power utility in the State was started at Ellensburg when the city in 1891 bought a power plant built by John Shoudy, who had founded that community and named it for his wife, Ellen. Electric service was to be provided to residents by a city-owned utility, just as water was being provided.

Since the technology for transmitting electricity any great distance had not yet been developed, "central station power" was limited to the urban and more populated areas. Thus, many of the early utility services throughout the nation were city publicly owned utilities. While they were a revenue supported proprietary business-like function, they were "government" forms of operation.

With the technological development of high voltage transmission, making transmission from remote power sites feasible, enterprising businessmen soon discovered that these city-owned utilities could be purchased and merged into larger operating utilities. Larger potential loads could be served by smaller utility investments because the peak-load periods of different customers occurred at different times of day. The service costs saved by interconnecting separate utilities could become handsome profits to the private business venture. Since city-owned utilities were limited to their own city limits under their "home rule" authority, they had no incentive to merge or seek larger utility service areas. The large Eastern holding companies saw their chance to make profits by purchasing and integrating many small municipal and private utilities, and they seized it.

Electric service is best provided by a monopoly. There is no "free competitive enterprise" for electric service because duplicate investment would be costly, and multiple poles and lines up and down the same streets would be unsightly and unbearable. A customer does not have a choice of suppliers. Electric service is provided by a privately owned utility operating under a public franchise granted by the people – or a publicly owned utility owned and operated directly by the people.

A private power company is financed like most privately owned businesses. Mortgage loans or bonds issued against the value of its properties, under normal circumstances, provide about 60 percent of its capital needs. It then issues stock to investors for the other 40 percent and investors earn a profit on their stock. The primary interest of the company is, of course, to make a profit for its stockholders. Since the company has a monopoly, there is conflict between the stockholder's interest in a greater profit and the customer's interest in good service and lower rates. To prevent undue monopoly profits, regulatory procedures have been established by the various state governments. Private power rates, the rate of allowed earnings, are set and limited. However, the company is protected against any arbitrary or capricious state regulation that would cause it to lose money. In effect, the company must be assured that it can charge rates high enough for it to be "competitive" enough in the money markets to attract investors. Since it has no competition for customers, that is akin to having a guarantee of profits under state regulation.

A publicly owned utility is operated on a not-for-profit basis. The customer is the owner of the utility, which is also operated as a monopoly. While the pressure between stock investors and customers over higher profits versus lower rates is absent, there is the continuing need for control over work efficiency and quality of service. A locally elected utility board or city council exercises this control. Rates, service, and operation of the utility are subject to election debate, review, and decision.

A publicly owned utility is financed primarily through issuance of revenue bonds. A few publicly owned utilities have been financed partially through issuance of general obligation bonds (bonds backed by local taxes). Revenue bonds are backed only by pledges against anticipated income of the utility. They are not liens against the utility's properties or the properties of the utility's customers.

One distinct difference between a private power utility and a publicly owned electric utility from the customer's standpoint is that under private power ownership, any increase in the value of the utility accrues to the stock investor, but under public power, any increase of value in equity (i.e., debt-free equity from paying off the revenue bonds) accrues to the customer-owner. This difference can be likened to the difference between a person's renting a house or buying a home. Under private power, the customer will always "rent" electric service. Under public power, as the revenue bond "mortgage" is paid off or reduced as related to total utility value, the resulting debt-free equity can be used to benefit the customer through lower rates or the ability to raise needed new utility capital without increasing rates. The customer "buys" electric service from a public power utility.

Experience has shown that in comparable service areas, the rates of public power utilities are lower than those of private power utilities. It is this economic leverage of building a debt-free equity in the customer interest which has mainly provided lower rates.

Seattle and Tacoma had established public power systems years before Initiative 1 was approved. Tacoma's started in 1893, followed by Seattle's in 1902. Tacoma voters authorized the takeover of the Tacoma Light and Water Company primarily to get a better water supply. Seattle's action came when its citizens could not get adequate streetlights at a reasonable rate from the private power company serving the city. The first residential customers were served by Seattle City Light in 1905. Seattle is one of the very few cities in the nation where duplicate and competitive electric service has existed. Seattle City Light finally purchased the private power lines of Puget Power in 1951.

By the 1920s, these two city light systems were prime examples of how public power could provide better service and lower rates. In the case of Seattle, it was a good example of public power's "yardstick" influence on a private power company. For many, many years, rates charged by Puget Power were lower in its Seattle service area, where they were measured by the yardstick of public rates, as compared to rates elsewhere on its system. (In the years to come, the entire strong local public power movement in the Pacific Northwest provided a yardstick influence which helped bring the lowest private power rates in the nation to this region.)

Using an existing State law under which mutual or private non-profit cooperatives could be formed, some of the more populous areas near the city limits of Tacoma started small electric utilities. While they could exist and operate on a member-ownership basis, returning any excess income over costs to their members, they were definitely limited in area and authority. Their nearest potential source of power was Tacoma Light then making further developments on the Nisqually River. In 1922, a young Farmer-Labor candidate, Homer T. Bone, was elected to the State House of Representatives from Pierce County. In the 1923 Session, he tried to get legislation passed that would allow Tacoma Light and other city systems to

The City of Seattle was served by both Seattle City Light and a competing private electric company from 1905 until 1951.

Courtesy Bonneville Power Administration

provide an electric supply to small mutuals, cities, and cooperatives on their borders outside the city limits without requiring the purchasers or sellers to be subject to any tax. The legislation was also drafted to assist Tacoma Light to move ahead on its Cushman hydro plants, but this ran head-on into Mark Reed and his company's timber holdings in Mason County. The legislation was not only defeated, but Reed and the private power companies had a law passed levying punitive taxes against any city light system building facilities or selling electricity outside of its city limits. This legislation was passed as Referendum Bill 3, which would go to the people for a statewide vote in the General Election of 1924. To counter this, the "Bone bill" was turned into Initiative 52, and enough signatures were collected to put it on the 1924 ballot also.

Bone took the issue to the Washington State Grange in annual session at Vancouver in June 1924. The matter so incensed the delegates that they not only passed a resolution to oppose the "Reed" Referendum Bill 3 law but to endorse the Bone bill. They added another resolution from the floor authorizing creation of public utility districts for the acquisition and development of hydroelectric sites. The 1924 statewide vote on Referendum Bill 3 was 99,459 For and 208,809 Against. The temper of the people against the private monopoly power trust was beginning to show. However, Initiative 52 was also rejected by a vote of 139,492 For and 217,393 Against.

At the June 1924 State Grange Session, representatives of the Super Power League, composed principally of organized labor representatives from the Electrical Workers Union, Local 46 of Seattle, also had presented a proposal to form a statewide public power organization to develop hydroelectric sites. Grange delegates instructed their state officers to meet with that League and pursue the matter. Thus, at the 1925 State Grange Session at Pullman and the 1926 Session at Kennewick, Grange delegates adopted resolutions endorsing passage of laws "to allow the same right of public ownership of electric and water utility systems enjoyed by city residents to persons living outside of corporate cities," which would allow formation of public utility districts. At the June 1927 State Grange Session at Auburn, a report of a Special Committee on Electric Power Development was adopted calling for drafting an initiative to the people to enact a PUD law, to be voted on at the 1928 General Election. However, at the 1928 Grange Session, State Grange Master Albert Goss reported that the Executive Committee, after prolonged study, had held up drafting the initiative. He recommended that it either now be submitted as a bill in the 1929 Session of the Legislature or submitted as an initiative to the Legislature at that session. Fear of private power political domination of the Legislature prompted the delegates to vote to go the initiative route, although Goss had pointed out that the effort would cost up to $4,000 and the proponents would need to gather 40,000 petition signatures – a formidable cost and task in those days.

There was more delay in preparing the initiative, but with the legal help of Homer Bone and James Bradford, a former corporation counsel of Seattle, the petition was filed on October 25, 1928, and was being circulated for signatures by early November. The statewide anger of the Grange members, now joined actively by members of organized labor, provided the needed thrust. Over 60,000 signatures were obtained in the two months before the legislative session. Initiative 1 to the Legislature was filed with both the House and Senate in the 1929 Session. Following a lot of debate and maneuvering, private power domination prevailed. The Senate defeated the measure 20 to 17, and the House took no action. Under the State Constitution's procedure on initiatives, since the Legislature refused to pass the proposed law, it went to a statewide vote at the General Election in November 1930.

While the private power abuses of charging exorbitant rates and denying rural electric service were stimulating State Grange activity for a PUD law, underdevelopment of the Columbia River cultivated another segment of State voter opposition to private power. As far back as 1918, a proposal had been made by William Clapp of Ephrata to construct a huge dam on the Columbia River at the north end of the great Grand Coulee to once again turn its water back into that coulee. The purpose was to reclaim and irrigate up to 2,000,000 acres of farmland. When Rufus Woods, Editor-Publisher of the *Wenatchee Daily World*, printed his first article on the proposal on July 18, 1918, the fight for Grand Coulee Dam was on. The private power holding companies threw everything in the book at the proposal. Washington Water Power, as a holding company pawn of the power trust, led the fight for underdevelopment of the river, sponsoring construction of a low dam at Kettle Falls on the Columbia River in 1925 which, if a license had been granted, would have precluded construction of the high dam at Grand Coulee since the Kettle Falls Dam would have been in the bottom of Grand Coulee's reservoir. To counter the drive for reclaiming farmland using Grand Coulee Dam water, Washington Water Power and its front organization, the Spokane League, proposed construction of a gravity system by diverting waters from other sources in Idaho and eastern Washington to flow across the State of Washington. Woods and Clapp, to offset findings of the Columbia Basin Survey Commission which came out for the gravity system, enlisted the help of James O'Sullivan, an attorney who had lived in Ephrata from 1910 to 1914 but had returned to Michigan to run his father's construction firm following his father's death. They asked him to draft a "construction report" on the feasibility of building a huge dam at Grand Coulee. O'Sullivan came west, made a study and report, and then, upon returning to Ephrata to live in 1929, became Executive Secretary of the Columbia River Development League organized by supporters of the big dam. The long campaign, as later described by Woods in words like "gigantic hoax," "misinformation," "threats," "deceit," "big money," and "intimidation," was indeed intense. Grand Coulee Dam, started as a State of Washington project, became a federal project by executive action of President Franklin D. Roosevelt in 1933 and was completed to its first stage in 1941.

$60,000,000 FOR DAM

THE WENATCHEE DAILY WORLD

PUBLISHED IN THE APPLE CAPITAL OF THE WORLD AND IN THE BUCKLE OF THE POWER BELT OF THE GREAT NORTHWEST

26TH YEAR, NO. 173 · OWNER OF THE ASSOCIATED BUREAU OF CIRCULATIONS · WENATCHEE, WASHINGTON, FRIDAY, JULY 28, 1933 · ASSOCIATED PRESS & UNITED PRESS LEASED WIRE REPORTS · · · PRICE 5 CENTS

ROOSEVELT AND PUBLIC WORKS BOARD APPROVE GREAT COULEE PROJECT

LATEST Wheat Control Bodies To Be Set Up

Franklin D. Roosevelt spoke at Grand Coulee Dam (under construction) in August 1934. The *Wenatchee Daily World* announced approval of the project July 28, 1933.

Courtesy BPA

However, the fight for Grand Coulee Dam in the 1920s welded together a coalition which helped pass the PUD law in 1930.

Actually, State Grange Master Goss and the Grangers were cool to the idea of reclaiming 2,000,000 acres of farmland, since new farmland and new produce would compete with present farmers. However, Grand Coulee offered much needed and desired low-cost electricity for the farms; so Grange support swung in behind the "pumpers" fighting for Grand Coulee, and while Woods and his *Wenatchee Daily World* did not support the initiative, many other "dam proponents" in return joined with the Grangers to help pass the "power bill."

The private power companies did not take a direct stand against the proposed law. Instead, they organized a Taxpayers League as a front for their opposition. It is interesting to note that during this campaign period, for the first time in the State's history, electric rates in the private power company areas started to be reduced. New "farm service consultants" were hired. Even a special electric section, paid for by the companies, began to appear in the *Washington State Grange News*.

However, private power abuses were still prevalent in the people's minds. Statewide voters approved Initiative 1 by a vote of 152,487 For and 130,901 Against. The initiative carried in 28 of the State's 39 counties with a statewide majority of 54 percent. Chapter 1 of the new law read, "The purpose of this act is to authorize the establishment of public utility districts to conserve the water and power resources of the State of Washington for the benefit of the people thereof, and to supply public utility service, including water and electricity for all uses."

Under the new law, the people, by local voter approval, could establish public utility districts to serve an area as large as a county for the purpose of providing themselves utility service on a publicly owned not-for-profit basis. Towns and cities could also be included in these service districts, which would be municipal corporations operating as a proprietary business governed by a locally elected board of commissioners. Hiring of professional management was mandated by the law. Once a district was formed, the people could use the right of eminent domain (condemnation) to take over the properties of the private power company serving the district if the company refused to sell its property to the people at a fair negotiated price.

A PUD was a new kind of utility structure. Unlike city light systems, it could cover a whole county. Unlike city light systems where the city council had to deal with many other governmental type issues, each district would have a special board dedicated solely to providing electric and/or water utility service. As can be imagined, this new law and its opportunities for

Page one of the *Seattle Daily Times*, November 5, 1930.

Homer T. Bone, author of the Washington State PUD law in the 1920's, cheers voter defeat of private power's Initiative 139 in 1940.

public power entities caused consternation not only among the local private power officials but in the offices of their Eastern holding company owners as well. This set the stage for some terrific political battles between the people and the entrenched private power trust, which left no stone unturned to hold onto their profitable power systems.

The Washington State Grange and its local Granges had merely won the first political battle in the private versus public power war as statewide voter approval was given for local people to have the right to form local public power districts. It was back to the trenches beginning in the 1932 General Election to form districts in particular counties. By this time, organized labor, urged on by the electrical workers' union, was also supporting the public power effort.

In 1932, local Granges sponsored signature petitions to get eight PUD formations on the ballot. The power trust hit back, and all but three were defeated—these being PUDs in parts of counties or small areas. The five county-wide attempts lost. One other PUD formation for part of a county was held off the ballot by a last-minute injunction which was the result of a private power legal challenge.

At the 1934 General Election, local Granges were successful in getting four PUDs approved. This was the year private power blocked three other efforts in eastern Washington (in Lincoln, Adams and Columbia counties) by use of court injunctions granted on technicalities. The court challenges had caused confusion in a number of petition efforts, blocking other PUD formation moves. Of the four approved, two were county-wide and two were to form PUDs in parts of a county, but these were in the same county (Mason), and because they both passed, the whole county could be served by public power.

A legal challenge by private power supporters against one of the new county-wide PUDs (in Benton County) was defended by the State Grange, and as a result the State Supreme Court validated the constitutionality of the entire PUD law in May 1936.

This court victory unleashed an all-out Grange effort to form PUDs in the 1936 election. Further, H.J.R. 10 had been submitted to the voters by the 1935 Legislature, which would add a constitutional amendment to allow State construction of electric transmission lines to carry public power from the two federal dams then under construction (Bonneville and Grand Coulee) to new local PUDs.

Twenty-six PUD formation elections were held in 1936, of which fifteen were approved by majority vote. One of the fifteen absorbed a small district formed back in 1932, so this brought the total of PUDs formed in the State to twenty-one. The constitutional amendment lost, whereupon the Grange shifted its support away from a State constructed electric transmission system to one to be constructed by the federal government.

Undaunted by defeat in the eleven unsuccessful efforts, fighting the power trust's tremendous financial opposition, local Grangers and local union members carried PUD formation in seven more county-wide votes in 1938 and followed those in 1940 with four more.

In that year, the statewide fight against private power's Initiative 139 detracted from some of the local formation efforts and six were voted down. By 1942, public attention and effort were swinging to the nation's all-out World War II needs, and PUD formation was put on the back burner.

With those successful efforts plus those where formation failed, the electric power political fights were turbulent during the ten years from 1932 to 1942. Since two of the PUDs shared a county, thirty-one PUDs had been established in thirty counties. Mason is the only county having two PUDs.

As of this writing in 1987, one more successful election in 1984 established a PUD in one more county. Twenty-seven of the thirty-two PUDs formed have been activated in twenty-six of the State's counties. Eleven serve electric customers only; four serve water customers only; ten have both electric and water utility systems; one has a water and a sewer utility; and one has all three types of systems, operating a small sewer utility in an unincorporated area by special legislative approval to answer the needs of a small town relocated as the result of federal construction of the John Day Dam. PUD electric service covers more than one-half of the land area of our State and serves about one-fourth of the State's electric customers.

Several of the PUDs formed in the 1930s have never been activated— they have never gone into either the electric or the water utility business. Private power companies found out early that to block activation of a PUD, they should elect "stooge" candidates to PUD boards. Many spirited commissioner elections have occurred over the years. Our present Public Disclosure Law reveals that even as late as the 1970s, private power gave financial support to such candidates. These elections of anti-public power candidates were bones of contention between the companies and the local people.

Several districts have not been activated because pressure for rural area service was eliminated when a number of rural electric cooperatives were organized. By using low interest federal funding, they built lines to the rural areas. This was definitely true in eastern Washington, where the urban areas are served by Washington Water Power. While this meant fewer PUDs, it did get electric service to rural areas. Further, while these cooperatives were a private organization in structure, they operated on a not-for-profit basis in the consumer interest like a PUD. They became strong allies fighting for federal public power dams and transmission facilities and receiving their power supply from those sources. The PUDs in return totally supported federal appropriations for the nationwide rural electric cooperative funding by Congress. Several of the more rural PUDs used this low-cost funding.

One of the first PUDs organized in 1932 was for a portion of Spokane County. While still existing, its area or size is not identifiable as the records were destroyed in a Spokane courthouse fire some years ago.

Following the many successful PUD formation elections in 1936, State Grange Master Albert Goss assembled a meeting at State Grange headquarters in Seattle on December 7. Thirty-four PUD commissioners attended. The meeting was chaired by Fred Chamberlain, long-time Grange public power leader. Also attending were Jack Cluck, Grange attorney, and R. W. "Bob" Beck, representing J. D. Ross, Superintendent of Seattle City Light. At the meeting, the Washington Public Utility Commissioners' Association was formed with adoption of by-laws and election of the first President, Charles Pederson, Whatcom County PUD Commissioner. Members of the new Executive Committee also elected included Phillip Terry (Douglas), Vice President; Malcom Moore (Pacific), Secretary-Treasurer; plus Commissioners Cardwell (Cowlitz), Spada (Snohomish), Reilly (Lincoln), and Worthington (Stevens).

Private power forces tried to hamstring the public power movement by sponsoring two statewide initiatives: Initiative 139 in 1940 and Initiative 166 in .946, which I will discuss in detail later. Finally, after quite a number of districts were activated, private power turned its political efforts back to the Legislature. Here they attempted, as in the initiatives, to get punitive laws which would make PUD operations inefficient or restrictively more costly.

The private power companies fought construction of the federal dams and federal transmission lines being approved by Congress and constructed in the 1930s and 1940s. They viewed them for what they are: publicly owned power facilities.

PUD Political Activist, 1935–1947

By 1935, the private versus public power political and legal fights were raging across the State and in the courts. That was the year I left my chokersetter job in a logging camp to take a federal office job.

I was residing in Stevenson, Washington (Skamania County), where my Dad, coming out of the Great Depression, was once again trying to make a living in lumber and logging. I had started as a "whistle punk" several years before and had progressed to "bull" chokersetter on a rigging crew for the Blue Ox Logging Company. A friend who worked as a political assistant to Doug Caples wrote to me saying that I might be able to get a job on the administrative staff of a new federal works program – the Works Progress Administration – being started by President Franklin D. Roosevelt. He asked that I submit three letters of recommendation.

I secured letters from George F. Christenson, owner of the Bank of Stevenson; H. E. Rogers, Superintendent of Stevenson Schools; and Walter Hufford, Mayor of Stevenson. I got my first taste of the political system when the telephone nearly rang off the wall with my friend yelling, "Look, this is a Democratic job and you have sent in letters from three of the biggest Republicans in southwest Washington. Doug says you can't have the job unless you can get some Democratic letters of recommendation." So I went to Ed Hollis, Chairman of the Board of County Commissioners (Democrat), and Clyde Linville, Prosecuting Attorney for Skamania County (Democrat), and got some more nice letters. I then discovered that each political party had a State Committeeman in each county. John Smith, a local barber at Carson, Washington, was the Democratic State Committeeman for Skamania County. When I approached him for a letter, he said, "Hell, kid, I can't write a letter. You write it and I'll sign it." I followed his instructions and got the job.

This led to my friendship with Caples, who introduced me to Senator Homer Bone in 1938 the evening he recruited me for the ranks of young political activists fighting for local public power against the "abuses of the private power trust." Bone helped me in another way by introducing me to J. D. Ross, longtime head of Seattle City Light, who had been appointed the first Administrator of the Bonneville Power Administration on October 10, 1937. Ross died in March 1939, so I knew him very briefly and only as a young person meeting him occasionally at political rallies. Starting with Ross, it became my privilege to know and work with every Bonneville Administrator to this date.

Ross was the person who started the federal electric transmission grid. Congress authorized construction of tie lines between the federal Grand Coulee Dam in northeastern Washington and the federal Bonneville Dam on the lower stretch of the Columbia River. A second line would provide backup capacity in case the first line was damaged. It would have been logical for both lines to run east from the Bonneville Dam up the Columbia River Gorge and then go north to Grand Coulee, but when Ross started to plan such intertie lines, the second bent quite a ways west (down the Columbia Gorge) and then north before curving east toward Grand Coulee, so that it just happened to go by way of Seattle. In later years during World

Skamania County PUD #1 was the first PUD to acquire the property of a private power company. It was activated in January 1940.

War II, this proved to be a very valuable "mistake" when the meandering line took needed power to Boeing for airplanes and to Bremerton for Navy ships. From the beginning, this line expanded the power grid in areas where activation of a new PUD would be made easier by having a power supply separate from that of a private power company which the PUD was trying to acquire either by condemnation or negotiating a purchase price. The availability of a federal power supply gave local public power an advantage over private power.

The voters in Clark County approved formation of their PUD in 1938 after we got the measure on the ballot. My Dad, still living at Stevenson, was active in getting a Skamania County PUD approved the same year. That one, incidentally, became the first PUD to be activated by taking over private power property when it acquired the properties of the West Coast Power Company. The first PUD in business was Mason County PUD No.

1, formed in 1934 to serve a small area of that county around Hoodsport. In 1935, this PUD took over electric service to the town of Hoodsport and the local lumber mill when a small mutual cooperative utility system converted to a PUD-type organization. The PUD law was more flexible than laws regulating mutually owned power suppliers, permitting line extensions to adjacent rural areas desiring service. Several other PUDs, using Rural Electrification Administration loans, had started to serve some rural customers in 1938 and 1939.

In 1940, the first statewide initiative against local public power was sponsored by the private power trust. As usual, the private companies arranged and paid for a front organization. Initiative 139 was a very cleverly worded proposed law. In essence, it would require voter approval before any revenue bonds could be issued by a public utility district. A PUD needed the right to finance its activities like any other business—the right to go to a banker when the need for money arose, and borrow the money on the prospective earnings of the business. Changing a normal business decision into a political decision, with the delays and opposition private power money would guarantee—as such a law would do—would diminish the prospect of activating a PUD.

A tremendous campaign to "Let the People Vote" flooded the State. Private power forces had already been able to get such a law on the Oregon books and later years were to prove that it was very effective in blocking several PUD activations in that state. Once again, the Washington State and local Granges, now joined by an all-out effort by organized labor, took to the streets. I was a very busy volunteer!

One factor in this election had been completion of the Bonneville Dam which provided federal public power to a new aluminum industry plant at Vancouver in December 1939. The Bonneville Project Act of 1937 had established the "temporary" federal power marketing agency called the Bonneville Project Administration, later changed in 1940 to the Bonneville Power Administration. Homer Bone and the other public power supporters in Congress, such as Republican Senator Charles McNary of Oregon, had placed a "preference clause" in the Act, providing that publicly or cooperatively owned utilities would have first rights ahead of private power to the low-cost federal public power. The voters of this State recognized that to get such low-cost power they should have a law under which they could activate and operate their PUD public power utilities in an efficient business-like way. They were not hoodwinked by the misleading "Let the People Vote" slogans. In the 1940 General Election, the "power trust's" Initiative 139 bit the dust with 253,318 For and 362,508 Against.

After this election, my personal involvement in public power issues slackened for two years. My federal job took me to Tacoma which, served by public power, had the lowest power rates in the nation. I transferred to private industry as a Safety Engineer for the Seattle-Tacoma Shipbuilding firm. Because of my past experience in logging, I was assigned to work with the riggers under the whirly cranes making the larger lifts. I returned to Vancouver in the summer of 1942, where my mother had moved following my father's death early that year. Since our nation had just entered World War II in December 1941, I anticipated going into the Armed Services.

I went to work for Kaiser Engineers at its Vancouver shipbuilding yard in personnel management, hiring and labor relations. I found my friend Doug Caples busy trying to activate the Clark County PUD. While most of the City of Vancouver was served by the Portland General Electric Company from across the Columbia River, and the rural areas were served by the Northwestern Electric Company (a Pacific Power and Light Company affiliate), little progress had been made to get the PUD into business. The war effort had placed attempts to activate some PUDs on the back burner. However, an opportunity arose in Clark County when, to provide living quarters for the many persons imported from the Midwest and elsewhere for the shipyard defense work, the Vancouver Housing Authority put up houses just east of Vancouver in a compact area called McLoughlin Heights, which was within easy reach of the Bonneville J. D. Ross substation. This housing project was a natural for PUD service, which was provided by the Clark County PUD beginning in August 1942. Yes, Caples just happened to be Chairman of the local Housing Authority and attorney for the Clark County PUD.

His anger at the private power companies was roused when, as Housing Authority Chairman, he wrote to both Northwestern Electric and Portland General Electric seeking bids to provide service to what would be a good electric load in a concentrated housing area. Northwestern Electric turned him down in favor of Portland General Electric, to force the Housing Authority to accept a one-bid monopoly price. Caples then turned to Clark County PUD which, though formed in 1938, had not yet been activated, but was negotiating to purchase the local utility properties. It had employed George Hibbert as a manager/consultant to work with a fiscal agent retained to deal with the holding company owners in Chicago and New York.

Thus, when Portland General Electric hit the Housing Authority, and through it the National Housing Authority in Washington, D.C., with a bid of $25,000 to provide the service, Clark County PUD countered with

Commissioner Heye Meyer of the Clark County PUD throws the switch to start electric service by that PUD in 1942.

an estimate that it could provide this service for $12,000. Hibbert, Manager of Clark County PUD, although not a graduate engineer, was a sharp and knowledgeable utility person, and when James Polhemus, President of Portland General Electric, made his exorbitant bid, it was Hibbert's work before the Federal Power Commission which tipped the scale in favor of PUD service. The contract with the Housing Authority put Clark County PUD in business, and the incident once again demonstrated private power monopoly abuse, while it set the stage for an all-out private versus public power war in Clark County.

In 1940, several other PUDs had gone into business. Some began to operate after successful condemnation cases against the serving private power company and others after negotiated sales of the private company's facilities to the public. Grays Harbor, Pacific, Wahkiakum, Cowlitz, and Mason No. 3 were a few. Thus activation of Clark County was viewed as a win for public power.

During the period when PUD activation commenced, starting around 1938, a division in public power ranks grew, not over whether PUDs should buy out private facilities, but over the procedure for buying them out. PUD commissioners, elected by the voters as they formed a district, felt they had an obligation to get into business. This could be accomplished by buying out the existing private power company. The two ways to do this were to negotiate a purchase price or, failing in that, to use the power of condemnation or the right of public eminent domain, which meant going to court and having the price to be paid set by a jury or by a judge. Two strong personalities, Jack Cluck and Bob Beck, were involved in this argument in PUD ranks as how best to activate a PUD.

Following the meeting at the State Grange headquarters in 1936 and formation of the Washington Public Utility Commissioners' Association, Jack Cluck, attorney for the Grange and principal defender of the PUD law in lawsuits being brought by private power, began to represent individual PUDs. Cluck's law firm, Houghton, Cluck, Coughlin and Henry (in later years Riley), became the leading and major provider of legal services to PUDs which wanted to acquire properties from private power by means of condemnation lawsuits.

R. W. "Bob" Beck, a close employee-associate of J. D. Ross, who had gone to Bonneville with Ross, was loaned by Ross in June 1938 to help negotiate private power buyouts here and in Nebraska. Cluck and Beck thus ended up on opposite sides of the controversy over the best method by which to activate a PUD, and this issue nearly split the PUD forces in the mid-1940s.

The chief architect in efforts to acquire private power properties for PUDs through negotiated purchases was a fiscal agent named Guy C. Myers. Myers' work in transferring electric utility properties from private ownership to public ownership had commenced a number of years before with his involvement when Wendell Willkie and David Lilienthal worked out similar sales in the Tennessee Valley Authority area. He was very active in pursuing negotiations for properties in Nebraska. Myers, who originally worked for the Montana Power Company, got involved in the municipal revenue bond markets when he assisted an irrigation district in Montana with some financing. From there he worked on other revenue bond financings for public organizations and became acquainted with heads of several Eastern holding company owners of private power utilities operating in the Pacific Northwest. He met J. D. Ross when Ross needed help to secure some municipal revenue bond financing in Wall Street during the depression years, and through Ross he became very active in PUD negotiated acquisitions in the State of Washington.

Guy Myers' winning formula for such negotiations was that he could offer the common stock owner a better price for his stock than its current value on the market. Since the common stock of most of the utilities operating in this region was owned centrally by one holding company, Myers knew he would usually be dealing with one person—the president of the holding company or the president of the local utility reporting to a holding company boss. The potential earnings of a utility property could be readily determined by looking at past revenues. Since the PUD would be financed by lower cost tax exempt revenue bonds and the overhead would be further reduced because public utilities were exempt from federal income taxes and were to be supplied with low cost power from new federal power dams, a good price on the outstanding common stock could be offered. The price always included a "margin" to allow for local rate reductions once public power took over, and since the voters had shown themselves to be opposed to private power, the PUD commissioners were in a strong bargaining position to move ahead on the deal. Myers' standard contract gave him a one percent commission on any purchase price. He paid his own expenses and those of engineering or other outside consultants when these people were needed.

One of the first purchases he negotiated was for the properties of the Grays Harbor Electric Company serving Aberdeen and Hoquiam. Since it was essential that this PUD operation be a success to prove that public power would benefit the ratepayer, it was vital that the new manager be someone trustworthy and qualified from public power's viewpoint. Myers and the local PUD chose Bob Beck for the job, and it was a good choice. Beck later organized an engineering consulting firm which earned acceptance and a reputation for reliability with the various investment bankers who participated in public power purchases negotiated by Myers in the states of Washington and Nebraska. R. W. Beck and Associates became a household word in public power and investment banking circles for doing all kinds of engineering analyses. Because private power nationwide was opposed to the Washington PUD movement, not too many bankers or consulting engineers would work for or be associated with public power.

The two schools of thought as to how best to get into business — condemnation or negotiation — caused dissension among public power advocates. Each method was promoted by well meaning persons who made their living by providing legal or engineering services or as fiscal agents or investment bankers, and PUD commissioners, elected to activate their utilities, began to argue the question of how best to achieve a goal on which they all agreed. Some felt the condemnation route was best — others were satisfied with negotiated purchase prices.

The argument came out into the open in 1942. The State Grange and those persons favoring condemnation found that acquiring a broad utility system one piece at a time was not only costly but time consuming. Thus, Initiative 12 to the Legislature was prepared by August 1942. The proposed law would allow two or more of the individual PUDs in the State to consolidate their efforts to take over all of the properties of a power company by condemnation. Enough signatures were obtained to present Initiative 12 at the 1943 Session of the Legislature, where it was passed. However, private power forces filed Referendum 25 against it and secured the necessary signatures to place it on the 1944 General Election ballot. The new law was rejected by a statewide vote of 297,191 For and 373,051 Against. One reason for the defeat was that public power support was divided. There were those persons, including yours truly, who were fearful that consolidation of individual PUD efforts through a statewide or large group organization under three appointed persons would result in loss of local control. I also had another reason for opposing the law.

I was and am a stalwart supporter of electric utility service under public ownership. Since such service must be provided by a monopoly, without the usual free competitive enterprise on which our capitalistic economy is founded, there is no reason in my opinion to allow private persons to make a guaranteed profit on a service for which competition is not practical. However, I was not then, nor am I now, a Socialist. My support of public power was as a means to an end — not a means for an end. I supported public power to eliminate the abuses of private monopoly power. The private power companies that operate in the Pacific Northwest today are a far cry from the holding company subsidiaries that operated here in the 1930s and 1940s. While I am not enraptured by some of the things they do today, they are providing proper electric service at rates that are reasonable private power rates. It would be better for the customers if they had their own public power utilities with undoubtedly lower rates, but today's private power monopoly abuses are not extreme enough to arouse local voters to take them over. It was a lot different in the early 1940s, when PUDs had yet to prove themselves workable.

A number of Socialists in this State were involved in the public power movement. Carl Thompson, Secretary of the Public Ownership League of America, became involved in the Grange effort to pass a PUD law in 1928. Later, Fred Chamberlain, stalwart Grange public power activist, served as President of the Washington Public Ownership League. Several counties formed local organizations of the League and, while all members were not active Socialists, these organizations played a strong part in circulating petitions and encouraging votes to form PUDs. In 1944, the League sponsored a candidate for a State Senate seat on the Socialist Party ticket and used the Washington Public Utility Commissioners' Association office in Seattle as a campaign office for the candidate. Many League members, while being good persons, favored public ownership not only of utilities but also of other businesses. Disagreement over socialism festered in public power ranks and intensified the division over Initiative 12 and Referendum 25.

This political action by the Public Ownership League, although its Socialist candidate was not elected, prompted a group of us from Clark County to form the Public Power League of Washington. The mainstays of this organization were Mable Johnson, Treasurer of the Clark County Pomona Grange, and Maude Swick, an elderly Republican precinct committeewoman and Grange Recorder for the *Vancouver Sun* newspaper. Mable was our first President and Maude our Secretary-Treasurer. From 1944 to 1948, the Public Power League of Washington represented those persons who supported public power but were not Socialists or socialistically inclined. As its President in 1947 and 1948, I became acquainted with people in public power circles statewide. The League helped make a change in the Washington Public Utility Commissioners' Association in April 1947. With the support of the League, one of my closest friends, Frank Stewart from Clark County, moved in as the Commissioners' Association's Managing Director. And "move in" he did, with assistance from several of us other young turks when we came to Seattle on a Sunday morning and physically moved the Association's office from the Alaska Building to the Jones Building.

The year 1946 brought another statewide private versus public power fight when private power forces sponsored Initiative 166, another cleverly worded initiative to the people. As in the Initiative 139 campaign in 1940, the slogan was "Let the People Vote" on revenue bonds. The difference between the 1940 and 1946 campaigns was that in 1946 there was a division in private power ranks, with Washington Water Power and Pacific Power and Light on one side and Puget Power on the other.

Chief support of the initiative came from Kinsey M. Robinson, President of Washington Water Power, joined by Paul B. McKee, President of Pacific Power and Light. Of course, the usual "citizens'" committee favoring the initiative appeared, and private power money to be spent in this effort was going to be substantial.

Following the Initiative 139 fight in 1940, the Federal Power Commission had issued its Opinion 59, analyzing the political activities of the private power companies in the Pacific Northwest from 1935 to 1940. This report showed that during that period they had spent in excess of a million dollars for political purposes. Worse still were the following findings: approximately one-half of those political expenditures were charged to their customers under the heading of "operating expenses"; proper accounting practices were violated and incomplete, misleading, and false records were maintained; utilities made large indirect and concealed political expenditures; the companies had their employees compile elaborate card indexes of voters and ring doorbells to campaign for the initiative, charging the ratepayers for their time; former public power advocates were hired and placed directly on private company payrolls; secret payments were made to prominent citizens; political advertising was charged to regular sales promotional accounts paid for by the ratepayers.

That these practices and policies were also used in later years was brought out in an independent analysis of The Washington Water Power Company made in 1950 by Stone and Webster, a renowned private power analysis firm. Howard Aller, President of AP&L which still owned all the common stock of Washington Water Power, ordered the study, after the FPC 1947 Report of The Washington Water Power Company showed that the company spent $179,242 on the Initiative 166 campaign in 1946. One recommendation of the Stone and Webster report was that political and propaganda expenditures could be reduced $300,000 per year without adversely affecting Washington Water Power's public relations. Aller wanted to know why the rate of return on the common stock was below normal. He found out.

However, in 1946, President Frank McLaughlin of Puget Power, with the approval of its holding company owner in Boston, was actively negotiating with Guy Myers over PUD acquisition of that company. Puget Power was under a threat of takeover stimulated by the competitive yardstick pressure of Seattle City Light and Tacoma Light on rates, and the company felt it could get a better price for its stockholders through a company-wide negotiated sale. Several recent condemnation awards to PUDs indicated that this was the case. Initiative 166 would block such a negotiated sale, so Puget Power was opposed to the initiative.

In Clark County we had a double problem. Heye Meyer, the incumbent PUD Commissioner and long-time Grange leader, was opposed by a private power "Trojan horse" candidate named Walden Higdon, who, if elected, would try to block PUD purchase of the remaining private power facilities in Clark County. Higdon was from a pioneer family of Clark County. In 1944, partly because of the division in public power ranks over Initiative 12 and Referendum 25, the private power forces had knocked out pro-public power Clark County PUD Commissioner Joe Ast with their candidate Elmer Deetz. However, Meyer and L. M. Jones, the third member of the Clark County PUD Board and a strong public power supporter, moved ahead in 1945 to condemn the properties of Portland General Electric in downtown Vancouver over Deetz' opposition. The jury award in November 1945, in a U.S. District Court, was probably the most favorable public power award ever made. Testimony by Clark County PUD had estimated the market value plus severance damage at $722,000. Portland General Electric's expert witnesses had testified that a fair price would be $1,475,000. The award was $801,000, which was less than two times the gross revenues in the last twelve months. Awards had normally been up to four or five times the annual gross revenues.

With that success, the Clark County PUD began planning condemnation proceedings against Northwestern Electric and its associate, Pacific Power and Light, which served the rest of Vancouver and rural Clark County. To block this move private power openly ran its candidate for the commission and supported Initiative 166. This really got action from persons such as myself. I took a two-month leave of absence without pay from my regular employer to coordinate the campaign to re-elect Heye Meyer and defeat Initiative 166. The Grange and organized labor were my mainstays. The Machinists Union furnished me a campaign office upstairs in a building diagonally across the intersection from the Northwestern Electric office. Each morning I would see carloads of Pacific Power and Light employees from Portland arrive, troop up the stairs, get their door-knocking area assignments, and hit Clark County. Our committee, by holding Grange socials and passing the hat, raised a respectable political pot of around $5,000 during the entire campaign. After the election, in talking to the man whose public relations firm handled the private power campaign in Clark County, I was told the company had spent around $65,000 plus the unreported time of employees from within and without the county.

Several of the incidents in the campaign make amusing recollections. One involved a trade fair at the Vancouver Housing Authority Auditorium in McLouglin Heights east of Vancouver, which had various company booths to promote business following the end of the war. Northwestern Electric's very large booth, which was right in the middle of the auditorium, went all-out for Initiative 166.

We had just formed our Committee Against 166, and although we had no money, we wanted to be at the fair. Booths lined the outside perimeter of the auditorium, and a double set, back to back, ran down the center of the room. By the time I could get some finances committed, all the booths had been taken. However, the manager of the fair let me set up a table at one end of the center row of booths. It wouldn't be a booth, but at least we could put up a sign and arrange our literature on the table. While I was having a cup of coffee with a local radio station reporter, we decided on a slogan: "166 Is Full of Tricks." A friendly sign painter prepared a banner. I built a "T" out of 1 x 2 lumber and nailed it to the top of the double booths behind us so that it stuck out about four feet overhead. From this, on colored ribbons, I suspended jokers from decks of cards and put up another sign that said: "Look for the jokers in Initiative 166." The jokers were at eye level or slightly above. The result was terrific. As the people came down one side of the center booths and turned the corner to go up the other side, they were brushed on the head by the hanging jokers, which directed their eyes to one sign and then to the other. On the second day, I was able to get some copies of Initiative 166, on which I circled the "tricks" before handing them out. The power company employees nearly went ape complaining to the manager, but he merely pointed out the pro-166 displays in their booths. Campaigning at the fair was fast, inexpensive, fun — and very effective. "166 Is Full of Tricks" was later picked up and used statewide.

The PUD law very specifically provides that a PUD manager cannot get involved in commissioner elections. George Hibbert was still the Manager of Clark County PUD. As far as I was concerned, he had been doing a good enough job, but we found ourselves at cross-purposes during the campaign. As campaign coordinator, I was merely a volunteer in the election fight. Many PUD employees, recognizing that this was a life or death struggle between the PUD and Northwestern Electric, came down to my campaign office and volunteered their services during off-duty hours. They worked like troupers in this fight.

Since Hibbert couldn't be involved officially, he would call me to his office every other day and demand to know what I was doing as campaign coordinator — and then waste my time telling me how he could not get involved. He didn't help the situation by continually riding me and the Monday before election he went too far. He called me to his office and laid it out that if the election went our way, he was to get the credit, but if we lost, I was to get the blame. I busted out of his office very angry and went down the street to Doug Caples' office. Caples was still attorney for the district and a guiding light for much of the PUD activity. I told him that based on my analysis, Heye Meyer was going to be re-elected and we would defeat 166 in Clark County. I also told him that after the campaign was over, I would work to get Hibbert fired. He cooled me down and I never took such action, but early in the following year, Hibbert was let go. The PUD Commission asked my opinion, as a public power leader, on who might make a good manager. I said that they had an electrical engineer by the name of Vince Cleaveland, and while I didn't know anything about his ability to be a manager, he had certainly pulled no punches in helping kill Initiative 166 and re-elect Meyer. I was glad when they gave him the job. He turned out to be a good manager – and later my boss.

Meyer was re-elected by a substantial vote – I stayed at the courthouse until 4 a.m. the next morning to be sure. The statewide vote on Initiative 166 was 220,239 For and 367,826 Against. Our local vote defeated it by a wider margin. Public power had beaten private power again.

Another public power experience touched my personal life in 1946. I was serving on the Ruling Board of Elders for the First Presbyterian Church in Vancouver. When the Portland General Electric properties, which had served the church, were taken over by the PUD, the church was then served by public power, although Northwestern Electric also served Vancouver. Cecil Root, a very fine man, superintendent of our Sunday School and a Northwestern Electric employee, served notice on Reverend John Pressley that he would resign, not only from his Sunday School activity but from the church, unless the church took its business away from "socialistic public power." When the matter came to the attention of the Board, the Elders suggested that the change not be made. To transfer service now would mean the church was taking a political stand for private power – where it had not been involved before. However, the three trustees, who actually ran the church's business activities and were all private power supporters, didn't agree, so the transfer was made. Pressley called me to apologize, saying he hoped the action would not alienate my service on the Board. I told him that while it hurt to see the church get involved in political issues, the action of the trustees would only increase efforts on my part to have the PUD take over Northwestern Electric.

One year later, in November 1947, this happened when a successful condemnation action was instituted. The jury award was made the same month and Cecil Root shortly was transferred to Yakima where Pacific Power and Light still serves today. I continued to go to church in Vancouver and somehow it seemed to me that its lights burned a little brighter after

March 1948 when the PUD took over service again. I chaired the Every Member Canvass the following year and did right well raising money for the church's budget. One of the largest contributors had been serving as a trustee in 1946.

A factor in the Northwestern Electric (Pacific Power and Light) condemnation was that private power supporter Elmer Deetz, by moving out of his commissioner district, had to resign from the PUD Commission in July 1947, and, with Higdon defeated by Meyer, the surviving commissioners, Meyer and L. M. Jones, returned public power supporter Joe Ast to the Board by appointment. Another plus for public power was that the Vancouver *Columbian*, which had been an arch PUD opponent in its editorials and news stories, following defeat of Higdon and Initiative 166, had joined the effort to "go all PUD and make it the best in the State."

On January 8, 1948, I attended my last public power function as a layman. As President of the Public Power League, I attended the membership meeting of the Washington Public Utility Commissioners' Association in Seattle.

Local PUD Employment, 1948–1951

In early 1945, with two other young married friends, I secured waiver of the draft deferment requested by my employer, the Kaiser Company, and volunteered for duty in the Armed Forces—hopefully the Navy. My two friends made it but I got a 4F turndown because of a substantial loss of vision in my left eye from an unfortunate bout with cornea ulcers in 1942. Unknown to me until I met the Navy doctor for my physical, I had been carrying a hernia since my logging days.

When World War II ended in mid-1945, Kaiser Company closed the shipyard and as part of its postwar endeavors entered the home construction market. I was assigned to that work and was promoted rapidly.

However, in April 1947, I received a call from the head office in Oakland saying that they were terminating their plans to build 1,400 homes near Beaverton, Oregon, in the Portland-Vancouver area, and that I would be transferred to Ann Arbor, Michigan, to work in their car industry headed by Edgar Kaiser. Many of the Vancouver shipyard administrative employees had gone to Ann Arbor when our yard won a competitive model car design contest against two other Kaiser shipyards. After discussing the transfer with my family, I decided to resign from Kaiser, draw my accrued bonus, and look for another job in the Pacific Northwest. One of the reasons for this decision was my continued involvement as a citizen-supporter of public power. I was President of the Public Power League of Washington, and I wanted to remain in the Pacific Northwest.

From April to October 1947, I managed the Piccadilly Inn, a lucrative beer tavern at 20th and S.E. Morrison in Portland which belonged to my brother-in-law. A family emergency that came up just as I got the call from the Kaiser head office prompted me to take the tavern job although it was completely foreign to my background, experience, and abilities – and I didn't even drink beer. However, it gave me an unbelievable income, which added to a small family financial base without which in later years I could not have remained in public power work. Taxes were low, and with pinballs, punchboards, and claw machines, the business was a winner. By October, my brother-in-law was real happy with his deal with me. Business had increased substantially and he suggested that he buy another tavern which I could also manage, but I told him this was not my idea of living, and that he should either sell Piccadilly or be ready to take it back to manage at the middle of the month.

From there I delved very shortly into the oil furnace business and then joined a pump firm to set up its retail outlets for farm irrigation systems in Oregon. This job looked good for the future, but it required a lot of travel away from home. Thus, when I received a telegram at Salem, Oregon, in March 1948 from Vince Cleaveland, Manager of Clark County PUD, stating they had taken over the properties of Northwestern Electric (Pacific Power and Light) and offering me work as Personnel Director, I took a cut in pay of $100 per month and went to work for public power.

When I arrived on my new job in April 1948, I found a new type of business world. While my work was to be in personnel management, employee job descriptions, utility jargon, work assignments, and technology were all foreign to me. To learn more about the field, I immediately enrolled in a University of Oregon Portland extension course in utility financing and in an apprentice lineman course at Clark College. For the first six months, I would leave my office at 5 p.m., go down to the King Street Substation, and hop into one of the servicemen's rigs to ride around with him as he performed his evening duties and answered his trouble calls. I had to learn the utility business in a hurry. On one occasion, the serviceman had to open a line switch to break the high voltage circuit so that a heavy line crew could work on the line at another location. The switch wouldn't open, so he put his climbing spurs on, went up the pole, and while I strained on the handle at the foot of the pole, he hit away at the switch gear above with a hot-line stick. I soon developed a tremendous respect for linemen.

Several incidents of note happened during my Clark County PUD employment. I had been there only two weeks when I was called into the offices of Guy Burch, Chief Accountant, and Ken Durgan, Auditor. They said, "You might as well know, we've decided that the 'little man in the corner office' [Cleaveland, the manager] must go." They then recited certain criticisms of his way of operating. I was indeed surprised, but I responded: "Since you have chosen up sides before I got here, just leave me out of it." I then had to sit on the sidelines and watch this war develop.

Vince Cleaveland, the man I had recommended to replace George Hibbert back in 1947, had been raised by a father who owned two small private utilities in the Dakotas. He was a graduate electrical engineer with a good background in utility service. The problem in our office could not be blamed entirely on Cleaveland. It was caused by the rundown state of the electric system the PUD had acquired from Northwestern Electric. For many years, anticipating a PUD takeover and meeting the costs of the war effort, the former private power owners had skimped miserably on maintenance. The "DuBois pike" was a joke among PUD crew members who had worked for Northwestern Electric. DuBois Lumber was a leading mill in town, and the DuBois pike was a two by four piece of lumber used to prop up some of the decaying poles around the county. To make things worse, when Northwestern Electric pulled out, they stripped the office of engineering maps, financial records, reports, and analyses. The Clark County PUD had no records on which to base its anticipated future. No one knew if we were making money or not. Vince was by nature a precise person, and in these circumstances he had to run a tight ship. When line crews asked for more equipment or accountants wanted a bigger budget, he would say "No—not until we get some idea of where we are financially." His department heads knew this—but instead of explaining it to the crews or the other employees, they would merely say, "The little guy in the corner office says No!" Bad feelings were brewing.

Finally, by August, I couldn't stand it anymore, so I went to Cleaveland and said, "Either you are not delegating authority to your department heads, or if you are, they aren't using it to work with you as a team." He asked what I meant and I explained how his department heads were undermining his decisions to the employees. The next thing I knew, he had Hugh Whisler, General Superintendent, in his office and smoke started to come out over the transom. Whisler made the mistake of rising to his feet, pointing his finger at Cleaveland, and shouting, "You've got to go." Whisler was fired, as could be expected, but then the other five administrative heads joined him in a petition to the Board of Commissioners, telling it to fire Cleaveland. The next night, I was called down to the home of Commissioner L. M. Jones, where I found Heye Meyer and Joe Ast, the other two commissioners. They asked my advice. I said that, while some of the fault did lie with Cleaveland, under no circumstances should they let a group of employees tell them who could *not* be the manager. If they did, the same employees would soon be telling them who *could* be the manager. Whisler, Burch, and Durgan were let go. The other three department heads remained.

With all of the financial department heads gone, Cleaveland asked if I had any ideas. I mentioned that during the Initiative 166 campaign I had made friends with Frank McLaughlin, head of Puget Power, so I might contact him to see if there were some potential top accounting personnel in those ranks who might be interested in these jobs. Vince sent me to Seattle, McLaughlin turned me loose on his staff, and we secured the services of three top finance persons who gave many years of good service to the Clark County PUD: Manley Brown, Dean Vail, and George Watters. Watters later became Manager of Clark County PUD.

The thought of raiding private power companies for their personnel gave me a chuckle many years later in 1967 when Charles "Chuck" Luce, working as the Undersecretary of the Interior in the Johnson Administration, called to inform me that he was going to accept work with Consolidated Edison in New York. Luce had been a Bonneville attorney in the 1940s and Bonneville Administrator from 1961 to 1966 before becoming the Undersecretary. Chuck said, "Several weeks ago three portly gentlemen wearing homburg hats came to my office and offered me the job of Chairman of the Board and Chief Executive Officer of Consolidated Edison of New York. I've decided to accept and, since it will be announced next week, I wanted to call a few friends out West to reduce their shock over the news." I laughed and he asked why. I said it was funny. Back in the days when we were trying to get qualified employees for public power ranks, we had to call on private power companies – and now, in his case, a private power company was calling on public power for a qualified employee. We both laughed, he on the way to a lot of hard work but also to the bank, and I going back to my work on that Saturday for public power.

My labor relations experience at Clark County PUD was very trying. Clark County has the only PUD in the State where the takeover from private power meant more than changing the name on the doors of the office and trucks and the color of the paychecks. Usually when a PUD took over private power properties, most of the employees stayed on and made good PUD employees. In Clark County, the PUD had started out serving the Housing Authority; then it acquired some property from Portland General Electric; and then finally it acquired the property of Northwestern Electric. This meant meshing three different groups of employees physically and mentally. Bear in mind, too, that there had been some hot political fights

Left to right: Clark County PUD Commissioners L. M. Jones, Joe Ast, and Heye Meyer in 1947, when their PUD acquired the last of the private power properties in that county.

Courtesy BPA

where local employees got involved during the intervening years. One big question concerned seniority in the line crews, and personalities clashed. The result was a lot of tension, which culminated in a strike by the electrical workers. In my opinion, this strike was not so much caused by dissatisfaction with management as by arguments in the workers' own ranks.

It had been statewide PUD policy over past years to favor organized labor because labor had supported local public power. Labor contracts were welcomed in PUD ranks while labor was still trying to get collective bargaining in private power ranks. Clark County PUD was one of the first ones to permit collective bargaining by its office employees. However, when the electrical workers went out, so did the office employees. We had some real tough days, as administrative employees, trying to keep the lights on. One major worry was a large synchronous condenser machine which at that time was used on electric systems to regulate and control electric output. If unattended, it could go out of control and actually explode. One night during the strike, Cleaveland and I went across the street about 9 p.m. to get dinner. We had just bit into our steaks when he asked what day of the week it was. I told him it was Wednesday. He looked funny and said, "My gosh, it's Ash Wednesday." He looked down at his steak and added, "I hope the Lord doesn't take it out on me by letting that condenser fly to pieces." Cleaveland was a devout Catholic and I was a member of the Masonic order. Eventually, after some long tough days and nights, it cost us another nickel per hour to settle the strike.

Sometimes life was not all work and no play. Thus, in 1949, attending a Northwest Public Power Association meeting in Spokane, I got to meet Kinsey M. Robinson, President of Washington Water Power and arch foe of public power in any form. Following our NWPPA business meeting, Mel Rooney, Cowlitz County PUD attorney, and I dropped down to the Early Birds Club in the basement of the Davenport Hotel to meet a long-time friend of mine, Hal Leffel, head of Kinman Business University. Hal and I had been quite active in the statewide work of the Washington JayCees. The three of us were sitting at the end of the bar, which curved out and then ran down the length of the room, when Hal said, "There's a good friend of yours, Ken, sitting down there." He pointed to two men seated about 30 feet from us down the bar. I asked who it was and he said, "That's Kinsey Robinson." I asked the bartender to serve the two men a drink, and when he told them who had bought the round, they raised their glasses to toast my hosting. Shortly the other man left and Robinson came up to our end of the bar to say hello to Hal, whom he knew as a Spokane businessman. He then turned to me and introduced himself. I said, "Before I tell you my name, I would like you to know that the best public power money in the State of Washington just bought you that whiskey." He said, "Now I do want to know who you are." I said, "I'm Ken Billington from the Clark County PUD down at Vancouver." He said, "Oh, yeah, Clark County — that's a pretty good utility." It was really my own money that had bought his drink, as public power people never had an expense account, but he then sat down and the four of us hoisted a few, arguing two against two over private versus public power. Later we all four went out east of Spokane for a good steak dinner – and this time it was on private power money at his insistence. We met many times after that – mostly as adversaries. The last time I ever saw him, we met on a friendly basis at the dedication of the Centralia steam plant in the early 1970s. He was rough and tough, as my later dealings with him were to prove.

One final incident of note in my life at Clark County PUD concerned an ice storm that came out of the Columbia Gorge in January 1950. I happened to be in Seattle serving on a statewide committee of managers, safety engineers, union business agents, and personnel management types working on a new Electrical Workers Safety Code for the State when the storm hit around 2 p.m., cutting directly across Clark County like a giant knife. By 5 p.m., 22,000 out of a total of 27,000 customers were without electricity. Poles were down everywhere. Meters were actually pulled off of houses by the weight of the ice on the lines. Telephones were also disrupted. Cleaveland did get a call through to me and since the Portland airport was closed, I grabbed a train going south from Seattle. We slept overnight in our coaches at Centralia, however, when the train was stopped by the storm. On arriving home about noon the next day, I had to dive in and hire contractor crews from anywhere in the Pacific Northwest I could find them. I also got crews from other utilities. The trick was to get them in and dispatch them ahead of any of the telephone repair crews which were rolling in from around the State. If telephone service was restored before electric service, we would be drenched with calls for service. In storms like this, the first order of business is to get the servicemen and line crews out and by opening main switches and actually cutting lines, you eliminate the danger of high voltage damage to life and property. Then you start restoring service from the high voltages down. Sixty-nine thousand volt transmission lines go back into business first; then perhaps, if you have them, 12,450-volt subtransmission lines and then 2,400-volt distribution lines. Those were the lines Clark County PUD had. It just so happened – and not by design – that PUD Commissioner Heye Meyer was one of a very few customers in his area served from a 12,450-volt line. When he got service nearly two weeks before all his neighbors served by the 2,400-volt circuit got theirs, one can imagine his chagrin and embarrassment and his neighbors' ire at his "special privilege." At the other end of the county, Commissioner Joe Ast was one of the last five customers to get service back – over six weeks after the storm. Here again, private power's bleeding of the system by delayed maintenance over the years before takeover caught the PUD short. But once we got all the lines up again, we had a practically new electric system.

I was called to Olympia during the 1949 Session to help lobby through some needed PUD laws allowing streetlighting districts in rural areas. Frank Stewart, Managing Director of the Washington Public Utility Commissioners' Association, was busy getting a new law enacted to allow joint action by PUDs to acquire private power property, which was needed to allow six PUDs to jointly purchase the remaining Puget Power properties under arrangements being negotiated by Guy Myers. This caused another political fight at Olympia so I was called in to work on laws to make it possible for utility districts to operate more efficiently. Clark County PUD loaned my services to the State PUD Association. The joint action law was passed but it was limited so that only negotiated purchases could be made jointly. There would not be any joint condemnation of private power properties.

Actually the law that emerged was a three-way compromise. The PUDs got their joint action law which simply said that two or more districts could do anything jointly which an individual district could do, with the exception of condemning private power properties, creating sub-districts, or levying taxes. A second part of the law established a three-person State Power Commission which Governor Arthur B. Langlie wanted. The third part required a PUD to continue to pay its proportionate share on any school bonds issued at the time of any private power takeover, in addition to paying the regular in-lieu school tax paid by the PUD under the regular PUD tax paying law.

After the experience of our first labor strike at Clark County, it became apparent to me that, while we could and did favor good contracts with organized labor, there were certain new elements being introduced into labor negotiations with PUDs which could disrupt orderly or fair bargaining. Breaking large utilities down into local county size units was good for the purpose of local control but, in a large utility, labor negotiations were conducted by a committee from labor and a committee from management at a location somewhat removed from the day-to-day operation of the employees. Employees decided to accept or reject contract provisions agreed to by labor negotiators by means of a mail ballot. When the PUDs were bargaining with the unions, day-to-day negotiations of the committees became tailgate issues the next morning on every work crew. The decision to accept or reject provisions came at hastily called night meetings at labor halls attended by a minority of the workers involved and usually dominated by the "tough guys" of the membership faction currently out of power who were critical of whatever the current union leadership did. Then, too, since labor was represented by a single union throughout most of the State, labor negotiators soon discovered that by playing one PUD against another and getting one benefit here and another benefit there, they made gains more easily. I do not say this in criticism of labor, but merely to state it as it was.

I was loaned by Clark County PUD to the PUD Association in an effort to coordinate labor negotiations among the PUDs and to seek a method of joint negotiations. We were not successful for various reasons, but the experience gave me additional knowledge and contacts among officials and managers of other districts in the State. It also taught me the strength, as well as the weakness, of local control in a PUD.

By the end of 1950, I had settled into my routine as Personnel Director for the Clark County PUD. Innovations, such as a newsletter for employees, *The PUD Echo*, were helping to bring a new team spirit to the different groups of employees. We started an employees' social organization, the PUDESO. We established a credit union and added all the embellishments of successful corporation employee practices.

The twelve years since Senator Bone had gotten me involved had not only been interesting to me as a lay volunteer political supporter of public power, but had now resulted in what I felt was a good and satisfying job in public power.

Looking back on those twelve years, I see that there were many private versus public power issues in which I was not personally involved but which I later would learn about as I served the districts statewide. They had been good years for public power and the people of the Pacific Northwest. The establishment of the Bonneville Power Administration, the continued construction of the federal dams on the Columbia River and its tributaries, the rural electric programs by both the PUDs and rural electric cooperatives, the Grand Coulee reclamation project of new farmland, and the lower and lower electric rates, not only in new public power service areas but also in the areas of the private power companies (encourged and forced by the competitive presence and pressure of the local public power districts), all came about during these years.

This then was my background and personal involvement before I stepped out on the statewide, regional, and national stage of public power service in 1951. And before going forward to describe the thirty years which make up the main part of this book, I will describe some of the things that happened during the 1940s which laid a foundation for my work.

2

Public Power Activity
State, Regional, and National

Power Wars of the 1940s

THE DECADE of the 1940s saw many battles between private power and public power as local people tried to activate their PUDs. Following the first negotiated purchase of a small mutual utility by Mason County PUD No. 1 in February 1935, several districts made use of federal rural electrification funds in 1939 to build lines to rural areas not being served by private power. Then, following the first county-wide takeover of a private company by Skamania County PUD on January 1, 1940, other PUDs were activated by condemnation or negotiated purchase of private facilities. Snohomish, activated in September 1949, was the last PUD to provide major or total county-wide coverage. Whatcom County PUD, which became active in 1954, serves only one electric load – a new industry which required public power in the area when Puget Sound Power and Light Company (Puget Power), serving that county, could not furnish the electricity.

Twenty condemnation cases were filed during the 1940s. In fourteen cases, the districts accepted the judge or jury award purchase price. Since three districts had two separate cases each, these fourteen cases permitted eleven of the districts to provide major service: Benton, Clallam, Clark,

Cowlitz, Douglas, Franklin, Grant, Klickitat, Okanogan, Skamania, and Pend Oreille. Eight others were activated by negotiated purchase of the major private power facilities serving their areas: Chelan, Ferry, Grays Harbor, Lewis, Mason No. 3, Pacific, Snohomish, and Wahkiakum. One other besides Whatcom, Kittitas, constructed power facilities in unserved rural areas and still serves only part of its county. Starting with Mason No. 1 in 1935, there are now twenty-two electric PUDs operating in twenty-one of the thirty-nine counties in the State.

In the rough court battles, private power used every possible legal delaying tactic to block takeovers. Appeals to higher courts, requests for review of decisions made, requests for new trials, and other legal maneuvers were used. The Okanogan County PUD started its condemnation suit against The Washington Water Power Company on December 21, 1939. It finally purchased the system on May 11, 1945. Clark County PUD had to go to the State Supreme Court twice to answer delaying appeals before it was permitted to take over Pacific Power and Light Company properties.

Certain good changes were made by the Legislature in the PUD law during the 1940s. PUDs would be allowed to pay a gross revenue tax which would replace the property taxes that had been paid by the private power companies before takeover. A compromise with city officials required the consent of the city before PUD facilities could be placed on their streets and in their alleys. This was to combat tactics used by private power supporters to scare city officials into blocking PUD activation. Employees who came to the PUD under private power takeovers would retain their former benefits. A PUD could not be denied a power supply, even by the private utility whose properties it had acquired. This provision made sure that such a company could not thwart the majority vote of local people to have local public power service by refusing to supply power. PUD commissioners would have six-year terms with staggered elections every two years. This provision emphasized the non-partisan nature of the office and provided stability by always having two experienced commissioners on a board. A public referendum on district policies and practices would be on the commissioners' election ballot every two years. The PUDs would have the right to issue revenue bonds in a businesslike manner, but to issue general obligation bonds beyond a set low limit, they must get voter approval. Commissioners would be paid a small per diem in lieu of salary, and actual expenses could be reimbursed if itemized on a public voucher. Needless to say, the fights were intense at the Legislature as private power opposed any law changes that would make the PUDs more efficient or more businesslike.

Many of the private versus public power political fights of this decade concerned the federal power program. After the death of J. D. Ross in 1939, Dr. Paul J. Raver came on the scene as Bonneville Administrator following two interim appointees. Raver had been head of the Illinois Commerce Commission, which regulated utilities in that state. While he was to head up the federal power transmission and sales program then developing in the Pacific Northwest, he did not anticipate the rough fight against it by the private power companies. Since Bonneville was to become the power supply department for many of the PUDs and rural electric cooperatives being formed and activated, he was soon leading his expert staff in the public power crusade. Issues such as establishing a Pacific Northwest power pool to coordinate power generated by the federal dams with power from non-federal utilities were of great importance. The private power companies either opposed the pool outright or tried to use it to get special power sales contracts with the government. Some of the larger publicly owned utilities which generated their own power did not want federal lines in their areas, fearing that they would lose the federal power loads they were serving. World War II, which increased the need for power at particular locations, such as shipyards and housing for military personnel, forced the issue. Sol Schultz, Bonneville Chief Engineer, and Dr. William Dittmer, Bonneville Power Manager, made good use of the War Production Board's powers to cultivate power pooling and interconnected transmission. Private versus public power issues got hot and heavy, and one of the hottest issues was whether Bonneville would have the right to wheel federal power over private power lines and substations to reach new PUDs or rural electric cooperatives seeking federal power supplies. Power supply was coming on line from the federal dams faster than newly activated PUDs and cooperatives needed it. Thus, private power companies were asking for power sales contracts with Bonneville. At the same time, several PUDs could not be served by Bonneville because Congress had failed to appropriate funds to build needed lines and substations. It took a defiant stand by Dr. Raver, at the urging of the Washington PUD Commissioners, to refuse to grant contracts for sale of federal power to private power companies unless these companies granted the use of their lines in the contract for wheeling to PUDs.

In 1946, control of the House of Representatives in Congress passed to the Republicans and some strong private power supporters took over key congressional committee chairmanships. Here in the Pacific Northwest the private power companies started to use the old divide and conquer routine on public power. Along with the larger public power utilities which owned generating plants, the private companies established the Pacific Northwest

Utilities Conference Committee, based on the so-called Tacoma Agreement Group, which coordinated operation of the non-federal power plants with the plants of the federal government. Bonneville Administrator Raver had encouraged formation of this group, thinking that such a committee would support Bonneville's building of backbone federal transmission lines. However, while the committee was purported to have been formed to handle technical and engineering aspects of coordination, it ended up being a political policy group that was anti-Bonneville and anti-federal power. Private power found a natural ally in the Tacoma city-owned utility which did not want Bonneville service in its area. Certain large federal loads, such as Fort Lewis, were then served by Tacoma Light, which did not want to lose that business. Then, too, bordering Tacoma were the several small mutuals, cooperatives, and small city systems served by Tacoma which would be eligible for Bonneville service under the preference clause in the law that said public utilities had first call on federal power. Tacoma fought Bonneville service to these utilities until well into the 1970s.

C. A. "Clif" Erdahl, Commissioner of Utilities for Tacoma, was selected Chairman of the new PNUCC. In 1947, Frank Stewart of the State PUD Association overheard a conversation between Kinsey Robinson, President of Washington Water Power, and another Spokane businessman in which Robinson told the businessman he was making a trip from Spokane to Portland to participate in a group of private and public power utilities to "head off the work of Bonneville Power." When the businessman questioned the advisability of "getting in bed with public power," Robinson assured him that the committee had a "friendly public power man, Clif Erdahl of Tacoma Light, as the chairman." The group was given greater credibility with public power people when Clint Hurd, President of the Northwest Public Power Association and Manager of the Cowlitz County PUD, joined.

Benton County and Klickitat County PUDs had acquired properties from Pacific Power and Light, so Paul McKee, President of Pacific Power and Light, proposed to Dr. Raver that Pacific Power and Light would sell power to the PUDs but at rates higher than the federal power rates. This would not only pay for use of the private lines, but it would also compensate Pacific Power and Light for having to run its costly oil-fired steam plants to serve its own loads. The matter came to a head in the hearing by Congress on Bonneville funds in the House Appropriations Subcommittee in early 1947.

Congressman Ben Jensen of Iowa was Chairman of the Subcommittee. Erdahl, as Chairman of the PNUCC, introduced himself as a "public power representative" and then called on the private power persons in the group to testify. Their strategy was to support the Bonneville backbone transmission lines, but to oppose one after another proposed Bonneville local service facility needed to serve a small PUD or cooperative, testifying that the service could be provided by a non-federal facility already in place or on the planning schedules. By preventing these small utilities from receiving federal power, private power meant to leave Bonneville with a surplus if Bonneville continued to refuse to grant power sales contracts to the private power companies. This play would also put a facility owned or controlled by a private company between Bonneville and the local utility. It was during these hearings that Congressman Jensen referred to the State of Washington as the Soviet State of Washington, implying that public power was un-American.

At this time a division in the congressional delegations from the Pacific Northwest occurred. Since the 1930s, active support for the federal public power program, as well as the local public power activities, had come from both the Republican and Democratic sides of the aisle by congressmen from Oregon and Washington. They all fought for authorization of Bonneville facilities and new dams for the Corps of Engineers and Bureau of Reclamation projects. Strong joint support also followed in the Appropriations Committees to get the dollars needed to move ahead on development of the Columbia River power resources.

However, the year 1947 found Republican Congressman Lowell Stockman of Oregon opposing Republican Senator Guy Cordon of Oregon over Bonneville appropriations. Stockman was from eastern Oregon where private power service was dominant. Cordon, joined by the strong support of Senator Warren G. Magnuson of Washington, fought for full Bonneville financing needs. Many of the House cuts were restored when the Senate conferees were instructed by a vote of the full Senate to take this action in the conference committee. However, some needed facilities were lost for this one year as the result of the misleading joint private/public power testimony of the PNUCC.

Over on the House side, strong public power voices, such as those of Congressman Walt Horan (Republican), Russell V. Mack (Republican), and then Congressman Henry M. Jackson (Democrat), were answering the Jensen tirades, and intense political fights over private versus public power in the Pacific Northwest were occurring in Congress.

Kinsey Robinson, appearing in May 1946 before congressional committees where public power people were trying to get Foster Creek Dam in Washington (later renamed Chief Joseph Dam) approved for construction, had said the dam was not needed and made his famous statement, "I have been in the power business since I was seventeen years of age and I always thought I was quite an optimist as far as being able to sell power. But there is a limit to the amount of power you can even give away in any area, particularly in Washington, Oregon, and Idaho with their small population." Within three years of that speech, the Pacific Northwest was faced with brownouts from a power shortage. Fortunately, the public power forces, led by Senator Magnuson in the Senate, and Congressman Walt Horan in the House, got Chief Joseph Dam under way over private power opposition.

With President Harry Truman's election in 1948, efforts to establish a Columbia Valley Authority, to be patterned after the Tennessee Valley Authority, surfaced in Congress. However, behind-the-scenes lobbying by the Army Corps of Engineers and the Bureau of Reclamation supported the private power opposition and the bills did not get too far. There was division even in public power ranks over the proposed CVA. A constant and growing concern of the public power utilities, which wanted to maintain local home rule, was that some of their authority might pass to federal agencies. Even the Northwest Public Power Association and the Washington Public Utility Commissioners' Association argued over certain federal involvement and influence in the late 1940s. In July 1950, the National Electric Light Association, an organization of private power companies, adopted a platform calling for the use of interstate compacts to market power from federal dams. Such compacts would eliminate the preference provisions, whereby power from federal facilities went to local public and cooperatively owned utilities first. Attempts to do away with these preference provisions led to a prolonged fight over a Columbia River Interstate Compact for the Pacific Northwest states of Washington, Oregon, Idaho, and Montana, in every legislative session from 1953 to 1965.

Fortunately, the PUD commissioners stood pat, even in the face of the 1947 defeat of Bonneville funding for facilities and, fortunately, Dr. Raver was strong in his determination not to be dictated to by private power political pressure. While a contract to sell Bonneville power to the private power companies on a joint basis was signed in 1947, the amount of power was limited and the contract was for only one year. It included wheeling rights whereby Bonneville could send power to public power utilities over private lines. Federal power reached the new utilities at federal power rates – and future Congresses funded the needed facilities. Private power benefited because for each firm (guaranteed) kilowatt-hour transmitted to a public or cooperative utility over private power lines by Bonneville, the company supplying the lines received two kilowatt-hours of interruptible power (supplied when it was available) from Bonneville. Since the private companies had backup steam plants and had formed an Inter Company Pool of power, they all had access to this interruptible power. In practical use, it was as good as firm power.

Even within one "family" of local public power there was controversy. In the Washington Public Utility Commissioners' Association there was internal bickering between those who were promoting acquisition of private power properties by condemnation and those who were promoting acquisition by negotiated purchase.

I use the word "promoting" for a special reason. Most of the effort to form, activate, and operate locally owned public power utility districts was made by dedicated local citizens who volunteered their services to the movement. All of the PUD commissioners in the beginning years served without any salary or per diem payments or even reimbursement for a lot of their expenses. Unpaid work was the foundation of local public power. However, it would be less than honest not to acknowledge that a great many dedicated people who worked in the movement were motivated by that good old American desire to "make a buck."

Guy Myers worked as a fiscal agent for the PUDs for a commission, and the holding company presidents encouraged PUD commissioners to move ahead whenever a negotiated buyout would make more money for their stockholders. The legal firms handling all the condemnation actions were being paid for their work and thus PUD commissioners were encouraged by them to move ahead with these actions. Consulting engineers were always needed by the districts, and they had their own need for income. As the years passed, more and more of the investment bond houses furnishing needed financing established local representatives to "call on the commissioners."

After saying these things, I ought to point out that the commissions, legal retainer fees, and engineering service costs—yes, even the financing margins—paid by the PUDs, were very much lower than fees for comparable services paid by the private power companies. I have a total of the fees paid to Guy Myers in his twenty-plus years as a fiscal agent for various PUDs and their projects. It does not come close to the salary and other financial benefits of a single private power president serving in the same period of time. And Myers paid all of his expenses out of his commissions.

The fact that there were two opposing camps on how to activate a PUD caused continuing conflict within the PUD ranks. In May 1942, the conflict forced the resignation of Harry W. Pierson (Grant County PUD), President of the Washington Public Utility Commissioners' Association. Pierson took a trip to Chicago and New York paid for by investment bankers favoring negotiated sales. This caused commissioners supporting condemnation of private power properties to challenge his fairness as a leader. Secretary of the Interior Harold Ickes became involved when he gave off-the-record instructions to the Bonneville staff to kill a negotiated purchase of Puget Power in which a Bonneville employee, who was later to resign, would have made a lucrative commission if the purchase had been consummated. Things were rather rocky inside the family, as well as from the outside, with all the private power fights.

By 1946, Guy Myers and Bob Beck had negotiated a system-wide purchase of Puget Power properties with Frank McLaughlin, Puget Power's President, and his holding company owners in Boston. One PUD, Skagit County, was to purchase the entire utility and then transfer properties to each of the other PUDs in whose areas the properties were located. The generating facilities and non-PUD area facilities would be operated by a joint board made up of members from the seven PUDs involved. The "Skagit deal" became an issue in the Initiative 166 campaign that year, having landed in the courts.

When the State Supreme Court failed to render a timely decision—taking over a year to decide following the hearing of the case—the Washington State Grange at its 1947 session complained about the delay. In a surprising response, the Chief Justice publicly criticized one Justice for not making up his mind. Evidently, the indecisive Justice had the deciding vote, and when he cast it, the decision came down five to four against the PUDs. That particular Justice was later accused of accepting large loans from pinball interests while a case involving slot machines was pending in the court, and he was subsequently defeated in his re-election effort. The majority opinion on the Skagit case was written by a Justice who had been secretary of the statewide Committee on Referendum 25 which private power had sponsored in 1944 repealing the law passed in the 1943 Session allowing joint PUD acquisition of private power property. It was a tough legal opinion against the PUDs.

In March 1943, Snohomish County PUD, with Jack Cluck as its attorney, had completed a condemnation case against Puget Power, but the established price of $9,500,000 was criticized by Dr. Raver as being too high and the PUD did not accept the award. Following the court decision against the Skagit purchase, Snohomish County PUD started to move ahead to accept the previously obtained condemnation award. This prompted McLaughlin to sell Puget Power distribution facilities in Lewis and Chelan counties in 1948 and in Snohomish County in September 1949. Puget Power was paid $16,500,000 for the Snohomish properties—nearly five times gross annual revenues—and certain public power voices, including mine, were very critical of Myers for paying $7 million more than the condemnation award, but history has proven that it was a good buy. This sale occurred after the Joint Action Law to open the way for negotiating a sale of the remaining Puget Power properties was passed at the 1949 Session of the Legislature.

The Chelan sale further demonstrated the fierce and intense pressures in the private versus public power fight. The 1948 negotiations between Puget Power and Chelan County PUD were proceeding with dispatch. Word got out that agreement was close and that the PUD would be approaching the bond market to secure funds for the purchase.

One effective weapon used by private power proponents was the last minute legal challenge, which would cast a shadow over bond issuance and thus block the sale.

Sure enough, in the last week of the Chelan purchase the negotiating group was tipped off to anticipate a "taxpayers' lawsuit" against the Chelan County PUD Commissioners. Similar lawsuits which had been filed previously as blocking efforts had been dismissed—but only after maneuvered court delays.

Here were three PUD commissioners, elected by majority vote of the people of Chelan County, who had voted in favor of having a public power district. They were negotiating in good faith and had secured an agreed upon price from the willing seller of the property, but they were now being faced by a fake taxpayers' lawsuit sponsored by an outside interest. Word had it that Kinsey Robinson was trying to block this sale to protect his generating plant at Chelan Falls.

The result of this suit was to turn honest elected officials into subpoena-dodging fugitives in order to carry out their sworn public trust. They hid out in three different locations, calling in to a central point, while necessary legal documents and revenue bond issuance documents were being drafted for their approval and signatures.

Billy McKenzie, one of the commissioners, told how he would call up the central point and ask, "Has the moon risen yet?" to thwart possible wiretapping, which was practiced even in those days. Upon being informed that it hadn't, he would hide out another day.

Finally, the moment came when everything was in order. The commissioners gathered, called an adjourned meeting back to order, passed the needed resolution, signed the documents to issue the bonds, completed the purchase, and adjourned the meeting. Deputy sheriff process servers were actually approaching as this took place. Since there was no substance in the legal challenge, it was immediately dropped by the persons sponsoring it. Even private power presidents did not like to pay useless attorneys' fees.

There were no holds barred in the private versus public power fight.

In the early 1940s, the Securities and Exchange Commission had issued a directive ordering the Eastern holding companies to dispose of their captive private power utilities in the Pacific Northwest. American Power and Light Company, which owned all of the common stock of Washington Water Power, Pacific Power and Light, and Northwestern Electric — plus several other utilities — started some maneuvering and negotiating which unleashed several hot legislative and court fights. First they attempted in 1947 to merge Washington Water Power and Pacific Power and Light. This merger was opposed by public power leaders, the State Grange, and State labor groups. The State Public Service Commission had helped by refusing to approve the merger when Chelan County PUD, in May 1950, filed a condemnation suit on the Merwin Dam owned by Pacific Power and Light. The dam was clear across the State from Chelan — but public power people were learning the lesson from private power people that hamstringing lawsuits can cloud financial deals. Following this merger defeat, the owner of Pacific Power and Light (AP&L) sold the common stock to a private underwriting group who could rightfully be called speculators. After holding the stock just long enough to avoid paying capital gains on short-term investments, the first group of private power stockholders sold the stock to new owners, and the value of the stock jumped from $10 million to over $20 million in just one year. Such financial wheeling and dealing was a good example of disregard of consumer interests by the owners of private power — but public power officials could not block the maneuver.

Disposal of ownership of Washington Water Power by AP&L also stimulated a rough fight. Howard Aller, President of AP&L, was looking for the highest bidder. Guy Myers negotiated an arrangement whereby three PUDs (Chelan, Stevens, and Pend Oreille) would acquire all the common stock of Washington Water Power, and stock held on Washington Water Power property in Idaho would go to a nonprofit corporation in that state. This arrangement unleashed legislative fights in both Idaho and Washington, SEC rulings, and federal appellate court fights. Actually the persons fighting for private ownership of Washington Water Power, headed by Kinsey Robinson, won when the SEC issued a decision making the sale of the stock to the PUDs subject to approval of the SEC. While the SEC law clearly stated that local political subdivisions, as well as the state governments under which they operate, were exempt from SEC jurisdiction, a federal appellate court refused to hear the case after being persuaded by the SEC that the issue wasn't ripe for court review. In other words, the mere issuance of an order by the SEC that the matter might come under its jurisdiction created a cloud over the financial dealings of the PUDs, yet they had no recourse to the courts to clear the issue. The negotiations between Aller and Myers stimulated a rough private versus public power fight in the 1951 Session of the Washington Legislature.

The efforts of the PUDs to acquire Puget Power also raised some differences between the PUDs and Tacoma Light. As stated earlier, Clif Erdahl, Tacoma Commissioner of Utilities, joined with Kinsey Robinson and other private power officials in the so-called Tacoma Agreement which was viewed as pro-private power. Thus in March 1948, when Erdahl recommended that Tacoma condemn the Puget Power generating plants at White River and Electron, his move prompted some overnight condemnation filings by two PUDs, since Tacoma's proposed action would block PUD purchase of those plants. Erdahl's proposal exacerbated the bad feelings among the PUDs against Tacoma which had started at the 1947 congressional hearings. Resentment against Erdahl erupted violently in the 1951 Session of the Legislature over the Spokane Power Bill which he supported and which the PUDs opposed because it was designed to kill the sale of Washington Water Power to the three eastern Washington PUDs.

While this book concerns the growth of local public power in this State and the Pacific Northwest and particularly in the public utility district movement, it should be remembered that the original initiative sponsored by the State Grange in 1930 called for "development of the water resources" to supply both electric and water utility service to local areas. Until the 1950s, no separate effective public water district law had been passed, and therefore local people used the PUD law to provide public water service in many areas. However, once a PUD was formed, it had all the powers under the PUD law, including the right to provide electric utility service.

As pressure grew in rural King County for water utility service during the early 1950s, a new law to allow formation of public water districts only was passed by the Legislature.

It was interesting to see how Puget Power would encourage new water-only districts throughout the area to avoid formation of a PUD to provide water service. It has been said that King County, Washington, ended up with more sub-public water and fire districts than any other county west of Cook County, Illinois.

The PUD law has been used to provide water service in Washington by creating sixteen PUDs operating one or more water districts, including several which provide water only and have never gone into electric service.

After a 1948 power shortage, local utilities looked for ways to augment federal dam power. Tacoma Light moved toward its Cowlitz River projects; PUDs commenced studying future dams on the mid-Columbia; and Idaho

Power proposed building low level dams in the Hells Canyon stretch of the Snake River. The latter move set the stage for intense private versus public power fights before Congress and the regulatory agencies in the 1950s.

Summary

The 1940 decade saw county-wide service by twenty of today's twenty-two electric operating PUDs; defeat of private power's "vote on bonds" statewide initiatives in 1940 and 1946; defeat of public power's 1943 joint condemnation legislation by a private power referendum in 1944; a victory for public power in Congress to get region-wide Bonneville federal power service to small PUDs and rural cooperatives, after a setback in 1947; the start of several new federal dams over private power opposition, but defeat of a Columbia Valley Authority concept by private power with the help of certain federal agencies; defeat of a Washington Water Power/Pacific Power and Light merger by AP&L, which resulted in the sale of Pacific Power and Light stock to new private power ownership at a substantially higher stock value; blocking of the sale of all of the Puget Power properties to PUDs by ongoing legal challenges; passage of a joint action and negotiated purchase law by PUDs in 1949, plus other needed improvements in the basic PUD law; and, finally, movement by PUDs to buy Washington Water Power from AP&L, which resulted in a 1951 legislative stand-off between private power and public power.

Money in Politics

Contrary to a prevalent view of the general public, the votes of individual legislators are not for sale.

I am aware of the attempt in 1951 to buy votes for the so-called Spokane Power Bill which was exposed by two pro-public power legislators from Pierce County and resulted in a jail term for the briber. I know that certain legislators were found to have been on a hidden payroll of a private power company for several years. Former legislator Bob Perry was indicted and went to prison for tax fraud and extortion and then later testified in a lawsuit exposing private power's use of political funds. A private power company retained the law firms of a senator and a representative which seemed to compromise their pro-public power position, and the manager of the old Olympian Hotel told me that the room bill for a particular legislator who sponsored anti-public power legislation was always sent to the private power lobbyist. I am aware of other instances, rumored and actual, which could make me sound like a Pollyanna, but I spent thirty years in the legislative arena and came out of the experience with the firm belief that if a vote is ever bought in Olympia, it is an extreme exception, not the rule.

Money talks in politics just as it does in business. Politics is business, the business of government. But if there is outright graft in this State, I am not aware of it. There is, of course, money to be made legally in politics. Individuals who support winning candidates are looked on favorably for State jobs, such as architects, special attorneys used by the Attorney General's office, legislative staff jobs, and many other administrative and management activities, and when a preponderance of either Republicans or Democrats are selected for these jobs, such selections can have the flavor of partisan politics. But such favoritism is no more prevalent in the political arena than in most of our private business activities. Because of the public visibility of elected officials, I personally feel that partisan hiring is less prevalent in government than it is in private business. I have been aware of certain legislation sponsored by a particular legislator which would result in a law that would benefit him or her financially, and there is no question that service in the Legislature attracts a good supply of clients to a practicing attorney or his or her legal firm. But my observation has been that the overwhelming number of persons who serve in the Legislature are honest, sincere, and of above average intelligence. Many who served during my period of involvement took a definite loss financially, because of time spent away from their private businesses, and made sacrifices and asked their families to make sacrifices for the sake and honor of public service.

During my years as a Washington PUD Association lobbyist in Olympia, I won a lot of crucial votes for public power although public power did not have money to spend on politics. It would have been illegal to spend ratepayers' dollars in that way, and as for private funds, I was having a hard time raising enough money to keep the PUD Association in business. Because the PUD Association was and is a private non-profit corporation (membership by a PUD is entirely voluntary), an early Attorney General's opinion cleared its right to lobby. Most certainly, the legal beagles of the private power companies would have challenged my political activity had there been any chance of winning a lawsuit that would stop it.

The PUD Association did have a small fund with which I could buy tickets to political fund-raising events, such as dinners for State political parties and candidates. I had to attend these functions just to get acquainted. But we made no direct contributions to campaigns, with one exception in 1972. The PUD Association did not even help out certain candidates by furnishing stamps to their campaign headquarters, a popular hidden form of support used by some groups. Since federal law prohibits the use of corporation moneys to support federal campaigns, I used my personal money to attend fund raisers of candidates for federal offices. When the small PUD Association allowance for state fund raisers ran out, I used personal money to attend legitimate fund raisers of State and local political election candidates, and I never received reimbursement for this by inflating my expense account. Looking back on my personal political expenditures on behalf of public power, I see that if it had not been for a frugal wife who could keep family expenditures down, plus previously accrued family financial resources, I could not have afforded to be the public power lobbyist as the Executive of the PUD Association.

The one and only contribution for a political purpose made by the PUD Association during my tenure as its Executive was $500 contributed in 1972 to the grass roots committee sponsoring Initiative 276—our State's present Public Disclosure Law. We made this contribution in June, after my friend, Mort Frayn, former Republican legislator and Speaker of the Republican controlled House in 1953, invited me to a breakfast meeting with a number of Seattle business leaders. Frayn said, "Look, these people are out of money and need help to get this initiative passed." My Board of Directors grumbled a little, but on my urging they agreed to make the contribution.

In 1976, during the campaign by the anti-nuclear power proponents of Initiative 325, I, along with the PUD Association, was accused before the Public Disclosure Commission of using public funds for political activity. We had not given money to the campaign, but were running some pro-nuclear power ads. We were cleared of all charges when we proved to the Commission that we had been running these ads for two years before the election, and their frequency had not increased during the campaign.

The use of my own personal funds in political campaigns was a personal investment in my professional pursuit. I made the investment in order to do a better job for the PUDs. One political cause I personally raised money for was the so-called Senator Bob Greive Fund which became quite a news media item in later legislative sessions. In the fall of 1956 before the general election, I received a call from the Senator informing me that he had just obtained a $250 contribution from Puget Power and wondered what the PUD Association could do to raise money for the election of some Democratic senators. He suggested that we contribute $10 per senator to the twelve senators running for election. I responded by saying that one of the twelve was a Spokane senator who had never voted with us and therefore I would not give him a dollar even if I had it. I also reminded him that the PUD Association did not make political contributions, nor had I done so personally since coming to work there, except to participate in tickets to fund raisers.

That day, I had lunch with Gene Hoffman, former Superintendent of Seattle City Light. I told him about the conversation with Greive. Hoffman was a Republican but definitely a strong supporter of public power. I recounted to him the difficulty we faced on having to compete with the money of the private power companies. That afternoon about 3:30 p.m. Hoffman walked into my office and laid down two $20 bills and a $10 bill. I asked what they were for. He said, "I thought you needed $110 for Senator Greive." I said, "Yes, I do but after all, this is to elect a Democratic Senate and you are a Republican." His answer was, "If we are going to stop the efforts of Kinsey Robinson and the private power crowd, we are going to have to have a Democratic Senate." I accepted the $50.

I called R. C. Rodruck, Sr., who, as a private businessman and a public power supporter, did participate in political fund-raising events, and he also gave me $50. I then wrote a personal check to Senator Greive in the amount of $110 using $10 of my own money and sent it on its way. Shortly, I got a copy of a letter which he had sent to eleven different senators, forwarding the $10 public power contribution to each of them. I have kept the cancelled check as a personal memento.

In later sessions, there was quite a public fuss made over the Greive Fund. Greive raised money for his friends because he was elected from a rather safe district and then asked the legislators he had raised money for to vote for him for Senate majority floor leader. He was a practical politician who made political trades, but he never used his office illegally or for personal financial gain. By the 1963 and 1965 sessions, however, he had a closer alignment with the Spokane senators who primarily supported private power. He told me, "I never get support from PUD County Senators for my Senate majority leadership vote." I assume that money for the Greive Fund continued to come from private power sources because 1956 was the only time I ever raised money for the fund. In conversation with Kinsey Robinson and Paul McKee at a Pacific Northwest Utilities Conference Committee meeting in the mid-1950s, I said, "I'd sure like to get into one of these political combats with you people with some dollars like yours." Public power had just lost the Stevens County PUD sellout election. McKee said, "Ken, we'll trade our dollars for your votes any day you want to trade." That supports my belief that individual legislators are not for sale. Financial contributions to political candidates are essential if we are to keep our free democracy. It is rough sometimes when you are on the side with little funds, but I would be the last one to criticize or complain about political contributions.

Sometimes when public power legislators were approached by private power lobbyists offering political contributions, the lawmakers would ask me what to do. I always told them, "Take their money and vote against them." Some of them did, I'm sure.

From our earliest days, we are cultivated as individuals to be a winner. As school kids in our essay contests and sports, we strive to be a winner. So we require our senators and representatives and other public officials to be winners. And they, too, as individuals want to be winners. In today's legislative races, with the larger populations in each legislative district, it takes mass media advertising to be a winner, to put across to a wide voter population that this candidate will pass the laws they want passed if he or she is elected. Advertising costs money and therefore the candidates and their political parties go after fund raising with a vengeance. All voters should respond, and while cash is important, volunteer work can also be of value. Your contribution will, as it should, make you known to your legislator, but I believe after thirty years of experience that it won't buy his or her vote.

Besides campaign contributions, lobbyists and others spend money on the established practice of wining and dining legislators and other public officials. Some go so far as to provide them with tickets or seats at sporting events or other entertainments. Most of these occasions are for no other purpose than getting some time alone with the official. During the legislative sessions, hundreds of lobbyists are vying for the legislator's attention to a particular problem. Using meal times or after adjournment time is one way to do it. I couldn't afford such entertainment simply because of a limited PUD Association budget, and it took a lot of effort to get equal time with a legislator to offset my private power counterparts with their very liberal use of such methods. However, the fact that I was able to get lawmakers to vote for public power bills without wining and dining them is additional evidence that their votes were not for sale.

Our whole political system is based on principles that all of us, including public officials, establish and support. Our two-party political system exists because Republican principles differ somewhat from Democratic ones. That legislator best represents his or her constituency whose principles agree most closely with those of the majority of voters. Thus a legislator from Spokane is likely to believe in private power and vote for its interest whether courted by a lobbyist or not, as a legislator from a public utility district is likely to vote in the interests of public power even after eating at Kinsey Robinson's table.

Legislators like political contributions and being wined and dined, but this merely proves that people in public office are human. People who have not participated directly in the political process and who complain, criticize, and view legislators and public officials as a bunch of crooks for accepting legal hospitality from lobbyists ought to examine their own human traits and ask themselves whether they would sell their principles for a good dinner, or whether they would think of it as a fair trade for an hour of their attention, with no further obligation incurred.

3

1951–1956 Era
Face-Off, Fights, and Failures

1951–1952

THE YEAR 1951 started with a bang in private versus public power affairs with battles being fought in the State Legislature. The Democrats had a 25 to 21 majority in the Senate, which nevertheless was controlled by private power when Democratic senators from Spokane joined in a coalition with the Republican minority to organize the committees. The Public Utilities Committee was headed by Senator Henry Copeland, Republican from Walla Walla and an arch-private power supporter. Of his committee of nine, six had supported private power in the past. These six included three Spokane Democrats. The three members who were pro-public power, one Republican and two Democrats, came from PUD counties. On the House side, a Democratic 54 to 45 majority retained Representative Charles Hodde as Speaker and selected a pro-public power Utilities Committee with a majority of 8 to 3. Hodde was a long-time public power supporter, having commenced his legislative work as a lobbyist in the early 1930s for the Washington State Grange. He was elected to the House in 1937, defeated in 1939, and re-elected in 1943, and rose to the Speakership by the 1949 Session.

With active negotiations going on for three eastern Washington PUDs to acquire the common stock of Washington Water Power from AP&L, the Idaho Legislature rushed a law through, under private power urging, making it illegal for any PUD to own property in that state. The law also established substantial penalties and fines for PUD officials found guilty of trying to acquire property for a public utility. In this State, efforts to block the PUD purchase took the form of legislation providing that the City of Spokane would have a vote on the matter. Proponents of the bill were claiming that public power was being "rammed down the throats" of the Spokane people who had never voted for public power. This legislation was supported by Governor Arthur B. Langlie, who came from the City of Seattle and as its former Mayor had been supportive of Seattle City Light, but felt strongly that local people should have the right to vote on whether they wanted public power. Backed by the Governor's support, the Senate passed the bill by a vote of 28 to 17. To offset this pro-private power legislation, the PUD forces sponsored a bill mandating that the City of Spokane would have the right to acquire such properties from the PUDs should the purchase occur, and that the city could make the purchase by condemning any such PUD-owned properties. The issues bounced back and forth between the Senate and the House by means of parliamentary maneuvers until March 7, when utter confusion arose over a statement on the House floor by a Pierce County representative that he and one other member had been offered a bribe to support the Spokane Power Bill. His accusations resulted in the investigation and jailing of the person he named although no direct link could be established between that person and the private power lobbyists who were suspected of being behind the bribe. The result was defeat of the Spokane Power Bill in the House 55 to 44 and passage by the Legislature of the PUD-sponsored legislation to make sure that if the PUDs' purchase went forward, the people of Spokane could take over the properties in that city.

It was during this legislative session that an event took place which changed my personal life. Frank Stewart had left the Washington Public Utility Commissioners' Association in early 1950 to pursue business developments in Brewster where construction of the Chief Joseph Dam had just started. Replacing Stewart as Executive Secretary was John McCauley, who had previously joined the PUD Association's staff as an editor of its newsletter. During House consideration of the public power sponsored bill, a vote on the House floor was scheduled for a Friday. On Monday of that week, McCauley sent a special notice to the various PUD commissioners around the State which included a list of House members whom Mc-

Cauley labeled as being ready to vote for the bill; a list of those opposed to it; and a list of those whose intentions were not known. He was urging the commissioners to contact the legislators on the "Not Known" list and ask for their support. On Friday, just before the vote, an opponent of the bill who somehow had obtained a copy of McCauley's notice arose and asked his fellow members if they would like to know how they were going to vote on the matter. He then proceeded to read off the lists. Fortunately, this embarrassing revelation did not hinder passage of the pro-public power legislation, but shortly thereafter McCauley left to join a congressional staff in Washington, D.C., and the Washington Public Utility Commissioners' Association was looking for a new Executive Secretary.

Because of my statewide work on the joint labor negotiations effort, my volunteer work with the old Public Power League, and the two sessions I had helped out in Olympia to get legislation passed providing for more efficient PUD operation, several PUD persons from around the State asked me if I was interested in the job. I was, I applied, I was interviewed, and I was hired. I moved my family to Seattle and started my new job in May 1951.

While I had been somewhat acquainted with the Washington Public Utility Commissioners' Association and its staff by means of its self-owned service corporation now called the Public Utility Clearing House, I was not aware of the sorry financial status of my new employer. When I arrived on the scene, I found about $300 on hand and some dead-horse bills from attorneys and a printing firm of several thousand dollars. The salary of my one employee, a very efficient and dedicated secretary-bookkeeper, was due. We scrounged around among the member districts who were still loyal to the Association and got enough money to stay in business, although I waited several times for my paycheck. On August 6, a special membership meeting which I requested was held in Wenatchee. Politely but firmly, I told the PUD commissioners and managers in attendance that it was not my Association and that if I had to spend my time running around the State encouraging the PUD membership to keep it alive, I would not have time to do the work I could see needed doing. I agreed to stay on until January 1952, and if necessary to use some of my own personal money, but I said that if at that time we were not a going endeavor, I would have to look elsewhere for work, since I had a family to support. Their reaction was terrific and from that low point the Association became a viable instrument of coordination and service on mutual projects and interests of the PUDs in the State of Washington, the Pacific Northwest, and the nation.

Facing my responsibility as Association Executive, including its lobbying work, I hoped there would be time to get up to speed by the 1953 Session. This would allow me to go through another election of all House members and some senators, giving me a chance to get acquainted with them. My luck ran out in August. A special session was called by Governor Langlie because of a financial crisis in the State government. I did not go to Olympia immediately, with the other utility lobbyists, because my entire effort at that time was in trying to keep the Association afloat.

I got a call from Larry Karrer, Vice President of Puget Power, advising me that an increase in the State utility excise tax was definitely being considered. This tax on gross revenues is levied on all electric utilities in a manner that prevents it from being immediately passed on to customers. Since a utility is a monopoly, whether privately or publicly owned, any taxes are ultimately passed on to the consumers, but in this case, the tax is not separated from utility revenues and any increase must be absorbed by the utility until a future rate adjustment can be secured. I left for Olympia at once.

As I walked into the balcony area running between the House and Senate under the Capitol dome, which is referred to as "Ulcer Gulch" by legislators and lobbyists, I was amazed to see the reaction of the other utility lobbyists. Here were persons representing all the large private power companies, the telephone companies, and the railroads. Each was representing a powerful separate group, but they were all waiting for the PUD lobbyist to get there.

The first question fired at me was whether or not I knew what was going on. I said I did not because I had just arrived, but that I knew a man who could inform me. I then placed a phone call through to Charles Hodde, Speaker of the House. I said I had just arrived and that I did not know my way about very well so I thought I might as well start at the top. Since both chambers were under call, he said he would meet me at the House north door and take me to his office. When he appeared, I could not help noticing the respectful envy in the faces of my fellow utility lobbyists.

I now knew why the other utilities had been waiting for the PUD lobbyist. Evidently, I had inherited substantial influence and power by virtue of being the only lobbyist who spoke for basic local public power in the State at the legislative sessions. It was indeed interesting and I later made up my mind that the only way to protect such courtesy was never to over-use, abuse, or flaunt it. This resolution was my guide thereafter, even when I have stood in the gallery watching fellow lobbyists move in and out of the chambers when they were not supposed to go in there. Possibly I could have done the same, but I never did. At any rate, once I was inside Speaker Hodde's office, he outlined the situation and told me his plan. He said under no circumstances could I divulge where this particular tax package was coming from—and most certainly, not over on the Senate side where his "presence" would be its kiss of death. I learned early and at first hand of the intense rivalry between the two equal bodies and how the leaders in each of them use other means to infiltrate and plant ideas which end up being the other guys' position and which in the final action can be viewed as a "compromise."

Hodde, being a strong public power supporter, believed in the benefits which low electric rates could bring to our State. Thus he wanted to avoid increasing the utility tax. His proposal was to substitute another tax package, including taxes on soft drinks and cigarettes. It did not occur to me at the moment but Hodde has never smoked although I've seen him drink an occasional soda pop.

Upon leaving his office, I took my fellow utility lobbyists into my confidence. We planned our assault on the Senate by assigning certain senators to each of us and away we went. It worked. The House passed one version of a tax package, the Senate had one of theirs (which included Hodde's ideas), and the compromise included a utility tax, but it was reduced from a proposed 5 percent to 3.3 percent. This was an increase of only .3 percent, and the increase had a definite termination date. I would not want to indicate that it was only our efforts which led to this result. There are many factors involved in the legislative process. Sometimes votes turn on events that have nothing to do with the issue at hand. I won a Rules Committee vote in 1967 against private power in just such a manner and I did not know how it really happened until 1972 when a private power lobbyist told me his side of the incident. Our effort in 1951 on taxes was only one of many that influenced the outcome. But at least for ourselves and for our bosses, the Hodde strategy to keep electric rates from being increased by higher taxes paid off.

The years 1951 and 1952 saw a lot of activity outside of the legislative arena for local public power and the PUDs. The City of Seattle, which had earlier dropped out of the joint purchase plan of Puget Power being worked on by Guy Myers, had separately negotiated a price with that company to purchase its properties in Seattle. Voter approval had been sought in November 1950 under ballot Proposition C, which failed at the ballot box, and the outcome could not be determined until the absentee ballots were counted. There was also some confusion over invalid ballots, so it was not until that matter had been settled that final count of all ballots resulted in approval by only 724 votes. Seattle City Light got the Puget Power properties for $28 million and completed the transfer in March 1951. It was a good purchase to knock out the wasteful competitive duplication of service, but it was a much more costly purchase when the duplicate and unusable lines of Puget Power had to be removed or integrated with the City Light facilities.

Trouble was also occurring in Guy Myers' negotiated PUD purchase of Puget Power. PUD commissioner elections in November 1950 had put new faces on PUD boards (Kitsap and Skagit), and these commissioners just happened to voice the same type of opposition to the purchase which Washington Water Power President Kinsey Robinson was voicing — although Robinson was not opposing it publicly.

Secretary of the Interior Oscar Chapman, under the Truman Administration, called for construction of a regional intertie between the Bonneville Power Administration and the Central Valley Project of the Bureau of Reclamation in northern California in January 1951. This set off the opposition alarm bells in PUD ranks. Loss of the low cost federal power to California was not acceptable.

A hearing was held in Spokane on February 24, 1951, by the Securities and Exchange Commission on the proposed purchase of the Washington Water Power common stock by the three eastern Washington PUDs. Following this, Guy Myers negotiated a sale to the PUDs with Howard Aller, President of AP&L, for $65,115,000, which was announced in January 1952. When the SEC reasserted jurisdiction over the matter in February, the PUDs attempted to get a restraining order from the 9th Circuit Court of Appeals but failed there. The sale was lost on March 28, 1952. The result was that AP&L was forced to distribute the Washington Water Power common stock among the AP&L stockholders. This established Washington Water Power as a new, separately owned private power company. Robinson had won his fight against Aller — and now moved harder against the PUD purchase of Puget Power. He began working on a merger of Washington Water Power and Puget Power using the same financial interests which had bought the Pacific Power and Light stock for a speculative profit in 1950. The PUDs earlier had made their offer to buy the remaining properties, including the generating plants of Puget Power, for $97 million with a proposed bond issue of $115 million. This deal also ran into trouble when the Whatcom County PUD dropped out of the joint purchase effort in September 1952.

Disposal of the Pacific Power and Light common stock by the speculators who had acquired it from AP&L in 1950 was completed in December 1951. This resulted in a tremendous rip-off profit which came to public view in the spring of 1952, and which I will describe later on. It was only the intervention of the Washington Public Utility Commissioners' Association which had prevented the intervening finance group from making an even greater profit. However, the sale established another new separately owned private power company based in the Pacific Northwest which later intensified the private versus public power political fights.

The year 1951 saw action by local utilities to boost the regional power supply by proposing to build their own dams. Pend Oreille County PUD filed for a Federal Power Commission preliminary permit to study what would become its Box Canyon Dam project. Idaho Power filed on the Oxbow site in January 1951, which set off the prolonged Hells Canyon Dam fight. Tacoma Light received its license to construct its Mayfield/Mossyrock Dams in November of that year; but, before construction could start, it would take a U.S. Supreme Court decision to overturn the Cowlitz River Sanctuary Bill, a State law which sportsmen and the State Department of Fisheries had persuaded the Legislature to pass in 1949. Chelan County PUD contracted with Puget Power to finance an extension of the Rock Island Dam near Wenatchee. Ground breaking took place on August 7, 1951. The extension increased the power supply for the Pacific Northwest and also allowed another new aluminum plant to be located at Wenatchee, responding to the need created by the Korean War.

In July 1952, Congress gave its approval for the five Pacific Northwest states to enter into an Interstate Compact to control the use of Columbia River waters. The private power forces seized on this compact as a way to eliminate the federal power marketing program, which gave preference to local public power and electric cooperatives for receiving federally generated electricity. Primary coordination of river and power development between federal and State agencies had been conducted through the Columbia Basin Inter-Agency Committee established in 1946, whose membership was made up of State representatives and representatives from those federal agencies dealing with power production, regulation, and transmission. But with this new states-only negotiating group, we weren't too sure what to expect!

An off-shoot of this drive to eliminate the federal marketing program was a Governors' Power Advisory Committee formed in 1953, which included the five governors of the Pacific Northwest states and federal agency representatives from the Corps of Engineers, the Bureau of Reclamation, the Federal Power Commission, and the Bonneville Power Administration. Governor Langlie and a pro-private power advisor of his, Holland Houston, were main proponents of the Committee, which had a strong flavor of states' rights versus federal rights. I anticipated a busy time being the eyes and ears and occasional voice for the PUDs.

The year 1952 also saw drafting of a new city charter for the City of Tacoma. One of my assignments in my new job as Executive of the Washington Public Utilities Commissioners' Association, which started in May 1951, was to heal the rift which had widened over the previous four years between Clif Erdahl, Commissioner of Utilities of Tacoma, and the PUD people. I tried; however, repeatedly, Erdahl made statements in the newspapers about the PUD purchase of Puget Power which aided and abetted the campaign his friend Kinsey Robinson was waging against the purchase. To protect myself, I gathered quite a file on Erdahl's published remarks, and got my Board's approval to become directly involved in the drafting of the city charter. My first effort, in which I was joined by Gus Norwood, my counterpart in the Northwest Public Power Association, was to lobby a charter provision whereby Tacoma Light would be administered by a utility board, separate and apart from City Hall. A staunch ally in this effort was State Representative A. B. Comfort, a local insurance man. Tacoma voters approved the new charter, with the provision we wanted, in November 1952, and Erdahl's office was eliminated. Later in 1953, as the new Utility Board sought a Director of Utilities, he was a strong contender for the job, and my involvement with the city's selection of a Director will be related in the next section, which covers 1953 and 1954.

Speaking of Gus Norwood of the NWPPA brings me to another interesting phase of my life in public power. I had met Gus in the 1940s before he was hired as NWPPA's Executive. He was very learned, very well educated, if not over-educated, with an all-out dedication to public power. He was as fanatical about it as I was to become over the years, perhaps even more fanatical. He had brains and courage – I had courage and political savvy. We were different, but we made a good team, and we have been long-time friends. However, our first relations as association executives got off to a rocky start.

Gus came out of World War II having served as an officer in the Navy. He had earlier graduated from the Naval Academy at Annapolis, and following the war, he did graduate work in public administration at Harvard. In Seattle, he became acquainted with the PUD Association staff and was hired in November 1947 as the first Executive Secretary of the NWPPA with offices in Vancouver, Washington, where I was first associated with him. NWPPA had been formed following a meeting of public power persons in Olympia on October 18, 1940. Its beginning purpose was to coordinate joint efforts of the larger public power utilities, several having generating resources of their own, but the membership was opened to include representatives from city systems, PUDs, and rural cooperatives in the four

Gus Norwood served as the first
Executive Secretary of the Northwest
Public Power Association from 1947
to 1966.

Courtesy NWPPA

Pacific Northwest states. In January 1941, the new group adopted a constitution and bylaws at Tacoma, and in August 1947, just before Gus was
hired, the association was incorporated at Longview.

I had accepted the job with the Washington Public Utility Commissioners' Association, had resigned my job with the Clark County PUD, and
was moving to Seattle when I became aware that some NWPPA members
wanted to abolish the PUD Association by consolidating the two associations. I spoke to Gus about this, and at the end of our conversation, which
clarified the issue, he recognized that there was a need for both groups, and
we agreed to give each other mutual support. Where our efforts would duplicate each other, this could only mean a stronger—not a competitive—
stand for public power. From there on, we worked in dual harness until he
was appointed the first Administrator for the new Alaska Power Administration in 1966 under the Johnson Administration. When President Nixon
took office, Norwood was of course relieved of that position, but as a federal employee, he was transferred to the Atomic Energy Commission near
Washington, D.C. In 1974, I ran into Gus in Washington, D.C. and he did
not seem very happy with his work. I suggested to Don Hodel, Administrator of Bonneville, that he "bring Gus home." He did so, assigning Gus to

write a policy history of the Bonneville Power Administration. As always, Gus did a brainy, thorough, and dedicated job.

When I arrived on the scene in 1951, the Washington Public Utility Commissioners' Association was a voluntary group interlocked organizationally with a private non-profit corporation originally named the Public Utility Research and Information Service. The officers and board of the Commissioners' Association automatically became the officers and board of the corporate structure. While almost every public utility district in the State belonged to the Commissioners' Association, which had low dues, not all of them used (and paid fees for using) the research and information services program. That was why the organization was failing financially. Although the primary purpose of participation had originally been to get the districts activated, now that they were in business, there was a greater need for the organization to address their operating problems. I thus proposed, in June 1951, that the corporate structure be renamed, and that its purpose and duties be refined. Amended articles of incorporation were filed in October 1951 establishing the Washington Public Utility Districts' Association. Then in June 1952, the Commissioners' Association took the new name of the corporation.

The Board included four commissioners from PUDs located west of the Cascade mountain range and four from the eastside PUDs. A president, the ninth member, was elected at large but the position was rotated each year between the westside and eastside PUDs. Board meetings were held monthly and two membership meetings were held each year in June and December. As the first years of my service rolled by, it dawned on me that the commissioners who were not on the Board met with the other commissioners only twice a year, so that while the nine persons on the Board were well informed and thus kept their districts aware of current happenings, the other districts had to depend on a biweekly newsletter for exchange of information. It became evident to me that strength would come by unity and unity could only come by participation. Thus, in June 1955, the membership adopted revised bylaws to allow any member district to name a representative to a statewide Board of Directors. Henceforth, if the district wanted to attend the monthly Board meetings and participate, it would have an opportunity to do so. If it wanted to stay home, at least it would have a choice. This change caused the districts to grow in strength and unity, which were needed because the attacks on local public power in the Legislature and elsewhere in the region and nation were mounting. The Association became an effective group to protect the interests of the PUD consumer-owners, and it also supported the city light systems and rural electric cooperatives where they needed assistance.

The year 1952 saw the activation of another organization for PUDs which was administered through the PUD Association office. Shortly after the PUD joint action law was passed in 1949, a number of the districts working through PUD Association committees began studying how the new law could be used for efficiency and savings. One committee looked at the possibility of joint purchasing of goods and services. At this particular time, a number of districts commenced having problems with their insurance coverage. Several had policies canceled overnight and others were finding out the hard way that the local insurance agents serving their needs were not too familiar with utility insurance. To meet this problem, the PUD Association Board in June 1951 approved establishing the Washington Public Utility Districts Power and Water Distribution System—a joint action entity for PUDs. In 1950 the Board selected Robert C. Rodruck, Sr., of the Pacific Underwriters Corporation to help organize it and establish a joint insurance program for its members. "Rod" Rodruck was a long-time public power supporter who had helped in the recall of the Seattle mayor who fired J. D. Ross, Seattle City Light's long-time Superintendent. As a result, Ross and Rodruck became close friends over the intervening years, and Rodruck became a lead supporter of local public power in all forms—including PUDs.

In May 1952, the Distribution System was formalized when the three districts of Skamania, Mason No. 3, and Douglas joined it for insurance coverage. I was designated Assistant Secretary so that the operation could be coordinated through the PUD Association office. Participation by the districts was entirely voluntary, and some joined while others did not. Over the years, the joint insurance program saved many dollars for those districts which did participate, and good sound utility insurance coverage was forthcoming. There was never any financial connection between the joint system and the PUD Association or between myself and Rodruck or his firm. However, Rodruck voluntarily contributed to needed efforts to help in PUD Association programs because he believed in public power.

In 1953, we wanted to issue a booklet titled *The County Light Story*, which told what a PUD was and how it was operated, to offset the sizable PR offensive that private power had mounted against us. The PUD Association was still struggling to keep my head above water—and thus it was Rodruck who footed the $1,200 bill for the booklet—unsolicited by me, voluntarily by him. His contributions were always made with no strings attached, except those of a developing and long-standing close friendship between us based on the high regard I have for this man.

In May 1952, I helped form the Electric Power Consumers Information Committee. Kirby Billingsley, Chelan County PUD Commissioner, was one of its instigators. A nationwide meeting had been called by national labor and farm leaders and consumer-owned utility representatives in Washington, D.C., to form a lobbying group to support the rural electrification program and federal multiple purpose development of river basins. Federal appropriations for these programs were under severe attack by the private power forces. Even the Tennessee Valley Authority, which had not yet received its self-financing authority, was having difficulty getting money and authorization from Congress for needed projects. It was the only time in my life when I found myself in the presence of a President in a small group. President Truman addressed the assemblage at the Willard Hotel, and afterwards, by invitation of Senator Warren G. Magnuson, who even then was a power in Congress, I was included in a small group that met with President Truman. I let my wife, who is a good Democrat, shake hands with me twice when I got home.

In the spring of 1952, further evidence surfaced about the "rape of the ratepayer" that had taken place in early 1950 when AP&L disposed of its Pacific Power and Light common stock. AP&L sold 500,000 shares of Pacific Power and Light stock to a private utility syndicate for $16,184,847; cost per share, $32.37. This happened after a public power syndicate's final offer of $16,325,000 negotiated by Guy Myers with AP&L President Aller had been rejected by the Securities and Exchange Commission on a technicality. The public power financing syndicate had publicly expressed its intent to acquire the stock and then sell the utility properties to local public power utilities — without profit and at a price which would allow lower electric rates to the consumers. It was interesting to see the SEC attorney who blocked the sale Myers had negotiated resign shortly after the sale to the private utility syndicate and go to work for the legal firm retained by Pacific Power and Light. Pacific Power and Light then increased the number of shares from 500,000 to 1,750,000 on a $3^{1}/_{2}$ to 1 stock split, and the cost or value of each share was thus $9.25.

On October 11, 1950, just as soon as a six-month holding period to avoid paying short-term capital gains taxes was up, the private utility syndicate sold 1,078,744 shares at around $13 per share.

Later, in July 1951, the syndicate sold 291,464 shares of the original divided block and then 27,000 more at $14.25. And, finally, on December 21, 1951, it offered 352,792 of the original divided shares at $15.875 per share with the prospectus stating that the original cost per share was $9.28.

Thus, on an original investment of just under $16,200,000 in 1950, the private power syndicate by early 1952 had a potential profit of just over $7,500,000, or 46 percent. The sad part is that this increase in the value of Pacific Power and Light would be reflected in the rate base and rate structures on which the private power customers would pay rates. The Washington Public Utility Commissioners' Association tried to prevail upon the SEC to stop or control such maneuvering but only received a curt telegram stating that the "original investors were entitled to a proper underwriting fee."

Two 1952 events led me into prolonged private versus public power fights outside of the legislative arena. The first was the transformation of the Stevens County Rural Electric Cooperative into the Stevens County Public Utility District, which filed a condemnation suit in September 1953 against the Washington Water Power properties in that county. The second event was the first Federal Power Commission hearing on Idaho Power Company's application for its license to construct Oxbow Dam in the Hells Canyon stretch of the Snake River. The hearing was held in Baker, Oregon, in July and ultimately led to formation of the National Hells Canyon Association, an organization one of whose leaders, Al Ullman, a Baker realtor, got his start in politics. Ullman ran for Congress in 1956, won, and remained in office until 1982.

Under date of July 1, 1952, I wrote to Gene Hoffman, Superintendent of Seattle City Light; Frank Ward, Superintendent of Tacoma Light; Owen Hurd, Manager of Benton County PUD and President of the Northwest Public Power Association; Commissioner Irv Woods of Okanogan County PUD (PUD Association President); and a number of other PUD managers and commissioners. The letter outlined the need for local utilities to develop hydroelectric plants to augment the slipping federal construction on the Columbia River and its tributaries. I had just witnessed the formation of the Pacific Northwest Power Company, a joint corporation wholly owned by four private power companies, created for the purpose of jointly building and operating large hydroelectric and other types of generating plants. In our local public power program, through formation and activation of county size PUDs, we had brought utility monopoly control closer to the people but we had also changed the centralized financial assets and strengths of a larger utility system into isolated autonomous smaller utilities. Looking at the future, it appeared logical to me that some kind of legal entity was needed by which we could consolidate the financial strength of these small utilities to construct some of the larger needed projects. Grant County PUD was very actively pursuing construction of the Priest Rapids

Dam on a mid-Columbia River site on which the Corps of Engineers had previously been authorized to build a dam. The PUD would need help to finance the project.

We met at Gene Hoffman's Seattle City Light office on July 9 and agreed to sponsor legislation at the next session of the State Legislature to enact a joint operating agency law. Working with Harvey Davis, Chelan County PUD attorney, and Dean Barline, Assistant City Attorney of Tacoma, we drafted a law that would permit two or more PUDs and/or city light systems to organize a separate municipal corporation to construct and operate generating or transmission facilities. The corporation would be under the direct control of the member utilities, but it would be separate and apart from them from the standpoint of any financial commitments or obligations. Our main goal was to create an organization to take over the construction of Priest Rapids in support of Grant County PUD. In early December, prior to the legislative session, we presented our proposal to Governor Langlie. Governor Langlie, who had strong states' rights views, had wanted a State Power Commission for some time, as an alternative to the strong and leading federal participation in river and power development.

The Governor agreed to sponsor a combination bill — one that would establish a five-person State Power Commission, by amending the unworkable law passed in 1949, and that would give legislative authority to city light systems and PUDs to form operating entities to construct and operate generating and transmission facilities. The proposed law evolved during the 1953 Session of the Legislature through some very tough bargaining between private power, public power, and the Governor's office.

Several other factors affected the private versus public power affairs in our State. Myers was still trying to consummate the purchase of the remaining Puget Power properties by those PUDs still cooperating in his scheme even as he had tried to get the Washington Water Power stock purchase. With Whatcom County PUD's withdrawal in September, the six remaining PUDs — Jefferson, Kitsap, Skagit, and Thurston, plus Snohomish and Chelan counties — as participating owners in the generating plants, offered $89,490,000. Current assets and operating funds would require a bond issue of $107 million. Whatcom's portion of the Puget Power system would remain with the private company until it was obtained by that PUD's condemnation or negotiated purchase. Whatcom County PUD had retained an engineering firm which was well known to Washington Water Power and this disrupted the bargaining between Puget Power and Whatcom County PUD. The joint PUD offer also set off a proxy fight among

Puget Power stockholders instigated by Kinsey Robinson. However, by an 84 percent vote on October 27, the Puget Power stockholders approved the sale. Prior to the closing date, punitive lawsuits were filed to delay the sale. PUD elections in Kitsap and Skagit counties centered on the issue and the spotlight of controversy swung to the 1953 Legislative Session. Robinson was pushing his merger move.

A sidelight to the 1952 maneuvering was an incident that occurred at a statewide Chamber of Commerce conference reception I attended at the Ben Franklin Hotel in Seattle on November 7. I had returned from a meeting of the Pacific Northwest Utilities Conference Committee in Tacoma and had been asked by a PUD manager to get in touch with his local Chamber secretary. Arriving at the reception, I met Clif Erdahl, Chairman of PNUCC, and while conversing with him and a former member of Senator Magnuson's staff, a man approached whom I did not know. He broke into our conversation to speak to Erdahl and asked him what he knew about a lawsuit to be filed the next morning in Thurston County by Archie Blair, a Tacoma attorney, to block the proposed purchase of Puget Power by the PUDs. He said that Blair had been retained, as he had been in the past, by Washington Water Power. The man didn't know me, and Erdahl seemed a bit flustered by his comments. Continuing, the man said, "We kicked Jack Jones off the PUD Commission in Kitsap County and elected an old man named Ferguson, ninety-two years old, who will do whatever 'Popcorn' O'Brien wants him to do." (O'Brien was the anti-Puget purchase PUD commissioner elected in 1950.) The man continued, "We're fearful that a lame duck session will be called before Ferguson gets on the board" in early December and thus they needed the lawsuit to delay action until the new board could meet. I later learned that the man was Cliff "Red" Beck, Manager of the Port Orchard Chamber of Commerce. Later, when Beck served in the Legislature from Kitsap County from 1961 to 1979, we got along very well, but in 1952 he was opposing the PUD purchase of Puget Power.

The year 1952 included many events affecting power development in the Pacific Northwest and in particular private versus public power development. On February 26, Pend Oreille County PUD became the first PUD in the State of Washington to get a license for a hydroelectric dam when it received Federal Power Commission approval for its Box Canyon Project. A private power victory occurred when the Defense Production Administration granted one of the first and also the largest "amortization certificate" for construction of a dam by a private power company in the Northwest to Pacific Power and Light, which was permitted to write off 75 percent of a $26,000,000 cost portion of its new Yale Dam on the Lewis River in southwest Washington. The use of rapid amortization write-offs against federal income taxes to stimulate new defense industries was then being practiced nationwide. But to apply such a write-off to dams in the Pacific Northwest was a sham and a pretense which granted untold millions of dollars of subsidies to the private power companies. Private power companies nationwide, financially supported by the Pacific Northwest companies, were carrying on a campaign against federal dams with the hypocritical claim that the dams were being paid for by the taxpayers. About local public power, they said that such utilities didn't pay *any* taxes, when they knew very well that PUDs paid a special gross revenue privilege tax in lieu of property taxes, and, in addition, the same 3.3 percent gross revenue tax the private power companies paid. While telling outright lies on the one hand, private power was putting federal tax dollars into its own pocket.

Portland General Electric got a 65 percent write-off of $22,260,000 on its Pelton Project, and Washington Water Power enjoyed 65 percent of $34,425,000 on its Cabinet Gorge Dam. The height of hypocrisy was reached when the Idaho Power Company, after the defeat of the federal high Hells Canyon Dam, received a 50 percent write-off for $20,047,610 of its Snake River Project costs plus a 25 percent write-off on $1,558,557 of its costs for needed transmission lines, which were put up to block construction of Bonneville lines in Idaho. There were those who maintained that the rapid amortization process, while reducing tax liabilities in early years, merely deferred payments to later years – and in some of the state regulatory processes in later years, a flow-through-credit procedure was adopted to protect the customers. However, the forgotten – or rather ignored – fact, which only persons familiar with utility accounting procedure recognized, was that the rapid amortization process in effect granted interest-free loans of those early retained dollars to private power, which over the years, invested in the companies at their fair allowable rate of return, earned more dollars than were later paid out as deferred taxes. The granting of this type of tax subsidy to the private monopoly power companies was abusive to their ratepayers. The question could be asked, "Why didn't public power people object to such chicanery?" Some of us did, but there were other more newsworthy events for the media to concern itself with and the Pacific Northwest did need more power resources to keep ahead of the loads being forecast.

In late 1952, the Pacific Northwest was faced with a power brownout caused by anticipated low water runoff in the river systems. The Defense Electric Power Administration was called into play and set up orders to curtail the use of electricity should the shortage occur. This required substantial negotiations among the utilities and Bonneville because of Bonneville's direct service to aluminum industries necessary to the war effort. The anticipated shortage also raised the issue of sharing of steam generation costs. The private power companies, as well as some of the larger publicly owned utilities which generated some of their own power, both hydro and steam, purchased power from Bonneville on a kilowatt-year basis. In addition, the private power companies were granted the right to establish an Inter-Company Pool whereby they could pool their total supply and take power from the pool when they needed it, before buying power from Bonneville. Because of the pool, Bonneville's rate for power to private companies was much lower than the rate paid Bonneville for firm power by utilities such as PUDs, which were dependent on Bonneville for their total supply. One of the factors in the lower cost to private power was the companies' oil-fired steam plants which made it possible for them to contract for less firm power because they had these plants to back them up in case of a power shortage. In wet water years, when there was plenty of hydroelecrtric power, the operation of the high cost steam plants was never required; however, in the winter of 1952–1953, these plants had to go on line. "Sharing of steam costs" became a regional issue between private and public power—with only one public power official, Clif Erdahl of Tacoma, supporting the private power side. Public power's position was "share benefits in wet years and we'll share steam costs in lower water years." It never happened but later became a factor in 1953 when the private power companies were granted long-term power contracts with Bonneville under the Eisenhower Administration elected in November 1952.

Mentioning the 1952 federal election brings to mind a number of federal elections from 1948 to 1956 in which the private versus public power issue was involved and on which it had an effect. With the election of Eisenhower, the so-called partnership power policy started to evolve. In simple English, this policy was to reduce federal participation in power development, and, since the federal power involvement in the Pacific Northwest was large, the policy did not bode well for public power people. A Republican-controlled Congress meant that persons from the East, the same ones or ones similar to those who controlled committees back in 1947, would once again be in power. Fortunately, Senator Guy Cordon of Oregon, a strong supporter of Bonneville, had been re-elected in 1948 and Senator Wayne Morse of Oregon and Senator Warren G. Magnuson of Washington, two strong public power supporters, had been elected and re-elected in 1950. Following that, in 1952, Congressman Henry "Scoop"

Jackson, running on a public power platform, had bucked a nationwide and statewide Republican wave and won election to the U.S. Senate.

Eisenhower did appoint Governor Douglas McKay of Oregon as his Secretary of the Interior, and while in later years McKay was to withdraw the Interior Department's intervention in the Idaho Power case before the Federal Power Commission, which in many people's minds caused us to lose the federal high Hells Canyon Dam fight, we were to have a Pacific Northwest man as the boss of Bonneville. However, public power persons underrated the influence which Ralph Tudor, another man who was familiar with Pacific Northwest river development but who hailed from California and had strong anti-federal public power views, would play in the new administration. Tudor, who was the Corps of Engineers' Portland District Engineer from 1943 to 1945, came back to government in 1952 as Undersecretary of the Interior. In July 1954, the year Cordon was running for re-election, Tudor administered the axe to the Bonneville staff by ordering 700 people laid off. The Oregon press went wild. Republican Senator Cordon, who had always been a friend of Bonneville, unfairly got the blame for acts of a Republican Administration, and was beaten by his Democratic opponent, Richard Neuberger, by a very small margin — and most persons attribute it to the pro-Bonneville and pro-public power stance which Neuberger took.

Two other federal elections, in 1956, are of note. Secretary of the Interior McKay resigned to return to Oregon and run against Senator Wayne Morse. Governor Langlie of Washington, ending his third term in that office, ran against Senator Magnuson. McKay and Langlie were outright supporters of the Eisenhower "partnership" power policy but, while Eisenhower was re-elected, his coattails did not carry supporters of his partnership policy. Magnuson and Morse, running on a strong program for federal regional comprehensive river development and support for public power, handily defeated them.

The year 1956 also saw Congressman Sam Coon of eastern Oregon, who had sponsored the John Day Dam partnership legislation, challenged by high Hells Canyon Dam supporter Al Ullman. Ullman by then was the lay citizen President of the National Hells Canyon Association, organized after McKay withdrew the Department of the Interior's opposition to Idaho Power's low dams in the FPC hearings. Senator Neuberger joined the congressional candidate debates over Hells Canyon and Ullman was elected.

While neither I nor the PUD Association ever got involved in partisan political races (I did use personal family funds to support federal candidates from both parties whom I believed in), we made certain that those candidates from either party who had supported local public power received direct "thank you" letters, and most certainly did not object if a candidate used our letters in his campaign literature.

One final note on 1952. After Governor McKay had been designated by President-elect Eisenhower to be Secretary of the Interior, rumors were rampant that Paul Raver was out as Bonneville Administrator – and guess who was being mentioned as his successor? Clif Erdahl, Commissioner of Utilities of Tacoma, where the voters had just approved a new type of city government eliminating his office. Several years before, I had been introduced to Governor McKay by a mutual friend, Judge Val Sloper of Salem, Oregon. My wife and I had gone to Salem to visit the Slopers, were invited to attend the State Fair, found Sloper in a cake baking contest with Mrs. McKay, and enjoyed the courtesy of the Governor's box at the fair. Thus, with my Board's permission, I sent a direct letter to Governor McKay taking issue not only with the removal of Raver but most certainly with Erdahl's appointment as Bonneville Administrator. Erdahl's support was coming from the private power side of the fence, and once again bore out what I had learned the hard way about Erdahl during my first two years on the job.

1953–1954

The 1953 Session of the State Legislature convened on January 12. It was my first full-time regular session as the public power lobbyist. Each of the three private power companies operating in the State had two full-time visible private power lobbyists (making six in all) to one for public power. I say "visible" because I was later to find out that two of the companies had "two on the Hill" and one or two downtown in Olympia. One Spokane legislator in the House of Representatives was an attorney who was retained by private power to do its legal work while he was supposed to be serving the people of his district. As I walked around in Ulcer Gulch, my fellow lobbyists all reminded me that this was the session where the private power forces were really going to take care of the PUDs. They were remembering the fight over the Spokane Power Bill in the 1951 Session where Democratic control of the House had severely beaten private power.

The 1952 election had seen the re-election of Republican Governor Langlie and a swing to solid Republican control in the Senate, 25 to 21, and in the House, 58 to 41. The 1953 Senate Republicans did not even need a coalition with the private power Democrats to control. Although it was historically true that the predominance of public power support came from the Democratic side of the political aisle, the movement had had some strong Republican support around the State. While PUD commissioners run and are elected on a non-partisan basis, my personal friendships and acquaintances with them would indicate about a 60 percent to 40 percent Republican flavor among them. After all, the PUDs were rural in nature with small town businessmen and farmers on their boards who many times while being non-partisan in office did have a more conservative attitude in politics. At any rate, word was out that Kinsey Robinson was riding high and would be running the show at the Legislature. I did not believe this, being aware of several things which I felt the private power forces were over-looking.

First off, Republican control in the Senate had come by electing eight "new" senators from PUD counties. Some of the newly elected senators had served in the Senate before and were returning after being re-elected following a previous defeat by a Democrat or another Republican. But in simple terms, a coalition of 8 Republican and 16 Democratic senators, or 24 votes out of the 46 total senators, materialized to block anti-public power legislation.

Following the election in 1952, the Senate Republicans had established a Committee on Committees composed of five senators. Three of them — McMullen of Clark, Wall of Chelan, and Dahl of Stevens — were from counties where active PUDs were in business.

Dale McMullen was a leading attorney from Vancouver and just happened to be a long-time personal friend of mine. Barney Dahl was the publisher of the *Chewelah Weekly* newspaper, a strong Grange member, and very independent. Harry Wall was a wealthy lumberman from Manson and very conservative. Wall turned into a pillar of strength for public power, and the metamorphosis was interesting to observe.

On the Friday night before the election, I received a call from Wilfred Woods, editor/publisher of the *Wenatchee Daily World*. He stated that Harry Wall, Republican candidate for State Senator, was in his office and had agreed to support public power. Wall was in a tight race with Art Garton, a Democrat. Woods said a special ad to this effect was to be run the following Monday just before the election. I said, "Fine, I hope he reads it again after the election." Wall was elected by about 50 votes, as I recall, and his ad gave me an avenue of approach.

During Wall's earlier terms in the Legislature, he had been a very strong supporter of private power. One story had it that when he was the Chairman of the Senate Utilities Committee, he had killed a pro-public power bill with a pocket veto. In those days, this meant that the Chairman would put the bill in his coat pocket and kill it by not allowing the committee to act on it. But he made his pledge and he lived up to it because that was what the people of Chelan with their new public power electric service wanted. During the 1953 Session, while he was stalwart for public power, I would get the impression that this stand went against his own personal feeling. I thought he probably cringed as he voted for public power. But as the session wore on, he became more interested in the facts about public power, and toward the end, he was quite a strong supporter although he still didn't take part in any floor maneuvering. By 1955, however, the man had changed completely. He took pride in being known as a public power senator, and his actions in the 1955 Session carried out his feelings.

At any rate, these three senators on the Committee on Committees played important roles as the following events took place. The Republican Committee named private power supporter Senator Henry Copeland of Walla Walla as Chairman of the Senate Utilities Committee. He had chaired this Committee in 1951 under "coalition" control, but in 1953 it was composed of eleven senators, six of whom were known to be public power supporters. On the Sunday before the Legislature was to convene, Senator Copeland went to the news media with the statement that the Public Utilities Committee would never convene until a change had been made in its make-up and that he intended to take this to the Republican caucus. The next morning "Stub" Nelson's story in the *Seattle Post-Intelligencer* was head-lined "Private Power Wins First Round at the Legislature." Sure enough, Senator Copeland's Committee had been re-constituted with thirteen senators, eight of whom were favorable to private power.

I stayed out at my motel that morning, calling PUD commissioners in the eight counties having Republican senators and operating PUDs. I said, "Go out and buy yourself a *P-I*, read the headline, and then call your senator in Olympia and gently scream in the phone, 'What in 'ell is going on over there!'" The calls had the desired results. As I entered the Governor Hotel for lunch, I met Senator Bob French from Okanogan County who said he had just been called by PUD Commissioner Irv Woods about the matter. He assured me that everything was all right and no one should get excited. Later I heard from the seven other senators. Thus a coalition of 24 senators to defend PUDs was formed – 16 Democrats and 8 Republicans. We couldn't pass anything because the agreement was only to defend against punitive bills – but private power couldn't pass anything against us either. The point to be made here is that by overplaying their hands, the private power companies forced action that solidified our side in the Senate.

Over on the House side, other things were taking place which private power lobbyists didn't recognize. They did not notice the strength and determination of three female legislators from counties having operating

PUDs. Ella Wintler from Clark and Eva Anderson from Chelan (both Republicans), and Julia Butler Hansen from Cowlitz-Wahkiakum (Democrat) were indeed to play important roles in defense of public power, each of whom saved the day for the PUD lobbyist on separate occasions.

There was no dearth of anti-public power bills introduced early in the session. HB-77 and its companion bill in the Senate, SB-54, were the million dollar babies of the private power companies. Passage would stop any future activation of a PUD in the State by blocking the right of eminent domain (condemnation) by such public bodies. The bill did not make condemnation illegal, as that would probably have been declared unconstitutional by the courts. It merely established a Catch-22 procedure to be followed by the PUD which would be self-defeating. SB-12 would provide a very easy method to dissolve both active and inactive PUDs, and included a "motherhood" clause assigning assets of dissolved PUDs to the public schools. SB-92 would mandate a referendum on any action taken by a PUD board, which would completely disrupt any attempts to run the utility in a businesslike way. SB-104, which was specifically designed to block purchase of Puget Power by a number of PUDs, would require public bids on the issuance of all revenue bonds. HB-148 and SB-261 would allow any city located in a PUD county to condemn the utility property of the PUD. Thus, by establishing city light systems, a city could cut the operating heart out of the PUD and make it impossible for the utility to serve the rest of the county. There were others, but these were the major ones.

HB-77, the big one for private power in the 1953 Session, was very cleverly worded. Its purpose, as put forth by its proponents, was to set criteria for PUD condemnation of any generation or transmission facility of a private power company. The bill provided that a PUD, in addition to getting a certificate of use and necessity from a court of law to enter a condemnation action against a private power facility, must get the approval of the Washington Public Service Commission. To give such approval, the Public Service Commission, following a public hearing, must find that "the loss of the generation resource will not disrupt, disturb or impair the ability of the condemnee adequately to supply existing users." Anyone could recognize that you could not take a single insulator away from a private power company without disturbing its ability to serve existing customers.

Clif Erdahl came to Olympia to talk with me on behalf of Kinsey Robinson, the chief proponent of the legislation. Chelan County PUD was moving ahead to condemn the Chelan Falls generating plant of Washington Water Power. There was strong feeling among the people that a local resource should belong to and be used by local people. Washington Water

Power had by that time lost its service area and thus its service responsibility in Okanogan, Douglas, and Grant counties. Erdahl and I met at the Governor Hotel, and he suggested that if I could find a way to accept HB-77, support for a joint action law, which the cities and PUDs were going to seek, would come from the private power forces. I explained that this was not possible. There was no way I could get my Board to approve a law which destroyed the rights of an individual PUD in trade for a law which merely granted joint action on a power supply. I stated that if the joint action law could not be accepted on its own merits as a way to help finance needed Pacific Northwest power generating projects, it should not be passed.

The next step on HB-77 was a public hearing scheduled in the House Judiciary Committee room under the control of the Public Utilities Committee. The turnout was terrific. Kinsey Robinson appeared, accompanied by his legal counsel, Allen Paine, and legal counsel for Pacific Power and Light, Allen Smith. Paine and Smith were two of the top utility lawyers in the Pacific Northwest and could be expected to effectively influence the committee members and other legislators.

I had my PUD Association president, Chauncey Price, a PUD commissioner from Skamania County, with me. Price, who was a former legislator with a law degree (although he never practiced law), would be no slouch in testifying. I also had Harvey Davis, a top PUD lawyer from Chelan County PUD, who would be strong for us.

The room was jammed with both pro-private power and pro-public power supporters and the shortage of space was to our disadvantage, as Representative Ella Wintler immediately recognized, because the pro-public power forces outnumbered the pro-private power supporters by a substantial number, PUD commissioners and managers having arrived from all over the State. Wintler proposed to the Committee Chairman that he postpone the hearing to see if we might use the House or Senate Chamber. He did so and word came back for us to move to the Senate Chamber. As we were moving, Joe Davis, Assistant to Ed Weston, State Labor Council President, came up to me and said, "Ken, do you need some help? I've got Ed primed." I said, "Do I! And see if someone can get Heinie Carstenson, State Grange Master, located." Well, it was quite a show with some hot and heavy testimony on the bill and off the bill, with the Chairman having to remind the speakers from time to time to stick to the subject. I had some strong public power voices talking that night. But, as could be surmised, the bill, although in substitute form, was voted out of the Committee and sent to the House Rules Committee. Our strategy was to fight the bill at every possible stage, so when it was reported from the Committee on its referral to the House Rules Committee, one of our supporters made a motion to indefinitely postpone it. This move was blocked by the Republican majority who called it a parliamentary trick sponsored by the Democrats, which it was – and the bill went to Rules. However, when substitute HB-77 appeared before the House on second reading, Representative John O'Brien (King County), Democratic Minority Floor Leader, raised a point of consideration, asking that a vote be taken on whether or not the House would consider substitute HB-77. A yea vote would be against public power and a nay vote for public power. The roll call result was 53 nays, and the substitute bill was killed.

This is where Representative Eva Anderson of Chelan saved the day. It happened this way: One of the 53 nay votes was Representative Ed Reilly, Spokane Democrat, former Speaker of the House and pro-private power, who had switched from yea to nay to be on the prevailing side. Of the 52 original nay votes, 37 were by Democrats and 15 by Republicans. Only 4 Democrats voted yea, and these were legislators from the Washington Water Power service area. Every Republican from a PUD legislative district, totaling 12, had voted nay. The other three Republicans who voted nay were from non-PUD areas, and their votes were secured by the direct effort of Anderson. Without them, public power would have lost the vote.

Now that the substitute bill had been killed, however, the House had before it the original HB-77. I met with several PUD area legislators outside the south door of the House, who were arguing over the next immediate move. Julia Butler Hansen, Democrat of Cowlitz-Wahkiakum, was insisting that a motion to indefinitely postpone should be made. She felt it was the only way to hold certain Democratic votes in place. Conversely, Representative Joe Lester, Republican of Chelan, expressed fear that since such a move had been defeated previously on a Republican versus Democratic strategy-issue vote, it would fail again. As a neophyte lobbyist, I did not know what to do, but they had to make a quick decision. At that moment the House was called back to order and they had to go inside. I sided with Hansen, saying that public power issues were not partisan even if the Republicans on the House side went against us. Since a motion to indefinitely postpone could kill the bill for the Session, as they had explained to me, then we should go for that – win or lose.

On consideration of the original bill on second reading, Floor Leader O'Brien moved to indefinitely postpone its consideration. Some hot floor debate for and against the measure then ensued. Just prior to the vote, Representative Kermit McKay, Republican from a PUD area legislative district, rose on a point of personal interest under a provision of the Constitution and was excused by Speaker Mort Frayn from voting on the issue. A roll call vote followed with 52 yeas, including a vote from Representative Ed Reilly. Public power had held and won. Then Reilly gave notice that he would ask for reconsideration of the vote at the proper time, which was his privilege since he had voted on the prevailing side. A lot of turmoil erupted at that point with more debate and argument. O'Brien and Charlie Savage, Democrat from Mason, Jefferson, and Clallam counties (PUD areas) pointed out that Ed Reilly, as Speaker in 1943, had ruled that any vote on a motion to indefinitely postpone was not subject to reconsideration. O'Brien then moved that reconsideration take place immediately, following which Savage moved that O'Brien's motion be tabled. The tabling motion prevailed by voice vote. The Speaker ruled the bill had been indefinitely postponed. By that time, all members were somewhat tired of the controversy and confusion. Most certainly from my place in the gallery, I, too, was confused, but I thought we had won. Since no move was ever later made on the House side to seek reconsideration, the private power's million dollar baby was defeated for the Session.

SB-12, the bill making it easy to dissolve any PUD in the State, was introduced by Senator Ed Flanagan of Yakima. The law would cover operating PUDs as well as non-active ones, although Senator Flanagan told Senator Wall that his primary interest was in dissolving the Yakima County PUD, where election of anti-PUD commissioners occurred repeatedly. He failed to mention, however, that Pacific Power and Light sponsored the petitions for nominating these commissioners and contributed the campaign funds they needed to get elected. The bill was attractive to some senators because it very cutely provided that any assets left over after PUD dissolution would go to public schools. As any thinking person would recognize, such a law would severely damage a PUD's ability to obtain business financing. We passed the word to Flanagan by way of the senators in the PUD coalition to block punitive PUD bills that SB-12 was dead. However, Senator Wall came to me and asked why we couldn't give Senator Flanagan a law which would take care of his Yakima situation but not hurt the other PUDs. I frankly could see no value in keeping that "captive" PUD in existence so, with the approval of my Board, I had Harvey Davis of Chelan County draft a PUD dissolution bill which exempted all operating PUDs and provided that any district which took action to become operational would be protected from dissolution for five years. With Senators Wall and Ganders (two pro-PUD senators), joined by Senator Flanagan, as sponsors, the compromise bill was introduced as SB-372. We also had it put in on the

House side as HB-484. What happened? Senator Flanagan then started to say, "We really don't want to dissolve our PUD. The people like to have it as a club over the head of the private power company to keep them in line on rates and service." Both bills died in committee.

But we didn't do all of that work for nothing. In 1969, when a truce was struck in the legislative wars between private and public power, one of the compromises was a bill to dissolve inactive PUDs. I dug SB-372 out of my files, and that is the bill that became law in 1969. Senator Wall thus kept his agreement with Senator Flanagan – 16 years later – and with both of them gone.

Two other bad bills, SB-92 and SB-104, were sponsored by Senator Jack Rogers of Kitsap County, an editor/publisher of a weekly newspaper in that county who was trying to block the purchase of Puget Power by the PUDs. As I recall, he stayed at the Olympian Hotel while in Olympia, where the lobbyist of Washington Water Power also made his headquarters. In later years, Senator Rogers returned to the Olympia scene as Executive for the Association of Washington Counties, and we enjoyed a good working relationship. But in 1953 he was out to stop local public power.

SB-92 was a cute one. The bill provided that any action taken by a PUD Board of Commissioners to acquire or improve any utility property would be subject to referendum and voter approval. One could easily see that under such a requirement no positive decision could be made by the elected commissioners and substantial political confusion could result. Some persons interpreted the proposed law as being so broad that even daily operating decisions would be subject to voter approval.

SB-104, whose purpose was to block the Puget Power sale, was even more devious. It hid behind the high-sounding purpose of requiring mandatory bids on any revenue bonds issued by a PUD, but the wording in the proposed law went far beyond that, establishing such complicated requirements for issuing the call for bids and receiving bid responses that in effect they blocked any possibility of issuing bonds. It was a very clever bill.

Senator Copeland, pro-private power Chairman of the Senate Utilities Committee, was so eager to get both bills passed that he had them reported out of his committee without holding public hearings on them.

As a young person still enthralled with the working of our democratic form of government, I was really burned up at such cavalier action. I had made arrangements for some qualified investment bankers to appear and testify at the hearing, and following Senator Copeland's abortive move, I hit the Governor's office. I guess my appearance shook Governor Langlie's secretary as she kindly got me in to see him without delay. I was a bit rash, but I was angry.

Now, never in my experience has a Governor given a pledge to veto a bill before it is enacted. Langlie did not do so on this occasion, and he and I did not see eye to eye on a number of things, but it was comforting to hear him say, "Ken, I would look long and hard at any bill coming on my desk with that kind of a legislative history. In the meantime, try to amend them and make them workable if you have to accept them."

SB-92 never made it out of the Rules Committee. The precedent it would set for all kinds of local government units would have been horrible and I later wondered how Senator Rogers would have viewed such a requirement for county commissioners in his later years of service to them.

SB-104 was another story. It cleared Rules and was placed on the Senate calendar. Senators Wall and Nat Washington and I worked until midnight the day before it was scheduled, drafting amendments. We had seven in total. I got them typed by 3 a.m., got some shut-eye and was back in the wings of the Senate by 8 a.m. I placed the amendments with seven different senators. When the bill went on second reading for amendments, Senator Wall presented one exempting emergency bond issues and short-term loans. Senator Washington offered an amendment to allow selling of bonds below par—a usual practice. Senator Rogers acknowledged that such amendments were proper. Just then, Senator Tom Hall of Wahkiakum offered our third amendment, which extended the bill to cover the State and all of its political subdivisions. Senator Rogers objected strenuously because he realized that with that amendment the bill would have the entire weight of the State agencies, port districts, school districts, and so forth, mobilized against it. He rose and asked if there were any other amendments that should be submitted to him in order for a compromise to be worked out on the legislation. Senator Albert Rosellini, Minority Floor Leader, looked up at me in the gallery and I shook my head "no" as vigorously as I could. Senator Rosellini then rose and stated that the amendments should be submitted to the Secretary of the Senate and reproduced for all senators to study.

About this time the four other senators having amendments rose out of their chairs and submitted them. A motion was then made by Senator Vaughn Brown to refer the bill back to committee. Senator Rogers moved that this motion be tabled, and the deciding vote was on. By 24 (15 Democrats and 9 Republicans) to 22, the motion to table failed. Then, on the original motion to refer, it carried 26 to 20. Public power won.

This crucial vote on the motion to table had an interesting sidelight. The roll call was proceeding when Senator Gerald Dixon from Pierce

County voted "yea" against public power. Senator Washington jumped out of his seat and crossed over to Senator Dixon to hurriedly explain what a "yea" vote meant. At the end of the roll call before the result was announced by the Senate President, Dixon changed from "yea" to "nay." Senator Zack Vane, also from Pierce County but voting at the end of the alphabetical roll call, also had voted against public power with a "yea." Senator Vane, a Democrat, had been appointed to take the seat of Senator Don Eastvold, who had resigned from the Senate upon his election as Attorney General the previous November. Senator Vane's appointment had been by a County Commission chaired by a strong public power supporter named Harry Sprinker. When Senators Vane and Dixon were asked after the voting was completed why they had gone against public power on the issue, they said they had asked Clif Erdahl, Commissioner of Utilities of Tacoma, about the bill and he said he saw nothing wrong with it. This was another instance when Erdahl seemed to side with Washington Water Power's Kinsey Robinson. On the final vote, public power picked up two more senators. One was Senator Vane and the other was Paul Luvera of Skagit County, one of the eight Republican senators from a PUD county, who had simply misunderstood what the tabling motion meant. Since the roll was called in alphabetical order, he voted before Senator McMullen of Clark or Senator Wall of Chelan, who were providing public power Republican floor leadership at the time. The senators from PUD counties, at my suggestion, informally agreed that in future crucial votes Senator Howard Bargreen of Snohomish as a Democrat and Senator Barney Dahl of Stevens/Pend Oreille as a Republican would register loud and audible votes in the chamber. I doubt if this strategy produced any results because one main ingredient in the American political system is the human ego of an individual legislator that causes him or her to make an independent decision on every vote cast – but it made me feel a trifle better in the tensions of the session.

HB-148 provided another private versus public power skirmish in the Senate, where it was called SB-261. The bill as originally introduced would have allowed any city or town located within or without a public utility district to condemn any utility properties within its borders even if they were owned by a PUD. When we approached the sponsors of the legislation in the House, they informed us that their interest was only for those cities and towns located outside of a public utility district. The purpose of the bill was to allow cities and towns in King and Pierce counties to acquire the Puget Power properties should some outside PUDs consummate a purchase. They wanted the same right granted to Spokane in 1951 when the PUDs were trying to buy Washington Water Power. However, the legislation, if passed as introduced, would block any future PUD acquisition of private power properties. It would also create a tremendous problem for any operating PUD by threatening its distribution system with loss to any local city or town that wanted to have a municipal light system. The bill was changed in the House to say that the property of a PUD could not be taken over by cities and towns located within a district, and it came to the Senate in that form. However, Senator Rogers was still carrying on his effort to block the Puget Power purchase by the PUDs, so when the bill came on the Senate floor for second reading, he proposed an amendment which would protect PUD ownership up to a date-certain, March 8, 1953. This simple amendment would have destroyed the Puget Power purchase because the threat of condemnation thereafter by any city or town within a district ac-quiring properties after that date would restrict issuance of revenue bonds by the PUDs to purchase the private power property. Here, once again, the Senate coalition to stop punitive bills against PUDs went into action. Rog-ers' amendment was defeated and the bill passed as sent from the House.

The big utility legislation passed in 1953 was HB-462, which provided a new State Power Commission and permitted two or more cities and/or public utility districts to establish a separate corporate agency to jointly construct and operate generating and transmission facilities. This compro-mise, or joint legislation, came after individual bills had been introduced by various parties for the same purpose. Glen Smothers, Manager of the Grant County PUD, which was interested in constructing the Priest Rapids Project, had asked for legislation which did not provide for a State Power Commission. I had asked for a joint action bill which had been sug-gested by a collaboration, beginning in July 1952, between the cities of Seattle and Tacoma and the PUD Association. A separate bill had also been introduced which would amend the 1949 law establishing a State Power Commission, a law that was ineffective and inoperable because of certain restrictions in the statute. After a series of meetings in the Gover-nor's office, HB-462 was drafted by the Governor's legal advisor. The Gov-ernor had agreed to wording whereby the five-person State Power Commis-sion would represent the various types of utilities then operating in the State. Appointments by the Governor to the Commission were to include one representative from the public utility districts, one from the City of Seattle, one from the City of Tacoma, and two representatives-at-large, to look out for the interests of the other utilities then operating in the State, namely, the private power companies. A hearing on the bill was held on Wednesday, February 25, 1953. The PUD Association supported the bill but requested that it be allowed to submit clarifying amendments. The fol-lowing day, I worked with Harvey Davis, attorney for the Chelan County

PUD, and John Davis, an attorney representing Puget Power, to draft proposed amendments. We met with representatives of the cities of Seattle and Tacoma and explained each of the amendments, which we were planning to submit to the House Utility Committee. It then occurred to me that, on a complex piece of legislation such as this, needed changes could not be secured by argument before a legislative committee. I therefore called the Governor's office and asked for a meeting for the next day, to which the representatives of the cities of Seattle and Tacoma would be invited. After the meeting was set up, it occurred to me that even the private power companies should be present. I called Alan O'Kelley, attorney for Washington Water Power, to advise him of the meeting but stated that I did not have the right to invite his people on behalf of the Governor. He called the Governor's office and secured approval for their attendance.

My Board instructed me to avoid any confrontation with the Governor over this legislation, if at all possible, because of the other anti-PUD measures then bouncing around the legislative chambers. The Seattle and Tacoma representatives agreed to our proposed amendments but did state that on one or two they would not support us if a fight arose in the conference with the Governor.

Attending the meeting at 11 a.m. on Friday, February 27, were Governor Langlie, Andy Anderson, his legal advisor, John Dierdorff of Pacific Power and Light, Alan O'Kelley of Washington Water Power, John Davis of Puget Power, Frank Ward, Superintendent, and Dean Barline, Assistant City Attorney, for Tacoma, Councilman Bob Jones for Seattle, Henry Carstensen, Master of the State Grange, and Harvey Davis and myself for the PUDs. Everything went well at the meeting. We lost only one proposed amendment to deny the State Power Commission the right to sell falling water. The Governor insisted on retaining that right and to avoid a confrontation we accepted that provision.

One of the interesting amendments we proposed which was accepted by the other conferees was deletion of the emergency clause which would have established the State Power Commission immediately upon passage of the bill by the Legislature and signature by the Governor. I proposed this amendment because the City of Tacoma had approved the new form of charter government which would establish a new utility board for the operation of its utilities, but the charter was not to become effective until June 1953, and I frankly did not want a lame duck city government, including Commissioner Clif Erdahl, to recommend or appoint the Tacoma representative to the new Commission. Striking the emergency clause would place the law on the books 90 days after the Governor's signature, and after the new city government took office in Tacoma. I am not sure others present were aware of my motive in wanting that amendment, but at this point, after spending two years trying to make peace and establish a friendship with Erdahl, I found it impossible to do.

We took our amendments to the House committee that night, they were accepted, and the bill was reported out for House consideration. The House Ways and Means Committee reduced the appropriation for the new State Power Commission from $200,000 to $100,000, and the compromise bill was passed by the House on March 5, 1953, and by the Senate on March 9, 1953. One provision we accepted was to cause us problems in the future—the proviso that formation of a joint operating agency by two or more cities and/or public utility districts would be subject to State Power Commission approval. Joining with the private power companies, we had made certain that the State Power Commission could not take over development of any project once a utility had commenced its development. First right of project development was to remain with the local utilities. We therefore were not unduly fearful of having to get State Power Commission approval for any joint operating agency formation. We now had a joint action law for the Priest Rapids Project.

Two more incidents that occurred in the 1953 Session should be noted. One was good, and one could have been bad for me personally.

In 1953, there were about 80 recognized lobbyists around the marble halls. Of that number, only one was a woman. She was a likable person but she got us into trouble by violating House floor rules by going into the House chamber when the House was in session. When a complaint was filed with Speaker of the House Mort Frayn, three of us were called to his office and told that, unless we could exercise some control over her activity, he would have to bar all of us from access to and from the chamber even before and after sessions. Ed Weston, President of the Washington State Labor Council, came up with the idea of establishing an informal organization of lobbyists within which we could openly discuss those matters mutually affecting all of us. We therefore established what is now known as the Third House. In 1953, we called it the Third House Breakfast Club and would meet once a week. During the first meeting, our lady lobbyist was present and heard a very strong discussion about protocol and the courtesy we had to practice in our lobbying activity. It was made clear to all that it would be the duty of every lobbyist to "affect the activities" of any individual lobbyist whose conduct placed all of us in jeopardy or under criticism. We established a dues structure for the organization to limit membership to those who were recognized as active lobbyists, and since we had no purpose for the funds, Weston proposed that some of them be used to buy a television set for a rehabilitation center where injured employees were being treated. We bought the television. Later on, a Third House project was to conduct a "Youth Legislature," for which we worked with the YMCA to hold a study session for young persons from throughout the State, and a mock legislative session which would be held each year. The Third House has also financed other worthy causes over the years. Working as an organization, we could all contribute to finance group social activities for the legislators and their staffs. This allowed all lobbyists to participate as well as attend such functions.

The second notable incident was a personal experience which taught me a good lesson in political warfare. During an evening late in the session when the Senate was at work and the House had adjourned, I was on the House floor talking to two House member friends when a woman named Pearl came into the chamber and over to where we were. I had been introduced to her in 1951 by a mutual friend and knew she was working as a secretary for one of the senators who was chairman of a committee. In those days, legislators only had a personal desk on the floor but committee chairmen had the privilege of a committee room office and their own secretaries. Other members had to rely on a stenographer pool, calling on such workers to come down on the floor before and after the sessions to take dictation for any necessary correspondence.

Pearl offered me a drink, whereupon I said "Fine—where at?" She said, "Why don't we go back up into the committee room where I know my boss has a bar?" I accepted the invitation in front of my two friends, so there was no thought that there was anything wrong in it. We proceeded to the committee room, had a drink, and had started on another when a question hit my mind about why Pearl, who was secretary to one of the most ardent anti-PUD senators and one who had been trying to get legislation passed which would damage the PUDs, had sought me out by coming clear over to the House side. By that time, the conversation had turned to "boy and girl chatter," so I left.

The next morning, getting on the House elevator, Stub Nelson, reporter for the *Seattle P-I* said, "You're a pretty lucky boy." "What are you talking about?" I said. He said, "Last night they had you set up, with a photographer outside the committee room, and were looking forward to getting some pictures of you and your 'hostess' as the evening progressed." I said, "I make mistakes, Stub, but I try not to be a damn fool." It kind of jarred me to think that some of those persons on the other side of the private/public power fence would stoop to those tactics, but it taught me a good lesson. I never saw Pearl again, and she never returned to future legislative sessions. I was very happy to see the 1953 Session adjourn at its 60-day limit on March 12, 1953.

One important thing my first full session had taught about the legislator/lobbyist relationship is that although individual legislators are well-trained in many particular fields, during a legislative session they will be faced by decisions to be made in many other fields. A lobbyist is welcomed and appreciated by a legislator. But seasoned lobbyists take care not to distort information for short-range gains. They know they will only lie once to a legislator before damaging the interest of those they represent. It is the legislator who casts the votes.

Coming out of the legislative session, the Association and I were plunged into another private versus public power fight. While Kinsey Robinson had failed the previous November to stop approval by the Puget Power Board for sale of its properties to the PUDs, he had been successful in forcing the Board to approve terms of a proposed merger of Washington Water Power with Puget Power. His support in the Puget Power Board came from some of the large investment bankers who owned common stock in both companies, including the same bankers who had made the substantial profits during disposal of the Pacific Power and Light stock by AP&L in 1951. The merger would be subject to approval by both the Public Service Commission of the State of Washington and the Federal Power Commission in Washington, D.C. Puget Power management still favored sale of the Puget Power properties to the PUDs but, because of its Board action, had to remain neutral in the proposed merger.

Our first step was to testify at the State hearings. In this, we were joined by the Washington State Grange and State Labor Council, and the five PUDs which had the Puget Power purchase offer on the table. In addition to testifying at the hearings, the PUD Association sponsored a public information program in western Washington to alert the electric ratepayers to the proposed takeover of Puget Power properties by Washington Water Power. Lengthy State hearings commenced on May 18, continued during the whole month of July, and concluded on August 13 after 2,000 pages of testimony. It became evident to those of us who opposed the merger that the greatest gains from such a move would go to Washington Water Power. Puget Power had become quite strong financially as a result of the cash it had secured from sale of properties to PUDs in previous years. There was testimony that the supposed gain in generating capacity, which Washington Water Power witnesses claimed would result from the merger, would be possible only if the Northwest Power Pool was dissolved and the two companies, upon being merged, operated as a unit. It became very apparent that those owning stock in Washington Water Power would gain substantially more than those owning stock in Puget Power. These facts were drawn out when top Puget Power employees, while remaining neutral, were subpoenaed for testimony by those of us who oposed the merger.

In early September, Kinsey Robinson started to contact some of the industrial customers of Puget Power on the west side of the State and gave every indication that he knew what the decision of the State regulatory body was going to be. Sure enough, on October 16 the merger was approved by the State Public Service Commission. Later, one was to wonder if it was pure coincidence when one member of the State Regulatory Commission became a top officer for Washington Water Power and one of the leading attorneys for the Commission joined the legal firm of Washington Water Power.

However, at that moment, all eyes swung toward the Federal Power Commission in Washington, D.C., which had scheduled hearings for November 9. When these hearings were postponed, the Puget Power Board, meeting on November 12, voted not to extend acceptance of the merger beyond November 19. Simultaneously, the Board withdrew its approval for the PUD purchase of Puget Power properties. In effect, the opponents of the merger, who had fought so hard arousing public support for Puget Power to block the merger and avoid a statewide private power monopoly, had provided a new lease on life for Puget Power. I received a telephone call from Frank McLaughlin, Puget Power President, shortly after his Board had taken action, telling me his company intended to stay in business under a new plan by which the Puget Power stock would be dispersed to new stockholders by the holding company. He stated that, with the new Administration in Washington, D.C., proposing long-term power sales contracts between Bonneville and private power, and with Puget Power's financial position being strengthened by the sale of certain properties to PUDs and properties in the City of Seattle, the climate favored their staying in business as a private power company. In effect, public power had won the battle against the proposed merger, but was about to lose the war on securing the remaining Puget Power properties.

As I recall, that merger fight required me to raise $20,000 out of the various PUDs around the State to pay attorneys and engineers to testify before the Public Service Commission to block this merger. Some of the money was used for our PR program against the merger in Puget Power's service area. Snohomish County PUD and Chelan County PUD spent in the neighborhood of $37,000 each, including fees to their own staff attorneys for working on this case. The costs were justified because that merger could only have resulted in the throttling of public power by private power statewide.

Another major issue that boiled to the surface in 1953 involved the high Hells Canyon Dam fight on the Snake River. In 1950, Idaho Power Company had proposed building five low dams on that stretch of the river. The Idaho Power Company had applied for a license to build a single dam at the Oxbow site. Then, in December of 1952, they had filed a revised license application for the construction of three dams, including one dam with some storage capacity. In the first hearings, in July of 1952, the Department of the Interior had intervened in defense of a large high federal dam at the Hells Canyon site. However, with the election of the Eisenhower Administration, new Secretary of the Interior Douglas McKay, on May 5, withdrew the Department's intervention. The Northwest Public Power Association had been leading public power's opposition to the low dams and support of comprehensive river development by building a high dam at Hells Canyon. I had encouraged all PUDs on the north bank of the Columbia River from Pasco to the ocean to intervene in the hearings, and they had done so. They supported the high dam not only for the additional power it would supply but also because there was a need for more adequate upstream storage against flood damages. The 1948 Vanport flood was still in the minds of the lower Columbia River people, including the PUD commissioners. A local organization called the Idaho-Oregon Hells Canyon Association had been formed earlier, but I helped form the National Hells Canyon Association, whose foundation was the Granges of Washington and Oregon and the State Federations of Labor of Oregon and Washington. This new association attempted to fill the public interest gap for a high dam in the Federal Power Commission hearings left by the withdrawal of the Department of the Interior. Senators Magnuson and Jackson of Washington, joined by Senator Morse of Oregon, introduced legislation to authorize construction of a high federal dam at Hells Canyon. Senator Magnuson also introduced a resolution in the U.S. Senate calling for an investigation of Secretary of the Interior McKay and the Federal Power Commission over the manipulation of certain federal procedures in the hearings. The Hells Canyon issue was to boil for a number of years.

In August, Governor Langlie made his first appointments to the new State Power Commission. The law had been worded so that one commissioner would come from the PUDs of the State, one from a city the size of Seattle, one from a city the size of Tacoma, and two (at-large) from other types of utilities operating in the State, namely, private power. The PUD Association sent three recommendations to the Governor. By nomination and secret ballot, we had selected, in order of the most votes received, Kirby

Billingsley, Chelan County PUD Commissioner; Earl Cole, Cowlitz County PUD Commissioner; Irv Woods, Okanogan County PUD Commissioner; and Tom Quast, Snohomish County PUD Commissioner. Billingsley came to me and said that even though he had received the most votes, he felt that Quast, who was a Republican and was from the largest PUD in the State, should rightfully be placed on the PUD list of recommendations. Because of that, he declined the nomination and we submitted the names of Quast, Cole, and Woods. Quast was appointed by the Governor for a four-year term. The Governor then appointed Bob Jones, Councilman from Seattle, for a two-year term; Roy Skill of Yakima, a former Pacific Power and Light employee, for a two-year term; and Otto Warn, an owner of a shoe store in Spokane, to a four-year term. The Tacoma appointment was left open. As stated previously, removal of the emergency clause in the State Power Commission legislation permitted the new city government of Tacoma to make recommendations to the Governor after Clif Erdahl left office as Commissioner of Utilities. Finally, in September, the Governor appointed Walter Gordon, a professional engineer of Tacoma, to be that city's representative on the new State Power Commission. It was a very fine choice, in my opinion, and Gordon later was selected to chair the new Commission. Erdahl, at about the same time, was appointed Acting Director of Utilities under the new city administration and utility board.

The City of Tacoma had approved its new council/manager government in November of 1952, with election of the new Council and Mayor in early 1953. Prior to the City Council election, Dick Haley of the candy firm Brown & Haley, son-in-law of the late Rufus Woods, who had led the fight for the great Grand Coulee Dam as editor/publisher of the *Wenatchee Daily World*, held a meeting with certain PUD personnel from Chelan County. He was aware of the poor relationship which had arisen between the City of Tacoma utilities people and PUD representatives from throughout the State over the past political battles in the State Legislature.

While I had been specifically assigned to improve relations with Erdahl and Tacoma when I was first hired, Erdahl had sided with private power so many times that I had already told my Board there seemed to be no way I could do this. With my Board's knowledge, I had sent a letter to Secretary of the Interior McKay opposing Erdahl's private power sponsored appointment as Bonneville Administrator. Therefore, when a second meeting with PUD people was arranged by Dick Haley, to which a number of Tacoma City Council candidates had been invited, as well as Kirby Billingsley, Wilfred Woods, and Frank Stewart from the Chelan County PUD area, I was also invited. Present that evening were other Tacoma persons, including Walter Gordon. There was no mention of Erdahl at the meeting. We merely urged the City of Tacoma to get back into an active fight for comprehensive multiple purpose river development and to distance itself from private power's opposition to the federal program. We emphasized that it would be good if Tacoma Light could cooperate with the local public power program in the State of Washington on matters involving policy decisions affecting the federal power program as well as the local PUD program.

Shortly after that meeting, following the City Council election and installation in office of Mayor Harold Tollefson, Haley called and asked if I would be willing to come to his office in Tacoma to meet the new Mayor and tell him about the poor relationship which had been growing between Tacoma Light and the PUDs. We met on May 22. I was cautious in this meeting because I didn't know how he felt about this matter or what his views were on the PUDs. Upon his assurance that his only interest was in getting the full facts, I related the specific actions Erdahl had taken against public power and told him how I thought PUD officials felt about them. He asked if I would put this information in writing, and I said that I would have to clear such a matter with my Board of Directors, but that I could certainly send him a copy of the letter I wrote to Secretary of the Interior McKay.

Following this first meeting, another meeting with the Mayor was arranged by Kirby Billingsley and the Mayor's brother, Congressman Thor Tollefson, for June 15, and Billingsley, Wilfred Woods, and I attended that meeting together. After clearing the matter with my Board in early June, I prepared a letter to the Mayor detailing Erdahl's activities in the private/public power fights. Later in June, Dick Haley and I, at his request, met with individual members of the new City Council and at each of these meetings I reviewed the previous relationship between the City of Tacoma and the PUDs and stated our hope that relationships would be improved in the future.

The new Utilities Board in Tacoma was appointed by the Mayor and confirmed by the City Council. Haley arranged a meeting for Woods and me with Gerrit VanderEnde, who became the new Utilities Board Chairman, in Seattle where, at Haley's request, I reviewed this matter in detail again. At the close of the meeting, VanderEnde asked whether I would be willing to meet with the other four members of the Utilities Board in Tacoma in order that they might hear the same information. He arranged this meeting for early September. By then, my letter to Mayor Tollefson had been made public by a radio news commentator and had caused certain members of the Legislature to become embroiled in the issue. After my one meeting with the Utilities Board in Tacoma, the only time I saw any member of that group was at Pacific Northwest Utility Conference Committee meetings, briefly. The Board selected Erdahl as Acting Director of Utilities, and I had no further formal discussions about him with Tacoma officials.

I went to Tacoma in December 1953 for an informal meeting with VanderEnde to talk about the resignation of Gene Hoffman as Superintendent of City Light and the appointment of Dr. Paul J. Raver as the new Superintendent. I pointed out that it was urgent that they make some type of move in Tacoma in support of public power development, even if they kept Erdahl, who then appeared destined to be named Director of Utilities. When VanderEnde assured me that it was Tacoma Light's intention to cooperate with the public power groups in the State, I made arrangements to return to Tacoma with Lars Nelson, Master of the State Grange, and Billingsley, for a meeting that would not be concerned with personalities but with dealing with the overall power program.

In January of 1954, on direct instructions by my Board, I sent a special letter to the Tacoma Utilities Board complaining about some underhanded statements Erdahl had made to the Spokane press, speaking as Acting Utilities Director of Tacoma. I received no response, but in early March 1954, I received a call from VanderEnde asking me to meet with him in Seattle. At the meeting he informed me that he and other members of the Utilities Board were being pressured by a member of the Washington Water Power staff, Archie Blair (the Tacoma attorney used by Washington Water Power many times in previous years for legal services), Reno Odlin, head of a local bank, and even some of his own savings and loan board members, to have Erdahl promoted from Acting Utilities Director to Utilities Director of Tacoma. He said that the private power people were saying, "Unless you keep Clif Erdahl on as Utilities Director in the City of Tacoma, you will kill private power in the State."

VanderEnde was also concerned because Tacoma had spent considerable funds in rebuilding its steam generation plant and the Utilities Board could not determine why this had been done, since the city had a new requirements contract from Bonneville. It finally came to light that the steam plant was rebuilt to supply power to Washington Water Power, but that on March 1, Kinsey Robinson had pulled the rug out from under Erdahl by canceling the power purchase contract. Thus Tacoma found itself with bonds issued for the steam plant that would provide certain benefits, but the time was fast approaching when the rates might have to be raised to pay for it.

VanderEnde was further concerned because the Central Labor Council had sent two men down to the last Utilities Board meeting and asked for a special meeting before any selection of a Director was made. I could see that, while Erdahl was having private power supporters on the one hand put pressure on the Utilities Board for his appointment, he was stirring up organized labor public power support also to bring pressure on the Utilities Board. VanderEnde said he could not expose Erdahl's strategy publicly, but that he felt it was wrong that the "labor boys didn't realize they were backing a phony public power man." I told him there was nothing I could do in the matter except give the information I had to Ed Weston, President of the State Federation of Labor, so that a true public power labor leader would at least know the facts about Erdahl before the meeting on selection of the permanent Director.

Later that day, I got a call from Ed Fussel, energy reporter of the *Seattle Times*, who confirmed that Erdahl was being pushed for the public power post of Utilities Director in Tacoma Light with the argument that it would be the only way to protect private power in the State. I called Weston, and he called Vernie Reid of the Tacoma Labor Council, who would be at the meeting, and cautioned Reid not to ask any questions on the retention of Erdahl that called for a "yes" or "no" answer. At the meeting, the labor representatives, ignoring Weston's advice, asked the direct question of VanderEnde: "Are you going to keep Erdahl as the permanent Director of Utilities?" VanderEnde replied "No, we are not." Erdahl was dismissed as Acting Director on March 17.

The following day, I received a call from VanderEnde, who was in San Francisco attending a business meeting, stating that he had been criticized by W. C. Gilman, consulting engineer for Tacoma Light, for discharging Erdahl. Gilman was quoted as saying that some of the men who were being considered for the post "aren't fit to be dog catchers, but Erdahl is eminently qualified for the post." I pointed out to VanderEnde that Gilman was very friendly with Kinsey Robinson, that he had been used by the Whatcom County PUD to oppose the Puget Power purchase by PUDs, that he had been used in support of the Washington Water Power/Puget Power merger attempt, and that we had often wondered how he became the consulting engineer for Tacoma Light. I said we felt it was only another incident where Robinson was influencing Erdahl.

There was a lot of excitement at this point. I received a call from Frank Ward, Superintendent of Tacoma Light, who wanted to know whether Mayor Tollefson had been in front of the PUD commissioners and had told them he was going to get rid of Erdahl several months before. As I told Ward, Mayor Tollefson had never spoken to the PUD commissioners to my knowledge and I had not seen him since early last year.

In early April, the Pacific Northwest Utilities Conference Committee met, with Erdahl as Chairman. I was there as a public power representative. The primary discussion was about the upcoming Senate appropriations hearings on the Bonneville budget, and we also talked about the federal power program as it pertained to Chief Joseph and The Dalles construction schedules. At the end of the meeting, Erdahl, after giving a short speech concerning the desirability of maintaining the Committee, appointed John Dickson, Manager of Wahkiakum County PUD, Acting Chairman, and turned the meeting over to him. All during the day there had been a lot of undercurrent discussion and whispering between Dickson, Kinsey Robinson, and Paul V. McKee, President of Pacific Power and Light. Members of the new Washington State Power Commission were present, and there was a rumor that they intended to back Erdahl for full-time Chairman in order to keep the Committee going, but this endorsement had been quashed by an objection from Commissioner Tom Quast. Dickson assumed the chair and many stirring testimonials to the qualities and usefulness of Erdahl followed.

The move to hire a full-time staff and make the position of Chairman a full-time job was rejected by a number of those present, including me. Puget Power's representative was also negative. I expressed the feeling that the Committee had served a worthwhile purpose but that the majority of our people would not want to participate in a formal organization that tried to serve both private and public power interests, although our differences could be subordinated to consideration of mutual operating problems in meetings such as this. When a stalemate seemed inevitable, a committee was appointed, but its members could not agree to hire Erdahl as a full-time Chairman with a salary. They proposed to retain him on a per diem basis at $75 per day plus expenses, and left the question of full-time employment to be decided later. All the private power companies and Seattle City Light (Councilman Bob Jones) agreed to share the temporary costs. Tacoma Light declined, and the Northwest Public Power Association, which had never contributed to the costs of the Committee, did not agree to do so this time.

At the next meeting of the Utilities Conference Committee in late May, a move was again made to hire Erdahl as the full-time Chairman. The matter again reached a stalemate, at which point Washington Water Power and Pacific Power and Light delivered the ultimatum that the Committee would have to retain Erdahl as a full-time paid Chairman if it were to continue with their participation. McKee, who had been outside the room conferring with Robinson, came back in and looking at Frank Warren, who represented the Portland General Electric Company, said, "Frank, I think I can speak for you. I have consulted with Kinsey and we have decided that we are going to continue the Committee and hire Erdahl, and those of you who want to go along with us are welcome to do so either on a sustaining basis or otherwise." Warren's response was, "Paul, I don't think our company is ready to go along to the extent that there is no other alternative to keep the Committee active." Bob Jones of Seattle then said, "McKee, the public power boys said they would be willing to go along even under a private power chairman, so why don't you keep it together until a decision can be made?" McKee said, "OK, you're all invited to a meeting at the Public Service Building in Portland, Oregon. John Dickson, you make the arrangements and invite the people." Whereupon the last words of the occasion were uttered by Robinson, "All right, we will make the decision then, and in the meantime we'll see that Clif doesn't starve."

The next meeting, arranged by Dickson, took place in Portland at Pacific Power and Light's Public Service Building on June 10, 1954. At this meeting, as at the previous meeting, a new strategy had been adopted whereby individual PUDs were invited to attend. Prior to the Portland meeting, the Northwest Public Power Association, the State PUD Association, Tacoma Light, and Puget Power had publicly stated opposition to participation in any committee which had a paid staff, but they expressed willingness to continue to participate in an informal voluntary committee, as in the past. When the Committee voted to have a full-time paid Chairman, and selected Clif Erdahl to fill the position, the Northwest Public Power Association, Seattle City Light, Tacoma Light, and Puget Power withdrew. A budget of $28,000 was adopted for the fiscal year July 1, 1954, to June 30, 1955, and Erdahl was to be paid $16,000 per year, $1,000 less than his Tacoma Utilities Director job had paid. It was of interest to note that for that year nearly 98 percent of the budget came from the three private power companies, Washington Water Power, Pacific Power and Light, and Portland General Electric. The only public power utility that gave money to the Committee was the Eugene Water and Electric Board, which contributed $300. The Washington State Power Commission contributed $350. Wahkiakum County PUD remained as a member of the Committee on a non-paying basis.

In June 1955, the Pacific Northwest Utility Conference Committee put on its usual show before Congress, which I attended. Erdahl began with the unanimity statement to which almost any utility could agree, and then made the point that 70 to 80 percent of the utilities in the Northwest were in support of the statement. He made no specific request for a new federal power project, and when the Senate Committee Chairman, Senator Carl

Hayden of Arizona, asked about the need to start on Ice Harbor Dam, the only federal dam which was ready for construction, Erdahl suggested that if the government wasn't going to build it, they should turn it over to local utilities to build. Following this, the PNUCC members present offered strong verbal support of a bill by Congressman Coon of Oregon to construct John Day Dam in partnership with private power. Erdahl, as Chairman of PNUCC, answered a question from Senator Hayden about the attitude of the people of the Northwest toward this kind of partnership by saying that some people were opposed to it, but many other public and private utilities were for it. The rest of the Committee's presentation emphasized the tremendous amount of money needed for new power plants and transmission lines, without mentioning the huge return being paid back to the federal Treasury by the ratepayers, including interest on previously invested federal dollars. Prior to the hearing and unknown to Erdahl, I had accidentally overheard via a speaker telephone his call to Alex Radin, Executive Director of the American Public Power Association, in which Erdahl stated that the Northwest was united on the power development program, that the statement to be submitted by PNUCC represented the views of many of the public agencies as well as the private companies, and that only a few of the PUDs and Puget Power were trying to make trouble.

Needless to say, when it was my turn to testify, my views were a bit different. I specifically requested a new start at Ice Harbor Dam, stating that we had not had a new federal start in the last four years. When I got home, my Board approved a mailing of a detailed report of the hearing to all our member districts. Only Wahkiakum County PUD continued as a non-paying member of PNUCC. Then in November 1956, when PNUCC was asked to arrange a meeting for State utilities and some federal agencies at the request of Assistant Secretary of the Interior Fred Aandahl, the PUD Association protested to Aandahl through three Republican Congressmen – Walt Horan, Russell Mack, and Thor Tollefson – and we received a written response stating that henceforth Bonneville would work directly with the public power utilities on any power meetings.

The battle continued into 1957 at the the federal appropriations hearings and culminated in a showdown between Senator Magnuson of Washington and Congressman Ben Jenson of Iowa, who chaired the Senate and House committees handling appropriations on federal dams. By this time, both the Northwest Public Power Association and the PUD Association were on record as unanimously favoring full federal dam new starts at Ice Harbor and John Day. Once again, the Pacific Northwest Conference Committee testified in support of construction of dams but did not go into who should be the constructor. Again, the members of the Committee from private power, after the written unanimity statement had been given, testified verbally to Jenson in favor of partnership construction of John Day Dam. Maggie insisted that it be constructed and totally owned by the federal government. In the congressional showdown, Magnuson secured an initial appropriation of $1,000,000 for the project as a federal project, and John Day Dam went under construction on that basis. PNUCC and private power lost that battle.

In July 1958, Erdahl resigned from PNUCC to run for Congress. His primary financial support came from the private power companies, but he was beaten in the primary by John Coffee. Shortly thereafter, Erdahl went directly on the private power payroll, as an employee of the Pacific Northwest Power Company, an entity formed jointly by the private power companies to construct dams.

In 1961, he returned to Tacoma as Utilities Director, and while a number of issues were to arise on the legislative scene, I never found any direct evidence that he became involved in them. By that time, there was substantial cooperation between private and public power working on the regional power supply, the California Intertie, and the Canadian Storage Treaty where our interests were compatible, and while he and I had a brief exchange over a statement he made in 1963 against Bonneville rates, I had no further direct personal or official problem with Erdahl as head of the Tacoma Utilities.

One act of his I didn't like was his refusal to permit the small mutuals and cooperatives located on the south edge of Tacoma, which had been relying on Tacoma for power supply, to secure their power from Bonneville. This, of course, was a political decision to be made in Congress, but because of Erdahl's private power connections, Bonneville was never able to get the necessary appropriations to build the needed facilities to grant such service. One basic attribute of Erdahl's was his determination to protect the interests of Tacoma Light. The construction of the two dams on the Cowlitz River would probably not have occurred without his tenacity as well as his abilities. While we had severe disagreements, we never had bad personal relations. We both shared the view that the other person was entitled to his opinion, so we just agreed to disagree.

Many other decisions affecting public power were made during 1953. Bonneville Administrator Paul Raver had instructions from Washington, D.C., ordering him to offer long-term power contracts to the private power companies. Under the original Bonneville Act, first call on federal power rightfully went to the consumer-owned utilities. Next in line for power were new industries, which could contract directly with Bonneville if the foreseeable energy needs of the preference utility customers were taken care of first. Low man on the federal power supply totem pole was the private power companies, who could contract with Bonneville only for one year at a time, since the federal government had never made a long-range commitment to supply power to the Pacific Northwest, and therefore couldn't know except from year to year how much power might be available from the federal dams. The new Eisenhower Administration sought to upgrade the position of the private power companies so that while they would still be second in line for federal power behind the not-for-profit consumer-owned utilities, they would be granted long-term contracts which must be fulfilled before Bonneville could serve any new industrial customers directly. We were not allowed into the negotiating sessions between Bonneville and the private power companies, but we learned enough about the new proposed contracts to make us quite upset in the early part of 1953.

One of the difficulties was that my Board had such a firm belief in the fairness and strong public power position of Paul Raver that they could not imagine that he would ever be a party to any kind of a contract which would undercut the preference clause. He never was, but my problem was that I knew he was under direct orders from Washington, D.C., where the entire trend was against public power, as exemplified in the person of Ralph Tudor, Undersecretary of the Interior. Even Secretary McKay, coming from the State of Oregon where most of the service was provided by private companies, while not lending himself to any violation of the preference clause, was interested in getting long-term power contracts for the private power companies. Finally, NWPPA and the PUD Association had to take the hard position that we would challenge the new contracts in court, and necessary changes were then made. Twenty-year contracts were extended to the power companies, incorporating a five-year pull-back provision to ensure that the needs for the preference utilities would be taken care of by Bonneville first as required under the preference clause. While the contracts were to run from 1953 to 1973, each September there would be a meeting between Bonneville and the private power companies where Bonneville would give notice five years in advance that it would be withdrawing from the supply specified in the contracts whatever power it felt was required to serve the growth needs of the publicly and cooperatively owned utilities, as well as to serve any existing direct service industry.

In 1953, the Washington PUD Association moved its offices and hired a third employee when the work load got heavy during the fight to prevent the merger of Washington Water Power and Puget Power. I had a very outstanding secretary-bookkeeper, a lady named Eleanor Hisey, who had previously worked for the Washington State Grange and was a devoted and dedicated public power supporter. She was very efficient, and up until 1963, when she resigned to get married, I cannot recall one day that she was absent from work. My second employee was Carlyn F. "Andy" Anderson, a young University of Washington graduate who had written his Master's thesis on public utility districts, and who proved to be another devoted and dedicated worker. Over my entire period of employment with the PUD Association, I was lucky enough to enjoy a small number of efficient and dedicated employees, who always made their boss look good. Andy came in 1953 and left after five years in 1957, saying to me, "I like the job, I like you, but I cannot see any great chance of promotion or growth in my capacity and, therefore, I must turn to another field." The PUD Association offered only one job higher than the one he held, and I was still quite young and vigorous in 1957. Andy joined the U.S. State Department, did considerable work overseas, and progressed very ably until he tragically contracted a tumor in his brain and died at a rather early age. Eleanor got married, adopted a daughter, and then became the mother of a second daughter. Eleanor and Andy were two of the best — but other good ones were to come later; I've been fortunate in my employees.

In September 1953, the Pend Oreille County PUD finally acquired the properties of Washington Water Power in that county, after starting a condemnation action in June 1947. These were among the few private power properties to be obtained by a PUD, following the sale of Puget Power properties to Snohomish County PUD in 1949.

Pend Oreille County PUD played an important role in getting Whatcom County PUD into the electric business even though Whatcom County served only one customer, an industry. I had been contacted by a longtime friend of mine, attorney Bob Graham of the Bogle and Gates law firm, who was representing a potential industrial customer seeking a power supply to build a refinery near Bellingham. Puget Power, which served that area, did not have the needed power, and Bonneville could not provide service until a later date when a new federal dam was due to come on line. I got in touch with Pend Oreille County PUD, which was then moving ahead on its Box Canyon Project, and got the Whatcom County PUD and the Pend Oreille County PUD people together, along with representatives of the new refinery. They negotiated a contract whereby Whatcom County PUD would purchase power from the new Box Canyon Project in order to serve the new industrial load. When the new federal dam was completed, the Whatcom County PUD transferred its power purchases to Bonneville.

On November 20, 1953, I received a call at my home from Gene Hoffman, longtime Superintendent of Seattle City Light. He said, "Ken, you will be the first person outside of my own family to know that I am resigning from my job at the end of the year. Monday morning, I am going to lay my resignation on Mayor Pomeroy's desk." I said, "Oh no, Gene, we need you at Seattle City Light." He said he felt it was time to make a change, that he had another business opportunity, and that he felt the program was rolling along at a time when he could step out following acquisition of the Puget Power properties in Seattle. He mentioned his assistant, John Nelson, as a potential replacement. My response was that Nelson was a very able person, but the position was one of leadership in the Pacific Northwest and we were in need of strong leadership.

After hanging up the telephone, I began to think of potential successors for Hoffman. It occurred to me that Paul Raver, who was still Bonneville Administrator, might just be interested in coming to Seattle as head of the largest publicly owned utility in the Northwest, if the rumors that he would be terminated by the Republication Administration were true. I called my friend Frank Stewart in Wenatchee and bounced the idea off him. His immediate response was very affirmative. I said, "You are closer to Mayor Alan Pomeroy than I am, and in the meantime I will try to locate Paul Raver." I found Raver in Washington, D.C., and learned that he would be returning to the West Coast the following Wednesday by way of Montana. Monday morning, Hoffman placed his resignation on the Mayor's desk. By Wednesday, we had prevailed on Raver to come home by way of Seattle to meet with Pomeroy. Mayor Pomeroy recommended his appointment and Raver was confirmed by the City Council on December 21, 1953, with his job to start January 15, 1954. Thus we retained the strong voice of Dr. Raver on public power's behalf in the Pacific Northwest.

Chelan County PUD filed for a Federal Power Commission preliminary permit on the Rocky Reach dam site in November 1953 and became the first PUD to file on the Columbia River, although Grant County PUD had been questing for its Priest Rapids site in Congress for a year by then.

In retrospect, 1953 was probably one of the most important years in private versus public power battles in the Pacific Northwest. In some ways it marked a turning point. From the 1920s and 1930s, on through the 1940s, public power had been on the move against private power, with the formation of the public utility districts, the activation of most of them, and the growth of the large federal public power program in the Pacific Northwest. The Eastern holding companies had disposed of the common stock they originally held in Northwest utilities, and while this had resulted in some strong independent private power companies remaining in the Pacific Northwest, they were at least more interested in Pacific Northwest power problems than their predecessors in the East.

Prior to 1953, the PUDs had attempted to take over Washington Water Power and acquire the Puget Power properties, and had won most fights in the Legislature. In 1953, the year that private power was supposed to beat public power in the legislative arena, but didn't, private power's merger to establish a statewide monopoly was defeated; the PUD purchase of Puget Power was rejected; local public power projects on the Columbia River with joint participation by private power and public power were started; Tacoma Light returned to the public power orbit; and Bonneville signed its first long-term power sales contract with private power. All of these events had a lasting effect. Looking back, one can recognize 1953 as the year that the private versus public power relationship here in the Pacific Northwest leveled off somewhat, even though the legislative fights and issues were to continue for many more years.

The year 1954 was busy on many fronts in the private versus public power conflict, but it also included a severe head-on clash between the Grant County PUD, supported by many of the consumer-owned utilities in the State, and the newly established State Power Commission. Arguments revolved around development of Priest Rapids Dam, which had been authorized as a Corps of Engineers dam by Congress in 1950. As federal development of power in the Pacific Northwest slowed down, local utilities turned to the study of potential dam sites it would be feasible for them to develop.

Glen Smothers, Manager of Grant County PUD, had been Chairman of the State PUD Association's Power Use and Conservation Committee for several years. His district had started a study of the Priest Rapids site in 1952, and in 1953, they commenced seeking congressional deauthorization of the site so that a non-federal entity could develop it. The Power Use and Conservation Committee had of course been very active in seeking legislation which would permit cities and/or PUDs to develop projects jointly. Actually, there was division in public power ranks over Grant County PUD's action because many of the local utilities still favored federal development of the remaining sites on the main stem of the Columbia River. However, under Grant County PUD sponsorship, a meeting was held in Ephrata on October 7, 1953, to study formation of a joint operating agency. Representatives of seven PUDs and two city light systems attended. A second meeting was held on October 9, 1953, attended by sixteen PUDs and seven city systems. Coming out of that meeting was an agreement by fourteen PUDs and seven city light systems to file a joint application with the State Power Commission to form a joint operating agency under the new law. Official signing of the application took place at Ellensburg on January 8, 1954, and it was filed on January 22, 1954. Disagreement immediately broke out between the utilities and the State Power Commission, which had just opened its new offices in Seattle and hired Frank Ward, Tacoma Light Superintendent, as its first Managing Director. A hearing on the application was held on March 26, 1954.

At the hearing, the State Power Commission took the position that before a joint operating agency could be formed, the project to be constructed would have to be cited. The local utilities took the position that formation was a first step. If a particular project was named in the application, approval of the application would mean endorsement of the project by the State Power Commission. The State Power Commission took no action on the application but announced its intention to make an overall survey of power needs and available projects. To counter this blocking action, five PUDs—Cowlitz, Grays Harbor, Mason No. 3, Douglas, and Grant—announced formation on April 1, 1954, of the Washington Municipal Power System under the 1949 joint action PUD law.

On July 13, Congress approved legislation deauthorizing the Priest Rapids site but changed the law which had previously designated Grant County PUD as the only potential constructor of the project. The Act made the range of potential developers so broad that it even included State agencies. In addition, Senator Cordon of Oregon struck out the part of the proposed law which provided that power left over after the local utilities' needs were met would be purchased by Bonneville. While the right of Bonneville to purchase the power was retained, funds to purchase it would have to be appropriated at a later date. An amendment by Senator Magnuson requiring that the power produced at the project be marketed in accordance with the federal statutes governing sale of power from a federal plant was defeated when this too was opposed by Senator Cordon.

Grant County PUD immediately (on July 14) filed an application with the Federal Power Commission for a preliminary permit to study construction of the dam. They had retained Harza Engineers back in November 1952 to do the necessary engineering work for the application. In a meeting two days later, the State Power Commission heard its Managing Director recommend that the Commission bypass the preliminary permit stage and apply immediately for a license whereby the Commission would construct the dam. When this was declared improper procedure, a hasty meeting was reconvened on July 20, just before President Eisenhower was to sign the enacted deauthorization legislation, and the State Power Commission decided to file an application with the Federal Power Commission for a preliminary permit to study Priest Rapids that would compete with the Grant County PUD's application. Tom Quast, as the PUD representative on the

State Power Commission, was the lone opponent of this attempt by the Commission to undercut the Grant County PUD.

My role during these many months, besides assisting in attempts to form a joint operating agency or joint action system, was to mediate between the State Power Commission and Grant County PUD. I was trying to avoid a head-on fight which undoubtedly would result in prolonged hearings before the Federal Power Commission and even lengthy court fights, thus delaying the project which, if load forecasts were accurate, was definitely needed in the Pacific Northwest. I arranged several meetings with Chairman Walter Gordon of the State Power Commission, his attorney, Frank Hayes, and representatives from Grant County PUD, including Manager Glen Smothers and Senator Nat Washington who also served as the local PUD's attorney. We got nowhere, and therefore in September I recommended to my Board of Directors that we ask the single PUD to challenge the State Power Commission in the State courts.

On the one hand, the State Power Commission was refusing to take action on the application to form a joint agency to let the PUDs and cities go ahead together on the project. They thought this would help block Grant County PUD from getting the project licensed by the Federal Power Commission, the project being too large for one small utility. On the other hand, in our opinion, the law was very clear that the State Power Commission could not take over any project which a local utility had actively started to develop. On September 16, Grant County PUD filed suit against the State Power Commission challenging the legality of actions taken by the Commission in connection with Priest Rapids. On October 8, Grant County PUD won its case in Superior Court by having a temporary restraining order against the Commission made permanent until the constitutionality of the State Power Commission law could be tested sometime later in the fall. Then on October 21, the Federal Power Commission granted a preliminary permit on the Priest Rapids site to the Grant County PUD. The PUD immediately started engineering work and agreed to furnish information to the State Power Commission with the proviso that, if the State Power Commission eventually were granted authority by the Federal Power Commission to build the project, the Commission would reimburse the PUD for engineering costs. Agreement was also reached that, if the State Power Commission constructed the project, the PUD would be guaranteed a share in the power output adequate to meet the power needs of its service area. The legal action then moved to the State Supreme Court.

Dr. Raver reported to his new assignment as Superintendent of Seattle City Light on January 15, 1954. Shortly thereafter, we had lunch and discussed various potential power problems of the Northwest. While Kinsey Robinson had been defeated in his effort to merge Washington Water Power with Puget Power, there was no question that Puget Power needed an additional source of power. Robinson had been using this as his main selling point for the merger. It became our mutual thought at this meeting that it might be well to surround Puget Power with four strong publicly owned utilities to form an umbrella of power supply to prevent attacks by Robinson. The utilities we selected were the city light systems of Seattle and Tacoma, the Snohomish County PUD to the north, and the Chelan County PUD to the east. Chelan County PUD and Puget Power already had a close relationship as a result of Chelan's completion of the Rock Island Dam. I broached the thought to both PUDs. Chelan County PUD immediately responded in the affirmative because it recognized the political need for this type of alliance. Snohomish County PUD was not too sure. It took several meetings with their commissioners and management to convince them of the value of this move, but when they agreed to it, the Puget Sound Utilities Council was established.

Prior to that, when Raver and I discussed potential engineering consultants, the name of Jack Stevens, a staff engineer at Bonneville, came up. Afterwards, I saw Jack in Victoria at a meeting of the Governors' Power Advisory Committee. During an intermission we got off to one side and he asked me what my thoughts were on the Utilities Council. He had been offered a job as consultant to the Council, but was rather hesitant to leave his long-time federal job. I told him that security was important, naturally, but that opportunities such as this didn't knock too often in a man's life. He would be backed by five of the largest and strongest utilities in the Pacific Northwest, and win, lose, or draw, he should have sufficient time in his new assignment to make other contacts as a consulting engineer. Upon his return to Portland, he called Dr. Raver and told him he would accept the consultant's job.

President Frank McLaughlin of Puget Power was a master of public relations who had been sent out here in the 1930s to clean up a mess made by the anti-public relations activity of a previous president. McLaughlin had done his homework very well. The newspapers in the Puget Sound region were filled with superlative editorials during April 1954, hailing the new Council as the answer for future power needs. Little did the editors realize that the purpose of the Council was to thwart a private power merger which could throttle public power in the State of Washington. The Council did serve other useful purposes. One thing it did was to inject a note of optimism into a region which had been twice shut down because of power shortages and brownouts. Later on, in the early 1960s, when it was no longer needed, it died a natural death.

Dr. Raver's presence at Seattle City Light made another change in the Pacific Northwest. At that time, only one main engineering firm was dedicated to serving public power in this area. R. W. Beck and Associates had always served so efficiently and solidly that certainly in my mind there was no need for another engineering firm. However, Dr. Raver pointed out to me that, as local utilities took over a greater share of power supply responsibilities, there would be a growing need for engineers. He meant, he said, no criticism of the Beck organization, but rather saw a need for broadening the field and bringing more active engineers into the Pacific Northwest so that they could become familiar with Pacific Northwest problems.

To implement this plan, he got in touch with Hank Zinder of H. Zinder and Associates, an engineering firm based in Washington, D.C. Zinder had been a former top staff person at the Federal Power Commission before forming his own consulting engineering firm which worked primarily with rural electric cooperatives throughout the nation. Zinder came to the Northwest, looked at the amount of engineering work which might be available, and opened an office in Seattle. To head the Seattle office he selected Sol Shultz, long-time chief engineer at Bonneville, who had been working with Dr. Raver since 1940. The presence of a competing engineering firm did not affect the Beck firm. It merely made available more top-flight brain power to serve the needs of the local public and cooperative utilities.

One of Shultz' first assignments was to handle the power marketing for Grant County PUD and its Priest Rapids Project. His work in 1955 resulted in a tremendous step forward for the Pacific Northwest regional power grid when he arranged for non-federally generated power to make use of the federal transmission grid.

Another major event in 1954 was that the Northwest Public Power Association sponsored federal legislation to establish a regional power corporation through which construction of federal dams and the extension of the Bonneville transmission grid could be financed. During the year, Douglas County PUD filed an application for a preliminary permit to do studies on the Wells Dam site. This meant that three major dam sites on the mid-Columbia River were being developed by PUDs.

The first draft of a Columbia Interstate Compact was agreed upon by the seven states participating in the negotiations, and the negotiators were planning to submit the proposed compact to their state legislatures in 1955.

At a special hearing held in Seattle in early December, where Washington members of the Compact Commission were to review the recently drafted compact, I presented the PUD Association's opposition to the document as written. We took exception specifically to the way the document allocated control of hydroelectric power development. We were afraid that if this regional resource were considered piecemeal, with individual states having control of different sections of the basin, comprehensive development of the river system would be destroyed. We specifically questioned inclusion in the compact of upstream states, such as Wyoming, Utah, and Nevada, which had been given three votes, or 27 percent of the total votes, while only 5 percent of the basin fell within their borders. In the first draft, the same states, although having 27 percent of the vote, would not be required to contribute together more than 6 percent of any overall compact budget. Under the proposed allocation of power, it appeared that 60 percent of the potential power of the region would go to the states of Montana and Idaho, while the states of Oregon and Washington, which had the largest populations, would become power exporters. This figure was derived from a formula proposed in the compact to determine how much power generated at downstream sites as a result of upstream storage would be returned to the upstream states. Needless to say, this inequity in the compact kicked off a conflict which would be fought in the various legislative arenas until 1965.

Late in 1954, when federal agencies started to study possible development at the Mountain Sheep and Pleasant Valley sites on the Snake River below the Hells Canyon stretch of the river, Governor Jordan of Idaho and Governor Langlie of Washington pulled out all stops to block the effort. It thus came as no surprise in November 1954 to see the Pacific Northwest Power Company, the combine of four Pacific Northwest private power utilities, file a request with the Federal Power Commission for a preliminary permit to study both sites. Once again, the Northwest Public Power Association and State PUD Association joined forces to intervene and block such action. The two proposed dams would eliminate any possible chance of constructing the high Nez Perce Dam which, as in the case of the high Hells Canyon Dam, would be a tremendous water storage dam. Such a dam would not only create needed hydroelectric power in future years, but would also provide fresh water storage for downriver reclamation purposes. Here, too, was the start of another long fight between private and public power.

Final activity in 1954 concerned the third draft of the proposed Columbia River Development Corporation bill being sponsored by the Northwest Public Power Association. A special membership meeting of the Association held in Spokane on December 10 approved changes which had been made in the first two drafts, and with the election of Dick Neuberger as U.S. Senator from the State of Oregon, a proponent of the legislation was to be seated in Congress. Meanwhile, following the filing of the lawsuit against the State Power Commission by Grant County PUD, I was busy drafting amendments to the joint State Power Commission and operating agency law which would remove the requirement that forming a joint operating agency must have State Power Commission approval. The amendments were being put into legal language by attorney Jack Cluck under the guidance of Senator Nat Washington and myself, and we had already started the lobbying effort to get the 1955 Legislature to make the needed changes.

While there had been plenty of private versus public power activities in the Northwest for many years, a major national fight between these forces surfaced in 1954. President Eisenhower had directed the Atomic Energy Commission to enter into a contract for some of its power supply in the Tennessee Valley Authority's service area from a proposed steam plant to be constructed outside the TVA area by a private power combine. This was the infamous Dixon-Yates proposal. The TVA people were astounded but recognized that this was the first step by the Administration to stop growth of the TVA even in its own service area. The corporate entity which was to build the plant proposed a financing arrangement of 95 percent bonded indebtedness with only 5 percent common stock. This type of leverage smacked of the old Samuel Insull holding company era. The utility companies that would own the plant were two holding companies and not even operating utilities. In the first twenty-five years, the power contract would cost TVA $139 million more than the same amount of power supplied from its new Fulton steam plant, and at the end of the twenty-five-year period, the private owners would own the plant, whereas under TVA construction, the government would own the plant.

While our major effort during the year centered on Northwest problems, we did spend considerable time working with and through our congressional delegation to block the Dixon-Yates proposal. This fight was the forerunner of TVA's move to seek self-financing legislation from Congress, and in the next few years, with my Board's approval, I made many a trip to and from Washington, D.C., in support of the TVA effort, to return the courtesy which those southern congressmen and senators would extend to the Pacific Northwest in our fight to protect our public power program in this region. Leadership of the TVA effort fell on the shoulders of an official of the Chattanooga, Tennessee, Electric Utility Board, named States Rights Finley. He had been given that name when he was born in South

Carolina, and had moved to Tennessee. States would call me and ask if I could come to Washington, D.C., on a given date, and I would catch a DC6 or DC7 red-eye out of Seattle flying all night in order to meet his schedule. He always stayed at the old Willard Hotel in Washington, D.C., and he always had a breakfast strategy meeting at 7:30 a.m. During a number of those years, the East Coast was on Daylight Savings Time when the West Coast was not and, therefore, a 7:30 a.m. East Coast time meant a 3:30 a.m. body time for me. Even though I was still a relatively young man, the seven-day weeks without vacations and holidays, topped by this kind of necessary body adjustment, were an interesting period of my life. But Congress did get the TVA self-financing legislation through after several years of work – and my loss of sleep.

1955–1956

In 1955 the State Legislature convened a session on January 10 that would be very busy dealing with electric utility issues. Besides the standing private versus public power fight, of major import was the conflict between the State Power Commission and Grant County PUD, supported by other local utilities, over construction of the Priest Rapids Project. The 1954 elections changed the face of the Legislature. While Republicans still had control in the Senate by a majority of 24 to 22, control of the House passed to the Democrats, who had 50 members to 49 for the Republicans. Public power still maintained its coalition strength in the Senate, and selection of Representative John O'Brien as House Speaker and Julia Butler Hansen as Speaker Pro Tempore assured that the House Public Utilities Committee would have a majority of public power supporters on it.

A flood of power legislation was introduced. Private power had the Senate looking at legislation to triple the PUD privilege tax, and a revised Spokane Power Bill was strangely worded but seemed to say that no properties of Washington Water Power could be acquired by public power without the approval of Spokane voters. On the House side, legislation to abolish the State Power Commission and another bill which removed the Commission's authority to develop hydroelectric projects were introduced. The PUD Association sponsored legislation to revise the procedure for forming joint operating agencies which would comply with established standards but would no longer require approval of the State Power Commission.

One bill of mutual interest was an amendment to the PUD law removing a three-year limitation on sale of power by a PUD to a private power company. It was recognized that, as individual PUDs attempted to construct large generating plants on the mid-Columbia River, they would need to market surplus power either to the federal government or to all operating utilities, including private power companies, in order to finance such projects in the absence of an established joint operating agency.

The "happy tax bill," sponsored by Senator Happy of Spokane, which would have tripled PUD taxes, was stopped in committee. However, when another bill dealing with clarification of State Tax Commission distribution of the PUD privilege tax came on the Senate floor, Senator Happy attempted to add his legislation by amendment. The result was some terrific debate on taxes but defeat of the "happy tax bill" by a 28 to 18 coalition vote. SB-208 was introduced to ratify the Columbia Interstate Compact which had been negotiated during the previous year and signed by all seven states in early January. The PUDs also had some housekeeping legislation needed to help improve efficiency.

Governor Langlie, in his State of the State address, set the stage for the big issue centering on the State Power Commission versus local utilities. He specifically supported the State Power Commission's wish to construct the dam at Priest Rapids, and asked for $1,000,000 for exploratory work on the project in addition to its budget request of $215,000 to meet its current expenses. The State Supreme Court had scheduled arguments on the Grant County PUD case, which the PUD had won in the Superior Court, for January 25. It was our decision in response to Governor Langlie to move ahead with the legislation we had drafted which left the State Power Commission in business but not in a position to block local utilities.

On February 18, the State Supreme Court rendered its decision in the Grant County PUD versus State Power Commission case, ruling in favor of the PUD, and finding that the State Power Commission had exceeded its authority in filing its competing application for the Priest Rapids site.

On February 22, Senator Nat Washington and I were called down to Governor Langlie's office, and the Governor asked me directly why we would not accept the State Power Commission as power supplier for the public utility districts. My answer was simply that whoever controlled the power supply could have a marked effect on, if not actual control of, the distribution utility. We would not agree to place our power supply in the domain of a politically appointed statewide commission which might become dominated by private power companies. I stated that it was our basic belief that any power supplier should be directly responsible to and controlled by the local distribution utility. I had previously been told by the Democratic leaders in the House, who were to write that year's appropriations bill, that I could assure the Governor that, "Unless agreement on the State Power Commission can be reached between the local public utilities and your office, we will not appropriate any funds for its continuance."

On the basis of this conversation, a series of conferences and meetings was arranged by Governor Langlie in his office between representatives of private power, representatives of the cities of Seattle and Tacoma, and myself. The sessions were for discussion of the amendments we had drafted for the State Power Commission law clarifying the rights of local utilities, both privately and publicly owned, to have first opportunity on power development. Accompanying me at the negotiations was Glen Smothers, Manager of Grant County PUD.

As was the usual case in these negotiations, private power representatives always sought to add amendments to curtail local public power. One proposed amendment would remove the right of a public utility district to condemn a private power generator installed at a dam constructed by the State Power Commission. I had a problem when Glen Smothers sided with the private power companies on this particular issue. I had to turn to him and say that, while he had every right to speak for Grant County PUD, I was authorized to speak for the other PUDs on the basis of what I believed to be their consensus. I told those present that, while I could rightfully negotiate on matters dealing with joint activity and joint powers of public utility districts, I could not agree to any changes in the basic PUD law which relinquished the right of an individual PUD. After some heated exchange, Governor Langlie turned to the private power representative and stated that this matter would have to be put aside.

Following several hard days of negotiation, Governor Langlie called a press conference to announce the changes on which we had agreed. He called our agreement a compromise. Coming out of the press conference, Stub Nelson of the *Seattle P-I* passed by me and said, "Some compromise! You got everything you wanted." That wasn't quite right, but it was a good feeling to know that we had secured most of what we needed.

However, I then had another problem. Democratic House leaders said they felt they could not take a chance on sending such amendments through the Legislature, including the appropriation for the State Power Commission for the next biennium, and then let the Governor have the last say by using his item veto. At that time, the Governor's veto power extended to details. Actual words, phrases, and punctuation could be vetoed. My first response to the leaders' fears was to have Max Nicolai, an attorney for the Democratic caucus on the House side, draft what we termed a reverse severability and veto provision. In essence, the provision stated that it was the legislative intent that such legislation be approved in toto and that to veto or change any particular section by veto would destroy its legislative intent and thus render the entire legislation, including the State Power Commission funding, null and void. It would have been interesting if we had included this provision. If we had, it undoubtedly would have been challenged in the State Supreme Court.

To avoid having to use it, I arranged a meeting between Governor Langlie and the House Democratic leadership. I remember walking down to the meeting with Democratic leaders O'Brien and Hansen, where the Governor pledged that, if the House would provide the $215,000 appropriation for State Power Commission operation and passed only those amendments which had been agreed to in our negotiations, he would not veto the legislation if it came to his desk.

On that basis, the House enacted HB-658, as amended, without the reverse severability and veto section, included $214,142 for the State Power Commission, and the matter was settled. We also obtained the other legislation, including SB-367, to allow long-term power sales contracts with private power companies and the omnibus bill for improving the PUD law.

One amusing incident occurred in the 1955 Session at an evening hearing on SB-208, legislation to ratify the Columbia River Interstate Compact. Congress in 1952 had authorized the states of Washington, Oregon, Idaho, Montana, and Wyoming to negotiate an interstate compact governing the allocation and use of Columbia River waters. Having watched the long and hard fight, including prolonged court action among the states involved in use and allocation of the Colorado River (Colorado, Arizona, and California), I felt that a solid compact negotiated at this time on the Columbia River, when there was not too much pressure over allocation or water use issues, would be of tremendous benefit to the Northwest states, so in 1953, I had recommended to my Board that we support negotiating such a compact. Little did I realize that within two years the private power companies would inject into the interstate compact debate and formulation some provisions which would hurt public power. This started us down the road to killing the compact by lobbying against its ratification by the Washington Legislature. While the private versus public power fight did stop the compact for a number of sessions, it was finally the State of Oregon, with a Legislature dominated by private power forces, which struck the final blow by killing it in 1965.

In 1955, I found myself trying to wear a white hat in support of a compact while being embroiled in a private versus public power argument about its provisions. We supported the compact for water use and allocation purposes but saw no need to extend it to cover power allocation issues.

For large or important hearings, it was the practice to use the Senate or House chamber. That evening's hearing in the Senate chamber drew quite a crowd, including a lot of reporters from the media. The Washington State Grange, the Seattle Chamber of Commerce, and the PUD Association opposed the legislation. When I appeared, two pro-private power senators saw some fair game in front of them in the person of a young public power lobbyist. Senator Bill Shannon of King County and Senator Ed Flanagan of Yakima County had been eating red meat. Shannon was a highly qualified engineer who had done work for Puget Power. In fact, the lake behind one of Puget Power's dams was named in his honor. Senator Flanagan, a conservative farmer and former baseball player, was a stalwart supporter of Pacific Power and Light. I had finished my testimony at the reading clerk's podium just below the Senate's presiding officer station when these two senators took off on me with questions not even pertaining to the interstate compact, but concerning the need and value of public power and PUDs in particular in our State. They were making some pretty stiff statements against public power, including false charges that PUDs didn't pay taxes. Senator Flanagan ended one of his tirades against public power and my presence with the direct question, "Tell me, why do you want to exist?" This got quite a laugh from the audience. I realized what they were doing, so my answer, given audibly and with force was, "Senator, you ask why I want to exist. It is primarily because my wife and two children love me." This brought down the house, and broke up the hearing, as the chairman rapped for order and adjourned.

The next morning as I walked on the floor before the session to see Senator Harry Wall, Senator Flanagan came over and said, "Harry, last night we really tried to get this young rooster's goat." I said, "Senator, I was so mad and I knew just what you were trying to do, but I was determined that you couldn't beat me down." From that moment on, while Senator Flanagan, who had served in the Senate since 1943 as a pro-private power senator, never gave me a vote or any help, we had a cordial relationship. Thereafter Senator Shannon, who started legislative service in the House in 1947, moved to the Senate by appointment in 1951, and was first elected to the Senate in 1952, always referred to me, until finishing his last session in 1961, as "my friendly enemy." They were tough but good guys and I liked them both, but I was once again happy to see the end of the sixty-day session on March 10, 1955.

With the end of the legislative session, activity picked up on the Priest Rapids Project. Grant County PUD had to move ahead under its preliminary permit and because of refusal of the State Power Commission to allow formation of a joint operating agency, the individual district was fast trying to firm up its application for a license. Any applicant for an FPC license had to demonstrate its ability to use and/or sell all power to be produced.

Sol Schultz, long-time chief engineer for the Bonneville Power Administration who had been selected to head the H. Zinder and Associates engineering firm, was retained by the PUD as a consultant, and one of his duties was to advise on power marketing sales. Grant County PUD had agreed that first opportunity for power purchase would go to the publicly and cooperatively owned utilities in Oregon and Washington. It immediately became apparent to Schultz that, without agreement on the part of the federal government through Bonneville to wheel non-federal power, those local utilities would have no chance of participating because they would not have the necessary transmission lines.

Several of the large private power companies waiting on the doorstep took the position that they would build their own lines to the dam if Grant County PUD would sell to them. In fact, Pacific Power and Light announced plans to build a twin circuit wood pole line from Priest Rapids to Union Gap near Yakima and then over an existing right of way to its Conduit generating plant on the White Salmon River. The line would then go to a new project to be constructed at Swift Creek in southeastern Cowlitz County and thence to Troutdale near Portland.

Schultz approached Pacific Power and Light stating that he felt the company could save considerable funds if it would approach Bonneville to secure federal wheeling of non-federal power. Pacific Power and Light turned him down. Schultz then went directly to Dr. Pearl, the Bonneville Administrator who had replaced Dr. Raver, and pointed out to him that even if Pacific Power and Light built its own line, the federal transmission line would actually carry the power. Electricity flows to the point of need through the line of least impedence. Thus, in effect, the federal government would be wheeling the power but would not receive any payment for such service. On the other side of the ledger, Pacific Power and Light would be making an unneeded investment which could only be paid for by higher charges to its customers. Pearl expressed a concern but said Bonneville had no authority to stop Pacific Power and Light's plans.

Schultz then told his story to Morgan Dubro, the Bonneville Manager in Washington, D.C., who arranged for Schultz to see Assistant Secretary of the Interior Fred Aandahl. Here again the argument was rejected and, in fact, Aandahl emphasized that the present Administration had a partnership program whereby local utilities were to be encouraged to build their own needed facilities. However, about then, local Bonneville officials did agree to wheel the non-federal power for other utilities in accordance with the Bonneville Act. A solicitor's opinion, citing the deauthorization legislation providing that Priest Rapids be integrated with the federal system, supported Bonneville's right to wheel the non-federal power. It was then that Undersecretary of the Interior Clarence Davis stepped in and made the wheeling of non-federal power over federal lines a departmental policy.

Schultz was still concerned that the building of the line by Pacific Power and Light was a waste to both the company and the federal system. He later approached Howard Morgan, new Oregon Public Service Commissioner under Governor Bob Holmes. Morgan knew that before Pacific Power and Light could build such a line, approval would have to be secured from the Federal Power Commission because the line would traverse federal lands. Further, since he was the regulator commissioner, approval for the investment would have to come from his office. There was a face-off between Morgan and Paul McKee, head of Pacific Power and Light, in 1957 when Pacific Power and Light wanted to move ahead but Morgan refused approval.

A contract for wheeling was signed between Bonneville and Grant County PUD in April 1956. This firmed up the opportunity for local public power utilities to participate in the Priest Rapids Project as power purchasers. Then, with settlement of the Pacific Power and Light issue, Bonneville commenced wheeling for private power also, setting a precedent for future major wheeling arrangements of non-federal power over federal lines.

One of the bad things which happened, I see in retrospect, was the failure of more of the local public power utilities to take advantage of the surplus power to come from the Priest Rapids Project. A diligent effort was made by Grand County PUD to market the power to local public power, and the local utilities had a hard decision to make. Bonneville power was still costing about 3 mills per kilowatt-hour. Priest Rapids power was estimated to cost 5 or 6 mills. This was 1956. By the 1970s, Priest Rapids power became a bargain. I recall very vividly the night Smothers and Schultz asked me to meet them downtown in Seattle to inform me that they had just returned from Snohomish County PUD, the largest PUD in our State, where they had been told that it was that PUD's decision to remain with the federal power supply. At that time, Grant County PUD had over $1,400,000 sunk in the project, which was neither licensed nor proven feasible. I told them that they had kept faith with our agreement and the project would have to go forward even if the power had to be sold under long-term power contracts to the private power companies. We needed the additional power supply in the Pacific Northwest.

In early March, identical bills to authorize a high federal dam at the Hells Canyon site were introduced in both houses of Congress. Senator Morse of Oregon introduced a bill co-sponsored by twenty-nine other senators, including Magnuson and Jackson of Washington, Neuberger of Oregon, and Murray and Mansfield of Montana. In the House, sponsors were Representatives Don Magnuson of Washington, Gracie Post of Idaho, Edith Green of Oregon, and Lee Metcalf of Montana. Hearings were scheduled throughout the Northwest in early April, and they were heated and heavy, with leaders of agriculture and organized labor on one side being opposed by Chamber of Commerce representatives and individual businessmen and attorneys representing themselves on the other. Governor Langlie of Washington and Governor Patterson of Oregon both opposed the legislation.

The issue of power partnership was to be joined at the proposed John Day Dam site. The PUD Association and the Northwest Public Power Association called for construction of a federal multiple purpose project at the John Day Dam site. At the same time, Representative Sam Coon of Oregon introduced a bill calling for a joint or power partnership construction of the project. The Coon bill proposed a $310-million project that would have a capacity of 1,105,000 kilowatts. Power output would go to the local utilities under fifty-year contracts in proportion to the amount of money they put up. Stepping up to finance the power portion were Portland General Electric, Washington Water Power, and Pacific Power and Light. While construction would be by the federal government and ownership would be retained in the government, the power would go to the private companies. It was a case of the federal government owning the cow but the private power companies milking her.

It was at this time that another decision was made on the Hells Canyon issue. The Federal Power Commission examiner recommended that a license be issued to the Idaho Power Company to construct one of the dams in the company's three-dam plan for the Hells Canyon region. This was an interesting decision. In it the examiner turned down two of the dams because the cost of power from the two would be so high no market could be reasonably predicted for it. He then stated that, undoubtedly, under federal development and a theoretical comparison, the high single dam would be superior to the three lower dams. While the examiner's decision would not reach the full Federal Power Commission for several months, a special message was sent from the U.S. Senate to the Federal Power Commission that such a decision should not be made until final hearings had been held on the Hells Canyon legislation.

It was in June that Chelan County PUD finally acquired the Washington Water Power properties in that county, properties they had been attempting to get since 1945. The generating plant at Chelan Falls was ac-

Chelan Hydro Project on Lake Chelan was constructed by Washington Water Power in 1928 and purchased by Chelan County PUD #1 in 1955.

quired along with the distribution properties surrounding the east end of Lake Chelan. Actual purchase was by negotiation, although an order was entered in the condemnation suit which saved the private power company from payment of taxes. This was another instance of private power's bragging about paying taxes on the one hand and then using any means to avoid their payment on the other.

In late August 1955, I was called to Stevens County to meet with the PUD Commission to discuss an agreement which they had made with Washington Water Power. Stevens County PUD had moved ahead on its condemnation suit to secure Washington Water Power properties in that county. However, Washington Water Power had countered with an offer that if the matter were submitted to a vote in November and the people voted for the PUD, Washington Water Power would sell the properties for $3,100,000. But if in the election 60 percent favored private operation, the present PUD properties would be sold to Washington Water Power for a price to cover outstanding debt plus $200,000. Under the law, the people could not sell their PUD properties without voter approval in an election. To all appearances the PUD had an advantage because 60 percent of the voters must agree before the public utility could dispose of its property. However, when I was shown this proposal, which already had been agreed to by the PUD Board, my response was, "Your local PUD has been lost." The Board was somewhat astonished, but I pointed out that rates, taxes, and service were all on the private power side, which was serving in the towns while the PUD, which had taken over the rural electric cooperative service, was serving the countryside. The result was lower private power rates in Colville as opposed to higher PUD rates at the end of the line. Washington Water Power had a generating plant located on the Spokane River in the south end of Stevens County. While this plant did not furnish the power for Stevens County PUD, Washington Water Power paid high property taxes to the county for this facility. Finally, electric service in the town areas was more reliable than it was out along the county roads the PUD served.

The campaign, which took off immediately, required my presence in Stevens County four or five days each week during October and November. The State Grange dispatched two Grange deputies and we had the support of local public power people. However, Washington Water Power put on a whirlwind campaign using Bozell and Jacobs, a large public relations firm. It was later documented that they used employees whose salaries were paid by the ratepayers for a countywide door-knocking campaign. They even hired linemen and dispatched them to Stevens County to help with the door-knocking.

When the vote was held on November 22, the voters by a 5-to-2 vote, or 71 percent, approved the sale of the PUD properties to Washington Water Power. The election attracted nationwide attention. Efforts of local people were overwhelmed by the all-out campaign of the private power company, in a battle between a $100 million private monopoly corporation with all of its resources and a $2.5 million publicly owned utility. It was a contest where the private power company could use every known method of disseminating political propaganda while the public agency, limited by state law, could only use a few official letters and factual advertising in the county's two weekly newspapers. False and misleading anti-PUD statements were made by Washington Water Power. But as I stated when I was first informed about this proposal, rates, taxes, and service in this particular instance favored private power, and it was therefore logical that voters, even if they had not been swayed by the intense propaganda, would want to sell the PUD properties to the private power company.

Later, Washington Water Power's annual report filed with the State Public Service Commission for the year 1955 showed Stevens County PUD election expenses of $66,671; payment to an advertising agency for services in connection with its business of $112,388; and contract payments to Bo-zell and Jacobs, the public relations coordinating firm used in the campaign, of $35,584. We never found out to what utility account the wages of the linemen who were door-knocking during the campaign in Stevens County were charged. Were they charged above the line and thus treated as regular operating costs, or were they charged below the line against company profits? If past practices of the 1930s and 1940s were followed, a lot of the costs of the campaign probably were charged above the line. The total spent by the pro-PUD forces, including cost to the PUD Association for my work and the Grange's cost for the two deputies, came to just over $8,000. One can visualize the difference in the two campaigns just by comparing the costs. Thus came about the only sale of PUD properties to a private power company since enactment of the PUD law by the people in the 1930 statewide vote.

Kinsey Robinson savored his victory over public power with great relish, spending time during the next year appearing at conferences and conventions of private power, talking about the Stevens County results and how they had been obtained. Actually, while the company had gained slightly more than 2,000 customers from the PUD in Stevens County, the year had resulted in a net loss to the private company when Chelan County PUD was successful in finally acquiring the 2,300 private power customers near Lake Chelan. In addition, Chelan County PUD had secured the Chelan Falls generating plant. To offset the bad news in Stevens

Box Canyon Dam on the Pend Oreille River was the first dam licensed to a State of Washington PUD, February 26, 1952. The Pend Oreille County PUD #1 put the dam into service in 1955.

Courtesy Pend Oreille County PUD #1

County further was the good news in next-door Pend Oreille County that the PUD had completed its Box Canyon Dam. In addition, on November 4, 1955, license was granted to Grant County PUD to move forward with its Priest Rapids Project, which now would be in the form of two dams, one near the original Priest Rapids Dam site contemplated by the Army Corps of Engineers and another further upstream to be called Wanapum, after the local Indian tribe located adjacent to the dam site. The year 1955 also

A group of Wanapum Indians attended the dedication of Wanapum Dam in June 1966.

Wanapum Dam on the Columbia River was put into service by Grant County PUD #1 in 1963. *Courtesy Grant County PUD #2*

closed out with a record eight rate reductions by PUDs, which included a reduction of 17 percent for the new Chelan County PUD customers taken from Washington Water Power.

Final good news for public power in 1955 was the announcement by the Office of Defense Mobilization that it was going to stop issuing certificates of rapid amortization on private power generating plants. However, before the December 31 deadline, a flood of private power tax write-off applications hit the department, including a broader one for Idaho Power Company for its three-dam plan in upper Hells Canyon. That was an application we planned to watch. A nationwide compilation by the National Rural Electric Cooperative Association showed that the value of rapid amortization to the private power companies under the program had exceeded all the federal dollars invested by the government in federal power projects and rural cooperative loans combined since the very beginning of those programs. Pacific Power and Light had just been granted rapid amortization on its proposed Swift Creek Project; federal taxes totaling 65 percent of the $63 million full cost of the dam – that is, $41,226,900 – could be withheld and paid later. Government subsidies over the $33^1/3$ years which would be needed to pay the withheld taxes (which acted as an interest-free loan) were computed as being nearly $37,000,000. Permitting double larceny was an Internal Revenue Service ruling that 50 percent of the stock dividends for Pacific Power and Light for 1954 was considered as a return of capital resulting from this rapid amortization subsidy and thus that percent of the stock dividends was exempt from the income taxes of the receiving stockholder.

The Pacific Northwest private power companies had certainly received their share of this federal tax dollar subsidy program. Of course, some of those federal tax dollars had been used by the local companies in support of their national organization advertising program against the federal dams and power lines being financed by the federal taxpayers. Thus, all of the dollars saved didn't go into their stockholders' pockets.

The year 1955 saw the death of two long-time commissioners. W. K. "Billy" McKenzie, elected in 1936 when the Chelan County PUD was formed, died on January 11. Preston Royer, who was elected to the Benton County PUD Board in 1936, died on April 1. Time was moving on and some of the original long-time commissioners were being replaced. I will have more to say about these public power pioneers in Chapter 9.

January 1, 1956 was the date of retirement of Appellate Court Judge Homer T. Bone. Thus ended his public service which dated from his first election to the State Legislature in the 1923 Session through his U.S. Senate service from 1932 to 1944 and then his service as judge on the Appellate

Court in San Francisco. Bone had been the main architect of the Grange initiative passed in 1930, the "compromise" which led to enactment of the Bonneville Project Act in 1937, and even while on the Appellate Court he retained a steadfast position in support of public power. He returned to reside in Tacoma during the remaining years of his life, and on one or two occasions it was my privilege to once again meet the man who in 1938 got me involved in local public power.

Another milestone which occurred in early 1956 was the January 6 announcement of Chelan County PUD's purchase of Rock Island Dam from Puget Power for $28,226,200. The PUD had earlier filed a condemnation action against the dam primarily to thwart condemnation action by another publicly owned utility from the westside of the State, and then later had, by contract, financed and constructed a second powerhouse at the project. Under the purchase plan, Puget Power was to advance $1,500,000 to finance the preliminary engineering on the Rocky Reach Dam. Stone & Webster was retained as the architect/engineer for the new project, and a license application was filed on January 25 with the Federal Power Commission. At this time over 2,500,000 kilowatts of generation were being studied, developed, or constructed by PUDs statewide. These included not

Rock Island Dam was the first non-federal dam constructed on the main stem of the Columbia River. It was constructed by Puget Sound Power and Light Company and put into service in 1933. Chelan County PUD #1 helped finance a second powerhouse in 1951 to serve a Korean War industry, a new Aluminum Company of America smelter (*shown in background*), and in 1956 the PUD purchased the dam from Puget Power.

only the dams on the main stem of the Columbia River but also many other projects throughout the State.

Shortly after the Chelan County PUD purchase of Rock Island, Puget Power and Douglas County PUD reached agreement on the Wells Dam. Both had filed an application for a preliminary permit on the Wells Dam site and the PUD had been awarded the permit. Puget Power had petitioned for a rehearing, and without agreement there could have been prolonged Federal Power Commission hearings and even court action. Puget Power agreed to withdraw its opposition to the preliminary permit if it would be given the first opportunity to buy power surplus from the Wells Dam after the PUD's own needs were met.

Effective April 1, Clark County PUD made one of the largest rate reductions it had ever made. It was estimated that its customers would save $345,000 in the first year.

Filing of the license application for Rocky Reach Dam by Chelan County PUD did aggravate a dispute between Douglas County and Chelan County over siting of the Wells Dam. At the same time, the Cowlitz County PUD challenged Pacific Power and Light over projects they both wanted to develop at Swift Creek, and here again active negotiations went forward to forestall a fight before the Federal Power Commission. Agreement was reached on July 16 with Cowlitz County PUD to construct Swift Creek No. 2 downstream from the major Swift Creek Dam to be constructed and owned by Pacific Power and Light. Pacific Power and Light would purchase any power the Cowlitz County PUD did not need. Meanwhile, construction contracts were being let on the Priest Rapids Dam and the first bonds had already been issued by Grant County PUD.

In 1952, during his campaign for the presidency, Dwight Eisenhower had expressed concern over federal government involvement in any type of power development. Later, in his first term, he had again expressed his preference that the federal government not be involved in power production or transmission. In 1956, just as his campaign for re-election was to commence, he made a statement that it might be well to examine the federal government's involvement in power development and possibly think about disposing of the Tennessee Valley Authority, as well as other federal agency power facilities.

By the time we had straightened out the issue on formation of a joint operating agency at the 1955 Session of the Legislature, Grant County PUD had progressed so far with individual utility contracts in order to prove its ability before the Federal Power Commission to construct the projects that we did not pursue formation of a joint operating agency. However, in discussing Eisenhower's evident opposition to federal power agencies, my Board of Directors, at its June 29 meeting, authorized the PUD Association to sponsor formation of a joint operating agency. We named it the Washington Public Power Supply System, and gave the individual PUDs an August 1 deadline to decide whether they would participate in this new joint entity.

By that date, seventeen out of the nineteen members of the PUD Association operating electric distribution systems had passed Board resolutions to join. Simultaneously, a ratepayer in the Clallam County PUD challenged that district's action in joining the new entity and making an advance for its financing purposes. This provided an opportune lawsuit as it was known that, before bonds could ever be issued under the joint operating agency law, the constitutionality of the law would have to be approved by the State Supreme Court.

In the law governing formation of joint operating agencies, it is required that once the application is filed with the Department of Conservation and Development, an advertisement must be placed in the legal newspaper of any county in which it is contemplated that a generation or transmission facility will be constructed or operated by the entity. Thus, following filing of our application to form the Washington Public Power Supply System, on October 8 we advertised in each of the 39 counties of the State of Washington. While the application indicated construction of a steam plant and several small hydros, our hidden purpose was that, should Eisenhower be re-elected in November and should he be successful in disposing of the federal power facilities, we would have a public power system standing ready and waiting to purchase all of the Bonneville transmission system within the State of Washington. In later years, there have been many speculations in the news media about the real reason the Supply System was formed. This, in fact, was the purpose we had in mind when we filed its application for formation in 1956.

On July 19 Congress finally took up the authorization legislation for a high federal Hells Canyon Dam. Private power opposition was rampant throughout the nation because Idaho Power Company, under the license previously granted to it, was actively working on the site. Although the license approval had been challenged in the Federal Appellate Court by the National Hells Canyon Association, the company moved ahead on construction. The National Hells Canyon Association won a U.S. Supreme Court order against the Idaho Power Company that the government would not be held responsible for money the company lost if a federal court decision reversed the Federal Power Commission's license approval.

The Hells Canyon legislation came to the Senate floor first and after substantial debate private power won by a vote of 51 to 41. After this defeat, the House took no action. Public power supporters of the high dam were stunned because it meant loss of one of the most valuable potential multiple-purpose projects on the Columbia/Snake River system.

Their response was to convene a meeting in Salt Lake City of persons and organizations who had supported the high dam. There they formed the Western States Water and Power Consumers Conference composed primarily of Western states persons and organizations interested in water resource development, along with national organizations which supported such development. In future years, this Conference would be convened every second year during an election campaign – presidential, gubernatorial, or congressional – which would provide rallying points around those candidates who supported the consumer interest in river development. John F. Kennedy, in his successful run for the White House in 1960, was to appear before the Conference at Billings, Montana, where he gave his major speech on reclamation and river development. But for now, even though the National Hells Canyon Association was to continue its court battle, the Hells Canyon Dam was lost. On October 8, the Court of Appeals upheld the license the Federal Power Commission had issued to the Idaho Power Company.

In August 1956, Klickitat County PUD filed on the John Day Dam site. In doing so, it stated that first preference was for federal construction of the dam but in recognition that the federal government appeared to be abdicating such effort, it felt that the project should be developed as a public power site under public financing.

By this time, the 1956 elections were warming up. Governor Langlie ran for the U.S. Senate against Senator Magnuson's re-election bid and Secretary of the Interior McKay had resigned to return to Oregon and run against the re-election of Senator Wayne Morse. State Senator Albert Rosellini of King County became the Democratic nominee for Governor, and Emmett Anderson, Lieutenant Governor to Governor Langlie, became the Republican candidate. While the Association tried to avoid partisan elections, we could not stand still when Langlie, in his prepared speech for an August 28 television appearance, took after Senator Magnuson over his support of the high Hells Canyon Dam. I prepared a statement for George Hamilton, Commissioner from Douglas County, and President of the PUD Association, and A. Lars Nelson, Master of the Washington State Grange, calling Langlie's statements "irresponsible." We pointed out that six of our present nine members of Congress, including three of Langlie's fellow Republicans, supported the high Hells Canyon Dam.

Later, when Langlie attacked construction of the Ice Harbor Dam, I was happy to see Herb West, Executive Vice President of the Inland Waterways Association, also pick up the cudgel against Langlie's statements. My telephone call to West's office in Walla Walla was not very expensive. Then, finally on September 17, in a television debate on power between Governor Langlie and Senator Magnuson in Spokane, Langlie denied a statement made by Magnuson that there had been a definite lack of new power project starts under the Republicans. Langlie's response was, "I want to inform you, Senator, we have plenty of new starts. Priest Rapids is going ahead and whether you like it or not, I can tell you that my leadership in the State Legislature is what made it possible for Priest Rapids and the PUD there to go ahead and build that dam." Two days later, Glen Smothers, Grant County PUD Manager, said publicly, "We are building the Priest Rapids Dam in spite of Governor Langlie's opposition rather than because of his leadership. Evidently, Governor Langlie's memory is a little short. He doesn't seem to remember that, when we were asking his support as Governor of the State to get federal enabling legislation, he told two of our representatives he wouldn't lend his name to a lost cause."

On the other side of the ledger, I received a call from Harvey Davis and Howard Elmore from the Chelan County PUD stating that they had heard that Emmett Anderson, who resided in Tacoma, had announced his intention to use Clif Erdahl as his power advisor. I immediately called former State Senator Virgil Lee, who was campaign manager for Anderson, and asked him to check the matter out because such action would certainly have an adverse effect among PUD Commissioners and other public power persons on Anderson's candidacy for the governorship. He called back shortly to say the story we heard was wrong and to arrange a meeting for us with Anderson, who in person denied such an intention. I pledged to see that the rumor was squelched in public power circles.

Although our practice had been not to participate in partisan elections, we had always forthrightly thanked members of the Legislature of both parties for any support they gave public power. It was interesting to note that Senator Rosellini included in his campaign literature quotations from one of my letters, which had gone to twenty-five other members of the State Senate with the same words. His announcement said, "Here's What They Say About Rosellini: From a public utility district official: 'On behalf of this Association, its member districts and the electric and water customers whom they serve, we wish to thank you for your confidence and support shown us during recent legislative sessions.' " The words were signed by

Billington, Executive Secretary, Washington Public Utility Districts' Association.

The result of the 1956 election was that President Eisenhower was reelected, Senator Rosellini was elected as Governor of the State, and the Democrats took the State House of Representatives 56 to 43. In the Senate, while we had been well treated in the 1955 Session under Republican control of 24 to 22, the Democrats scored an upset victory of 31 to 15. What was more important was that certain senators who had been most vicious against public power from both sides of the aisle were knocked out of their seats. When time came for organizing the committees on the Senate side for the 1957 Session, Senator Nat Washington, a strong public power supporter, had a great deal to say about who would be on the Public Utilities Committee. We looked forward to the 1957 Session with a little bit more security.

In December 1956, I hired John McCarthy as a replacement for Andy Anderson, who would be leaving at the end of January 1957. We had located McCarthy at the School of Communications at the University of Washington, where he was a graduate student, and felt very fortunate to hire him. I was to be lucky again to have on board a very good employee as my Administrative Assistant.

Summary

If a one-word description of the private/public power war during the 1951–1956 era were needed, it would be "leveling" or perhaps "equalizing."

The period saw private power attacks on public power in the Legislature beaten back. A private power move to merge two companies into a statewide company was blocked. Private power's move for a "partnership" project with federal power at John Day Dam was stopped. Private power did win an election permitting it to buy the Stevens County PUD, but the PUD purchase of Washington Water Power distribution properties at Lake Chelan and its generating plant at Chelan Falls restored the balance of power. Public power failed to purchase all the properties of Washington Water Power and Puget Power, and these companies won independent ownership status from Eastern holding companies, as Pacific Power and Light had done previously. Public power lost the only direct congressional vote on high Hells Canyon Dam, which permitted Idaho Power Company to move ahead on construction under its Federal Power Commission license. While another attempt was to be made in 1957 to secure the federal dam, it was lost when Congressman Jack Westland, the only congressional opponent from the State of Washington, blocked House Interior Committee approval of the legislation.

PUDs started construction on some local public power hydro plants, but this construction was financed by power sales to the private companies. Private power had to accept the Bonneville federal grid for power transmission purposes, and new starts were made on federal public power dams. Both private power and public power utilities won first rights to develop power sites ahead of the State Power Commission. The period, as one would say at a prize fight, ended in a draw, but the legislative conflicts were to continue.

4

1957–1962 Era
The Calm
and the Storm

1957–1958

HAVING WORKED in two previous legislative sessions where I watched
the friends of private power stack the Public Utilities Committees against
public power, I moved ahead just after the 1956 elections. One never counts
votes until they are "cast in concrete," but one can get a fair idea about a
particular legislator's attitude on a given issue from conversation, contact,
and study of the legislator's performance on the job or in the campaign.
Thus a particular stand on the private/public power issues would label a
legislator as being pro-public power or pro-private power.

In 1953, the Chairman and a majority of the House Public Utilities
Committee were pro-private power. In the Senate, it was even worse. In
1955, there was a public power "flavor" in the House and a private power
flavor in the Senate. Several pro-private power legislators from the House
were defeated in the 1956 election and thus the House retained its public
power flavor. In the Senate, even though our defense coalition of 1953 and
1955 was still present, the Senate Utilities Committee, at the insistence of
Senator Nat Washington, had a public power flavor.

Another hopeful sign as we went into the 1957 Session was that, while our last three years had made us an "opponent" of the Governor of our State—not only over the State Power Commission's action at Priest Rapids but also over Hells Canyon and other river development issues—we now found a strong public power supporter in that office. Governor Albert D. Rosellini was a breath of fresh air. In my opinion, he rates among the top governors, if he isn't the best, this State had during my active involvement in State politics from 1938 (Clarence Martin) to 1981 (John Spellman). There have been other governors who have done a good job, and my high rating of Rosellini is based on more than his support of public power. He demonstrated a special ability to select good department heads and appoint good judges. In only two instances did he make bad appointments, and the failure of these officials to serve well cannot be attributed to the Governor. The State had good and efficient administration during his two terms in office.

On January 14, 1957, when the 35th Session of the Legislature convened, I was backed up by the PUD Association's first special legislative committee, which the Board had appointed on my recommendation, and which was made up of commissioners and managers from the PUDs throughout the State who would meet in Olympia at regular intervals during the legislative session so that I could consult them about the feeling of the PUD on issues as they came up. One of the difficulties I had faced in the previous two sessions was serving nearly 100 bosses. I felt a responsibility to each of the three commissioners from each PUD and their top management, and sometimes when a fast legislative decision had to be made, I felt a bit lonely in having to decide for all of them. At that time, lobbying of the Legislature by individual PUD officials was prohibited, and while they were free to come to Olympia, they could not contact legislators officially except at the direct request of the Legislature. We shortly started having our monthly Board of Directors meetings, as well as the area Association meetings, in Olympia during the legislative session, and while no reimbursement of expenses could be made for any direct lobbying, certainly it seemed to be within the province of individuals to call upon their legislators from home if they happened to be in the town.

Our main thrust during the 1957 Session was to improve PUD efficiency, and we sponsored certain bills designed to do this. We had wanted for some time to nullify the false argument by private power that PUD activation would mean a loss of tax income to local areas, but we had been afraid to get into this matter during the intense private/public power fights in previous legislative sessions. This time, we sponsored and secured passage of legislation which simply stated that regardless of the amount to be paid by a PUD under its privilege tax (a gross revenue tax established in the early 1940s that the PUDs would pay in lieu of the property tax private companies had paid on facilities the PUDs took over from them), this tax would have to equal or exceed the property taxes paid under regular tax levies on any utility properties which the PUD had acquired in the previous taxpaying year. In other words, we put a floor on the PUD privilege tax to wipe out the argument that activation of a PUD would mean loss of tax revenue to the county, cities, and schools.

Next on taxes, we were approached by the local county commissions who pointed out that present wording in the PUD tax law limited their use of PUD taxes for specific county purposes. We broadened the law to state that a county could use such moneys for any established "State purpose." Since this was a State levied tax, a constitutional provision required the moneys to be limited to State use, but the new law gave the local county commission far more leeway in deciding how to spend those taxes than they had under the old law.

Finally, we had found as we commenced construction on the large hydro projects on the Columbia River and its tributaries that the influx of construction workers posed special problems to schools and other taxing districts. We therefore sought and got enabling legislation to allow us to make special tax payments both for operation and maintenance and for capital expenditures for construction of schools. A special formula was established to cover the cost of providing for construction workers' children in the public schools.

We were able to increase the annual maximum per diem payments to commissioners from $2,500 to $3,500, but since per diem payments were established by each local board, and State law forbade a public official to raise his own salary, the increase could not benefit any present incumbent PUD commissioner. However, in this same legislation, we were able to remove a $15 limitation on reimbursement of expenses and thus allow reimbursement of actual expenses claimed on an itemized public voucher. A mileage allowance limitation was also stricken by this bill, leaving it up to each local board to establish a mileage allowance for itself and its employees.

Another improvement which we sought and obtained was the right of the local utility to establish its own treasurer if it wanted to do so. The law had said that the PUD must use the county treasurer, which had not only complicated the paperwork for the county treasurer, but had also taken control of any reserve funds away from the PUD, since its reserves would be mixed in with other county reserve funds for temporary investments. Giving the PUD Commission the right to administer its own funds, even though its selection of depositories was limited and it must have proper bonding to protect the funds, led to greater efficiency. Since the law made a separate treasurer optional, several of the smaller districts continued to use the county treasurer's office.

The big power legislation for the 1957 Session centered on abolishing the State Power Commission. At our membership meeting the previous December, my recommendation to table a resolution calling for the Legislature to abolish the Commission had prevailed. I had already discerned such tremendous anti-Commission feeling on the part of individual legislators that I felt they would abolish it even if we wanted to retain it. However, at our January Board meeting, our people were so incensed that they passed a resolution calling for its abolishment.

Substitute SB-280 abolished the State Power Commission and made further corrections in the law to prevent arbitrary blocking of the formation of joint operating agencies. This bill would allow new projects to be started by a majority of a joint operating agency's membership, rather than requiring unanimous consent. It extended the right of joint operating agencies to own coal-bearing land and make contracts for mining and marketing the coal. It put limitations on a joint agency's bond financing procedures, including requiring public bids on bonds instead of negotiated sales.

Just as the bill came to the Senate floor for second reading, debate, and possible amendment, it dawned on me that in abolishing the State Power Commission, we would be wiping out certain powers granted to an established joint operating agency by cross reference to the original State Power Commission law. I made a hasty exit out of the Senate gallery down to the floor and called Senator Washington to the door. Washington recognized the problem immediately, and quickly drafted a floor amendment which simply stated that a joint operating agency would retain all of the powers, and be subject to the same restrictions, formerly granted to or placed on the State Power Commission. His floor amendment prevailed.

A companion bill, SB-281, established a new Division of Power Resources in the Department of Conservation and Development, and provided for transfer of all records of the State Power Commission to the new Division. It also permitted continuation of studies by the State on the matter of power resources. An advisory committee of five persons to be representative of the power industry from all parts of the State would be available to the new Division to provide it with information and advice.

In the meantime, on the House side, HB-47 was enacted, appropriating $275,000 for the new Division of Power Resources to do engineering studies to design a steam plant. The bill limited the studies to the Cle Elum-Roslyn coal-fired steam plant proposal, and while it provided for State construction of the plant, if that proved feasible, it also provided that before the State started the project, a notice of intent would be published so that any utility or group of utilities could appear before the Department and by demonstrating its intent to proceed with the project would be given the first opportunity to construct and operate the plant. This legislation specifically prohibited the State from purchasing or acquiring transmission and distribution systems or other generating plants. It limited the State to construction and operation of this one steam plant.

Another minor bill was SB-359 which allowed a PUD to establish a loan guaranty fund for issuance of local utility district bonds to make improvements. A PUD had the right to establish a local utility district within the larger public utility district for a special project, such as a small water system or a streetlighting improvement project. A guaranty fund, while being secondary to other district obligations, would provide more security for the local utility district special bonds.

One final bill was special legislation designed to allow the City of Seattle and Pend Oreille County PUD to jointly develop a project on the Pend Oreille River. To block a move by Washington Water Power to get the excess power from Pend Oreille County PUD's Box Canyon Dam, Seattle City Light, through its City Council, signed a contract to buy that surplus power. Now attention was turning toward construction of another dam downstream. Since the PUD held property rights to the Z Canyon site, it was felt that the next dam constructed could be owned jointly by the PUD and the city system. This legislation was essential for such a plan to be pursued.

While the 1957 Session was a busy one, and a number of anti-PUD bills had been introduced by individual pro-private power legislators, we spent our time on the "improvement" legislation and on getting rid of the State Power Commission.

One of the first non-legislative activities important to public power which took place during the legislative session was the first official act of the new Director of Conservation and Development, Earl Coe, who on January 31, 1957, approved the formation of a joint operating agency called the Washington Public Power Supply System by its member PUDs. The application had been filed the previous October. Since the PUD Association was coordinating this action, the organizational meeting of the Supply System took place in the Association's office in Seattle on February 20, 1957. Present were fifteen representatives of the seventeen member PUDs. When space in the small office proved too limited, the meeting was adjourned to

Director of Conservation and Development Earl Coe approves formation of the Washington Public Power Supply System in January 1957. *Left to right:* A. Lars Nelson, Master, Washington State Grange; Clyde Riddell, President, Washington PUD Association; Grover Greimes, Clallam County PUD Commissioner and Chairman of the Joint Operating Agency Organizing Committee; Jack Cluck, attorney for the Washington PUD Association; Claude Danielson, Manager, Mason County PUD #3; and Roy Sheldon, Commissioner, Pacific County PUD #2.   *Courtesy BPA*

the nearby Roosevelt Hotel, where the organization was completed. As a convenience, for a number of years, the Association provided secretarial services for the new joint operating agency, including the preparation of meeting notices and minutes.

The new group selected a Managing Director. Strange as it may seem, one of the candidates sponsored by several of the districts was J. Frank Ward, who was fresh out of a job as Managing Director of the abolished State Power Commission. On second thought, this was not strange because Ward had a distinguished record in utility management: first as a staff member of the Bonneville Power Administration, second as Superintendent of Tacoma Light, and finally as Managing Director of the State Power Commission. His tenacity and ability could be recognized, even though they had been used to oppose the local utilities.

Another candidate was Owen Hurd, Manager of the Benton County PUD, who also had a very good record of performance in the utility field. He originally started with Pacific Power and Light, then transferred to the Bonneville staff, and finally became Manager of the Benton County PUD. Hurd was well known in public power circles, having served as President of the Northwest Public Power Association. I personally favored Hurd because, while I recognized the ability of Ward—something you do sometimes when a person is opposed to you—I felt the greatest need at this time was an individual who could pull the districts together in a joint action agency.

It should be recalled that the reason we thought we needed the new joint action agency was that after the re-election of President Eisenhower, we were afraid the federal government would sell the Bonneville transmission facilities within the State of Washington, and if this should happen, we wanted to be able to purchase them so that they would not go to the private companies. I felt Hurd's presence could greatly assist in bringing the rural electric cooperatives and city systems into such a deal should it become necessary. The fifteen representatives voted by secret ballot, and when as Recording Secretary I counted the ballots in the presence of one district sponsoring Ward and one district sponsoring Hurd, the selection was Owen Hurd. He would be available to fill the job full time in October.

Shortly after the legislative session, Governor Rosellini appointed Senator Francis Pearson from Clallam, Jefferson, and Mason counties to the Washington Public Service Commission. I was very supportive of this appointment and in the early years had great respect for the performance of Pearson. In fact, on two occasions, which will be reported later, he gave me information or insight which was valuable in understanding certain events. However, as the years went by, I sensed and witnessed a change in this man which bothered me. Pearson was blind but had the ability to more than offset such an impairment. He could "see" more than most men ever could, but his constant exposure to the management types of the privately owned utilities of power, telephone, and gas in my opinion altered his outlook, which in the beginning favored the consumer and the public interest in utility service.

There is an element in the process by which we regulate privately owned companies which concerns me. Simply stated, the human factor common to us all causes a flaw in the system. I have watched individuals who served on regulatory commissions, where they made the decisions affecting the rates, services, and financing of the private utilities, move off such commissions to become employees of the utilities they had formerly regulated. Top staff employees as well as officials of regulatory commissions have done this. Robert Yeomans left the Public Service Commission to re-enter private law practice, following approval of the Washington Water Power/Puget Power merger by the Commission on which Yeomans sat, and shortly thereafter accepted a top administrative job with Washington Water Power. Kinsey Robinson came over to the westside of the State one month before that decision was rendered, and contacted some of the leading industrial customers of Puget Power to inform them that he was the man with whom they were to deal. Frank McLaughlin, President of Puget Power, called me and said he had been told this by some of his industrial customers.

Bob Simpson, who was a top staff attorney for the Public Service Commission through the Attorney General's office, has done good legal work in later years with the law firm serving Washington Water Power. Ralph Davis, who was Chairman of the Public Service Commission under the Langlie Administration, ended up as Secretary, then President, and finally Chairman of Puget Power.

A regulatory commissioner plays two roles. First he renders semi-judicial decisions about rates and services for the private utility companies — power, telephone, and gas. Then, once a decision is made, he administers it. This involves day-to-day contact with the same private power officials or their representatives. He occasionally has lunches or dinner meetings with them, and it has been known for a commissioner to go on fishing trips with them and be a guest at other social and sports functions they pay for.

In the mid-1960s, a top private utility lobbyist told me he was called at 1 a.m. by a regulatory commission member who told him to get down to a leading downtown Seattle restaurant and pay the bill so the commissioner could go home with his party. I also recall that questions were raised to me about how a utility commissioner who had a set public salary could afford certain property investments or a heated swimming pool.

It is not my purpose here to question any individual's honesty but rather to cite the type of influence which a human being is subjected to in the role of a utilities regulatory commission member. I have often wondered if I had been thrust into such a job, whether I would have been able to remain objective about what was in the interest of the consumer.

In later years, just prior to completion of Pearson's last term on the Public Service Commission, it hurt me personally to have to face him in argument before the Washington State Grange Utilities Committee at a Grange Annual Session. He defended the pro-private power side and I defended the pro-public power side. But in 1957, we were pleased to see a man with a consumer interest in utility service appointed to the State Public Service Commission.

In May of 1957, the PUD Association started printing its newsletter, which had formerly been mimeographed. A special public relations committee had recommended that we do this the previous year, and we had included the cost in the year's budget. Whereas the bulletin had previously gone only to commissioners and managers of PUDs, the new printed newsletter was mailed to all PUD employees as well as the officials. There was a definite need for better public understanding of the PUD program to withstand the private power advertising attacks being made against public power.

In June, the U.S. Senate held confirmation hearings on the reappointment of Jerome Kuykendall to the Federal Power Commission. While he was from the Pacific Northwest, and ordinarily we would welcome having someone from our region on any important regulatory commission, the action by the Commission under his chairmanship on Hells Canyon had so aggravated public power supporters that we felt an obligation to oppose his nomination. I had to leave the American Public Power Association conference being held in New York to get to Washington, D.C., to speak against his confirmation, but our opposition was futile since the Senate has a long tradition of confirming a President's choice unless the person appointed is clearly unfit to serve.

In April, Senator Kefauver's anti-monopoly committee had revealed that the Office of Defense Mobilization had granted a tax write-off certificate of over $65,000,000 to the Idaho Power Company on its Hells Canyon projects. The subcommittee pointed out that on April 17, a week before the ODM had announced its decision to the public, Idaho Power Company stock on the New York Exchange had enjoyed a big spurt of trading. The ODM then admitted turning over the certificate to Idaho Power Company on April 18, one week before it made its public announcement. Pending before Congress at that time was another bill to authorize high Hells Canyon Dam in place of the three lower dams of Idaho Power Company. To counter support for the legislation, Idaho Power Company turned back the certificate in August. On this one, public power had won but that victory did not set the matter to rest because in a later year we had to fight a special arrangement between Bonneville and Idaho Power Company whereby Bonneville would pay for wheeling rights over Idaho Power Company's transmission lines, providing another backdoor subsidy to that company.

In August, Director of Conservation Earl Coe announced the appointment of Truman Price as Supervisor of the Conservation Department's new Division of Power Resources. We had joined with others behind the scenes to secure Price's appointment, so the announcement met with great favor in our ranks. Price was the son of long-time PUD Commissioner Chauncey Price. He was an outstanding electrical engineer who had worked for Pacific County PUD following graduation from the University of Washington.

In September, the Supply System filed an application for a preliminary permit to study the Ben Franklin Dam site just north of the Tri-Cities area on the Columbia River. With Owen Hurd aboard as its new Managing Director, I participated in negotiations between the Supply System and Douglas County PUD to allow the Supply System to take over the construction, ownership, and operation of the Wells Dam. By the end of the year, I had negotiated a possible settlement between Douglas County PUD and the Supply System which would permit Douglas County PUD to withdraw power from the project for its own purpose equal to that which I knew it could retain if it owned the dam and sold any excess power to the private power companies. We reached this informal agreement the day before Hurd was to speak at the Bridgeport Chamber of Commerce.

I was leaving Wenatchee by bus that evening to return to Seattle when I learned from Manager Kirby Billingsley of Chelan County PUD that Guy Myers and Puget Power had instigated a well-organized campaign among local people calling for Douglas County PUD to go it alone in the construction and ownership of Wells Dam. Myers was slated to be fiscal agent on that project, as he was then serving on the Rocky Reach Dam for Chelan County PUD, although my personal opinion was that we didn't need him. At any rate, arriving in Seattle that evening I called back to the Cascadian Hotel in Wenatchee and talked to Hurd, who was spending the night there on his way to Bridgeport for the Chamber of Commerce luncheon the next day. I urged him to propose in his speech that should the Supply System take over the project his recommendation to the Board would be that a minimum of 200,000 kilowatts would be earmarked for Douglas County PUD's withdrawal. Hurd did not agree with me, saying that he felt the local PUD would be acceptable to Supply System takeover of the project without any specific power allotment commitment.

Sure enough, he proceeded to Bridgeport the next day and made a very good speech urging that the local PUD accept Supply System presence on the Wells Project, but as he finished, a very respected local orchardist-businessman, Ross Heminger, rose in the audience and, while being very complimentary to the Supply System, made an urgent appeal that Douglas County PUD go it alone in the construction of Wells Dam. The issue bounced around for several months but in February 1958, the final decision by Douglas County PUD was that the PUD would go it alone on the construction and operation of Wells Dam, financing the work with long-term power contracts to the private power companies. Later, since the reservoir from Wells Dam would inundate property in Okanogan County, the Okanogan County PUD was given a share of the power output to be used when that PUD needed or wanted it.

It had been interesting to watch the negotiations for the power sales contracts to the private power companies as the PUDs continued to construct dams on the Columbia River. At Priest Rapids and Wanapum dams, which were the first to be constructed by PUDs, pull-back provisions were substantially more favorable than those which were negotiated for the Rocky Reach Dam and after that the Wells Dam. In each case the portions and pull-back provisions seemed to get worse for the local public utility district.

My final action in 1957 was to issue the draft of a proposal on power for the Pacific Northwest, suggesting that we amend the Bonneville Power Act so as to make Bonneville the marketing agency for power produced by states and their political subdivisions. The proposal, of course, did not fly because the private power companies had already found that they could fill their power supply needs from projects financed by local public power. Some of the public power people were still pushing real hard for a federal Columbia River Development Corporation which would provide financing for power facilities from federal revenues, and there was the honest interest of local districts that fought to retain ownership of a local falling water resource for the benefit of local people.

The State Legislature did not meet in 1958, but it was a busy year. It was a bad year for me personally because it involved some rather emotional events which terminated my two special long-term friendships with Glen Smothers, Manager of Grant County PUD, and Frank A. Stewart, an independent consultant to a number of public power utilities, particularly the Kittitas County PUD in its study of a proposed coal-fired steam plant at Cle Elum.

The year started when the Federal Power Commission in January denied the Pacific Northwest Power Company's license application for the Mountain Sheep and Pleasant Valley dams on the Snake River. The FPC ruled that such dams were not best adapted to the comprehensive development of the river system. However, in March, PNPC filed an amended application asking for up to ten months to study a High Mountain Sheep Dam plan plus a plan for a second dam on the Salmon River. Since the National Hells Canyon Association and the Northwest Public Power Association had intervened in the previous license fight, they were most active in fighting the new application, and this indeed involved my office.

Also in March, the National Reclamation Association came forward with a proposal to establish a Pacific Northwest account whereby reclamation could be funded from power revenues. For the first time, they proposed the direct use of Bonneville revenues without tying a particular reclamation project to a specific dam. They were thinking particularly of rebuilding an irrigation project east of Spokane, but what concerned us was that tying one project directly to Bonneville revenues instead of tying it to a specific dam would set a precedent for unlimited and uncontrolled use of power revenues. These irrigation projects could be not only many miles distant from the federal dams which were primarily being constructed in Oregon and Washington, but they could be in areas where federal dams were opposed, such as Idaho and Montana, and even as far away as the fields of Texas.

We wanted to support the Spokane project but we could not sit still for a blank check approach to reclamation. Previously, we had agreed that reclamation subsidies would be provided for irrigation water from revenues of a specific federal dam. We altered this by agreeing that a reclamation project could be subsidized out of revenues from a particular dam even though that particular reclamation project did not use water stored or backed up by the dam. This initial move in 1958 kept us involved in this issue until the mid-1960s when we finally, under the leadership of Senator Henry M. Jackson, pounded out a compromise on power revenue use for reclamation purposes.

In 1958, federal legislation to establish a Columbia River Development Corporation was first introduced. Study had started on this proposal in 1954 and then, with Senator Richard Neuberger as its lead proponent, a bill was introduced in 1958 after many drafts had been revised. While the Northwest Public Power Association furnished the leadership in pushing this bill, the PUD Association gave it strong active support.

We heard of a proposal for Bonneville to sell several of its substations in the Stevens County area to Washington Water Power for $37,000. We registered a strong protest, and under public scrutiny the sale was consummated, but the price was raised to $152,000.

In July, we discovered that an appropriation had slipped through the House for Secretary of the Interior Fred Seaton to use to make a limited study of the Pleasant Valley site on the Snake River. Development of this site would have put another block in the road to development of the Nez Perce Dam. By some very fast work on the part of the Senate Appropriations Committee, of which Maggie was a member, the appropriation was changed to cover the entire basin, and it required coordination of the study with the ongoing Army Engineers 308 Review.

In August, following the resignation of Clif Erdahl from the Pacific Northwest Utilities Conference Committee, the Committee was reorganized. It reverted to its former status as an informal study group with a chairman designated from an operating utility. At my August Board meeting, I presented an outline of the new reorganization and suggested that individual districts might consider once again participating in the Committee.

Following rejection in February by Douglas County PUD of the Supply System's plan to take over the Wells Dam, the Supply System, in April, had filed a preliminary permit application to study the Packwood Lake Project in eastern Lewis County. We recognized shortly after the joint system was formed that, in addition to proving that the law under which it was formed was constitutional, we needed to embark on a project requiring revenue bonds to establish it as an ongoing entity and put it beyond the reach of those who would like to destroy this joint PUD effort. Thus, we selected this small project. The preliminary permit was approved in October by the Federal Power Commission.

Culmination of the fight for the high Hells Canyon Dam came on June 2, 1958. The House Interior Committee killed the high Hells Canyon authorization legislation in its Reclamation Subcommittee. The only congressman from the State of Washington who opposed the high Hells Canyon Dam was on that committee, so if credit or blame is due to any one person, it rightfully goes to Congressman Jack Westland.

In July, hot controversy broke out in the Grant County PUD over the management of Smothers. I had met Smothers back in 1947 before I ever went to work for public power, when I was serving as President of the Public Power League of Washington and he was Chairman of the PUD Commissioners' Association Power Use and Conservation Committee. While I was Personnel Director at Clark County PUD, Smothers and I served on a statewide committee working on safety rules for electrical workers. When I came to work for the PUD Association, he was even then active in power supply matters. We developed a close personal friendship over the years. He was a man with a terrific personality; he had a natural ingenuity for organization and getting things done. He was not a graduate engineer, but from practical experience he had developed an engineering ability which was second to none. He early recognized the need for local utilities to help develop power to meet forecasted load growth, and this caused him to be interested in the Priest Rapids Project. It can be rightfully said that without this man's abilities, tenacity, and drive, the dams might never have been constructed—or at least not as soon, at such low cost, and under local utility ownership. He faced and beat some terrific problems and strong opposition—some with my help, such as when the State Power Commission tried to stop him. He was a real doer.

However, certain things occurred which bothered me as early as 1955. First had been our split in the Governor's office when we were working on

The first concrete was poured for Priest Rapids Dam on the Columbia River April 25, 1957, by Grant County PUD. *Left to right:* Glen Smothers, Manager, Grant County PUD; R. B. Jackson, Construction Superintendent; Senator Henry M. Jackson.

the amendments to the State Power Commission-joint operating agency law. He had sided with private power, and I had to face him down in front of the group. Additionally, during the 1955 Session, I would find him saying one thing to legislators while I had to say something else. Fortunately for me in that session, he got into a personal problem with the local police force over alleged drunken driving. I maneuvered through My Haskett, that year's Association President and local Thurston County PUD Commissioner, to have him released, but the police served notice that, while they would let him go, he would have to stay out of Olympia except during the daytime for the rest of the legislative session. I got a chuckle out of the situation when he would drive to Seattle from Ephrata and call me in Olympia to find out how things were going. I would urge him to come on down and stay over so I could explain and show him the action. He would always decline.

Another thing that bothered me cropped up when I was having lunch with him one day where he outlined a proposal of a group to build some dormitories and a restaurant with a liquor license adjacent to the construction site at Priest Rapids, to take advantage of the at-site payroll of the construction workers. He offered me a chance to buy in, but I declined, emphasizing that if the proposal was pursued, he should be very careful and make certain that the District was not embroiled in it in any manner. Later, I became aware that Smothers, being interested in keeping his project moving ahead, wanted to close the power sales contracts quickly, and therefore wanted to favor the private power companies. Luckily Sol Shultz was involved in the Priest Rapids Project, fighting for federal wheeling of non-federal power. He held out for giving some public utilities a chance to contract for Priest Rapids power and thereby slowed down Smothers' desire to go with private power.

On a Saturday in February 1957, when I was working in my office, having left Olympia after spending the week at the Legislature, I received a call from Bob Beck of R. W. Beck and Associates. His question was, "Isn't Glen Smothers still the Manager of Grant County PUD?" I said, "Yes, he is, and in fact they have just raised his salary to $25,000 a year and made him the highest paid public official in the State of Washington." This exceeded even the Governor's salary. Beck then informed me that his firm had been representing the City of Fairbanks, Alaska, in a generating project and that a cost difference had arisen with the Elliott Machine Company, manufacturers of the generator. The matter had to be arbitrated, and the representative of the Elliott Machine Company sent to meet with Beck was none other than Smothers, who informed Beck that he was representing the Elliott Machine Company as a consultant.

I didn't give this much thought until later that year when I got direct information that Smothers had been retained by Harza Engineers to write the marketing report on a Belgian Congo project which Harza was engineering. This upset me somewhat because Harza Engineers was the chief design and construction engineer on the Priest Rapids Project, and this retainer smacked of payoff. As soon as I could, I drove over to Ephrata and got Smothers to go down to the project with me alone. As we drove along, I asked him about the Elliott Machine Company consulting work. He said, "Yes, I am taking private consulting work on the side as long as the projects involved are outside the continental United States" (Alaska was still a Territory at that time). I then asked him if he was doing this consulting work for Harza Engineers and he said "Yes, and while I have only received $1,000 from Elliott Machine, I am thinking of charging Harza Engineers $5,000 for its marketing report on the Belgian Congo project."

I pointed out to him that even though the work might be bona fide, it raised a question of ethics which the general public would misunderstand if it were known. I also asked him whether or not his Commissioners were aware of this special side work of his, since he was a full-time administrative employee. He stated that he had never cleared it with them. I told him that I would have to inform his Commissioners.

It took me some time to do this because the press of other duties did not afford me a chance to attend to this one specific matter. I first talked to Bill Schempp, Commissioner of Grant County PUD. Schempp was astounded and said that certainly it should not be permitted. Later, I had lunch with George Schuster at one of the Board meetings of the State Association in Seattle. When I told him of it, his reaction was the opposite. He said he thought it was a great compliment that a worldwide engineering organization like Harza would pick their PUD manager to write a marketing report on a large project like the Belgian Congo. This time, I was astounded. The tie would have to be broken by Fred Arlt, the third Commissioner, but before I could talk to him, Arlt went to Honolulu for a vacation and had a heart attack, whereupon I did not feel it proper to involve him in this argument.

This brought us around to February 1958. One morning, I received a call from Senator Nat Washington who was the attorney for Grant County PUD. Washington said Schempp was in his office with a strange tale to tell. Schempp said an equipment salesman accompanied by a friend of Schempp's had come out to his ranch on Sunday, the day before, and asked: "Do I have to go along with this 5 percent deal?" When Schempp asked him what he meant, he said that he had been approached by Frank Bell, Jr., the nephew of Frank Bell, Sr., a close confidant of Smothers during all this period of dam construction. The salesman said that Bell, Jr., had informed him that, if Bell was designated as a local representative for a 5 percent commission on the sale, he could assure the salesman that he would get the contract for some butterfly valves involved in the fishways. I asked Washington, "Who is awarding the contract?" He said, "Merritt-Chapman-Scott, the general contractor on the dam." I told him there was nothing anyone could do about that kind of wheeling and dealing by a private contractor. But his concern was that these valves were supposed to be part of the material and equipment which under the contract were to be purchased and furnished the contractor by the PUD. I told Washington to get over to the PUD office at once and find out just how the general contractor had, in that case, been permitted to award such contract. He called me back later that day and said that it looked like some special change orders had been issued permitting Merritt-Chapman-Scott to do this. My next question was, "Did the PUD Commission approve the change orders?" and his answer was, "No, there is no official record. Smothers signed the change orders without any Commission approval." Washington said he was coming over the next day, and I suggested that he meet with Lars Nelson, Master of the Washington State Grange, and me to see what could be done.

I have always wondered why Smothers signed those special change orders without the approval of his Commission. His Commission was supporting him 100 percent in his work on the construction of the project, and if he had merely secured the official approval of the PUD Commission for the change orders and entered them in the official minutes, probably no question would ever have been raised concerning the matter. In the meeting the next day, it was decided that an effort would have to be made to have Smothers removed as Manager.

Time moved along and it wasn't until July 1958, when Nelson and I attended the Democratic State Convention in Yakima as observers, that the matter came to a head. Washington came to our hotel room and informed us that the decision had been made in favor of Smothers, since Arlt was siding with Schuster even though they recognized that Smothers had violated the law on the change orders. Washington had prepared a twelve-page indictment of the management policies of the PUD, including a reference to the change orders. He said he was hesitant to put it out because as the attorney for the PUD he should not criticize his client. Nelson and I pointed out that he was also a State Senator and that if he didn't put out the report then we were obligated to do so.

Washington returned to Ephrata, put out the report on July 17, and following exchanges in the public press with Smothers, was fired July 26. This inflamed the local ministerial association and others who started to demand a Grand Jury investigation of Grant County PUD. The ministers had gotten into the situation because Smothers previously had been involved with some publicity out of Las Vegas where evidently in his presence one woman had stabbed and killed another woman. He was not involved in the killing incident except as a witness, but the headlines shook local people. Over the weekend the demand for a Grand Jury got so intense that Smothers came in the following Monday morning and hurriedly resigned, thinking that this might stop the investigation. It didn't. He shortly left the area and my last information was that he died in late 1961 in Costa Rica where he had been working on a reclamation engineering job.

Here was a man who had great ability without formal education. Here was a man who could have been commended by his fellow men for the successful construction of two major hydroelectric projects on the main stem of the river. Here was a man who could have had a salary well above that which many persons earn and who could have remained there as Manager of Grant County PUD and as a leader until his retirement. And yet, here was a man who for one reason or another turned off the right track and got mixed up in the wheeling and dealing which is evidently quite commonplace in situations such as this. I always felt that Smothers, while being bright in one area, was gullible to have been taken in by his friends. The influence which Bell, Sr., had on this man was terrific. Smothers reflected the view that earning not necessarily a dishonest dollar but rather a fast dollar is an accepted thing to do. In other words, get on the inside and make a deal or use your inside position to make a deal – no bribery, no corruption, no graft, no illegality – but simply have knowledge of a coming event which could result in a profit to you as a person. While I had never used inside information, I am aware that it has been used, not only in this instance but in others, including some in government, for personal gain.

The eventual Grand Jury investigation and court trial found Merritt-Chapman-Scott, the general contractor, guilty of bribery. It also brought out that money had flowed to Bell, Sr., and thence to Smothers for various consultant and other business relations with persons directly associated with the contractor.

Smothers was intensely loyal to his friends. A good example of this was the episode in Las Vegas. The grapevine had it that a high official of a construction company was present at the time, but that it was Smothers who stayed put and took the publicity. He was the type of guy who would stand his ground to help someone else or keep his given word, right or wrong.

I doubt if either Nelson or I could have prevailed upon Washington not to divulge what he had found even if we had wanted to keep things quiet. However, my only request to Smothers previously had been that he not get the District involved in something illegal, so I couldn't protest when Washington exposed the change order caper.

The second personal circumstance in 1958 that I regret struck on September 15 as I was traveling to Ephrata, having been summoned to appear before the Grand Jury. Frank Stewart was a very important person in my life in public power. Our close friendship dated from 1942 and involved our families as well as our business relationship.

Frank was very intelligent – business wise and politically wise. He was a Democrat by development and choice. In early years, I felt he would become one of the top men in our State. Had he not gotten off the track, as I felt he did, he surely would have made it. He was honest, as far as I know, but he had an insatiable drive to make money. There is nothing wrong in that, if that is a person's choice, but in his case, that choice placed me in the position of having to force him out of a position where he was providing what I felt was a needed and valuable service for the public utility districts.

He furnished a stimulant to PUD progress, but he couldn't or didn't bring to his job understanding of moral responsibility to those for whom he worked.

We met in 1942 while both of us were holding near-top executive jobs with Kaiser Engineers at Vancouver, Washington. Frank had been with the company at Grand Coulee when it was being constructed. However, in 1946, he got crossways with some of his bosses over something about which I don't know the details, and left his job. He entered a public relations consulting service with a mutual (and very good) friend named Milt Bona, just at the time the Washington Public Utility Commissioners' Association was being divided over the issue of negotiated sales versus condemnation as a means to acquire private power property. This was also the time of the Initiative 166 political fight and the Public Ownership League versus the Public Power League. Frank accepted the job as Managing Director of the Association and its service organization, the Public Research and Information Service. We were all involved, but I was still playing my public power political activist role as a layman.

Frank did a terrific job for the Association and the PUDs. He pulled them back together again during some of the most terrific fights in the legislative arenas in Olympia and Washington, D.C., and in the courts. From August 1948 to January 1949, he served as Director of Conservation and Development in Governor Mon Walgren's Administration. In October 1949, he took a leave of absence to enter real estate sales and business property development near Chief Joseph Dam which was just then going under construction. In 1951, he again served the PUDs in fighting the Spokane power bill at Olympia. When his business pursuits didn't pan out, he went with Chelan County PUD as an industrial development consultant. Kirby Billingsley, long-time public power leader and one of the principal people to get Frank involved in the Association years before, resigned from his Chelan County PUD Commissioner's office and was appointed Manager of Chelan County PUD in December 1953. The two were again working side-by-side and were helping me strengthen the PUD Association.

One of Frank's assignments was to negotiate with Lawrence Harvey, head of Harvey Aluminum, regarding a new plant which might be brought to the Wenatchee, Chelan County PUD area. I remember Frank's call one evening to my office where I was working a little late. He asked if I could join him for dinner at the Ben Franklin Hotel. His eyes were glowing as he told me about spending the previous evening sitting outside Harvey's home overlooking Beverly Hills and Los Angeles. He was enraptured.

However, shortly thereafter, he started to cause problems in the negotiations with Harvey. Billingsley and Guy Myers, as the fiscal agent for Chelan County PUD, were trying to pin Harvey down on the contract for power purchase. Frank started to try and get the Commissioners involved. While everyone recognized that they must be involved eventually, it would have been a poor thing to do until Harvey got more definite on what was to be agreed. In any contract negotiations, whether it be a labor contract or a business contract, it is advantageous to the person doing the negotiating at the preliminary stages to have to "go back to my bosses and see if this is acceptable." Such delay allows second thoughts. It is similar to having a car salesman see if he can "sell" your deal to his sales manager.

The next thing I knew, I had a call from Billingsley saying he had gotten a report that Frank had been doing some consultant work for Harvey Aluminum and asking if I knew anything about it. I said, "No, but I'm headed for Wenatchee right now." I drove over that evening and met Frank downtown at the Night and Day Cafe. I asked him a direct question: "Have you done any work for Harvey Aluminum?" He answered directly: "Yes." His explanation was that he had taken several public relations assignments and had gone over to Skagit County and to The Dalles, Oregon (where Harvey was interested in an aluminum plant), but had done the work on weekends. I could see that he didn't recognize that working for two parties to a negotiation constituted conflict of interest, and that Chelan County PUD would take a dim view of this. I told him I had been asked to meet with Billingsley and the PUD Commissioners for breakfast the next morning and would have to tell them what he had told me.

I met with them and told them—but I also spent some time criticizing some of Billingsley's past actions which I felt had led to this bad situation. When Billingsley took over the managership of Chelan County PUD and brought Frank aboard, there was, at least in my opinion, some strong inferences that Frank would be appointed Assistant Manager. Whether this was only an implication or a definite pledge, I wasn't sure. But when Billingsley left Frank with only the rank of industrial consultant, he felt that he had the right to accept other consultant work. Of course, Frank had failed to recognize that working for Chelan County PUD would morally preclude his accepting such work from Harvey. At any rate, this breach of moral responsibility terminated Frank's association with Chelan, and he then pursued his power-consulting work elsewhere while still living in Wenatchee. I helped him locate other work and made several calls commending his work to various utilities at his request. I felt the PUDs could use the brains of a promoter and doer. There was a lot of maneuvering going on regarding new generating plants and further PUD actions to acquire private power property, as well as at the Legislature. I welcomed his presence.

He put together a deal for Douglas County PUD with Kaiser Engineers, who by now were operating the Kaiser Aluminum plants at Spokane which had been acquired after World War II. Douglas County PUD, which was trying to move ahead with the preliminary engineering on the Wells Dam, had been faced with a challenge from Puget Power and with a disagreement with Chelan County PUD over the location of the Rocky Reach Dam about how its reservoir level could encroach on the Wells site. Kaiser agreed to finance the legal and engineering costs for the small district in return for some of the Wells Dam power. Kaiser was also thinking of building a new aluminum plant in Douglas County. Frank served as consultant for Douglas County PUD with his retainers being secured by the PUD by the contract between the PUD and Kaiser.

In December 1955, it was reported in the *Wenatchee World* that an Advisory Committee for Chelan County PUD was being formed, sponsored by Vic McMullen, local Democratic leader. When I read this, I suspected that the hand of Frank was striking back at Billingsley and his Commission. Several strong Democrats were criticizing the local PUD in language which sounded a lot like the propaganda being used by private power around the State and nation. I sent Frank a strong personal note that ended with the comment, "I would caution you away from personal bitterness because programs are bigger than men and this last action isn't good." I also talked to George Hamilton, President of the Douglas County PUD Commission who had just been elected 1956 President of the State PUD Association. Both he and Frank assured me that the Advisory Committee proposal was not at Frank's behest. Frank answered me in a beautiful letter written on a Sunday morning which I have retained and treasured. And, thinking about it now, McMullen's Advisory Committee move failed. It probably wouldn't have if Frank had been masterminding it.

Everything was going along okay as far as I knew on the financial arrangements with Kaiser, although I found myself sitting between Chelan and Douglas in their disagreements over the power-producing relationship of the two dams. In 1956, Bill Nordeen, Douglas County PUD Manager, furnished me a copy of a letter he had written to his Commission about a State Examiner's report which questioned Frank's expense vouchers to Douglas County PUD. Certain mileage claims could not be substantiated, and certain telephone calls could not be justified. While the District was not out the money, since it was reimbursed by Kaiser, the legal issue from the State Auditor's standpoint was with the District. The matter was settled as far as I know.

Then, at the November 1957 Association's Board meeting, Commissioner George Hamilton of Douglas County PUD, who had been my President the year before, pulled me aside and said, "Ken, I don't know what we are going to do about Frank." I said, "What do you mean?" He said, "His costs are driving us crazy and we just can't afford them." My question was, "What do you mean? I thought all costs on the Wells Dam were being covered by Kaiser." He said, "No, they bowed out last June, and we have been going it alone since then."

I invited Frank, who was at the meeting, to go to dinner at Pancho's with Bill Nordeen and me, without anyone else on my Board being present, and he told us what had happened. When he confirmed what Hamilton had briefly told me, I was a bit upset. I told him I had made it very clear that promoters and supporters like himself were essential in a lot of PUD cases, but I had also made it clear that he shouldn't charge the small PUDs for his per diems and other expenses. The large ones like Snohomish, Clark, Cowlitz, and so on, could afford to hire specialists and they sometimes needed them—but the little ones couldn't afford them.

The discussion got so hot that if Nordeen hadn't stepped in, there probably would have been a fist fight. It wasn't good and I felt bad, because here again I was facing off with a person whom I had had as a close personal friend, as well as a business friend. And he had helped me many times.

On December 8, Frank submitted his resignation to Douglas County PUD. During this period, he had continued as a consultant to Skamania County PUD, Cowlitz County PUD, and Tacoma Light. My thoughts flashed back to the calls I had received at Olympia during the 1955 and 1957 sessions when Frank was there with me. I received calls from each of those clients asking me what Frank was doing at Olympia. My response was always, "He's your man, ask him." I was aware that he was sending a per diem voucher to each of them for each day he was in Olympia and I did ask him if submitting per diem vouchers to different clients for the same day was proper. His answer was that one works more than an eight-hour day when in Olympia, which is surely correct, and thus vouchering more than one client for the same day should be all right. I felt it was none of my business, but it seemed wrong.

In April 1957, Frank called me to say he was in Skamania County to help with formation of a county-wide industrial promotion group. He said such action was necessary to save some of Skamania County's local resources. When he couldn't demonstrate the emergency of the situation—he was referring to hydro on the upper Lewis River, the proposed Swift Creek development of Pacific Power and Light—I declined his request to get involved. I did point out to him that Cowlitz County PUD had already

Swift No. 2 Plant on the Lewis River generates power from falling water. It was financed and constructed by the Cowlitz County PUD #1 and put into service in 1958.   *Courtesy Cowlitz County PUD #1*

reached agreement with Pacific Power and Light and that such action might pit one PUD against another.

He moved ahead and the next thing I knew I had a call from Chauncey Price, Skamania County PUD Commissioner, saying Frank was urging them to file a condemnation suit against Pacific Power and Light on the project. I urged Price to immediately call Commissioner Earl Cole of Cowlitz County PUD to straighten things out. After talking to Cole, Price agreed that Skamania County PUD would not get involved, but his decision stirred up the severe local argument which ended in the attempted recall of Price in May 1958. He held his office by nine votes, and the recall attempt caused a lot of bad feelings in later years. Frank disavowed any involvement in the attempt and I believed him because I found out later from Milt Bona that Frank had asked for his help in saving Price. Milt's help was probably the determining factor in the vote result. But Frank stirred up the industrial development movement which caused the recall attempt.

My final involvement in Frank's public power activity concerned his consultant work for the Kittitas County PUD when that PUD was thinking of building a steam plant using Cle Elum coal. Following its action to dissolve the Washington State Power Commission, the Legislature had appropriated some funds to pursue the project through the Department of Conservation and Development. It was logical for the local PUD to carry out the preliminary work and be reimbursed from State funds, and a $25,000 allotment had been made for that purpose. However, I received a call from the Department asking me to verify just what work Frank was doing for the PUD. I tried to get details but couldn't be sure, and the amounts going to him didn't seem exorbitant.

Then on September 15, on my way to appear before the Grant County Grand Jury relative to some Grant County PUD activity on the Priest Rapids Dam, I stopped at the Kittitas County PUD office to make a courtesy call. The Manager told me that the local Commissioners had asked him to verify some of the conferences reported on their consultant's vouchers, and that my name was on the one for August. For August 27, a per diem was charged for a conference with Jack Stevens, Puget Sound Utilities Council, and Ken Billington, Washington PUD Association. This shook me.

The only consultation Frank had with me on August 27 was when he stopped briefly at a table in the Marine Room of the Olympic Hotel where Stevens and I were having lunch. He had eaten lunch with some other people. Then later, as I left, he was in the lower lobby. We walked back to the Washington Athletic Club together, and I proceeded on to my office. We talked about our families, not about power matters. I couldn't lie, and didn't lie to the Kittitas County PUD Manager. Shortly after that, Frank's consultant contract with Kittitas County PUD was terminated.

Leaving the electric power development and service field, Frank turned to real estate and property development, and as far as I know did tremendously well. He became involved in various major developments throughout the country and eventually moved to New York. I was contacted only once after he left his public power work. A man who identified himself as a private investigator had been retained to check on Frank to see if he should be issued a security license. While I had no answers, some of his questions which were prompted by others to whom he had talked related to "double clients," "double per diems," and "questionable conferences on per diem reports." I told him that I had always felt Frank had produced good results for his clients and while such actions may or may not have taken place, it was my feeling that if push came to shove, he would find that Frank was not dishonest.

When Frank left the power field, he never contacted me again. It was with a shock that on July 30, 1974 (my birthday), I read in the *Wenatchee*

World of his death in Montana on July 17. Evidently, he had returned to the Pacific Northwest. In 1975, driving through Montana from the East Coast, I talked to Joe McElwain, then President of Montana Power (whom Frank had introduced me to many years before), and he told me that Frank had talked to him just before his death. And thus ends what I have to say about a guy with whom I had a lot of personal, as well as business, dealings but whose friendship I lost. Good or bad, he did perform some vital services to local public power, and he never faltered in support of our program.

1959–1960

The year 1959 got under way at the November 1958 election. This was the first State General Election since the Legislature was redistricted by people's Initiative 199 in 1956. The initiative provided for 49 Senate members from each of 49 districts. The House would have 99 members, two from each of the 49 districts and one additional member from the 31st District. The last time the Legislature had been redistricted was in 1933, and since then there had been a growing resentment against the strength of the rural districts by the more populous districts in the growth areas around Seattle and Tacoma. However, as is the usual case in redistricting, the Democrat-controlled Legislature in 1957 amended the people's Initiative 199, and the amendments were approved by a two-thirds vote of both houses of the Legislature. When the State Supreme Court upheld the amendments, after a court challenge had been mounted against them, the 1958 election was held according to the new apportionment. The amendments had not changed the number of districts but only certain of the boundaries established in the initiative. The 1958 election increased Democratic control in the Senate from the 1957 level of 31 to 15, to 35 to 14. Over on the House side, Democratic control jumped from a 56 to 43 ratio to 66 to 33.

One personal sidelight of the 1958 election occurred in my home district, No. 46, where I had moved to a new home in June. A young Republican legislative candidate had come knocking at my door and I was impressed by his directness. I asked if he had a sign which I might put in my front yard which sat up somewhat from neighboring yards, and so, in the November 1958 election, I displayed a "Gorton for State Representative" sign, for young Republican candidate Slade Gorton. While I was and am normally a Democrat, I worked very hard to sustain a nonpartisan political position because of my nonpartisan political job as an executive for the PUDs. But in this particular year, the Democrats did not have acceptable candidates from the 46th and I was impressed by Gorton. He won, and I supported him in his many elections to come, making personal financial contributions when he ran for Attorney General. However, in 1980 when Slade decided to run against Senator Magnuson, I wrote him that if he were running against any other person, I could support him, but I would not ever change my support of Maggie, whom I considered, along with Scoop Jackson, to be best for our State. I received a very kind and courteous letter from Slade stating that he recognized and honored my attitude toward Maggie but hoped that if he was successful in his election challenge, we could once again enjoy our political friendship. Following the 1980 election, I wrote him a congratulatory note and suggested that he now start "re-earning" the yard sign location in my front yard.

The regular 1959 Session convened on January 12. With Democratic control, we maintained a public power flavor in the utilities committees and rules committees. Since we had a friendly Governor, Rosellini, my main effort was again to get laws passed to improve PUD efficiency.

In 1956, prior to the 1957 Session, I had enlisted the brains and good will of John Dawson to prepare amendments to that portion of the PUD law pertaining to the issuance of revenue bonds. Dawson was one of the lead partners in the renowned bond counsel firm of Wood, King & Dawson of New York. The firm and John had been of great value to many of the PUDs in issuing bonds for acquisition of private power properties in the 1940s, and for financing of some of the mainstream dams then under construction by PUDs. He had done what I felt was a masterful job, and while there had been division in our ranks, I should have gotten the bill passed in 1957 but failed because of a log jam in the Senate Rules Committee in the closing days of that session.

In late 1958, Kirby Billingsley sent me a personal note which he had received from Dawson complaining that Dawson had worked hard in preparing the amendments but found that a legal counsel for one of the leading bond firms had said such tedious amendments were not necessary, that a very brief bill could make the changes, and that Guy Myers was definitely against opening up the PUD revenue bond statutes. Thus Dawson wondered why it was worth anything to try and help people to better themselves. This note placed SB-219, Dawson's amendment to the PUD revenue bond statute, at the head of my list. I was successful in getting it passed and from that date on the State of Washington PUD law included what I felt was the most efficient revenue bond issuance statute in the nation.

We had a number of other minor housekeeping bills to be passed, including a clarification of the PUD privilege tax that would avoid penalizing a district using its own self-generated electricity. By special statute, we provided for the sale of a water distribution system by Snohomish County

PUD to the City of Everett. We obtained payment for relocation of power lines occasioned by highway relocations, and while we stood aside on a bill sponsored by Grant County to allow that PUD to have a five-person commission instead of the established three-person commission, we made certain that the legislation could apply only to a district which held a Federal Power Commission license for a project for which the estimated cost of construction was $325 million or more. Since all the other districts in the State were opposed to a five-person commission, we kept peace in the family by letting Grant County PUD move ahead in a manner which local people deemed necessary to rectify abuses the Grand Jury found in its investigation of the previous management policies at the PUD. We also secured a law to allow PUDs to have private pension plans in districts that did not have State retirement coverage for PUD employees.

We had to obtain several of these bills by attaching them to other legislation because our basic omnibus bill got tangled up in a private versus public power fight, one of the most interesting fights in which I have ever been involved because we won it on a tie vote in the Senate. Actually, we got into that fight by accident, but it turned into a donnybrook. It centered on a private power bill, SB-365, governing the matter of territorial limitation aimed at the cities of Seattle and Tacoma rather than the PUDs, and the story unfolded as follows.

Early in the session, as a result of a conflict between the City of Centralia and the Lewis County PUD, we introduced legislation which would have provided a reciprocal arrangement between PUD Commissioners and City Councilmen. Under the existing law, a PUD could build facilities inside the city limits only with the approval of the City Council. Therefore, we wanted to extend this law to provide that a city-owned utility could not build its facilities out in a county under the jurisdiction of a PUD Commission without the approval of the PUD Commission. The City of Centralia had been pirating certain Lewis County PUD customers because the City's electric rates were lower than the PUD's. About the same time that this occurred in Lewis County, Seattle City Light and Puget Power started to compete for a service area near Tukwila on the south city limits of Seattle. The result was that Puget Power had SB-365 introduced.

I mailed copies of the bill to Jack Cluck, attorney for the State Association; D. Elwood Caples, attorney for Clark County PUD; and Harvey Davis, attorney for Chelan County PUD. I asked one question: "Would enactment of this legislation stop the activation of any future PUDs within the State of Washington?" All three responded with a definite "yes." We had no alternative and thereupon took our position against SB-365.

This alarmed Puget Power, who then approached me to say that they would be willing to make substantial amendments to the legislation which would exempt coverage of PUDs and the future activation of any PUDs. They said their fight was against the city systems. By this time, however, I had alerted our forces statewide and taken a position against the legislation. This, incidentally, demonstrates one of the problems of lobbying for a group as broad as public utility districts. In the case of a private power corporation, the president of that organization working with his lobbyists can make a fast decision and by placing two telephone calls he can coordinate with the presidents of the other power companies interested in the State of Washington legislation. We had to coordinate 21 such utilities and keep the city systems and cooperative systems aware of our position. A private power president merely has to pick up the telephone and call his head lobbyist in Olympia and give him the new position for the company. We couldn't work that way. We had to first advise all our bosses, then hold a meeting to try to ascertain what the majority viewpoint was, and then go to the legislators with our position. On SB-365, we had sounded the alarm bells when it was first introduced and warned the people who made decisions that the legislation would have stopped any further PUD activation. We did not have the time or the opportunity to consult with them about amendments.

Further, we usually favored the city utilities when their interests conflicted with those of private power. There is always a balance of power in the Legislature among the three elements of private power, municipal power, and the PUD. It had taken the combined effort of the PUDs and municipals to offset the private power position in many previous fights. I therefore urged our members to stay with the city systems in their defense against this territorial legislation. Of course, this meant we had splits in the PUD ranks. Lewis County PUD wanted some type of territorial legislation to protect them against inroads by the City of Centralia. Additionally, several of the PUDs working very closely with Puget Power on construction of mid-Columbia River dams actually lent the services of their attorneys and others to contact individual legislators on the issue.

When SB-365 came up in the Senate, it passed by a two-vote margin. However, in a fast move, opponents switched their votes and gave notice that reconsideration would take place on the following day. The vote on the next day to reconsider ended in a tie. Now the Lieutenant Governor as the Senate's presiding officer can cast a vote to break a tie on procedural matters but not on the final passage of any legislation. Lieutenant Governor Cherberg as Senate President cast the deciding vote that the bill could be reconsidered. Following various maneuvers to reassign the bill to committees, which failed, a roll call vote was called for final passage and this vote once again ended in a tie. Cherberg couldn't vote to kill the bill, but by very quick thinking announced, "Senate Bill 365 having failed to obtain a constitutional majority is declared lost." He rapped his gavel and killed the bill before any of the proponents could switch their votes in order to move for reconsideration. It was probably the first time that a power fight had ever been won on a tie vote, and credit must go to Lieutenant Governor Cherberg. His abilities, fairness, and firmness as a presiding officer were a marvel to behold. In this instance, he saved my skin, but I have seen that man in many situations not involving me do an outstanding job as the presiding officer in the State Senate, even in those years when the opposite political party had control of the Senate leadership.

One interesting sidelight was that as Senator Wib Hallauer from Okanogan, Senator Jerry Hanna of Chelan-Douglas, and I left the legislative building on that tense evening after the bill was killed, and approached my car, Hallauer looked down and said, "Billington, that license plate is prophetic." Sure enough, I was driving a car with the license number 365.

After the 36th Legislature ended its regular session on March 12 under the 60-day constitutional limitation, a Special Session of 15 days to end on March 27 was called. During this time, I tried to dig out our omnibus bill, but the Senate leadership turned me down because the title was so broad they felt it could invoke another SB-365 fight. The 1959 Session was a turning point in the private versus public power fight. Heretofore, Puget Power, because of its close alliance with Chelan County and Douglas County PUDs in the construction of dams on the Columbia River, its vicious fight against the merger sponsored by Washington Water Power, and its cooperative efforts with public power through the Puget Sound Utilities Council, had not joined forces with Washington Water Power and Pacific Power and Light, the main proponents of anti-PUD legislation. Coming out of the 1959 Session was a realliance of all three private power companies in their political and lobbying activities at Olympia. I immediately began to notice this. Another shift was that Kinsey Robinson began to change the stance of Washington Water Power. While still principally supporting the election of Republican legislators and more conservative Democrats from Spokane, Robinson, when elevated to the position of Chairman and Chief Executive Officer of Washington Water Power, selected Democrat George Brunzell as the company's new President over Lou Thrailkill, a very efficient utility vice president of the company who moved in Republican circles. Also in 1959, Jeremiah "Jerry" Buckley, who was to turn into a dominant and strong lobbyist for Washington Water Power, showed up on the scene. While in future years Jerry was to become one of my most vicious opponents, we developed a very good personal relationship. We didn't agree about politics and we didn't see each other socially, but I sincerely liked the guy and felt he liked me even though he was against public power.

It was in 1959 that I received a call from Commissioner Fran Pearson stating that he had been informed by Robinson that Brunzell's salary was going to be increased substantially and that Brunzell could use moneys in excess of the additional income tax he would have to pay on the salary increase to fund the election of Democrats.

In July 1959, following defeat of SB-365, the territorial limitation legislation, Puget Power filed a request for rate increases for its service area which incorporated special lower-rate buffer zones surrounding the cities of Seattle and Tacoma. This was a good example of the so-called yardstick influence of public power on private power rates. But it meant that customers served in other Puget Power service areas were going to have to subsidize the lower, if not below-cost, rates which Puget Power was going to collect in areas such as Renton, Tukwila, and Federal Way bordering on the service areas of Seattle City Light and Tacoma Light. The grapevine had it that this rate request meant that Ralph Davis was favored over long-time executive vice president Larry Karrer as a potential replacement for the current president of Puget Power.

It was about this time that the law firm of Durkan & Durkan, whose member Senator Martin Durkan was one of the lead proponents of SB-365, began doing legal work for Puget Power. This extension of legal work carried over into 1960 when, during the Public Service Commission hearings on the Puget Power rates, I was to receive a call from Commissioner Pearson asking if I knew what State Representative Len Sawyer, as an attorney, was doing in the Puget Power rate hearings. Pearson stated that, while Sawyer wasn't at the table with the regular lawyers of Puget Power, he was attending every daily session, sitting in the front row, and receiving copies of each daily transcript. In 1961, during the legislative session, I was to find out what this meant but I could not give Pearson an answer on the matter in 1960.

One 1959 political footnote was that when I attended a testimonial dinner late that year on behalf of Governor Rosellini with my usual one-person ticket, I was impressed by the number of private power executives and lobbyists who were there. The Puget Power people took up a whole table. I pointed this out to my Board at its November meeting.

The 1959 federal legislative scene was also quite hectic. Senator Scoop Jackson had been very busy pushing for a new production reactor at Hanford. He was trying to make it a dual-purpose reactor which would produce plutonium for defense purposes and use the waste steam to generate electric power. Following the resignation of Clif Erdahl and the reconstitution of the Pacific Northwest Utilities Conference Committee in August 1958, that Committee was asked by representatives of the Atomic Energy Commission to assist in a study to be made by the engineering firm of Stone & Webster on the feasibility and advisability of a steam plant to be constructed in conjunction with the plutonium reactor. On January 20, 1959, I got a call from Scoop stating that he had met the previous day with John McCone, Chairman of the AEC, and had been informed that the PNUCC was to help with such a study. Scoop was concerned that public power would not be well enough represented within the Committee, and he anticipated that Stone & Webster's findings would not favor the steam plant. I immediately sent a wire back to Scoop naming the public power individuals who would be serving on the PNUCC study committee: Owen Hurd, Managing Director of the Washington Public Power Supply System, and Kirby Billingsley, Chelan County PUD Manager. He in turn forwarded this wire to McCone stating that, in Scoop's opinion, these men would assure that public power would be represented satisfactorily. However, it wasn't to work that way.

Sure enough, the following September, I got an SOS call from Scoop. He stated that the Stone & Webster engineering report had said construction of a steam generating plant in conjunction with the reactor was not feasible. He wanted to get another engineering report on the project and this time for the Joint Committee on Atomic Energy of Congress. His question was, "Do you know of any good public power consulting firm where they have Q clearances?" I said, "What's a Q clearance?" He explained that this was a special clearance granted by the Atomic Energy Commission to allow individuals access to classified data on nuclear energy. Scoop stated that the principal of one firm which had been suggested could not get a Q clearance because of his wife. I recognized the touchiness of the situation but told Scoop I would try to find such a firm. I called Bob Beck at his Columbus, Nebraska, office and asked him if his firm had any Q clearances. He stated, "Yes, I have one, Herb Westfall has one, Bill Trommershausen has one, and Dr. Emerson Jones, who we are using on a proposed nuclear plant here in Nebraska, has one." I called Scoop back and said, "You've got your engineering firm with their Q clearances." R. W. Beck and Associates was retained for a second study of the Hanford Generating Plant with a resulting finding that such a plant, while having potential problems because of the low pressure and wetness of the steam, was feasible under established engineering principles and concepts. The study was completed in March 1960 and bolstered by further reports from the General

Electric Company and Burns and Roe, Inc., constructor and architect-engineer, respectively, for the new reactor. The Beck report was further supported by findings of the Federal Power Commission staff. The report led to the federal legislative fights centering on authorization and construction of the Hanford Generating Plant by the Washington Public Power Supply System in the period 1961 to 1966, and was a definite turning point in the construction of that plant which has, since its completion in 1966, served as a very valuable power-producing asset to the Pacific Northwest.

The year 1959 saw another federal legislative fight, and this one caused a big family fight within local public power here in the Pacific Northwest. It centered on proposed amendments to the Federal Power Commission law governing payments to upstream dam owners for use of their stored water by downstream power generators. Under the law, federal dams were exempted from having to pay upstream benefits to non-federal dam owners. Conversely, non-federal dam owners operating downstream projects located below storage dams owned by either the federal government or non-federal owners were required to pay the upstream owners for the release of stored water which increased generation at the downstream plant. Here were the new run-of-river plants being constructed by Pend Oreille County PUD, Chelan County PUD, Grant County PUD, and Douglas County PUD. Here were all the downstream federal dams from Bonneville on up, which with the exception of Grand Coulee did not have any established storage capacity. But also present in various river systems were a number of private power storage dams, such as Montana Power's Kerr Dam on the Missouri River, and even Washington Water Power's storage in Lake Pend Oreille.

Thus, when S-1782 and HR-5309 were introduced in Congress, the family fight broke out between the public power owners of dams and the public power utilities which relied on the federal power supply. Here in the Pacific Northwest, the difficulty was intensified because none of the federal power agencies — Bonneville Power Administration as a marketing agency, the Corps of Engineers as constructor and operator of downstream dams, or the Bureau of Reclamation controlling the storage or reclamation dams — would get involved in the issue. Thus, it fell to Gus Norwood as Executive for the Northwest Public Power Association and myself to pick up the cudgel to defend the federal dams' exemption. This upset the members of the PUD Association constructing or operating dams because, while their arguments for the legislation centered on the need to have federal dams and non-federal dams treated equally, the legislation itself went far beyond that, so that the downstream federal dams would be paying benefits to the upstream private power dams. I can recall one meeting at the Eastern Washington PUD Commissioners' Association where Percy Campbell, Manager of Pend Oreille County PUD, rose up out of the audience, pointed his finger at me, and called me a "saboteur."

But to Gus and me the principle involved was a great deal more important than the issue of coordinating waterflows and power generation. When a non-federal developer of a given dam site is either a private corporation or a publicly owned utility, such development is always for the individual utility's benefit. When a site is developed by the federal government, it is for the general public's benefit. We therefore felt we were obligated to oppose any change of the Federal Power Commission Act which would give extra benefits to an individual utility whether it was privately owned or publicly owned. Conversely, it was our feeling that the investment in a federal dam came from the general public for an overall public benefit. Therefore, any gain which an individually owned dam would secure from a general public investment dam should rightfully be paid for by whoever was making profits from the general public investment.

Then, too, there was the matter of equity. The legislation would require that payments be based on the cost of the dam. Thus, since investment costs were considerably lower for federal dams than for private power dams, the federal payments to private owners would be higher than non-federal payments to a federal dam. The issue was to rage for several years with some very severe family fights. What made it doubly difficult was my feeling that the four PUDs were being stirred up and used by the private power companies primarily because those companies were the main recipients of power from the PUD dams, with the exception of Pend Oreille, and thus those companies would get the most benefits from the change in the law. On top of this, since this was a federal law, it affected public power throughout the nation, making the issue nationwide. The American Public Power Association and National Rural Electric Cooperative Association were drawn into the fight when the private monopoly power companies sought clarification of Federal Power Commission regulation under the anti-trust laws. While a change was needed to allow monopoly utilities to coordinate operations and make contracts with each other, the wording being sought would have opened broad gaps in other nationwide anti-monopoly regulatory control.

With the election of President John Kennedy in 1960 and a change in the Administration, there was more aggressive leadership on behalf of the federal power agencies, and here in the Northwest a coordination agreement was eventually negotiated. Finally, some strong federal agency voices were raised on behalf of the non-generating public power utilities which relied entirely on Bonneville for their power supply and would have to bear part of the cost of paying upstream storage benefits.

The year 1959 also saw a split in public power ranks over the proposal to establish a federal regional corporation to finance federal power facilities in the Pacific Northwest. Previously, under the principal leadership of the Northwest Public Power Association and following the election of Senator Richard Neuberger from Oregon, bills had been introduced and hearings had been held on legislation to create such a corporation. S-3114 in the previous Congress had been introduced by joint sponsorship of all senators from the Pacific Northwest states of Oregon, Washington, and Montana. This year, when the bill was re-introduced as S-1927 in May, only one senator, Neuberger, sponsored it. The primary reason that Senator Neuberger acted alone was that the new bill included a provision that Oregon would receive a special allocation of power to come from the John Day Dam then under construction. This, of course, was not acceptable to many of us in public power because it violated the basic preference clause in our eyes, and it also was not acceptable to Senators Magnuson and Jackson.

The year 1959 saw final passage of the Tennessee Valley Authority self-financing legislation on which I had worked for many years. On this bill I lost the vote of Washington Congressman Russell Mack, from the 3rd District, who had long supported public power. For some reason, and I never found out why, at the very last minute he supported amendments which would have crippled the legislation. My only solace was that with my Board's approval, I sent a rather stringent letter to the Congressman. Fortunately, the bill passed without his vote, and when the Senate completed work on it in July, we were very happy to see both Magnuson and Jackson in the forefront helping our friends from the TVA area secure this needed legislation. President Eisenhower signed the act and TVA was permitted to secure its future finances on a businesslike basis instead of having to go the uncertain political route.

The kick-off year for another large power proposal, the Pacific Northwest-Southwest Regional Intertie, was 1959. While the matter had been proposed first in 1950 by Secretary of the Interior Oscar Chapman, it was immediately stomped on by Senator Magnuson at our urging. In 1959, it resurfaced in the form of a proposal between Bonneville and the huge Pacific Gas and Electric Company in California. We had been aware that negotiations were being carried on in the pro-private power atmosphere of the Eisenhower Administration and thus when the matter came up in April, we had to take action to block the arrangement.

One of the best ways to block action by a federal agency is to require that agency to make a broad study of the matter. Thus, we threw our support behind Senator Jackson's action via a Senate Interior Committee resolution mandating a full and comprehensive study of regional interties by Bonneville. The proposal put me, along with other public power persons, in a dilemma. We supported the concept of regional tielines as envisioned by Leland Olds, long-time leader and disciple in public power consumer benefits. Olds came out of the Franklin Roosevelt hierarchy of New York State and served many years as head of the Federal Power Commission. He visualized construction of large centralized plants which would provide power to broad regions by means of interties.

I had gotten into substantial arguments within the public power family with those who felt the Pacific Northwest should remain aloof and apart from other regions and thereby keep our low-cost public power benefits at home. The problem was that we were operating a river system which was uncontrollable because of our failure to build adequate upstream storage to save the spring runoffs for needed generation during the low-water months in the winter. We had tremendous surpluses of electricity in the summertime which could enrich our finances if we could find a way to market it. Thus, I favored interties and received considerable criticism from good friends, such as even Kirby Billingsley, who had a very provincial outlook, not only for keeping power generated by the dams located in his region of the Columbia River at home, but also for keeping power generated in the entire Pacific Northwest out of California.

An argument against an intertie that would send our power to California was the fear that the large publicly owned utilities in California, such as Los Angeles and Sacramento, could by once getting the lines in place, like the camel that got its nose under the tent, then exercise the national federal preference clause as public power utilities and take away that power contracted for sale by the government to the private power companies in the Pacific Northwest.

We did not object to the long-term power sales contract to private power in the Pacific Northwest by Bonneville, as long as we were certain that the federal power could be pulled back with five years' notice to serve the increasing loads of the small publicly owned utilities. The reservoir for power to serve Wahkiakum, Skamania, Mason, and Ferry PUDs, along with other smaller utilities, was lodged with the private power companies in the Pacific Northwest until we needed it. Get the tielines constructed and that power might go to California. Therefore, I had many occasions to tell Senator Jackson that we wanted to support the tielines as an economic benefit to the Pacific Northwest with the sale of surplus power, but that we could not do so until we were assured that we could be protected against loss of federal power to the public power utilities in California. Kirby Billingsley argued that once the tielines were built, even though we put in the legislation that only surplus power could be sold in California, the tremendous strength of the California delegation in the House of Representatives could repeal such a law. I countered Kirby by saying that if the four Pacific Northwest states with their eight senators could not defend against such a change in the law, then we deserved to lose.

The credit for solving this problem goes to Senator Jackson. I was in his office in April 1959, agreeing that the way to block the special interest tieline between Bonneville and Pacific Gas and Electric Company would be a Senate Interior Committee mandate for a broad study by Bonneville when we again discussed how to protect the Northwest against California acquisition of federal power. He said, "Ken, have you ever heard of the Dartmouth case?" Not being a lawyer, I said, "No." He outlined it for me. It was one of the earliest cases decided when John Marshall was Chief Justice of the Supreme Court. It was decided on the constitutional protection of contracts, and while I have never known the details, he stated that it established that Congress could not abrogate a valid contract between the government and a citizen without due recompense. I returned to the Northwest from that trip and at a Bonneville Advisory Committee meeting, following adjournment, talked to Dr. William Pearl, Bonneville Administrator, and Don Tilson, Works Manager of the Aluminum Company of America's Vancouver, Washington, plant. I told them that at the Senator's request this was not to be discussed publicly or extensively, but that it appeared to be the one way we might get needed regional preference for federal power locked down by a contract arrangement rather than just by a statute.

It is interesting to think back now on the intervening years before Public Law 88-552 was finally enacted in August 1964 under Senator Jackson's authorship and direction. It is a three-section law. The first section set up its purpose, namely, that federal power needed in the Pacific Northwest could not be sold by the Secretary of the Interior outside of that defined area. The second section defined the area. The third section said the Secretary should insert the provisions of the first two sections in all the power contracts in the Pacific Northwest. This was the section being most closely watched by Senator Jackson and myself when it went through. Shortly after passage of the law, contract amendments were proffered to all Pacific Northwest power purchasers by the Bonneville Administrator at the direction of the Secretary of the Interior. We knew that even if the twenty-six congressional members from California ever repealed the law, the contractual provision would remain at least until all contracts had terminated.

I was invited to a meeting called by Dr. Pearl on June 25, 1959. A portion of the Senate resolution ordering Bonneville to study the intertie proposal had directed Bonneville and the Bureau of Reclamation, operator of the Central Valley Project in northern California, to consult with certain representatives of state utility commissions and utility organizations. From that meeting, a broad consultation committee was established out of which a subcommittee composed of twelve West Coast persons was selected to follow the study. I was to represent the interest of local public power in the Pacific Northwest.

In the meantime, on another front, support was stimulated for a regional intertie. Sol Schultz of H. Zinder and Associates had contacted the governors of Washington, Oregon, and California (Rosellini, Holmes, and Brown), suggesting that it might be well to have an independent study made of the intertie to make certain that findings coming from Bonneville would not center on the small tie between Bonneville and the Central Valley Project in northern California. Governor Pat Brown of California commissioned a study.

I supported Schultz in his suggestion primarily because of my belief in this man's abilities, as well as his strong support of public power. Schultz had come to Bonneville as its chief engineer when Dr. Paul Raver arrived in 1940. He coupled an outstanding engineering ability with refusal to be satisfied with what other men had done in the construction and design of high voltage transmission systems. His experiments with better ways of doing things resulted in tremendous advances in the technology of transmission towers and systems while he was at Bonneville. It was this leadership which brought together a staff of engineers in Bonneville unmatched by any other utility, privately or publicly owned.

It was Schultz' leadership and daring which actually resulted in lowering the cost of transmission towers and transmission lines at a period when all other things were moving up in cost. These cost savings in technological improvements made a great contribution to the Pacific Northwest because appropriated dollars from Congress came hard and by stretching them, more facilities were made available to the Pacific Northwest. He even had the courage to test certain types of equipment by deliberately short circuiting actual Bonneville lines to prove a new piece of equipment was functional. What he did took guts, but his cost-cutting was used to break up monopoly bidding by several major electrical supply firms. Later, after he left Bonneville, he was instrumental in securing federal wheeling of nonfederal power.

He was now saying that, while a small capacity tie between Bonneville and Pacific Gas and Electric Company might be feasible, the presence of such a small tie should not preclude a major tie between the Pacific Northwest and the Southwest which could bring tremendous benefits to both regions. Schultz' findings and report recommended construction of two 500,000-volt lines as opposed to the Bonneville report which suggested one 230,000-volt line. Meetings in January of public power people were critical of the Bonneville report when it came out, using Schultz' report as a basis for disagreement.

Looking back now, it seems to me that it was this separate effort by Schultz backed by the governors which culminated in construction of the major tieline. The Bonneville study report spent considerable space justifying the initial tie between Bonneville and Pacific Gas and Electric Company, but reacting to public power criticism, it evolved into a document that supported the larger interregional ties.

We had established a Pacific Coast Power Coordinating Committee composed of public power representatives from the three Western states and the Province of British Columbia, which formed a strong nucleus for the tielines. We came to agreement in April 1960 on a law which would provide a contractual protection for the Pacific Northwest as originally outlined to me by Scoop Jackson.

Under date of June 9, 1960, I drafted a special letter to Senator Jackson reflecting what became my Board's position. The letter proposed that the Bonneville Administrator be granted the authority to require clauses in contracts with both outside purchasers and Pacific Northwest customers to provide pullback safeguards on both power and energy upon notice which could range from 30 seconds up to but not to exceed five years.

There were to be a lot of twists and turns in the intertie road but 1959 was the kick-off year.

We were still trying to come to an agreement on subsidies to reclamation projects from power revenues. The argument still centered on the Spokane Valley Irrigation Project when the Reclamation Association tried to have the subsidies paid from surplus Bonneville funds. We wanted the project to go forward but felt that permitting federal power revenues to be milked in this way could not be acceptable. We compromised by agreeing to tie the project to Chief Joseph Dam, even though there was no direct relationship between the two projects. The rationalization which we used to forgive ourselves for abandoning our position that a reclamation project had to be directly associated with the particular dam from which it got its subsidy was based on the fact that the existing irrigation project in the Spokane valley would give up its existing water rights and thus the water flow-ing on down the river would generate additional power at Chief Joseph Dam. Sometimes one had to reach a long way for logic, but we were still faced with the danger of a national reclamation account tapping federal power revenues out of the Pacific Northwest to put water on a Texas irrigation or reclamation project.

The first power from the Priest Rapids Dam was generated in early October 1959, and then on November 17, voters of the Grant County PUD approved having a five-person Board of Commissioners. The first two new persons on the Board were appointed in January 1960 subject to being retained or replaced by the voters in the next General Election.

A happy event of 1959 was the annual conference the American Public Power Association held in Seattle during May. This meeting provided a good public relations forum for public power. It featured the Governor of our State giving an outstanding speech which we wrote for him on public power and the benefits it had brought to the consumers.

Ongoing during this year, and extending into future years, was the dispute between private power and public power before the Federal Power Commission over the High Mountain Sheep Dam (private) versus the Nez Perce Dam (public). Before the FPC, private power was represented by the Pacific Northwest Power Company, and public power by the Washington Public Power Supply System.

While 1960 was a non-legislative session year, it was a very busy one. Many of the major issues which arose during 1959 spilled over into 1960. Coming out of the 1959 Session of the Legislature was a directive to the Legislative Council, made up of members of both parties in both houses to make studies when the Legislature was not in session, to conduct a study on taxes paid by all utilities in the State, primarily in response to continued complaints by the private power companies that public power was not paying its fair share of taxes and that private power rates were higher because of tax payments. I had expressed support for such a study, feeling that the PUDs would not come off too badly in a factual tax comparison which involved not only actual tax payments made but also actual rates charged. Such a study might show that the city light systems were not paying their fair share of taxes, since they do not pay the State privilege tax in lieu of a property tax which the PUDs pay, but I also knew that the fight would be between the private power companies and the PUDs, so the spotlight would not rest on the city systems.

Thus, when the Subcommittee on Revenue and Taxation of the Legislative Council opened its hearings in September 1959, we were ready to go. Although the Legislative Council's directive had limited the study to state

Priest Rapids Dam (*above*), the first main stem Columbia River dam built by a PUD, was put into service by Grant County PUD #2 in 1959 and dedicated June 2, 1962 (*below*). C. J. Miller, Master of Ceremonies, is at the podium.

Courtesy Grant County PUD #2

and local taxes, private power immediately tried to have federal taxes included. We suggested that if the scope were widened that much, then a study should be made of the interest-free loans the private companies had secured from their rapid amortization certificates, and of the amount of federal taxes they were permitted to withhold after collecting them from their customers under the new liberal depreciation schedules afforded them by the Internal Revenue Service code. And finally, we suggested that if federal taxes were to be included, it would be proper to make a comparison of rates. Using the year 1958, we demonstrated that total taxes paid by private power—federal, state, and local—during that year amounted to slightly over $8 million, but if they had sold the same amount of power in 1958 at the average rate that public power charged, they would have left more than $15 million in the pockets of their customers which more than offset their total taxes. We also noted in our outline that the actual cost of energy to the private power companies was lower than the cost to the PUDs. We thus demonstrated that higher taxes were not what caused the private power companies to charge higher electric rates.

By the middle of 1960, we did another tax comparison to show the Legislative Council. We selected six PUDs with comparable service areas to those of the private power companies and recomputed the previous year's electric bills of the schools, city government, and county government in the PUD areas using private power rates. The comparison showed that these tax-supported entities had saved a lot of money by being served by a PUD instead of a private company. To this saving we added the actual dollars received by the schools, cities, and counties from the PUD privilege tax paid in place of a private power property tax. Then, using a formula provided us by the State Tax Commission, we computed the property taxes they would have received if the PUD property in their area had been privately owned. It was clearly demonstrated that the direct tax payments received by tax-supported groups from the PUD privilege tax, plus the savings which such entities enjoyed on their PUD electric bills, greatly exceeded revenues they would have received from a private power property tax after deducting the cost to them of the higher private power rates. We were also able to demonstrate to the Legislative Council's subcommittee that, while the private power companies might have in the early 1950s paid higher taxes than other local businesses because their property, which crossed county lines, was evaluated by the State Tax Commission resulting in higher values than those established by a local county assessor who sets county tax values, there had been an ongoing systematic reduction of the state equalization rates for the companies during the preceding eight years. The result was that private power taxes had not kept pace with either their increase in rates which brought in higher revenues, or with rising local property values. I do not recall ever seeing a report from this Legislative Council Subcommittee on Revenue and Taxation but neither can I recall further claims by private power that PUDs were not paying their fair share of local and state taxes.

In April 1960, when the Public Service Commission approved rate increases for Puget Power and Washington Water Power, two things were brought to light. First, Puget Power had secured approval of rate buffer zones adjacent to the cities of Seattle and Tacoma where the rate increases were much less than elsewhere in the Puget Power service areas. In fact, the standard electric rate for residential service in one of those zones was actually lower than that of Seattle City Light. Since the state regulatory process involves approval of a company-wide rate of return, it was easy to recognize that losses in a particular rate zone would have to be offset by higher rates charged in other service areas of a company. In other words, some of the Puget Power customers, like those in Thurston County or Skagit County, or even in eastern King County, were going to have to have higher electric rates to offset the lower competitive rates to be charged in the buffer zones. It was an odd method of establishing rates for an overall utility company, and our grapevine indicated that credit for the idea would go to Ralph Davis, former Chairman of the Public Service Commission under the Langlie Administration, who had gone to work as Secretary of Puget Power but would be rewarded by the Board of Directors by being made President of Puget Power in 1962.

In Oregon, where Pacific Power and Light had a similar competitive problem with local public power, such as in The Dalles, the regulatory commission had approved a company-wide rate of return and then said if the company wanted to adopt local zones as rate buffers against public power such loss of revenue must be taken by the stockholder rather than being shifted to other customers of the company.

However, a greater rate penalty against customers took place in these 1960 private power increases. I was unaware that the 1959 Legislature, acting on the recommendation of members of the Public Service Commission, including Chairman Francis Pearson, had amended a longstanding law dealing with the private power rate of return. Since the 1930s, there had been a statute on the law books which supposedly said that any earnings of a private power company which were in excess of the approved rate of return of the regulatory commission would have to be set aside and refunded to the customers of the private power company. In 1959, the law was amended to say that any moneys coming from earnings in excess of the established approved rate of return, but which the company could demonstrate had been invested in facilities for the consumer interest, would no longer have to be returned to the customer. I knew that in rate proceedings, while the regulatory commission sits in judgment on the case, its staff supposedly represents the public interest in the rate hearing, and I was aware that in several rate cases the commission staff had tried to invoke the requirement that excess earnings be refunded or credited to the customers. I also was aware that the staff had never won such an argument. Now, with the new law, it would be hopeless to ask for refunds because in essence the law would provide that, should a company have earnings in excess of the approved rate of return, the money could be used for new consumer facilities and thereby increase the value of the utility for the benefit of the stockholder rather than the customer.

While neither of these rate issues regarding buffer zones or diversion of excess earnings directly affected any of the operating PUDs, the issues once again stimulated efforts in local non-operating PUD areas to get the PUDs activated. Ever since the failure of the total Puget Power purchase in 1953, the Thurston County PUD had made efforts to acquire the Puget Power properties in that county. To offset this, a committee named We Want To Vote On PUD had been organized, undoubtedly backed by the efforts of Puget Power. Thus, in October 1960, a letter from this committee went forward to the Chairman of the Subcommittee on State Government of the Legislative Council presenting four proposed bills to be considered at the 1961 Session of the Legislature. The bills would require that a popular vote be taken on condemnation, that a PUD could be dissolved by popular vote, that all PUD decisions would be subject to initiative and referendum procedures, and that the use of moneys for a survey must be approved by district voters if a tax levy was involved. We immediately recognized that our work had been cut out for us for the 1961 Session.

In June 1960, Senator Magnuson addressed the State Grange Session at Pullman, where I served as Recorder for the Public Utilities Session Committee. Following Maggie's speech, we were walking together toward the luncheon in his honor when he asked if I had ever considered going to Washington, D.C. Irv Hoff, his long-time administrative assistant, had left to join the Lyndon Johnson for President Committee and I knew that several close friends of Maggie had suggested me as a replacement. I told him he didn't have enough money in his staff budget to afford me. He said, "How much are the public power boys paying you?" I said, "No, that isn't it, and I'd be highly honored if you asked me to work for you. However, I have two lovely children in Roosevelt High School, and it would take a lot of money to get me to pull them out of the Pacific Northwest." The subject was not pursued.

At the urging of the Northwest Public Power Association and State PUD Association, the Supply System filed application with the Federal Power Commission to build the huge Nez Perce Dam on the Snake River in March 1960. After losing high Hells Canyon Dam for lack of a sponsor, public power wanted to make certain that the Nez Perce Dam would not go by default in the same way. Our people had already objected to the construction application of the Pacific Northwest Power Company at High Mountain Sheep Dam.

In July, we had to challenge the State Fisheries Department for printing a report with taxpayers' money which directly opposed the Nez Perce Dam but supported the High Mountain Sheep private power dam. We suggested to Governor Rosellini that, if the State Fisheries Department was to oppose Nez Perce on the fish issue, then the Department of Conservation and Development or the Department of Economic Development of the State should intervene in favor of the dam because it would provide additional low-cost power for economic development.

Another 1960 crisis arose after we finally prevailed upon those PUDs who were asking Congress to repeal a particular section of the Federal Power Commission Act that affected upstream-downstream benefits to agree to certain amendments to the legislation they wanted. These would grant but strictly limit exemption from the normal anti-monopoly regulation to let the private power companies coordinate their uses of the river. The difficulty came up in a House of Representatives committee when the chairman reported that the PUDs supported the measure, but failed to mention the agreed-upon amendments. Public power nationwide was opposing the legislation, and it took quite an effort to clarify in the minds of our State's delegation what was required to make the legislation acceptable to us.

In 1960, we coined the new word "taxocrisy," combining the words "tax" and "hypocrisy," to describe the hypocrisy of private power in its propaganda which claimed that private power paid more than its fair share of utility taxes. In fact, the 1958 dividends of Pacific Power and Light had been ruled 100 percent tax-free based on the rapid amortization and accelerated depreciation practices of that company. Pacific Power and Light had been joined in 1958 by Washington Water Power, 89 percent of whose stock dividends had been declared tax-exempt. "Taxocrisy" seemed to us a quite appropriate word, and was another of our arrows in the ongoing war between private and public power.

The year 1960 was bad for us because we lost some strong public power personages to death. Senator Dick Neuberger of Oregon died in March; on August 3, Leland Olds, long-time public power leader from the Franklin Roosevelt era, died; and Guy C. Myers died on August 20.

Myers died at age seventy-one at his retreat in the Barbados Islands. At the time, he was still serving as fiscal agent for Douglas County PUD on construction of its Wells Dam. Myers was an active and strong force in public power circles for many years. The fact that his interest was primarily financial did not detract from his basic belief in the benefits of public ownership of utilities. I will have more to say about him in Chapter 9.

October 1960 saw the death of J. Chauncey Price, Commissioner of Skamania County PUD, public power pioneer who is also described in more detail in Chapter 9. He had played a very strong role in my public power service — many times more like a father than a boss. He was on vacation touring in Hong Kong when he died. One of the bitter chapters in Chauncey's life occurred when Clyde Riddell, a fellow Commissioner, opposed him in Chauncey's recall election. Riddell was one of the three persons serving on the special State Grange Committee in 1927 and 1928 which drafted the PUD initiative law and, thus, when these two old-timers fell out, the whole program was shaking, from my standpoint. Clyde had died the previous December 30, having left the Commission after Chauncey won the recall election. I would hope they would be friends again in the Hereafter.

On November 24, the Merritt-Chapman-Scott Construction Company, which had constructed Priest Rapids Dam for Grant County PUD, pleaded *nolo contendere* to the indictments brought as the result of the Grand Jury investigations and was fined $50,000. Previously, Frank Bell, Sr., had been found guilty of perjury in the problems which had surfaced in the matter. Thus ended a sorry chapter in that history of local public power. Some fallout reaction would take place in 1967 over the retention of a particular attorney by the Grant County PUD Commission and a recall election over the issue.

The November 1960 election saw the re-election of Governor Rosellini and brought Democratic control in the State Senate to 36, with 13 Republicans, but in the House, Democratic control dropped from 66 to 59, with 40 Republicans, or a gain of 7 on the Republican side. While I thought that continuance of Democratic control by legislators elected from the PUD areas would result in a safe and sane 1961 Legislative Session, I did not recognize that private power's influence among certain of the individual Democratic legislators was having a strong effect. The election also promoted one of public power's strongest State legislative weapons, Representative Julia

Butler Hansen, long-time legislator from Cowlitz-Wahkiakum counties, to Congress from the 3rd District. She filled the seat of long-time Congressman Russell V. Mack, who died earlier in the year.

1961–1962

The 37th Session of the State Legislature convened January 9, 1961. The previous election had established a Democratic majority in the House of Representatives of 59 to 40. In the Senate, the Democrats held a majority of 36 to 13. The session was to see the roughest legislative fight that had ever occurred between private and public power in the State of Washington. The fight was over HB-197 introduced by the private power supporters, and when it reached the floor of the House of Representatives on February 21, the 44th day of the session, it placed the House under call for four days and nights during which there were 45 roll call votes and participation in debate by 61 members. It was the only session in my legislative experience when I slept overnight on a davenport in the Judiciary Committee room which was just off the floor of the House of Representatives.

The issue centered on private power's attempt to get a so-called right-to-vote bill. They had tried to get a right-to-vote law in 1940 through a statewide initiative, and then again in 1946 with a second statewide initiative. Having failed in both attempts, they conducted public opinion surveys each year during the 1950s which convinced them that there was too much public favor for the lower public power rates to win by the statewide initiative method. Thus, they had turned back to the legislative arena, and HB-197 was their vehicle.

Starting in 1959, they commenced to make inroads on the Democratic side of the Legislature to counterattack the basic strength in the Democratic party in support of public power. The 1959 legislative fight over territorial protection for Puget Power against the city light systems had been led in the Senate by Democrat Martin Durkan who had been elected from a new 47th Legislative District in 1958 and who was growing in power in Democratic circles. I was also to find out that Representative Len Sawyer, also becoming a power in Democratic legislative circles, had done legal work for Puget Power in its rate case and then traveled throughout the State in the previous November elections to give financial support to newly elected Democratic legislators from PUD counties. I was astounded to find that Jack Burtch and Eric Anderson, new legislators from Grays Harbor County, actually felt that HB-197 had merit until the PUD Commissioners from that area and I sat down with them and pointed out the problems with the legislation. The bill also had solid support in Thurston County where Puget Power the previous year had organized a We Want To Vote On PUD Committee and by substantial expenditure of political funds in the PUD Commissioner race had elected a candidate who supported that position.

Another developing strong legislative leader, who later worked very closely with Durkan and Sawyer in legislative strategy and action, was Representative Augie Mardesich. Coming from a PUD county, he was basically a public power supporter and later was very positive in helping me — but in this particular session, he was cooperating with those supporting private power to work out strategy and organize House votes.

The kick-off on the issue came when, behind the scenes, the pro-private power Democrats tried to dump Speaker John O'Brien. They failed by one vote; however, Representative Dick Kink of Whatcom County was selected as Chairman of the Public Utilities Committee which had a hairline division between pro-private and pro-public power membership. I found out later that Kink had been working for Puget Power during the intervening months since the previous legislative session, as had some of the other Democratic legislators. I was not too surprised to later discover that Representative Bob Perry, who became the leader from the Democratic side of the aisle in support of HB-197, had actually filed a report with the Secretary of State, who required legislators to show financial involvement exceeding $1,500 per year with any particular corporation, naming the Washington Irrigation and Development Corporation as one of his clients. This was a wholly owned subsidiary of Washington Water Power whose management officers were the directors of the captive corporation. Perry remained with WIDC until it was to be used as the coal-mining operator at the Centralia coal-fired steam plant in the late 1960s. It was evidently at this time that the Tyee Construction Company, an electric line contracting group, became associated with Washington Water Power through Perry.

At any rate, HB-197 was introduced January 23 under the sponsorship of Representative Harry Lewis, new Republican legislator from Thurston County; Representative Margaret Hurley, Spokane Democrat; and Representative Avery Garrett, Democrat elected in 1958 from the new District 47, the same district and election that had moved Martin Durkan from the House to the Senate. Another new representative from the 47th was Dick Poff. It was interesting to note in later roll call votes on crucial issues that Sawyer and Poff voted consistently with private power's position. Garrett would side with the majority of the Democrats supporting public power views on certain of the roll call votes, but would deviate and stay with private power's side of the issue on crucial attempts to kill HB-197.

HB-197 was a very cleverly worded piece of legislation, having all the flag-waving appeal of the right to vote. In essence, it would require a local PUD commission to submit its proposal to condemn the properties of a private power company to the voters of its district prior to taking such action. While a person could argue that this particular requirement of elected officials had merit, the details of the legislation were far from fair in this regard. Simply put, it was a "heads I win, tails you lose" proposal in favor of private power.

Simple logic explained the deficiency and unfairness of the measure. In any condemnation action, one goes before a court of law and asks for a decision from either a judge or a jury. Each of the parties to the suit has the right to testify about the value of the properties to be condemned. In past public power condemnation suits, the private power company would come in, testify about how much it would cost to replace the property and demand substantial additional amounts for severance damages. On the other side, the public officials could come in and testify about the original cost of the facilities less depreciation, or they might use the values established by the State Tax Commission on which the private companies paid their taxes. These tax values were always substantially less than the values used by the private companies to ask for higher rates. Somewhere in between the figures offered by each side, the judge or jury would make a suitable award.

HB-197, while it would require the PUD Commissioners to submit the issue to the voters, would also require them to include the estimated price of the acquisition. This naturally would force the PUD Commission to set the ballot price relatively high in order to make certain that, should the voters approve the action, the approval would provide enough money to consummate the purchase. However, this would also reveal to the private power company what the Commission might be willing to pay. It would utterly destroy the PUD's ability to testify in court for a lower value and leave some leeway for compromise. Should the PUD Commissioners set the ballot price at what they would normally ask for, and the judge or jury award was one dollar in excess of the amount approved on the ballot, the entire condemnation case would be voided. It was indeed "heads I win, tails you lose" for the private power companies.

The bill was reported from the Public Utilities Committee on a 13 to 12 signature vote with one signer being Representative Chet King from Pacific County PUD. From there, it went to Rules. Here, some of the public power legislators felt they had 9 of the 18 votes to hold it in Rules. I found out differently from a strange source.

On Thursday, February 16, I attended a small reception at the Benson Hotel in Portland, given by leaders of utilities from throughout the Northwest to welcome new Bonneville Administrator Charles "Chuck" Luce. George Brunzell, President of Washington Water Power, also was in attendance. During the evening, in friendly conversation with me, he said they had two "labor" votes on the House Rules Committee and could "pull" HB-197 any time they wanted. I found out later that he was absolutely correct. Previously, Ralph Davis, who was then Secretary of Puget Power and heading up its lobbying activity, passed me in Ulcer Gulch stating that they had 59 votes in favor of the legislation on the House side. My rejoinder to him was that he ought to recount their votes as I did not get the same tabulation.

When I returned to Olympia the following Monday, I checked with Speaker O'Brien about Brunzell's statement. He made no comment but did inform me that because of a previous pledge to Representative Hurley, he had to allow a secret ballot on HB-197 in the Rules Committee. I learned that Brunzell had been correct when the bill popped out of the Rules Committee by an 11 to 7 vote to appear on the second reading calendar for Tuesday, February 21.

While there were fluctuations on the various roll call votes taken during the four-day fight, the ability of private power to pass the bill or public power to kill the bill hinged on getting 50 votes, with neither side winning that crucial one-vote margin. Clayton Farrington (Democrat) from Thurston County was both ill and feeling heat from the 1960 private versus public power PUD election and activation issue. He was conspicuous by repeated but excused absences during the debate and roll call votes. This created the 49 to 49 standoff in the House.

Our strategy was to kill the legislation outright, but shortly after it had been introduced, working with attorney Jack Cluck and Representative Shirley Marsh from the Cowlitz-Wahkiakum legislative district, who was also a PUD attorney, I had prepared eight basic amendments to attempt to remove specific provisions which would unduly penalize public power. Several of these provisions would also establish guidelines for future political fights between private and public power over the issue of activating public utility districts.

Public power did not lack for leadership, having House members such as Representative Norman Ackley, a promising young attorney who had worked for Judge Homer T. Bone in the Federal Appellate Court at San Francisco; Representative and attorney John Goldmark of Okanogan County; attorney Mark Litchman from King County, who was the Democratic floor leader; and fellow Representative-attorneys Bill Klein, Dan Brink, Bob Schaefer, and Wes Uhlman. There also were strong non-attorney Grange leaders, such as Horace Bozarth and Paul Holmes. The 40 Republicans were voting as a block, with the exception of Representatives Ella Wintler from Clark and Bob McDougall from Chelan-Douglas, although on several procedural votes McDougall followed his caucus instructions. The minority floor leader was Dan Evans of King County, backed by the legal advice of Representative Slade Gorton of my own legislative district.

Debate opened with strong statements for and against the bill. Strategy re-referral motions were made and debated. Several motions to adjourn had been defeated on roll call votes by the private power supporters. When it became obvious to Speaker O'Brien by 7 p.m. that tempers were flaring and order in the chamber might not be maintained, he recognized a motion to adjourn, called for a voice vote, declared that it had carried, broke his gavel while ruling it had passed, and abruptly turned and walked out of the chamber and into his office. Legislators were swarming in the aisles. It was a tumultuous time.

The next day, to hold against passage of the legislation, a filibuster was mounted in the form of myriads of amendments or motions to re-refer the bill and then demanding an oral roll call vote on each one. Opponents of the legislation had enough votes to support demand for a roll call, and they could further stretch out the long, tedious votes by taking turns at unexcused absences which held up the House proceedings until the absent members had been located. The most extreme instance of this occurred when a representative near the end of the alphabet sneaked off the House floor and was finally located by the sergeant-at-arms at the top of the stairs in the Capitol's dome.

In the meantime, we were attempting to locate that 50th vote by every possible means. On the second full day of debate, following adjournment, meetings were held at which our eight amendments to clean up the bill were presented by Shirley Marsh to Dan Evans and Slade Gorton and others supporting its passage. Thus, on the third day, in between the delaying strategy motions and roll calls, there was an attempt at compromise. By this time, severe hard feelings were developing among individual legislators throughout the chamber. My fellow lobbyists were getting fed up with me because each day that the legislators were tied up on this particular bill meant one day less for other lobbyists to secure passage of their desired bills. Probably the person who showed the greatest strength during this ordeal was Speaker John O'Brien who was still smarting under the attempt by the pro-private power Democrats to unseat him at the beginning of the session.

One of the highlights of the fight was when Representative Norm Ackley exposed a very cleverly worded part of the bill. He showed that if private power won the first vote required by the proposed law, any future attempt by a PUD to seek a second vote or reversal of the first vote would be automatically blocked. Another "heads I win, tails you lose" for private power. Representative Slade Gorton, who was acting as a principal legal advisor to proponents of the bill, sided with Ackley. The two of them worked out a clarifying amendment which passed. Ackley's revelation did demonstrate that the bill had been drafted to do more than provide for a simple vote of the people.

Even the State congressional delegation got into the act with Senators Magnuson and Jackson sending Speaker O'Brien a strong telegram opposing the bill on the third day of debate.

On the fourth day, it looked like business as usual, namely, fighting for amendments to compromise the legislation, but that effort bogged down over an attempt to add provisions which would forbid political participation by both public and private power utilities and their employees. Finally, Representative Avery Garrett, one of the three sponsors of the original bill, moved that it be re-referred to the House Rules Committee. Up to this time, while he had voted with opponents of the legislation for amendments to improve the legislation, he, as one of the original sponsors, had voted against any motion to re-refer the legislation.

When the House recessed for lunch, I was in Ulcer Gulch when Representative Morrill F. Folsom, Republican from Lewis County, approached me. We had consistently lost four of the six Republican representatives coming from PUD counties operating electric utilities. He and his seat mate were two of them. He stated that he had stayed with the Republican caucus leadership on their assurance that a compromise could and would be worked out on the legislation. I told Representative Folsom our difficulty was that the request to compromise was similar to a situation where persons entering a foot race were asked whether they preferred a ten-pound weight to be tied to their right leg or their left leg. One could not compromise on a basic issue. I said this law would be like saying to legislators, "While we, the people, elect you to come to Olympia and pass laws and make decisions on our State government, you cannot adopt budgets or propose programs or carry out your elected responsibility without bringing the matter back to the people who elected you and getting their approval by a second vote on the matter." I also showed him how the provision was doubly onerous because it would give private power one-sided and definite financial advantages. Folsom then said that he would vote to re-refer the bill back to the Rules Committee.

Even though the House was under call when it came back into session, I was able to get a note to Speaker O'Brien that a 50th vote was present for re-referral. Folsom got up and stated he had stayed with his caucus on the assurance that a compromise would be made, but that it couldn't be done. Now he was going to vote with his local people and their PUD. Upon demand of the previous question being sustained, the Clerk called the roll on Representative Garrett's motion that HB-197 be re-referred to the Committee on Rules and Order. The motion was carried by 51 yeas and opposed by 47 nays, with one absent or not voting. Voting on the prevailing side was Minority Leader Dan Evans. I think he voted on the prevailing side so that he could ask for reconsideration, but another fast gavel on the part of Speaker O'Brien moved HB-197 back to the Rules Committee where it remained for the rest of the regular session and the short special session called thereafter.

The intense private/public power fight was over, but it planted seeds which the 1963 Session would reap. As the result of this tough fight, much of the pro-PUD legislation which we had sponsored was denied or defeated. I had previously been informed that one of the last demands made in the Democratic caucus by Representatives Sawyer and Mardesich, when attempts were being made to remove O'Brien as Speaker, was that Representative Dick Kink be given chairmanship of the Public Utilities Committee in the House.

The PUD Association had sponsored SB-177 for the investment of surplus funds as merely a housekeeping measure. The Senate approved it 44 to 1, more than four weeks before the session adjourned. After the defeat of private power on HB-197, the private power lobbyists informed me that they were going to "kill your SB-177." Each time I asked Chairman Kink to give me a hearing or committee meeting on the bill, I was put off. He evidently was practicing the art of pocket veto. When this became obvious beyond doubt, I located a bill, HB-363, dealing with investment of county funds which had passed the House and was over on the Senate side in a committee. It had a broad title. Very quietly, with the assistance of a few persons, I arranged for it to move—move fast, be amended by the Senate to include PUDs, and be passed. The House concurred with a vote of 84 to 0. Representative Kink also voted for it. HB-363, as amended by the Senate, accomplished practically the same thing as SB-177 which was still located in the Chairman's pocket file at the end of the session—having been killed by the private power lobbyists.

I must confess enjoyment during the last three days of the session, watching them kill a bill which had already been passed. On the other hand, other legislation which we had sought, concerning improvement in our public bid law, clarification of the joint ownership of property by PUDs and city utilities, increase in Commissioners' per diems which was long overdue – all died as a result of the intense private versus public power fight. We were able to block ratification of the current Interstate Compact draft which again included a power allocation among the states and which would have worked against local public power. We secured one other improvement, namely, clarification legislation to provide that employee benefits would be continued by a PUD that acquired a private company. This had been one of the most tiring legislative sessions in which I had ever been involved.

Coming out of the session, I had hoped to catch my breath but soon found myself embroiled in another legislative fight which would run for a year and a half. This was the fight in Congress over the Hanford Generating Plant. When the new production reactor had been authorized by Congress in 1958 at the insistence of Senator Jackson, the convertible facilities, whereby waste steam could be used for power production, had been included in the design. I first became involved when Jackson asked me to help him secure reputable engineers to make a second feasibility study on the project and I had secured R. W. Beck and Associates which had the necessary "Q" clearances.

Thus, when new President John F. Kennedy requested authorization by Congress for the power portion as a federal plant, it seemed like a simple step toward getting this needed facility for the Pacific Northwest. We underestimated the terrific legislative fight which the private power companies, the Coal Producers Association, and some of the railroads would mount against this project. I testified on May 17 before the Joint Committee on Atomic Energy in favor of the plant, and it appeared at that time that favorable action by Congress could be anticipated.

Once again, all the load forecasts in the Northwest pointed to the danger of a power shortage just a few years ahead. On July 13, 1961, HR-6744 was taken up on the House side, and by a vote of 176 to 140 they refused to authorize the steam plant portion of the new reactor. The Edison Electric Institute, the nationwide organization of the private power companies, had mounted a tremendous campaign against House approval. On July 18, primarily because of Jackson's influence, the Senate approved authorization of the power plant by a 54 to 36 vote; however, Representative James Van Zandt of Pennsylvania, representing the coal producers' interests, joined by Representatives Craig Hosmer of California and Ben Jensen of Iowa, responding to private power opposition, had the House instruct its conferees to stand pat and reject the project. On September 5, the Senate approved a compromise which would have reduced the size of the power plant to 400,000 kilowatts and limited the use of the power to the Hanford Reservation, but on September 13, by a vote of 251 to 155, the House rejected this compromise and the plant was dead.

On that particular day, I happened to be sitting in the office of Earl Coe, Director of the Department of Conservation in Olympia. Truman Price, his power division supervisor, came into the office and informed us of the House defeat. Coe looked at me and said, "Why don't we build it ourselves?" and I said, "We have just the organization with which to do it." On September 22, Governor Rosellini asked the Department of Conservation to make a study of the feasibility of non-federal construction of the steam plant. This study was endorsed by the State Power Advisory Committee and bolstered by a ruling from the Attorney General's office. The law that was passed when the State Power Commission had been abolished in 1957 had authorized the State to construct one steam plant. While the effort at that time had been directed toward a coal-fired plant at Cle Elum, the Attorney General ruled that the law was broad enough to let the State pursue construction of the Hanford Steam Plant, and the law still had the provision that once such a steam plant was declared feasible by the State, any utility or grouping of utilities could take over the project to avoid actual State construction and ownership.

In the meantime, I had gone into high gear seeking a resolution from my Board of Directors calling upon the Washington Public Power Supply System to construct the power facilities at this reactor site. On October 20, 1961, the Executive Committee of the Supply System passed a resolution endorsing the suggestion and instructing its Managing Director to proceed with plans for carrying it out. Owen W. Hurd immediately went to work, and, with the help of the staff of the Atomic Energy Commission, members of the Federal Power Commission, and other necessary agencies, drafted a proposal whereby the government would sell waste steam to the Supply System which in turn would finance and construct the steam plant. All during this period, the Pacific Northwest private power companies were not making any public statements about the project. However, at our December 1961 annual meeting, Alex Radin, General Manager of the American Public Power Association, in his address to our group revealed that Ed Vennard, the head of the Edison Electric Institute, who appeared on a joint panel in Mexico City with Alex, told him in conversation that the private power companies in the Northwest were absolutely opposed to the project. When Alex asked him why the Edison Electric Institute was opposing the project when the Pacific Northwest private power companies were not doing so, Vennard stated that he had personally made a survey of the leadership of private power in the Northwest before the Edison Electric Institute took its stand against the legislation, and that they were definitely opposed to this project. Basically, the nationwide private power opposition was to a federal steam plant, which they feared might open the door for expansion of the federal power system in the Pacific Northwest the way the Tennessee Valley Authority had expanded.

Private power opposition did not alter our determination to have the Supply System construct the plant as a non-federal project. However, on July 6, 1962, the General Accounting Office issued an opinion that the Atomic Energy Commission did not have the legal authority to sell the steam and negotiate with the Supply System in construction of the plant. I found myself in early July in Washington, D.C., with Owen Hurd. One day, as I was sitting in the audience of a hearing conducted by the Joint Committee on Atomic Energy, Scoop Jackson came into the hearing room through the door behind the seated Committee members, and motioned for me to come up out of the audience and join him in the area where the Committee sat. He said, "Ken, the only way we can get this plant approved is to make a deal. I am going to propose that one half the power from the plant be sold to the private power companies." My response was an audible, profane expletive. I was embarrassed as the Committee members who had overheard me kind of glanced up. I then whispered, "Let me get hold of Owen Hurd who is downtown at the APPA offices before you do this." He agreed, and I went to a pay phone and called Owen to the Hill. We met with Scoop and asked for twenty-four hours to call back and check with some of the public power leaders in the Northwest about the idea. He agreed and we spent the next few hours talking to quite a number of public power people. The consensus was that the project was very much needed in the Pacific Northwest, and while the compromise would be a bitter pill to swallow, for the good of the region, we should accept it and go forward. We thought this would stop private power's opposition to the project. We were to be proven wrong.

On July 11, Jackson made his offer that one-half of the power to be produced at the Hanford plant by the Supply System would be allocated and sold to the private power companies in the Pacific Northwest. Under the legislation, the power would be traded to Bonneville for federal power. Bonneville would integrate the steam power with the federal hydro power and then sell it back to the utility. While I did not recognize the intricacy of this arrangement at the moment, it turned into a second benefit for private power at the expense of public power involving this particular plant. What it eventually came down to was that in order to cover the cost of the plant, a higher rate per kilowatt-hour had to be paid for power generated by the facility, and thus this higher cost power would be traded for lower cost power from Bonneville. For instance, the six-mill power from the Hanford Generating Plant would be traded for Bonneville three-mill power, and thus the utility making the exchange would actually get back twice as many kilowatt-hours as it gave in trade. Figured this way, the 50 percent of the Hanford Generating Plant which went to private power ended up being about 80 percent in actual kilowatt-hours. This meant that private power was going to get a greater share of the federal power in the Pacific Northwest. However, at the moment, we agreed to the arrangement in order to get authority for the Atomic Energy Commission to participate.

At this same time, Glenn C. Lee, conservative Republican publisher of the *Tri-City Herald*, had sent his editor, Don Pugnetti, to Washington, D.C., to try to find out how the legislation was going to be treated in Congress. Pugnetti called me one morning at the American Public Power Association office and asked if I knew whether or not Kinsey Robinson, President of Washington Water Power, was in town. I said yes, he was, and I knew because I had seen him and John Burke, President of the Pacific Northwest Power Company, just the night before on the plane I took to get here. As I told Pugnetti, they had been flying first class and I was flying coach, as usual. I had declined an invitation by Burke to ride downtown with them because Radin was picking me up at the airport. Evidently, when Pugnetti called the hotel and got Burke on the telephone, Burke told him Kinsey Robinson was not in town, and this lie rather upset the newsman, as one could imagine. From then on the *Tri-City Herald* swung over to the public power side of the fight with a vengeance. On July 17, the House voted down the 50-50 compromise by 232 to 163 votes. On August 1, the Senate, by voice vote, approved the project.

One change had occurred in the opposition. Representative Craig Hosmer of California, who had been an ardent opponent of the federal steam plant, had swung completely over to support construction of the plant by the Supply System. This gave us a strong voice among the Republican leadership on the House side. Lee and Pugnetti made three trips to Washington, D.C., during this legislative fight, to work the Republican side of the House primarily, and on August 27 they prevailed upon Governor Rosellini to join them on their second trip. They flew all night in order to reach Washington, D.C., the next morning, and while they worked the Republican side of the aisle, Rosellini was very busy working the Democratic side. Thus, on August 29, when the opponents of the plant tried to get a House motion to instruct their Conference Committee members, they lost, and on August 30, the House voted to commit the project to a free conference, where the Committee members would make their own decisions. The project was back in the running. Just before the final vote in September, Lee and

Pugnetti went back to Washington, D.C., for the third time, and this time they found out where exactly the opposition was coming from. Of course, during all this time, we of public power were making innumerable trips to and from Washington, D.C., and providing necessary information to the supporters of the bill, which included every congressman and both senators from our State, plus those of Oregon and Governor Mark Hatfield of Oregon. When the free Conference Committee report came before the House on September 14, a motion to strike out the Hanford Generating Plant was defeated 186 to 150. On September 26, 1962, President Kennedy signed the bill approving this needed plant for the Pacific Northwest to be constructed by the Supply System.

A sidelight to all this was that on September 24, 1962, when Glenn Lee appeared on the program for the Bonneville Advisory Committee in Spokane, he delivered a terrific speech outlining the fight for the Hanford Generating Plant and including some caustic comments about the action of Kinsey Robinson in heading up the private power opposition to the plant. That night after dinner, I dropped down to the Early Bird Club for a nightcap and met Robinson. He appeared to have been having a few and his words were, "Ken, who is that s.o.b. who came into my town and criticized me?" I said, "That's Glenn Lee, publisher of the *Tri-City Herald*, who refers to himself as a conservative Republican supporter of free enterprise and who fought the battle of Hells Canyon Dam in the Tri-Cities on behalf of private power." That moment made up for a lot of hard days and nights during the previous year and a half; and the Pacific Northwest was to get the 800,000 kilowatts of electricity from a plant to be built by the Supply System which, on many occasions in the future, would be a Godsend for the power users of this region.

Other happenings of note for 1961 and 1962 included the completion of the Priest Rapids Dam in 1961, plus first power from the Rocky Reach Dam in June. Seattle was awarded a license for its Boundary Dam which set off continuing conflict with the Pend Oreille County PUD over its plans to construct the Z Canyon Dam.

In April 1961, coming out of the legislative session, I could see the need for bolstering public understanding of public utility districts. I prepared a written outline to all PUDs in April, suggesting that they establish a PUD Progress Committee. This would be a local committee, made up of leaders throughout the community. Three times a year the Committee would be invited to meet with the local PUD Commissioners and Manager to hear about current PUD actions and involvements. If we included all established community organizations, we would avoid the accusation of hand-

Rocky Reach Dam on the Columbia River was put into service in 1961 by
Chelan County PUD #1.

picking the Committee in each area. I never got this idea across, but it at
least stimulated thinking on the part of the local PUD officials about the
need for a greater effort to let the people know about the good points of
public power. The 1961 legislative fight did stimulate my Board to ask for a
special study of ways we could mount a stronger program to get public
power bills passed by the Legislature and to defeat anti-public power bills.

Following a meeting in May 1961 with Undersecretary of the Interior
James Carr on the California tie protective legislation, which would ensure
that California could not take power out of the Pacific Northwest that was
needed here, Charles Luce, as the new Administrator of Bonneville, came
out in July with a written proposal for protective legislation following the
outline given to me by Senator Jackson back in 1959. This was the first time
Senator Jackson's suggestion that we protect our supply with pullback
clauses in the contracts surfaced as an official proposal.

In June 1961, D. Elwood Caples, my long-time friend who took me out
of the logging camps, was appointed by Governor Rosellini to be the State's
representative on the Columbia Interstate Compact Committee. He would

serve with two senators and two representatives for further negotiations. A special meeting of that group and my Executive Committee, attended by the federal, Montana, and Idaho representatives on the Compact Committee, was held on August 4, 1961. I outlined the objections which we had to the previous drafts of the compact, and later detailed these in a letter to Caples.

In August 1961, George Faler, a young Assistant Attorney General working for Attorney General John O'Connell, appeared before my Board to outline a lawsuit to be brought against some electrical equipment manufacturers for what appeared to be antitrust bid-rigging practices. My Board instructed me to give full support to the action, which I did by helping to compile information on past equipment purchases among the PUDs. Several years later, I was chagrined and unhappy over having done so when I found out that Faler had left his public employment but had been retained by O'Connell as a private attorney to pursue the work at a much higher fee than Faler's public post had paid him. What made me doubly angry was also to learn in later years that the Attorney General's office had retained a second private attorney, Mr. Aliota of San Francisco, one of the nation's leading antitrust attorneys, to work on the case, and that a fee-splitting arrangement was made. It hurts when people one considers friends do such things, but it hurts doubly when you feel such friends have used you in doing them. The only good feeling I got from this incident was that if antitrust bid rigging was going on, and from the records I saw it appeared to be, the challenge by the Attorney General was in the public interest.

In September 1961, I was alerted to a statewide public opinion survey that was apparently being conducted by the private power companies. Following defeat in the Legislature of their one-sided right-to-vote proposal, they had announced their intention of once again submitting it as an initiative in the next election. I never got to see the results of the survey, but evidently what they found was not to their liking because in February 1962 the companies announced that they would not be sponsoring a statewide right-to-vote initiative. This indicated to me that the people had finally begun to recognize the jokers in the legislation considered by the 1961 Legislature under the high-sounding phrase "right to vote."

In early 1962, I became directly involved in working on a new payout proposal for Bonneville and federal power projects in the Pacific Northwest. During the three previous fiscal years, Bonneville had run a deficit, but fortunately a substantial surplus built up from overpayments during earlier years had kept them out of the red so far. It was obvious, however, that without a change the Pacific Northwest would be faced with a substantial rate increase. Working on a subcommittee of the Bonneville Advisory Committee for the Seattle area, we proposed a "rolling maturity," or joint pool system payout procedure. This was adopted May 10, 1962, by the full Bonneville Advisory Committee and we were once again off to Congress to get it approved.

Heretofore, each federal dam was required to pay for itself from its own revenues. Additionally, facilities constructed for Bonneville were on a strict repayment schedule. For example, the repayment schedule of the Bonneville Dam, completed in 1946, was set up so that the power portions of the project would be repaid with interest by 1996; yet, as anyone could recognize, there would continue to be substantial earnings from sale of power to be generated by that project for many years thereafter. Under the individual or isolated repayment schedule, such revenues could not be used to amortize other federal dams or power facilities but would go into the federal Treasury. We therefore proposed that all federal appropriations for power portions of federal dams, plus appropriations for transmission facilities constructed and operated by Bonneville, would be repaid on a rolling maturity payout schedule whereby each power facility must be paid out in the fiftieth year of its last appropriation, but revenues from power dams paid off in earlier years would be applied to paying off dams or added portions of federal power projects built in later years.

In February 1962, the House Interior Committee began hearings on several reclamation projects outside Bonneville's service area. It was proposed that reimbursement of costs beyond the irrigators' ability to repay would come out of Bonneville revenues. I immediately sent telegrams to the House Committee, as well as the Department of the Interior, opposing the proposal, and this became a running gun fight until August 17, 1962, when we won it by tying the Mann Creek Project in eastern Idaho and the Baker Project in eastern Oregon to the southern Idaho reclamation dam revenues, and the Spokane Valley Project to Chief Joseph Dam revenues.

In March 1962, Thurston County PUD had a special election. This was the district that had sparked the 1961 right-to-vote legislation. Puget Power had got Vic Francis elected to the Commission in 1960, to serve with two pro-PUD Commissioners, Harvey Thompson and John McGuire. McGuire died in the spring of 1961 and Francis and Thompson were deadlocked when it came to appointing a successor. It looked as if there would be a standoff until the next PUD Commissioner election in November of 1962. However, when Francis abruptly resigned effective February 15, 1962, the remaining Commissioner Thompson, in accordance with the law, called a special election which had to be held between forty and sixty days following the resignation.

An all-out campaign ensued. Two candidates supported by Puget Power ran on a platform which said that they would not acquire Puget Power properties in that county without submitting the matter to a vote of the local residents. They were opposed by two candidates who forthrightly stated their intentions to carry out their responsibilities under the present law, which would be to acquire the properties and activate the PUD. It was once again a case where the candidates favoring private power seemed to have substantial funds for the campaign, while their opponents more or less passed the hat. The result was election of the two pro-private power PUD Commissioners.

It is possible that had McGuire lived, he and Thompson could have initiated condemnation action in 1961, but, based on past experience, it is reasonable to believe that Puget Power could have delayed the suit in the courts until after the November 1962 Commissioners' race, whereupon, if the people of Thurston County felt the same way as they did in the March 1962 election, a second pro-private power Commissioner would have been elected and, as in Yakima County, where the private power company had dominated the PUD Commissioners' elections over the last twenty years, the result would have been the same. The special election in March 1962 served the purpose and Thurston County continued under private power service.

In April 1962, the Washington delegation to the Interstate Compact Committee under Chairman D. Elwood Caple's guidance submitted a proposal to remove power allocation from the proposed compact and to include a new provision that the compact would not affect federal laws governing the sale of power.

It was also in this month that a conflict between the Pend Oreille County PUD and the Inland Power and Light Cooperative reached the boiling point. The PUD sought to condemn the properties of the Cooperative and this caused severe disagreement and consternation in consumer-owned utility ranks. The PUD had previously been petitioned by customers residing in that county being served by the Cooperative to provide them service. Following a long period of attempted negotiation for such properties and such customers, which efforts failed, the PUD turned to the courts. The PUD was to lose, however, when the court found that since the Cooperative owed money to the federal government in its loan program, the federal government had an interest in the utility facilities, and while a PUD might condemn non-publicly owned power facilities, it could not exercise the right of eminent domain against the federal interest in such properties.

In March 1962, the Federal Power Commission staff recommended the Mountain Sheep Dam be licensed instead of the Nez Perce Project, but ruled that the Supply System should receive the license instead of the Pacific Northwest Power Company. This recommendation placed the issue before the Federal Power Commission. Then, in June of that year, new Secretary of the Interior Stewart Udall came out in support of High Mountain Sheep over the Nez Perce Project. He took this position to protect the salmon fisheries in the Salmon River. We issued a protest to the action, stating that intervention of the Secretary of the Interior at this time, when the Federal Power Commission was making its decision, was certainly untimely in view of the fact that the Department of the Interior had withdrawn its intervention in the Middle Snake issue many years previously.

In May of 1962, John McCarthy, my Administrative Assistant, gave notice of his intent to resign. I had been very fortunate in having Jack, as well as his predecessor Andy. However, once again, an employee was expressing satisfaction with the job but needed to look elsewhere since there was no chance of advancement, there being only one higher job, namely, mine, above his.

In 1959, I had seen Gus Norwood of the Northwest Public Power Association fill a secondary position in his organization with a qualified woman. This was many years before the strong women's movement or equal opportunity program commenced. It seemed like the job did not have a high enough salary to induce a man to stay in it, but it would be a better-than-average job for a woman in those days. Thus, after discussing it with my Executive Committee, I posted notice of the Administrative Assistant position as being open to either a male or a female applicant.

Gus had hired Vera Edinger, who graduated magna cum laude from Linfield College in 1951 and had work experience in issuing publications. She became editor of his *Public Power News*. I was surprised one month after my posting to receive a call from Vera asking what my response would be if she filed an application for the job! I immediately drove to Vancouver to meet with Gus and Vera. She said she wanted the job in Seattle so that she could continue her education at the University of Washington and get a Master's Degree in public administration. With agreement all around, she applied for and got the job.

Once again, I was to be very lucky. While future years were to give me many accolades and compliments on my work performance from my bosses, as well as others, I always had to insist that it was in great part because of dedicated and efficient employees who always made their boss look good. Certainly, Vera Edinger Claussen (she married one of my Commissioner bosses in 1966) was at the top of that list until my retirement. Over the years many Association activities and projects were initiated and administered by her brain power and abilities. I became an early disciple and supporter of women's rights and equality in the workplace.

In September 1962, I proposed establishing a Managers' Section of the PUD Association. I felt it would strengthen our joint activity by providing a discussion and study forum four times a year for the managers from throughout the State. Top management personnel could get together and share their experiences and plans for carrying out the policy decisions made by the individual Commissions, and I would get a better understanding of those problems being faced by day-to-day management, as well as have an opportunity to provide them, as full-time employees, with current information on outside matters affecting all districts. I got a big boost in this direction on October 12, 1962, when the infamous Columbus Day windstorm hit western Washington, knocking practically every utility down. This brought forth a tremendous cooperative effort to restore service, and a mutual aid program establishing a three-party contract among all districts using the State PUD Association as the center post. One contract with the PUD Association would tie an individual district to all other districts, initiating third-party contracts. The contract established dispatch centers to alert as well as send repair crews across county lines for emergency storm damage repairs. This, incidentally, was one of the first major assignments given to Vera as Administrative Assistant and was thereafter primarily administered under her direction. Actual approval by my Board to establish the Managers' Section came later at the November Board meeting.

A significant milestone in PUD history took place on October 19, 1962. Held in conjunction with our Board of Directors meeting in Aberdeen was a banquet celebrating the occasion on which Grays Harbor County PUD became the first debt-free PUD in our State. At the banquet, where Undersecretary of the Interior James Carr was the guest speaker, a final check of $255,000 was presented to the bond house in payment of the last outstanding revenue bonds for the District. In 1939, just prior to the District's takeover of the property, average use of residential electricity was 652 kilowatt-hours per year at a cost of 4.6 cents per kilowatt-hour. In 1961, the previous year, average residential use was 10,585 kilowatt-hours at a rate of 8.8 mills, or less than one cent, per kilowatt-hour.

Thus, the years 1961–1962, which produced such torrid fights in the legislative arenas, were to end on this high note of PUD history-making.

Other PUD customers throughout the State were still enjoying the rate reductions between 1959 and 1961 which totaled in excess of $1.3 million per year. This was in the same period when the private power companies were securing approval for higher rates through the regulatory commission in excess of $5,000,000 per year. It was having that kind of knowledge in one's mind which helped offset the rough times in the legislative fights.

Two other events also had helped. First was the takeover of BC Electric, the private company serving British Columbia, by the public power utility which was now named British Columbia Hydro and Power Authority. This action was going to speed up settlement and construction of the upstream storage dams on the Columbia River system. Second, an agreement on the rolling maturity and joint system power payout on federal dams and the Bonneville transmission system in the Pacific Northwest was secured in Congress. The tempo and interest of the time were reflected in the Association's Annual Meeting held December 6 and 7 where we had the largest turnout ever. The pace seemed to be getting ever faster for me as we closed out the year.

Summary

The era from 1957 to 1962 saw elimination of the State Power Commission; establishment of the Washington Public Power Supply System; public power victories in three tough legislative battles over private power, including the construction of the valuable Hanford Generating Plant (but with definite advantages to the private monopoly power companies); continuation of public power rate reductions as private power rates were increased; and the start of the interregional power programs, including future Canadian storage dams and tielines to the Pacific Southwest. But the political fights were to continue.

5

1963–1968 Era
The "Balancing Act" Years

1963–1964

WHILE THE 1961 Session of the Legislature was perhaps the most tiring and stressful at which I was to serve, the 1963 Session which convened on January 14 was one of the most interesting. Following the all-out legislative fight over the so-called right-to-vote bill in the House in 1961, the special election in the Thurston County PUD in March of 1962 had put pro-private power PUD Commissioners in office and thus placed that local issue at rest. However, the Democratic State leadership made this one of the campaign issues in 1962, and, with the support of the strong pro-public power Democrats who were elected to the Legislature, Governor Rosellini passed the word that a right-to-vote bill similar to HB-197 would not be looked upon with favor if it reached his desk.

Finally, the 1962 elections had made some changes in ratios. The Republicans had gained eight seats in the House but they still were faced with a 51 Democratic majority. Some pro-private power Democrats in the 1961 Legislature – Art Avey, Jim Leibold, and Dick Poff – had been defeated by pro-public power candidates Ken Rosenburg, Dan Jolly, and Gary Grant, respectively. Representative Mardesich had been elected to the State Senate.

But private power still had support from at least six Democrats in the House.

Late Sunday evening, the day before the Legislature convened, the grapevine informed me that some dissident Democrats, who had failed in their attempt to oust Speaker John O'Brien in 1961, were meeting with Republican leaders. It is the procedure in the House for the Chief Clerk to call the new session to order and to preside during the election of a Speaker. Nominations are always made from both sides of the aisle, but this time there were two Democratic nominees and one Republican nominee.

When the Chief Clerk called for nominations, Democratic Representative Bob Schaefer (Clark County) nominated Representative John O'Brien (King County). Then, Democrat Margaret Hurley (Spokane County) nominated Representative Bill Day (Spokane County). Republican Representative Damon Canfield (Yakima County) nominated Representative Dan Evans (King County). On the first roll call vote, O'Brien received 45 votes, Day 6, and Evans 48. The six Democrats voting for Day were himself, McCormick, King, Kink, Hurley, and Perry, all leaders in the 1961 private power attempt to disrupt the PUD law.

On the second roll call, Representative Bill O'Connell (Pierce County) swung to Day and the vote was O'Brien 44, Day 7, and Evans 48.

On the third roll call, all but one of the Republican side of the House swung to Day, plus three other Democrats from the original O'Brien vote. The result was O'Brien 41, 57 for Day, and 1 for Evans. Representative Dwight Hawley insisted on staying with his Republican nominee.

Day was thus declared Speaker of the House. The coalition then proceeded to nominate Republican Representative Ella Wintler (Clark County) as Speaker Pro Tem. The Democrats nominated one from their side. The vote was Wintler 54 to 45 for the Democrat.

This coalition which primarily grew out of the 1961 private/public power fight, controlled in the House. Many of the major committees in the House were chaired by Republicans. The coalition Democrats also got chairmanships or places on the strong Rules Committee. From a private power/public power standpoint, the Public Utilities Committee and Rules Committee were overwhelmingly flavored in favor of private power. Democratic Representatives Perry, Hurley, McCormick, O'Connell, King, and Kink — coalition members — were placed in the front leadership seats on the Democratic side of the aisle. Evans retained his front seat as the Republican floor leader. I thus could see an interesting session opening up.

The first issue was an effort to increase the PUD privilege tax. Blocking this took a lot of work on my part but it was indeed fun. During the Legislative Council study, between 1959 and 1961, comparing private power taxes with public power taxes, I had been able to demonstrate that the cities, counties, and local schools in comparable PUD service areas were better off than they would have been if they had been served by private power and received private power tax payments. The PUD privilege taxes paid to these local entities, plus the savings they made on their electric power bills under the lower PUD rates, greatly exceeded the revenue they would have taken in from the private power company property taxes minus the higher private power electric bills. I sent this information to the entire House membership, and the legislation to increase PUD privilege taxes never cleared its committee.

Another fun bill was one repealing the joint action law placed on the books in 1957 so that Seattle City Light and Pend Oreille County PUD could act jointly. The bill to repeal was for no other purpose than to satisfy the whims of a private power lobbyist, and I killed it by a parliamentary maneuver. The law, which probably would never be used by Seattle City Light and Pend Oreille County PUD, was so restrictive that it could not be used for any other purpose than jointly building a dam. I felt that the private power lobbyist wanted it repealed primarily to demonstrate just what complete control private power had over the House through the coalition leadership. Very late in the session, the bill jumped from the Public Utilities Committee by a vote of 10 to 2 and immediately moved out of Rules to the calendar. I was informed that Representative Perry was pushing it. It was thus my thought that this being the case, we should let private power work as hard as they could for the bill, even though it was of very little benefit to us to defeat it. When a move came to boost the bill from second to third reading and final passage, many of the pro-public power legislators objected and on an electric roll call the required two-thirds vote was blocked. The bill had to go back to Rules where it died by the clock on the deadline. It was a minor victory, but good for our morale to win.

The big one for the 1963 Session between private power and public power was HB-43, a bill to ratify the Columbia Interstate Compact. It was reported out of the House Water Resources Committee and then passed through the Rules Committee like a bullet. We prepared certain correcting amendments and when this became known to the sponsors, they moved the bill to the Ways and Means Committee. There it was indefinitely postponed by a vote of 19 to 17, but the private power lobbyists went to work. A special and unprecedented meeting of the Ways and Means Committee, under the chairmanship of Chet King, coalition Democrat from Pacific County, was held at 10 p.m. on Tuesday, February 26. Proponents of the bill were all on hand but opponents were not even alerted to the meeting. The

FINANCIAL BENEFITS TO SCHOOLS, COUNTIES AND CITIES FROM PUD ELECTRIC SERVICE

District	Actual Electric Bills (1)	Bills At Private Power Rates (2)	Savings from PUD Rates (3)	Taxes Paid By PUDs (4)	Total Benefits from PUD Service (5)	Estimated Private Power Property Tax (6)	Extra Benefits from PUD Service (7)
Benton	$154,696	$240,303	$ 85,607	$ 76,273	$161,880*	$102,713	$ 59,167
Clark	414,425	580,976	166,551	212,735	379,286	334,384	44,902
Cowlitz	212,725	447,567	234,842	86,895	321,737	182,418	139,319
Franklin	236,106	321,298	85,192	48,249	133,441	92,820	40,621
Grays Harbor	222,775	527,240	304,465	102,094	406,559	154,666	251,893
Lewis	109,232	206,050	96,818	55,135	151,953	77,245	74,708
Mason No. 3	25,047	59,059	34,012	34,105	68,117	39,763	28,354
Skamania	43,144	71,174	28,030	10,810	38,840	13,247	25,593
Snohomish	976,230	1,861,926	885,696	395,643	1,281,339	991,761	289,578

*Does not include special City Taxes paid by the PUD and absorbed in rates. This amounted to: Benton PUD, $77,964; Clark PUD, $9,148; and Snohomish PUD, $116,380.

(1) Actual PUD electric bills for schools, cities and the County.

(2) These same PUD electric bills, recomputed, using the adjacent or comparable private power company rates.

(3) Savings to the local tax-supported entities as a result of PUD electric service with lower PUD rates.

(4) Actual PUD direct taxes, paid in place of a property tax, and received by schools, cities and the County.

(5) Total benefits to the tax-supported entities from PUD lower rates and PUD taxes.

(6) Estimated property taxes which would have been paid under private power company service. (Computed using a formula furnished by the Washington State Department of Revenue.)

(7) Extra annual benefits which the schools, cities and County receive as a result of PUD electric service with lower PUD rates, as compared to private power service.

(Study For The Year 1969)

1963–1968: The "Balancing Act" Years ❈ 197

bill was thus reported out by a 22 to 6 reversal of the previous action to indefinitely postpone. It was read into Rules and bounced out immediately on the Thursday calendar for second reading. At this point, Speaker Bill Day ruled that the compact was a treaty, and that any and all amendments were out of order. This resulted in a substantial uproar in the House but the Speaker ran the bill into Rules to make it ready for a third reading. Sure enough, it bounced out for third reading the very next day and was passed 55 to 41 with all but one of the coalition voting for it.

One of the interesting sidelights on House action on the compact has been known up to now by only three persons: U.S. Senator Warren G. Magnuson, State Senator Mike McCormack, and myself. Representative Bill McCormick, Democrat from Spokane, and supporter of the private power position in favor of ratifying the compact, had visited Senator Magnuson in Seattle just the day before the House was to consider the measure to discuss the need for ratifying the compact. Maggie responded by saying he would send a wire down in support of the action. The evening of February 20, I got a telephone call at my motel from State Senator McCormack informing me that he was in receipt of a telegram which had been sent by Senator Magnuson to Representative McCormick, but because there had been a misspelling of the last name, "mack" instead of "mick," the wire had been delivered to him. I said, "Have you opened it?" and he said, "Yes, I did before I noticed the error in delivery. What should I do?" I said, "Meet me at the Olympia library parking lot and I will take it off your hands." We met and Mike gave me the telegram. It read, "Hope you can continue. Interstate pact serves a very good purpose in our resource problems. Your leadership very helpful."

I did not deliver the telegram to Representative McCormick. I kept it, and on my first trip to Washington, D.C., following the legislative session, hand delivered it to Senator Magnuson pointing out to him that there was substantial Democratic opposition throughout the State to ratification of the current draft of the compact. He said, "Ken, you yourself have said you were in favor of a compact, and I thought with Elwood Caples now chairing the Committee, that the thing was straightened out." I told him that, in the opinion of many persons, the proposed compact had been improved but it was far from being fair to the State of Washington. The matter had been put to rest in this legislative session and we would continue to work for a proper compact which we could all support.

The compact had been substantially improved from a power allocation standpoint primarily because D. Elwood Caples, my long-time friend, was Chairman of the Negotiating Committee from the State of Washington.

However, there were so many deficiencies left in the compact that we had no alternative except to oppose it. It did not provide for flood control storage in upstream areas which would have been of benefit to Washington as a downstream state. It lacked effective pollution control powers which were of great importance to Washington as a downstream state. It would have placed control of diversion of water out of the Columbia River system in a sixteen-member Commission instead of in the respective state legislatures, and it continued a voting procedure which was stacked against our State. It still contained wording which could have been used to obstruct federal participation in river development. It provided for no ceiling or control on future appropriations which would have to come from regular tax moneys to support the Compact Commission. Finally, there was no method by which a state could withdraw from the compact once it had joined.

When the bill arrived in the Senate on Sunday, March 3, a floor fight ensued over which committee it would be assigned to. In this instance, the pro-compact backers, including the private power legislators, won, and it was referred to the Committee on State Government which by analysis seemed to have members who would favor ratification of the compact. However, the Committee was chaired by Senator Al Henry from the PUD counties of Clark, Skamania, and Klickitat. Thus, he sought and secured a favorable ruling from Lieutenant Governor Cherberg as Senate Presiding Officer that the legislation would be treated as a regular bill rather than a treaty before the State Senate, and would therefore be subject to any proposed amendments to be made by the Committee or on the floor. Hearing was held in the Committee and the bill was reported to Rules by a 7 to 5 vote. Proponents of the legislation, at a time when two senators were absent, made a parliamentary move to enact the legislation. Opponents thereupon availed themselves of parliamentary maneuvers to delay the legislation from reaching the floor of the Senate for action until the two absent senators had returned, in order that consideration could be given the legislation by the full membership of the Senate, and so that there would be time to prepare essential amendments. The press reported that 60 to 100 amendments had been prepared, but actually there were only 13. Opponents of the compact felt the deficiencies should be pointed out and corrected before passage. During the last day of the regular session, there was considerable maneuvering behind the scenes by both proponents and opponents of the legislation. By noon of that day, it became apparent that there was a strong question about whether the proponents had the necessary 25 votes to pass the legislation. It had become evident that a number of the proposed amendments which were essential would receive substantial support. It was also recognized that taking time to adopt even one amendment in the Senate would doom the legislation because time would run out before it again could be considered in the House. On this basis, agreement was negotiated by a particular senator to leave the legislation in the Senate Rules Committee with no floor consideration, but to continue the Compact Negotiating Commission during the next two-year period. Thus, ratification of the compact was defeated, but we knew it would come up again in the next session.

When the coalition had been established in the House by stacking the Public Utilities Committee on that side, the Senate reacted by establishing firm public power control in the Senate Committee. They added one more pro-public power senator to their Utilities Committee and rejected by a 29 to 17 vote private power's attempt to add three of their friendly senators to it. One piece of legislation which was essential was a bill to allow sale of three water systems by Snohomish County PUD to the City of Everett on an optional basis and under terms agreeable to the local Commission. As the bill moved through the Senate, an amendment was added which would also permit the construction of a sewer system in Klickitat County by the PUD to take care of a situation created by the construction of the John Day Dam and relocation of a small unincorporated town in that area. PUDs were not in the sewer business and did not want to be in the sewer business, but this was the only way that this problem could be met. The bill became somewhat entangled in power politics in the House, and for a while a move was planned to add certain PUD dissolution amendments which would have made it necessary to kill the legislation. Senate sponsors of the bill, however, were quite firm in their position that other legislation of interest to the House leadership would be treated accordingly or not at all on the Senate side unless the bill was passed in a form acceptable to the sponsors. It passed the House by a vote of 98 to 1; the only dissenting vote was from Speaker Bill Day.

The only bill which the State PUD Association had sponsored was one to clarify certain provisions of the PUD purchasing law. It met with instant opposition from the pro-private power forces in the House Public Utilities Committee, and word was given me that this was in retribution for our refusal to accept a compromise on the right-to-vote issue. This sort of retribution had occurred several times, and at least one of those times, getting back at us was self-defeating for private power. A special bill which would permit refinancing of outstanding bonds on the Rocky Reach Project by Chelan County PUD was killed in the House Public Utilities Committee. This legislation would have saved up to $70,000,000 over the life of the project and would have undoubtedly meant lower costs for the power purchasers of that project, who were primarily private power companies. But the House Committee killed this legislation because we would not accept a compromise on the right-to-vote issue, which we could not do. It was indeed a very interesting session and on balance we had to feel quite good.

On January 10, 1963, the first meeting of the new Managers' Section of the Washington PUD Association was held at the Ben Franklin Hotel in Seattle. Sixteen Managers were present, and Kirby Billingsley, Manager of Chelan County PUD, was elected Chairman of the Managers' Section for 1963. This group became a very effective force in continuing operation of Public Utility Districts because four times a year it allowed those persons responsible for management to get together and analyze the events and activities affecting management of the districts, providing better coordination among the districts.

One interesting sidelight of this particular meeting occurred when Jerry Buckley, top lobbyist of Washington Water Power, contacted me after the meeting in Olympia. Jerry and I had developed a good friendship since his arrival on the scene in Olympia as a private power lobbyist in 1959. We naturally disagreed violently over our private/public power views, but I found him to be a nice guy, and his abilities around the legislative chambers were starting to be felt. Jerry came to me and said "Ken, this isn't any of my business but a fellow came to me and said that he saw you and your new female Administrative Assistant entering the Ben Franklin Hotel and going up in the elevator in the early afternoon last Friday. The guy hung around and said he didn't see you come back down and he is evidently trying to make something out of this situation." My response was, "Jerry, it so happens that the first meeting of our new Managers' Section was held at that hotel on that particular date and time. We were going up to the 12th floor conference room, but you can do me a favor by telling your informant that I learned a long time ago that business and pleasure do not mix, and while I know I have a very attractive female assistant, you can be quite certain that there will be no occasion such as that supposed by your informer."

Recounting this reminds me of what I said to Vera Edinger when she joined my staff. She was an attractive young lady and I stated very forthrightly at the beginning that her private life was entirely her own but that I would have to insist that should any red-blooded Commissioner or Manager attempt to become involved with her or show her special favor, it just could not be. Vera had been tragically widowed by the unfortunate death of her husband before she joined our staff, and I just didn't want any misunderstandings to arise. However, I did not reckon with the election of an eligible bachelor Commissioner in 1964. Thus, by early November 1965,

Vera approached me to ask whether my rule applied to single Commissioners. It seemed that Commissioner Al Claussen of Grant County PUD, a graduate of the University of Washington, followed the practice of buying four season tickets to Husky home games and she had been invited to attend with him. My response was, "Hell no, I merely wanted to avoid any wrong type of involvement." The result of that first date was a marriage the following August 1966 and my loss of a very efficient and dedicated employee.

But it would be for only a short period, as it happened. Vera had worked since graduation from college in the early 1950s. She had held full-time jobs since that time and therefore when she left us to return to being a housewife, even though she had two children, staying at home was not enough for her personal satisfaction. I went ahead and hired a new Administrative Assistant, Joan Whinahan, who was also very efficient.

Then, in October 1966, the Managers' Section directed me to hire someone to do research on our PUD labor contracts to find out the best way to coordinate them. George Doty had just retired from Seattle City Light as Personnel Director and I approached him for the job. On the same day I had completed my arrangements with Doty, he called and stated that he had changed his mind and could not accept the assignment because he had entered retirement for the purpose of getting away from the pressure of labor negotiations. The very next day, Vera called just to find out how things were going in the Association, and I told her that I needed someone to do research on labor contract work. It then occurred to me that she could do that kind of research in her home in Soap Lake with an occasional trip to the Seattle office. When her husband Al agreed to this, she once again became of service to the Association.

Then, in September 1967, one year after being hired, Joan resigned because the Association job required her to travel extensively throughout the State to various PUD meetings and functions which interfered with her own family obligations. This really threw me a curve, especially as we were moving toward our annual meeting which always required a great amount of planning. Again, thanks to Vera's willingness to help and Al's agreement, Vera said she would serve until the end of the year or until I had time to replace her. However, when the annual meeting was over, she wanted to stay, and we certainly wanted to keep her, so she returned on a full-time basis as Administrative Assistant. Thereafter, she was promoted to Assistant Executive Director, and she held that position until she left the Association in 1979, one year after my retirement.

Speaking of various personnel changes, it was in late 1963 that my long-time, very efficient employee, Eleanor Hisey, decided to resign. Eleanor was there when I arrived in 1951. One could never have found a more dedicated employee. She gave solid support to public power and worked side-by-side with me in the hard years to keep the Association in operation. She resigned because she intended to get married and did not want a full-time job. Once again Lady Luck looked over my shoulder, and in December 1963, Phoebe Haworth joined my staff as secretary-bookkeeper. She was to be with the Association for 14 years. While having an English name, she had an Italian temperament; not only was she very efficient and dedicated, but she was also rather stubborn and strong willed when she needed to be.

The year 1963 saw the death of Dr. Paul J. Raver on April 6. Public power lost one of its strong leaders and I lost a very close friend and advisor.

In May, Donald A. Pugnetti, the managing editor of the *Tri-City Herald*, who had played such an essential role in getting the Hanford Generating Project authorized, received the Thomas L. Stokes Award for 1962. This was a national award which consumer-interest and public power groups presented each year to a newspaperman who had written articles to promote the wise and proper use of the nation's natural resources. We were delighted that a Pacific Northwest person would receive this recognition and in particular a person who had helped us get the new generating plant.

Dedication of the Rocky Reach Dam was to follow on July 20, 1963, and finally, after many years of fighting, the Bonneville Power Administration won approval to provide service to southern Idaho in September of 1963. It was also in September that President John F. Kennedy journeyed to Hanford for the groundbreaking ceremonies for construction of the Hanford Generating Project.

In November 1963, Bonneville announced a rate increase of 8½%, the first rate increase in the twenty-five-year history of the agency. The kilowatt-year rate was to go from $17.50 to $19.80, effective December 20, 1964.

The Coordination Agreement between Bonneville, the Corps of Engineers and the ten generating utilities in the Pacific Northwest was completed. This would provide a means of substantially firming up the power supply throughout the region, and would provide for necessary and fair payments between upstream and downstream dams, as well as payments to other generating plants tied to the integrated regional transmission system.

We were still experiencing difficulty in getting a proper law to provide protection for our region if we agreed to export and sell power to California. Senator Scoop Jackson had secured Senate approval in April 1963 by a 51 to 36 vote for S-1007, the regional preference protection legislation. When the bill came before the House Interior Committee in July, Con-

Earl Coe was Director of the Washington Department of Conservation and Development from 1957 to 1964. Following his death in 1964, the Washington PUD Association established the Earl Coe Award, "Dedicated to outstanding leadership in the conservation and development of the power and water resources of the State of Washington and the Nation."

Courtesy BPA

gressman Jack Westland insisted on inserting words requiring specific congressional authorization of any federal lines to be constructed for regional interties. We tried to stop the action but failed, and the legislation passed the House in August 1963 with the Westland amendment.

We ended the year 1963 with our annual meeting in December, the highlight of the meeting being a salute to Earl Coe who by that time had begun his losing fight against cancer with several trips to the Mayo Clinic, and who was finishing out many years of public service to our State as a State legislator, Secretary of State, and now Director of Conservation and Development.

The year 1964 commenced with final approval of negotiations on the Columbia River Treaty in January. It had first been approved in 1961 by the United States, but ratification had been held up in Canada because of the fight between the British Columbia province and the dominion government. Negotiations had now been completed, and the treaty was to be ratified on June 10, 1964, in Canada.

The Federal Power Commission reaffirmed its award of the High Mountain Sheep Dam license to the Pacific Northwest Power Company which it had granted by overruling its staff's recommendation that the license go to the Washington Public Power Supply System. This followed a rehearing. The Supply System then served notice of its intent to appeal the decision to the federal courts.

Regional support was mustered for congressional passage of legislation connecting the Pacific Northwest to the Pacific Southwest by an intertie. A four-line package was being sought, including a direct current line. The legislation had progressed to the House of Representatives Rules Committee where we found it being stalled by Representative Bernie Sisk of California at the insistence of northern California Representative Harold "Biz" Johnson. Johnson was insisting that 400 megawatts of power be furnished to the Central Valley Project in northern California from the Pacific Northwest because the dc line was going to be built directly from the Pacific Northwest to southern California. The ac (alternating current) lines from the Pacific Northwest in northern California would be owned by private power — Pacific Gas and Electric — which would try to keep all imported power for itself.

I was in Washington, D.C., at the time, when Chuck Luce, Bonneville Administrator, came out of a meeting and informed me of this problem. He telephoned Bernie Goldhammer, Power Manager for Bonneville in Portland, to see what might be done, and they agreed that the Pacific Northwest would furnish such non-federal power to northern California. Goldhammer had located a potential source through the BC Hydro Authority. This agreement was the only way to break a deadlock where we were insisting that the regional preference protection legislation on federal power must be passed before we would agree to authorization of tie lines to southern California. Representative Sisk stopped blocking the interregional tie line legislation in the Rules Committee, and it was finally adopted on August 14, 1964. A week later S-1007 — Scoop Jackson's bill — was passed without Westland's amendments. It became Public Law 88-552, providing regional preference on federal power. Regional ties would now be constructed.

One sidelight was that, in seeking Senate authorization of the tie lines, Senator Carl Hayden from Arizona insisted that a second dc line be included in the legislation. This line also would start at Celilo just east of The Dalles, Oregon, but would run to Phoenix, Arizona. When this was agreed to by Senator Magnuson, the legislation was approved. Bonneville would own the dc line throughout the State of Oregon with the Los Angeles De-

Packwood Lake Hydro Plant was put into service in Lewis County, Washington, in 1964 by the Washington Public Power Supply System.

Courtesy WPPSS

partment of Water and Power Board constructing the portion south of that in conjunction with several of the private power companies. On the ac line, Bonneville would have one section and the Portland General Electric Company, in conjunction with its Pelton Project on the Deschutes River, would have a segment connecting with Pacific Power and Light and Pacific Gas and Electric lines towards the south.

In August 1964, in a continuing effort to stem the growing private power control in the State Legislature, an organization called the Washington State Power Users' Association was incorporated. Principal participants were the Washington State Grange, the PUD Association, the State Labor Council, and a number of individuals from around the State. Its main purpose was to provide a better coordinating effort among those groups supporting the consumer interest in utility service. Also in August, dedication of the Packwood Lake Project, the first project to be completed by the Supply System, was held on the 27th.

In the fall of 1964, the last PUD condemnation suit against private power was filed. When the Grays Harbor County PUD went into business in 1940, it acquired only the utility properties in the western part of that county. Puget Power was still serving the Oakville area in eastern Grays

Harbor County. Repeated attempts had been made to negotiate for the purchase of the property from Puget Power, but every time the PUD request had been rejected. The PUD rates were substantially lower than the private power rates, and the resident citizens of Grays Harbor were demanding that they be provided with PUD service. Finally, Grays Harbor County PUD filed its suit against Puget Power.

As usual, Puget Power's attorneys and expert witnesses testified to the tremendous value of the properties, while the PUD countered with State tax valuations and original costs less depreciation valuations. I called Paul Coughlin, the attorney handling the PUD case, and tipped him off to the fact that Puget Power recently had purchased the Northwest Improvement Company, a small private power company located adjacent to Cle Elum, for a price of approximately four times the company's yearly gross revenue. When Coughlin introduced this evidence at the trial, it sounded logical to the court and jury. Thus, the PUD acquired Puget Power's property on the same basis, for $231,500, substantially less than Puget Power had been asking.

November of 1964 saw the election of Dan Evans as Governor of the State of Washington. Looking ahead to the forthcoming 1965 Legislative Session, we issued a white paper on the Columbia Interstate Compact. I did it for two purposes. First, to establish definitely in the Governor-elect's mind those portions of the compact which were deficient from the standpoint of our State and, second, to make up with my long-time friend Doug Caples, who felt I had let down when he, after being successful in cleaning up the compact as regards the power allocation portion, still found the PUD Association and the Washington State Grange opposed to the compact. I had to point out to Caples that, while the power portions were very important, the basic PUD law also required that we conserve and develop the water resources of our State, and when it came to flood control, pollution, and water allocation there were still tremendous deficiencies in the compact favoring the interests of upstream states over those of downstream states.

In 1964, I made one of my dumber mistakes. In September 1961, when Vince Cleaveland, my first public power boss, resigned his Clark County PUD managership, that Commission had asked me for replacement suggestions. I arranged for the Commission to meet with Durwood W. Hill, Manager of the Tillamook PUD. I had observed Hill at various public power meetings and liked the way he handled himself. Clark County PUD hired him and he was doing a very good job. But in early 1964, when Alex Radin, Executive Director of the American Public Power Association, asked if

I had any suggestions for a possible replacement for Ray Schatt, Manager of the Nebraska Public Power District, who was retiring, I again mentioned Hill, who had originally come to the West Coast from the Midwest. At Radin's request, I called Hill and talked him into going to Nebraska for an interview, saying it was the second biggest public power job in America and he owed it to himself to take a look at it. Hill came back home and told me that he was going to stay at Clark County PUD. I was delighted. But two months later, Nebraska must have upped the ante, because when I called my office, my secretary told me Hill was trying desperately to get hold of me. When I called him, he said he was going to take the job. I said, "Oh, (expletive)!"

On March 13, I received a letter from Ed Evans, President of the Clark County PUD Commission, asking me to consider applying for the job as Hill's replacement. Since this was the district where I first started in public power, by helping it organize in 1938 and then going to work in 1948 as Personnel Director, and since it was large enough that I could hire the technical brainpower to run a model utility, the offer did intrigue me. However, I declined and suggested that they interview others. I did say that, if after doing so they still wanted me to apply, I would consider it. I was very happy where I was although the salary at Clark would have been higher. I did just the opposite of what I had talked Durwood into doing. Fortunately, the Commission selected George Watters as the new Manager. He was one of three top finance persons I had helped Vince Cleaveland hire from Puget Power back in 1949 when we had the local palace revolt by the superintendent, chief accountant, and auditor. George proved to be a very effective manager and did a very good job for "my" PUD.

In the latter part of 1964, the State PUD Association retained J. Ward and Associates to conduct a statewide public opinion survey. It was the one and only survey ever made during my tenure as Association Executive. The results were very gratifying, showing a strong public awareness of the benefits which ratepayers derived from the lower public power rates and local policy control. However, while the survey indicated that the voters could be aroused to take our side in a statewide political issue between private and public power, individual people didn't seem to know whether they were being served by public or private power when they flipped a switch. They favored public power theoretically, but they did not see it as a crusade as voters had in the 1930s, 1940s, and 1950s.

Following the death of Earl Coe, whom we had saluted at our 1963 Annual Meeting, because his public service of many years had been tremendous in behalf of the people of our State, the Association established the Earl Coe Award, and at the December 1964 Annual Meeting, the first Earl

Coe Award was made to Charles "Chuck" Luce in recognition of his outstanding work in finalizing agreement on building the upstream dams on the Columbia River system in Canada. The award reads, "Dedicated to outstanding leadership in the conservation and development of the power and water resources of the State of Washington and the Nation." Earl Coe had served well in this regard and Chuck Luce certainly deserved the award.

Getting the Canadian dams under way under the new treaty had involved long and tedious negotiations which brought forth the Columbia Storage Power Exchange, a non-profit corporation organized under State of Washington laws, which issued $250-million-plus tax-exempt revenue bonds to advance construction funds to Canada for the dams. Members of the Exchange represented various utilities that had power supply interest in downstream generating plants. The arrangement was complicated but the added power supplies to come from the upstream water storage were very beneficial. In addition, upstream storage for downstream flood control protection was essential.

The year 1964 had an upbeat ending, but I wasn't too sure what the next legislative session would be like with a brand new Republican governor and Democratic control in the Legislature.

1965–1966

The regular 39th Session of the State Legislature convened on January 11, 1965, under very interesting circumstances. First, the 1964 election had seen Governor Daniel J. Evans, Republican, elected for the first of his three terms. But at the same election, while the Senate Democratic majority remained at 32 to 17, the same as it was the previous session, the Democrats in the House had regained 9 seats, giving them a 60 to 39 edge over the Republicans. Two coalition Democrats of the 1963 Session from Pierce County had been defeated by two regular Democrats who were friendly to public power. This placed another coalition beyond the reach of the six remaining dissident Democrats who were still strong supporters of private power. Having nothing to do with partisanship, a federal court had ordered the Legislature to redistrict the State before it could enact any other law in this session.

Representative Bob Schaefer, Democrat of Clark County, was elected Speaker of the House. The pace was hot and heavy in the first few days, although we were relegated to the sidelines of the redistricting issue. The Senate Democratic majority enacted a redistricting bill hoping that the Democrat-controlled House would approve it and it would be placed on the outgoing Governor's desk before the new Republican Governor was sworn into office. The effort failed. Then a redistricting bill was passed by the House, approved by the Senate, and vetoed by the new Republican Governor. Activity on other measures was restricted to introduction, with no committee action. Finally, when the federal court clarified its order and stated that other legislation could advance to third reading and final passage before the redistricting law was passed, things started to move ahead.

We had our usual array of improvement bills seeking better laws under which to operate public utility districts, and they were met by the full force of the private power lobbyists' opposition. As usual, the ratio of lobbyists was 8 to 1, with 3 from Washington Water Power, 2 from Pacific Power and Light, and 3 from Puget Power, to 1 for public power. The big issue for this session was going to be ratification of the Columbia Interstate Compact. Our previous letter to Governor-elect Evans in late 1964 had been widely circulated. But even with the obvious deficiencies which we maintained were still present, it appeared that ratification would occur. At a special meeting of the seven-state negotiating committee for the compact in Portland on January 29 and 30, Oregon presented two amendments. First, it proposed a court procedure to enforce pollution control and second, reinstatement of flood control criteria that would ensure that any flood of the magnitude of the one that occurred in 1894 could be controlled. It was the goal of the member states to build enough upstream storage to control river flow to 600,000 cubic feet per second at The Dalles, Oregon. When Montana objected to the flood control criteria, Oregon dropped its request. D. Elwood Caples had resigned from the Compact Negotiating Committee prior to this meeting, and our State Representative did not offer any amendments, which indicated to us that the PUD and State Grange recommendations to our representative had fallen on deaf ears.

Ratification of the compact was attempted by the introduction of HB-606 on the fortieth, or last, day for introduction of bills. The bill was referred to the State Government Committee and its proponents demanded a quick hearing. The hearing was denied on specific instructions of the Speaker of the House. On Tuesday, March 2, the bill was reported from the State Government Committee on an 8 to 4 vote, and when it came on the floor a move was made to refer it to the Ways and Means Committee. This motion was defeated by a 51 to 48 vote, and the bill went to Rules. Word was out that Rules was holding it by either a 10 to 7 or a 9 to 8 vote. Rumors flew fast and thick.

On March 4, it became apparent to me, in watching the various maneuverings of the private power lobbyists and the legislators with whom they were working in various conferences and cloakroom conversations, that action to get the compact ratification legislation out of the Rules Committee was scheduled for that day. Opponents of the legislation also reported this to me. Up to this point, strength against ratification of the compact had come from the regular Democrats headed by Speaker of the House Schaefer. As the pressure built up on the Rules Committee, I wondered what could be done.

At 10:30 a.m., I called James Dolliver, Administrative Assistant to Governor Evans, and asked for an opportunity to see him for a few minutes. I had originally met Dolliver when he was an administrative assistant to one of our State congressmen, and he had always been direct and fair in his dealings with me. He granted my request for a meeting, and I went to Dolliver's office. My opening statement was simply that the compact was very much alive in the House Rules Committee; that it appeared that we were going to be unable to hold it any longer; and that unless something was done, the compact, as it was presently worded, was going to be lying on the Governor's desk within about four days. The Governor would then have the unenviable job of making up his mind whether he was going to sign the ratification of this deficient compact.

I asked whether any detailed studies had been made by the Governor, his legal advisors, or anyone else on the actual wording in the compact. I asked whether they were aware of the disadvantages to the State of Washington in this compact which we had cited to the Rules Committee and to others. Dolliver said he had not made such a study personally, whereupon we went through the compact practically word for word. I pointed out the unlimited budget with mandatory allocation and responsibility for raising revenues to meet the budget that the member states would have; the loophole undermining effective pollution enforcement by the use of the word "may" instead of "shall" in one particular important reference; the voting veto which could be used against our State by the upstream states; the flaws in the provisions governing the protection of Pacific Northwest waters from raiding by the southwestern states of California and Arizona; the absence of any flood control criteria; and the open-ended use of this Compact Committee for special interest lobbying purposes and intervention before regulatory groups and commissions.

Our meeting ended by Dolliver literally scooping up the compact, copies of my remarks before the House Committee, and other information and saying, "I'll take these in to Dan right now." There is no way that I can know what took place thereafter, but I was well aware that the all-out push to blast HB-606 out of the Rules Committee on that date fizzled and cooled down before the Committee even had a meeting. Late that evening, Representative Bill McCormick of Spokane, who had been the prime pusher for the compact in the House, told me that it was "dead for the rest of the regular session." I was sure this was true if he said so, and we then looked forward to the Special Session.

As the Special Session of the Legislature started, you could see that another attempt would be made to get the compact ratified. Just a few days after convening, the pressure mounted again in the House Rules Committee, and on the crucial day when action was anticipated by everyone, proponents and opponents, I again contacted Dolliver by telephone to inform him that the situation was getting critical again. He asked if the pressure was "hot." I said, "Most certainly." Then, again, as the day proceeded, I could sense a cooling off. I do believe that by that time there was enough indication on the House floor that, while the votes were there to ratify the compact, such substantial amendments would be made to the draft that all the other states would be required to once again ratify the compact as amended.

Later, toward the close of the Special Session, John Sweat, Executive Secretary of the Compact Committee, showed up again in Ulcer Gulch. Jokingly, I said, "John, I guess I'll have to get the troops out again." He responded by saying, "No, that won't be necessary. I am not here to push the compact. I am actually here to see what might be done in the next two years relative to continuing negotiations." He continued, "I think probably the State of Washington might as well adopt the compact to their own liking and leave it up to the other states whether or not they will accept it." He then asked me whether I would support ratification of the compact if all of the amendments which I had proposed were adopted.

I told him that he placed me in the same position Representative Jack Hood did on the night of the hearing when he asked me that question, and that I had to say no, simply because it would be impossible for me to agree to any compact until I got back to my Board and found out what its view would be. I stated that we wanted a compact which was limited specifically to water allocation and pollution control and which used regular State budget procedures to finance it and regular State agencies to administer it. We did not want a compact which would be administered by a central staff and have a central unlimited budget, and whose decisions would be subject to influence by lobbyists. I added that if they accepted all the amendments which we had proposed, I would be very willing to try to sell the amended compact to my Board and the other PUD Commissioners and Managers. John made one parting remark. He said, "I feel that we did not get as strong support out of Governor Evans as we should have anticipated by his election. He campaigned in favor of the compact. Governor Smiley of Idaho came into the State and campaigned for him. But for some reasons unknown to me, he would not accept this compact." I told John that I was sure that the Governor was sincere in his viewpoint, that he was in favor of a compact, but that he felt the way we did, namely, that the present draft did contain some serious deficiencies and because of them he could not sign it in good faith for the State of Washington. There was no further action on the compact during that legislative session.

Another full-scale private versus public power legislative battle erupted over a measure to provide bond refunding by public bodies. The bill was designed for use by all public bodies, including the State of Washington, and should not have been occasion for any private versus public power controversy. It passed the Senate by a 48 to 0 vote. However, when it was considered in the House Local Government Committee, Larry Hall, lobbyist for Puget Power, appeared and submitted an amendment in the form of a new section which would, in effect, require that no refunding bonds of an electric generating plant owned by any public body (city light or PUD) could be issued without the prior approval of any utility or person which had contracted for 5 percent or more of the power and energy from the generating plant. While the amendment sounded logical, it would have established by law the right of a private corporation to override the discretionary powers given to local public power by the Legislature. Further, by requiring prior approval, it created a Catch-22 situation. Under the wording of the amendment, you could not exercise any powers granted by the law without getting prior approval, and yet you could not seek the prior approval until you had exercised powers of the law in order to submit a proposition to the outside private corporation. The issue erupted into a hot floor debate and there was a lot of maneuvering, but public power lost, and SB-417 was approved with the amendment attached by 51 to 47.

We immediately did some fast work in the Senate, which refused to concur in the House amendment and sent the bill back with the request that the House recede therefrom. Just at this time, two pro-public power representatives had to be absent, one because of an auto accident and the other because of illness. The House refused to recede. Speaker of the House Schaefer then appointed as conferees two persons who had voted for the bill, including the amendment, on final passage, and one who had voted against the bill with the amendment attached. However, all of these just happened to be from public power areas and had voted against the amendment when it was being added to the legislation. A challenge was raised to the Speaker by several private power supporters on a point of order, and a lot of argument and discussion followed, but the Speaker held his ground and the House conferees were appointed.

The bill then went back to the Senate in order that a conference could be granted with conferees appointed from that body. The Senate conferees included two of the bill's original sponsors plus a pro-private power senator from Spokane. The punitive amendment deadlocked the bill in the Conference Committee, and it looked as if this otherwise good bill was going to die. I then came forward with a substitute amendment which removed the stigma of the original House amendment by not granting private power veto rights over the discretionary policy decision of public body officials. Next, my amendment forced the negotiating procedures between the public body and the private power corporation back to the level of the power contracts; and, finally, it provided that any savings from a refunding bond issue would be returned to power purchasers in an amount proportionate to the amount of power which they were taking from the project during any particular year. With a 4 to 2 ratio in favor of public power in the Conference Committee, the substitute amendment was adopted. The bill was approved in this form and placed on the Governor's desk.

In the meantime, as a result of these various fights, our housekeeping legislation went down the drain, reflecting the gathering strength of the private power forces in the legislative arena which had been growing since 1959. When the Legislature adjourned on May 7, 1965, it had been in session for 114 days — the regular session plus a Special Session, the longest session in the history of our State to that date.

In the three direct instances where there had been a private versus public power disagreement, the public power position prevailed. These were the Columbia Interstate Compact ratification legislation, the refunding bond act, and a Senate bill establishing a Nuclear Energy Division in the Commerce and Economic Development Department, where private power had attempted to incorporate amendments to eliminate public power participation in nuclear energy development. Legislation to change PUD elections to odd numbered years was amended in the Senate, so that PUD elections were to remain as provided by the basic PUD law. It was a long and arduous session.

Sometimes in the private versus public power political wars, there would be occasion for laughs and personal enjoyment. One such occasion for me was a Chamber of Commerce luncheon in June of 1965. Under Governor Evans' leadership, a number of business leaders from throughout the State made an industrial promotion tour of New York, Boston, and Philadelphia in late spring. We were fortunate in having Commissioner Bob Keiser of

Chelan County PUD in the group. Much of the expense for the tour was borne by the Seattle Area Industrial Council and I imagine the Seattle Chamber of Commerce. In return, arrangements were made for the leaders to come back and stage at this luncheon an actual demonstration of the program they used to sell the State of Washington as a good place in which to do business. As the PUD representative on the Seattle Chamber of Commerce Resource Development Committee, I was invited to attend. Now each of the participants in the industrial tour wore a special blue jacket. Besides the Governor, who did the main selling job, Walter Straley, President of Pacific Northwest Bell, provided his very able services. He was a master in many regards. The agenda of the local show was just like it had been in New York and elsewhere. We arrived at a Chamber of Commerce luncheon at around 11:30 a.m. for a pre-luncheon martini if we cared to have one. We were then seated as though we were industrialists or business-men in New York or Philadelphia or Boston.

On that particular morning, I got tied up with Bill Hulbert of Snohom-ish County PUD and Bob Beck and Herb Westfall of R. W. Beck and Asso-ciates in a conference on the proposed Bonneville rate increase. At 12:05, it dawned on me that I was supposed to be at the luncheon. I grabbed a cab and got to the Chamber of Commerce after everyone else had been seated. A friend in the State's Department of Commerce and Economic Develop-ment came up and guided me to a seat.

The tables were round, with eight people at each table. I sat down with Bud Donohoe of the Seattle Chamber on my right and, two places from me, Ralph Davis, President of Puget Power. I was looking forward to an interesting luncheon conversation. About this time, my friend came back and said, "Ken, the seat on the left of Governor Evans is open. Would you like to take it?" I asked, "Don't they have a head table?" And he said, "No, that's not the format, and if you want the seat it is available." I agreed, whereupon he escorted me clear across this large luncheon room and brought me to the seat of honor on the Governor's left. Just as I sat down, after being cordially welcomed by the Governor, I looked up and at two adjacent tables, wearing their little blue jackets, were two high officials of Washington Water Power and Pacific Power and Light. You should have seen the looks on their faces.

There it was, a seat next to the Governor left vacant as though it was being saved for a very important person; a public power man enters the room as a late arrival and is escorted clear across the room and seated there. The implication was that it had been planned that way and I was the special person for whom the seat had been saved. It was truly an enjoyable occasion. I not only had a good conversation with the Governor and enjoyed the very well-done program, but I also enjoyed the glances of my private power counterparts who were watching like two hawks. It was well worth the $5 which I paid to get into the luncheon. I laughed all the way back to my office.

On the other side of the feelings ledger, there were some bad moments. Thus in June 1965, I issued a white paper to the PUD Managers and officials in criticism of Francis Pearson, Chairman of the Washington State Utilities and Transportation Commission. As I stated earlier, he had become a friend of mine as a State Senator from Clallam County. He had been instrumental as a local Grange Master in formation of the Clallam County PUD. His first few years on the regulatory commission as an appointee of Governor Rosellini had been spent very much in the consumer interest. But as the years passed, he seemed to become more amenable to and directly supportive of private power positions. By 1965, he had become the spokesman of private power in criticizing public utility districts.

We met head-on at the June convention of the Washington State Grange. Later that week, I was informed by a rural cooperative leader that Pearson had also attended a Western Conference of Utility Regulators at Sun Valley at which Clyde Ellis, General Manager of the National Rural Electric Cooperative Association, had given a forthright speech on the need for effective regulation. Pearson had given a rebuttal, becoming quite emotional as he denounced alleged activities by public utility districts in his State. His speech included claims that if these activities were made public they would be worse than the Insull scandals (1929–1932) during the Great Depression. It was evident that he was trying to court favor with the private power companies looking towards reappointment under the new Republican Administration when his term expired. I had no alternative except to label him for what his actions showed him to be, namely, a person who was performing some very valuable acts in the interests of private power. This was one of the duties of my job which I did not enjoy.

The years 1965–1966 marked the halfway point in my tenure as Executive for the Washington Public Utility Districts' Association. During my entire period of service, it was my privilege to have the close confidence and support of two of the best senators this State will ever have, in my opinion. During the 1950s, I had witnessed the abilities and strength of Senator Warren G. Magnuson. Most of the credit for today's low cost federal hydroelectric power in the Pacific Northwest is rightfully due Senator Magnuson. Without his efforts, many of the major federal dams on the Columbia River system would never have been built, and many times when appropriations for the federal transmission grid were in jeopardy, it was his work which

Left to right: Senator Henry M. Jackson, Ken Billington, Senator Warren G. Magnuson, Washington, D.C., 1962.

secured money for continuing needed construction. While his presence and strength were to continue until he was defeated for re-election in 1980, the 1960s saw the rise of Senator Henry M. "Scoop" Jackson as a strength and power in behalf of our State and the Pacific Northwest. His success in getting the dual purpose reactor and the Hanford Generating Plant authorized in the early 1960s was creditable, and while the presence of both Senator Magnuson and Senator Jackson was to be very important in the 1970s for needed federal legislative action on Pacific Northwest power matters, Senator Jackson's legislative abilities were best demonstrated to me in the years 1965–1966, when I got to play a part in his behind-the-scenes activities.

In June 1965, while in Washington, D.C., I discussed with Senator Jackson and his Administrative Assistant, Sterling Munro, the authorization legislation for the Third Powerhouse at Grand Coulee. This legislation also would approve a new federal power payout schedule which was vitally needed for Pacific Northwest projects. The Secretary of the Interior had approved a payout schedule in 1963 which provided that reimbursement of appropriations made for Pacific Northwest power facilities would be repaid from revenues from all of the facilities system-wide, instead of each individual project being required to pay for itself. However, we needed to get that payout schedule under statute law. Private power forces were opposing such a move. The legislation had cleared the Senate committee. Congressman Wayne Aspinall of Colorado, Chairman of the House Interior Committee, was a strong advocate of Western reclamation projects. While indicating support for the measure, including the payout schedule, he had informed Senator Jackson that the measure would also have to include provision for a basin account whereby power revenues would automatically subsidize new reclamation projects.

The picture was further being clouded because the total Idaho delegation was now asking for a new broad Southern Idaho Reclamation Project which would be paid for by large subsidies from Pacific Northwest power plants. Finally, the issue of water diversion from one river basin to another was being pushed by California, which was looking at the Columbia River system. The Central Arizona Project legislation had specific provisions endorsing a study of river diversion into the Colorado River, and the American Public Power Association in its national conference had just endorsed the Central Arizona Project.

Basically, what was needed was to keep all the various factions in the Pacific Northwest united. That meant those interested in the lowest possible power rates, industry and organized labor, would have to sit down with those interested in reclamation projects and agree on a formula which would limit power revenue subsidies to reclamation and not interfere with a system-wide power payout procedure, but which would be fair and acceptable to both sides. Senator Jackson said, on the water diversion issue, that the nationwide public power group should stay together and that control of any studies should be under legislation then being proposed to establish river basin commissions. He pointed out that the use of a properly constituted River Basin Commission in the Pacific Northwest could take the place of a Columbia Interstate Compact. He suggested that the PUDs and their Association, which was devoted to low cost power as well as water development, might be an effective force to seek agreement among Pacific Northwest factions.

I pointed out that we certainly wanted to go with the system-wide payout procedures, but that we were at odds with certain portions of those procedures which would be considered in the new proposed Bonneville rate increase. There were two major points at issue. The first was in establishing a reasonable period of time for amortization of federal facilities. The Secretary of the Interior was using fifty years to pay off federal generating projects but only forty years for the transmission system. We felt that all federal facilities should have a fifty-year amortization period. The second point at issue was whether to include in the payout requirements the use of replacement annuity reserves, in the form of charges to current electric ratepayers for specific reserves to be set aside to cover the cost of replacements of the facilities. We felt that it would be better to appropriate money for replacements and additions as they were needed, and then to amortize reimbursement for the new appropriations just as the costs of the original facilities were amortized. I did agree to try and clarify the American Public Power Association position on river diversion studies.

By February 1966, the American Public Power Association's Legislative Committee was turned around when I submitted two resolutions. One specifically endorsed the power projects included in the Central Arizona Project, but the second called for any river diversion studies to be confined to a nationwide river basin study conducted by representatives outside of government under legislation introduced by Senator Jackson. Senator Jackson had already been successful in including in the River Basin Commission legislation specific prohibition against studies for the diversion of water from one river basin to another.

In March 1966, I submitted a recommended position paper to my Board on the Southern Idaho Water Development Project. When they adopted it, I sent it to the State of Washington congressional delegation as a statement of our basic position. It proposed that Congress should place a limit on the percentage of any reclamation project which was to be paid for out of power revenues and adopt a policy whereby repayment of reimbursable costs of reclamation projects coming from power revenues would be postponed until the power system repayment obligation to Congress had been fully met; that Congress should make the payback period for appropriations for power portions of multiple purpose projects more realistic; that Congress should place a ceiling on the use of federal power revenues to assist irrigation; and that Congress should authorize construction of a federal transmission line to southern Idaho. With Board approval, this policy position was the basis of my continued negotiations with the reclamation interests.

In April 1966, I submitted a report to my Board on the Aspinall amendment to the Third Grand Coulee Powerhouse legislation. The amendment was good in some respects and terrible in others. First, it was bad because it reversed congressional procedure on authorizing power revenue subsidies to reclamation projects. Henceforth, any reclamation project authorized by Congress in the Pacific Northwest would automatically be eligible for power revenue subsidies unless such eligibility was specifically denied it by Congress, whereas formerly any new reclamation project had to be related to a specific federal power dam. The amendment was good because it did not set up a separate account to be administered by the Bureau of Reclamation, but provided that the Bonneville Administrator would pay for such costs directly, leaving control of power revenues with the Bonneville office. It tied down the fifty-year payout period by statute, which could be good if it also applied to transmission facilities but bad from the standpoint of actual amortization scheduling on power facilities, which would have a much longer service life than fifty years. It did provide for joint system payout, which was definitely being opposed by the private power companies. Of great concern to us was that the Secretary of the Interior was to make an annual report to Congress on the total power revenues without specific reference to the individual reclamation projects and in such a manner that one could immediately see the sponsors of reclamation projects in other parts of the nation smacking their lips. One simple amendment to strike the term "Pacific Northwest" would make these gross power revenues available to reclamation projects nationwide. However, a plus was that Aspinall had specifically defined the Pacific Northwest.

I suggested to the Board that this might be an acceptable amendment for a compromise between our Governor and the State of Idaho—that Idaho might agree to accept a River Basin Commission in place of the Columbia Interstate Compact if other legislation by Senator Jackson could limit diversion of power revenues for non-power purposes.

On April 21, I was contacted by Sterling Munro. I told him I had been invited to a meeting to be held in Spokane on Wednesday, May 4, by George Crookham, Chairman of the Idaho Water Commission, who was heading a committee composed of Reclamation Association people from five states. The purpose of the meeting was to study language which could clarify the Aspinall amendment. Sterling said he would furnish me a draft of the language which Senator Jackson was working on. I introduced this draft at the meeting, along with the position paper approved by my Board on the Southern Idaho Reclamation Project, and doing so placed me in the hot seat between George Crookham, on the side of the supporters of reclamation, and Norman Krey, head of Kaiser Aluminum of Spokane, who ended up as leader of Bonneville's industrial customers.

Crookham was a large man with a dominant personality, a potato farmer from Caldwell, Idaho. He was direct and courageous. At times he had even tangled with the Idaho Power Company over certain service policies in that state. Krey was also a dominant personality and very tough minded when it came to anything which might increase power costs for Bonneville.

Between May 16 and May 20, I found myself in Washington, D.C., shuttling in and out of Senator Jackson's office on the Senate side and Congressman Tom Foley's office on the House side, dispatching ideas to and from Crookham and Krey. Foley, leaving Senator Jackson's staff, ran a successful race against Walt Horan, long-time Republican Congressman from Eastern Washington's 5th Congressional District. It was his first session in Congress beginning his many years of strong leadership service to our State and nation. On May 23, I sent Crookham a copy of the current draft language to be used to clarify the Aspinall amendment to the Third Powerhouse legislation. In the meantime, Senator Jackson was holding up Senate concurrence on that legislation pending word from the Northwest that we had agreed on clarifying language. At the American Public Power Association Annual Conference, we had secured passage of the resolution endorsing the power dams included in the Central Arizona Project but calling for studies on any diversion of waters to be made by a National Water Commission composed of citizens outside of federal government service, as proposed in Senator Jackson's bill S-3107. Time was getting tight on the Third Powerhouse legislation. Work on the facility could not start until it was passed because no appropriations could be made until it was authorized.

On May 31, I sent a night letter to Senator Jackson and Representative Foley recommending that the Third Powerhouse legislation, including the Aspinall amendment, be accepted if a mutually agreeable but definite limitation on diversion of federal power revenues for reclamation purposes could be enacted within the near future by other statutory law. On June 1, I was able to get Governor Evans to send a night letter to Senator Jackson also supporting the Aspinall amendment unchanged, but stating that specific reclamation limitations should be enacted during this session of Congress by other legislation.

Then, on June 15, a meeting was convened by Crookham attended by reclamation supporters, state resource board representatives, industrial power users, and private power and public power representatives. It was agreed that Crookham and I, with the assistance of Bill Burpee, attorney for the Bureau of Reclamation, Region No. 1, in consultation with the industrial customers and others, would work on the proposed statutory language which I had submitted on May 4 as amended by the May 9 draft. We would consider some method to build allowances for inflation into the limitation we wanted; grant additional funds for reclamation if power revenues from upstream storage dams were increased; include language to allow the older reclamation projects to receive the same irrigation assistance from power revenues as any new reclamation projects; and finalize the statutory language providing a limitation on the use of power revenues.

On June 23, our agreed-to statutory language was unveiled in the form of a telegram from Crookham to me, which I sent on to Senator Jackson, who included it in an amendment to S-3034, a law separate from the Third Powerhouse legislation, but which amended the act and was known as correcting legislation. The Third Powerhouse legislation was approved on June 14, and the correcting legislation was finally approved in late August. The Jackson correcting legislation to the Third Grand Coulee Powerhouse Act to which Congressman Aspinall had attached his basin account law, provided: Present and future reclamation projects in the Pacific Northwest would have to be scheduled so as not to cause increases in Bonneville rates; financial assistance for reclamation projects must come from "net revenues"; and irrigation subsidy assistance could not exceed an average of $30 million annually in any period of twenty consecutive years. This provided for up to $600 million of reclamation assistance from power revenues, and meant that the region could have a substantial reclamation program without unduly penalizing power users. And, oh yes, the required annual report on Bonneville revenues to the entire Congress each year by the Secretary of the Interior would not be necessary.

In late July, I received a personal letter from Senator Jackson telling of his success in getting the amendment which we had agreed upon added to the second measure. The second paragraph of his letter read, "After many long hours of hard work, marked with the spirit of friendly cooperation, interested parties in the Northwest joined in supporting the Basin Account Amendment which foresees expanded water resources development in the Northwest but provides that such development shall not cause increases in the rates and charges of the Bonneville power system." A copy of the letter had gone to many of us who had been involved, but on the margin of that paragraph on my letter were the words, "Am I telling you this? Many thanks for the fine job you did, Ken!" As I have stated earlier, the State was very fortunate to have a man of his ability in the congressional arena. Credit should also go to his staff members who, along with the staff members of Senator Magnuson, were among the top professionals around Washington, D.C. With all my other Association involvements, this issue had kept me very busy.

It was at the 65th meeting of the Columbia Interstate Compact Negotiating Committee in Spokane on August 3, 1965, that our fight on the compact came to an end. Way back in the early 1950s, we had constructively approached the possibility of and need for a compact. After witnessing the long drawn-out court fight between California and Arizona over the waters of the Colorado River, I had felt that a properly constituted compact would be of great assistance to the people of the Pacific Northwest. In the years after the turn of the next century when actual allocation or use of such waters might be controversial, a good compact adopted now could be of benefit. However, when the private power companies, nationwide and here in the Northwest, tried to use the Interstate Compact as a means to offset federal power projects and change federal power marketing policies in their favor – when they dominated drafting of the compact here in the Pacific Northwest – public power had no alternative except to oppose and try to defeat it.

Following the Oregon amendments to the compact on pollution control enforcement and flood control criteria that state had proposed the previous January, the Attorney General of Oregon issued an opinion which sustained several of my main criticisms of the proposed compact. He agreed that it contained no effective pollution control procedure, that the voting arrangements favored the upstream states over the downstream states, that the unlimited budget of the compact could encumber individual member states with drains on their tax revenues, and that the Compact Committee itself could become intervenors or lobbyists in regulatory and legislative arenas. On August 3, 1965, the State of Oregon submitted a letter to the Compact Negotiating Committee announcing its withdrawal effective as of that date, and renouncing any further financial encumbrances. The Attorney General's letter also provided, "That the Compact would be ineffective to prevent diversion of water from the Columbia River system." The Oregon letter had been approved by a vote of 7 to 3 in its Commission on Interstate Cooperation which handled negotiations on the compact for the State of Oregon.

Nearly simultaneously with the demise of the Interstate Compact, Senator Jackson secured an amendment to S-21 which became Public Law 89-80 and which provided for federal river basin commissions composed of federal agency representatives and governors of states located within a given river basin area. The law prohibited any studies for the diversion of water from one river basin to another. He had accomplished by federal law what could not have been accomplished by the compact.

The year 1965 saw some events which affected me personally. In January, Gus Peters, one of the strong old-type public power pioneers, died. While he had left his active role as a PUD Commissioner from Lewis County some years before, even in his waning years I made it a point to seek him out and talk to him on current issues and problems. Then Truman Price, who had been head of the Power Division in the State's Department of Conservation and a strong public power supporter, left his job when the new Republican State Administration came in. Truman moved to Washington, D.C., to work for the Department of the Interior. I'd miss his advice and presence.

Perhaps the most important event which would affect me later was the replacement of the Manager of Snohomish County PUD – the largest District in the State. A. S. J. "Syd" Steele had become Manager of Snohomish County PUD shortly after the District acquired its Puget Power properties. Syd was a Texan imported for private power administrative work by Frank McLaughlin, long-time Puget Power President. When the District took over the Puget Power properties, a known liberal Democrat was Manager. With a change of the Commission he was let go and Syd got the job. Syd was a typical Texan by nature and a very good utility manager, but he didn't like me at all and made it known to me and others at PUD Managers' Section meetings and elsewhere. Simply put, in Syd's mind, I was a public power fanatic, and while he worked for public power, he had been with private power too long to take much of a liking to me – and in truth, the feeling was mutual.

At any rate, I found several of the newly elected Commissioners from Snohomish ending up with the same attitude toward me – and I would later find that the poison seemed to come from Syd. Fortunately, the strong person on the Board was Tom Quast, who said what he thought when he disagreed with me, but became quite close to me during the days of State Power Commission controversies.

Two new Commissioners were Walt Jones and Bill Hulbert. Both came on board suspicious of me. But as time passed, they started to judge me on what they saw instead of what they had been told, and in both cases, I must have passed muster because in friendships as well as work relationships, I found them to be two of the nicest and sincerest guys I ever met. While Walt seemed to be somewhat of a conservative Democrat, Bill was indeed a Republican. I found out that Bill came from a long-time Snohomish County family, and he was evidently quite wealthy in his own right.

When Syd Steele notified his Commission of his intention to retire at the end of 1965, it commenced looking for a replacement. A nationwide search began, as this was a top public power job. One day in July, when I was coming away from a lunch meeting, Walt was standing by my car in the parking lot. He said, "Ken, do you know who would like to be offered our Manager's job?" I said, "Who?" He said "Bill Hulbert." I said, "You're kidding. He's a successful businessman in his own right. I understand he has quite a bit of money. Why would he want to be a PUD Manager?" Walt said, "You know, Ken, he told me he would like the job because he would like to do something on his own. All his life, and he is successful, his father always seemed to be in the background. Bill just wants to do something of his own without feeling his father was involved."

I had been raised by the same kind of man—severe but loving. Many times when I was addressed as "Mr. Billington," I would unconsciously look over my shoulder expecting to see Mr. Billington. I said, "Walt, give him the job. He has the education and business ability needed. He certainly has turned into a very strong Commissioner and I think he'd do a good job just because of the reason he wants it."

I don't know if that helped Bill get the job, but on August 31 he resigned as commissioner and was hired as the Administrative Assistant to the Manager, Syd Steele. Bill took over as Manager for the Snohomish County PUD on January 1, 1966. Sometimes persons who convert to religion are stronger than those raised in religion. Bill Hulbert became one of the strongest local public power leaders I ever had the pleasure of working with. We had differences, which was to be expected, but I always knew where Bill stood and he always knew where I stood. Most of the time we stood together. He was accepted nationwide in public power circles, serving many years on the Board of the American Public Power Association and then serving a term as its President in 1974–1975. Shortly thereafter, I submitted his name to the APPA's Awards Committee as a nominee to receive its Distinguished Service Award. I overlooked the fact that immediate past presidents serve on the Awards Committee, and Bill rejected my recommendation. However, he wasn't an "immediate past president" after one year, and I put his name up again. The Board of Directors acted, he received the award, and he deserved the award. He also was a very good friend of my very good friend Senator Scoop Jackson, being raised in the same town but on different sides of the track.

In October, I was invited to address the Accounting Section of the American Public Power Association which was meeting in Wenatchee that year. I had a pretty good speech prepared on the benefits coming from the PUDs of our State. Then, lo and behold, Chuck Luce, Bonneville Administrator, speaking the afternoon before I was to appear on the program, unleashed some very hard words criticizing PUDs for overcharging their customers. Actually, the speech that hit the news media was not the speech Luce gave. What short-circuited the event was that an early draft had been leaked to the *Seattle Times*, and he did some substantial editing before delivery.

However, the speech he delivered was severe enough that even the *Wenatchee World*, long-time supporter of public power, editorialized against us in that day's edition. Needless to say, I took off my gloves and after calling Chuck proceeded to set the record straight. He understood and I understood – but it didn't stop there.

KIRO-TV and radio was trying to gain public attention through a series of management editorials. Sure enough, the unedited Luce speech was the basis of one of these, and again the PUDs were put down unfairly. Worse than that was the KIRO editorialist's unwarranted praise of Puget Power.

KIRO was, just at that time, in the midst of seeking renewal of its license from the Federal Communications Commission. I secured my Board's approval and took out after them in Washington, D.C. My contact there was Ken Cox, Federal Communications Commissioner and a long-time friend I met through Senator Magnuson. A. Lars Nelson, State Grange Master, also got into the act. We made our rebuttal to the editorial when I appeared as a guest editorial spokesman on KIRO on December 30, 1965. Previously KIRO's editorial genius Lloyd Cooney had criticized those of us who fought and defeated the deficient Columbia Interstate Compact, so this second shot at local public power had to be challenged. I ignored my dad's advice never to get into a particular type contest with a small striped animal because I felt the step was necessary. It was a satisfactory closeout for the year 1965.

The year 1966 saw transition to thermal plant construction intensify. In July, it became apparent to me that a new era in power generation in the Pacific Northwest was approaching. Commencing in the 1930s and going on through the 1940s, the primary construction of generating projects had been the responsibility for the federal government with its multiple-purpose dams. Then in the early 1950s, under the Eisenhower Administration, some of the responsibility for constructing generating plants passed back to the local utilities.

During the 1950s, because of the political strength of the private power companies, the local public agencies were forced into partnership projects with them. In effect, this allowed the private power companies to drive a wedge between the publicly owned utilities that generated their own power and those that were wholly dependent upon the federal power system for their power supply.

In the late 1950s, some local public agencies, especially the three PUDs on the main stem of the Columbia River, were even used as a spear point by the private power companies to seek amendments to the Federal Power

Commission law regarding the payments to upstream dams for storing water that when released would generate power in downstream dams. Negotiations for a coordination agreement between upstream and downstream dams pitted the non-federal generating utilities, both private and public, against the federal power system.

Negotiations to build Canadian storage dams brought the same divisive factors into play when individual persons, in the name of both private and publicly owned generating utilities, formed the joint Columbia Storage Power Exchange group, a non-profit corporation.

Looking at the situation in July 1966, we saw that the big problem was to mesh the tremendous hydroelectric potential of the federal dams with steam plants to be built by non-federal utilities, with a view to constructing facilities in the Pacific Northwest that would produce the lowest cost power. Frankly, the best way to do this would be for non-federal publicly owned utilities to use public financing to construct the facilities in place of the private power companies whose reason for existing was to make profits and who therefore would have to charge higher rates than a non-profit utility.

Another divisive factor was that while the non-federal utilities had been building generating projects, their participation was always based on the needs of their own service areas. The federal government, through Bonneville, had been the mainstay in keeping power supply ahead of load growth requirements to promote industrial growth and thus help the whole region economically. But it seemed that another attempt would be made to split the publicly owned generating utilities from the non-generating ones in negotiations with the federal power system on what steam plants would be constructed and when.

In July, I approached Howard MacGowan who headed Corporate Services, a service organization that promoted and coordinated private/public power joint action in the hydroelectric projects, the Canadian storage development, and the dam coordination agreement. I suggested to him that the time might be right to get all non-federal utilities to agree to share all power supplies, with the one exception that if people in any particular area formed their own local publicly owned utility, they should have the right to a power supply that was in no way controlled by the private power company their PUD was replacing.

Mentioning Howard MacGowan reminds me that of the many interesting persons I met in my public power service, Mac would come close to topping the list. I would not know nor could I tell of all his exploits, but he was unique. His background was in newspaper work. I hear that he and Ross Cunningham, longtime editorial page editor of the *Seattle Times*, were very active in getting Warren G. Magnuson elected to the State House of

Representatives from the 37th District in 1932 – and then later to Congress – and that after Maggie's appointment to replace Homer Bone in 1944, Mac remained a close personal friend and political advisor for all the Senator's long service. I met Mac in Maggie's 1950 re-election campaign when Mac was Collector of Customs in Seattle in the Truman Administration.

With the election of Eisenhower, Mac was out of a job. It was then that he decided to form a service firm called Corporate Services. With my full knowledge and agreement, and with Senator Magnuson's knowledge, Mac was of service to both private power companies and public power utilities with his intimate knowledge of how utilities worked and his contacts in Washington, D.C., including the senior senator from our State.

I can recall very vividly when Maggie said during the Hells Canyon Dam fight, "Look, Ken, Mac is in and out of this office but you can be sure he isn't going to deter me from my support of public power." I was never uncertain of what Mac was after in a given situation, because he would always level with me even when performing ably for his clients. Mac was distinctive looking because he wore a patch over one eye that he had lost the sight in. But, boy, he earned his nickname of "McGooselin Mac-Gowan." Our one joint venture was the MacGowan Salad which I devised at lunch with him one day at the Olympic Hotel. We made it out of lime-stone lettuce, crab and shrimp meat, and the hotel's excellent Italian house dressing.

MacGowan was the one sponsoring me as a possible replacement on Maggie's staff when Irv Hoff resigned. It was this background which prompted me to discuss with Mac what I felt should be done on a future regional power supply – I was willing to deal private power into the plan if local people reserved the right of self-determination on electric utility service.

On July 29, I approached George Brunzell, President of Washington Water Power, along these lines. Later, I talked to Larry Karrer, Executive Vice President of Puget Power, and still later to Frank Warren, President of the Portland General Electric Company.

In the meantime, I sent up a trial balloon in a letter to Senator Jackson, copies of which were widely distributed among utility people. It outlined the following proposals:

1. The private power companies would be granted requirements contracts with the federal power system. This, in effect, would nullify the preference clause because we would share the federal power supply with them to the limits of their requirements.

2. The local utilities, private and public, would ask for a law whereby the federal system would purchase non-federally generated power, integrate it with the other power supplies of the federal system, and sell it under the requirements contracts to both private and publicly owned utilities. This, of course, would give the federal power system control over transmission grids and make the federal government the marketing agency for all power being generated in the Pacific Northwest, with the exception of the individually owned plants then in existence or to be built in the future for local utility use.

3. Non-federal steam plants would be constructed by a State of Washington municipal corporation which would have the right to finance the plants with revenue bonds under a businesslike law. This, of course, would strengthen local public power.

4. A formal control commission comprising representatives of both private and public power would determine the size and location of the needed steam plants and would decide when they would be built. The commission would work in conjunction with the federal power system.

It immediately became apparent that the private power companies were not going to accept these proposals. Instead, they were going through the divide-and-conquer routine again—proposing to form a coalition of the publicly owned generating utilities plus one or two more large non-generating PUDs, or a private/public partnership task force designed to control the construction of steam plants and to dominate negotiations with the federal power system in this transition period.

A meeting was held by Corporate Services in September 1966 in which this idea was advanced, the need to work with Canadian utility people to install generators at the Mica Dam being used as the immediate incentive.

In late September at the PUD Managers' Section meeting at Ocean Shores, I spoke rather definitely about the need for regrouping the PUDs and other publicly owned utilities before joining alliances with the private power companies. However, at all times I acknowledged their presence and the need for their participation in Pacific Northwest power supply planning.

About this time, David Black returned to the Northwest as Bonneville Administrator, and immediately urged cooperation between private and public power in this steam plant transition period.

In early October, I made a trip east to speak in the Tennessee Valley and then went on to Washington, D.C., where I met with Senator Jackson, Senator Magnuson, and new Undersecretary of the Interior Chuck Luce. I told them it was my intention to try to regroup the publicly owned utilities to prevent the private power companies from dominating and controlling the negotiations on steam plants.

I arrived back in Portland, Oregon, on October 12, just in time for a morning meeting called by Bonneville Administrator Black for October 13, which would be attended by both private and publicly owned utility representatives. At this meeting, Black announced formation of a Bonneville task force (later called the Joint Power Planning Council) for the steam plant transition, and again served notice that Bonneville was going to insist that private and public power people work together.

In the meantime, a letter had gone out over the names of the managers of the publicly owned generating utilities (Chelan, Douglas, Grant, Pend Oreille, and Cowlitz PUDs), Seattle City Light, Tacoma Light, and Eugene Water and Electric Board, inviting other publicly owned utilities to join them for a meeting in Portland on the afternoon of October 13 at 1:30 p.m. I also learned that Corporate Services had scheduled a meeting to be held at the Portland Hilton Hotel at 3 p.m. at which the private power companies, plus the generating utilities, were going to "sit down again on the Canadian power topic."

It was evident to me that the play would be to gather in the interested publicly owned utilities at the 1:30 p.m. meeting and then move across the river in Portland to the Corporate Services meeting at 3 p.m. and solidify the private/public coalition for steam plant construction.

At the 1:30 p.m. meeting, by asking some pertinent questions, I more or less shamed the public power people for thinking in terms of a coalition with private power which in my view would inevitably end up in conflict with the federal power system. The meeting was rather interesting. It started off with about six of the public power generating utilities representatives speaking highly of the need for working with the private companies, etc. My remarks were strong enough that representatives of three of the PUDs which were being courted to join the private/public power coalition (Snohomish, Clark, and Grays Harbor) came to me immediately after the meeting and said they would not go across town to meet the other group.

I found out later that the 3 p.m. group was all set. On two different occasions during their meeting a representative of the private power companies proposed the formation of a task force composed of private and public power utilities. As usual, Tacoma and Eugene were all for the idea. The group even had a name selected, and a news release that was ready to go. Fortunately, the real public power supporters present held firm and said they would not move ahead to form such a task force until the other public agencies were consulted.

Later, at the October Board meeting of the State PUD Association in Wenatchee, I gave those who attended a history lesson on the struggles between public and private power in this State. I was lecturing on how to behave like public power people, and the outline of my remarks follows:

OUTLINE OF REMARKS BY KEN BILLINGTON
Executive Secretary, Washington PUD Association
to
Board of Directors Meeting
Wenatchee, Washington
October 21, 1966

I. History and Background

1939–1952 – Start and growth of the federal public power system.

Growth of local public power systems. Reference to "local public power" includes cooperatives, which are an essential part of the team.

1952–1966 – Local public power development, hydro.

1. JOA law and WPPSS formation.
2. The partnership story, PUD hydro projects. Cooperative needs between private and public power (non-federal).

The Basic Fundamental: The lowest cost power possible plus an abundant available supply to be used as an economic tool to promote the economic growth of the Pacific Northwest.

II. Private Power Role During This Era

1940 – Opposition to the federal regional transmission grid.
1946 – Opposition to additional federal dams.
1947 – Killed appropriations for feeder lines and substations for smaller utilities (appearance of so-called public power people who actually not only supported but also fostered the private power opposition to federal public power – still around today).
1952–62 – Sharing of steam costs; threat to preference clause in long-term private power contracts; partnership proposal for John Day Dam; attempts to control through State Power Commission; killed Rocky Reach bill; Hells Canyon fight; Nez Perce-Mountain Sheep issue.
1962 – Opposition to Hanford Steam Plant.

III. Situation Today – New Era

Steam plant transition.

August 18 trial balloon, letter to Senator Scoop Jackson by Executive Secretary.

Analysis of proposal to Senator Jackson (four parts):
1. Requirements contracts to private power. (Benefits private power.)
2. Specific statutory legislation to use BPA as power marketing agency for non-federal power-revolving fund legislation then before Congress. (Implied authority to purchase; direct authority to exchange.) (Benefits public power.)
3. Use WPPSS or other revenue bond issuing entity to construct and operate plants. (Benefits public power.)
4. Control by local utilities, private and public. (Benefits both private and public power.)

Reactions to letter: Accusations against Executive Secretary of
1. Attempting to kill WPPSS.
2. Formerly promoting cooperation with private power, now opposing it.
3. Undercutting federal power system.
4. Weakening public power financing.

IV. Diversified Activity on Grouping Utilities for Steam Plant Studies and Construction

Corporate Services.
NWPPA Power Supply Committee.
WPPSS.
BPA Task Force.

September 16 meeting, Corporate Services

BPA Task Force, 9:00 a.m., October 13, 1966.

Public Agency Meeting, 1:30 p.m., October 13, 1966.
Opening remarks by generating utilities.
Questions asked by Billington.

1. Some confusion as to wording of the letter of invitation. "If you are interested in joint utility effort," you are invited to

attend. Inference was that meeting was to formulate joining with the private companies. Is that why we are here?

2. Does presence here denote decision to accept this idea?

3. Have the utilities and their policy boards, whose names appeared on the invitation letter, approved this proposal to join the private power companies for development of a future power supply?

4. Wouldn't it be better for local public power to get themselves together on joint planning prior to an approach with the private companies?

5. Are we, as local public power people, agreed on a public power approach to a regional power supply?

6. Will power be used as an economic tool for regional industrial development? Who will build a surplus power supply on which to base regional industrial development and replace the former efforts of the federal public power system?

V. The Basic Issue

Federal public power main promoter of regional power for industry (1939–1966) now will diminish.

Use local public power to promote regional power. Whereas a private power company cannot devote its resources to a regional need beyond its own service area, a publicly or cooperatively owned utility can do so.

Emphasize preference clause relation to federal power by local public power.

Basic need: group local public power. Eliminate division between generating and non-generating utilities brought about by partnership on hydro with private power.

Need for PUDs to adopt regional attitude.

Size of local public power: large enough to do the job alone. Cannot agree with the view that we *have* to include private companies because their load growth potential is essential to finance plants. Direct attention to Hanford Steam Plant. Private power did not exercise its option of 50 percent of the output of the plant given to them by Congress until the publicly and cooperatively owned utilities had over-subscribed to take the output to 103 percent.

Need for engineering and legal research based on local public power needs as related to transition problems.

Control by local public power where regional needs are involved.

Should be done prior to alliance with private power where attitude could be based on anti-federal power position.

Does not preclude working with private power, but separation on policy issues should be between private and local public rather than between private plus some local public versus other local public, or along the lines of the past hydro generating and non-generating division.

Summary:

1. The basic need is to use the joint resources of local public power to assure the availability of low-cost power for industrial development on a regional basis. This to replace present source of regional industrial power as the federal public power system phases out on construction of hydro power plants.

2. Let us re-analyze what I am saying: up to now the basic regional planning for industrial power development has been done by the federal system. The PUDs through the Supply System and with the support of other local public and cooperative power utilities have done some work in this direction. However, the main effort has been federal.

3. Major efforts of local utilities, both public and private, have been to provide for individual utility service areas. To illustrate: Dams, "slice of cake" contracts, coordination agreement, CSPE.

4. Distinguish between public power and private power on joint regional promotion. Private power must think only in terms of its own service needs.

   Not said in criticism: Private power management should not or cannot divert financial resources from stockholders and dedicate them to a regional power supply.

   The private companies are already joined and whether or not you recognize it, they have a basic interest, namely, don't strengthen public power in any form—federal, local or joint local (WPPSS). Not said in criticism: They have to do this to protect their self-interest.

Therefore, development based on their needs will not promote industry for the whole region, and will not promote the use of public power, which is the road to low-cost power.

5. Let's look at ourselves during this period. Let's look at ourselves today. Some of the things I am going to say won't make me friends, but someone has to say them.

First, to the so-called public power generating utilities.

To meet your needs on your local hydro plants you have had to work with the private power companies. This is recognized and no one is criticizing you. You will have to continue doing so on your hydro. Some of your actions, because of the negotiating techniques, have appeared to be anti-federal public power.

Examples: upstream benefits bill, anti-California interties, co-ordination agreement, anti-trust legislation. You appeared to be taking benefits away from federal public power.

Federal public power *is the power supply for the non-generating* local utility. Thus the non-generating utilities have feared your motives and efforts.

Somehow you must assure them that while you must continue to deal as partners on your hydro plants, you can join local public power for regional power planning and construction of the steam plants.

Now for the non-generating utilities.

Your efforts have centered in WPPSS, and that is good. However, WPPSS is a construction and operation entity. It is not necessarily a planning body or a policy body. It could be, but it isn't.

It does not have all PUDs as members. It poses problems from the standpoint of participation by a large utility (non-PUD) such as Seattle City Light, or small utilities like the cooperatives, which are organized as private non-profit organizations.

Further, whether intended or not, WPPSS now appears to have its mind made up on where, when, and how the next plant is to be built. This is not immediately acceptable to some of our generating utilities which must mesh their hydro plants with this steam transition effort.

On the other hand, I despair when I hear good public power PUD people say, "We can't use the WPPSS at this time because the private power boys won't accept it." Who cares, or who should care, what private power will or will not accept or use?

Federal system — issues which must be studied.

Preference clause: need to clarify as it pertains to industrial contracts.

Implied authority to purchase power. Specific authority to exchange power.

Industrial sales: industrial customers should share in any higher regional costs of new steam plants.

To deal with federal public power on these questions, all local public and cooperative power utilities should be together or grouped.

Suggestions for action:

1. Group local public and cooperative power utilities for the purpose of taking over the responsibility of building a regional power supply, this to include power above and beyond their own service area needs to be used to promote regional industrial growth in cooperation with the federal public power system.
2. Establish a local public power task force or grouping to evaluate the needs and potentials of the local public power utilities regarding a future power supply. Deal with the federal power people as public power people, based on policies which reflect the needs and views of local public power utilities. Engineering and legal studies should be made by pro-public power firms if outside engineers or attorneys are used.
3. Cooperate with any private power task force. but base such action on the needs and potentials of local public power, not on the needs or policies of private power.

Shortly after my Board meeting, I called Dave Black to arrange a dinner meeting and found that he was going to Washington, D.C., to prepare his budget request. In the conversation, he said that we were working at cross purposes. I disagreed and said we were together if he meant what he was saying. He pooh-poohed the idea that the private power companies, "being only four in number," could dominate the situation. It was apparent to me that, while he was a brilliant young man, he was certainly naive and didn't know the basic fundamentals of public and private power relationships. I told him so in no uncertain terms and when I got through (it took about 50 minutes on the telephone), he said, "Well, I can see that we can't settle this on the phone so when can we get together?" I said we could meet at his earliest convenience. He said he would be back on November 3 and wanted to speak with me then because he was going into immediate conference on this matter.

I met with Black and Russ Richmond, his assistant, on November 3. We spent nearly two hours reviewing the whole history of power development in the Pacific Northwest. On every occasion, I had been arguing that the publicly owned utilities should regroup into some sort of a council in order to have a unified voice in this matter of steam plant transition. I gave them the outline which I had presented to my Board at the October meeting and stressed to them that, while it was essential that the private power companies participate in overall planning, we should never let ourselves get into the position of needing their approval to move ahead on needed power projects.

It was a good constructive meeting for all of us.

The previous weekend, October 29, I sat down in Portland with Hank Alderman of Ruralite Services and Gus Norwood of NWPPA to try to heal a breach between their two organizations relative to the cooperatives. I used the weekend to work with Owen Hurd to pull him back from his position, which seemed to me to be "don't confuse me with the facts, my mind is already made up," about the next nuclear steam plant – when and where it should be built.

In the next week, on Tuesday, Bob Gillette, Manager, and Bob Ries, Power Manager, of Grant County PUD came into my office and we started to set down on paper a proposal to form a public agency power council. During the following two days they carried this to a number of utilities: Seattle City Light, Tacoma Light, Cowlitz County PUD, McMinnville Water and Light, and others.

On November 3, following my meeting with Dave Black, we had an evening meeting in Portland attended by Owen Hurd, Gus Norwood, Hank Alderman, Bob Gillette, Bob Ries, Fran Scarvie, and myself, in which we hammered out the additional details on forming the Public Agency Power Council which would be discussed at the special meeting of all utilities to be called in Seattle November 10 by the Northwest Public Power Association.

As I saw it, we needed to draw Seattle City Light into a close alliance with the State of Washington public utility districts to eliminate the pro-private power influence exerted on Seattle City Light by Clif Erdahl of Tacoma Light and to offset the same pro-private power viewpoints in public power circles of Byron Price of the Eugene Water and Electric Board.

The final decision of the November 10 meeting was that a temporary executive committee would be established composed of twelve persons with four each from the cooperatives, city systems, and PUDs. Selection of these persons was very important. I definitely felt that Snohomish County PUD should be represented, being the largest PUD and situated adjacent to Seattle City Light. I felt that one PUD out of the three central Washington PUDs with the large dams should be represented in this group, preferably by Bob Gillette, who was well-accepted by most of our people. Bob's appointment incidentally was agreed to by the Chelan County PUD and Douglas County PUD people whom I had talked to earlier.

Next, we found Owen Hurd of the Supply System insisting that one of his Board members be placed in the group, and he proposed Commissioner Ed Evans of Clark County PUD. It was then logical that the fourth member of the PUD group come from the State of Oregon. I approached the Central Lincoln PUD representatives and suggested Bud Albright, who was First Vice President of the Northwest Public Power Association and would be President the next year. I ran head on into what must have been a split on the Board because three of the directors did not agree and proposed Don DeFreese, another director. I stated that my only interest in the matter was in having a man from their utility as the fourth PUD representative. However, to head off any fight, I approached Alan Jones, who was then acting as temporary chairman, and suggested that he appoint Bud Albright to chair the PUD caucus. This would preclude his being nominated and pave the way for DeFreese.

During the luncheon on November 10, it dawned on me that we had not asked anyone to make these nominations. I immediately got Owen Hurd to contact Glenn Walkley to nominate Ed Evans; I then went to Bob Archer of Clark County and suggested that he put the name of Bill Hulbert in nomination; I then went to Kirby Billingsley and said it would be nice if he would nominate Bob Gillette as the north central Washington representative; and, of course, we had the Central Lincoln PUD thing ready to go. The meeting was called to order and the three groups—cities, cooperatives and PUDs—were instructed to caucus and each pick four representatives for the temporary executive committee.

Well, this was the fastest caucus ever held. The PUDs had their representatives selected within three minutes. There were, of course, some mutterings from some of the PUDs which felt they should have had their people on this temporary executive committee. But you couldn't have everyone on it, and we had to move ahead.

In the interval between November 10 and December 15, when the formal organization was to take place in Vancouver, it was suggested that we change the name to the Public Power Council, and this suggestion was accepted.

By this time the publicly owned utilities were starting to pull together. During the latter part of October and early November, I had spent considerable time with John Nelson, Superintendent of Seattle City Light, driving into his mind that as a successor to men such as J. D. Ross, Gene Hoffman and Paul Raver, he had to assume the responsibility of leadership in the Northwest. I pointed out to him that many persons in utility circles felt that Tacoma Light with Clif Erdahl, a pro-private power man, was actually running the city utility show and Erdahl's policies were affecting him. I also arranged for John to meet with Bill Hulbert, Manager of Snohomish County PUD. Bill emphasized the need for public power to close ranks and Seattle City Light started to swing its influence toward supporting public power goals.

An interesting sidelight to this period was that coming back from lunch one day, I got to thinking that most of the PUDs and public power organizations used consulting engineers for advice. There were two engineering firms in the Northwest which more or less competed with each other: They were R. W. Beck and Associates and H. Zinder and Associates headed by Sol Schultz, the former Chief Engineer of Bonneville who had also been used by the City of Seattle and the cooperatives. My thought was that if I could get these two engineering firms to cooperate with each other, this would automatically be a good example to their clients. I first had lunch with Bob Beck and sounded him out—on the history of public power, the current need to unify us, and the future of public power. I then broached the possibility that he might want to cooperate with Schultz. He was very willing to do so. The next day, I had lunch with Schultz and discussed the same idea with him. He was very amenable. The third day, I had lunch with both of them. It was not only a gratifying occasion, but of considerable interest.

Both of these men were deans of public power from long service. I appealed to them by saying simply that someone had to weld the public power utilities together again and lessen the influence of private power in our ranks which had split us. Both of them insisted on the ethical position that the interests of their individual clients would remain uppermost. But both of them could see that regrouping public power would serve the ultimate interests of all their clients, and I am sure they did help out – off the record.

To me, the year 1966 was very important for public power in the Pacific Northwest. It was a busy five-month period from July 15 to December 15.

The growing strength of the private power forces in the State Legislature from 1961 on made it apparent that we would have to increase our legislative efforts. We made the one and only state-wide public opinion survey during my tenure with the State PUD Association in late 1964. Its findings were very much in our favor, showing strong public support for public power throughout the State, being even stronger in PUD areas than in the city light system areas. We had thought this might be so for many years, since we were aware of the yearly public opinion surveys which the private power companies had been making. However, this public support was not being translated into individual legislator's actions. Thus, on my recommendation the State PUD Association approved a special research and information budget which would give me some direct additional help both in the legislative arena and in the public opinion effort. In early 1966, with the increased budget, I hired two attorneys, Dan Brink, a former Democratic State Representative, and Newell Smith, a young Republican who was active in the Dan Evans 1964 election. I hired as our public relations consultant Bill Holloman, a qualified long-time newspaperman recommended to me by former Speaker of the House John O'Brien. Most certainly, when the 1966 elections gave control of the House to the Republicans 54 to 44, this additional help was welcome. A number of the new Republican legislators came from public power areas, but I knew that chairmanships of the important committees would undoubtedly go to legislators who supported private power positions in previous sessions. The 1967 Session of the Legislature was going to be interesting.

1967–1968

The 40th Session of the Legislature convened on January 9, 1967, with solid Republican control in the House, Democratic control in the Senate, and Republican Governor Evans facing his second regular session. The House eliminated its longstanding Public Utilities Committee and informed me that PUD bills would be referred to the House State Government Committee. While I had learned a long time ago the old adage "to the victor belong the spoils," I was a bit chagrined to find that from a total committee of fifteen, I had a potential of five friendly legislators on a private/public power issue. My chagrin was heightened somewhat when I found that the secretary for the new Speaker, Don Eldrige, came from a top office of Puget Power. Secretary is a good position in which to control access to the Speaker. I nearly gagged when I heard Representative Margaret Hurley (Democrat) of Spokane defying the Republicans for eliminating the use of secret ballots in Rules. She reminded them that back in 1961 a bill in which the Republicans were very interested could not have gone out of the Committee to the floor without a secret ballot. She was referring to the time when Speaker O'Brien let her have a secret ballot to get HB-197, the anti-public power bill, out of Rules.

As for the Senate Committee, we were informed that it appeared we would have an edge of two votes, Senators Gissberg and Mardesich from the Snohomish County PUD area. A Republican move to enlarge this committee by two pro-private power senators was rejected by the Democrats, but I noted that Senator McMillan (Democrat) from the PUD areas in northeast Washington voted in favor of this attempt. The Republicans used as their reason that there was a 10 to 3 ratio of Democrats to Republicans on the Committee, but it included all the Democratic senators from Spokane, who always just seemed to be on the Public Utilities Committee in the Senate, and responsive to the needs of Washington Water Power.

It was very apparent that the private power lobbyists and supporters were confident of their strength in the Legislature. The private companies had announced their intention to build a coal-fired steam plant in Lewis County, and there were many statements and rumors that they needed special legislation to protect the plant from a PUD takeover. I repeatedly sent messages that it was our hope not to have a private/public power fight and that if, indeed, the private power companies had a problem relating to their coal-fired steam plant in Lewis County, we would try to work out some type of compromise for legislation agreeable to both sides. I was given to understand that there were two pieces of legislation drafted by private power attorneys. One incorporated some drastic restrictions on PUD activity as well as providing for the joint ownership of the steam plants by private and public power. The second was a bill pertaining only to joint ownership. There was a lot of talk about the danger of PUD condemnation of the steam plant, which did not make sense because public power could build a steam plant for less money than it could acquire one by condemnation, which would require payment of severance damages.

On Friday, January 27, in the company of Newell Smith, one of our legislative legal consultants, I met with Governor Evans for an hour. He expressed the view that the private power companies should be entitled to finance, construct, and own steam plants. I stated that we of public power did not have any disagreement with this; however, I did point out to him in some detail that the consumer would be the loser in the long run because private power's fixed charges on their investment were substantially higher than those for publicly owned plants. I emphasized that we very definitely wanted to cooperate with them in planning for generation of electricity to serve the needs of the whole region. He stated that he did not know exactly what they wanted. They had come to see him and he had made it rather plain that he didn't want a private/public power fight in the Legislature. I stated that it was not our purpose to start a power fight, but that we could not stand by if the basic principles of the PUD law were attacked. I expressed a willingness to cooperate and see if we could not work something out. He then stated that he would contact the private companies and see what could be done.

As we left the Governor's office, Newell handed me a draft of the proposed legislation which the private power companies were considering. He had been given this by John Ellis, attorney for Puget Power, just that morning. I could not see anything in it that would cause consternation except that they wanted private and public power to own the steam plants jointly.

At 8 p.m. that night, Leroy Hittle of the Associated Press called me at home from Olympia and said that the *Spokesman Review* was going to carry a story about a bill to be introduced the following Monday which would spark a private/public power fight. The news story said that there were provisions in the bill which would eliminate the right of a PUD to condemn generating plants. I explained to him that condemning a steam plant did not make sense, because a PUD could build one as good and a lot cheaper than it could buy one under condemnation procedures. The next Monday, January 30, SB-283 was introduced, providing for joint ownership of the plants.

The next day I attended a meeting in Tacoma composed of attorneys from PUDs, city system and private power companies, and Bonneville. Through Dick Quigley, attorney for the Washington Public Power Supply System, I had asked permission to meet with the PUD attorneys after the other meeting adjourned. Dan Brink, our other legislative legal consultant, accompanied me to Tacoma. The alleged purpose of the meeting was to work on regional power planning legal problems, so I was a bit surprised to find that the group had concentrated on this joint ownership legislation. I pointed out to the attorneys that this issue had not gone before any of our policy people as yet and until this was done, I could not take a position for or against the legislation.

It was apparent to me that at no particular spot, from committee to floor to conference committee to Governor's office, could I be sure of blocking the legislation. My only hope was to threaten a private/public power fight which the Governor and some leading Democratic senators, primarily Senator Martin Durkan, did not want because of statewide political races they would be entering the following year, so this threat was the only possible way to seek and obtain compromise in the form of amendments or a substitute bill.

The following Friday, February 3, a joint meeting of the Southwest and Eastern PUD Associations was held in Olympia. On my recommendation public power took the position of being opposed to the bill "in its present form." I was instructed to remain constructive in an attempt to see what could be worked out. I was also authorized to call any of the PUD attorneys who desired to attend a meeting on Wednesday, February 8, in Seattle.

Thirteen PUD attorneys and two city attorneys attended that meeting, and we started to work over a redraft of the legislation prepared by Jack Cluck as the State PUD Association's legal advisor. I had repeatedly instructed Jack to merely pull the teeth from this bill and not spend any time trying to make it a good piece of legislation. The previous Saturday, Jack had forwarded the original draft to John Dawson, a New York City bond attorney, for comment, after he had taken the legislation and tried to turn it into an act which would provide for a special and separate entity or organization. I pointed out that this did not meet the problem. The bill did not call for a joint "entity," but for separate joint ownership.

On Thursday, February 9, I met with Dave Black, Bonneville Administrator. Black very emphatically stated that he felt joint ownership was necessary to meet the cost of building plants large enough to serve future growth of loads in the Northwest. On that same day in Seattle, Harvey Davis of Chelan County PUD, Jack Cluck, Art Lane, attorney for Seattle City Light, and Paul Nolan, Tacoma Light attorney, went over the changes in Cluck's draft we had made the previous day.

On Friday, February 10, without any warning, Senator Mardesich called a meeting of the Public Utilities Committee and put SB-283 on the agenda. There was complete consternation in everyone's ranks over this, with the result that all I could do was go to the meeting and say that we opposed the bill in its present form. I outlined how we had had a difficult time getting a copy of the bill and analyzing it, since it had been introduced only two short weeks before. I emphasized that the private power companies had been working on this for three months and had waited three weeks into the session before they introduced it. I stated that we were trying to be constructive. Mardesich told me that I would have until the following Tuesday to come up with some changes or else the original bill would start to move. Private power lobbyists and supporters flung some very caustic words at me as the meeting adjourned.

Jack Cluck, Harvey Davis, and I worked long and hard over the weekend and then on Monday, February 13, I went to Vancouver to a hearing before Senator Magnuson on a bill before the Congress. Meeting there, after the hearing, were John Ellis of Puget Power, Allen O'Kelly of Washington Water Power, Hugh Smith of Pacific Power and Light, Harvey Davis of Chelan County PUD, John Riley from the State PUD Association law firm, Newell Smith for the State PUD Association, Art Lane of Seattle City Light, Paul Nolan of Tacoma Light, and myself. A compromise substitute bill was agreed upon, incorporating certain changes which deviated from Jack Cluck's last draft. These changes were to be relayed to Cluck by John Riley late that afternoon and early evening. I told my attorneys that I had to go before the Committee at 3 p.m. the following day so I wanted any necessary changes before then. I heard no further word from them.

I went before the Public Utilities Committee on Tuesday, February 14, and took the position that we would not oppose the bill in its substitute form but that certain PUDs and certain groups would undoubtedly be opposed to the basic concept of joint private/public power ownership. The following day, February 15, I heard nothing from our legal advisors until 10:15 that night. At that time, Jack Cluck called me and pointed out that two of the changes made in Vancouver were incorrect and should be improved upon. He dictated some material over the telephone to me which, after analysis and some discussion with him, proved unworkable. He then stated that it would be his intent to give this his attention the first thing the next morning and advise me of changed wording.

At 10 the next morning, I received an envelope at the State Auditor's office which showed that Jack Cluck, prior to any discussion with me on the previous evening, had taken it upon himself to redraft legislation and send it out to all PUD attorneys. This draft included the unworkable portions which I thought were discarded in our telephone conversation the previous night. I was not sure he had not also sent copies to legislators, which might provoke a fight. I immediately called his office and found that he was headed toward Olympia, I thought to see me. He never showed up. I found him at 8 p.m. that evening, meeting with a group of my Commissioners.

My analysis of the legislative situation was as follows: I knew the private power companies had the more restrictive bill still in mind. I could not find any definite place in the Legislature or in the Governor's office to block outright punitive legislation against us. The only factor working in our favor was the desire of the Governor and potential gubernatorial opponents in the Senate to avoid an all-out private versus public power fight during this session. The Governor had told the private power companies that they could not introduce their more restrictive bill. However, if we picked a fight in the State Senate over SB-283, the private power companies could go to the Governor and tell him we were uncooperative and unwilling to accept even a bill which had no direct harmful effect on us. Further, they had indicated a willingness to accept the changes proposed by us. The companies could then take either the original bill or the bill in the substitute form, as it came out of the Vancouver meeting, pass it in the Senate by at least a margin of 26 or 27 to 23 or 22 votes. Over in the House of Representatives, where they had absolute control, they could put punitive amendments on the bill (a vote on revenue bonds, restrictions on condemnation, territorial limitations, and so forth). It would come back to the Senate for a mere majority vote on concurrence. They already had the votes and would secure the blessing of the Governor because the "PUD's had thrown the first rock." That is why I continually said that, while not agreeing with joint ownership in principle or concept, our job was to pull the teeth in this bill and let it pass, not try to make it a workable or good bill.

I was certain by now that Jack Cluck's intent was to try to stir up a fight and defeat the bill by amendment. I had great respect for Jack. He had been in the private/public power fight since the 1930s; he had a sharp legal mind that could analyze accurately how legislation affecting public utility districts would work. Because of all that, I was willing to let him express himself on policy, as well as give legal advice. But in this instance, he kept getting confused on the concept of the bill. He kept visualizing that the bill would create something similar to a joint operating agency or a new non-profit corporation, or some type of an entity, rather than joint tenancy in a common ownership structure financed by individual utilities.

I presented my recommendations and position to my Legislative Committee and Executive Committee on Friday, February 17. Right in the middle of that meeting, when Commissioner Ed Taylor of Mason County PUD No. 3, said, "When Jack called me . . .," it dawned on me that Jack Cluck, who was supposedly my legal counsel, since I was Executive Secretary of the State PUD Association, had been very busy the previous 48 hours lobbying my committee members and other PUD Commissioners against my recommendations, analysis, and judgment on this legislation.

Frankly, I lost my temper, which was about the first time this had ever happened in my legislative history. I didn't necessarily object to what Jack was doing but, rather, to the way he was doing it. Had he come directly to me and said, "I think your decision is wrong; I think your judgment and analysis of the political situation are wrong; I think this bill is wrong, even in the amended form; and with or without your permission I want to talk to your Legislative and Executive committees," I would have gladly given him permission to do so. But when I found that he had spent all day Thursday and Friday morning going behind my back, while supposedly working as my direct legal counsel on the technical aspects of the legislation, I had to oppose him and meet him head on before my Legislative Committee and subsequently my Board of Directors.

I also found that Paul Holmes, Deputy Grange Master, had been involved in this same maneuvering. My Board meeting was quite heated on Friday, February 17, 1967. Ted Lloyd, Deputy Grange Master, spoke for the Washington State Grange against the bill. Certainly I could honor his opinion. Jack Wynne, Clark County PUD attorney, spoke for that PUD against the bill. Jack Cluck got up and was permitted to make an eloquent statement against the legislation. It was at this time that I had to take a definite stand. I did, when I gave the Board the Legislative Committee report. Just prior to this, I had left the room, called my wife in Seattle, and said that if I was not sustained by the Board of Directors, I would be home that evening after resigning my position.

The Legislative Committee had agreed that the Board could take one of three positions in view of the political strategy in the Legislature: we could either endorse the bill and support it; we could oppose the bill and try to kill it; or we could decline to oppose the bill in its substitute form. It was the latter which I had recommended to avoid an all-out private versus public power fight and the risk of losing what support I felt we had. The Board of Directors, by individual district and using a secret ballot, sustained my recommendation by a 16 to 4 vote.

Jack Cluck had taken the position in the Legislative Committee that he was the attorney and legal counsel to the Board of Directors and was not responsible to the Executive Secretary. I recalled that he had taken the same position when he was legal counsel to the Supply System and disagreed with Owen Hurd, its Managing Director. I would never take the position that he could not talk directly to the Board of Directors, but as long as I was responsible for the legislative conduct and activities of the State PUD Association, our legal counsel would not make policy decisions.

At any rate, substitute SB-283 moved out of the Senate Utilities Committee on Saturday, February 18, 1967. Following the regular procedure, it was read into the Rules Committee at 9 a.m.

To indicate the pressure that was behind this bill and the influence the private power companies had, the legislation appeared on the next calendar after it was read into Rules. However, the Senators made a gentlemen's agreement that while it would appear on the calendar February 20, it would be held over for one day. This came about primarily because the Washington State Grange opposed the bill and had prevailed upon some of the strong senators for this extra time, during which an attempt was made to check the constitutionality of the legislation with the Attorney General's office.

On Monday night, February 20, the regular dinner meeting of the Washington State Power Users' Association, which was held each week, convened at the Bailey Motor Inn. This was one of the roughest sessions I have ever had to undergo. Attending were A. Lars Nelson, Washington State Grange Master, Ted Lloyd, Deputy Master, Paul Holmes, Deputy Master, Jack Cluck, and other good public power supporters. House of Representatives member Dan Jolly was there for a while but did not stay when the accusations against me got a little personal.

My good friend Rod Rodruck of Pacific Underwriters Corporation, who had just been elected President of the Users' Association, presided. He asked me to lead off, and so I reported as factually as I could the position of the Board of Directors of the State PUD Association and told why it had been taken. Next was a response by Lars Nelson. His remarks truly did hurt because what he said in effect was that I had failed to consult with or advise his deputies during the legislative deliberations on this legislation. I could see that Ted Lloyd and Paul Holmes had gone to him and sold him on the idea that I had been negligent in consulting with them. I did not consider this to be factual.

It was possibly true that I was not running to them every minute, but time and again I would talk to them, either at the dinner meetings of the Users' Association or occasionally in the halls of the Legislature. Time and again I had asked them when Lars was going to get back to the State because I realized that they could not make a decision or take a public position on this legislation until he got back. The Grange deputies deal with the same legislators with whom I have the best contacts. But certainly they had no effective contact in the Governor's office, which was essential in trying to bring this matter under control.

Paul Holmes spent some time justifying his opposition to the legislation before the February 3 meeting of the Southwest and Eastern PUD Associations. Although the Grange had not taken any position, he was opposed to the legislation and he felt that if it went through, it should go through over our dead bodies. He also spent time justifying the fact that he spent the previous week lobbying my own State PUD Association people behind my back. Ted Lloyd got quite personal when he stated that I was one of the biggest compromisers and fixers and one of the best in the business, but what was needed was the backbone of the Grange. My only comment at that time was that I wished someone, including the "backbone" of the Grange, could show me where the votes were located to control or kill this measure.

I then could see the drift of it, so I thought I might as well wade in. I caustically pointed out that Jack Cluck as my legal counsel had gone off on a policy binge and frankly had tried to "cut my throat behind my back." I pointed out how close this issue had come to dividing the State PUD Association, which we had been trying to make stronger and better unified.

When I asked for some specific objections to the bill, the only ones made were that the bill was bad in principle, and that the private power companies had not justified this type of legislation. I respectfully pointed out that they did not have to justify it because Dave Black, Bonneville Administrator, was doing it well enough for them. I was a little bit shook by one statement made by Ted Lloyd, "The Grange needs this type of fight," because I, too, am a Grange member and honor the organization. It seemed to me then that Lloyd's motivation was to stimulate action in the Grange for a Grange purpose, and not necessarily to protect the public utility districts and the consumers of these districts. I told them rather emphatically that they were free to move ahead and do anything they wanted to do as the Washington State Grange, as individuals, or as individual PUDs, but as far as I was concerned, I was going to take the position of my Board of Directors and that was to state openly that I was not opposed to the legislation in its final substitute form.

The bill was considered on the evening of February 21. A motion was made to substitute the substitute bill for the original SB-283. This was approved by voice vote. At that time, an amendment was offered by Senator Nat Washington which had been drafted by Jack Cluck and furnished to Senator Washington by the Washington State Grange. In effect, the amendment would have tightened the provision whereby each participant in a joint ownership project would pay for its own financing costs, to make certain that such financing costs could not be considered a part of the operation and maintenance costs which would be allocated among the participants in the project. Actually, the amendment was acceptable from our standpoint but it had been given to me so late, it was impossible to get agreement around the entire circuit, including private power attorneys, for its acceptance as a Senate amendment. A motion to table the amendment was made by Senator James Keefe of Spokane after a response by the other sponsor of the bill, Senator Lewis, against the amendment. This carried by vote of 31 to 16, with two absent and not voting.

Senator Washington then proposed a second amendment, which would require public bids on the entire project, not just the part financed by cities and PUDs. In effect, this would subject the private power companies to the public bid and bond performance requirements of public agencies. Here again, a motion to table was made and this was carried by a voice vote as the strength of the previous tabling motion indicated how the vote would go.

A motion was then made to advance the bill from second to third reading in order that it could be voted on for final passage. This ended up with 31 voting yea and 16 voting nay, whereupon Senator Keefe made a hurried trip back to Senator Morgan of Kitsap County who changed her vote from nay to yea. This met the necessary 32 to 15 two-thirds requirement for advancement. The vote for final passage was 31 to 16, with two absent and not voting. Those absent were Senator John McCutcheon, who left the floor just before the final vote was taken, and Senator John Stender, who had been excused previously.

There is no doubt that an all-out fight might have brought an additional five or six votes to the defense of public power, but this vote clearly indicated the strength that private power had when it came to the basic issue of passing the law. The absence of Senator McCutcheon, a strong public power supporter, just at the time the bill was to be voted on, would indicate this if nothing else did. The change of vote by Senator Morgan in order to advance the bill would also support my theory. House action was very routine. Private power had full control. I took the same position there of not being opposed to the substitute bill, but opposed to any amendments. The bill went directly through and was signed by the Governor.

This was one of the toughest periods I personally have ever experienced in the Legislature. It hurts when well intentioned but politically unknowledgeable public power friends criticize you for having sold out. I could only recall that old adage, based on my knowledge of legislative strength in this session, "He who fights and runs away lives to fight another day."

The State PUD Association had sponsored three pieces of legislation. The first was legislation to allow an optional small salary for PUD Commissioners in operating districts. The second was a bill which would clarify an ambiguity in the current law to make certain that changes in the boundaries of a PUD Commissioner district could be made only by a PUD Commission. Two previous Attorney Generals' opinions had come into conflict, one saying that PUD Commissioner districts had to abide with county commissioner districts if the PUD was county-wide, thus a change in the boundaries of county commissioner districts would automatically change the boundaries of a PUD commissioner district. We wanted PUD Commissioner districts to be under the control of the PUD Commissioners. The

third bill was to clarify the law that tax levies in small special districts created to furnish streetlights or small water districts could be used for operation and maintenance purposes, as well as installation of facilities.

I had made one strategic error in SB-309, the legislation to clarify establishment of PUD Commissioner district boundaries. The State Constitution provides that any time a section of a law is amended, the entire law, as
previously enacted, must be contained in the proposed bill. Thus, when
SB-309 was drafted, it contained a number of sections of the current PUD
law. The particular amendment pertained to only one small paragraph of
the law. My error was in using a broad title which left the bill wide open for
any type of amendment pertaining to public utility districts.

Senator Bill Gissberg of Snohomish County wanted to change the
PUD law so that vacancies on the PUD Commission would be filled by
appointment by county commissioners. While PUD Commissioners in
Snohomish County, as in all counties, did not run under party labels, there
had been some intense undercover competition between Republicans and
Democrats in that county. During the 1950s and 1960s, Commissioners
more or less of a Republican flavor had continued to be elected. The result
had been appointment of Managers of a Republican flavor and the use of
law firms with a Republican flavor. Gissberg, who was a strong Democrat,
felt that appointments being made by a county commission could result in
Democratic appointees for any vacancy which might occur on the PUD
Commission, since Snohomish County at that time had a Democratic controlled county commission.

Thus, when my SB-309 came through the Senate the first time, Gissberg was successful in hanging his SB-321, County Commissioner Appointment Powers, on our legislation as an amendment. When it got to the
House, I was able to negotiate a compromise on the issue whereby, to fill
any vacancy, the remaining local PUD Commissioners would have the
right of appointment for the first 60 days, but if such appointment was not
made by that time, the county commission could step in and make the appointment. When the bill failed to clear the House before the end of the
regular session, it was returned to the Senate Rules Committee to await the
Special Session. I had secured Senator Gissberg's agreement to my compromise.

I was rudely jolted by the idea that all was not well when the bill came
out of the Senate Rules Committee at the request of a senator who supported private power. Since the bill would be on third reading and up for
final passage, it was necessary to move it back to second reading to put my
compromise in it. This required a two-third's vote suspending the rules.

When this was attempted, the action was defeated and SB-309, as amended with the Gissberg bill still attached as in the regular session, was repassed by the Senate on a vote of 30 to 17, with two senators being absent. Senator Jerry Hanna, fearing this would happen, had voted on the prevailing side and gave notice that he would call for reconsideration of the Senate action on the bill to try and hold it in the Senate. When, on the next day, this time arrived, he asked that the bill be set over until the following Monday as a special order of business immediately following lunch. This carried by a bare majority as a courtesy to the senator. On Monday, the motion to reconsider was voted down 26 to 22, with one senator being excused. The bill moved to the House.

By this time we had determined, not only by direct conversation with representatives of private power but through other means, that the main intent and purpose of moving this bill out of the Senate over to the House was to take advantage of the broad title of the bill in order to add an amendment which undoubtedly would spark a private/public power controversy.

On Monday, April 17, 1967, SB-309 came before the House of Representatives. A floor amendment sponsored by Representative Tom Copeland of Walla Walla and Representative Bill Day of Spokane did three things: It provided that no property owned by an electrical company could be condemned without first submitting the question of condemnation to voters of the utility district; it required that the estimated cost of condemning such property would be included in the vote; and, finally, it required that no sum in excess of the estimated cost as approved by the voters could be paid without further approval of the voters.

Here again was the same old fight we had faced in 1961. While submitting the question of a condemnation action to the voters might be proper, even in view of private power's unlimited political expenditures, the requirement that an estimated price be submitted destroyed the fair rights of the Commissioners in the court of law where the condemnation award would be made. A motion to hold SB-309 over until the next day was defeated 52 to 43. When a motion was made to delete the last sentence, which required submission of the price to a vote prior to establishment of the price by a court, it was defeated 54 to 43. The amendment was then adopted 56 to 39, with four being absent. A motion to advance it to third reading for final passage failed to get a two-thirds' majority vote when 42 voted against it. But the bill came back on the floor on April 19 for a third reading and passed on April 20 by a vote of 58 to 39, with two absent and not voting. Private power was riding high.

The bill, as amended by private power, was immediately transmitted to the Senate, but three days elapsed before it was read in. It got lost between the House and Senate. When it was finally read in, Senator Perry Woodall, Republican of Yakima County, moved that "the Senate do concur in the House amendments." He then asked that it be made a special order of business at 2:00 p.m. on April 26, the day following.

At that time a call of the Senate was ordered and debate was started. Senator Jerry Hanna raised a point of order, citing Rule 62 of the Senate Rules which provided that when a Senate bill was amended substantially by the House of Representatives to the extent of changing its scope and object, the returned bill would have to take the route of a regular bill and be assigned to an appropriate committee. Argument was made by Senator Woodall and Senator Harry Lewis, Republican of Thurston County, that this was not the case. The Presiding Officer, Lt. Governor John Cherberg, then ruled in favor of Hanna's point of order. Senator Woodall then moved that the bill be referred to the Committee on Rules and Joint Rules. Senator Hanna countered by stating that the bill should follow the course of a regular bill and be referred to the Public Utilities Committee. Another senator raised a point of order as to whether or not, if the bill was sent to Rules and then returned to the floor, the subject of the scope of the bill would again be before the Senate. Lt. Governor Cherberg stated that such a ruling would have to be made at that time. Senator Wib Hallauer then moved to amend the motion by Woodall and refer the bill to the Public Utilities Committee. Lt. Governor Cherberg then ruled that the referral to the Rules Committee was in order, and the vote was taken on the proposed amendment by Senator Hallauer. It was defeated by a 26 to 23 vote, whereupon the original motion to refer it to the Rules Committee was called for and was passed by a 26 to 23 vote. The strength of private power on the Senate floor was again proven.

From that moment on, things became quite hectic. Since three senators from PUD counties had voted with private power, it became apparent that the only way the bill could be killed would be in the Senate Rules Committee where vote was by secret ballot. We were working all over the place, including in the Governor's office, on the issue. Our early-session gentlemen's agreement with Governor Evans to avoid any private/public power fight had caused him to cool off the private power people who were against us, and on my recommendation the State PUD Association had not opposed the joint ownership bill sponsored by private power. We had kept our word and now it was going to be up to the Governor to deliver the goods and help avoid the private/public power fight.

The day before I knew the bill would come up again in the Rules Committee, I had Newell Smith, our young Republican legislative legal consultant, talk to the Governor and his Administrative Assistant, Jim Dolliver. Smith reported that the Governor did not want this bill on his desk.

The next morning, I called on Senator Ernie Lennart, a Republican from Whatcom County serving as a lame duck from District 41, who was a member of the Rules Committee. Senator Lennart was an older man, and in his early years he had actually been a PUD Commissioner in Whatcom County. Somewhere along the line, however, he became disenchanted with public power. He would never outline to me the reasons for his changed feelings, and while he would always remind me that he was a former supporter of public power, I never once got his vote on the floor. I reminded him that he and I had been there around the legislative halls a long time. We talked about 1953 when the Republicans controlled the Senate, primarily because of Senators from PUD counties. We talked about the basic issue involved in this amendment on SB-309, whereby it was a "heads, I win — tails, you lose" proposition for private power. I then said, "It is my understanding that Governor Dan Evans does not want this bill on his desk, but most certainly the votes have already indicated that if it comes out of the Rules Committee, it will pass." I told him the best I could do on the floor was 23 votes and I was doubtful that two of those would stay. He asked me how I knew the Governor was opposed to the bill. I said that I did not know that the Governor was opposed to the bill, but that he certainly did not want it on his desk. He asked if I would mind if he called the Governor and I said, "Certainly not." I offered to step out of his office while he made the call, but he told me to stay seated because, as he said, "I won't tell you what the Governor tells me anyway." He placed the call to the Governor's office, and while I could only hear one side of the conversation, I know that he definitely got the same word. When I asked him what he had been told, he said, "Substantially what you have told me."

At 9:30 a.m. on that morning, the Rules Committee met. I had gone to Joe Chytil, the Senator from Lewis County, and our only Republican supporter on Rules. I stated there was a possibility that Ernie Lennart would be voting with him that morning. Chytil was to later verify that in sounding Lennart out, he got this definite impression, but the important part of this matter is that when the Rules Committee came out, Senator Wib Hallauer and Senator Jerry Hanna, two PUD supporters, immediately came to me and asked, "Who did we lose this morning on that vote? The vote was only 9 to 8 to hold it in Rules."

Senator Hallauer then told me that Senator Lennart, sitting directly on his left, flashed his secret ballot to Senator Hallauer just before he passed it to the Presiding Officer, and the word "no" was on it. We had won the crucial vote because, as Hallauer also said when it came up the second time, and it did very shortly afterward, the vote went 10 to 7 in our favor.

It looked to me as if one of our people who had evidently dropped off on the crucial vote, thinking that this would have let the bill out of the committee, climbed back on board on our side, but Lennart saved the day. Credit would go to Governor Evans for keeping his word to me that if I would go along with the joint ownership legislation of the private power companies, he would hold against an all-out private/public power fight. Being an astute politician, he would also recognize that had the law passed with this damaging amendment on it, he would have the hard decision about whether to sign it or veto it. If he signed it, the strength of the State Grange and organized labor would get it referred for statewide voter consideration at the 1968 General Election when he would be facing the State voters on his first re-election try. During the remaining days of the Legislature, private power on several occasions tried to break the bill out of the Rules Committee, but by then the votes had solidified and they could not do it.

One last episode concerning SB-309 with the private power punitive amendment attached occurred on the very evening that the Special Session adjourned. Lt. Governor Cherberg offered the Governor's supporters another chance to get to an important bill establishing a Department of Transportation which the Republican members of Rules had been pushing. To do so, he would have to call a meeting of the Rules Committee, but before he did that, he wanted assurance that the private power forces would drop their attempts to bring SB-309 out of the Rules Committee. Presiding at the rostrum, he said, "The Senate will stand at ease and the members of the Rules Committee are invited to my office for a cup of coffee." Everyone knew what was happening, but shortly thereafter word was passed to me that all the Lt. Governor was doing was serving a cup of coffee, meaning that even then the private power companies would not let up on their attempts. Thus the bill which the Governor wanted on the Department of Transportation also died in the Senate Rules Committee that night.

It was a hot session and a hot issue, even getting down to personalities. Ward Bowden, who had been Secretary of the Senate for many years and was a close personal as well as political friend, was threatened with ouster by a Republican senator after Bowden passed through Ulcer Gulch and inadvertently made a joking comment as I was sitting there. A private power lobbyist heard him and relayed the story to the senator. I would add that it is the Senate Secretary who receives House passed bills to be "read in" in the Senate. The viciousness of private power was a wonder to behold, but I guess they could only think in terms of pressure rather than reason; and this was 1967, 15 years since my first full-time legislative responsibilities began.

Five years later, in 1972, I heard another version of that crucial 1967 vote in the Senate Rules. I was having a drink with Jerry Buckley, top lobbyist for Washington Water Power, and we were reminiscing about the rough private versus public power legislative battles we had fought. He stated that I had lost two votes, not one, on that morning. I asked which ones, and he said they were Chytil, Republican from Lewis County, and Gissberg, Democrat from Snohomish. I then asked who I had picked up besides Lennart. He said Ryder. Now, Senator John Ryder, Republican, was from my own legislative district, a very good senator who had never given me a vote in any private versus public power issue. Buckley explained that he was not voting for me but was voting against him. Evidently, Buckley had gotten involved in a banking bill which favored the commercial banks over mutual banks. Ryder reflected the mutual banks' interests, and was only getting even. I have no way of proving or disproving what Buckley told me, but it reminded me of another lobbying rule I always followed: if it doesn't involve public power and the PUDs, leave me out of it. Conversely, the private power companies, as private corporations, would get involved in management versus labor issues, corporate tax issues — and evidently banking issues. A lobbyist wins some and loses some for some very strange and unpredictable reasons.

The Special Session adjourned at 11:47 p.m. on Sunday, April 30, 1967, just two days short of the lengthy 1965 Session. I was ready to go home.

Coming out of the 1967 Session of the Legislature, I found that my role and responsibility in local public power politics were undergoing a change. I would not recognize it until after my total retirement in 1981, but the turning point occurred around 1966 as I completed my halfway period of service with the State PUD Association.

Through the 1950s and early 1960s, I was still primarily a young political activist, supporting public power. But as the years rolled by, many of the old-time Commissioners were leaving their service and most of the Managers I had served when I was first hired had also left. The result was that I was becoming what might be termed a senior statesman in public power. Senator Jackson implied this when he asked me to coordinate opposing sides on reclamation subsidies. I filled this role again during the formation of the Public Power Council in 1966. Gus Norwood, who had served longer than I had as a public power association Executive, moved on to become the first Administrator of the new Alaska Power Administration in 1967.

Even my own bosses, the PUD Commissioners and Managers, must have sensed my changing status because in January 1968 the title of my position was changed from Executive Secretary to Executive Director. I had never been affected by titles, so I gave the change no thought at the time. In retrospect, however, the title change reflected a change in my status among the public power leadership in the Northwest and the nation.

In May of 1967, I received the Harold Kramer Personal Service Award presented by the American Public Power Association at its Denver Conference. When first word of this was sent to me by Alex Radin, Executive Director of the American Public Power Association, I responded by requesting that his Board reconsider the matter, saying that public power awards should more rightfully go to officials and management types instead of those of us serving as Association employees. Thinking back now, it was obvious that I had gained stature and acceptance as a public power leader rather than just a trade association staff employee. My activities during the remainder of 1967 were to bear this out.

On Monday, May 1, following adjournment of the Legislature which killed the private power-sponsored amendment, I received a call from Ferris Gilkey, Bonneville Area Manager at the Seattle office, who said he wanted to sit down and talk with me at length. I invited him up to the office but he said no, he would prefer a more relaxed atmosphere. I suggested Wednesday lunch. Shortly after that, Dave Black was on the telephone stating that he understood I was having lunch on Wednesday with Gilkey and he wondered whether he and Russ Richmond could horn in? I stated that they would be more than welcome.

Shortly thereafter, Gilkey came to the office and proposed that in my next meeting with Black, instead of lecturing him or criticizing him for his previous stand, I take a more temperate view. Gilkey was alluding to two previous meetings. The first had been on November 3, 1966, when I served notice on Black that my first priority was to bind the local public power utilities together before I would support establishing a task force to study joint action of the public utilities with the private power companies and the Bonneville staff. It was true that at that meeting I found myself more or less lecturing the new Bonneville Administrator on the history of public power from 1938 on. Again, in January, I had gone down and had another quite positive conversation with Black about his habit of accepting the private power viewpoints and then trying to force the public power utilities to go along with what private power said they would have to have. For example, the private power companies were saying they would not go for any more "Hanford formulas" in construction of a steam plant by a public agency, and that they did not want any more "slice of cake" contracts like those they had with the PUD dams on the Columbia River. They claimed that these types of contracts had first claim on their revenues, thus undermining their outstanding stocks and bonds and affecting their financing. They were insisting that the only way they could participate in future steam plants was by investing their own private capital in them.

Black had accepted this without arguing in defense of the lower power rates which public agency financing permitted the companies to charge their customers. He had been spending a lot of his time telling the public power utilities that they had to knuckle under and go along with the joint ownership approach. In the January meeting, I had told him that we would go along with the joint ownership legislation, provided no gimmicks were put into it by private power to undermine the basic principles of the PUD law.

At any rate, we met for lunch on Wednesday, May 3. It was a congenial meeting and Black made no bones about his feeling that we had been double-crossed by the private power companies at the Legislature. I told him that the first major thing which had to be settled was how Bonneville was going to deal with its direct industrial customers and add new industrial customers in view of the future higher regional power costs. I said that the PUDs and other local public power utilities would not ask their customers, either residential or industrial, to absorb higher-cost steam plant power and let the direct service customers of Bonneville enjoy the lower-cost federal power. We discussed a possible method of handling this situation by setting up a new rate for the direct service industries which utilities could not take advantage of because it would be for interruptible power that could be pulled back anytime Bonneville's other customers were threatened with an outage. In this way, the direct service industries would be a repository of regional reserves because they would agree to shut down, shed their loads, in the event of an emergency. Not all industries could do this, but those that could would be eligible for the special rate.

The next point I made was that joint ownership was going to be very difficult to sell, that I thought it would be far better for Bonneville and the local public power utilities to set up a program and start moving on it, knowing full well that while the private power companies would verbally object, they would rush in at the last moment and participate.

It was at this lunch that I proposed a new concept to balance the interests of the large public power utilities against the small public power utilities. It had been my thought that if we could tie Seattle City Light with the Washington PUDs in some manner, we would have a combine of local public power large enough to provide the needed regional leadership. I had previously asked John Nelson, Superintendent of Seattle City Light, to attend the Managers' Section meeting of the PUD Managers in March where a lively discussion had taken place on the overall subject of power supply.

Seattle City Light would not be permitted by the Seattle City Council to join an operating agency composed of 16 PUDs where the voting would be 16 PUD votes to one Seattle City Light vote. Therefore, at this lunch, I proposed to Black that we think in terms of special JOAs for particular plants and that we make the Supply System a member of the new JOA. For example, if a plant were to be built on the Puget Sound rim, a new JOA with Seattle City Light, Snohomish County PUD, and the Supply System could be organized. Thus, the smaller utilities could participate in a specific plant under the umbrella of the Supply System. I said that in the lower Columbia River area, you might have a JOA composed of Clark County PUD, Cowlitz County PUD, and the Supply System. Black said he hoped that Clark County PUD and Cowlitz County PUD would come up with an alternative to the Portland General Electric Trojan site. It could be on the north bank and, under public financing, would produce lower-cost power.

As we finished lunch, he stated that he planned to be in Denver at the APPA Convention for two days the following week. I asked him if he would object if I arranged a small informal off-the-record meeting in Denver where some of the leading management representatives of the larger PUDs and Seattle City Light could sit down with him and see if we could bang out some kind of plan for a regional power supply which would permit participation by all concerned, but which would not make joint ownership mandatory. When he accepted this suggestion, I arranged for a meeting at the Denver Hilton Hotel on Tuesday, May 9, 1967.

The meeting convened at 2:30 p.m. In attendance were Dave Black, Bonneville Administrator; Russ Richmond, Assistant Administrator; and George Toman, Manager of the Washington, D.C., Bonneville office. Utility representatives were John Nelson, Seattle City Light; Bill Hulbert, Snohomish County PUD; Owen Hurd, Supply System; Glenn Hittle and Bob McKinney, Cowlitz County PUD; George Watters, Clark County PUD; Kirby Billingsley, Chelan County PUD; and myself.

It was at this meeting that Black informally outlined a new plan for the regional power development program. He envisioned six plants, starting with the coal-fired plant in Lewis County. In this plant he wanted public power to have at least 50 percent of the joint ownership to permit Bonneville to secure 425 megawatts for the Central Valley Project power commitment. The second plant, which would be the first nuclear steam plant in the Pacific Northwest, would be owned totally by public power. It would be built under the Hanford formula—namely, an exchange contract arrangement with Bonneville—but it would not incorporate that part of the Hanford formula which required 50 percent of the power to go to the private companies. The third plant would probably be a private power nuclear plant. The fourth plant would be another publicly owned nuclear plant, and it would be financed on the Hanford exchange contract arrangement up until the date of insufficiency, the time when Bonneville could no longer guarantee enough power to meet its customers' load growth. Bonneville felt that its study showed that under this plan, the date of insufficiency for the public agencies could be shoved back from 1980 to approximately 1987.

Black also outlined Bonneville's first thoughts about the new industrial rate and the type of power which would be sold under it.

The session lasted two hours and fifteen minutes with a good free-for-all discussion by all those present. Later it was said that this meeting was a turning point in getting the program under way to provide the new steam generation for a Northwest power supply. It definitely was a rallying point for local public power that made us feel closer to each other and able to take more positive cooperative action with the federal power system representatives.

One person who was present in Denver but conspicuous by his absence from this meeting (because I did not invite him) was Clif Erdahl of Tacoma Light. Erdahl's full efforts had been behind putting the public agencies in partnership with the private power companies through joint ownership of power facilities. It was amusing that when the coal-fired plant matter came up, George Watters moved that we let Erdahl and Tacoma Light take the 50 percent joint ownership with Bonneville of the plant, and everyone in the room from the local public power utilities raised their arms, voting aye. Black looked rather glum at the moment. We assured him that others would cooperate to make good on our California commitment. But the concept of special JOAs for special plants and the Supply System as a center post meant that our basic philosophy of getting power to the customer at the lowest possible cost would once again be a major criterion in power supply planning.

On May 16, 1967, a special election in Grant County PUD put three new Commissioners in office following recall action against current Board members in a dispute over their decision to retain a special attorney to handle a settlement with the contractor who had constructed Priest Rapids Dam. The problems uncovered by the Grant County Grand Jury investigation that began back in 1958 were continuing. My only solace in the matter was that the recall once again illustrated that control by local voters was still an effective force in PUD operation – regardless of which side one happened to be on in the dispute.

On June 5, 1967, the U.S. Supreme Court vacated the Federal Power Commission license granted to the Pacific Northwest Power Company for the High Mountain Sheep Project in a 6 to 2 decision. The Court not only remanded the matter to the Federal Power Commission but directed the Department of the Interior to reconsider constructing a federal dam at this site. It was a major victory for public power. We had used the Supply System first to seek permission to construct the Nez Perce Dam and then agreed that if the dam should be denied us by the Federal Power Commission, the Supply System would build the High Mountain Sheep Project. The irony of the original Federal Power Commission license to the Pacific Northwest Power Company was that the license awarded to that utility combine was to construct the High Mountain Sheep Project as designed by the Supply System. The Supply System had taken the issue to federal courts and had lost in the Appellate Court on March 26, 1966, which sustained the FPC licensing to private power. This reversal by the Supreme Court reaffirmed the law which said that preference in licensing the use of a public resource – falling water – should go to public power.

However, all was not well in public power ranks when this announcement was made at the Managers' Section meeting in June. Several of the larger districts wondered how long we should continue to pay attorneys' fees in a continuing fight against private power at this site if the federal government would be taking over the project. It was here that I suggested a possible negotiated agreement whereby the federal government would construct and own the dam, but public and private power would finance it and split the power resources of the project.

One factor which was starting to muddy the water was that the Supply System, under the strong leadership of Owen Hurd, had been moving ahead quite strenuously and there was a growing feeling on the part of the Bonneville staff, as well as certain of the PUD management staffs, that the tail was starting to wag the dog.

In July, I became aware of a conflict between Bonneville and the Supply System Board over adoption of the new Hanford Generating Plant budget for 1967–1968. To govern this relationship between the two independent entities, an operating agreement had been signed. However, Bonneville was objecting to including in the new budget money to make power planning studies. It did not want Hanford revenues being used to finance the High Mountain Sheep controversy. Conversely, it was a proper position of the Supply System that activities dealing with new steam plants in the North-

Hanford Generating Plant on the Hanford Reservation was put into service by the Washington Public Power Supply System in 1966. *Inset:* John F. Kennedy at the groundbreaking ceremonies in 1963.

Courtesy WPPSS

west would undoubtedly involve the Hanford Generating Plant. Sitting in a position where I could listen to both sides, I perceived that the conflict was due to a breakdown in communications rather than the intention of either side to take advantage of or force its position on the other.

Thus, in July, one of my behind-the-scenes activities was to issue a white paper to my Board of Directors on the Hanford operating budget. It settled the argument by clarifying for each side the other side's responsibilities and authority.

However, the stress between the staff and Board of the Supply System and the Managers of its member utilities became more intense and, in October 1967, I issued a white paper titled "The Analysis and Reevaluation of Using the JOA Law." We were seeing the first breach between the Supply System and its member districts. On one side, the Board of the Supply System was stating forthrightly that "Managers are not to make policy decisions" but, conversely, the Managers of the member districts were stating "Supply System policy members pay no heed to member districts' power supply needs or requests." It was in this white paper that the distinction was made between management's prerogatives and policy decisions, and it was here that the first proposal was made that the larger PUDs have more votes on operating procedures than the smaller PUDs since they served more people.

In August 1967, Dave Black transferred from his post as Bonneville Administrator to Undersecretary of the Interior, to replace Chuck Luce. Luce had resigned to accept the post of Chief Executive and Chairman of the Board for Consolidated Edison of New York City. Appointment of the second Undersecretary of the Interior from the Pacific Northwest was strong evidence of the political strength Senator Magnuson and Senator Jackson enjoyed in the Johnson Administration. What I liked best about the letter Black sent me saying farewell was his penned note reading, "Special thanks, Ken, for your help during my short stint. While we have disagreed on occasion, our objectives are the same. The public power movement in the N. W. has benefited immeasurably by your able representation. Good luck. Dave"

In October 1967, following Gus Norwood's resignation from Northwest Public Power Association to accept his new job in Alaska, a move was made to consolidate NWPPA and the State PUD Association with me as the head of the new organization. While this occurred at a time in my personal life when I could have moved away from Seattle without difficulty, I did not instigate the idea. The proposal caused argument among public power leaders. Therefore, I wrote a fast letter suggesting that instead of arguing as to what might be done by reducing the activities of either association, we think in terms of more, not less, and if we could not do this, then just get the best replacement for Norwood that could be found and keep both associations strong, there being plenty of work for both. Henry "Hank" Curtis from Idaho was hired to replace Gus. He was an ex-newspaperman who had worked in Olympia earlier with the Associated Press. Now he had his own public relations firm and was doing work for some of the Idaho rural electric cooperatives in their ongoing skirmishes with the Idaho Power Company at the State Legislature. Hank proved a very good teammate in our continuing efforts to promote public power. I recall that at the American Public Power Association Legislative and Resolutions Committee meeting in Washington, D.C., in early 1968, where I was introducing Hank to my fellow public power association executives from around the nation, Oakley Jordan, a rather crusty public power crusader from Arizona, came up and asked if I thought "this guy" (Hank) would do okay. My response was, "Oakley, how old are you?" He said, "Sixty-two." I said, "Yes, and I'll be 52 this year and Hank is 42. The answer to your question is that he'll do okay because I'll make him a success whether or not he knows anything. We need younger guys coming along to fill our shoes, as we won't be around forever." Oakley grinned and said, "Let's drink to that." Hank did okay and not necessarily because of anything I offered.

The year 1967 closed out with Senator Magnuson holding hearings on Bill S-1934, the so-called Reliability Act, on December 20. I joined representatives of Bonneville to testify for the State PUD Association in favor of some specific federal laws requiring better coordination among separate utilities to provide more reliable service to our customers. The bill was opposed by Corporate Services, which orchestrated a number of public power utilities and all of the private power companies. Their alternative to the bill was a voluntary organization called the Western Systems Coordinating Council, whose purpose, as stated, was to provide coordination and thus greater reliability among the generating utilities serving in the Western states. The federal law was later dropped as these kinds of voluntary councils started to spring up all around the country. The sad part was that this alternative left in place the natural inclination of each separate utility, private and public, as well as even the federal agencies generating and transmitting power, to make plans to supply its own customers and protect its turf. The result would be construction of costly transmission lines designed for the benefit of the individual utility, making what was best for the customer secondary. No one liked or wanted domination by federal laws, but where monopoly utilities were involved, establishing standards, especially in planning and constructing intertie transmission lines, would have benefited the public. It did not happen.

Failure to get this law passed did not dim our high regard for Senator Magnuson for his many years of devoted service in getting low cost power for the people. Maggie was the second recipient of the Association's Earl Coe Award, on my recommendation. Presentation of this award to him was the highlight of our annual meeting in 1967.

The year 1968 was to see formulation of the first phase of the Hydro-Thermal Accord. It was a very busy time for me personally and I was able to play a role which contributed greatly to the outcome.

On January 4, 1968, the Supply System and the Pacific Northwest Power Company filed a joint application with the Federal Power Commission to construct the High Mountain Sheep Dam. These long-time opposing litigants before the Federal Power Commission had agreed to do it this way following the Supreme Court's rejection of the license to Pacific Northwest Power Company earlier. Time was running short. The power supply would be needed soon. However, the picture clouded again when, in June, Secretary of the Interior Stewart Udall called for a federal dam on the Snake River at that location.

The Clark County PUD and Cowlitz County PUD purchased land near Kalama for a thermal plant in February 1968. They contemplated a

Senator Warren G. Magnuson (*left*) receives the Earl Coe Award from Ken Billington, Executive Director of the Washington PUD Association, at the association's Annual Conference in December 1967.

nuclear plant but the site was on a mainline railroad, which made a steam plant fired with imported coal a reasonable alternative. With the load growth increasing at 8 percent per year, all utilities were scrambling around trying to put a power supply program in place.

Local public power had come through in late 1966 by establishing the Public Power Council to block the attempt to get some of the larger publicly owned utilities to join with the private power companies to negotiate with Bonneville on a regional joint power supply program. In October 1968, the Council was staffed using funds from a central budget.

During 1967, there had been considerable study and discussion about how to proceed. Bonneville was encouraging individually sponsored but jointly owned plants, looking at the possibility of selling some of the services which would need to come out of the federal hydro system to the non-federal steam plants, payment for which would be in the form of power from the steam plants. Backup reserves could come from the federal hydro. Transmission of steam plant power could be wheeled over federal lines, and the federal system could supply power to meet peak loads over and above the base loads met by the production schedules of the thermal plants. Russ Richmond, the new Bonneville Administrator, thought that such an arrangement for power exchange would give Bonneville access to a large enough block of power to promote additional direct industrial sales. However, a problem arose with this plan because the consumer-owned utilities under the preference clause had first claim on any federal power, including any non-federal power which would be exchanged for Bonneville services.

The Marketing Committee of the Public Power Council had been in prolonged negotiations with the Bonneville staff trying for some kind of an agreement on a future Bonneville industrial sales program to avoid the head-on priority conflict between the preference clause and industrial contracts. Under the Bonneville Act, Bonneville could not sell power to privately owned power companies without including a five-year pullback provision in the sales contract. Bonneville could enter into long-term industrial contracts, but only whenever the foreseeable power supply needs of the consumer-owned utilities could be provided. Foreseeable time had been defined as that period of time which would be needed by a public agency preference customer to secure an alternative source of power. At that time, it took from five to seven years to plan and construct a power plant, so industrial contracts could not be renewed or new ones signed if Bonneville could not serve the foreseeable needs of its preference utility customers. It thus became apparent that a new plan would have to be adopted if Bonneville were to expand its direct industrial sales.

Another dilemma faced by the public power and cooperative utilities was how to participate in the thermal plant program without being penalized. When a new plant came on line, a participating utility would have to back off the low-cost federal hydro power and take the higher-cost steam plant power into its own individual system. Even certain public power utilities which had invested in the Centralia Steam Plant to provide public power for the Central Valley Project were having trouble because, while such steam power was to be sent to California from 1972 to 1982, to fulfill the commitment made on the regional intertie legislation, the participating public power utilities wanted protection against having to absorb the high-cost power into their own systems in 1982, in the event lower-cost federal power was still available.

The Bonneville Act did provide a means for Bonneville to directly coordinate the federal system with the local public power systems, but the private power companies did not want to accept this approach which was similar to the original Hanford formula and would mean substantial benefits to public power for financing purposes. However, everyone recognized that a totally integrated regional grid would require the financial resources of all utilities in an effort to construct thermal plants to meet foreseeable needs.

From the discussions between the Marketing Committee and the Bonneville staff, the concept of net billing arose. Under net billing, a publicly owned steam plant would be constructed and power from that plant would be purchased under contract by a local public power utility. Coinciding with this, the local public power utility would sign an exchange power contract with Bonneville, whereby Bonneville would purchase the power which the local utility would get from the new steam plant. Bonneville would pay for this purchase by reducing, or "net billing," the regular Bonneville power bill to that local utility in the dollar amount the local utility paid the constructor of the steam plant for the power which it purchased and passed on to Bonneville. This steam plant power would be melded with the federal hydro power and sold by Bonneville under all of its established power sales contracts. The result would be an increase in the overall cost of Bonneville power to all of its customers, but no individual utility would be penalized for participating in a new steam plant by being forced to take the higher-cost steam power into its individual system at a time when lower-cost federal power was still available. Under this arrangement, the direct service industry customers of Bonneville would help pay for the higher-cost steam power.

On July 22, 1968, I met with Russ Richmond at his request just after he returned from Washington, D.C. He outlined certain ideas which he said he "might present to the private power companies." Immediately after the meeting, I left for the Tri-Cities area in order to attend a meeting of the Supply System's Board of Directors. I was later to become a little upset to find that while he had told me he was outlining possible offers for the private power companies, he had already made the offers to them.

At the Supply System Board meeting, I was handed a copy of a letter which Richmond had written Kinsey Robinson, President of the Pacific Northwest Power Company, dated July 10, 1968. It incorporated a great many of the ideas which he had outlined to me. Immediately after the Board meeting, I had to fly to Washington, D.C., on another matter. Calling back to public power Managers Bill Hulbert of Snohomish County PUD and John Nelson of Seattle City Light, I found that they were not aware of these offers which Richmond had already made to the private power companies.

Actually, an amusing sidelight to this incident was that the Supply System, having been criticized quite severely by a number of the public power utilities for climbing into bed with the Pacific Northwest Power Company on the new joint license application for a Middle Snake Project, in reality had a pipeline to the private power sector. The Kinsey Robinson letter from

Richmond had gone to all presidents of the four private power companies comprising the Pacific Northwest Power Company. The copy received by Don Frisbee, President of Pacific Power and Light, was reproduced for in-house distribution. Hugh Smith, Pacific Power and Light attorney, but also attorney for Pacific Northwest Power, gave a copy of the letter to Owen Hurd, Managing Director of the Supply System. Hurd reproduced it for his Board's meeting, and that is how I got it.

At any rate, regardless of my confused feelings, shortly thereafter I was invited to a meeting in the office of Bernie Goldhammer, Power Manager and Assistant Administrator of Bonneville, where he outlined a two-part plan for a thermal plant program to Henry Alderman of Ruralite Services, Henry Curtis, new Executive Secretary of the NWPPA, and me. The first part of the plan was that Bonneville would agree to take surpluses from a privately financed plant into the Bonneville system on a direct exchange account basis. The private power company could "bank" surplus kilowatts and kilowatt-hours with the federal system during the early years of power production by the plant. The company then could draw kilowatts and kilowatt-hours out of its bank account in accordance with a previously agreed upon schedule. It would be a power exchange instead of a dollar exchange. The other part of the plan was that Bonneville would net bill from publicly financed plants for the life of each plant. Part of this power would be used to repay the privately financed plants on their "banking exchange" and the other part would be used to furnish Bonneville with a supply to take care of the load growth of the preference utility customers and supply power for new industries.

I presented this plan to my Board of Directors in the middle of August at Goldendale, Washington. It was then that things started to happen. Dave Black, Undersecretary of the Interior, was the guest speaker at the Wells Dam dedication on Saturday, September 7. I got Black and Russ Richmond off to one side for a very brief but hard-hitting conversation to the effect that regardless of who won the election for the Presidency on November 5, 1968, there undoubtedly was going to be a change of personalities in the office which could involve marking time until new people were brought into the Department of the Interior program. I strongly urged that Richmond, as Bonneville Administrator, come out with an overall program, a Hydro-Thermal Accord that private and public power could agree to for the good of the region. It would be a four-part package.

First, the Middle Snake Project would be a federal dam constructed and operated mostly by non-federal public financing, and providing a 50-50 split of power to private and public utilities.

Wells Dam is the only dam on the main stem of the Columbia River to use a columbine-type structure (joint spillway and powerhouse). It was put into service in 1967 by the Douglas County PUD #1. The fish hatching ponds in the background replenished the stock of fish whose spawning was interrupted by construction of the dam. All PUD dams were required to have fish passage facilities for upstream migratory fish as well as hatcheries.

Second, the public agencies participating in the Centralia coal-fired steam plant would have the option of net billing that power when it returned from the Central Valley Project. In addition, a second generating unit would go into the Centralia plant which would be financed by the private power companies to raise their rate base by investing in mortgageable property, and secure certain tax benefits for their stockholders by private investment as opposed to purchase of power from a publicly financed plant.

Third, the thermal program would allow exchange of surplus power with the private power companies for short terms and the long-term net billing of power from publicly financed plants.

Fourth, a new formula would be established for computing and paying the costs of the necessary backup reserves needed in the construction of a non-federal steam plant. A new formula was needed because, since the major backup reserves had to come from the federal hydro system and would have to be purchased by the non-federal plant owner, under the existing coordination agreement formula, the cost would be high and possibly prohibitive in the early years. Black agreed with me and also urged Russ Richmond to move ahead on this.

Leaving the dedication area, I met Kirby Billingsley and Owen Hurd for lunch. Hurd told me that according to his pipeline to the Pacific Northwest Power Company, there were indications that certain members of the Bonneville staff were making some other kinds of offers to the private power companies. One of the rumored offers was some kind of sharing on the output of Asotin and Ben Franklin dams. I, of course, hit the ceiling because these were to be federal dams coming under the preference clause. While Bonneville had been talking about a split of 50-50 on the Middle Snake Project, which we had been agreeing to, I could not see why other federal dams had to be brought into this package trade with private power.

On the following Monday I said this to Bonneville staff member Ferris Gilkey, and Ferris arranged for Russ Richmond to meet with me on the following Wednesday, September 12, 1968. Richmond assured me that he had made no offer of a deal with private power on other federal hydro projects. We did agree that it might be well if he, as the Bonneville Administrator, could sit down with public power representatives and discuss some of these proposals which he would then take to the private power companies.

On the following day, I received a call from Richmond asking whether I had the authority to call together a group of public power managers as an informal off-the-record sounding board for his ideas about what might be offered private power. He suggested September 23, 25, or 27 in Seattle. I was tied up on September 27 and I found that the first man I called, John Nelson, Superintendent of Seattle City Light, was leaving on September 25 for eight days on American Public Power Association business. I, therefore, arbitrarily picked September 23, Monday, as the date to hold the meeting. I called my President, Lloyd McLean, and Vice President, Arnold James, and told them what Richmond had requested. They approved and told me to proceed. I then dispatched a personal invitation to around 27 top level public power management personnel, widely representing municipals, cooperatives, and the PUDs. Twenty-four persons showed up, including Russ Richmond and three members of his staff: Ken Kaseberg, Bonneville attorney; Hector Durocher of the Power Managers Division; and Ferris Gilkey.

At this meeting, Richmond outlined the proposed package settlement. This included the federal dam, non-federally financed on the Middle Snake River for which he suggested a four-year moratorium on FPC license hearings. Private power was to get 50 percent of the power production of that development, which was to be non-federally financed, preferably by a municipal corporation using tax-exempt revenue bonds. The second unit of the Centralia coal-fired steam plant would be authorized and, if necessary,

Bonneville would take the output of that unit for the first year on a net billing basis. The first nuclear steam plant would be the Portland General Electric plant at the Trojan site, with that company having the right to bank enough power surplus with the Bonneville system (on a declining banking basis) to meet the needs of all the private power companies in the Pacific Northwest. In exchange for this, the private power companies would support Bonneville in its net billing arrangements with the publicly financed thermal plants under the presently existing authority of the Bonneville Act. Finally, an amendment was attached to the coordination agreement which would more equally amortize costs of backup reserves for non-federal thermal plants. The program was accepted off the record by the public power management personnel.

On the following Saturday, September 28, 1968, I talked briefly with Russ Richmond at the John Day Dam dedication ceremonies. He informed me that he had met the previous Thursday night with the private power company representatives and that they seemed to be pretty much in accord with the package settlement proposal. He said they had blinked a little when he proposed a four-year moratorium on the Federal Power Commission license hearings for joint construction of High Mountain Sheep or an alternative project. He said that when he reported the outcome of the meeting to Dave Black, when he said that private power's only concern was whether the Federal Power Commission would accept a postponement of the license hearings, Black assured him that the FPC would be more than willing to accept a postponement.

Russ Richmond was scheduled then to go to Washington, D.C., on October 7, where he would lay this program before the Bureau of the Budget, Department of the Interior, and certain congressional leaders, including representatives of the Appropriations Committees of both the House and the Senate. We had previously scheduled a meeting of the PUD Managers' Section for October 11 and I, therefore, proposed that he come back to that meeting, if he could make his arrangements on travel, and report his findings on the Washington, D.C., trip. He accepted.

In the middle of that week, I received a telephone call from Richmond, saying that his proposal had met with overwhelming acceptance, that agreement had been reached to seek a six-month postponement of the Federal Power Commission license proceeding on the High Mountain Sheep Dam in order to let all parties work on federal legislation along the lines of the settlement proposed. He asked whether we could invite cooperative and municipal representatives to our PUD Managers' meeting. Upon checking with Bob Gillette, Chairman of our Managers' Section, I told Richmond we could, and we did so.

After that, the Joint Power Planning Council announced the first phase of the Hydro-Thermal Accord, and at the Bonneville Advisory Council meeting, further information about the plan was made public.

There followed a lot of behind-the-scenes action on the Middle Snake Project settlement, some of which was amusing. Saturday morning, October 12, the day after my Managers' Section meeting, I received a call from Owen Hurd who said that they were planning a large public function in Portland, Oregon, on Friday, October 18, at which Secretary of the Interior Stewart Udall, Kinsey Robinson, Chairman of the Board of Pacific Northwest Power Company, and the Supply System officials would make a public announcement on the Middle Snake Project settlement. He asked if Lloyd McLean, my President, and I could attend the occasion. This conflicted with our established Board meeting, and I called McLean to suggest that the date of our meeting be changed.

On the following night, Sunday, October 13, I got a call from Jim Klein, Public Information Officer for the Supply System, who said that they had canceled their plans for a large blowout and had settled on a press conference at the Portland airport for Friday night, October 18. The Secretary of the Interior, Kinsey Robinson, and Owen Hurd would make brief statements, followed by press questions to the Secretary on the settlement, after which a small, informal dinner would be held for the Secretary. For this, the Executive Committee of our Association had agreed to move our Board meeting in order that McLean and I could participate.

On Monday, October 14, I met with Hugh Smith and Clem Stearns, of PNPC, and Jim Klein to select the public power people to be invited. However, on Tuesday morning, just before I was to send out a notice to move our Board meeting, I received a call from Owen Hurd to say that on the preceding evening at 11 p.m., Clem Stearns, Public Relations Officer for PNPC, had called Jim Klein and said that Kinsey Robinson had canceled the whole thing.

At our Managers' meeting, I had jokingly said to Russ Richmond that we of public power did not have to bow and scrape or save face or do anything on the Middle Snake compromise, as long as it was for the benefit of the region. I told him that he had our blessing to make any kind of arrangements to give any kind of a celebration and put anyone at the head table that Kinsey Robinson or anyone else wanted in order that any of the private power boys could save face or whatever they had to do to look good in the public eye. We just wanted a good project, constructed at the lowest possible cost to the ratepayers.

I might also add that at this time I ran into another problem. Elections were coming up and a certain candidate for U.S. Senator, namely Frank Church of Idaho, did not want the settlement to be announced. He felt it would cause confusion and stir up controversial public statements, pro and con. I also found out later the private power ranks were having considerable internal problems. Kinsey Robinson, after fighting all these years for private power development on the Middle Snake, was now in the position of agreeing that it would be a federal dam, constructed and operated by the federal government. Russ Richmond told me that the real statesmen of private power were Glen Jackson and Don Frisbee of Pacific Power and Light. These men were gung-ho for private power, but they also recognized the needs of the region.

A great amount of credit goes to Russ Richmond for negotiating and getting the settlement on a regional power supply under way as Bonneville Administrator. I recognized that in his position of having to deal with private power and public power, and especially with public power zealots such as myself, he had some problems. Why he talked to me on July 22 about what he thought he would propose to the private power companies, when he had already sent a letter dated July 10 incorporating most of the proposals, is beyond me. But I would also recognize in fairness that sometimes one had to make such moves to placate extremists on both sides of the fence. I had never considered myself an extremist, but I guess in some people's minds I was one in 1968.

At any rate, Russ Richmond is a thoughtful kind of guy who took time to scribble a little personal note to me, thanking me for putting together, by mere use of the personal prestige I had been fortunate enough to build up through my service to the PUDs, the sounding-board meeting of public power management leaders. This gave him the backing to sit down and make his proposal to the private power companies. I am sure that any other person serving in my capacity would have done the same and possibly would have done it better, but this, indeed, was a very interesting period in my role as Executive Director for the PUDs of the State of Washington. The Hydro-Thermal Accord had taken off and was moving ahead.

Another interesting 1968 sidelight was a visit I had in late June from Ira D. Cox, a special agent of the Intelligence Division, Internal Revenue Service. He said he was investigating the political activities of the Puget Sound Power and Light Company. He emphasized that the IRS was not concerned with whether these activities were legal, but rather with whether the company had spent on these activities money they took off their income tax as business expenses. For example, he said the company had reported a substantial amount of money for stamp purchases. I commented that since most of the official mailings of the company would presumably go out through postage meters, purchase of stamps might be one way of supporting candidates for political office.

I told Cox that I had discussed Puget Power's political practices with certain political figures. He asked for specifics and I recounted statements given to me by Bob Ray, a jeweler in Renton, who was a committee clerk for Senator Gordon Herr in the 1967 Session. According to him, public power was in deep trouble. He said he had met Lloyd Smith, lobbyist for Puget Power, at a printing firm when Smith was dropping off 25,000 envelopes to be printed for Avery Garrett. Ray said that Puget Power had not only the envelopes printed but a brochure as well, and that their employees addressed and mailed the envelopes. But I told Cox that the best way to find an answer to his question was to talk directly to the parties involved, because I got my information secondhand and had no way of proving or disproving it. I found out later that one of my Commissioners had sent Cox to me after being contacted by him. There was no question in my mind that substantial political financing was given by the private power companies to their favorite candidates or persons from whom they were soliciting support, but there was no law against it unless such expenditures were being charged as operating expenses of the utility instead of as a political expense chargeable to the stockholders.

A second incident involving mailing and postage meters hit me in the early fall. Jerry Buckley, head lobbyist for Washington Water Power, came up to me at a fund raising dinner for Representative John Rosellini in West Seattle and said, "I don't want to get mixed up in this, but I want to talk to you about a certain thing. Certainly I wouldn't want it known that I have come to you, because the Senator involved would cut my throat." He said that someone up in Pend Oreille County had sent Senator Sam Guess of Spokane an envelope which had a meter postage stamp on it. The person had cut his name off the envelope but made the accusation that this was metered mail and that there had been three county-wide mailings made on behalf of three different candidates by the Pend Oreille County PUD. The three candidates were Charles McCain, one of the PUD Commissioners running for the Legislature in the primary; Bruce Wilson, from Okanogan County, running against incumbent State Senator Dave McMillan who had been supporting Washington Water Power; and one other statewide candidate. Buckley did not name the statewide candidate but I thought it must be Martin Durkan in his primary campaign for Governor.

State Senator Sam Guess was a bitter opponent of the PUDs. He was so conservative that I would rank him as a candidate for the John Birch Society, if he did not carry such an ID card. He, of course, was trying to "raise hell," as Buckley put it, and had written a letter to the Attorney General's office accusing the PUD of expending public funds for political purposes. Buckley said that he had tried to dissuade the Senator from doing this but, "Couldn't you just get to the PUD and get them to reimburse the money or pay for it some way so that the thing could be hushed up?" He said he did not like to see this kind of an attack being made and the headlines would probably be quite big.

My immediate and honest response was simply that if the PUD was spending public funds for political purposes, then as far as I was personally concerned, they should get their knuckles rapped by the Attorney General or the State Auditor's office or whoever could get to them. Most certainly, all PUD people knew that you couldn't do this and if they were doing it, they should be stopped. I guess my response startled Buckley a bit, but nevertheless I thanked him for his kindness in tipping me off as to what was going on. Inside I was concerned because, first, I couldn't believe that anyone would be quite that dumb, but I also knew that once Sam Guess got this in the Attorney General's office he would make hay out of it, and every PUD in the State would be tarred with the brush of spending public funds for political purposes.

The next day, I put a fast call through to the Pend Oreille County PUD. George Kennett, the Manager, was absent so I talked to Albert Strayer, the Auditor. I said, "Al, I have this report. I am not going to tell you where it comes from, but you are being charged with using a PUD postage meter to mail out political mail. What is going on over there?" He said, "Ken, I don't know what it's all about but, first off, the PUD does not have a postage meter." He said the only postage meter in Newport was owned by the National Bank of Commerce, Newport Branch. He understood that as a public service, the bank would let any political candidate come down there and pay the amount of the postage and then they would run the envelopes through their postage meter. He said the PUD had permitted certain types of organizations, such as the Red Cross or the United Good Neighbor funds, to use the PUD addressograph plates for county-wide mailings, and that this same courtesy had been extended to any political candidate of any party who wanted to use their own staff to do the work and who furnished their own envelopes. I told him that I would have hesitated to permit this use of PUD mailing lists, which I knew it was the practice of most every other PUD to deny. He said Pend Oreille was a very rural area and everyone knew everyone else's business, so there were no secrets in either Republican or Democratic circles about this practice. He did agree that he would take it up with his Commission the next time and perhaps, as a public policy, they would discontinue the use of their mailing lists for any purpose. Well, the joke was really on State Senator Sam Guess. I immediately called the Attorney General's office and the Division of Municipal Corporations of the State Auditor's office and said I was aware of the Senator's complaint and that if it went through, it should be thoroughly investigated, but that the easiest and best answer to this phony charge that a PUD was spending public funds on political purposes by sending out metered mail from its postage meter was the simple statement: "The Pend Oreille County PUD does not have a postage meter."

The November 1968 General Election saw Governor Daniel J. Evans re-elected for his second term and the increase of Republican control in the House of Representatives by two additional seats, for a total of 56 to 43 Democrats. On the Senate side, the Republicans picked up two additional seats, reducing the Democratic majority to 27 to 22. While several changes from R to D and vice versa in PUD counties did not bother us, there were several changes on the Senate side from D to R in counties being served by private power which did concern us. After the fierce and close fight in 1967, the coming 1969 Session of the Legislature seemed ominous.

The 1968 election also saw the defeat of Democratic Senator Wayne Morse of Oregon by Republican Robert Packwood, thus terminating a long-time strong pro-public power voice in Congress.

The year 1968, in July, saw one sad event. R. W. "Bob" Beck died. Perhaps the most astonishing thing for me to read at that moment was that he was 72 years old. I just couldn't believe it and yet at the same time, I had known this man for so long and knew of so many projects he had worked on in public power development, stretching from the 1930s through the 1960s, that perhaps I should have realized that he would have to be that old. Bob Beck, however, was a unique person, and God evidently had given him a young body as well as a young mind to use and perform his dedicated work to public power. I have more to say about Bob in Chapter 9.

Summary

During the era from 1963 through 1968 the transition from hydroelectric power to the use of thermal plants for base energy needs began. The Hanford Nuclear Generating Plant was completed by the Supply System in 1966. Public and cooperative utilities regrouped in the Public Power Council to join with private power companies, Bonneville, and Bonneville's direct service industry customers to negotiate the Hydro-Thermal Accord.

A Columbia Interstate Compact which would have favored private power and the upstream states was rejected, but the Columbia River Treaty with Canada providing for substantial upstream storage in Canadian dams with financial support from Pacific Northwest utilities was a big step forward.

Beneficial federal legislation approved a major regional intertie with California that had safeguards to protect the Pacific Northwest against loss of federal power generated here, that limited power revenue subsidies to Northwest reclamation projects, and that provided for a rolling maturity system payout on federal power facilities.

In the State legislative battles, public power won some very close and crucial votes but could see the continuing growth of private power political strength.

It had indeed been an era of "Balancing Acts" between private and public power in the Pacific Northwest.

6

1969–1974 Era
"Peace Pipe and Joint Efforts"
with Private Power

1969–1970

THE 41ST SESSION of the State Legislature convened on Monday, January 13, 1969, signaling a new era in the legislative arena from several viewpoints. The House and Senate chambers and the offices of the legislators had been extensively renovated. The press desks, which had formerly been at the front of the chamber, were moved to the sides, with extra desks for reporters in the first row of the north gallery on the House side in case of overflow. Where, heretofore, many of the House members' desks had been pushed together in groups of three, which caused a rather tight squeeze for a man or a woman sitting in the middle, there were now only two such desk arrangements in the House chamber, and these were placed at the rear on the outside so that access to them was easy. Of principal concern to the lobbyists was that there would no longer be a way to contact a legislator directly by telephone from outside the chamber while he or she was on the floor. Formerly, one could call either the House or Senate chamber and have a page go to the floor and tell a legislator he or she had a telephone call.

This would provide a direct and most often immediate contact. Now, however, even though each legislator had a telephone at the desk, it was connected to a personal secretary. A lobbyist could call the secretary who could relay a message, but could not put the lobbyist on to talk directly to the legislator.

The 1968 elections had caused a large turnover in individual legislators, although the parties were not affected much. There were 13 new senators out of 49 and 21 new representatives out of 99. The Democrats controlled the Senate and the Republicans controlled the House. Governor Evans served notice that it was his intention to call the Legislature back in 1970. Dan Brink was still with me as my Democratic legal advisor but I had replaced Newell Smith, who wanted to spend more time in his direct law practice, with former Republican legislator Pat Comfort as my Republican legal advisor.

As I watched the organizing of the committees, I became concerned. The Senate under Democratic control consolidated the former Public Utilities and Commerce Committees into a new committee called the Commerce and Regulatory Agency Committee. While the chairman was Senator Augie Mardesich, Democrat from Snohomish County, the Committee numbered 19 members, of which—it appeared to me from past association—10 were solid for private power and 2 were potentially for them. When I looked at the Senate Rules Committee composed of 16, including Lt. Governor Cherberg as Chairman, it appeared that 8 of the senators would certainly favor private power on any private versus public power issue, and 2 others might do so. Over on the Republican-controlled House side, utility legislation would again be handled by the State Government and Legislative Procedure Committee as it was in the 1967 Session. It appeared to me that out of the 16 members, 9 by previous activity indicated solid support for private power. Further, on the House Rules Committee, out of the 17 members, 8 were solid supporters of private power. I could see that in any private versus public power legislative conflict my work was going to be cut out for me, but this did not deter me from moving ahead with proposed legislative improvements which would make the public utility districts, which were totally subjected to established law, capable of giving more efficient service.

The 1969 Session of the Legislature turned out to be the one in which peace on private versus public power legislative issues was established. On Tuesday, February 25, I dictated for my files a blow-by-blow account of how this happened based on the information I had at the time. On March 2, I added to this report. The following section is taken from those file records.

Legislative Highlights— 1969

This is being dictated on the evening of Tuesday, February 25, 1969. The purpose is to report some highlights in the movement of legislation affecting public power during the past month.

During the early part of the session, HB-140 and SB-178 were introduced by the private power forces. This legislation seemed to be a minor amendment to the joint action law of the public utility districts, but it was very puzzling and, in fact, our own attorneys could not determine what its import or purpose was.

I quizzed the private power lobbyists and I also had the sponsors quizzed by Pat Comfort, our Republican legislative consultant. We were told that it was to stop the use of PUD revenues to promote public power in non-PUD areas.

Such an amendment did not make sense because (a) we had never done this and (b) we did not intend to do it.

Later on I was told that the act was directed against use by the PUD Association of Paul Holmes, Deputy Grange Master, to campaign in the Renton area where a PUD formation effort occurred.

I passed the word quite firmly that this cooperative program with the State Grange had been discontinued over a year ago and that the PUD Association no longer had anything in its budget for such a purpose.

It was in the latter part of January that things picked up with a flourish. I returned from Washington, D.C., early on the morning of January 30, a Thursday, to attend a meeting arranged by Pat Comfort with Governor Dan Evans. At 11:30 a.m., Pat and I were with the Governor going over our plans and programs for the legislative session, and the Governor informed us that as far as he knew the private power companies had no basic issue for this session.

Little did he know that at that very moment, a skirmish and maneuvering were taking place on the Senate floor over the introduction of two vicious anti-public power bills, SB-303 and SB-304.

SB-303, which provided that city light systems could not serve one additional customer in an area served by the private power companies without the prior agreement of the private power companies, was directed against the cities of Seattle and Tacoma.

SB-304 was a dissolution bill which would abolish all PUDs except those which were presently operating electric utilities, but it had trick wording which would have precluded activation of any future electric PUD under any circumstances. It was truly the most vicious anti-PUD measure I had read since coming here as a lobbyist.

During the skirmish on the Senate floor over referral of SB-303 to a committee other than the Commerce and Regulatory Agencies Committee, which would normally handle such a bill, it became evident that private power had a majority vote on the floor. It looked as if private power had launched an all-out attack against public power and, according to every political analysis, private power appeared to have the votes to severely damage us.

No place in the legislative process in the movement of a bill did we have a "stopper" against this punitive anti-public power legislation. Since the last session, public power had lost Senators Hallauer, Hanna, and Chytil (two Democrats and one Republican) off the Rules Committee, and the replacements for those senators favored private power two to one. During the last session, it was the Senate Rules Committee which blocked an anti-PUD measure, and by only a one-vote margin.

On the House side of the Legislature there was no possibility of stopping anti-public power measures.

The first thing I did after getting the bad news was to return to the Governor's office and tell him that while we were being positively told that no private power attack on public power was going to occur in this session, an all-out attack was commencing in the Senate, one floor above.

Later on, as events unfolded, I had the feeling that this private power action irritated the Governor and that he served notice on some of the private power companies to lay off their attempts to start a controversy.

At any rate, during the following week of February 2 to 8, there was not much activity on these bills. My main effort was to alert the various districts throughout the State to what might be happening.

At this stage of the game, I became suspicious that the private power lobbyists were going beyond the top management policy of their companies.

Thus, on Sunday afternoon, February 9, while working in my Seattle office, I decided that if we couldn't beat them in the Legislature, we might as well make the record clear on the outside.

I placed a call to Russ Richmond, Administrator of the Bonneville Power Administration, at his home in Vancouver, Washington, and told him that I had about 72 hours before A. Lars Nelson, Master of the Washington State Grange, and Joe Davis, President of the Washington State Labor Council, would approach me and ask whether or not we were faced with an all-out fight on this issue. I told Russ that if we were, the individual legislators would freeze in their positions and the lobbyists would be at a stand-off, with the likely result that, after a terrific fight in the legislative halls, private power, with its evident voting strength, would pass a severe anti-public power piece of legislation. The only recourse we would have then would be a referendum by the State Grange and State labor which would lock the State of Washington into a private versus public power political fight until the General Election of 1970.

Most certainly, I told Russ, this open fighting would carry over to the Congressional Committees before which he would be appearing, possibly even as a lame duck Administrator, trying to sell a cooperative joint regional power supply program.

Russ, of course, was concerned, as he should be. He asked if I would call Don Frisbee, the new President of Pacific Power and Light Company in Portland. I stated that while I had met Frisbee, I was not personally very well acquainted with him. Russ stated that he was a new type of private power manager who had a live-and-let-live attitude rather than operating from a gung-ho anti-public power position.

I agreed to call Frisbee, and did so at 7 p.m. that night. His initial reaction to my concern, after he had recognized me and greeted me warmly, was to dismiss the issue. His position was that the bills dealt with a local matter and, after all, "we try to get things some sessions and you try to get them the other sessions." He emphasized that the regional power plan was far above the state level, and people concerned with regional power shouldn't become embroiled. I politely but firmly pointed out that if we had guts and blood in the legislative halls at the Washington Legislature, the ill will between the two factions would undoubtedly carry over and affect the cooperative attempts between private power and public power on the Centralia coal-fired steam plant, as well as any type of arrangements before Congress.

I stated that it was clearly impossible for strong PUD Commissioners — and I used Harry Swenson of Grays Harbor County PUD as an example — who were strong Grange members as well, to allow their Districts to participate in the coal-fired steam plant at Centralia at the same time the private power companies were cutting the heart out of the basic public power law.

Frisbee said that Pacific Power and Light was having problems in financing because the presence of inactive PUDs in their service territories increased the cost of borrowing money. I pointed out that by "inactive" they meant those PUDs which were not in the electric business, but as far as we were concerned, any PUD that was in operation with the smallest of water systems was active.

I then explained just exactly what SB-304, the dissolution bill, did and how it would effectively block the activation of any future PUD as an electric utility. He responded by saying that he was not as close to these bills as he perhaps should be, that his men had attended a conference of the private companies on their legislative needs, and that his only interest was in dissolving the inactive PUD in Yakima County.

He then said that he would get in touch with his men and get back to me.

After talking to Frisbee, I called Bill Hulbert, Manager of the Snohomish County PUD, and John Nelson, Superintendent of Seattle City Light, who I knew were going to meet with Russ Richmond at Sea-Tac Airport on the next day, Monday, February 10, to discuss a possible application by the two utilities to construct a thermal plant on Puget Sound.

I emphasized to them that they should point out to Russ the impossibility of cooperating with private power if we were going to be under attack in the Washington Legislature.

The next morning, I got to thinking about my conversation with Frisbee and wondered whether he might misinterpret it. My purpose in calling him, as I had explained to him, was to determine whether or not this severe action at the Legislature was truly top management policy and to explain to him that if it was, we might as well gird up for an all-out war. Even though I might concede that they could win in the legislative arena in this particular session, my position, of course, was that we would then take them to a referendum vote across this State.

My fear was that he would think my call was an act of weakness based on a desire to avoid a fight. I therefore called Russ Richmond again and said, "If you have a chance to talk to Don Frisbee, be sure that he doesn't misinterpret the reason for my call." I emphasized to Russ that public power would gain by an all-out fight because such a fight would focus attention on the various aspects of private and public power in our State, to our benefit.

He said that he was just at that moment about to return a call to Frisbee and that he would be sure to inform him that my call had not been based on fear of a fight. Jokingly, and as an aside, I told Russ that if we did have a terrific fight, I would probably get a bigger raise afterward.

The meeting between Russ Richmond, John Nelson, and Bill Hulbert took place in Seattle at noon on February 10. They agreed that Nelson would try to set up a meeting between the top management of the private power companies and the five public agencies who were working on the Centralia coal-fired steam plant.

This meeting was held on Friday, February 14. Attending the meeting for private power were George Brunzell, President, and Kinsey Robinson, Chairman of the Board of The Washington Water Power Company; Ralph

Davis, President, and John Ellis, attorney and Board member, of the Puget Sound Power and Light Company; and Don Frisbee of Pacific Power and Light.

On the public power side were John Nelson, Superintendent of Seattle City Light; Clif Erdahl, Director of Utilities for Tacoma Light; Bill Hulbert, Manager of Snohomish County PUD; Glenn Hittle, Manager of Cowlitz County PUD; and Jack Stein, Manager of Grays Harbor County PUD.

I had previously touched base with John, Bill, Glenn and Jack and encouraged them to hit the thing pretty hard. Incidentally, John Nelson called and discussed whether or not it would be advisable for me to be present at this meeting and we agreed that I should not be there because my absence would keep the discussion clear of any political matters and certainly keep me out of the position of having to compromise on any particular legislation.

Reports of this meeting came to me from Jack Stein that afternoon and Glenn Hittle the following Monday morning. Bill Hulbert left on vacation to get some rest following the strike at Snohomish County PUD that had lasted for nearly 30 days. I did not hear from John Nelson.

Evidently the meeting had been quite positive in the sense that the public power people served notice on the private power management that a continuing conflict in the State Legislature could jeopardize joint ownership of the Centralia coal-fired steam plant. However, there was evidence that it had been what I would term a "three martini summit meeting," a lot of loud talking resulting in no definite agreement.

On the following Monday, February 17, at 3 p.m., I was called to a phone booth in the Third House, or Ulcer Gulch, area of the State Capitol by Dale Traylor, lobbyist for Puget Power. He stated that Larry Hall, one of the chief lobbyists for the private power forces who works out of the Bellevue office of Puget Power, was on the telephone and wanted to speak to me.

Larry asked if I would be willing to meet for dinner that night with Ralph Davis, President of Puget Power. He said Ralph was trying to make arrangements to have Brunzell, Washington Water Power President, and Frisbee, President of Pacific Power and Light, come to Seattle to meet with me. I said that it would be impossible to meet unless I could get some of my own people to join with me, but that I would try and call him back at 4 p.m. to either accept or turn down the invitation.

I called Arnold James, State Association President, but found that he was still down with the flu, having been in bed for five days at this time. I then called Ed Fischer, Commissioner of Clark County PUD, Chairman of our State Association Legislative Committee, to see whether he could make the meeting. He said he would check the airlines and if there were no flights he could even drive up, if he left immediately, and get to Seattle by 7 p.m.

I then called Glenn Hittle and Jack Stein, the two PUD Managers who had attended the previous management summit meeting. Hittle had a Board meeting that afternoon, so he was not available, and Stein said he thought perhaps it would be better if those who attended the previous meeting were not present at this one.

I then located Commissioner Ed Taylor of Mason County PUD No. 3 at his bank in Shelton and prevailed upon him to join us. I picked Ed Fischer up at Sea-Tac Airport at 6:15 p.m.

We met Ralph Davis; Wendell Satre, Executive Vice President of Washington Water Power (Brunzell was ill); and Don Frisbee at the Washington Athletic Club in Seattle at 7 p.m. After a congenial dinner, we immediately got into discussions and negotiations.

Don Frisbee said, "When we go to New York to raise funding, the bankers say they have to charge us higher rates because two votes in that Yakima PUD can 'cut the heart out of your service area in Washington.' " I responded, "Don, you control that PUD because you elect those stooge Commissioners." He said, "You know that and I know that—but the bankers use the PUD as an alibi to charge us higher interest." I said, "We don't like bankers charging your customers any more for your money than we like them to charge PUD customers higher interest rates. Let's think in terms of a different approach."

That afternoon, after the call from Larry Hall, I had done some thinking about what might be done, and had discussed it with Pat Comfort, our Republican legislative consultant.

Prior to leaving Olympia that afternoon, I contacted both Lars Nelson, Master of the State Grange, and Joe Davis, President of the State Labor Council. Both men assured me of their backing. As I drove north to Seattle, I pondered why our operating PUDs took so much legislative abuse to protect the captive PUDs of private power, such as Yakima, Lincoln, Kitsap, etc. Therefore, to set the stage, I told Davis, Satre, and Frisbee that if they pushed through any law which violated the basic PUD law as it now existed—and that I felt that they had the votes to do it—I could assure them that the Grange and Labor Council would help us refer such a law to the people. We would be locked in a private/public power political fight for 18 months (until the 1970 election), and private power might even win the election, but in the meantime the Centralia plant would go down the tube as a joint ownership plant, and the hydro-thermal program would also die. I said I wasn't saying this as a threat but just to outline to them what would happen beyond the control of any of us.

I said to them that what I was going to propose had not been discussed with anyone and, in fact, Ed Fischer and Ed Taylor, my two Commissioners present, had not heard this before. I then outlined this position. Any public utility district which was not in the electric business as of this date would have to go back and get a mandate majority vote from the local people before it could go into the electric business. The one requirement would be that it not be a "gimmick" vote. There would be no vote on condemnation, no vote on cost of acquiring private facilities, and no vote on bonds. It would be a direct ballot issue, stating, "Shall Public Utility District No. _____ of _____ County construct or acquire facilities for the generation, transmission, or distribution of electric energy? Yes _____/No _____." The question would be placed on the ballot either by the local PUD Commission already formed but not yet in the electric business, or by a petition signed by 10 percent of the qualified voters in a district, which was the way a PUD was formed in the first place under present law.

Ralph Davis responded immediately that this proposal might have some merit. I then stated that on the dissolution bill, we might as well understand each other: that the PUD Association made a distinction between a totally inactive PUD and one which provided water but didn't provide electricity. I stated that if they were going to insist that Stevens, Thurston, and Skagit County PUDs be dissolved just because they were operating water districts only, we might as well end the meeting, walk out of the room, and get ready for the fight in the Legislature.

On the other hand, I said that if I could wave a wand and get rid of the Yakima County PUD, I could care less because that district was a sham. The people might think they had a PUD, but as long as the private companies elected stooge Commissioners, they never would have a PUD in reality.

I recounted how we had drafted a bill in 1953 which would have let the Yakima PUD be dissolved using a petition signed by 10 percent of the voters to get it on the ballot but requiring a majority vote of the people to complete the dissolution.

This seemed to interest them. They responded by saying that undoubtedly there were some legislative bills which we were interested in getting enacted. I had previously made a mental list of five legislative changes we wanted, but I led off by saying there was nothing before the Legislature that we couldn't walk away from without regret and that, frankly, we had nothing with which to trade. But, on the basis of what we were now looking at in the Legislature, we could use clarification in the redistricting of PUD

Commissioner districts and we wanted to correct an inequity in PUD Commissioner salaries which now existed.

I stated that we were also interested in the issuance of revenue bonds to prepay power bills. This proposal met with immediate negative reaction from the private power presidents, and we got into quite a discussion of this issue for about 40 minutes. I could see that their approach was entirely emotional and the arguments they cited against the concept appeared fallacious. However, I stated, "Let's put that aside then. I merely wanted to call your attention to one of the things we are interested in doing."

The fourth legislative item of interest to us, I stated, concerned whether or not a tax would be paid by the Hanford Steam Plant. I said that we were in the midst of negotiating on this, but would prefer that the private power companies not turn it into a private versus public power issue.

Finally, I stated that it had come to my attention very recently that an informal letter from the Attorney General's office was raising the question of whether the PUDs could participate in the Public Power Council. Evidently, there was feeling in some quarters that the present statute prohibited this.

At this point, Ralph Davis said, "Why don't I get our attorneys to get something down on paper so that we might all look at it?" And on that note, the meeting adjourned around 11:45 p.m.

The next morning, it dawned on me that we ran the danger of doing the same thing again, of having the president have the attorney do something, who in turn would instruct the lobbyist, and I was fearful that with each layer of interest from the president to the attorney to the lobbyist, we would find ourselves again disagreeing about what it was exactly that I had said the previous night. I therefore went to my office early on Tuesday, February 18, and got out the old 1953 draft of dissolution and improved it. Not only would the bill prevent dissolution of any PUD operating any type of utility properties, including water and electricity, but it would also prevent dissolution of any PUD which had taken material action or made material studies toward constructing or acquiring utility facilities.

I then drafted wording concerning the activation vote, patterned on my outline of this the night before. Besides requiring presently existing PUDs to get a mandate before going into the electric business, I also said in this draft that any PUDs formed hereafter would have 10 years in which to get into the electric business before they would be required to get a second mandate from the people on a ballot which could be petitioned for by the local electors of an existing district.

I then attended a conference at the Olympic Hotel being held to tell the press and others about the Centralia coal-fired steam plant. At the noon luncheon, I gave my drafts to Ralph Davis, who handed them over to John Ellis, his attorney. Sure enough, Ellis said he had called Bob Simpson, the attorney for Washington Water Power, that morning because Simpson had been the one who had previously drafted the dissolution bill for the companies.

I returned to Olympia at 2 p.m. for a conference with people from the cooperatives over legislation they wanted to introduce that would hurt the PUDs.

Following this conference between my Legislative Committee members and the cooperative representatives, Jerry Buckley, lobbyist for Washington Water Power, contacted me and said that Bob Simpson, their attorney, was coming over the next day and they would like to meet me at 9 a.m. I said, fine, and on that basis I stood by until I heard from Jerry the next morning, when he said they needed a little more time and couldn't meet me until 12:30 p.m.

At 12:30, joined by Pat Comfort and Dan Brink, our legislative consultants and both good attorneys, I met with the representatives of the private power companies at the Tyee Motor Inn. These included Jack Lansing from the Portland office of Pacific Power and Light; Bruce Beaudoin, Pacific Power and Light; Dale Traylor, Puget Power; Jerry Buckley, Washington Water Power; Larry Hall, Puget Power; and the two attorneys, John Ellis, Puget Power, and Bob Simpson, Washington Water Power.

We went over the material and agreed on the activation bill and the dissolution bill. We then agreed that they would accept our salary bill and our redistricting bill as our attorneys had drafted them.

The final issue was the clarifying amendments to the PUD law to permit us to participate in the Public Power Council. I stated that I would immediately get in touch with some of our attorneys and get to work on this. Thursday, February 20, the attorneys of the Public Power Council met in Vancouver, Washington. I had previously told Shirley Marsh, attorney for Cowlitz County PUD, that I wanted some type of amendments.

That night I had a meeting of my Legislative Committee at the Tyee Motor Inn in Olympia at which time representatives from the attorney groups that had met in Vancouver came back and said that they had taken a position not to trade or compromise with the private power companies, that they did not feel they needed any changes.

I pointed out to them that maybe they didn't feel they needed any changes, but nevertheless we had a golden opportunity to get some broadening of the study powers of the PUDs, and we might even be able to get some amendments to give us a little broader power on other activities.

They tried to say that we would have to trade away the legislation allowing prepayment of power bills by issuance of revenue bonds, which was being introduced in the Legislature.

I had, incidentally, insisted that if this legislation was introduced, I would not call for a hearing or try to move the bill without agreement with the private power companies. I should also remark at this time that at the Monday night meeting, Ralph Davis had insisted that Puget Power wanted a territorial agreement bill which they would be introducing. I countered by saying there were certain changes which we had proposed when the same legislation was before the Legislature in 1967, and that, unless they incorporated these changes, we would have to stand opposed to it. But if they did make the changes we recommended, we would stand aside and, while not being in favor of the legislation, would not go out and actively fight it.

At our Legislative Committee meeting on February 20, I detailed all the past happenings and negotiations, and by a five-to-one vote, the Committee recommended that it be accepted and referred to the Board for approval on the following day.

February 21, Shirley Marsh, attorney for Cowlitz County PUD, came to Olympia and, working with Dan Brink and Dick Quigley, the WPPSS attorney, started to draft amendments to the omnibus PUD law bill which was now being prepared. They worked and reworked this draft over the weekend, and on Monday I brought it down and had it sent to the bill drafting room under the auspices of Representative Bob Charette of Grays Harbor.

Today, Tuesday, February 25, has been a rather busy one. I started at 7:30 a.m. working to get this legislation cleared. I have taken it through the Division of Municipal Corporations; discussed it briefly with the Attorney General's office, although Ken Ahlf was absent due to his father's illness; and presented it to the private power company lobbyists, who immediately placed me on the phone to Herb Schwab of the Pacific Power and Light legal staff and Bob Simpson of the Washington Water Power legal staff. Both of them accepted our amendments after prolonged discussion with me.

The Puget Power attorney, John Ellis, was not available that day, but I was to be advised if there was any problem with the wording which I proposed.

If the wording is accepted, then a substitute bill will be prepared to include our redistricting measure, the activation vote measure, the watered-down dissolution measure, the correction in the PUD Commissioners' salary measure, and this last broadening of the right of PUDs to participate in regional studies.

The substitute bill will take the place of the present wording of HB-140, which was originally introduced by the private power companies.

A hearing has been tentatively scheduled for the afternoon of Friday, February 28. In the meantime, I have discussed the substitute bill thoroughly with Joe Davis, President of the Washington State Labor Council; Lars Nelson, Master of the Washington State Grange, who sat in on my Legislative Committee meeting; and other Grange leaders. They agree that under present circumstances this is about the best we can do.

This brings the matter up to date to this moment. Whether or not the bill will hold together and move on through the Legislature is still to be determined. But it has been an interesting lesson on legislative activity to find that when one does not have the necessary votes inside the Legislature, one can move outside and try to find other avenues to stop legislation which might have been passed and surely would have damaged the public power program.

And thus, good night at 11:40 p.m.

This is being dictated on March 2, 1969.

As stated previously, I had submitted the last section of the proposed omnibus bill to the private power companies on Tuesday, February 25. I had, incidentally, dug out former HB-188, a bill introduced by the PUD Association in 1965 to amend the law to allow the PUDs specific rights to advertise and promote the sale and distribution of electricity and water. This bill had been resoundingly rejected by the private power lobbyists in 1965 on the basis that it would permit us to hire special employees to carry on a political campaign in the inactive PUD areas. The argument was fallacious but it was convincing enough to scare the legislators and the bill was defeated.

I decided that, while the omnibus bill was going through, and since the Division of Municipal Corporations had previously told us that such a change in the PUD law would eliminate the grey area on the matter in State examinations, I would insist that this amendment go into the omnibus bill.

However, just before noon on Wednesday, February 26, I received a call from Larry Hall of Puget Power, who was greatly concerned over the wording which we had proposed in this new section. From there on, for the next 24 hours, there was a battle by telephone calls with practically every private power attorney in the Pacific Northwest.

On Thursday afternoon, after I had journeyed to Seattle and spent the full morning negotiating directly with the Puget Power people via telephone, I returned to Olympia and met Shirley Marsh, attorney for Cowlitz County PUD, who had come north to assist. We worked all afternoon and by 5:30 p.m. we had finally come to a negotiated settlement on this section.

It dawned on me as I drove back to Olympia that what had happened was that Schwab, the attorney for Pacific Power and Light, had given his approval first, followed by acceptance by Bob Simpson. Then perhaps they realized that they might have been too hasty in accepting our wording. It was then left up to John Ellis, attorney for Puget Power, to get them off the hook.

I thus found that in the negotiations we were being bounced back and forth among the companies. However, the final settlement was satisfactory and we then went into high gear. On Friday morning, I put the omnibus bill together in order to appear at 1 p.m. before the House Committee on State Government and Legislative Procedures.

Since the bill comprised amendments to the PUD law, I made the presentation. I was accompanied to the hearing by Arnold James (Lewis County), my State Association President; Ed Fischer (Clark County), Chairman of our Legislative Committee; and two Committee members, John Toevs (Grant County) and Walt Jones (Snohomish County).

After my presentation, the private power companies seconded and endorsed the bill. It moved very rapidly out of the Committee.

One amusing but highly acceptable sidelight was that in preparing the part of the bill to have the salary of a PUD Commissioner specifically set by the Legislature, we had not changed any of the conditions or amounts in the salary or per diem from those in the original bill. When I was questioned about this, I stated we had not wanted to cause any controversy, but I did highly recommend that the amounts be increased, since a previous survey showed that the people favored an increase. Therefore, before Substitute HB-140, which was the bill to be scalped and have the omnibus bill tacked on to it, came out of the Committee, the Committee on its own initiative increased the per diem of PUD Commissioner compensation to an allowable maximum of $35 per day and $5,000 per year. This came entirely as a surprise to me. Yet I imagine there will be those who will say that the PUDs sold out to the private power companies, trading the requirement for a vote to activate a district and a dissolution statute for a bigger per diem and a specific salary for PUD Commissioners. Nothing could be farther from the truth, since all Commissioners insisted that there be no trade on any of the "housekeeping" matters in the Legislature, including their own compensation.

This had indeed been a very interesting three weeks and, on balance, I think it has meant some specific gains for public power.

First, it has now removed one of the propaganda points which could be made by the private power companies: that the law provides no way to dissolve a PUD once it is formed. To the uninformed person, this was a big issue during any PUD formation election.

Second, the requirement that a majority vote be secured to activate an electric PUD is truly in the public interest, when we consider that formerly, to activate an inactive PUD through the election of new Commissioners meant that the people in a given district had to win two elections based on personalities and people rather than on issues. Now, they have a specific activation vote which can be demanded by local people by means of a petition signed by 10 percent of the electors of the district. I hope we will see moves for some activation votes.

At any rate, this law takes the propaganda slogan of "the people's right to vote" away from the private companies, who sought to use it as an umbrella to cover condemnation rights and to set a floor under the price of acquiring their property.

It will be rather hard for them to ever go back and amend the law and insist that the price, or bonds, or some other thing, be included in the activation vote rather than making it a separate ballot issue. And most certainly, the broader powers of the PUD to participate in regional surveys and other contracting matters benefit us.

It's been a good session so far.

———

Thus ended my personal file dictation in 1969. Substitute HB-140 passed the Legislature in record time with both private and public power lobbyists behind it. It was agreed to on February 27. A hearing was held on February 28 in Committee and the bill passed the House on March 5 by an 88 to 6 vote. Over on the Senate side, the bill was heard in Committee on a Saturday, March 8, reported in and out of Rules on Sunday, March 9, and passed by the Senate March 10 by a 46 to 1 vote at 5:40 p.m. just before a 6 p.m. cut-off deadline. The House concurred with some minor amendments made in the Senate on Wednesday, March 12, by a vote of 92 to 0. When Governor Evans signed Substitute HB-140 on March 25, a legislative compromise was reached that ended the long-time legislative fights between private and public power. Within a year, we were to find ourselves as allies on the legislative scenes in Olympia and Washington, D.C.

Governor Daniel J. Evans signs Substitute House Bill 140, the compromise legislation that ended private/public power fights in the Legislature. *Left to right:* Ken Billington, Executive Director, Washington PUD Association; Arnold James, Commissioner, Lewis County PUD, and Association President; Governor Evans; Ed Fischer, Commissioner, Clark County PUD, and Chairman of the PUD Association Legislative Committee.

On May 2, just before the adjournment of the First Extraordinary Session which had followed the regular session, Ward Bowden, Secretary of the State Senate, died of a heart attack. I remembered his fairness to me in 1967 when I needed help in the terrific legislative fight private power was waging against public power. At my request he provided a delay in the reading in on the Senate side of a House-passed pro-private power warped bill on which I needed time to work out a defense for public power. He was criticized for this by some, but he knew that I had been double-dealt on the issue and he wanted to be fair.

One sidelight to the 1969 Session and the "peace pipe" between private and public power in the legislative arena was my relationship with Representative Bob Perry. Perry was a very effective legislator — bright, forceful, and tough. He had joined private power early after his arrival in 1959, at the 36th Session, and was still with them when he left after the 44th Session in 1976. There will be later reference to my part of the "Bob Perry" legislative story — but suffice it to say, he was a tough opponent until the 1969 Session. Following the declaration of peace between private and public power, it was Perry who maneuvered a salary increase for the PUD Commissioners, but what was of more personal interest was what he did when he learned that my wife and I were going to the Far East—Japan, Hong Kong, etc.—to meet our son who was to get his first R&R leave from his Vietnam war duty.

Our son, Brad, was a young doctor who had received special training by the Army to do wartime orthopedic surgery. Brad called me in the spring of 1968 and, not finding me in Seattle, located me in Senator Scoop Jackson's office. He asked me to find out while I was in Washington, D.C., how he could apply for this special training, since he was single, would be going to Vietnam, and wanted to go as an orthopedic surgeon. Scoop overheard the conversation and when I explained it he offered to take care of it. I told him that in all the time I had known him, since the early 1940s, I had never asked him for a personal favor. His response was that it wasn't a personal favor: they needed doctors in Vietnam. At any rate, Brad spent the whole year of 1969, except for his 10 days of R&R in September, at the 27th Surgical Hospital at Chu Lai, right off the front line helicopter pad.

When Bob Perry learned that we were going to Hong Kong, he insisted that he would get in touch with a Sam Lee, a Korean gentleman who had been helping Bob's employer, Tyee Construction Company, secure construction work in the Far East, including Vietnam. We met Brad in Tokyo and then progressed to Hong Kong, where my wife and I had a lovely dinner with Lee and his wife. Little did I realize that this was the man who would turn up in the accusations, indictments, and prison terms involving Perry and Jerry Buckley, my Washington Water Power lobbyist friend, in later years. But at least, I have firsthand knowledge that there was a Sam Lee in Hong Kong in 1969.

One additional chore I was called upon to do in 1969 was to allocate representation among the PUDs, rural electric cooperatives, and city light systems on the Participants Review Board established by Bonneville to provide it with input from the utilities about budgets, costs, activities, and other matters dealing with the plants being constructed by the Supply System under net billing arrangements with Bonneville. Here again, I found myself in the role of senior statesman reasoning with the multitude of utilities in the four states that would receive power from the projects—who were all in the same boat. My allocation proposal was presented to the Public Power Council in Idaho Falls on June 19, 1969—and was accepted by it and thence by Bonneville. Since only municipal corporations of the State of Washington could become members of the Supply System, the Participants Review Board seemed like a logical and fair way for Bonneville to give other utilities the chance to review plant construction progress.

Phase I of the Hydro-Thermal Accord had been announced to the public and Congress just before the 1968 elections, and was formalized in April

1969, with seven proposed steam plants included – two coal-fired and five nuclear. With the election of President Nixon, the question was whether the new Administration would approve it. It was with satisfaction that the Secretary of the Interior, Walter Hickel, on October 27, 1969, approved the Pacific Northwest regional power supply program. Pacific Northwest utilities could breathe a little easier for the moment.

A closing highlight of 1969 for the Association and me was our presentation of the first William T. Elmgren Award. Bill Elmgren had been a long-time public power cohort of mine. We were serving together on the Ruling Board of Elders of the First Presbyterian Church in Vancouver in 1946 when the church got entangled in the private versus public power fight. Later, Bill went to work as I did for the Clark County PUD. When he retired, he was elected as a Commissioner for the PUD, serving from December 1954 to August 1963, when he resigned for health reasons. He served as the Association's President in 1961. Following his death, his family proposed that an annual award be made by the Association in his name to a PUD employee nominated by any district for volunteer public, community, and church service. The Association's Executive Committee and Executive Director would select the winner from those nominated. Tough decisions were to follow because so many outstanding PUD employees who were active in the community were nominated for the award.

The year 1970 was to see a new procedure in the Legislature. Ever since the convening of the first legislative session of our State on November 6, 1889, different Legislatures had found the need to hold what is termed an Extraordinary Session. The State Constitution had limited the legislative session to sixty calendar days but there had been occasions in the past on which by pulling the flag over the clock, members had extended a regular session beyond the constitutional limit. When challenges began to be made to this practice, the Legislature, as government became more complex, would adjourn on the required constitutional date and then immediately go into an Extraordinary Session.

Starting in 1959, these Extraordinary Sessions seemed to be a regular need. I don't know if getting new individual offices in 1969 encouraged the legislators in this trend, but 1970 saw the convening for the first time in our State's history of a Second Extraordinary Session. While it was to last only thirty-two days, it was a full-blown session and very important from the utilities' standpoint.

Following the legislative peace-making between private and public power in the 1969 Legislature, action on the construction of the coal-fired steam plant at Centralia proceeded with dispatch. The four public power utilities of Seattle City Light, Tacoma Light, Snohomish County PUD, and Grays Harbor County PUD signed on as joint ownership ,partners earmarking 28 percent of the power to be generated for export to the Central Valley Project in California. This made good on the Pacific Northwest's commitment made back in 1964 when the federal legislation authorizing the interties was enacted.

However, many licensing headaches followed. A multitude of state permits and licenses and approvals had to be obtained for the construction of a plant. All this paperwork was confusing enough, but in addition we found direct conflict between various State agencies as to which had jurisdiction over the various licenses and permits. The utilities recognized that this would be one of many such plants to be constructed in the State of Washington and felt that there should be some way of establishing a one-stop procedure whereby all State agencies with authority to issue licenses and permits could get together to grant a utility one certificate covering all approval required from the State to build a given plant on a given site.

About this time, strong movement was occurring in the environmental protection field. The Washington Environmental Council had been organized and John Miller, a young attorney, was lobbyist for the Council. Later, he was to serve on the Seattle City Council and then be elected to Congress in 1984 from the 1st District. The Council comprised those persons and organizations promoting improvement and protection of the general environment, the fisheries, and wildlife. Many requests from environmentalists had landed on Governor Evans' desk and shoulders and, therefore, the special Second Extraordinary Session of the Legislature was going to see a number of Governor Executive Request 'bills to deal with these and other special needs of the State. While the environmental groups were asking for a new Department of Ecology, the utilities were asking for a one-stop licensing procedure governing the construction of thermal plants. The efforts of these two interests were to meet head-on in the legislative arena, but in this instance private power and public power were working together.

A new procedure had been adopted by the Legislature that allowed bills to be filed prior to the convening date of the session so that public hearings could be scheduled during the very first week of the session. It was a bit odd to receive at my home on Saturday, January 10, a notice that a public hearing would be held on the afternoon of Thursday, January 15, on a bill which would not be introduced into the Legislature and available for us to study until January 13, 1970. This posed a problem for me because there was no way to determine the policy or position of the people I represented when I couldn't even tell them what the bill was all about. I lucked out on this particular bill because my Legislative Committee and a number of the managers had to be in Olympia on another matter on Tuesday, January 13, and could give me my marching orders.

To shorten this Second Extraordinary Session, a joint rule limited introduction of legislation to a one-week period, but over 180 bills were introduced on each side on the last day. One of the Executive Request bills, HB-49 and SB-49, would govern procedures for the location of thermal plants. In the meantime, the Washington Environmental Council came up with a bill to accomplish the same purpose. After an initial meeting of the utility people, it was decided that a third bill in the form of a substitute for the Governor's legislation would be drafted, and we started work on this bill immediately.

On Monday, January 26, a joint discussion session for representatives of the Governor's office, the environmentalists, and the utilities was held before the House and Senate Joint Committee on Nuclear Energy to sort out any differences which might remain over the three bills. To meet a legislative deadline, the Senate passed an amended SB-49, the Thermal Plant Siting legislation, on January 31. This was changed substantially from the original Executive Request bill.

In preparation for House action, the Joint Committee on Nuclear Energy asked representatives of the Governor's staff to draft legislation, the environmentalists to draft theirs, and the utilities to draft theirs. At a meeting the Committee accepted the utilities' substitute bill as the one it would recommend. Following that, all groups were called back before that Committee, at which time the Governor's representatives definitely stated that the Governor would not compromise the basic concept contained in his original Executive Request bill. The Joint Committee then stated that it would assume the responsibility of coming up with a draft that would be acceptable to all of us.

Some terrific behind-the-scenes activity took place on negotiations. I was having lunch with Len Jensen, attorney representing the Rural Electric Cooperatives in this matter, when Senator Mike McCormack, member of the Joint Committee, came by our table and hurriedly dropped off a draft, stating that he had to have it back by 1:45 p.m. and that if we wanted any changes, we would have to make them before then. We made a hasty exit back to my motel, went through the draft as hurriedly as we could, and marked certain changes which we felt were essential. I then returned the draft to McCormack.

At 8 p.m., we were furnished a draft of the so-called Committee Amendment to SB-49, the Governor's Executive Request legislation. After one final revision session the bill was reported out of the Senate Committee and placed in Rules. On Saturday, January 31, it went through the Senate. There had been a shift in action because it was first contemplated that the measure would come from the Republican-controlled House to the Democratic Senate, but this was reversed in order to assure the Governor that the Republican-controlled House would have the last shot at the bill. By this time we had resolved all our differences with the Governor's office, with the exception of a finality phrase we wanted in the severability clause to ensure that once a certificate was granted for construction to go forward on a project, the conditions of the certificate would be final, not subject to challenges or changes.

The Joint Committee then went into executive session and came forth with a complete House Committee amendment to SB-49. The Committee had accepted all of the utility recommendations. It was then brought to our attention that while we had provided an exemption in the act for the Centralia coal-fired steam plant, we had overlooked exempting the presently operating Hanford Plant. Our only method of correcting this was by a floor amendment which would be rather difficult to pass after everyone had agreed on the Committee amendment. However, we asked that the amendment be attached and secured the support of the two representatives from the Benton-Franklin area. The bill was scheduled for House floor action on Thursday, February 5. The Governor at this point called the president of one of the private power companies and got the president's agreement to withdraw his insistence on retaining the finality phrase in the severability clause. I checked on this and learned that while the Governor had not proven to the president that the phrase was unconstitutional, the president felt that it would be of little value to oppose the Governor's position. Actually, the Governor could have removed the finality phrase by the item veto method anyway. I checked with our attorneys from Snohomish County PUD and Grays Harbor County PUD, and while they were reluctant to have the phrase removed, they agreed that politics would decide what was done at this stage. One of the other private power companies, upon being contacted, said it wished to keep the finality phrase, but upon reflection joined the view that opposition to the Governor on this particular point was not essential. I therefore told the Governor's representative that two of the privately owned utilities would concede the point and that the PUDs would join them in this position. I emphasized that the Governor should understand that this conditional severability clause had been strongly supported on the Democratic Senate side; I also stated that we could not answer for the municipals or the cooperatives other than to say they would want to keep the phrase, and that one of the privately owned utilities had not been contacted as yet.

At this stage of the game, one of the flukes which can happen in legislative halls occurred. Since the House was under call, there was no way for us to contact legislators to advise them of our change of position. Thus, when SB-49 was considered, the first floor amendment, which was to cover the Hanford exemption, was adopted. When the next floor amendment, to delete the finality phrase from the severability clause in line with the Governor's position, was presented, Representatives Dan Jolly and Bob Perry, both of whom we had been unable to contact because of the call, took the position that the utilities had not agreed to this, which, in fact, had been the case up to about one hour before. The House rejected the proposed amendment 80 to 16. SB-49, as amended by the House Committee and our one floor amendment, was then approved 96 to 3. The Senate then concurred in the House amendments to the bill and it was forwarded to the Governor's desk with the severability clause worded as we had originally requested it. Fortunately, at that time, the Attorney General came forth with an opinion that the finality phrase was constitutional, after which the Governor's office signaled his willingness to sign the legislation, and he did so.

This was to be the first State in the Union to enact legislation covering all the ramifications of thermal plant siting. The law balanced environmental needs and concerns with the needs of a utility to get a final answer and full licensing and permit procedures in place.

Another very important piece of legislation was passed in this session from the Democratic-controlled Senate. In the final hours of the session, a compromise was effected between the Governor's request for a Department of Environmental Quality and the Senate version asking for establishment of a Board of Appeals and more citizen participation in environmental matters. The Governor was trying to consolidate a number of existing State departments, at the same time that the environmentalists wanted to maintain lay citizen representation on environmental commissions. The result was a new Department of Ecology with a strong director, which consolidated a number of co-departments which dealt with water and area resources, a lay advisory commission composed of seven citizens, and a formal appeals board. The new department was a compromise for all parties, with the Governor, environmentalists, and a Democratic Senate each getting a part of their request. Since the new department would have to participate in the new Thermal Power Plant Site Evaluation Council as one of a number of State agencies from which a utility applicant for a thermal plant site could secure total and final state approval, the utilities felt that establishment of this new department was proper.

Since the 1969 Legislature, the privately and publicly owned utilities had been cooperating on matters of mutual interest. It was rather difficult for a person such as myself to adjust to this state of affairs. After 31 years of some of the most vicious anti-public power fights brought on by the private power people, it was a bit strange. I could look back on the many months of the legislative sessions in the last twenty years when my own personal, physical, and mental resources were taxed to the breaking point from trying to stem the tide of private power attacks on public power. The management personnel of the private power companies were all very accomplished individuals. They were very intelligent and they had a lot of resources, especially money, when it came to playing politics.

I thought back to 1953 when there was a delicate balance in the Legislature between private and public power. In that session, public power won a basic issue in the House by one vote. Over in the Senate, public power could not pass anything it wanted, but it had 24 votes with which to block private power's efforts to hamstring the public power laws. While public power was in a somewhat better position in 1955, because a Democratic majority had been elected to the House of Representatives on a public power philosophy and platform, it could not do much more than hold the line. In 1957, public power was strong in both the House and the Senate, and we elected a Governor who had run for office on a public power platform and who had even used a personal endorsement from me in his election bid. The sessions in 1957 and 1959 saw the most constructive work on improving the basic PUD law. These covered taxes, purchasing, creation of subdistricts, and the excellent revenue bond financing amendment passed in 1959. Then, in 1959, private power started to make inroads on the Democratic side of the political aisle and, by 1961, private power had started to gain control of the Legislature. We held the line until 1967, but by 1969 it became apparent that private power finally had secured majorities in both the Senate and House. Only by use of outside pressures on top private power management had we been able to force the compromise settlement and thus start the "new look" in cooperation on legislative matters. By 1970, we were working jointly on the thermal plant siting bill.

However, in May 1970, I spent a very interesting morning session in a conference at the Portland General Electric conference room in Portland, Oregon. The purpose of the meeting was to discuss what steps should be taken on some federal legislation, S-940, the Snake River moratorium bill of Senators Jordan and Church, as it landed in the House of Representatives. The bill had been referred to the Committee on Interstate Commerce.

Seated around the table that morning were the top level lobbyists of the investor-owned utilities in the Pacific Northwest: Bob Short of Portland General Electric; Joe McElwain of Montana Power; Jerry Buckley of Washington Water Power; Ralph Milsap, Public Relations Director of Portland General Electric; Clem Sterns of the Pacific Northwest Power Company; Hugh Smith, attorney for the Pacific Northwest Power Company; and several other political wheels of private power.

It was interesting to see how they operated. Their attitudes were very severe and at times somewhat sarcastically critical of each other. What jolted me even more was the matter-of-fact manner in which they worked on their agenda, made their assignments, discussed individuals, etc. They were just like generals mapping out battle plans. I was a little bit dismayed by their cynicism when they spoke of members of Congress.

For example, if they needed the support of a congressman from a particular part of the country, their method would be to get hold of a private power executive in that area and talk as if the congressman were owned by the utility. While I recognized after many years in the legislative field that things do not work in just that manner, it kind of scared me to think that corporate strength might be exercised this way.

It is true, however, that I had heard strong labor leaders talk about certain legislators in the same way.

Just before the noon lunch, I thought I would have a little fun with them. Looking across at Hugh Smith, who had been an arch opponent of public power for many, many years and whose father, Allen Smith, was one of the first antagonists I tangled with at the State Legislature in 1951, I said, "Hugh, I have often wondered when I have had so many bloody ears down at the State Legislature just how you fellows gathered your strength to go on the offensive. Today I have had the right to sit in' the inner council and really see you guys operate. If I were a younger man, or if I felt the old private/public power fight was going to erupt again very soon, frankly, this would scare me." Hugh's response was simply, "Ken, while you were bleeding about the ears, we were bleeding all over. In fact, when Buckley was hired at Washington Water Power, he was instructed to go in and study the methods and manners of Billington so that he would become a success in the legislative lobbying field."

While I don't know how much truth there was to that, certainly it was, indeed, an experience to watch those top private power political wheels turn. But their style and tactics were not mine, and thus I found myself somewhat out of step with private power in our mutual lobbying efforts under our new truce. It was harder in the old days but I did not have to operate in circles where sarcasm and cynicism about our elected officials seemed to be the general attitude. Thinking back now, I believe that corporate arrogance was probably one of the reasons public power had done so well with less money and fewer paid lobbyists and no "subsidized prominent citizens."

Coming out of the Second Extraordinary Session of the Legislature on February 12, 1970, the utility industry in the State was faced with the problem of participating in the organizing of the new Thermal Plant Site Evaluation Council and the adoption of rules of procedure by that Council. Already there was considerable action by persons opposed to the construction of nuclear power plants in the State. A lot of this opposition was concentrated in Grays Harbor County where the Supply System was studying the feasibility of constructing a nuclear plant at Roosevelt Beach, north of Hoquiam.

State Senator Mike McCormack had served as Vice Chairman of the Joint Committee on Nuclear Energy during the legislative session and had been of much assistance in mediating the differences between the utilities and the environmental groups on the final draft of the new legislation for thermal plant siting. McCormack had also given strong legislative support for a number of years to defeating the Columbia Interstate Compact. Word was circulating that he might be a Democratic opponent of Republican Congresswoman Catherine May when she came up for re-election. He worked as a research scientist for Battelle Northwest on the Hanford Reservation, and it was clear that if continued in that job, he would be more or less limited to that local area. He approached me and suggested that I make use of his services as a consultant, which I readily recognized as being worthwhile. He could help greatly in getting good rules adopted by the Siting Council and in carrying the message in favor of constructing nuclear plants west of the Cascades.

I therefore placed a call to Congresswoman May on February 17, stating that McCormack had approached me on this matter and that I could make good use of his services, but that the word was circulating that he might be an opponent of hers in her coming election next November. I have always admired the lady's response. She said, "Ken, if it isn't Mike, it will be someone else, because no one will get a free ride in the coming election. Most certainly, if you can use his services, don't hesitate to do so. There is a lot of misunderstanding these days on the use of nuclear energy for power plants.

So go right ahead. Mike is a good guy." I assured her that if we used his services, it would definitely be with the understanding that on the day he announced his candidacy for Congress, we would terminate his contract.

We retained McCormack as a consultant. He resigned his job at Hanford, and while he was worth more than we paid him for the work he did for us, there is no question in my mind that being free from a routine day-to-day job out on the Hanford Reservation afforded him the opportunity to get organized with statewide contacts to run in the November election against Congresswoman May. McCormack announced his candidacy on July 15, and I terminated his contract. He was elected to Congress. Several times from around the State, local Commissioners and Managers were hit by Republican leaders with the question of what the Association was up to with McCormack. I told them to refer the leaders to Catherine May, who understood the matter and had given her blessing to the arrangement.

The year 1970 was to see local public power witness another eventful step, the reorganization of the Supply System to make its management more effective as it started its nuclear plant construction program. As a result of the reorganization, the larger public power systems, such as Seattle City Light and Tacoma Light, joined the Supply System, and I found myself in the difficult personal position of having to buck my long-term friend Owen Hurd, who was Managing Director of the Supply System.

We had successfully come through the 1970 Legislative Session and had obtained a one-stop procedure for State certification of thermal plants. The Supply System had responded to a request of the Public Power Council that it replace Eugene Water and Electric Board's plant in the Hydro-Thermal Phase I schedule and become the sponsor and constructor of the first thermal plant totally owned by public power. The Eugene voters had blocked their plant's construction. The Supply System was trying to get a permit to locate a nuclear plant at the Roosevelt Beach site, north of Hoquiam. Simultaneously, Snohomish County PUD and Seattle City Light purchased a potential nuclear plant site on Kiket Island in north Puget Sound. Clark County PUD and Cowlitz County PUD had already purchased property on the north side of the Columbia River near Kalama as a potential thermal plant site.

I could sense that unless an effort was made to consolidate the individual efforts of local public power to construct thermal plants, some of the larger utilities would be splitting off and, in my opinion, thereby fracturing the financial backing we would need to contruct these large plants. Conflict had arisen previously between management of the individual utilities and management of the Supply System, and we had been able to resolve it, but there still seemed to be a need to balance the participation by a large utility with the participation by a small utility in any joint undertaking to construct a thermal plant. Under net billing, a plant could pay for itself out of its revenues once it was operating, but the necessary preliminary costs were substantial and therefore participation by all of local public power was essential in my opinion.

Therefore, at my June 19, 1970, Board of Directors meeting, I issued a white paper calling for substantial reorganization of the Supply System. At that time, the Supply System had 17 public utility districts and the City of Richland as members. One problem I could see coming was the composition of the Board of Directors. Under municipal corporation laws, which governed PUDs and the Supply System, only the Board could take final action on the awarding or changing of contracts, the setting of budgets, and the approving of expenditures. There had been times in the construction of the large dams on the Columbia River by the public utility districts that the Board of Commissioners was in daily sessions to make the necessary decisions. It therefore appeared that a more streamlined system of control would have to be established in order to efficiently operate the Supply System in its construction of the large thermal plants.

In my white paper, I proposed that a new Board of Directors composed of five representatives be established. The change was extreme, but it emphasized the need to balance a large utility interest with a smaller utility interest. I suggested that one Board member be from Seattle City Light; one from Snohomish County PUD; one that would represent the other municipals, such as Tacoma and Richland; one that would represent the three public utility districts of Cowlitz, Clark, and Grays Harbor; and one that would represent the voluntary members of other State of Washington public utility districts.

Needless to say, my white paper evoked considerable comment for and against my proposal to reorganize the Supply System. The result was a special meeting in early July of various PUD people from throughout the State, at which a consensus proposed that a special Supply System Board meeting should be called to consider adoption of a resolution establishing a committee to review and revise the rules whereby the restructuring of the Supply System would take place. The decision was made that a total Board, composed of one representative from each member of the Supply System, would be retained, but that a strong Executive Committee, numbering no more than seven, would be delegated broad policy powers and the right to take action by the Board. By mid-August I was called upon to allocate the seven positions of the new Executive Committee among the public power utilities in the State.

Based on the number of customers, gross revenues, and annual kilo-watt-hour sales, I proposed that the new rule establishing the Executive Committee designate one member for the Snohomish County PUD; one for the City of Seattle; one for Tacoma and other municipal systems which might join the Supply System; one for the five western Washington PUDs of Clallam, Grays Harbor, Lewis, Mason No. 3, and Pacific; one for Cowlitz and Whakiakum PUDs; one for Clark, Skamania, and Klickitat PUDs; and one for the PUDs located in eastern Washington. This latter assignment raised questions about why only one member was allotted to the eastern Washington PUDs, but as I pointed out, the only two PUDs of any major size which would be requiring a substantial power supply were Benton and Franklin PUDs, since the others already had a substantial potential power supply. Another issue raised at this time was that the City of Seattle and the City of Tacoma had not affiliated with the Supply System, but as I pointed out, the only way those two larger utility systems would participate would be if they felt they would have a significant role in the decision-making process on thermal plant construction. The rule adopted provided for a five-person Executive Committee that would be increased to seven if Seattle and Tacoma joined. To make certain that these positions would be reserved, this allotment rule was assured for a minimum of five years.

Following completion of the reorganization, I immediately launched a campaign to get the City of Seattle and the City of Tacoma to join. In 1971, the City of Seattle joined by unanimous action of the City Council over the objection of Mayor Wes Uhlman. It was not until 1972, when Aldo J. Benedetti had replaced Clif Erdahl as Director of Utilities in Tacoma, that Tacoma joined the Supply System.

I have no way of knowing whether this reorganization hastened the retirement of Owen Hurd from his position as Managing Director of the Supply System, but he did retire in June 1971. I always hoped the change was not responsible for his retirement, but it was made without his endorsement or support. This reorganization meant that future participation by local public power in the Hydro-Thermal Accord would be stronger with Seattle and Tacoma joining the efforts of the PUDs.

In early October 1970, Owen Hurd and I were meeting with Russ Richmond, Bonneville Administrator, in Portland when Hurd received a call from a member of his staff from Olympia, where the Supply System was preparing for a site certificate application before the Thermal Plant Site Evaluation Council for the Roosevelt Beach site. The staff member relayed that in a conference with the State Fisheries Department he was informed that they were going to require an upfront appropriation of $2 million and a postponement of the construction of the Roosevelt site for six years so that they could undertake an extensive study of the effect a thermal plant would have on the clam population at the coastal site.

The information shook all three of us, because in no way could we contemplate, under the then forecasted power needs, a postponement of six years in the construction of this thermal plant. I can't recall who said it first, but one of us said, "Let's move to Hanford." I recall that Richmond said he would like to alert the congressional delegation to the change, and we agreed to do that. It was also at this meeting that Richmond outlined to us the current "equal opportunity" policies of the federal government which encouraged smaller contracts and more contractors. I told Richmond that this would be no problem. Under the law governing mandatory public bidding by PUDs and operating agencies in the State of Washington, any amount of work or equipment in excess of $10,000 would require competitive bids. I did not realize that this policy would be one of the future headaches of the Supply System. At that moment it permitted us to say to the federal government, "We cannot only do the job but we can do it better from your standpoint."

On November 7, the Supply System Board authorized construction of Nuclear Project No. 2 on the Hanford Reservation, after which they filed a site application with the new Thermal Plant Site Evaluation Council in early 1971.

Three other events of note occurred in 1970. First, new Attorney General Slade Gorton appeared before my Board on January 16 with bad news about the fee-splitting by the lawyers who prosecuted the antitrust bid-rigging lawsuit against electrical equipment manufacturers started back in 1961 under Attorney General O'Connell. A settlement of $16.3 million had been made, and an original fee of $1 million to the special counsel retained for the case had been increased to $2.3 million prior to Gorton's assuming the office in 1969. I was in near shock as were many of the other public power people in the room.

The second event was publication of the new interpretations by the Treasury Department regarding the use of tax-exempt revenue bonds to finance power producing and transmitting facilities. In 1969, Congress had passed laws to curtail and control the issuance of tax-exempt revenue bonds by local governmental agencies which used the proceeds to finance and build facilities for private corporations. The primary abuses of the agencies' right to issue bonds were in the issuance of so-called industrial development bonds. Here in the State of Washington, a clause in the State

Constitution prohibiting any grant of public funds for private use was controlling and limiting the practice, but nationwide this tax loophole needed to be closed. However, when Klickitat County PUD started to issue some revenue bonds to finance a major substation to sell electricity to a new industrial load, its use of tax-exempt financing was challenged.

About then, a question was raised over the issuance of municipal tax-exempt revenue bonds by the public power utility partners in the Centralia coal-fired steam plant.

I was drawn into the matter by the bond attorneys, who asked if I could secure congressional support to make sure the new regulations did not destroy the right to use tax-exempt financing for legitimate public power utility purposes. This gave me another chance to witness not only the political strength of Senators Magnuson and Jackson of our State, joined and supported by the strength of Congresswoman Julia Butler Hansen, but also the strength of the other six senators from the Pacific Northwest states of Oregon, Idaho, and Montana. One of my treasures is a copy of a letter dated September 17, 1970, addressed to Secretary of the Treasury David M. Kennedy and signed by Magnuson and Jackson, joined by Senators Mansfield and Metcalf of Montana, Senators Jordan and Church of Idaho, and Senators Hatfield and Packwood of Oregon. I was writing letters of thanks for this letter to Magnuson and Jackson on October 8, 1970. The rightful use of tax-exempt municipal revenue bonds by city light and PUD utilities would continue.

The third event was a plus. Tension had been mounting in parts of the State in the form of territorial disputes between the rural electric cooperatives and certain PUDs. We had already lived through the unfortunate dispute between Pend Oreille County PUD and the Inland Power and Light Company. I had gone through several legislative sessions where private power had tried to pass restrictive laws under the guise of territorial limitation but in words which would forbid any extension of public power in the State.

In 1969, however, based on private power's strength in the legislative arena and our making peace, a law was enacted which provided that public utilities (private power, PUDs, and city systems) and rural electric cooperatives could enter into voluntary territorial agreements on service areas. It did contain wording which the city systems didn't like, stating a "legislative intent against duplication of lines," but it did not contain any wording affecting the right of a PUD to take over private power lines.

To augment this law and relieve growing tension, I contacted the Executive of the Washington Rural Electric Cooperative Association and suggested we work out a contractual agreement to govern territorial conflicts. Since the cooperatives served more rural customers than the PUDs, they did have higher rates in a number of joint service areas. Thus, some cooperative customers would demand of their local PUD that they be granted PUD service. Sometimes the PUD and co-op lines were just across the road from each other. Actually, the PUD didn't have the right to refuse service to a local resident of the District, and if there was a legal challenge, the PUD would have to give such service. Thus, a territorial service agreement between my State PUD Association and the Washington Rural Electric Cooperative Association was approved and signed on December 2, 1970. While the agreement could not bind anyone, it set up an orderly procedure for arbitration in those instances where territorial conflict arose when consumers demanded a change in service.

The year 1970 had indeed turned into an eventful year.

1971–1972

The 42nd Session of the State Legislature convened on Monday, January 11, 1971. Democrats in the previous election had gained some seats, making their Senate majority 29 to 20. Over in the House the Democrats had gained four seats, but still left Republicans in control 52 to 47. Republican Speaker Don Eldridge had been appointed to the Liquor Control Board in March of 1970, and Representative Tom Copeland of Walla Walla, being Speaker Pro Tem, served as Interim Speaker. However, there was a dispute in the Republican caucus over selection of the Speaker, and Representative Thomas A. Swazey, Jr., of Pierce County was elected Speaker by a 51 to 48 vote. It looked to be an interesting session, although since smoking the peace pipe with private power in 1969, we would be pushing mainly for legislation that would improve efficiency in the districts.

The issue of redistricting was hanging heavily over the legislative body with threats of court challenges to the 1965 redistricting which had been done under Democratic control after being ordered by a court. This issue, while it did not directly affect me, did cause a lot of pressure on other legislation, and even though this session with two Extraordinary Sessions would create a new record of a total of 164 days, it would take another court fight commencing in July of 1971 and ending with a U.S. District Court establishing legislative districts in April of 1972 to settle the matter. State government was getting more complex as demonstrated by the increasing number of days it took to complete each session. When I first started as a lobbyist in the early 1950s, many of the sessions held to the constitutional limit of 60 days, with an occasional Extraordinary Session making the total days in a two-year period 70 to 80. However, in 1965, it took 114 days of legislative action, 112 days in 1967, and 152 days each in 1969 and 1970.

I was in good shape from a lobbying standpoint, having secured the services of former Speaker of the House Charles Hodde as my legislative consultant. Our main effort was to get a law which would allow us to require certain qualifications for contractors doing work for the public utility districts. Several districts had bad experiences under the mandatory granting of the lowest bid, and all work in excess of $5,000 had to be put out to public bid. We wanted to eliminate any fly-by-night contractors.

The other main issue involved taxation of thermal plants. We had agreed that it would be proper to subject thermal plants constructed by a joint operating agency to the same type of taxes paid by public utility districts on their generating plants. However, unlike hydroelectric sites which are automatically located where Mother Nature put the water, thermal plants would be built at various locations throughout the State. These plants could create substantial tax revenues to a local area from power sold elsewhere in the State and the Pacific Northwest. We also had the other problem whereby plants constructed by private power companies would pay a property tax which, because of a large concentrated investment, could affect total tax revenues to local areas. The utilities came to an agreement that they would attempt to seek a uniform tax law for thermal plants. In this instance, Charles Hodde, being one of the best tax experts in the State, would be of great assistance. We had insisted, however, that the Hanford Generating Plant previously constructed by the Supply System should be covered by a grandfather clause in the law because of the special contractual arrangements between private power and public power whereby any increase in the cost of power would automatically result in the private companies getting a larger share of federal power under the Bonneville/Hanford plant exchange arrangements.

Many bills dealing with environmental issues were introduced, and the first open meetings law was considered. However, with Hodde to keep an eye on the Legislature, my major efforts during February and March would center on Washington, D.C., and the Nixon Administration's cut in the budget and the shutdown of the N Reactor at Hanford, which would force closure of the Hanford Generating Plant and would come when the power supply in the Pacific Northwest was shaky. The following is based on an outline dictated February 28 and April 8, 1971, stating my personal views on the proposed reactor shutdown and my involvement in the argument over it.

Hanford Generating Plant – 1971 Shutdown

My first direct personal involvement in the Hanford Generating Plant shutdown threat occurred on Tuesday, January 26, 1971, at 5:30 p.m. at the Embassy Row Hotel in Washington, D.C., when Glenn Lee, publisher of the *Tri-City Herald*, and Sam Volpentest, Executive Vice President of the Tri-City Nuclear Council, came through my hotel room door. Both men were very upset because of day-long sessions with staff members of the Atomic Energy Commission and other federal government employees from whom they got strong rumblings that the N Reactor was to be closed down as a result of budget cuts.

Worse, word seemed to be that the shutdown would happen immediately and the funds appropriated for the 1971 fiscal year ending June 30 would be used to shut the plant down and lay off employees.

Various contacts which I made during the next several days with our congressional delegation and other governmental employees seemed to bear out what Glenn and Sam had told me.

Thursday morning, following completion of the APPA Conference, which I had been attending, I went to Congressman Mike McCormack's office and there read for the first time the news release which was to be put out that afternoon. The N Reactor was to be shut down immediately.

Along with Mike and Owen Hurd and members of other congressional staffs, we started to draft a letter to Congressman George Mahan, Chairman of the House Appropriations Committee, asking him to make a direct appeal to President Nixon to stop the shutdown.

I spent the balance of Thursday in the offices of other members of our State's congressional delegation asking them to sign the joint letter.

My next involvement was on February 3. I was back home preparing for a hearing before the State Senate Commerce Committee concerning the power supply situation in the Pacific Northwest. The hearing had been scheduled sometime prior to the Hanford closure announcement. Senator Mardesich had asked me to work out some of the programming to be presented that night, and I was attempting to do this. When I contacted private power lobbyists at the Legislature, they informed me that Clif Erdahl, Tacoma Director of Utilities, as former Chairman of the Pacific Northwest Utilities Conference Committee, was going to handle the situation. They said that Clif had arranged to have Maury Hatch, Vice President in Charge of Power Supply of Washington Water Power, and Dave Knight of Puget Power, appear. Senator Mardesich asked me who could represent Bonneville, since an emergency meeting of the Congressional Joint Committee on Atomic Energy forced Russ Richmond, Bonneville Administrator, and Bernie Goldhammer, Power Manager of Bonneville, to fly East. When I checked, I learned that Henderson McIntyre would represent Bonneville at the State Senate hearings.

When I suggested to the private power representatives that perhaps we should get together for dinner before the hearing and coordinate our testimony, they declined saying they thought they should get together by themselves. Later, when I proposed to a Seattle City Light lobbyist that if John Nelson, their Superintendent, was going to be present we ought to have dinner, he stated that Clif Erdahl, through his lobbyist, also had requested a dinner with John.

Later, when I was talking to John Nelson on another matter, he asked whether we could get together for dinner, and I agreed. Walt Jones, Chairman of our Legislative Committee, was going to be down in order to attend the hearing. When the private power boys and Erdahl's representative found that John and I were to have dinner, they called and wanted to know if we could all meet for dinner. I said that was what I had proposed in the first place. We were going to have dinner at the Jacaranda, and anyone and everyone was welcome to attend.

At the dinner meeting, it was made quite clear that Clif Erdahl should run the show, which was fine as far as I was concerned, even though I knew that Senator Mardesich was still expecting me to at least arrange the order of the speakers. During the dinner, the attitude of Clif and Maury Hatch was that the loss of Hanford was of no great consequence. After all, they said, their firm power loads and their resources as outlined in the 1970 Utility Conference Report showed that they could meet the utility requirements.

I voiced strong objection to both Hatch and Erdahl on this, stating that for the first time in over ten years we had an aroused public concerned with power supply, and while they could possibly take the technical position that under good water conditions we could meet our power load requirements, they all knew that we were skirting the brink of brown-out.

At any rate, we went to the hearing and the list I gave to Mardesich showed Erdahl leading off, followed by Hatch, followed by McIntyre, followed by me, the final speaker to be Norm Krey, representing Bonneville industrial customers.

I had warned Erdahl and Hatch that if they took the tack that they were proposing, there would be headlines in the next day's papers saying power people feel there is no emergency as a result of the Hanford shutdown.

Maury Hatch proceeded to give his technical opinion and, sure enough, the next morning an AP news story carried throughout the State said just exactly what I had warned these men the press would say. My first call came from Carrol Clark of the *Tri-City Herald*. I had not even seen the article, so I asked if I could have time to find out what it said. Shortly thereafter, I was called to the telephone by Jerry Buckley, lobbyist for Washington Water Power, who was talking to George Brunzell, President of that company. Brunzell was a very, very angry man. He stated that just two days before, he had taken the position that his company was 100 percent behind having the Hanford Plant reactivated, that he had seen to it that his position was well-known, and that Hatch had come over to Olympia and cut the rug out from under him. I told him the private companies should issue an immediate denial.

I then called Clif Erdahl and told him he had better get in touch with Maury Hatch to see if they could clean up the mess in which they had placed us.

Just at that time I received a call from Neil McReynolds, Press Secretary for Governor Evans, asking whether or not I would serve on a special Task Force as a public power representative to go with the Governor to Washington, D.C., and present an appeal for reversal of the shutdown order. I accepted.

Shortly thereafter, however, I recalled the remark that Clif Erdahl had made the previous night at the dinner table to the effect that if there was going to be any task force to negotiate a power supply for Tacoma Light, and certainly Tacoma Light had a part of the Hanford Plant, he was going to be on it.

I immediately called Larry Bradley in the Department of Commerce and Economic Development and informed him that if they were going to have persons such as Clif Erdahl on the Task Force, I did not want to serve. He said, "Let me call you back immediately." He did so shortly in the presence of Dan Ward, head of that department. I repeated the same statement to him, whereupon he read me the list of those requested to serve and said that this would be the full complement. Ralph Davis, President of Puget Power, was to be my counterpart for private power.

An amusing thing happened the next morning, February 5. I picked up a *P-I* to see the morning news on the matter and read the list of those to serve on the Task Force. My name was not there. Since I had told my Executive and Legislative Committees the night before that I had been asked to serve and had accepted, I called Neil McReynolds to find out whether or not I was to be on the Task Force.

Neil was very embarrassed and brought me a copy, in fact his copy, of the news release they had given to the press. A secretarial error had inadvertently omitted my name from the list. (Ha, ha!) I laughed and told Neil that this did not bother me in the least because I was not interested in receiving publicity, but in getting the job done.

Later that day, I was contacted by a secretary in the Governor's office informing me that a special meeting of the Task Force would convene on Tuesday, February 9, at 2 p.m. in the Governor's office to start working on the proposal.

One other little flurry of activity on February 3 followed the congressional Joint Committee on Atomic Energy hearings. Owen Hurd had come out of those hearings optimistically and had called his office with plans to put out a news release saying that the reactor would be restarted.

When I asked Deputy Administrator Don Hodel of Bonneville whether he had gotten the same readings, he was stunned. I then called Jim Klein on the public relations staff of the Supply System and fortunately found that he had watered down Owen's superlatives. It would have been a very bad publicity move if the release had gone out as Owen originally conceived it.

At any rate, at 2 p.m. on February 9, all the members of the Task Force went into a meeting with the Governor. We were given a preliminary outline or draft of the proposed appeal we would make to the Office of Management and Budget. When we came to the power portion of it, I could see that it contained close to the same terms which had gotten Clif Erdahl and Maury Hatch into difficulty with the press. I pointed out to the Governor that the Pacific Northwest Utilities Conference Committee report merely took into consideration the firm power loads of the utilities, and did not properly reflect the industrial interruptible loads which were a very important part of our economy. When I demonstrated this fact to the Governor, he asked that we change the report so that it would more truly reflect regional power load needs and not just those of the non-federal utilities. At that time, I insisted that any talk on increasing payments to the AEC by the Supply System should include the requirement that the AEC provide more reliable steam service and a definite amount of steam. Then the Governor asked what we should do after making our presentation. I said it was my opinion that we should hesitate for just a moment to see what reaction we got from the other side. After all, it had been their decision to shut the reactor down, so if they wanted to reconsider they should give us an indication.

He dismissed my recommendation, saying that he was the type that went in with a definite offer, the best offer he thought could be made, and then he fought for it.

It was then agreed that each of us would work over the draft and submit our recommendations to John McCurry of the Governor's staff, who was coordinating and preparing the proposal.

The next day I went to John McCurry's office and offered him some suggested wording changes, such as "cooperative scheduling" to meet power needs or requirements as steam was made available. I also asked for the insertion of a sentence pointing out that the present power emergency was a result of prior federal budget cuts which could not be compensated 'y any action of the non-federal utilities.

In the meantime I got involved in a mix-up of meetings between the Bonneville Administrator and an ad hoc committee appointed by the Public Power Council to work in conjunction with the Hanford Plant and the Supply System. I discovered this when I talked to Russ Richmond, Bonneville Administrator, who said he had a meeting on Friday, February 12, in Portland with the ad hoc committee. When I asked him if the Supply System was going to be present, he said he assumed so. Then I had to point out that the Supply System was holding its Board meeting on that particular day, and the staff would be at Seattle. After a lot of telephone calls, it was finally resolved that the ad hoc committee would move its meeting to Seattle, and the Bonneville Administrator would be invited to come there.

That Friday, I came to Seattle to sit in with the ad hoc committee. The Supply System Executive Committee and Board were meeting in the same building but I did not get to their meetings until just before they adjourned.

The ad hoc committee was chaired by Byron Price, General Manager of the Eugene Water and Electric Board. The committee spent most of the day finding out how the power supply would be affected by the Hanford shutdown, and getting information on the actual operating condition of the reactor. It decided to support a dual-purpose operation or nothing, since the cost of operating it as a single-purpose steam generating plant would be prohibitive. It was also felt that the operation should be for a minimum of three years, and preferably for up to five years. Price gave eloquent statements for not increasing our payments to the AEC for use of the steam generated by the N Reactor. At the close of the meeting he asked the members of the committee if they would have any objection if he joined the Governor's Task Force and they responded in the negative. Price asked whether or not I would have any objections to his coming along. I told him that others had been trying to get invited to the Task Force and I didn't feel free to tell the Governor of the State of Washington that he should be included, but that if he just happened to be on the plane, I would introduce him to the Governor and that, since he was President of the Northwest

Public Power Association, I would try to see that no one objected to his participation. Later he came to my office and informed me that he was going to ask Governor Tom McCall of Oregon to request that he be added to the Task Force.

During the afternoon I was informed by Bob Gallup of R. W. Beck and Associates, who was going to Olympia with Owen Hurd to work with John McCurry on a further refinement of the power section of the proposal, that the actual drafting of the power section had been done under the auspices of Ralph Davis of Puget Power; that Davis had cleared it with all the private power companies; and that therefore Davis was a little hesitant to have it changed. I told him that somehow everyone seemed to be overlooking the public power people in drafting the proposal, but that if the draft didn't meet our satisfaction, why, the easiest thing for me to do would be to decline to participate as a member of the Task Force.

Saturday evening, February 13, around 5:30 p.m., I got a call from Owen Hurd who stated that Dan Ward had called to advise him that Bernie Goldhammer, Byron Price, and Ralph Davis had agreed that they could offer the AEC up to $15 million for increased steam payments and that he, Owen, was calling me to seek my concurrence. I blew up and pointed out that this would run the annual cost to over $20 million, and that the bulk of this would fall on the public power people through Bonneville rate increases.

In the meantime, I had already found out from the Friday meeting that Bonneville, under the 20-year contract entered into with the private power companies in 1953, which used a five-year roll-ahead estimate of the amount of power which the federal government would provide the private power companies, was locked in on definite power commitments to the private companies until September 1973. Without the Hanford Plant, Bonneville might have to go out and purchase anywhere up to $25 million of power, to furnish the private companies at Bonneville rates, for each of the next two winter seasons, depending upon water conditions on the hydro system.

Owen, who was in his usual manner determined to get the Hanford Plant going at practically any cost, was a little hard to turn around during our Saturday evening conversation. But when I told him that unless they started at a lower figure or could justify offering these increased payments by getting something definite in return from the AEC, he had better just tell Dan Ward that I would not participate any further in the Task Force.

I then tried to get in touch with Price because he had made such a definite stand the day before that increased payments could not be justified. I was also amazed that Bernie Goldhammer, Bonneville Power Manager, was agreeing to this in light of Russ Richmond's strong stand on the previous Friday that increased payments could be made only if we had some control over scheduling to see that steam was available to meet power requirements.

Monday, February 15, I received a call in Olympia from Owen Hurd who said that, after checking out the matter with Russ Richmond through Ray Foleen, he felt there was a disagreement between Bernie Goldhammer and Russ Richmond. Richmond was saying that they would not agree to any increased payments without something in return. Bernie was saying to Dan Ward that they could afford to increase payments for the steam.

I called Dan Ward and told him that it appeared that the Administrator and the Power Manager of the Bonneville staff were taking different positions, but I still took the position that unless the proposal was changed to include a definite requirement that we get something in return for a cost increase, I would not agree to it. Further, under those circumstances, if the Governor thought it best that I should stay home, he should tell me to do so. Ward said that they had been trying to coordinate with everybody, but I told him that as far as I knew, the power section of the Governor's proposal had been prepared without any consultation with the public power people. We had had no opportunity to try to change it until after it had been prepared. At any rate, I said that unless I heard differently, I would be at the airport between 8:00 and 8:30 the following morning.

Coming home that evening from Olympia, I heard on the radio report that Congressman Mike McCormack was saying that he was "convinced" that the decision to reactivate the reactor had been made and that the reactivation order had been prepared and was on the President's desk for his signature. Mike, as a freshman congressman, had an insatiable desire for publicity in his district, and especially on this matter.

The next morning, Tuesday, February 16, I went to the airport and placed a call to Scoop Jackson from the Red Carpet Room, where others of the Task Force had gathered with the exception of the Governor. My call from Senator Jackson's office was returned about fifteen minutes before plane time and just as the others were moving out to go downstairs to the gate. Sterling Munro, Administrative Assistant to the Senator, was on the line because the Senator was not available. I asked him what the situation was and what the basis was for Mike McCormack's comments, stating that it was not my intent or desire to make a long trip just for the purpose of a political show. He stated that they had not received any response or word from the White House, and that as far as he knew no decision had been made to reactivate the reactor. He stated that Congressman Wendell Wyatt of Oregon had consulted with the White House and the Office of Management and Budget the previous week and reported to both Scoop and Mike that he was "encouraged." It seemed that Mike had interpreted this to mean Wyatt was "convinced." I said, "Okay, I will continue on the trip, but I still haven't reached agreement with the Governor's position."

When I arrived at the gate, there evidently had been an exchange between Mike McCormack and the Governor before the press. I noted that the Governor was looking a little bit stern and I found out that Mike was on the same plane as we were. We had all agreed that we would use the flight going East for the purpose of comparing notes and revising the proposal if revision was needed. However, the Governor passed the word that since Mike was present, we could not distribute the proposal drafts.

I was still concerned that the Governor did not truly understand that if costs of power at Hanford were increased, a definite benefit would accrue to the private power companies at the expense of public power.

We all agreed that a work session would be held that night to go over the final proposal.

During the flight, John McCurry let me read my copy hurriedly, following which I told both John and Stu Bledsoe that I had a problem with the wording and that, unless it was changed, I just could not participate. The wording proposed up to $15 million in steam payments with no mention of what we were to get in return. John had accepted several of my recommended word and phrase changes, and my definite requirement that cooperative scheduling would have to be part of the deal.

During the flight, I sat with Mike for a short period and asked him what he was basing his press reports on, and found that it was just exactly what Sterling had told me.

At any rate, that night in Washington, D.C., we commenced our work session, going over the proposal line by line. When we came to the power section, I noted that new computations on power deficiency had been prepared. Figures had been compiled for average water years, which were termed "normal" water years, and all power loads had been cranked into the load estimates, including industrial interruptibles. I recognized that, while use of average water years might fit negotiation, planning and operation would have to use critical water years.

Page seven of the proposal was my greatest concern. On the plane coming in, I had quite a heated discussion (with me generating most of the heat) with Bernie Goldhammer. I told him in effect that it was rough to find out that Bonneville had committed itself to the private power companies under the 20-year contracts, using Hanford as a resource, when Hanford could never be used as a resource in any of our other planning. I told him that henceforth he could be certain that members of the Public Power Council Technical Committee would be sitting in on any future negotiations involving Hanford power. I suggested that if he had an opportunity, he should emphasize to the Governor the need of including in the proposal a definite demand for increased control in return for any increase of payments.

When the power section of the proposal came up, I outlined to the Governor just how this 50/50 split of power from the Hanford Plant benefited the private power companies at the expense of public power anytime the cost of power was increased. Owen Hurd, Bernie and I also emphasized that we could not increase steam payments without going back to the bondholder. We also emphasized that it was the practice of the AEC to bill us for extra cost beyond steam. It was on this basis that page seven was rewritten to say that increased payments up to $15 million of a "total aggregate" amount would be made in return for specific availability of steam to generate a minimum of four billion kilowatt-hours to be dispensed by cooperative scheduling. Upon this final agreement on language, the Governor assigned various portions of the proposal to each Task Force member. I was given the assignment of emphasizing that industrial interruptible power had to be included in our load forecast. I also took that portion in which we required that the Office of Management and Budget set up a definite federal appropriations request schedule for federal dams then under construction so that the non-federal utilities could plan ahead by knowing how much power must be generated by their own steam plants to meet the needs of the region each year.

The next morning at 10 a.m. we went to the Office of Management and Budget and met with Dr. Nice, Bill Young, and Don Claybill. Dr. Glenn Seaborg and his assistant, Quinn, of the AEC, and James Watt, representing the Assistant Secretary of the Interior, were also there.

The presentation was well made. Looking back on it, however, I know that the credit goes to the drive and determination of Governor Dan Evans when he finally understood the position which I had to take representing public power. Recognizing the problems in that position, he did not hesitate to incorporate them into his proposal. It would have been easier for him if he could have proposed paying up to $15 million without asking for anything specific in return from the AEC.

When the Governor's Task Force returned from Washington, D.C., we went through a period of watchful waiting. During that time, there appeared to be a growing desire among the utility people to backtrack on the offer and let Hanford go down under the Office of Management and Budget directive.

At a meeting of the Joint Power Planning Council in Portland on Wednesday, March 3, Ralph Davis and Byron Price reported on the trip. I did not participate since I was not invited to do so.

One of the main things we wanted to do at this meeting was to seek speed-up of the Jim Bridger Steam Plant in Wyoming in order to pick up some of the slack in power supply caused by the Hanford closure.

In the meantime, I had gone to a number of PUD meetings and contacted a number of other publicly owned utility groups, pressing upon them that the "up to $15 million" offer was acceptable. I also found myself very busy offsetting remarks being made by Price that the N Reactor would be very costly to convert and that the best thing to do was to let it lie. It was very interesting to note how two men, Owen Hurd and Byron Price, who attended a series of meetings with the AEC immediately after the Governor's Task Force, visited with the Office of Management and Budget and came out of the same conferences with different views of what went on.

Owen seemed to lose his fight regarding the issue, and I found myself more or less filling his position of refuting the broad innuendoes and inferences which Price seemed to be spreading.

At any rate, under date of March 11, 1971, a response came to the Governor from Don Rice of the Office of Management and Budget. When I read it, I was astounded. It was apparent that the OMB was either deliberately trying to make conditions so completely unacceptable that we would reject them and thus get the blame for the closure of Hanford out here in the Pacific Northwest, or else we had just failed completely to get through.

The Governor called a meeting of his Task Force on Monday, March 15. In preparation for it, Jack Cluck, attorney for the Supply System; Bob Gallup, engineer of R. W. Beck and Associates; and I journeyed to Portland on Sunday, March 14, to be present early in the morning in Russ Richmond's office at Bonneville. Owen Hurd joined us.

At this meeting it was stressed that the Supply System representatives should stay in the background in all of this to preserve their position as possible legal challengers to the AEC over the abrupt closure of the plant. We also spent considerable time deciding that the plant was needed to meet Bonneville's commitments to the private power companies for the next two years.

A special meeting of the Public Power Council Hanford Ad Hoc Committee had been called for noon at the Evergreen Inn in Olympia. Byron Price had chartered a plane to get there. Owen Hurd, Jack Cluck, Bob

Gallup, and I drove north, leaving at 11 a.m. to arrive at the Evergreen Inn for the meeting.

Our purpose was to get public power's signals straight before a 2:30 p.m. meeting of the Task Force in the Governor's office.

As usual, the public power people were unhappy because they still rankled over the 50/50 split of Hanford power based on cost, under which any increased cost would mean that a greater amount of federal power would go to the private companies.

We came out of the meeting with a mandate to back the Governor to either reiterate his former offer or to reject the Office of Management and Budget counteroffer. The Public Power Council Committee was strong in its insistence that this decision not be made by the Joint Power Planning Council, and Byron Price agreed with this position, so later in the Governor's office, when Ralph Davis proposed that the matter be referred to a special meeting of the Joint Power Planning Council, I was surprised to find Price immediately joining with him in this proposal.

During the Governor's meeting, I pointed out the complete unacceptability of the proposed Bonneville rate increase in view of the contracts which were now in existence.

We analyzed each of the Office of Management and Budget's proposals and it became apparent that the OMB had misinterpreted the information which we had given it. For example, the Governor reported that in his first conversation with Rice at the time the proposal was being discussed, the Office of Management and Budget had made a telephone survey of surrounding utilities to ask what "excess capacity" they had. Naturally, every utility reported some excess "capacity" but, as we pointed out to the Governor, it was an energy shortage, not a capacity shortage, which we faced in the next few years.

The Governor then said he would like to have the Joint Power Planning Council take a look at this matter. On that basis, a special meeting was called in Portland for March 18, a Thursday. It was rather interesting to see that this time I was specifically invited to be there and to be one of the persons reporting. It had evidently become apparent that Price was not getting across to the public power people.

On Thursday morning, prior to the Joint Power Planning Council meeting, a meeting of the Public Power Council Executive Committee came together at which time a full report was given by Price and myself on the Office of Management and Budget offer and the Governor's Task Force meeting. We agreed on what should be done at the Joint Power Planning Council.

Our position was that we would accept and endorse Governor Evans' original offer and ask that he reiterate it to the Office of Management and Budget.

The previous day, John McCurry of the Governor's staff, who had been the primary person preparing communications to Washington, D.C., had shown me a draft of a counterproposal from the Governor. The power portion was completely unacceptable. Since the private power people had written the first draft back in February, I told John that I would take a crack at this second one.

I completely redrafted the section on power, and when I gave this to the Public Power Council and Joint Power Planning Council on Thursday, the 18th, it was accepted with a few refinements and incorporated into the Governor's response. This was prepared and sent on to Don Rice by the Governor.

The following week, on Wednesday, March 24, Owen Hurd, Bob Gallup, and I met with John McCurry. The day before, John had told me that the Governor wanted to send a small Task Force East again, and that from some source he had determined that I was more able than Byron Price to get through to the public power people. When we met on Wednesday, John stated that the Governor had decided to send only two technical men from the power side. I immediately said that Bob Gallup should be sent.

Earlier, on March 18 at the Public Power Council meeting, Byron Price had been rather critical of the R. W. Beck and Associates firm, stating that it had a special interest in keeping the Hanford Plant going because it was the original engineer which had certified that it was an economical project back in the early 1960s. Bob Gallup is not only a fine engineer, but he is hard hitting in negotiations, so I recommended him to McCurry to spite Price but also knowing we would be well represented.

Dave Knight of Puget Power was to be the other technical electrical man. Ray Dickeman and John McCurry were to go for the Governor to discuss the computations and figures submitted by the Office of Management and Budget on the operations of the reactor. To make certain that Bob would go in place of someone else, I personally called Alan Jones, Chairman of the Public Power Council, as well as Russ Richmond of Bonneville, and told them that this was my recommendation as a member of the Governor's Task Force. They agreed to it.

This sub-Task Force then went East for a meeting with the Office of Management and Budget on March 30.

In the meantime, Russ Richmond called me and said that his staff had refigured the amount of power Bonneville might be required to purchase to fulfill its contracts during a critical water year. It appeared that under critical water in the year 1971–1972, Bonneville would be required to purchase up to $20 million worth of outside power to serve its private power and other firm power commitments. In the draw-down year of 1972–1973 (from fall to spring when the dams had to draw water from storage), this amount ran to $33 million. When Harry Garretson of the Bonneville staff called me for Russ and informed me of this, it made me think that maybe the public power people would have to budge off their position of approving only up to $15 million to get the Governor's negotiations with the Office of Management and Budget off-center.

I therefore drafted a letter to the Hanford Ad Hoc Committee of the Public Power Council on Sunday, March 28, in which I played the devil's advocate just to stir up the committee's thinking. I proposed that we might go as high as "up to $18 million" based on the reasoning that even though this would not be fair to public power, for a three-year period the average we would have to pay for outside purchases could be that amount, being $53 million divided by three.

I stated in the letter that maybe this was the price we would have to pay to get the 50/50 division of the Hanford power albatross off our necks — where private power could trade their 50 percent for many more kilowatt-hours of federal power under the Bonneville/Hanford power exchange contracts. I also pointed out that this might be the way we could put pressure on the private companies during the third year of shortage, at the time when their Bonneville contracts had run out, to get agreement on what we were going to do with the Hanford Plant after it was shut down. I also suggested in this letter that maybe we could get the industrial customers to underwrite some direct power purchases from the Hanford Plant to offset such increased cost. After all, the industrial customers would have to buy power from outside the region if they couldn't get it here, and it would be better from our standpoint if they could buy it inside the region.

This letter left my office on Tuesday morning, March 30, and it turned out to be quite a coincidence that about 2:30 p.m. on that day, I got a call from John McCurry in Washington, D.C., who stated that I was going to receive a call very shortly from Governor Evans, who was then in Seattle, and John wanted me to be up to date on what had happened in Washington, D.C. He related how that morning he and Ray Dickeman had worked with the Office of Management and Budget man in charge of AEC appropriations, and Bob Gallup and Dave Knight had worked with the Office of Management and Budget man who handles Bonneville power appropriations, both teams having met with much success.

Incidentally, on the previous Wednesday, March 24, when we were meeting with John McCurry, I saw one of the sharp negotiators in this Hanford effort at work. I had never met John McCurry before becoming associated with this endeavor, but he divulged information to us at that Wednesday meeting which was unbelievable. Frankly, the Office of Management and Budget had used a figure for the cost of operation for the N Reactor which seemed to be completely out of the ballpark. And from some sources which I did not ask for, and he did not divulge, he had shown us where the operational figures submitted by Douglas United Nuclear to the AEC field office had been ballooned before going to Washington, D.C., and then further ballooned by the AEC in Washington, D.C., before they went to the Office of Management and Budget. In other words, it became apparent that federal bureaucracy was inflating the actual costs and that the Office of Management and Budget was dealing with these inflated figures.

Evidently, at the Tuesday meeting in Washington, D.C., Ray Dickeman and John had exposed the falsity of these figures to the Office of Management and Budget to the great anger and chagrin of the AEC. At any rate, just about noon, Washington, D.C., time, Don Rice of the Office of Management and Budget called John McCurry to his office and asked how they could settle this matter. John responded to Don that they were not back there to negotiate but merely were authorized as a fact-finding and technical group to reconcile the differences between the Office of Management and Budget thinking and the Governor's Task Force thinking. Rice said he wanted to move ahead on the matter and he had to get a decision, whereupon he picked up the telephone and called the Governor out at Seattle and they got into quite a discussion. Rice agreed to give up the conditions in his offer which had been unacceptable, namely, the immediate Bonneville rate increase; payment for steam at a time when we did not need it until June 30, 1972; the blank check of paying full out-of-pocket expenses on the N Reactor operation; and the requirement that the utilities out here pay the non-recurring costs on the N Reactor as determined by the AEC. Rice was insisting, however, that he get a higher price on the operation of the reactor from the Northwest utilities.

John told me that they had deadlocked at $22 million but that after he and the Governor had talked, he had gone back to Rice and had determined that Rice would accept a lower figure but "it would have to start with a 2."

About this time Bob Gallup and Dave Knight came on the line with John, and Dave Knight outlined his thinking about industrial customers. It had become apparent in refiguring the power resources with Hanford on the line that there was a slight surplus of firm power for the region. It was therefore thought that instead of making industry go outside the region in August and September (the early draw-down months) to purchase power at a 5-mill to 6-mill rate for the purpose of maintaining reservoirs, arrangements might be made for industry to pay that amount for the power in the Pacific Northwest. The arrangements would be for industry to make a payment to the Supply System of $3 million for the right to purchase one billion kilowatt-hours from Bonneville at established Bonneville rates. In other words, this would be 3 mills per kilowatt-hour to the Supply System and 2 mills-plus to Bonneville, or 5 mills-plus for the power. This would then reduce the $20 million compromise figure to $17 million that the utilities would have to pay. Arrangements would still be conditioned on the availability of steam for generating kilowatt-hours.

I mentioned to Bob and Dave that "great minds run in the same channel" because my letter went forward on that same day to members of Alan Jones' Public Power Council's Hanford Ad Hoc Committee.

I thereupon stood by and waited for the call from the Governor, which came very shortly thereafter.

My immediate task then was to try to locate Alan Jones and the bulk of the public power leaders here in the Northwest. Ralph Davis of Puget Power had been contacted for the investor-owned utilities and, of course, it would be rather easy for him to contact the four other companies and get a decision on their side. I was faced with the task of trying to clear with the majority of the leadership of around 100 consumer-owned utilities.

Fortunately, there was a Power Crisis conference at Wenatchee, sponsored by the *Wenatchee Daily World*, and I knew that Russ Richmond, Alan Jones, Byron Price, John Nelson, Howard Elmore and others were over there. I immediately called for Alan Jones but found that he had left and was flying home to McMinnville with Russ Richmond. I then got hold of Charlie Hodde, our legislative consultant who was on the program over there, and asked him to round up a number of the public power leaders and get them on a conference telephone at Howard Elmore's office. (Elmore was Manager of the Chelan County PUD.)

The Governor, in the meantime, had given me his private telephone number at the Governor's mansion so that I could consult with him if I ran into difficulty. When he had called me at 4 p.m., he had emphasized that the deadline for a decision was 10 a.m. on Wednesday the next morning. I told him that it was impossible for me to move ahead unless I got hold of some public power people.

That evening, when it became apparent that I was not getting through to enough people, I tried to contact the Governor to state that we just could not meet that deadline. Failing to get him direct, I called John McCurry in Washington, D.C., and John finally located the Governor who then called Rice and got an extension on the deadline until 12 noon Thursday, April 1, Pacific Standard Time.

In the meantime, I got through to Alan Jones and explained things to him, and he agreed to call a meeting of the Public Power Council on Thursday, April 1, at 9 a.m., in Portland. Finally, at 9:40 p.m. on that Tuesday, I got a conference call back from Wenatchee. Present at their end were Byron Price, John Nelson, Hank Curtis, Ken Dyar, and Howard Elmore. When I outlined what was being proposed, Price immediately objected. He said there was no reason to do it, that the plant should be shut down, etc. He made a great speech about protecting public power. This kind of burnt me because I was later to find that he had been talking to John McCurry during the same afternoon and at that time had sounded affirmative. I found the same thing in a private conference on the following day with Governor Evans, who remarked, "Price seems to say different things to different people." At any rate, in that Tuesday night's conference call, I had to get quite rough and tell him that I didn't give a damn what they did but I was getting tired of always being put in the position of trying to interpret their arguments.

Byron Price, John Nelson, and Bill Hulbert were going to Washington, D.C., for a special meeting on the Liquid Metal Fast Breeder Reactor on Thursday, April 1, so they could not be at the Public Power Council meeting.

But, at any rate, the meeting went on.

On Wednesday, March 31, around 11:30 a.m., I got a call in Ulcer Gulch from the Governor's office to inform me that he wanted to see me. I went down and for the first time in many years had a good hour and a half alone with Governor Evans. We went over all of the power issues relevant to the Pacific Northwest: the hydro-thermal program; the effects of increased costs of Hanford; the fact that public power could go all out in the first two years of the three-year period of the Hanford proposal, but we had reservations about the third year; and the fact that industry would have to come in and support us or I could not possibly sell the $20 million figure to the public power people. I told him I would let him know by noon the next day what could be done.

Thursday morning at 5 a.m., I left Olympia and drove south to be at the airport in Portland in time to pick up Quigley and Billingsley of the Supply System and Bob Gallup, who had flown back the night before from Washington, D.C., to Seattle. Gallup had called me around 9:30 p.m. the previous night, and just to sharpen his wits and make him re-examine what was being offered, I took a rather strong devil's advocate position against the proposal. I know I upset Bob, but sometimes a man can get into the spirit of compromise and go too far, and I wanted to be certain that he had rethought this thoroughly. I was sorry that I did this because the next morning when I met him at the airport in Portland, I learned that after my rough talk to him on the previous evening challenging some of his assumptions, he had arrived home to find that his father had died. I would certainly have to commend him for being dedicated enough to come to Portland on the next day in the face of that event.

Driving down that morning, I had tried to go over in my mind what might be done to get the public power people to go along with the proposal.

The Public Power Council Executive Committee convened with Russ Richmond and members of his staff present. Bob Gallup gave his report and did his usual excellent job.

I noted that there was a settling down among the public power people. While there had been the usual mutterings about private power "taking us to the cleaners" before the meeting, you could sense at the table that they were going to listen. In some respects, I think it was the letter they received from me the previous day which had kind of set their thinking that maybe public power should not just get angry over past happenings, but should think in terms of the future and the region's need.

At any rate, following Bob's report and some remarks by Russ Richmond, they asked me to make some comments. That is when I outlined the position which I thought they could take and which I had jotted down as I drove south that morning.

My first recommendation was that they accept the offer of the Office of Management and Budget for the operation of the N Reactor for three years, on the condition that the Bonneville industrial customers would agree to participate by paying $3 million directly to the Supply System to offset the increased cost of $20 million the Supply System would have to pay the AEC. A second condition was that public power would have the right to review whether the plant should be operated in the third year, and furnish the Office of Management and Budget with a decision prior to June 30, 1972. This would allow us to work out either larger contributions from private power to pay the increased steam costs during that third year, or a settlement more favorable to us than the 50/50 split on what could be done with the turbines and generators at Hanford after the third year.

I also had included as a condition for accepting their offer the specific cancellation of those unacceptable portions of the Office of Management and Budget's first proposal.

During a recess to have the resolution typed, Russ Richmond and I got on the telephone to Dan Ward and John McCurry of the Governor's staff in Olympia. We reported on the attitude of the group, and I promised to call back as soon as action was taken.

When Russ and I returned to the meeting, we found that it was going in the wrong direction again. So once again I dived in and pointed out the essential elements of any acceptable agreement.

For example, they were going to accept the offer for two years and then look at the third year. I pointed out that the Office of Management and Budget would like to see the plant shut down and would rush at the opportunity to accept only a two-year proposal. I stated that as a utility person I could not see how we could possibly have an 800-megawatt generator plant not operating out here in the Pacific Northwest when we were crying power shortage. I also pointed out that this year alone we were going back to Washington, D.C., seeking $400 million worth of appropriations to provide our 3-mill and 4-mill federal hydro power, and it was pretty hard for these federal people to understand why we were turning our backs on a $20 million figure for the operation of Hanford which was only in the neighborhood of 5-mill or 6-mill power. I also pointed out that we were a little bit inconsistent when we were fighting like tigers to get Hanford Plant No. 2 on the line in 1977 at a $6\frac{1}{4}$-mill power rate and turning our backs on a lower cost power supply.

It was then decided that a subcommittee composed of Hank Curtis, Northwest Public Power Association; Ken Dyar, Public Power Council; Dick Quigley, attorney for the Supply System; Bob Ratcliffe, of the Solicitor General's office; and I would draft a new resolution, which we did during the lunch hour.

The Executive Committee came back and by unanimous action adopted it. I immediately went to the telephone and called it in to Dan Ward and John McCurry. The Governor had asked that I call him at 3:30 p.m., saying that he would be out of his office until then but wanted to hear from me. I merely told John that there was no use bothering the Governor, that they could relay the resolution to him and then, if he needed me, I could be reached at the Evergreen Inn in Olympia because I had to drive back very fast in order to handle a meeting of my own Executive and Legislative Committees.

I left Portland at 2 p.m. and arrived back in Olympia at 3:30 p.m. Just after I arrived, I got a call from John McCurry who stated that the Governor was a little concerned about our hesitancy on the third year. I stated that there was no need to even mention that to the Office of Management and Budget, that it was an "in-house" reservation without which the public power people just would not have gone along with it. I suggested that the Governor merely tell the Office of Management and Budget that we were going to move ahead. Incidentally, John McCurry again showed his talent as a negotiator when, in the morning conference call from Russ Richmond and myself to Dan Ward and McCurry, he read us a work draft letter which Don Rice was preparing to telephone to the Governor. John had the letter even before the Governor had told Rice that we would accept the Office of Management and Budget's offer.

On Friday, April 2, at 9:30 a.m., John called me and said that they had come to an agreement on the wording of the Rice response and he read it to me. As far as I could see, it was acceptable. He stated that the Governor was just then releasing the letter to the press, and that the N Reactor was back on the road for a three-year period.

A lot of people played parts in keeping the N Reactor active, and I did my share of the work on it. It would be impossible to say any one person deserves the most credit, but I certainly have a greater appreciation for Governor Dan Evans after watchimg him work and working with him on this. I have the greatest respect for the abilities of John McCurry, who is the Deputy Director in the Office of Planning and Management here in State Government. It was uncanny to see that man contact people and get information and reconcile the different views being fed into him.

Bob Gallup of the Beck firm definitely demonstrated his sharpness, not only as a technical man and a negotiator, but also as a "salesman" when he had to present the idea to the Public Power Council.

One other name should be mentioned; namely, Alan Jones, Superintendent of the McMinnville Water and Light Department and Chairman of the Public Power Council. Certainly his quiet presence and cool head which kept him from getting stampeded or angry over issues helped greatly. Of course, while I'm mentioning people, Russ Richmond as Bonneville Administrator again demonstrated his tremendous ability to mediate between private power and public power. As a known Democrat, it was difficult for him to operate in a Republican administration, not because he is partisan in his job, but because of the partisan opposition to him by local Republicans. And, of course, when you think of the Bonneville Power Administration, you have to think of Bernie Goldhammer who is truly a mastermind when it comes to putting together power supply arrangements. And, right alongside of these, but on the negotiation sidelines, were Glenn Lee and Sam Volpentest of the Tri-City Nuclear Council knocking on AEC and congressional doors.

There are many more, of course, as I stated previously, but I mention these men because they were the primary leaders in getting the N Reactor reactivated for the Pacific Northwest in 1971. It's been a good effort.

———

After we solved the Hanford Generating Plant shutdown problem, I spent full time winding up the legislative session. Adjournment finally came at 4 a.m. on May 11. We were able to get a law saying that joint operating agencies would pay the same kind of taxes as PUDs, but the Hanford Generating Plant would be excepted under a grandfather clause. We got our qualification procedure for electrical contractors, and also a compromise with the Electrical Line Contractors Association and the Division of Municipal Corporation to clarify and improve the PUD purchasing provisions. We failed to get a uniform tax on future thermal plants, but did get an exemption in the Shoreline Management Act, which was to accompany Initiative 43 to the voters as a referendum, for steam plants which were certified under the thermal plant site certification law. We passed a bill to permit county local improvement districts to be used for initial installation of underground electric service as well as conversion to it. The open public meetings law was passed, but it was substantially changed from the initial bill as introduced, which was thought to be unworkable. We supported the concept of an open meetings law but this law was too rigid to be practical. A later Attorney General's opinion caused confusion about whether even two members of a three-member PUD Commission could ride together to attend a joint meeting of other Commissioners without risking court challenges to decisions made at the meeting. I was not unhappy to see the long session end.

The Supply System was the first applicant for a site certificate under the new Thermal Plant Site Certification Law, filing in the last week of January to construct a plant at Hanford. Owen Hurd, the first Managing Director of the Supply System, announced his impending resignation as of the end of June 1971. Under the revised rules of the Supply System, the Executive Committee would hire his replacement. I found that, without my solicitation, I was being sponsored as a replacement for Owen by a substantial number of the employees of the Supply System. I also heard that several community leaders in the Tri-Cities area were suggesting my appointment to the job. Such confidence and support were good for my ego, but I did not think of myself as the type of person who should head up an organization faced with the construction of a nuclear plant. I therefore spent time putting that idea to rest.

I was somewhat surprised when the Executive Committee selected one of its own members, Jack Stein, Manager of Grays Harbor County PUD, for the job. I had no problem with Stein's ability as a PUD Manager because he had done a commendable job at Grays Harbor. But in my opinion, he did lack certain regional and national vision which I felt the head of the Supply System should have. Also, while he had established a record of running a very tight ship in his District financially, I wondered whether this quality could lead to not hiring the expertise which would be needed to build the nuclear plants. Many years later, I was reminded by Don Pugnetti, editor of the *Tri-City Herald*, of a letter I wrote to him in support of Stein but which had raised these questions. I thought of this again when Stein returned after renegotiating the contract with Burns and Roe, architect/engineer, on Plant No. 2, where he was delighted to report a substantial savings on the contract to the Supply System. I wondered whether, during this period when there was severe competition among many utilities for the services of architects and engineers, Burns and Roe would assign first-rate engineers or those with second-rate ability.

Under the reorganization of the Supply System in August of 1970, a five-person Executive Committee had been established, which would be automatically increased to seven if Seattle and Tacoma should join. I had prepared a series of white papers providing information to Mayor Uhlman and members of the Seattle City Council about the benefits to be gained from Seattle's participation in the Supply System. In late 1970, I became aware of the opposition of certain of the Mayor's staff members and thus issued another white paper on the matter.

Superintendent John Nelson supported membership in the Supply System by Seattle City Light. Thus, in January 1971, a resolution was introduced in the City Council to approve Seattle's membership, and the City Council approved it by unanimous vote, but the ordinance was returned by Mayor Uhlman unsigned on February 22, 1971. The cover letter by the Mayor contained some misinformation which Council member George Cooley responded to by quoting from the white paper I had previously prepared. If Seattle City Light joined the Supply System, it would in my opinion strengthen the public power program and fend off the advances Puget Power was making to the City of Seattle for a closer alliance with that utility.

It was my hope that Tacoma would exercise its option to become a member, but Clif Erdahl was still Director of Utilities, and that city did not join until after his retirement in 1972 when the new Director, Aldo J. Benedetti, was appointed by the Tacoma Utility Board.

Since the Supply System had been selected as the main construction agency for the power plants being requested by the public power utilities, I felt it was essential that Seattle and Tacoma join with the public utility districts in activities of the Supply System by direct participation.

In July of 1971, the PUD Association availed itself of an opportunity to participate in the Public Employees' Retirement System. Previously, the Legislature had enacted a law providing that associations composed of municipal corporations of the State could become members of the State Retirement System. This had been jokingly referred to as the "Biesen Bill," primarily because long-time Executive of the Association of Washington Cities, Chester Biesen, was about to retire and the move was made to provide a retirement program for him. The State PUD Association had previously, in the early 1960s, established a private pension program for me and the other employees. I also had personal investments to finance my eventual retirement. However, since all the public utility districts, with the exception of one, were participating in the State Retirement program, it was logical for the Association to affiliate with it. In later years, this action was to provide the frosting on the cake of my retirement income. But in 1971, I accepted it as an indication of the sincere regard which my "bosses" held for me and which, indeed, made me feel good.

In December of 1971, Mayor Uhlman would have the chance to reappoint John Nelson as Superintendent of City Light or to appoint a new superintendent. My Board went on record with an endorsement of John's reappointment. Following my Board's action, I called John and told him I had an appointment on Saturday morning at 10:30 a.m. with Mayor Uhlman, whereupon he informed me that he had an appointment one hour earlier on the same day. When I arrived at the Mayor's office and stated my Board's recommendation that he reappoint John, Mayor Uhlman informed me that he was not going to reappoint Nelson and had so informed him just before our meeting. He then asked, "Would you be interested in the job?" My response was, "I came down here with my Board's endorsement to reappoint John Nelson. That is the purpose of my visit. However, since you have informed me you do not intend to reappoint him, then I must reverse your question: 'Would you be interested in me?' " He said he would, and then went into quite a discourse about his feeling that City Light should be more closely aligned with the Mayor's office.

He commented that in the hiring of consultants and the selection of necessary financial agents and bond attorneys, there should be coordination between the Mayor's office and the Superintendent of City Light's office. I frankly was not too clear about what he meant, but I did make it clear to him that, should I be selected, I would be the Superintendent of City Light and have the authority to operate it as a utility, not as a political arm of the city government. His final request was that I think it over and not close the door on being considered.

The matter became somewhat embarrassing in the following few weeks. First, my own family was absolutely opposed to the idea, saying, "Why do you want to start another career now, when you could retire at any time, even though you are only in your mid-50s?" What bothered me more, though, were rumors coming out of the Mayor's office, one of which I heard from Bud Donahue of the Seattle Chamber of Commerce, when we met on an elevator at a hotel. Bud said, "I know who is going to be offered the job of Superintendent of City Light, and I wonder if you will accept it." My main hope was that the appointment would be a person supportive of local public power. Evidently, word got out east of Lake Washington, to the Puget Power area, that I was being considered. I heard that Gerald Grinstein, former Administrative Assistant to Senator Warren G. Magnuson and now a member of the Preston, Thorgrimson, Ellis law firm, was attempting to find other candidates in order to counteract Uhlman's consideration of me. I laughed because he was doing a good job in shooting me down from a job which I did not particularly want.

In early January 1972, I had returned from a trip to Washington, D.C., when I received a call from Mayor Uhlman asking if I could come to lunch in Seattle and meet with him and Dick Ford, whom he had settled on as a potential appointee. I had heard that Grinstein put Ford's name in the running. We met for lunch, and I assured Mayor Uhlman that Dick Ford in my opinion most certainly had always been a very fair person and well qualified for administrative work, even though his primary background was with the public ports. However, I certainly would support him in his role as Superintendent of City Light after his frank statement to me that he was willing to work with local public power on joint projects. Later, the Ford nomination got into some problems before the City Council and was withdrawn. Final selection for the new Superintendent was Gordon Vickery, longtime Fire Chief of Seattle. I did not know Vickery very well but, again, when he assured me of his willingness to work jointly with other local public power officials, I took his word for it, and he proved to be a very effective person in local public power ranks.

The Second Extraordinary Session of the Legislature convened on January 10, 1972. Once again we found ourselves in Olympia. Our main interest was in securing correcting amendments to our purchasing law. We wanted to clarify the right to use our own crews for direct construction work costing up to a certain amount which would be fixed by the law, and clarify the right to purchase by negotiated sale, within a given period of time, articles or equipment costing up to a certain amount. We were successful in securing that law. The balance of our time at the session dealt with amendments to the State Retirement Law (which we were not sponsoring, but we wanted to be certain these amendments did not adversely affect the program); fighting off efforts to increase utility taxes; and negotiating changes in the State Electrical Code, which originally required inefficient work procedures.

Adjournment came at 12:30 a.m. on Wednesday, February 23, 1972, without the Legislature reaching agreement on a redistricting bill, the main purpose for the Special Session. Since the Legislature couldn't agree on redistricting, the U.S. District Court drew the legislative district boundaries for the State, effective April 21, 1972.

Attendance at legislative sessions is not all work and no play. One does have to find time to relax, and one place to relax is the political fund-raising receptions to which one buys tickets. Fund-raising is a necessary function in American political life. We lobbyists also had our Third House organization since 1953, not only to police our own lobbying activity but to raise funds for worthwhile community projects like the Youth Legislature and other events. When Dorothy Morrell, volunteer lobbyist on behalf of environmental protection causes, made application to the Third House for membership, Joe Brennan, a good-hearted Irishman and highly qualified lobbyist for a leading bank, who was serving as our Third House Officio, turned her down. I therefore organized "An Evening With Dorothy" fund-raising event for a "Candidate for the Third House" whose platform was Open Meetings—Good Environment—Popcorn; to be held at the Governor House, Olympia, Washington; Time: 6:00? Date: Sine Die Minus One. "No Host—Non-profit Election Committee: Beaudoin, Benfield, Billington, Blume, Buckley, etc., plus Brennan." (The other names were those of all the lead utility lobbyists.) Price: "Donation 50¢."

We sold a total of 82 tickets—or at least I collected $41—and on the committee's recommendation covered the cost of ticket printing of $20, and by letter tendered the balance of $21 to Brennan by letter dated March 1, 1972. In the letter, I explained my absence during the closing days of the session and proposed that the $21 be used to cover Dorothy's 1973 dues of $15, and that the balance of $6 be used to place on the desk of the 1973 legislators 150 popcorn balls suitably wrapped in cellophane. Brennan's response dated March 11, 1972, pointed out that the 1973 dues would be $25; that his receipt of my check made payable to the Third House might cause members to demand a financial report; that he had deposited the check to the Third House account; and that the Third House directory, going to the printers that day, would have a new special category showing Honorary Members, and under that listing would be one name: Dorothy Morrell. As Brennan wrote, "I trust that this course of action will get all you 'B's' (which I assume means bleeding hearts) off the hook and that in the future the Third House can settle down to such mundane affairs as the wining and dining of ourselves and occasionally a legislator."

I found out later that Joe had refused Dorothy membership in the Third House because, in tendering her dues check, she had written five conditions or requirements on it. This made it non-negotiable and impossible to accept. She was a very independent person entitled to her views—but in this instance her demands were too extreme for even good-hearted and jovial Joe. Non-negotiable checks didn't sit very well with a bank lobbyist. She later joined as an "unconditional" member like the rest of us in the 45th — 1977/1978 — Session.

Senator Scoop Jackson was moving ahead on his quest for the presidential nomination and I secured approval of my Board to join the so-called Scoop's Troops for a tour of the State of Wisconsin in February 1972. While we still guarded quite jealously our position of non-partisanship, it certainly seemed the least we could do, after all this man had done to secure federal power legislation for the Pacific Northwest. While the tour involved some personal expense, it helped me "get even" for a kind deed Jackson had rendered our family four years previously by helping our son in his medical career.

An interesting sequel to the saving of the Hanford Generating Plant in early 1971 occurred in 1972. Since public power had accepted continuation of the plant for the first two years of the three-year extension because Bonneville was locked into power supply to private power for those two years, it behooved public power to insist that extension for the third year and thereafter be analyzed and evaluated by Bonneville, the private utilities, and itself.

Coming out of the PUD Association's Managers' Section meeting in September 1971 was a direct request for the Public Power Council to move ahead on that analysis. As the review progressed, it became evident that unless contracts were changed, the 50/50 split of Hanford power required back in 1962 when the plant was authorized would end up as an 80/20 or even a 90/10 split in favor of private power, since the power would be exchanged with Bonneville on a cost basis and as the Hanford power costs increased, the companies would get more lower-cost Bonneville power in trade. While this did not increase the cost to public power, which was already receiving Bonneville power at Bonneville rates, it would greatly increase the proportion of Bonneville power which the private companies would hold on to.

By the next spring this situation was further aggravated when Senator Magnuson and Congressman Mike McCormack, in rightful pursuit of keeping the plant in operation, started building up political support for keeping the plant in operation beyond the agreed-upon three years ending in June 1974.

I called both of them and sent a confidential letter to Maggie under date of April 21 outlining how the increased costs would favor private power. On May 12, 1972, I sent a second letter and this time sent a copy to Congressman McCormack. As I emphasized, private power had presented two proposals for extending the plant. One was to convert it to a power-only operation, and the other was to rebuild it by adding a new high-pressure topping turbine. Under the existing contracts, if the plant were converted, the private companies would get nearly twice the amount of Bonneville power, through exchange, as the plant would produce, and if the plant were rebuilt, they would get 955 megawatts of the potential 957 megawatts to be produced. In the first instance, public power would be stuck paying about $25 million, or one-half the annual costs, for a loss of federal power to the private companies, and in the second, public power would pay $25 million per year for 2 megawatts of power. As I wrote, "there are going to have to be some substantial changes made in contractual arrangements. If not, one 'helluva' private/public power fight is going to break out all over the ballpark."

Fortunately, Bonneville Administrator Russ Richmond displayed his usual artful ability to mediate between private and public power. His plan, dated May 25, 1972, proposed conversion of the Hanford Plant to a power-only operation, adding a topping turbine and equitable sharing of such power up until 1996; construction of another 1100-megawatt plant by public power to be operable in 1981, with private power being entitled to 30 percent of the power produced; and a 10 percent sharing by public power in Portland General Electric's proposed Boardman plant.

I informed Maggie and Mike on May 26 that Russ' plan looked okay in principle, and I would leave it up to the power supply experts to finalize. It later proved unfeasible to rebuild and add a topping unit at the Hanford reactor. Because of that, a second new nuclear plant was placed under construction by public power in which private power residual rights under the original Hanford contracts of 1966 would be retained if Hanford was shut down.

In June of 1972, I was invited to a breakfast meeting by my friend Mort Frayn, former Speaker of the House, with a number of leading business persons of Seattle. Mort stated that the Coalition for Open Government, which was then sponsoring Initiative 276 to establish the Public Disclosure Commission and further improve the open meetings law of our State, was in difficulty. It appeared that without financial support from other sources, this group of sponsors was not going to be able to get the initiative before the voters.

Following the meeting, I presented the matter to my Board of Directors and they approved a donation by the Association of $500 toward the effort. It was the only time during my term of service with the Association that they made a political contribution. Later, after the initiative was passed and it was found that certain personal financial disclosures by all political candidates was required, I heard about my recommendation from a number of my PUD Commissioner "bosses." It rankled several of them that they had to subject themselves to making certain of their personal holdings public. They had no objection to disclosing any political money they used as candidates. However, after the many years I had to buck the private power political dollars, I was glad that we did make this little effort toward what I felt was better government.

In July of 1972, my Board gave me another gift. Back in 1966, I had attended a conference on our State courts. Coming out of that we established a Citizens' Committee on Washington Courts that had proved effective by establishing an appellate court system and improving the juvenile court procedures, and it had now embarked on making further improvements in our courts. I spent some personal time on volunteer work for the Committee, and when I was asked to accept the chairmanship, I naturally had to secure my Board's approval for the work because, while it was purely voluntary, it would involve a certain amount of my business time as well as a lot of my personal time. The Board approved my acceptance of the assignment.

In August of 1972, the Internal Revenue Service filed new rules which markedly affected financing arrangements for the public power plants to be built under the Hydro-Thermal Accord. The ruling that the federal government would no longer be considered an "exempt person" from taxes meant that public power could no longer use the net billing arrangement with Bonneville for underwriting power plant financing. To continue the net billing arrangement, taxable bonds would have to be issued to finance those plants. This meant that direct contractual relationships between local utilities and the Supply System would be required in order to finance the two plants, No. 4 and No. 5, which would later be placed under construction at the request of the Public Power Council as twin units of Plants No. 1 and No. 3.

In the fall of 1972, I became involved in one of the best projects the State PUD Association undertook during my service with it. I had returned home on a Sunday afternoon from our beach house when the telephone rang and I recognized the booming voice of former U.S. Senator C. C. Dill. He stated that following the death of his wife he had no other living relatives to whom he could will his remaining assets, and he wondered whether the Association would be interested in accepting money from him to establish a trust fund for the purpose of sponsoring oratorical contests among high school students in PUD counties. He stated that he wanted the students to learn how to speak publicly and that he thought such contests might cultivate their ability. I thought it was perhaps an older man's Sunday afternoon conversation, but shortly thereafter I received a letter from him confirming his desire to establish such a trust fund.

This project started me down a road which, during the next three years, would take considerable time and effort, including an all-out "shooting war" with the Internal Revenue Service over establishment of the trust.

1973–1974

The 43rd Session of the State Legislature convened on January 8, 1973. Each legislative session was unique and challenging, but this was to be one of the most unusual. While in many previous legislative sessions an Extraordinary Session had been called after the regular session, and in some years even a Second Extraordinary Session, this legislative session was the first in the State's history to be followed by three Extraordinary Sessions. Not only that, but a practice referred to as "continuing legislative sessions" was tried. Here, while the sessions were recessed, all of the standing committees would meet for what was termed "legislative weekends," and thus a number of days would be spent on legislative activity by the legislators meeting in their separate committees, but these days were not counted as legislative days because neither house was called to order. The previous 42nd Session of the State Legislature had used 164 days, mostly without a recess. There was concern that such long periods of service were changing the nature of our "citizens' Legislature." A number of the states of the nation had gone to full-time legislators and it was the hope that by using "continuing legislative sessions" enough leeway could be granted elected legislators to continue their chosen work or professions away from Olympia and thus keep ours a citizens' Legislature.

A second factor that made this session unusual was uncertainty about the federal budget. Without knowing what federal funds might be received by the State, it seemed impossible to adopt a budget for a two-year period. A third factor was that in the 1972 elections, Democratic control in the Senate had increased to a 31 to 18 vote margin, and over on the House side a Democratic majority of 57 to 41 had reversed from Republican control in the 1971 Session. Thus, a Republican Governor, Daniel J. Evans, was faced with a solid Democratic-controlled Legislature. A final matter, which caused loss of time in getting the Legislature organized, was that longtime Majority Leader Senator Bob Greive's position was challenged by Senator Augie Mardesich, and Mardesich won. On the House side, Representative Leonard Sawyer was elected Speaker.

While leadership in the houses did not concern me in 1973, it was a culmination of the drive toward legislative leadership which had started way back in 1961, provoked by the private power challenge against the Democratic leadership in the House at that time. The triumvirate of Durkan, Mardesich, and Sawyer had won legislative dominance. Since private and public power were now approaching the Legislature on a cooperative basis, power matters were of no great issue. The one major bill I had introduced at the request of my Legislative Committee was to amend the joint ownership law passed in 1967 allowing joint operating agencies, such as the Washington Public Power Supply System, to participate in joint ownership.

In 1967, when the private power companies had the joint ownership legislation passed, they made certain that it did not permit joint operating agencies to become joint owners because they were still opposed to the concept of joint action by PUDs. However, in making plans to start construction of Plant No. 3 of the Supply System, which was to be owned 70 percent by public power utilities under Bonneville's net billing process and 30 percent by the private power companies, all parties agreed on the need for an amendment to the joint ownership law. The bill was introduced on the House side as HB-502 and on the Senate side as SB-2402. Incidentally, this was the first year that a new legislative procedure was adopted whereby all House bills would be numbered consecutively as introduced starting with number 1, while all Senate bills would be so numbered starting with number 2001. The bill was not considered in the regular session, but this did not concern me because assurance had been given by legislative leadership that it would be acted upon in the Extraordinary Session. When that session started, the bill moved so fast that I had a hard time keeping up with it. A lot of the credit for its speed is due Charles Hodde who was still my legislative consultant and whose legislative lobbying ability was indeed an art to behold.

True to its word, the House leadership placed the bill on the first third-reading calendar for March 13 floor debate. However, it, along with the rest of the calendar, ran head-on into a conflict with committee meetings previously scheduled for the same day and was thus moved over to March 14. Since the Senate companion measure SB-2402 had already moved out of the Senate Transportation and Utilities Committee to the Rules Committee, our strategy was to get the Senate to give this bill special treatment and permit HB-502, when passed by the House, to bypass the Senate Transportation and Utilities Committee and go immediately to the Rules Committee. This procedure is a bit unusual but entirely proper when a bill has full understanding and strong support by various Senate leaders. I had planned on using Wednesday afternoon, March 14, for the purpose of arranging this action with the Senate leaders. At 11:30 a.m., I received an SOS call from Charles Hodde to the effect that HB-502 had been moved ahead on the House calendar and passed by a 93 to 0 vote, and on a motion by Majority Floor Leader Bob Charette of Grays Harbor-Pacific counties, it was being immediately transmitted to the Senate.

Needless to say, I had to go into high gear on our efforts to have it handled in a special manner in the Senate. Fortunately, the Senate had recessed for several hours which gave me enough time to seek out and get audiences with some of the necessary people. At 2 p.m. on that day, HB-502 was read into the Senate, whereupon Senator Damon Canfield (Republican) of Benton-Yakima counties, supported by Senator Dan Jolly (Democrat) of Franklin-Walla Walla counties, moved that the bill be referred directly to the Rules Committee. This action was approved by the entire Senate and HB-502 bypassed the regular standing committee.

The Senate adjourned at 2:30 p.m., and a meeting of the Rules Committee was held immediately. Senator Bob Bailey of Pacific-Grays Harbor and Senator Don Talley of Cowlitz-Wahkiakum were alerted to my desire for early Rules Committee consideration. They never got a chance to consider it, because Lt. Governor John Cherberg at the first opportunity and as presiding officer of the Senate and Rules Committee stated, "I am pulling HB-502 on behalf of Senator Dan Jolly." It thus appeared on the Senate calendar for March 15, moving from final passage in the House to the Senate Rules Committee and then on to the Senate calendar in a four-hour period, which must have come close to some kind of a legislative procedure record for any bill which would have to be classed as "routine legislation." Once the bill was placed on the Senate calendar, we were sure of consideration and although there was a two-day delay because of an unrelated Senate procedural dispute, final passage by the Senate by a 48 to 0 vote took place on St. Patrick's Day, March 17, 1973. I got to the Governor's legal advisors before the bill arrived at the Governor's office and was assured that the Governor would sign it as soon as it reached his office.

Other legislative activities in which we participated during the regular and First Extraordinary sessions were amendments to the open meetings law to make it more workable. These would allow executive sessions not open to the public for acquisition of real estate by lease or purchase; allow executive sessions when planning or adopting strategy or the position to be taken during the course of any collective bargaining or professional negotiations, grievance, or mediation proceedings; eliminate that portion of the open meetings law which had granted expenses, including attorney's fees, to a person bringing an action against a public official; and, finally, clarify the right of members of a governing body to travel together or attend other meetings together, provided they took no official action as defined in the open meetings law.

A second issue was introduction of legislation extending to a PUD as large as Chelan County PUD the right to have a five-person board. With the approval of my Board, we took the position that we would not oppose such legislation provided it did not compel other PUDs, which did not see the necessity of a five-person board, to enlarge their boards from three to five members. This bill was eventually killed during the legislative session by opposition from organized labor. Another bill to compel all PUDs to expand their boards to five members did receive our opposition.

In the legislation enacted to allow the State to issue waste discharge permits in conformity with the Federal Water Pollution Control Act, we had to make some fast moves to make certain that the Thermal Power Plant Site Evaluation Council or the one-stop procedure on licensing thermal plants would be the issuer of any waste discharge permits to thermal plants.

My major legislative work in this session occurred between the adjournment of the First Extraordinary Session on April 15, 1973, and the convening of the Second Extraordinary Session on September 8. In late July, a copy of a letter addressed to Howard C. Elmore, Chairman of the Pacific Northwest Utilities Conference Committee, from E. F. Timme, Director of Coordination of the Northwest Power Pool, came across my desk. Timme was alerting Elmore to an upcoming shortage of power from the hydroelectric reservoirs throughout the Pacific Northwest. The letter stated .that present reservoir conditions indicated a shortage of 19,000 megawatt-months over the anticipated 20½-month drawdown period. This was roughly 16 billion kilowatt-hours short of the necessary electricity to meet the firm power load estimates for the two-year period 1973–1974 and 1974–1975.

In response to an invitation from Elmore, Timme appeared at a meeting of the ad hoc committee of the Pacific Northwest Utilities Conference Committee which had been formed to work on the long-range power program from 1981 to 1994. The meeting occurred on August 1, 1973, and it was an eye-opener for me. Some of the representatives of the Oregon utilities mentioned legislation which had been passed by the Oregon Legislature at the session just recently completed which set up a program under the Public Utility Commissioner of Oregon which would exempt utilities from liability for damage claims which might result from customer losses as the result of mandatory curtailment of power caused by a shortage. The program required each utility to submit to the Commissioner a plan showing the order in which particular types of loads would be curtailed and then, upon his approval, if the plan was placed into effect, the utility would be exempt from liability. One defect I could see as it related to the current energy crisis being reported on by Timme was that the law did not go into effect until January 1, 1974.

As the meeting broke up, I called together attorneys from various utilities, including Alan O'Kelly of Washington Water Power; Doug Beigle, Puget Power; Parker Williams, Snohomish County PUD; Art Lane, Seattle City Light; and Paul Nolan, Tacoma City Light. I told them that the information on the Oregon law intrigued me and I wondered what protection the State of Washington utilities might have in case of mandatory curtailment. I thought it essential that the attorneys of the State of Washington utilities immediately examine the law books to find out where we stood on such a matter. I also stated that, since legislative committee meetings in conjunction with the anticipated mini-session to be held in September 1973 were to be carried on this coming weekend in Olympia, it would be my purpose to get copies of the Oregon law and alert various legislative leaders to the possible need of mandatory curtailment legislation for the State of Washington. I was able to get copies of the Oregon law from Norm Stoll, an attorney from Portland who had been working for the Public Power Council. I sent these to the five attorneys, along with some comments on what the PUDs might be thinking of proposing.

The first idea of major importance was that the curtailment must be administered by some authority other than the Washington Utilities and Transportation Commission, which did not have jurisdiction over the city light systems, PUD utilities, and rural electric cooperatives. We did not want to come under that Commission's authority in any way, as to do so would destroy the basic concept of local control of a utility. We recognized that to be protected against liability and lawsuits resulting from damages which might occur as a result of mandatory curtailment orders to an electric power user, a utility would have to be responding to direct instructions to curtail power from state government. We did not want the Washington Utilities and Transportation Commission to have the authority to give the consumer-owned utilities that order. Eventually, as we worked the law out, the Governor would give the order, and the Washington Utilities and Transportation Commission would administer it for the private utilities.

During the legislative weekend of August 3, 4, and 5 at Olympia, I called together the lobbyists for the private and public power utilities and explained to them what I saw as our need and immediately started to alert various legislative leaders. At that time, I hoped to keep the matter from becoming public until a more definite decision could be made on the need for such legislation. On Sunday morning, August 5, I met with Representative Bob Perry, Chairman of the House Transportation and Utilities Committee, along with Charles Hodde, my legislative consultant, and Jerry Buckley of Washington Water Power, and went through the report. I told them it would be my intention to get back to the Legislature as soon as we could determine if some kind of law was needed.

At 10:30 a.m. we moved into a Committee hearing on another subject, and, without any warning to me, Chairman Perry started to tell the other members of the Committee and all those present, including the press, what the trouble was, and then said, "Mr. Billington, would you mind making a report to the entire Committee on this?" Needless to say, I was somewhat flabbergasted, but I went ahead trying to be as conservative as I could. However, the headlines of the next day put the issue right out in the middle of the street. From there things began to pick up in a hurry, culminating in a full public hearing on August 15, again using the Pacific Northwest Utilities Conference Committee as the forum. I had been instructed by the Joint House and Senate Committees to get back to them as soon as it was determined if legislation was needed. I agreed to furnish their committees with some current information on the matter, and I did so.

I was called to a meeting between the officials of the Chelan-Douglas-Grant PUDs and their legislators on August 22 at the Crescent Bar Restaurant in Grant County. We spent considerable time going over the situation and discussing the fact that while these three districts had large generating plants of their own, the output of those plants was dedicated to regional needs and therefore their local districts would have to share in any curtailment program. At this meeting, I enumerated some of the basic essentials which I felt were necessary in the mandatory legislation; namely, that it not be administered by the Washington Utilities and Transportation Commission, that authority be vested in the Governor, that utilities be granted exemption from liability claims resulting from losses from curtailment, and that utilities should be deeply involved in planning the program. Senator Nat Washington, who was then serving as Chairman of the Western Council of State Governments, said he thought it was essential to get legislative leaders from the Western states together at a special meeting in order to start coordination on power curtailment between the legislative branches of government in the different states.

The next day, August 23, he called me in Richland where I was attending a Tri-City Nuclear Council meeting, and stated that he was moving ahead and would hold a meeting in Seattle at the Sea-Tac Motor Inn on September 5. Following the August 15 meeting, I tried to get some kind of an answer out of the Legal Committee of PNUCC. They evidently discussed the matter a lot but they took no action. Finally, on Monday, August 27, I began to get a little panicky because a Senate Transportation and Utilities Committee meeting was scheduled for the next day and we were fast approaching the day the special mini-session would be called on September 8. No one seemed to be moving ahead on plans for a mandatory curtailment law. I therefore placed a call to Ralph Davis, President of Puget Power, but, finding that he would be absent until after Labor Day, got in touch with Larry Hall of that organization. As we discussed the matter, he agreed that we should start moving. I told him that Hodde, our legislative consultant, already had a draft of the law in the typewriter, and we agreed to meet the following morning, August 28, at the Puget Power offices. We met and pounded out some basic fundamentals on the type of legislation which we felt was necessary. By 10:30 a.m. that morning, Hodde and I made a fast dash to the Senate Committee meeting and arrived there just after that Committee had adopted a resolution recommending that legislation be enacted to instruct the Washington Utilities and Transportation Commission to take over and administer the curtailment program.

Senator Gordon Walgren, Chairman of the Committee, singled me out of the crowd and asked me directly whether I thought this was the proper way to go. I could immediately see that it was important for me to turn the thing around because we certainly did not want to put the PUDs and city light systems under the Washington Utilities and Transportation Commission in any way. To gain a little time for thought I went into the background on the power energy situation and then, while speaking, decided I might as well meet the thing head-on. I stated that in my opinion it was improper to have the Washington Utilities and Transportation Commission order a curtailment program because, as the regulatory agency for the private utilities, it would have a conflict of interest, or at least be in a compromised position, in trying to deal later with any financial problems the private companies might have as the result of a curtailment which the Commission had ordered. The Committee got the message loud and clear and then stated that it would like to have a bill drafted by the utilities at the earliest possible date. I stated that I had already called all interested utilities to a meeting the following Thursday, August 30, at the Hyatt House, at which time we would try to coordinate our thoughts and draft legislation. I stated that we would try to complete this on August 31 and get it to our principals for approval, and that I could assure the Committee that on September 5 we would present it with a draft.

The following day, August 29, while I was in Olympia, I contacted Don Moos of the Governor's staff, and again had to plant the viewpoint very firmly that the Washington Utilities and Transportation Commission was not the proper group to order curtailment. We met on August 30 and started to draft legislation. This work was carried over to August 31, and in the meantime I once again touched base with Don Moos. Upon his recommendation, we got in touch with Don Brazier, Chairman of the Washington Utilities and Transportation Commission, who was to meet that afternoon with the Governor regarding this situation. Following some very hard drafting of legislation all day, we were about ready to adjourn with what we thought was a proper version at 6 p.m. when we got a call from the Governor's office asking whether or not we would be willing to meet with a "task force" that evening to work on the legislation. We agreed to stand by and, from 7:30 to 11 p.m. that evening, we had to take the Governor's representatives through the details of our position. One of the problems starting to surface was that the Governor wanted an "Executive Request bill," and we had already assured the Democratic-controlled Legislature that we would furnish them with a draft of legislation. I closed the Friday meeting by stating to Don Brazier that I would send a draft of our legislation back with him to the Committee Clerk and that he would be free to present it to the Governor to use as his Executive Request if he wanted to take our draft.

In the meantime, it seemed that everyone was trying to draft a piece of legislation to deal with mandatory curtailment. Senator Washington, who was coming up to the September 5 meeting of the Council of State Governments, had his research clerk working on it. The staff of the Joint Committee between the Senate and House Transportation and Utilities Committees was busy at work. The Washington Utilities and Transportation Commission was trying to get into the act, even though we had headed them off somewhat, and here we were as utility representatives trying to get approval from our principals of the bill which we had drafted.

On September 4, I received word that the Governor had accepted the utilities' draft with several minor changes. The Senate and House Joint

Committee had scheduled a meeting to be held immediately after adjournment of the Council on State Governments on September 5, at which time we were to present the utilities' draft. All the legislative leaders were present at the Council on State Governments Committee meeting on September 5. My problem was to avoid a partisan fight between the Republican Governor and the Democratic-controlled Legislature. It was rather amusing because the Democrats kept insisting that the utilities present their draft first before the Governor's representatives would be given a chance. I tried to sidestep this by letting the Governor's man take over, but they knocked this down and insisted that I proceed first. I did so, outlining the utilities' drafted legislation and explaining those portions which we felt were essential to administer mandatory curtailment in the State.

By agreement between the Governor and the legislative leadership, a mini-session, the Second Extraordinary Session, was convened on September 8, 1973, and adjourned eight days later on September 15. It was primarily concerned with budget matters and all other legislation was more or less pushed aside. However, based on recommendation of the Legislative Select Committee on Power Supply, which had been established in August, SB-2967, the Emergency Curtailment Act, was enacted. It had an automatic expiration date of July 1975. Under the legislation, the Governor was to administer the matter of electrical curtailment, using an advisory committee appointed by him of representatives of the utility industry.

In October 1973, the world was hit with the Arab oil embargo. Considerable confusion reigned in energy circles. Here in the Pacific Northwest, where the basic energy source was electricity, it seemed logical to go full out for a total electric power supply. In a number of meetings of utility people, prompted by support from civic and business leaders, the words "Go all electric and sink the Arabs" were heard. Many of the generating plants that would be discarded or canceled in later years were started because of this urgent situation.

In the intervening months before the Third Extraordinary Session of the Legislature was convened on January 14, 1974, under the "continuing legislative sessions" practice, work commenced on drafting comprehensive curtailment of energy legislation, including matters pertaining to gas and oil supplies. When the Special Session convened, it started off with a bang. With standing committees already in place, nobody had the usual two or three days' leeway to get ready during committee organization. Because this was to be a brief and limited session, cut-off dates for introduction and consideration of legislation were established. The cut-off date for introduction fell at the end of the week. However, under the rules adopted, every bill which had been introduced from the beginning of the regular session back in January 1973 was alive and active.

All in all, it was very hectic. It was a hard-working session for the legislators as well as the lobbyists. Charlie Hodde and I were involved in committee hearings and meetings stretching many days from 7:30 a.m. to 11 p.m., and while the session did not labor on Sunday, except for one weekend, a full six-day weekly schedule was followed.

The pace and confusion can be illustrated by telling about one particular bill which I had to do some work on in order to clarify the mandatory fire district contract payments bill which had previously been passed. The bill was passed in the House of Representatives on Monday, February 4, transmitted to the Senate, referred to a committee which I could not even locate by the computer, given a hearing, read in the Senate Rules late Tuesday afternoon, February 5, and reported out of Rules at 7:30 p.m. on the same day for the next day's calendar. I finally located it by asking a casual question of the fire district lobbyist as I came out of a hearing room for a brief moment at 10 p.m. that evening. Needless to say, I did some very fast work from that point to past midnight, early next morning, and up to 1 p.m. the next day. My work involved stopping the bill, preparing a needed amendment, getting it set to go on the floor, finding another way to go instead, withdrawing our amendment, passing the other bill, and turning my attention to the next issue.

When the Legislature got to the deadline it had previously set for adjournment, it could not get agreement with the Governor to be reconvened in April. Therefore, instead of adjourning sine die, the Democratic-controlled Legislature adopted a special concurrent resolution allowing the Extraordinary Session of the Legislature to recess to a date certain. The State Constitution provided that the House of Representatives and the Senate could each recess for up to 72 hours without the approval of the other body, but only with joint approval could they recess for longer periods. This procedure raised a point of interest because, unless legislation has an emergency clause to place it into effect immediately, legislation enacted by the Legislature goes into effect 90 days after adjournment of a session. Thus, some bills' effective dates were automatically delayed by the recess procedure. Also, the Governor had only five days to consider whether to approve or veto any bill while the Legislature was in session, which it was, even though it was recessed. After adjournment, the Governor at that time had ten days in which to make his decision.

When the Third Extraordinary Session of the Legislature convened again on April 15, 1974, we were informed that the new substitute SB-3170, the comprehensive energy curtailment legislation, would not be enacted. This left our present electrical emergency allocation and curtailment law in place with its expiration date of June 30, 1975.

Early in the 1973 Session, two legislators from Chelan County had introduced legislation for the purpose of providing their PUD with a five-person Commission. We had not blocked it except to state that should the bill start moving, we would attempt to amend it to restrict it to Chelan County PUD only. When we checked on why it was moving out, the Chairman told us that he had been unfairly criticized for holding the bill and had not received proper support from certain groups which had opposed the legislation. They had asked him to hold the bill and then later told other people that they were not opposed to the legislation. I went to the sponsors of the legislation and told them that had we known it was to move in this last reconvened session, we would have submitted the rewording which would clarify the ballot vote issue and also remove the term "districts of the first or second class." The bill was passed in the House, and in the Senate Committee our proposed changes were accepted with the support of the House sponsor. However, the bill was reported to the Senate Rules Committee and left there, so that adjournment came without its consideration.

The 43rd Session of the State Legislature adjourned on April 24, 1974, following three Extraordinary Sessions and one period of recess. While the total days of all the sessions during this two-year period were only 147, as compared to the previous two-year period with 164 days in session, our activities and involvement with the legislative branch of government had broadened greatly under the new practice of "continuing legislative sessions."

In January 1973, while at the Legislature, I received a letter from former U.S. Senator C. C. Dill, about the telephone conversation I had had with him the previous fall in which he proposed that the PUD Association establish a trust fund whose earnings would be used for prizes in a statewide public speaking contest for high school students in PUD counties. He planned to leave the money in his will. Thus, in March 1973, the Association enacted a resolution establishing the C. C. Dill Public Speaking Trust Fund. Then, later in early 1974, the Senator again contacted me and stated he did not want to wait until his death but would like to move forward on the trust grant. The trust fund was finalized in the fall of 1974. Details of this entire transaction appear in Chapter 9.

Stimulated by the sudden power shortage, Governor Evans established by Executive Order the State Power and Energy Council, to study and establish "basic concepts for discussion on power supply." Charlie Hodde, our legislative consultant, was one of those picked by the Governor to serve on the Council. During the various exchanges between public power and private power representatives, along with representatives of the direct service industries served by Bonneville, it was becoming apparent that some changes would have to be made in the way Bonneville was financed. Bonneville to this point had been treated like any federal agency, with all revenues paid to the agency being returned to the federal Treasury, so that it had to seek yearly appropriations not only for its construction program but for the ongoing operation and maintenance costs of the agency.

In October 1973, Undersecretary of the Interior John C. Whittaker instructed Bonneville to commence drafting legal language which would permit it to finance itself by issuing revenue bonds. The language must also cover the use of funds for operation and maintenance costs of the regional transmission system. In the early 1970s, the federal government had adopted new procedures for the use of committees by federal agencies which required that any consulting committee could be formed only by posting a notice in the Federal Register, going through the necessary public hearings, and establishing precise ground rules under which the federal agency would use any committee it set up. Such a committee would be totally subject to public purview. It was immediately recognized that this would throw deliberations of the Joint Power Planning Council open to public view with wide open news media coverage, not only of the actions taken, which, frankly, nobody would object to, but also of the heated exchanges about differences which still occurred between the three parties involved in the joint regional power supply.

To establish a different planning forum, we agreed to use the Pacific Northwest Utilities Conference Committee organization. While individual utilities could still maintain membership in the organization, the Public Power Council would join so that all consumer-owned utilities and the direct service industries could be members and participate in the PNUCC. Thus, during the early part of 1974, whenever I wasn't working at the State Legislature, I found myself serving on a legal committee (although I was not an attorney myself) composed of the top utility and direct service industry attorneys in the Northwest, helping to draft legislation for congressional consideration which would make Bonneville a self-financing agency. The legislation that resulted was the Federal Columbia River Transmission System Act enacted by Congress in October 1974.

December 1973 marked a very important meeting among the utilities and direct service industries in Seattle where, besides agreeing upon Bonneville self-financing, we agreed to participate in Phase II of a Hydro-Thermal Accord. Since the Phase I plants were to cover the anticipated load growth from 1972 to 1982, Phase II would cover planning for the next 10-year period to 1992. However, there had been so much disagreement about Phase I—the threatened shutdown of the Hanford Generating Plant, with studies to revise the plant for power-only operation, and the turn-down of the Eugene Water and Electric Board's nuclear plant by the voters in May of 1970—that many of the utilities were skittish about joining in a 10-year program. It was thus agreed that we would concentrate on a 5-year program, planning for those plants that would be essential to meet the forecasted load growth from 1982 to 1987. Since the net billing method was no longer available because of the change in Bonneville's status under the tax laws and because the financing capability of this method had been used up by increased costs of plants then under construction, we came up with a trust agency arrangement between Bonneville and the public power utilities. We agreed that the plan to rebuild the Hanford Generating Plant would be discarded in favor of construction of a totally new nuclear plant adjacent to the first Supply System plant at Hanford, the new plant to be known as Plant No. 1. And finally, we agreed to build an identical (twin) plant (No. 4) beside No. 1 and to construct twin plants (No. 3 and No. 5) side by side.

At this time, nationwide studies still indicated that nuclear plants were cost competitive with coal-fired plants. Additionally, nationwide studies and the experiences of other utilities involved in the construction of nuclear plants indicated that twinning plants and starting construction on the second one approximately 18 months from the time the first was started would mean substantial savings for the constructing entity. Part of the Phase II agreement was that the percentages of ownership participation in Plant No. 5 and in the proposed nuclear plant to be sponsored by Puget Power in Skagit County were changed. Instead of Seattle City Light, Tacoma Light, and Snohomish County PUD participating in the proposed Skagit nuclear plant to be built by Puget Power, that plant would be totally owned by private power, and Plant No. 5, instead of being owned 70 percent by public power and 30 percent by private power, as was the case with Plant No. 3, would have the private power ownership reduced to 10 percent. Only Pacific Power and Light would remain in Plant No. 5, with the other 90 percent being owned by consumer-owned utilities.

A settlement was negotiated in which the benefits and obligations still residing in the Hanford Generating Plant under the original contracts on the 50/50 power split back in 1962 were agreed upon. The new Plant No. 1

would be totally consumer-owned, and would be constructed and operated by the Supply System.

In March of 1974, we increased the staff of the PUD Association and I was able to hire another good employee, Ed Blakemore, as Administrative Assistant. Loyalty is a cardinal virtue in any employee, and Ed was to prove his loyalty in short order. Because I had two meetings scheduled for the same day, I dispatched him to a meeting of the Northwest Public Power Association in Vancouver, British Columbia, where one of my PUD Commissioners took him aside and tried to recruit him to secretly report to the Commissioner about certain activities the Commissioner thought were going on in my office. As a new employee, Ed was somewhat confused but had the loyalty and courage to come directly to me, and then, with his agreement, I secured a meeting with the Commissioner and one of his fellow Commissioners, who happened to be President of the Association during that year. The four of us had a rather direct discussion. I told the Commissioner who had spoken to Ed that the Association office was open, especially to Commissioners, and that he could examine any detail of our operations. I told him that if he had any question of any kind he could ask it now or prepare it and submit it to me later, but that if I ever heard of him trying to intimidate or cultivate one of my employees to become a stooge, I would disclose the matter to every other Commissioner in the State and I would do it by personally trying to knock him on his butt. After several years, Ed was able to move on to a better job with one of the public utility districts, and I was very happy to recommend him when questioned about his abilities.

One of my last personal actions in 1974 was to send a letter to Congresswoman Julia Butler Hansen who had announced her intention to leave Congress at the end of the year. She had been a pillar of strength, first while serving in the State Legislature and then later for the Pacific Northwest power program while serving in Congress. When it came to federal appropriations, we enjoyed a one-two punch with Senator Magnuson on the Senate side and Julia Butler Hansen on the House side. She was a great lady who could out-politic most men. I was elated when my Board approved my recommendation that she receive the Earl Coe Award from the Association, but I was chagrined to learn that she would be unable to attend the December 12 banquet where it was to be awarded. Thanks to tape recorders, when I met with her a week before the banquet and presented the award ex-officio, she made a very humble but responsive acceptance speech which I played at the banquet. As Chair of the House Appropriations

Committee's Subcommittee on Public Works, she had to be in Congress in actual session at the time the banquet was held in Seattle.

Summary

The era from 1969 through 1974 brought peace between private power and public power in the legislative arenas.

Joint legislative efforts worked out the first one-stop State certification for thermal plant siting in the nation, which was adopted by the State of Washington. The first and second phases of the joint Hydro-Thermal Accord were agreed upon. Major thermal plants were placed under construction.

Important federal legislation provided self-financing for Bonneville using federal power revenues to back federal bonds issued for financing purposes.

A successful joint effort kept the Hanford Generating Plant in operation, and a reorganization of the Supply System permitted the Seattle City Light and Tacoma Light systems to join the Supply System.

7

1975–1981 Era
Power Supply and Regional Power Act

1975–1976

THE 44TH SESSION of the State Legislature convened on January 13, 1975. It was to be one of the most interesting sessions during my service with the PUDs. It was strongly controlled by the Democrats with a Senate majority of 30 to 19 and a House majority of 63 to 35. What was of most interest was that in the Senate there would be 14 new faces. Although several of these were former House members who had moved to the Senate, there were also quite a number who had not served in either house before. Following the 1973 and 1974 sessions, many of the long-time and powerful senators had not run for re-election. Senator Greive had been ousted from his long-time majority floor leadership in 1973 by Senator Augie Mardesich, and in 1974 his seat was won by a good-looking, as well as intelligent, Republican lady by the name of Nancy Buffington. Other long-time and strong members absent from the roster included Atwood, Canfield, Connor, Dore, Durkan, Peterson (Ted), Stender, Wetzel, and Woodall, to name a few. This session would also be interesting because it was the last one in Governor Dan Evans' third term, and word was out that he would not seek re-election.

Another new young Democratic legislator who would become personally important to me later, though I did not realize it at the time, was Jim Boldt, 24 years of age, from the 8th District (Benton and part of Yakima counties). The next year, in the spring of 1976, Representative Boldt was a lead speaker for the Hanford Student Tour which the PUD Association was then conducting. This project brought high school students from PUD and city light areas throughout the State of Washington to the Tri-Cities area for first-hand observation of the Hanford Generating Plant in their introduction to the use of nuclear energy to generate electricity. The tour was part of a seminar that provided two days of study and instruction about this and other new energy sources for electricity. Vera Claussen, my assistant, had started the Tour and Seminar for the Association in May 1971. It became an annual highlight of my job. It was a pleasure to meet and greet the students and observe their reactions to the use of nuclear energy to supply power.

I recall picking up my President, Commissioner Bob Archer from Clark County PUD, at the airport the morning in 1976 when Jim Boldt was to make his speech before the students. As we drove in, I told Bob it would be well to observe this young man in action because one of these days it was my intent to take early retirement, and the Association would be in need of a replacement. I had already become acquainted with this man's forceful abilities by watching him at work at the Legislature. But in 1975, he was just a new young legislator who had to be taught the ropes on dealing with public power legislation.

The 1975 and 1977 legislative sessions also represented a high point in the influence by private and public utility lobbyists. Since making peace in 1969, we had cooperated on legislative matters affecting utilities. In 1970, we had jointly secured the one-stop site certification act for thermal power plants. The legislative leaders were closely identified with either private power utilities or public power utilities. When combined, our lobbying influence would be awesome and yet, on occasion, we would still have our differences.

Another item of interest of the 44th Session was its length. As required by the Constitution, the first session ended on March 13, 1975, but a Special Extraordinary Session was immediately convened on March 14, to run until June 9, 1975. This totaled 148 days of continuous legislative sessions. After convening a Second Extraordinary Session for three days in July, the Legislature met in August and September for two short one-day and two-day periods and then reconvened on January 12, 1976, to run for 75 days. The final total for the 44th Session was 229 legislative days, the longest in our State's history.

To understand private/public power happenings at the 1975 Session of the Legislature, one would have to go back to the 1974 Session. The big bill which local public power was interested in was an amendment to the joint operating agency law to clarify once and for all the right of the Washington Public Power Supply System to construct and operate generating facilities outside the State of Washington. In late 1973, just prior to the 1974 Special Session, I had talked to Don Frisbee, Chairman of the Board and Chief Executive Officer of Pacific Power and Light. He said he agreed that we needed this amendment, and stated that, as far as he was concerned, any proper law which would allow local public and investor-owned utilities to cooperate to construct generating plants was essential because of the financial crunch utilities were facing nationwide in trying to raise enough capital to build such plants.

While we still had underlying differences, since the year 1969 public and private power had been working cooperatively on a regional power program. Don said he would contact the heads of the other investor-owned utilities to see if they supported the amendment we wanted. In the 1974 Session, we introduced our legislation to clarify the "within and without the State of Washington" issue only to find ourselves crossways with Wendell Satre of Washington Water Power and Ralph Davis of Puget Power. In order to avoid an all-out private/public power confrontation in the legislative arena, we canceled a hearing on the legislation and backed away from it.

Following adjournment of the 1974 Special Session, I traveled to Spokane to sit down with Wendell Satre and talk with him directly about this issue. Present was Jerry Buckley, who still headed their lobbying activities after being promoted to Secretary of Washington Water Power. We had a forthright discussion and my summation was very simply that we would either get this authority by means of a direct amendment to our present law; reinstitute a court test and seek a legal declaratory judgment, a decision which we felt would favor us; or, as a third alternative, seek the same result by a statewide initiative. As Jerry drove me back to the airport that evening he said, "I doubt if Wendell actually understood your last statement and I will go back and make sure that he does."

Passing laws by initiative in the State of Washington is a very effective weapon the citizens have when the Legislature refuses to act on some of their interests. On one or two occasions, initiatives have been passed which have not been altogether for the public good, but, in the main, this has been a good means whereby the citizenry can write a law which a majority of them feel is badly needed. The private utilities, back in 1940 and again in

1946, tried to use the initiative method to block the expansion of local public power. Here the consumer interest in utility service prevailed and the initiatives were defeated. Then for many years during the late 1940s and the 1950s when private power was attempting but failing to get punitive legislation passed in the Legislature, I was always afraid that they would try to get laws we blocked there passed via the initiative route.

What I did not know was that the investor-owned utilities were having continuing public opinion surveys made by Central Surveys of Iowa, and in each survey, they found that even when they had a classy sounding slogan to push the initiative, such as "let the people vote," there was strong basic built-in support for public power because of its low cost. Thus, they felt that, if they ever got into a direct statewide voter issue with local public power, they could lose as they had in 1940 and 1946.

I think it was apparent to Jerry that while investor-owned utilities, by means of their political financial support, had obtained the attentive ear of a majority of both the Senate and House of Representatives in the State Legislature, they could not be too certain of what would happen if they got into a general statewide private/public power fight. Before the 1975 Session of the Legislature, I again contacted Wendell Satre who, at our meeting in Spokane the previous April, had agreed to sound out the heads of the other investor-owned utilities about a clarifying amendment to the joint operating agency law. It was rather interesting to see how we approached each other's legislative requirements. One side would never ask the other side to support its legislative needs. We would only ask each other to "understand" our particular needs.

Thus, I found myself at lunch at the Sheraton Hotel in Portland with Ralph Davis and Wendell Satre. I again stated that it was my intent to move ahead on this amendment and that I hoped they would understand. It was at this luncheon that they told me they were joining the telephone and gas companies to get amendments in utility regulatory procedures. When Davis said that maybe this legislative session would be an occasion to have a two-way street as regards support of each other's needs, I understood what they were proposing, and stated that while I would not be able to support the legislation they outlined, I could agree that in no manner would I become involved in their issue if they would not become involved in our legislative program. I enumerated several of the laws on which I would be working. The lunch ended with no overt agreement or support for each other's legislative needs or legislation, but with a good, fair understanding.

In the 1975 Session, I found myself handling seven bills for the PUDs. One, sought since 1974, was the amendment to permit the Supply System to construct within or without the State. However, just as we got started on that we ran into another problem associated with the construction of nuclear plants. When the Supply System failed to receive a single bid from a supplier of uranium ore (yellow cake), we had to broaden the authority for a joint operating agency to acquire and even mine land-bearing energy resources. This resource might be coal, which was already in the law, but it also needed to cover uranium and geothermal or any other known or unknown energy resource.

I already had the "within and without" bill introduced on the Senate side, so I decided to have a broadened bill introduced on the House side. I was delayed in the bill drafting room because of a clerical error when a conversation with Representative Robert Perry took place. Bob Perry, Democrat from the Seattle area, was one of the original six Democrats who became private power supporters in the HB-197 fight during the 1961 Session. Suffice it to say that Representative Perry became connected to the investor-owned utilities through being employed by the Washington Irrigation and Development Corporation, a subsidiary of The Washington Water Power Company.

During the 1960s, he had been an ardent pro-private power legislator. Frankly, he still was and certainly showed that in his support and handling of their bill, HB-435, the investor-owned utility amendments to regulatory procedures. I ran into Perry outside the cafeteria in the basement of the legislative building, and he said, "Where in hell is your bill?" I told him that I had fouled up in the bill drafting room because of a clerical error and that I did have this other amendment which had to be added. He said that he had been meeting just that morning with the private power lobbyists and while Washington Water Power and Pacific Power and Light had indicated their willingness to go along with our legislation, Dale Traylor, lobbyist for Puget Power, had said that his utility couldn't. Evidently, Dale hadn't received any direct word from his top management. Bob said, "I told him that he had better watch his p's and q's because they certainly, while not expecting your personal support for their legislation, should be well aware that if you fought them they didn't have a ghost of a chance to pass it." I chuckled internally hearing this come from Bob who had spent many previous years trying to knock my head off legislatively.

Bob Perry was one of the most astute political animals I have ever met, so I knew he recognized what could happen if local public power should get into a fist fight over this private power bill. He said, "Get your bill in and get it in fast because I want it just one step ahead of their bill during this whole session. That way there can't be any doublecross. I want it down on the

Governor's desk before we start on their bill." Well, from that moment on, we went into high gear and even though our "within and without" bill, HB-544, was introduced substantially later than HB-435, it always seemed to be one step ahead of HB-435.

The lobbyists for the investor-owned utilities kept the word of their presidents. While they were not asked for, nor did they give any visible support to our legislation, they very honestly told their ardent supporters in the legislative arena that they were keeping hands off, and if the legislator wanted to support it he could. As a result, we obtained the support of some very definite pro-private power legislators.

On the night the House was to hold a hearing on HB-435, I found, on returning to Ulcer Gulch, that Jerry Buckley had called. When I responded, Jerry said, "Just a moment, I would like to put Bob on the line to you." Representative Perry came on and said the hearing was scheduled that evening at 7:30. He asked if I would be willing to appear and testify in support of the legislation. I told him that my agreement with the private power companies was that I would not oppose it nor would I become involved in it. I said that when I discussed the legislation with my legislative committee, we could see some merit in the "construction work in progress" issue since we recognized the need of raising capital in such large amounts for needed generating plants. I stated that we also could see some value in obtaining for our Pacific Northwest investor-owned utilities those federal tax incentive write-offs which were given to other private power companies in the nation by the federal Treasury. This was the procedure where federal tax payments would be postponed by the Treasury even though they had been collected from the private power ratepayer. On the other hand, I told him that there were some things in the bill which I did not agree with, but that I would stay out of it because of the understanding that I had with Satre and Davis. I told him I was planning to attend the hearing, but I did not care to testify. He asked if I would be willing to explain how PUDs financed generating plants if the question came up. I agreed that if this was brought up, I would respond to a request from him to explain it to the Committee.

I attended the hearing that evening accompanied by Commissioner Ed Fischer of Clark County PUD and J. Wiley Bowers, Executive Director of the Tennessee Valley Public Power Association. Wiley was in the Northwest for an American Public Power Association meeting and had come down to Olympia to visit me. We purposely sat in the back row to avoid the hot and heavy fireworks between the companies—electric, gas, and telephone—in support of the legislation, and the Washington Utilities and Transportation Commission which was very definitely opposed to it. Sure enough, the question came up from one of the Committee members about how the PUDs financed their generating plants. Representative Perry as Chairman spoke up and said, "Mr. Billington of the PUDs is here tonight, and I would like to have him come forward and explain it."

At that stage of the game I would have preferred to stay seated, but since he made a definite request, I had no alternative to speaking. In my statement I made it very clear that we were not involved with this legislation and that we would take no position from an official PUD Association standpoint. I outlined the method used by the public power organizations to finance their generating plants. I closed with a frank statement that it was my personal knowledge, because we were cooperating with the investor-owned utilities on the financing of a regional power supply, that a large number of investor-owned utilities in the nation were hard pressed to raise dollars for internal cash flow purposes, as well as capital construction costs. I stated that certainly, if adjustment was necessary in regulatory procedures to allow them to raise the money they needed for the good of the region, then the Legislature should examine the entire matter. Later, some of my consumer interest friends interpreted my remarks as being an endorsement of the legislation. It honestly wasn't, but merely, perhaps, a damn fool statement as I look back at it. It was just an attempt on my part to be honest.

Later, during the legislative deliberations when individual legislators would approach me about my personal position on HB-435, I stated very forthrightly that the PUD Association took no position on the measure, but I expressed my view that some work-in-progress costs should be incorporated into the rate base as the project was being constructed, and second, that I had personally changed my position about retention of federal tax moneys by the investor-owned utilities. It was true that under their proposal, federal taxes would be charged to their customers in the rate payments, and, thus, when the companies kept these dollars and did not pass them on to the federal Treasury, this meant the investor-owned utility was being financed by federal tax money collected from the customer. But if this was going to be our nation's policy, I felt the investor-owned utilities in the Pacific Northwest should have the same financing privileges as investor-owned utilities elsewhere in the nation.

HB-435 came through the House without too much trouble. But when it arrived in the Senate Transportation and Utilities Committee, it ran into quite a storm. Chairman Gordon Walgren was opposed and it took some pretty hard arm twisting by lobbyists to bring it out of that Committee and then out of the Senate Rules Committee. I had to be absent from the legislative arena during those days because of a previously scheduled American

Public Power Association conference and a personal family requirement. For this I felt fortunate because it would have been awkward to be present during the tough lobbying period.

The bulk of the opposition to this legislation came from my friends of the consumer groups. It wasn't easy for me when they approached and I had to turn them aside or even directly support certain portions of the legislation. The bill got to Governor Evans' desk but, on July 2, 1975, he vetoed it. That was a real shock to the private power, telephone, and gas companies. However, he had some time previously signed HB-544, our big one which Representative Perry put on his desk ahead of HB-435.

The 1975 Session of the Legislature was very beneficial to local public power. We did have to drop one of our bills, which sought payment of fire district contract costs out of the established PUD privilege tax. We got crossways with the Association of Counties which felt that this would mean fewer dollars for the county commissioners from the PUD privilege tax. In effect, it would have meant this, but it was the honest thing to do. However, the fire district representatives favored the county commissioners' side in the argument, and we dropped the matter for this session.

One of the best bills which we got passed was HB-410. We were sponsoring another bill, HB-276, which would have extended errors and omissions insurance for public officials to all local government entities. A bill previously passed in the 1973 Session which would have done this had left a gray area. In studying the errors and omissions insurance problem, Omar Parker, attorney for Grays Harbor County PUD, called my attention to the indemnification provided to school board members under established law. I got the law out and found that it was very important, so we incorporated it into HB-410. Both of these bills caused a lot of confusion and a lot of hard work. Ever since the Watergate episode in Washington, D.C., there had been the suspicion, especially in the minds of legislative people, that any time you tried to get a law to protect a public official, you were trying to rip off the public. I had to really work hard on the indemnification law, which actually merely said that if a PUD Commissioner, other public officer, or employee of a PUD was sued because of errors or omissions while carrying out his or her official duties, he or she was entitled to be defended by the public utility district, which would pay attorney's fees, a settlement, or a judgment. The one exception to this privilege would be an official about whom a court would find that he or she had not acted in good faith.

Another bill which was passed that interested me personally was HB-664, which dealt with required thermal insulation in residential structures. Several years previously, the electric utilities working through the Electrical

Safety Code had clarified the need for installing either substantial insulation or electric heat equipment with substantial heating capacity in a given house. The matter had become intense because a number of California contractors had come into the Pacific Northwest under some federal financing provisions to build a large number of residential structures. Practically all of these structures were heated by electricity. However, after the first winter, all the utilities were hit with storms of protest by the residents of these new structures. How could they have such high bills in a region with the lowest electric rates in the nation? The customer who complained of high bills was also a cold customer. Even with high bills, they could not get their residential structures warm. Following the Arab oil embargo which hit the world in late 1973, a great surge took place to insulate the older homes. Boiling into my office one day came a young man by the name of Doug Canoose, a young insulation contractor in Vancouver, Washington. He was aggravated because, as he stated, there were a lot of fly-by-night Portland insulation contractors coming across the bridge into the State of Washington, going to the houses of local residents and scattering some gravel in the attic, getting paid for a poor insulation job at a high price, and then retreating back across the Oregon border. Doug wanted a law to control such activities.

The interesting part to me was that Doug was the son of my friend Conner Canoose, who, while working for D. Elwood Caples back in 1935, had secured my first office job which took me out of the logging camps. Doug Canoose had been named in honor of Douglas Elwood Caples by his father. Canoose had already persuaded Representative Al Bauer from Clark County to introduce HB-664, a bill to help correct the problem. I contacted some of the power-use personnel from the PUDs and private power: Ron Harper at Snohomish County PUD, Ken Crow at Grant County PUD, Floyd Keller at Clark County PUD, and Byron Swigert from Puget Power. We drafted a substitute House Bill which could be more effectively administered. Needless to say, this brought a horde of building contractors out of the sky to land on our attempts to get proper insulation installed in electrically heated residential structures. The building contractors, as well as the general contractors, have always had a potent lobby at the State Legislature, so that it required the united strength of all of the electric utility lobbyists to get the legislation passed. However, we overlooked one thing: Governor Evans had established an advisory commission to work on a new statewide building code. We failed to contact him about our bill and when he was advised that the statewide building code would be dealing with this matter, he vetoed our bill. By the time I got to his office and explained what was behind this legislation, the only solution was to go back to the next legislative session in 1976, with the Governor joining forces with the utilities, and re-enacting the law. Here again, it was not legislation which would control the building industry, but, rather, legislation which would provide that contractors would install equipment with sufficient electric capacity, plus a proper matching amount of insulation, to keep a house warm in the different areas of the State. After this bill passed, it was hoped that a utility would no longer be faced with a high bill complaint from a cold customer.

One of the biggest legislative fights in which we were not directly involved but about which we were very definitely concerned was Senator Augie Mardesich's move to revamp the public pension systems. Up to this time, the individual systems for teachers, cities, firemen and other public employees had been administered separately. Each had used a leapfrog approach at the legislative sessions to gain particular benefits or larger retirement payments by playing one system against the other. Mardesich insisted that these programs be consolidated and have limits placed on them. While some people, rightfully or wrongfully, were critical of Senator Mardesich's legislative activities, I personally know that it was this man's political strength and determination which closed the door on certain pension activities and provisions which were getting out of hand or becoming too liberal. He undoubtedly saved the State and its political subdivisions many millions of dollars in future years on pension costs.

My non-legislative public power activities in 1975 and 1976 were quite hectic. From the spring of 1975 to the end of 1976 I was for the first time directly and personally involved in a gubernatorial election. I had been very careful in past years not to get involved in partisan political elections because the PUD Commissioners were non-partisan, and I served them through the Association. My involvement this time was not exactly partisan because it had to do with supporting a primary candidate on the Democratic ticket. I stopped campaigning after Dr. Dixy Lee Ray won the September 1976 primary over Wes Ullman and Marvin Durning. I had become progressively disenchanted with Mayor Ullman and the way he dealt with Seattle City Light. My disillusionment with him was not caused by the incident in late 1971 and early 1972 when we danced around the circle about whether he would appoint me as Superintendent of Seattle City Light. I did not want the job anyway. But it did start then when his intention seemed to be to pull Seattle City Light more directly into the executive branch of city government.

Since he came in during a change in the form of government for the City of Seattle, I did not clearly understand what was happening. Seattle City Light had for many years under strong superintendents such as J. D.

Ross, Gene Hoffman, Paul Raver, and then John Nelson, been operating more or less separately from city government as a revenue-supported business. Its operations—from the standpoint of cost per customer for various utility functions, administration, accounting, distribution, etc.—were very efficient when compared to other utilities, either publicly owned or privately owned. While there had always been the tendency on the part of the city government to try to milk the revenues of Seattle City Light, the superintendents, backed by the State Auditor's office, had prevented too much diversion of Seattle City Light revenues to general city purposes. However, under the new form of government, with a strong Executive versus a strong Council, and a Mayor interested in helping to select consultants, bond attorneys, and other specialists, a change started to take place in Seattle City Light. For example, it was easy to have Seattle City Light purchase a large computer system, but to require that the system be available for other city functions. The money Seattle City Light spent on the City Attorney's office was always substantial. For many years, the vehicles in the Seattle City Light fleet were purchased and maintained by Seattle City Light personnel. The new government consolidated this fleet with general city vehicles and charged each department for purchase and maintenance of the vehicles its employees used. It was interesting to hear from Seattle City Light employees about excessive work order charges. Even the cost of changing oil in the vehicles seemed to go up substantially. I felt very strongly that publicly owned utilities, being supported by earned revenues instead of taxes, should be operated like a private business. I should add that I never disliked Wes Ullman personally. He always treated me fairly and, as far as I know, he was honest. It was the system of government which led to the change in Seattle City Light and which, in my opinion, reduced the business efficiency of the utility.

But back to the gubernatorial race of 1976. My involvement commenced in the spring of 1975 when I was having lunch with Ruth Howell, editor of the editorial page of the *Seattle P-I*. Having lunch together was a custom we enjoyed every so often just to visit. Ruth was a wonderful person, intelligent, direct, and honest. She was very interested in the Nature Conservancy Program, and earlier she had secured my personal support for the program, both financially and as a speaker. Ruth died about six months later in November, and the world suffered a tremendous untimely loss.

At lunch she spoke in her usual full-speed-ahead style. My opener was, "What are all these stories and the small editorial concerning one Dr. Dixy Lee Ray returning to the State of Washington and running for Governor?" She countered by saying, "You think the *P-I* now has its candidate?" I said it certainly looked like they had. She said, "Would you really like to know who more or less encouraged Dr. Ray to come back to the State of Washington and get involved in the Governor's race?" When I responded in the affirmative, she asked that I keep it a secret and I pledged to do so at least until I got back to my office. She said it was "Eddy Carlson of United Airlines." This was rather interesting, primarily because Carlson had been more or less associated in my mind with the Establishment. When I asked why, she responded that Carlson had expressed his intent to return to our State after retirement and was just interested in having good leadership for the State, and he felt that Dr. Ray could provide it. At that point, the matter was dropped and we discussed various power supply needs and environmental challenges that were being raised.

My personal awareness of Dr. Ray had grown through the years while she was with the Atomic Energy Commission. I had met her of course when she was head of the Pacific Science Center. While she was with the AEC, I became better acquainted with her, once meeting her in New Orleans at the airport when she went down to address the American Public Power Association. On occasion, I would see her in Washington, D.C., but beyond that we had no personal contact. A few days after my lunch with Ruth, I called Dr. Ray at her Fox Island home to welcome her back, and encouraged her to look at the gubernatorial race. As far as I was concerned, she was a very intelligent and direct person, and it seemed to me that the State could use someone of this type, even though she might not have experience in State government, which seemed to be a prerequisite to becoming Governor.

In early October 1975, I was contacted by former State Senator Wib Hallauer. Wib told me that he and his brother were closing out their orchard and packing plant business in Okanogan County and that he was going to have a little money and some time, so he was wondering what my attitude would be toward his running for Governor on the Democratic ticket. My response was that he should meet other potential candidates who were already more or less in the field, particularly Dr. Ray. I put him in contact with her and a dinner meeting was arranged, to be held on November 5 among Dr. Ray, Hallauer, Max Nicholai (a leading attorney who had worked with the Senate Democratic caucus in Olympia), and Ernie Conrad of the University of Washington.

I got fouled up on that particular night and couldn't be present primarily because of a hearing before the State House Committee on a nuclear energy moratorium bill which had been introduced in the Legislature.

Following the Special Session of the Legislature in 1976, I became directly involved in the campaign on Initiative 325, the anti-nuclear proposal. I therefore was not too active in the gubernatorial primary, but I did support Dr. Ray to the best of my ability. I realized that she had turned to some of the Establishment for her financial support. I also heard that Wendell Satre, of Washington Water Power, and the other power companies had contributed to her campaign through their Fair Competition Council political action committee. I was aware that the aluminum companies were definitely supporting her, as, of course, those industries associated with nuclear energy were. She did not raise any great amount of money but ran a good campaign, even though it was in some respects one of an amateur.

I was amazed to see how other candidates in the Democratic primary and then later in the campaign of the Republican candidate fell into one deadly trap of attacking her strongly by name. The campaigns of Marvin Durning and Wes Ullman did it in the primary and later John Spellman did it in the General Election. Dixy Lee Ray enjoyed name recognition throughout the State. The name itself was rather unique, and it was interesting to the ear. In my opinion, any person, when asked whom they are supporting for Governor, never wants to be without an answer. No one wants to appear dumb. In this case, it was pretty easy to remember at least one person who was running for the office. When the Durning ads would start off with, "Hear What Dixy Says," they might as well have dispensed with the copy below. Frankly, the ads were meant to tear her down on her positions on oil tankers, nuclear energy, and other issues. But just by putting her name at the top of the ad, even though they filled the ad with anti-Ray statements, they contributed to her name recognition. I was surprised but satisfied when she beat Ullman and the others in the primary.

After the primary, I went back to the sidelines, but I was somewhat concerned over the abortive effort by some of the more liberal Democrats to pull back and start a campaign for Martin Durkan on an independent ticket. I met him at a fund raiser for John Cherberg and asked him directly if there was any seriousness in it. He responded by saying "no." I then got in touch with Neil Cheney, State Democratic Chairman, and gave him a lecture on the need of the Democrats, instead of standing back and fussing because their chosen candidate had not been picked, to get hold of the Dixy Lee Ray campaign and, as a united party, go forward with the candidate. I felt she definitely had a chance to beat Spellman. It was interesting to see the maneuvering to unite the Democrats. About this time, I was contacted by Lou Guzzo, Dr. Ray's campaign manager, asking that Charles Hodde assist in her campaign. I told him that he should contact Hodde directly, since Hodde was not an employee of the PUD Association but was only retained as a consultant. He contacted Hodde, who kept me informed on what he was doing in coaching Dr. Ray on taxes, school financing, and other issues of the campaign.

The campaign came to its conclusion, as is known, with a resounding victory for Dr. Ray, and shortly after that Hodde found himself in a "kitchen cabinet" of about four to seven people surrounding the new Governor-elect to try to help her get started on her new administration. Hodde came to me and said it might be that he would join her staff, in which case I would have to look for another legislative consultant for the PUD Association.

On November 10, I had to fly to Washington, D.C., on a business trip and found myself on the same plane with the Governor-elect and Lou Guzzo. It was at this time that Guzzo told me they would like to have Charlie Hodde on their team. My response was that they could not get a better man, or one who was more knowledgeable about State government, but that, if they were going to do it, they should move ahead promptly so that I might get prepared for the legislative work.

Hodde kept me advised on the various discussions, and on December 12 he came into my office and said that Dr. Ray had made her offer to him to join her administration. Her first request of him was that he take on the Department of Social and Health Services reorganization and he said there was no way that he would do that. He said, "I responded by stating that there were only two things that I would do in her administration." And her response was, "Take your choice." He told me, "I didn't know exactly what to do at that point but I think I am going to—." I interrupted him by saying, "Do me a favor and don't tell me what you are going to take because if it gets out to the newspapers which are trying to make all the guesses now on who will be in her cabinet, you will always think I'd slipped it to the press." Thus, while I had received definite word he was going with the administration of Dr. Ray, it was not until I read it in the newspaper on the day of the announcement that I found he was going to be Director of Revenue. In the meantime, there were a lot of grapevine rumors and phone calls as to who might get this job or that job in the Dixy Lee Ray Administration. A number of persons kept calling me. I guess that they thought because Charlie Hodde was in, I would have some influence. Frankly, I did not get involved because I had found over many past years that those who get wound up on appointments always find themselves the losers in the long run, even if the person they recommend makes it.

I did get a little involved in who should not be appointed. The National Association of Railroad and Utility Commissioners had its big annual conference in Hawaii and, of course, all the private utilities went over to attend. Some of them brought back the rumor that former Commissioner of the Washington Utilities and Transportation Commission, Fran Pearson, had expressed an interest in returning to become Chairman of the Commission again. Later, there were a lot more hot and heavy recommendations for the Washington Utilities and Transportation Commission. The name Bob Perry hit my ears. Following the 1969 settlement of the political conflict between private power and local public power in the legislative arena, Perry, while still being very close to the investor-owned utilities, had assisted me in our legislative work. However, I could not forget that he was one of the first Democrats in 1959 to sell out to private power, having found very early that the political dollars were on their side of the fence. To me, appointing Pearson or Perry would have seemed like asking a fox to guard the chicken coop. Thus, taking an opportunity to speak directly to Lou Guzzo, I hit the subject head-on. It was comforting to hear Guzzo say, "Look, Ken, I spend a lot of time just throwing those kinds of names in the ash can for Governor Ray." As I told him, I had no candidate but I seemed to be more interested in just fending off the political pros in the hope that Dr. Ray could come through with a good administration.

Going into a Democratic party Christmas fund raiser, I met Dr. Ray as I came through the door with Virginia, and the Governor-elect introduced us to Neil Cheney saying, "Here are two of the people that were with me early on in my campaign." With that kind of an introduction, I then went and sought out Joe Zaspel and Duayne Trecker, two of her new staff members. To both of them I said that it was my hope that she would not use old political types or former appointees in her new cabinet. They responded by saying the only one of that type that they were aware she would be appointing was Charlie Hodde. I was heartened to hear this. It merely verified what I had felt all along—that she was direct and honest.

Several persons who I knew would have the ear of Governor Ray came and asked whether or not I would accept an appointment, one for the Regulatory Commission. I declined for two reasons. First, I did not want to chance ending up the way other persons have, namely, forgetting my commitment to the consumer; and second, at this point, I did not want to start another full-time career.

Charles Hodde's birthday is exactly to the day ten years before mine, but he was ready to bite off and go after it again. I was starting to think of retirement in about a year and a half. I was happy to note that one person in the new administration was going to be former State Senator Wib Hallauer who would head up the Department of Ecology. Following the dinner which I had helped organize a year before, he had joined the new Governor's campaign team and thus was to be rewarded. But the good part of it was that he would bring not only a good business head to the department's affairs, but also that his approach would be in the public interest.

It seemed like the latter half of 1975 found me in more arguments and controversies than usual. In early July, I became aware that Chairman Nassakis of the Federal Power Commission had instructed the General Counsel of the FPC to take the position that the FPC not only had the authority to approve Bonneville rates, to make sure they would be sufficient to meet congressional payback requirements, but also had the authority to approve the way the rates would be structured. He was basing his position on FPC oversight of rates for the Southeast Power Administration and the Alaska Power Administration. Both of these agencies had been established under a different law or executive order and such FPC oversight was allowed. In Bonneville's case, the same law that permitted the FPC to approve the Bonneville rate schedule stated very clearly that the FPC would not have jurisdiction over establishing the Bonneville rate structures. I immediately got in touch with Senators Magnuson and Jackson. In their usual very adroit manner, they got the matter clarified. I was pleased to receive a letter from Scoop stating that a meeting had been arranged between the FPC and Bonneville on the subject and that he had been assured that a full clarification of the FPC's authority would be forthcoming. I alerted Governor Evans to the problem and was a bit surprised to receive a return letter from him stating little concern for the FPC's action. I fired off a second letter just to reinforce his thinking that there had been more to the FPC move than most persons would recognize. It was also my information that Chairman Nassakis' action was being promoted by California utilities, who were trying to force a lower rate on the power being sold over the intertie. We won.

My second controversy centered on an editorial by Glenn Lee of the *Tri-City Herald*. Ever since Lee had supported public power's fight for the Hanford Generating Plant back in 1962, he had been a stalwart booster in construction of added nuclear plants, but only if they were to be built on the Hanford Reservation. A decision had recently been made by the Supply System to construct its second proposed nuclear plant west of the Cascades at the so-called Satsop site. Anti-nuclear plant sentiment had been growing and rumors were prevalent that a lot of the controversy west of the Cascades was being stirred up by persons or organizations in the Tri-Cities area, hoping that such controversy would force abandonment of westside nuclear plant sites in favor of the Hanford Reservation. The *Tri-City Herald* hit with a very damaging editorial on July 15, 1975, opposing westside plants, and a jarring exchange of correspondence between the Tri-City Nuclear Industrial Council, the *Tri-City Herald*, and the Washington PUD Association occurred.

My next controversy centered on the Corps of Engineers' report on mitigation costs for the Snake River dams. Anyone could recognize that a dam could not be constructed without having some effect on the shorelands, but it did seem a little obvious to me that the power users were going to pay a lot of mitigation costs for dubious purposes. First the report insisted that hatcheries be constructed upstream above the dam to replace fish lost because of the dam's construction. We had long favored the construction of hatcheries, but felt that building them above dams only increased the problem. Second, part of the mitigation cost would pay to purchase land from which fishermen could launch boats or which they could wade alongside of to fish for steelhead. The question was, Did fishermen have such facilities before the dams were built? The worst demand, however, was that mitigation costs cover purchase of lands for a hunting preserve and a game bird farm to stock such "compensation lands." While it was true that waters from the dam would inundate certain land formerly used by wildlife, it seemed odd that electric ratepayers were going to have to buy such land and stock it for the future. We lost this argument on all three points.

Probably one of the most interesting controversies facing me arose in September 1975. Senator C. C. Dill had donated $16,000 to the Association which we had placed in a trust fund, all the proceeds of which would be used for prize money in oratorical contests among high school students. All administrative costs of the program were to be borne by other Association funds. All at once the Internal Revenue Service challenged the trust fund and designated it as a type which must pay a certain amount of the principal to the government each year. When I had spent a lot of time and effort arguing with the local IRS representatives without getting anywhere, I got in touch with Senator Magnuson in Washington, D.C. He was as astounded as I that the government would not agree to let us have a trust fund of which every dollar from the fund's earnings would be given away to students. In defense of the IRS, the problem evidently arose because Senator Dill, in making the contribution of the funds, had taken it as a deduction on his personal income tax report.

Many past incidents had caused me to admire the ability and efficiency of Senator Magnuson, but I never had a better opportunity to see him in action when his personal feelings were also involved. I will never forget the day I received a call back from him, saying, "Ken, I couldn't believe you when you told me that the government was insisting that a trust fund held by a non-profit organization such as yours would be subject to taxation. It didn't make sense that you couldn't have a gift of money held where all the earnings would be given away to students, but that's what they told me when I first called about the matter. However, I have now gone to the top, and I understand that upon second study, they have now determined that the trust falls under a different regulation. You'll get a letter shortly stating so." On December 5, 1975, I received a letter from the Internal Revenue Service stating that the C. C. Dill trust fund would not be subject to regulations whereby a portion of the principal of the trust would have to go to the government each year. Maggie won and future student orators had won.

In December 1975, I sent a letter to Governor Evans in his capacity as Chairman of the Pacific Northwest River Basins Commission, to rebut statements made by a representative from an environmental group complaining that there had been no citizen participation in power planning matters. In that letter, I pointed out that there was substantial participation in power planning by the many consumer-owned utilities which had duly elected citizen boards. In this letter I once again urged him to seek a way to extend Pacific Northwest control and influence over Bonneville. Seven years later, I received a copy of the letter mailed back to me by Governor Evans after he had been appointed to the new Pacific Northwest Power Planning Council, with a note reminding me of my early position on the matter.

One of my last efforts of 1975 ended disappointingly. Jack Stein, Managing Director of the Supply System, had notified his Executive Committee and Board of his intention to retire. I was aware that there had been some controversy about whether construction on the Supply System generating plants was progressing on schedule. Stein's retirement meant that the Executive Committee would have the job of seeking a replacement. Sam Volpentest, Executive Vice President and Manager of the Tri-City Nuclear Industrial Council, gave me the name of Tom Nemzek. Nemzek had been head of the Research and Development Administration activity on the Hanford Reservation for a number of years, but had been promoted and moved to Washington, D.C. He was in a top job as the Director of the Division of Reactor Research and Development of the Energy Research and Development Administration. After the running gun fight between the Tri-City Nuclear Industrial Council and the PUD Association in July over the Glenn Lee editorials, Volpentest suggested that it might be well if Nemzek's name was proposed by another source. I was very happy to take that suggestion because I was aware of the man's ability and performance while at Hanford. I therefore secured Tom Nemzek as a speaker for our 1975 annual conference program. He came to Seattle not only for the purpose of making the speech but also, at my suggestion to both sides, to meet with various members of the Supply System Executive Committee and

Board. I was chagrined when Ed Fischer, Chairman of the Executive Committee, stated that he personally would interview Nemzek. I had hoped that others of the Executive Committee could be present. However, it was a one-on-one meeting and when Nemzek was asked what salary he would request, and the figure he named was substantially higher than was being paid at that particular time, Fischer ended the interview. The salary requested was substantially higher than the one that was then being paid Stein, but it actually was about one-half the salary which would be paid the new managing director in 1980, a man who had worked for Nemzek. I was disappointed that Nemzek did not get the job, but it was not within my province to say who should or should not be hired by the Supply System.

The year 1976 was very important in power supply matters in the Pacific Northwest because many events occurred in that year which had a marked effect on future years. My first involvement was to cover the continuing legislative session which reconvened January 12, 1976, for a Second Extraordinary Session, and ran through March 26, 1976, for a total of 81 days. One change that occurred on the legislative scene was the resignation of Speaker Len Sawyer at the insistence of the Democratic House members.

On January 23, 1976, the Bovee/Crail contract was canceled by the Supply System, I understood due to dissatisfaction with their performance. This was a major contract on Plant No. 2, and the cancellation caused a lot of conflict and delay in the construction schedule. It was to set the stage for one of the first major lawsuits involving the Supply System and also to directly affect my work at the Legislature in 1977. This case became a factor in my early retirement in July 1978.

A 1972 ruling of the Internal Revenue Service had eliminated the use of net billing sale of power produced by generating plants financed by means of tax-exempt municipal revenue bonds. Bonneville could no longer buy power from such plants. This meant that the two new plants built by the Supply System would have to get their revenues from direct sales contracts to individual utilities. Seattle City Light had commenced an energy study in 1975 which was completed in early 1976 and indicated that Seattle need not participate because it had access to other power sources, such as power it could obtain by raising High Ross Dam, and because its confined utility service area had a substantial residential electric heat load. By applying conservation measures, it could not only reduce load growth but possibly have its own "in-house" power supply source by reducing present residential usage with insulation and other conservation measures. While several other utilities elected not to participate in these new plants, Seattle City

Light was the first major utility in the Northwest to turn away from joint construction of generating plants.

On January 29, 1976, Cowlitz County PUD took first action to explore the possibility of taking over Pacific Power and Light's Merwin Dam license, which was coming up for renewal. The old private versus public power political pot began to heat up.

A major event of this year was Initiative 325, sponsored by the Coalition for Safe Energy (CASE). This was a direct challenge to all nuclear plants, and a campaign to oppose the initiative was organized. The problem for local public power was caused by the open meetings law, which specifically prohibited the use of any public funds for political purposes, but also severely limited the involvement of elected officials in political campaigns. I first attempted to get a clarification from the Public Disclosure Commission about what would be proper behavior for a PUD Commissioner whose public office obligation required him to support new generating plants in order to meet anticipated power needs of the district, while he faced a political initiative which, if passed, would bring to a grinding halt construction of new power plants. This was an ongoing dilemma during the campaign. While the PUD Association, as a private non-profit corporation, would not be subject to the requirements that public officials would, it was deemed essential that we adhere to the spirit of the open meetings law because our purpose was to serve the public. We ended up walking on eggs during the campaign. As we could have anticipated, the proponents of the initiative challenged the PUD Association, and we had to face a hearing before the Public Disclosure Commission on October 19. Our accusers specifically challenged some nuclear power plants ads, although we had been running these ads for a number of years before the initiative was proposed, and we felt that we were entitled to proceed as long as we could demonstrate that we had not increased their frequency or length. During the hearing, the Association and I were absolved of charges that the ads violated the law.

On the other hand, the private power utilities were not under the same restriction, and they mounted a strong campaign against the initiative, which, to our relief, the voters of the State rejected in November.

In June 1976, Bonneville Administrator Don Hodel issued a notice of insufficiency to all public and cooperative utilities being served by Bonneville, which stated that, as of June 1983, Bonneville would no longer be responsible for the power load growth needs of the local utilities. It also stated that at that time, should Bonneville's power supply be insufficient to meet those needs, there would be an allocation among the public and cooperative utilities of whatever power supply Bonneville then had. He also stated that Bonneville direct service industrial contracts to aluminum and other companies would not be renewed as they expired. Eighty-five percent of these industries were located in public and cooperative utility service areas. This encouraged many of the utilities to sign direct purchase sale contracts on the two new plants to be constructed by the Supply System. Eighty-eight utilities oversubscribed the plants' output to a total of 133 percent.

At this time the State of Oregon was giving substantial publicity to the formation of a Domestic and Rural Power Authority. DRPA would be a state agency which would try to purchase power directly from Bonneville under the preference clause. As outlined, it would contract to use the private power transmission and distribution lines up to the service drop leading to the meter. From this point, DRPA would own the wire and the meter, with the power then being sold to the customer by the "public power DRPA." One could see a tremendous lawsuit overshadowing the federal power supply in the Pacific Northwest with a fight through the U.S. Supreme Court. We felt confident we could win for public power against this perverted use of the preference clause. A recent case in California gave us support. However, this disruptive fighting among the utilities and states of the Pacific Northwest could seriously affect our ability to meet the anticipated power shortages.

On December 6, 1976, in Spokane, Senator Scoop Jackson met with major representatives of all utilities in the Pacific Northwest, along with representatives of the direct service industry customers of Bonneville and direct representatives of Bonneville. It was agreed that unless we could obtain specific federal legislation to clarify the use of federal power in the Pacific Northwest, as a base for future power supply needs, the joint regional efforts would fall apart. We decided that the utilities and other major power supply users would commence drafting federal legislation to provide specific joint regional power supply efforts. The work would be coordinated by the Pacific Northwest Utilities Conference Committee, which had become the center for joint power supply planning efforts among the utilities and major Bonneville industrial customers.

It had indeed been a hectic year and one which saw many events affecting power supply. One major event was the first C. C. Dill public speaking contest held by the PUD Association. We held our regional eastside and westside contests in October and November, so for our December Annual Conference we had the four student winners appear on a luncheon program. We asked speech instructors from three major universities to act as our judges to pick the statewide winner. It was a happy occasion for us and the students.

1977–1978

The last five years of my life in public power centered primarily on the Washington Public Power Supply System and its growing array of troubles and problems. I was also involved in passage of an act by Congress dealing with the Pacific Northwest regional power supply. The kick-off for this law took place at the meeting in Spokane on December 6, 1976, with Senator Jackson. The utilities and direct service industries agreed to seek passage of a federal law providing a formal method to plan and construct needed power plants for the Pacific Northwest centering in the Bonneville Power Administration. With the White House passing to a new Democratic President and Democratic majorities controlling the Senate and the House, we thought we could get such a law without all-out partisan political infighting. It also seemed to be a suitable time to seek some stabilization in the nuclear regulatory action which was causing considerable consternation and difficulties among all the utilities, including the Supply System, which wanted to construct nuclear plants.

On January 14, 1977, I participated in a small meeting with Dr. James Schlesinger who, word had it, would become the first Secretary of Energy if a proposal to establish this new cabinet level position were accepted. At the time, he was heading what was termed the White House Energy Office. The meeting, held in Washington, D.C., was attended by David Freeman and Katherine Schirmer who worked on the Carter/Mondale transition staff; Lee White, representing the Energy Task Force, Consumer Federation of America; Ellen Berman of the Energy Task Force, Consumer Federation of America; Alex Radin, Executive Director, American Public Power Association; Bob Partridge, General Manager, National Rural Electric Cooperative Association; Jack Sheehan, Industrial Union Department of the Steelworkers of America; and Rubin Johnson, National Farmers Union. I attended in my capacity as Chairman of the Western States Water and Power Consumers Conference, as well as Executive Director of the PUD Association.

The purpose of the meeting was to seek information on the new Carter Administration's plans with regard to energy supply and development. My particular portion of the conference dealt with criticizing the federal nuclear regulatory process. I pointed out to Dr. Schlesinger that the continued failure to stabilize regulation in the construction of nuclear plants was causing terrific increases in the cost of the plants. This was not due to the safety procedures being required, but was happening because one after another of the requirements would be altered during plant construction, necessitating substantial renovation or rebuilding of work already done. I pointed out that the failure of our nation to standardize its regulations for plant design had resulted in unrestricted development of plants by hired architects and engineers leading to building a new Cadillac instead of a proven Ford. While the response and assurances from Dr. Schlesinger showed that he agreed with me, the situation did not change, resulting in what happened later to America's nuclear power plant program. It became a debacle for many utilities.

The 45th Session of the State Legislature had already convened on January 10 and with Democratic control in both the Senate and the House, and a new Democratic governor, I was anticipating a smooth-running session. This proved to be the case, but I also unknowingly participated in the legislative enactment of a law which in succeeding years would, in my opinion, contribute a great deal to the difficulties of the Supply System.

Following cancellation by the Supply System of the contract of Bovee & Crail, one of the lead contractors on Plant No. 2, in January 1976, the firm sued the Supply System for $24.5 million and the Supply System countersued them for $45 million. In the fall of 1976, I was called into a conference with the staff and lawyers of the Supply System to discuss the extent to which change orders could be issued on public contracts. It was a natural occurrence that, once a complex project was undertaken, certain change orders could be issued to alter the contract. By past practice and precedent, it was the attorneys' feelings that they could defend a challenge of the right of the Supply System Board of Directors to issue such change orders. This practice would be supported by what had happened in the 1950s during the construction of the large dams on the main stem of the Columbia River by PUDs. However, the changes being made in the nuclear regulatory provisions, the fast-track construction where design of the plant was just ahead of actual construction, and the total confusion throughout the entire nuclear industry about materials and supplies, with severe competition throughout the entire nation for obtaining such items, were forcing the Supply System into change orders of a size which might not fit "past practice and precedent."

It was thus agreed that a specific State statute should be secured to make the right to issuing change orders clear. At that conference and subsequently during the period when the legal staff was drafting the proposed statute and in testimony before both the House and Senate committees which would later deal with the proposed new statute, it was repeatedly emphasized that the size of the change orders involved would be in the range of $200,000 to $300,000. In the House I had it introduced as HB-852. I secured as sponsors on the House side Representatives Boldt and Kilbury, legislators coming from the Tri-Cities area where the Supply System was headquartered, along with powerful legislators from both sides of the aisle, to demonstrate non-partisan support. On the Senate side, I secured sponsorship by the two top Democratic leaders, Senators Walgren and Bailey, along with a Republican leader, Senator Seller. I do recall Senator Walgren commenting, after he had studied the bill in detail and signed on as a sponsor, that this appeared to mean work would be performed "about 20 percent under bid and 80 percent under change order." I responded, "Absolutely not. Change orders under this bill will be limited to a small size, but they are needed to make certain that a legal challenge cannot be raised on necessary changes resulting from new requirements of the Nuclear Regulatory Commission."

Actually, the law was worded so that change orders could be made to comply with changes in government standards and changes in specifications by the project architect/engineer for safety purposes, or to expedite project completion on the most advantageous terms in the public interest. It was this last clause which I failed to recognize for what it turned out to be. At any rate, after prolonged testimony to the effect that it was a needed statute and that the change orders would not be of any major size, the bill was passed in the House by a vote of 90 to 0. It proceeded through the regular Senate committee in proper order.

On May 4, I got an urgent call from Jack Cluck, attorney for the Supply System, asking if there was any way this legislation could be enacted and signed by the Governor as soon as possible. Evidently, in preparation of the lawsuit between the deposed contractor and the Supply System, there had been indication that one of the arguments by the contractor was to be that there was no specific statutory language allowing change orders by the Supply System. While the particular contractor had been removed from the project, other contractors were receiving change orders.

I contacted Senator Walgren as Floor Leader and explained the need for immediate passage of the law. That day happened to be one of the established deadline days whereby at a certain time the House or Senate must have enacted a bill or it would be considered dead. On that particular day, many senators were interested in passing Senate bills only. However, as a sheer courtesy to me based on many years of service around the legislative halls, Senator Walgren got the House bill out of the Rules Committee and placed it at the foot of the Senate calendar for that day. Previously, I had taken the legislation to Senator Mardesich who, upon reading it, told me that while he could not support the legislation, since he felt that it might be opening a Pandora's box in favor of contractors, again in deference to our longstanding political friendship, he would not oppose it.

At 3 in the afternoon, just two hours before the deadline on passage of Senate bills, Senator Walgren called up my House bill. There was considerable controversy for a few moments because the Senate was taking action on a House bill. Senator Walgren prevailed and stated that this legislation was needed, and that it had been passed unanimously in the House and approved unanimously by the Senate Utilities Committee. The bill was advanced from second to third reading by voice vote and on a roll call vote was passed 48 yeas and no nays. There was one absent and not voting. That was Senator Mardesich who, glancing up to me in the balcony as the bill was brought up for consideration, took a puff on his cigar and walked off the floor in order not to vote against my interest. The bill was signed by the Governor on May 16 and, with the emergency clause, became effective immediately.

In June 1977, one of the first change orders issued by the Supply System under the new Act was to an electrical contractor in the amount of $747,000. I was jarred because it was more than twice as large as testimony to me and to the Legislature claimed the bill allowed. Shortly thereafter, another change order in the amount of $450,000 was issued. About this time, I received a call from Bruce McPhaden of Kaiser Aluminum Company. He had been very active in the election campaign of Governor Dixy Lee Ray and had more or less kitchen cabinet status in the new State administration. He asked, "What in hell is going on down at Hanford?" I said, "To what are you referring?" He stated that he had just come from a Board of Directors' meeting of a large local bank on which he served and one of the other members of the board, a contractor, was making open comments to the effect that he was now in "Fat City," having just secured a substantial contract at Hanford in the construction of Plant No. 2 for the Supply System. He was stating that this was a "contractor's heaven," whereby a contractor once he got the job could then get substantial change orders primarily because of the changing regulations under which the plants were being constructed. These changes would void a lot of the standards under which a contract would have been bid and let. I told him I was not too close to the actual construction practices but was greatly concerned that, instead of facing up to the actual problem and seeking a law whereby the difficulties of constructing a nuclear plant under a public bidding process could be reduced by allowing the owner to negotiate work contracts directly, and thereby exert greater control, the Supply System staff had got me to secure a law which would merely offer a way out of a bad situation after the contractor got on the job. Imagine my chagrin in October 1977 when a $96.7 million change order was issued by the Supply System.

It was also in October 1977 that I verbally informed members of my Executive Committee that I was strongly contemplating retiring from my position as Executive Director on July 1, 1978. While this change order action was not the reason for my retirement, it was a contributing factor. It had been my plan for quite some time, based on family requests and suggestions, to seek early retirement. My 62nd birthday would come in July 1978. I also had a strong feeling that Association activity could be better carried out by a younger person.

The First Extraordinary Session of the 45th Session of the Legislature adjourned on June 22, 1977, after 102 days. This was the latest date of any adjournment of a special session. While a total of 229 days had been used during the 44th Session and its Extraordinary Sessions, this was the latest date of adjournment in a continuing session which had commenced on January 10. It had been an extremely productive session for our legislation. Other than the change order legislation, we secured a law providing for a primary election in PUD Commissioner races when more than two persons filed for the office and a special law allowing one district to construct several needed sewers. When the law was proposed that public holidays would be held on particular days of the week, we provided that the number and designation of such holidays would be set by the local boards and not by the State Legislature. In addition, we secured a salary increase for Commissioners, the first since 1969; a law to allow Chelan County PUD to have a five-person board but not affecting the other districts; a code reviser bill which eliminated all references in the joint operating agency law to the defunct State Power Commission which had been abolished in 1957; and a law requiring specific insulation in new residential construction. In legislation granting emergency energy allocation powers to the Governor, we made certain the utilities would not be liable for any damages resulting from mandatory curtailment.

The years 1977–1978 were very hectic from a personal standpoint as we worked on the Regional Power Act that came out of the initial meeting with Senator Jackson in late 1976. The utilities and direct service industries thrashed out what they wanted the law to say in the Pacific Northwest Utilities Conference Committee, and there were many, many tension-filled tough meetings among interests which had some very strong philosophical, political, and economic differences regarding power supply and its use. In later years, I chuckled a little when the news media, quoting persons who opposed passage of the legislation, kept calling all of us "large utility and industrial interests which are jointly using their powerful lobbying forces to dictate how these resources will be used for their own special purposes." They were not present in our discussions and did not hear the direct and many times rough arguments over this legislation in the four years it took to put it together.

The pressure on me arose from some very severe family fights inside public power. Three months into 1977, we had pounded out certain basic concepts. First, the direct service industries were agreeing to release to the Bonneville Administrator their present contractual rights to low-cost federal power prior to contract termination, in return for new long-term contracts based on new legislatively granted authority to Bonneville. This released federal power would then go to the investor-owned utilities, and residential and small farm customers, on an exchange arrangement between Bonneville and the investor-owned utilities. There would be no fiscal impact on, or loss of power supply to, any of the local public power utilities. They would also get new extensions of their requirements contracts. The preference clause and policy would remain intact.

One unsettled question which provoked a later fight was how new public agencies once formed could participate. Self-financing was to be sought for Bonneville using the total federal power sales resources to underwrite needed federal dam facilities. These federal revenues could also be used to purchase cost-effective region-wide conservation, energy from small hydro and other renewable energy power plants which were also cost effective, and, finally, the output of additional or new large thermal plants needed to meet regional power loads. Congressional reenactment of the preference clause, and new contract extensions, would assure that the region would have first call on Bonneville power. An organization representative of the utility industry in this region would plan for the power needs of the region. One of the concepts hard to reach agreement on was that individual utilities would subordinate their right to make decisions on power plant construction to a regional decision wherever regional financing or underwriting was to be used to construct the plant. Up to this time, it was the prerogative of either an individual utility or a group of utilities to start individual plants.

Another concept we agreed on was that we would provide joint utility action regarding the fish versus power issue, particularly as it pertained to the use of power revenues for protection of the fisheries resource. The first draft of the legislation was finished in the spring of 1977. Much of the foregoing was accomplished by establishing three separate rate pools of federal power and the Pacific Northwest Electric Planning and Conservation Organization, or PNEPCO, composed of utility representatives only.

A strong disagreement broke out in public power ranks when Snohomish County PUD took exception to the size of Rate Pool A which was to provide power supply to the preference customers. This resulted in a severe family fight inside the American Public Power Association at its Toronto conference in June and later at a specially called meeting in Denver in August.

The power planning organization was constituted only of utility representatives because of the honest and sincere feeling on the part of the utilities that if they were going to be held responsible for the failure or success of a regional power supply, then they should have the right and responsibility of planning the power supply. Local government and state officials expressed strong opinions that there should be non-utility representatives on any planning council. We of public power did not object to this, as we showed in our later agreement that the planning organization should be changed to include non-utility representatives. But we were also quite strong in our position that any such planning body should then be assigned the responsibility for the success or failure of the power supply program. Further, we definitely were insisting that local representation through duly elected persons be maintained as a positive right of local people.

The State of Oregon Legislature, under the urging of Governor Bob Straub, enacted a law to establish a Domestic and Rural Power Authority. To me, this seemed to be done in bad faith because the proponents were promoting it with the claim that it would bring lower electric rates to the domestic and rural electric users in the State of Oregon. How any honest and logical person who thought in terms of keeping in place the total private power capital and operating costs up to the last few feet of electric service, and then superimposing the necessary cost of a state bureaucracy to administer the DRPA program, could still promise lower rates to the electric consumers of Oregon, was totally beyond my comprehension. The proposal was dishonest and illogical in my opinion. The economic facts denied that it could be done.

This move by the State of Oregon caused Utility Commissioner Francis Ivancie of the City of Portland to get into the act by demanding that the low-cost federal power be shared with the people of his city. This forced me to ask the question: If the low-cost federal power was going to be shared among all electric customers in the Northwest, why didn't we share the substantial amount of low-cost public power coming out of the PUD dams on the Columbia River, the major portions of which went to the private power companies and in particular to those serving the City of Portland? The controversy reached its extreme when the City of Portland filed a lawsuit against the new Secretary of Energy, Dr. Schlesinger, and the Bonneville Administrator challenging the net billing contracts which had been used to underwrite the public power plants or portions of plants then under construction. It was really becoming a mess.

Finally, in September, Senator Jackson introduced S-2080 and Congressman Lloyd Meeds introduced HR-9020 in Congress. Simultaneously, they both submitted special amendments to satisfy the objections being raised by the Snohomish County PUD. Hearings were scheduled to be held throughout the Pacific Northwest by a House subcommittee chaired by Congressman Meeds in December. I could see that a lot of trouble would arise if we couldn't find a solution to the in-house public power differences. Therefore, in early November, I issued a white paper proposing changes in the rate pool size whereby the pool reserved for use by preference utilities would be increased to include the total anticipated energy from any federally financed generators, suggesting that this rate pool be available to new as well as existing preference utilities. I proposed adjustment in the price of the federal power which would reflect the cost of net billed power previously purchased by the federal system and the use of secondary (non-firm) power sales revenues on a proportionate basis between different rate pools; and suggested further, that any changes in federal anti-trust provisions be very carefully evaluated to make certain that the basic laws were not destroyed in adjusting for needed protection for collaborative action on a regional power supply in the Northwest by private power companies. Finally, I took the public position that non-utility public representatives should be placed on the regional power supply planning organization provided that no disruption was caused in the utility decisions and actions necessary to furnish a reliable regional power supply and conservation program at the lowest attainable cost. The white paper was later referred to as the "Billington balloons," which these suggestions were. Sitting between and among warring public power utilities, as well as fighting off the moves of the Oregon DRPA and the lawsuit filed by the City of Portland, I was not leading a very happy life.

My testimony before Congressman Meeds in Seattle on December 9 was, in my opinion, a display of the art of walking a tightrope. Coming out of all of this was the so-called GOAT or "Get-Our-Act-Together" Committee, established in early 1978 by the Public Power Council. I was asked to serve as Chairman. Members included Bill Hulbert, Snohomish County PUD; Al Benedetti, Tacoma Light; Larry Cable, Eugene Water and Electric Board; Vince Slatt, Inland Power and Light Company; Ed Schlender, Jr., Elmhurst Mutual; Alan Jones, McMinnville Water and Light; Ken Dyar, Central Lincoln PUD; and Frank Lambert, Clark County PUD.

The foremost concerns of the GOAT Committee were the treatment of new preference customers, the composition of the PNEPCO Board, and the conservation program. However, in concentrating on these three areas, we found it necessary to name 12 changes which should be made in the bill to secure public power support for it.

Following acceptance by the Public Power Council, the plan was released at a public meeting in Seattle on March 24, 1978. The major change was that PNEPCO would have 9 utility representatives and 9 appointees of the 4 Northwest state governors, with the right of any 5 of the 18 persons to veto any action. While this plan brought public power forces together again as a unit, it did not satisfy all parties involved in the effort. Thus, when hearings were resumed in April, it was evident that the region was divided and therefore no action was taken on the legislation.

The non-utility locally elected officials increased their insistence that non-utility people be represented on PNEPCO as well as placing greater emphasis on the need for conservation. Their push for representation on the body culminated in a special hearing by the State Legislature's Senate Utilities Committee in June 1978 where it became evident to me that there would be a change in PNEPCO, but where I was still trying to insist that whoever was given the authority for making plans on future regional power supply should also rightfully accept the responsibility for its failure or success.

In late summer, new legislation, S-3418 and HR-13931, was introduced in Congress. These were the so-called kitchen table drafts. Word was that, without benefit of any utility representation, other than the presence of Bonneville personnel, the legislation had been drafted over a weekend at the kitchen table of Senator Jackson. The strong presence of Bonneville in this was understandable because Don Hodel had resigned from being Bonneville Administrator in December 1977, and Sterling Munro, long-time Administrative Assistant to Senator Jackson, after certain arm-twisting efforts by the Senator as well as myself and others, had accepted appointment as Bonneville Administrator on January 1, 1978.

By this time, Congressman Jim Weaver of Oregon had mounted quite a campaign against the proposed legislation. Weaver had introduced his own version of a regional power bill the previous year, in March 1977. It was so extreme in concept, directly controverting the basic preference clause, that it was given no chance of passing. It did stir up strong controversy over this new legislation when a House hearing was held in October. I was attending the hearings in Washington, D.C., and when it became apparent that House action was so disrupted, former Congressman Wendell Wyatt of Oregon and I, as representatives of the Public Power Council, personally requested that Senator Jackson stop action on the Senate side. He did so, bringing the legislative process on this bill to a standstill.

At the request of the Public Power Council, I secured a special meeting with Senator Jackson on December 20, 1978, where he told those attending that the Public Power Council should prepare needed public power amendments as it definitely was his intent to proceed with regional legislation. This concluded our action for the year.

There were many other important events that affected me personally during 1977 and 1978. First, Ed Blakemore resigned from his Administrative Assistant's job in February 1977 to accept work with Mason County PUD No. 3. Here again, I saw that a younger person had to turn to outside employment because of no room to advance within the Association. But here again, I was successful as always in having good employees. I was able to advance Martha "Marty" Dresslar to the position of Administrative Assistant and secure the services of Pamela Morton as her replacement. Pam later turned into a jewel because in August of 1977, Phoebe Haworth, our Administrative Secretary/Bookkeeper, retired after nearly 15 years of good service to me and the Association. In January 1978, I submitted a formal letter of retirement/resignation to my Board of Directors and a search was begun for a replacement. A number of highly qualified persons applied and, while I took no part in influencing the Board's decision, it certainly met with my approval when Jim Boldt, the former young legislator who became an employee of the Supply System, was hired as the new Executive Director, coming on board May 1, 1978, to become Executive Director July 1, 1978. At my Board's request, I agreed to remain as a legislative consultant for the three years ending June 30, 1981 to help in the needed transition, as well as to work on the regional power legislation and to work at the legislative sessions.

The 1978 American Public Power Association Annual Conference held in Atlanta was a very happy occasion. I was presented the APPA's Distinguished Service Award. My longtime friend Durwood Hill – now from Nebraska due to my dumb "mistake" back in 1964 – made the presentation. What made me happy was to be able to state to a nationwide audience of public power leaders that the award was really in honor of the many fine men and women who had served and were serving as my "bosses" in their locally elected offices as PUD Commissioners, and to my very loyal and efficient employees "who always made their boss look good."

Tension increased between Bonneville and the Supply System in 1978, centering on Bonneville's oversight of Supply System activity. While the contractual relationship between the two agencies was quite specific on Bonneville's right to approve major contracts and changes, there had been continued argument over how far such oversight extended.

At the American Public Power Association Annual Conference in Atlanta, I set up a meeting between John Goldsbury, President of the Supply System Board of Directors; Ed Fischer, Chairman of its Executive Committee; and Neil Strand, its Managing Director; and prevailed upon Sterling Munro as the new Bonneville Administrator and long-time personal friend to attend to see if we couldn't cool the issue. Coming out of the meeting was what I thought was agreement that the two agencies would jointly select an outside consultant to review the entire matter and recommend some guidelines for Bonneville oversight. I was somewhat surprised one month later when Bonneville unilaterally retained Theodore Berry and Associates, a renowned consulting firm, for a substantial management performance audit of the Supply System.

I felt that Munro had been encouraged to do this by Senator Jackson and thus, in August, I found myself in the Senator's office being quite verbally critical of the unilateral action by Bonneville after what I thought had been an agreement to make a joint study of their relationship. Scoop's answer was, "Ken, the problems out there in the State are not within my province and I can't get involved, but I'm getting enough comments from others that indicate something is not right. I wouldn't serve on the Board of Directors of the Supply System without having ongoing management performance audits conducted." My response was, "What do you mean by management performance audits?" He explained to me that the practice in large corporations, such as those in automobile manufacturing or shipbuilding, was for a board of directors to have an established or retained work force performing audits of its line management's performance. The purpose of the audits would not be to interfere with line management's rights and prerogatives to proceed, but merely to give the board of directors a way to evaluate the procedures and practices of its line management to see that they were not only in keeping with the board of directors' directives but also were carried out by the most efficient methods.

I recognized that he was correct in stating that the problems which were then surfacing about the Supply System did not and could not involve congressional members. I didn't recognize that what he was giving me at that time was a concept of legislation which I would use in the 1979 Legislative Session when a great argument broke out in the State of Washington Legislature over the Supply System.

The Theodore Berry and Associates report came out in December 1978. The way it came out caused more legislative heat and public argument than the contents of the report itself.

The matter came up at my annual Association meeting in early December. Bonneville, which had commissioned and would pay for the report, furnished copies to the Supply System Board on the condition that it would not be made public until it was released by Bonneville. When the Supply System Board attempted to meet in executive session to study the report and to honor Bonneville's condition, one of the most artful jobs of news media overkill I have ever seen took place. The Supply System was challenged under the open meetings law provisions with the result that the report went back to Bonneville without study and became an issue of controversy instead of a useful evaluation to improve relationships between Bonneville and the Supply System.

I, personally, was somewhat puzzled when I noted that several key findings were in words nearly identical to previous management studies which the Supply System itself had commissioned. I was never to feel that the unilateral spending by Bonneville of nearly $300,000 of ratepayers' money had accomplished what a joint evaluation, as agreed to in Atlanta, might have accomplished. Things were to get worse instead of better.

Two strong public power leaders died in January of 1978. Senator Hubert Humphrey and Senator C. C. Dill, about whom I have more to say in Chapter 9. Senator Humphrey's funeral ceremony brought to mind the way I met the Senator many years ago.

One early morning when I was to leave the Spokane airport on a West Coast Airline DC3 for a flight to Portland, Oregon, the plane was late taking off, and I learned later that Senator Humphrey had flown all night on his way from Minneapolis to Spokane to connect in Spokane with the DC3. I recognized him, of course, but I had never met him. Our flight proceeded to Yakima and then started toward Portland, whereupon we encountered one of the heaviest storms in which I have ever flown. The pilot could not go above the storm and he didn't dare try to go below it because of the Cascade Mountain range to the west. We had to go directly through the storm, as he told us over the intercom. The plane rocked all over the sky but finally we broke out under the clouds over Clark County, Washington, about 20 miles north of the airport. At the Portland airport, as we taxied to the landing, I noticed a welcoming committee which included Senator Maureen Neuburger, U.S. Senator from the State of Oregon, with whom I was personally well acquainted. She had succeeded her husband, Senator Dick Neuburger, following his death. I had been friends of the Neuburgers for many years.

When we started to deplane, I saw a rather interesting sight. Senator Humphrey was crawling up and down the aisle looking for his shoes, which he had removed as the plane took off from Spokane in order to catnap before his arrival in Portland. I got down on my hands and knees and crawled up and down the aisle to help him. I found one of his shoes, and he found the other. He put them on, straightened his clothing, and departed from the plane to the welcoming ceremony. I came off the plane about the same time and was recognized by Senator Neuburger. She introduced me to my traveling companion, who then jokingly told her that I had helped him find his shoes. He had evidently traveled to Oregon for a political fund raiser on behalf of Senator Neuburger. I didn't see him again until September 28, 1968, when Vice President Humphrey, a candidate for President, was speaker at the John Day Dam dedication. I was also an invited guest and seated on the speakers' platform, which gave me a chance to again shake hands with Vice President Humphrey. Even though people always talked about his terrific memory for names and places, I was astonished when he recognized and remembered me as "the chap who helped me get off an airliner by finding my shoes." And that is exactly how I met one great man!

In 1978, local residents of Skagit County secured enough petition signatures to require a vote on activating their PUD for electric service. It has always been the policy of the PUD Association that while we could give information and guidance and advice, we could not actively instigate formation or activation of new PUDs. Actually, it was usually when the private power companies which naturally opposed such efforts came in with broad and false public statements damaging to all PUDs that we would get directly involved. Such was to be the case in Skagit County PUD.

The Puget Sound Power and Light Company put out a white paper which was so extreme that we felt it necessary to get involved and thus by order of the Board and new Executive Director Boldt, I prepared an answer to the white paper which we made available to the local area. I also participated in several local election meetings. The attempt to activate the PUD lost at the November election. It was the last PUD activation effort I participated in before my full retirement on June 30, 1981.

1979–1980

The 46th Session of the State Legislature convened on January 8, 1979. Following the regular session, which would adjourn sine die as required by the State Constitution on March 8, 1979, a First Extraordinary Session would be convened on March 21, 1979, with final adjournment after 73 days of the Extraordinary Session at 3 a.m. on June 2, 1979. This would be a very hectic session from my standpoint. First, I would be in my new role as legislative consultant working under the direction of our new Executive Director, Jim Boldt. He was the boss. Second, while the Democrats retained a workable control in the Senate, the House in the 1978 election had evenly split 49 to 49 between Republicans and Democrats. The result when both sides held firm without forming a coalition, such as the coalitions which had been formed in several previous legislative sessions, was that the House adopted rules to provide for two speakers—John Bagnariol would continue as Democratic Speaker and Duane Berentson would be Speaker for the Republicans. The office at the southwest corner on the third floor of the legislative building, usually used by the Speaker Pro Tem, was appropriated and converted into an office for the Republican Speaker of the House. If I were asked to describe this legislative session in one word, the word I would be tempted to use is "weird."

While credit must be given to the co-speakers for doing a good job under the circumstances, the arrangement did result in some unusual legislative events that one would not normally anticipate or expect when there is majority control by either party. A single legislator from either side could exercise disproportionate influence on the fate of any particular bill merely by indicating his or her intent to bolt the leadership. Then, if a particular piece of legislation was sufficiently controversial to disrupt the solidarity of either of the caucuses on a major and unrelated issue, such as the budget, this controversy more or less condemned the unrelated legislation to death. Under normal circumstances, when a single party controls the committee structure and elects one of its members as Speaker, most bills have their final drafts prepared in individual committees and few amendments are allowed to be presented on the floor. In this session, many bills could not come out of their committees without an agreement to allow the entire House to consider the legislation as a Committee of the Whole, where a multitude of floor amendments would be allowed to be proposed and voted on. This happened to practically every bill considered by the Committee of the Whole. Since neither party and no coalition was in control, bills were often held in the Rules Committee to avoid loss of control by the cooperative leadership when it could be discerned that a substantial number of floor amendments would be proposed. Lobbyists soon learned the art of walking on eggs.

A third factor that made this a somewhat stressful session for me was that the problems of the Washington Public Power Supply System were escalating at a tremendous rate. Costs of nuclear plants were skyrocketing. Anti-nuclear activity, which broke into the open following the Three-Mile

Island nuclear incident at Middletown, Pennsylvania, was becoming more fierce. Supply System Board meetings and Executive Committee meetings were becoming three-ring news media circuses as the press took full advantage of the open meetings law. Bonneville versus Supply System arguments were becoming more intense.

In the midst of all this, Representative King Lysen underwent a transformation from a strong pro-Supply System supporter in the Legislature to a tough and hard opponent of the Supply System. In 1977, as Chairman of the House Utilities Committee, he had assisted me greatly in securing the change order legislation for the Supply System. He, of course, felt as disappointed as I did when the Supply System used that law in amounts different from the way they said they wanted to use it when we were trying to get it passed. Even in early 1978, Lysen was still a strong supporter of the Supply System, using that view to oppose enactment of a Regional Power Act by Congress. In 1978, he asked me to arrange an interview with the top management personnel of the Supply System as a representative and employee of a particular engineering consulting firm. I arranged the interview because most certainly if the Supply System needed an engineering consultant and the work could be done by a supporter, then there should be no objection as long as the firm was qualified. Lysen was interviewed, but I was informed by the top management of the Supply System that the particular type of engineering work which he was seeking for the firm was not the kind the Supply System needed. With his election to the Senate in 1978, however, he became one of the most vociferous legislative opponents of the Supply System.

There was, indeed, considerable turmoil and argument revolving around the Supply System centering on the media coverage. It really intensified when we sought legislation to allow the Supply System to establish a security force, which was one of the requirements for getting a license from the Nuclear Regulatory Commission. I proposed a force patterned after the public port authorities' security forces. I did not anticipate that local law enforcement agencies would join forces with the anti-nuclear people who were claiming the Supply System intended to establish a "police state." Even so, we made good progress on the legislation but did lose it at the last of the session because of the problem of leadership control in the House. The Democratic Speaker had to lock it up in Rules in order to maintain needed Democratic support on some other major legislation, namely the budget. This session got hot and heavy, especially on Supply System matters.

I recalled my conversation the previous August with Senator Henry Jackson and his explanation of how ongoing management performance audits helped a board of directors make certain that line management was performing on a proper level of efficiency. I spoke to Senator Ted Bottiger, then serving as Chairman of the Energy and Utilities Committee, who asked that I have a law drafted to establish an Administrative Auditor for the Supply System Board of Directors. I contacted Jack Cluck who wrote the draft using the concepts I outlined. This auditor's staff would perform audits of the work of line management, not for the purpose of argument or challenge to line management, which would be totally free to set its own style, but for the purpose of informing the Board of Directors about whether the procedures and methods of line management got the job done the way the Board of Directors wanted it done.

My first thought was to find some way to make the audit reports public and thereby increase public confidence in the Supply System Board. The logical way, to me, would be to have them filed with the State Auditor's office. I approached that office on the idea.

Our State Auditor was Robert V. "Bob" Graham. He had earned broad statewide confidence as evidenced by his successful re-elections after he had succeeded long-time State Auditor Cliff Yelle in 1965. He was a friend of public power whom I met and worked with while he served as Chief Examiner of the Division of Municipal Corporations under Yelle, which annually audited every PUD as a municipal corporation. Bob was tough but he was fair.

Years before, a local PUD Manager had called my attention to a habit one of his Commissioners had of stretching the use of his Commissioner's per diem by showing up repeatedly at the Manager's office and requesting that the two of them "go inspect some lines." After each cursory trip, the Commissioner would submit a voucher for a per diem payment. I would hasten to add that this practice was an extreme case, as most Commissioners were honestly and very carefully avoiding any possible statewide smear from the private power forces.

I told the Manager to forget he even called me, and that I would take care of the one bad apple in the barrel. It took only one call to Bob Graham. I don't know what happened but the practice stopped abruptly, as the Manager confided to me later.

At any rate, first draft of the law required that the audit reports be filed with the State Auditor's office. When I proposed this, I was not aware that it would be controversial. Back in 1973, the State Legislature had established a Legislative Budget Committee with its own auditing staff, primarily so that the Democrats, who controlled the Legislature, could oversee the use of budgeted funds by a Republican governor. There had been a growing feeling that once the legislative body appropriated the funds, it could not be certain that they were being used efficiently in the administrative or executive branch of government.

While the State Auditor was primarily concerned with fiscal matters, there had been a growing nationwide trend for state auditors to widen their scope and make management performance audits. Legislators didn't like this, so when our bill proposed that the State Auditor's office have anything to do with performance audits, there was adverse reaction from the Legislative Budget Committee and its auditing staff. I made it clear that I did not want to be involved in this fight between the legislative and executive branches, and that I did not care where the reports went, but I was seeking some way of making reports by the Administrative Auditor retained by the Supply System public, so we could eliminate some of the growing public concern. Senator Bottiger accepted the legislation as we drafted it, and it was introduced.

This happened just as the Theodore Berry & Associates report was made public by Bonneville. This report contained not only constructive compliments for the Supply System and its staff, but also some specific recommendations for changes. The report caused considerable controversy within the family of local public power. The immediate reaction from line management of the Supply System was to oppose the bill, and some very hot discussion sessions within the PUD Association Board of Directors took place. Senator Bottiger helped me substantially when he appeared at one of the Board meetings to recommend support of his legislation creating the position of Administrative Auditor. HB-1075, the Administrative Auditor legislation, which was finally passed, met opposition every step of the way. When it finally landed on the Governor's desk, it had a confusing new section which had been added as a Senate floor amendment. The amendment would have extended the open meetings law to small committee meetings of Supply System employees, but what constituted such a meeting was not made clear. Under the amendment, any legal action in which it could be proved that the open meetings law had been violated could jeopardize an entire project. Such a broad brush amendment would have made the law unworkable.

Combatants in the in-house family fight of local public power met head-on in the Governor's office. The President of the Board of Directors of the Supply System sent a letter, undoubtedly at the instigation of its management, requesting outright veto of the law. Those of us who felt the presence of ongoing performance audits would strengthen the Supply System management, as well as assure Board oversight of performance, had to support veto of the second section of the law but approval of the first part. I felt somewhat comforted when I got a call from the Governor's office asking if I could help prepare a proper veto message for just the second section.

I was indeed heartened to read an editorial on May 8, 1979, stating that Governor Ray supported the legislation as passed the previous day. However, the issue did not stop with the partial veto of the law and approval of the rest of it by the Governor on June 20, which made it effective on September 20, 1979. A special committee was established by the Board of Directors of the Supply System in early July to get ready for the new law, and three separate meetings with legislative leaders were held by that committee to make certain that the committee was moving in the right direction.

In September, when the law became effective, the Supply System advertised for applicants for the job of Auditor and received 140. By the time they had boiled these down to a total of six, it was early December and a special joint meeting of the Senate and House Utilities Committee requested that the Supply System Board appear before it, as a provision in the new law required. When the Board complied on December 13, 1979, the legislative leadership accused the Supply System of having "purposely dragged your feet" on implementing the new law, and the matter boiled on into the Second Extraordinary Session which was convened in January 1980.

I was positive that there had been no "foot dragging" on the part of the Supply System committee, as it had been chaired by Paul Nolan, Director of Utilities for Tacoma, who was sincerely trying to make certain that what was done met with legislative leadership approval, as well as insisting that the new post of Administrative Auditor be filled by a person well qualified to adequately perform for the Board of Directors. There was indeed growing concern inside the Board of Directors that management of the Supply System needed bolstering. The result of the 1980 Session was that Senator Bottiger, who had been a long-time strong supporter of local public power, instructed his staff to draft legislation which would eliminate the Board of Directors of the Supply System and place administration of the Supply System under a three-person commission appointed by the Governor and confirmed by the State Senate.

This was not acceptable because we felt that if the Supply System was to be taken over by the State, there should be a State takeover of financial responsibility for the projects. Under the legislation, while control would pass to the new State commission, any financial responsibility would still lie with the local participating utilities. Again, it boiled down to my conviction that the party with responsibility for making decisions should be the party with responsibility for providing the financing.

The fight over SB-3266 in the 1980 Session was intense and pitted friend against friend. The law was blocked by some very astute lobbying. When this occurred, Senator Bottiger went before the Senate Rules Committee and asked that a Senate inquiry into the Supply System be instituted with the power of subpoena. He even agreed to grant bipartisan control with the right of the minority party lead representative on the Utilities Committee, Senator Susan Gould, to veto any subpoena issued. He requested and secured an appropriation of $323,000 to cover the cost of the inquiry. Prior to that, the Supply System Board of Directors had accepted the resignation of its Managing Director, Neil Strand.

It is the custom for any lobbyist, when a legislative session commences, to seek an appointment with the Governor, not only to say "hello" but also to outline any legislation the lobbyist wants. I made an appointment to meet with Governor Ray, accompanied by Executive Director Boldt. As the three of us sat down, she turned to me and said, "Ken, Neil Strand has to go. He is a nice person, but, frankly, I don't think he's up to handling the job he is supposed to be doing." My response was, "Governor, I came to that conclusion nearly a year ago, at the time we were arguing over the Administrative Auditor legislation, but it's not in my province to say whether he stays or goes. Frankly, Jim here is sitting in the hot seat because there will be an all-out family fight in the PUD Association over this issue. So whatever action the Association takes is going to be up to him." As we left the office, Jim turned to me and said, "I'm ready, because I think we are to a point where we can no longer defend against some of the criticism being raised." I then said, "Okay. Let me see if we can put together a meeting of certain members of the Executive Committee which under the Board rules of the Supply System has the authority to hire and fire Managing Directors."

I called Paul Nolan, Director of Utilities at Tacoma, and Joe Recchi, Superintendent of Seattle City Light. I placed a call to Bill Hulbert, Manager of Snohomish County PUD, but finding him on vacation, talked to Jim Maner, his assistant. I then contacted Bob McKinney, Manager of the Cowlitz County PUD, whose representative on the Supply System Executive Committee was Don Hughes. A meeting was convened February 9 in Paul Nolan's Tacoma office. McKinney and Hughes from Cowlitz, Maner and Commissioner Stan Olsen of Snohomish County PUD, Joe Recchi and Deputy Mayor Bob Royer from Seattle, Jim Boldt and I attended. After thorough discussion of what was going on on the legislative scene, as well as the Governor's direct remarks and other concerns about progress of Supply System projects, we agreed that Strand would have to be terminated. I was to leave the next morning for Washington, D.C., to work on the Regional Power Act, but was asked to stay over and prepare a written statement to justify our action to the full Board of the Supply System. This I did, and Bob Royer came by my home on late Sunday afternoon to pick it up.

I also placed a call to Ed Fischer, Chairman of the Supply System Executive Committee, and told him that there appeared to be four votes to request the termination of Strand. His response was to make it five because in the last two months there had been a number of occasions on which he felt certain questions he raised had not been suitably answered.

The following morning, Monday, I flew off to Washington, D.C., and called back on Wednesday to find out that when Strand was called into an executive session of the Executive Committee, he saw the handwriting on the wall and tendered his written resignation to avoid mandatory termination. The result was a substantial uproar on the Board of Directors of the Supply System which the press referred to as the "sagebrush rebellion." Many of the Eastern Washington PUD Commissioners serving on the Board were upset over the termination of Strand. While it was recognized that the Executive Committee did have the authority to fire Strand under Board rules, there was considerable conflict over the issue.

When Strand submitted a letter of resignation, the written outline which I had carefully prepared, knowing that it would have shown all the Commissioners that it was necessary to make a change, never surfaced. The time was rather turbulent, but the search committee set up by the Board came up with an outstanding replacement in the person of Robert L. Ferguson, who had been one of the top people in construction of the fast-flux test facility at Hanford. Work progressed on what was beginning to be a more difficult goal of getting the plants completed and on line. As could be seen, most of our legislative lobbying activities during the 1979–1980 session were defensive, attempts to protect member districts in the Supply System against punitive legislation. Probably a measure of success would be the number and types of bills that were defeated. In this regard, Jim and I succeeded in our work, but we carried it on in an adverse legislative climate.

In April 1979, a startling event occurred. Representative Bob Perry, the long-time proponent of private power in the legislative arena, had not returned to the Legislature for the 1977 Session. After the 1975 arm-twisting session on HB-435, which Governor Evans had vetoed, it had been his decision to pursue other avenues of endeavor. When the Democrats had regained control of the House in 1973, they reversed the previous action of the Republican House, which had abolished the Utilities Committee and established a new committee which consolidated two of the most important areas of legislative consideration into the Transportation and Utilities Committee. Perry chaired this very important Committee from 1973 through 1976 in both the 43rd and 44th Sessions of the Legislature.

There had been some rumors, both private and public, that certain retainer fees were being paid for special design engineering on a West Seattle Bridge under contracts issued with the approval of the Legislature. A federal Grand Jury got interested in the matter in early 1977. Perry disappeared. On April 30, 1979, Perry returned to Seattle accompanied by Shelby Scates, long-time political columnist of the *Seattle P-I*, and surrendered himself to federal marshals. He stated that he had left the country in July 1977 with the assistance of The Washington Water Power Company, which had secured work for him in Mexico with the Ebasco Company. Evidently, a secret indictment had been issued against him in December 1978. He was arraigned before a federal court on May 10, 1979, and went to the federal penitentiary. I dropped Perry a note, in care of the federal marshals in Seattle, stating that while I could not condone or agree with his past actions, I certainly congratulated him on being man enough to face the situation and take whatever penalty was invoked. A lot of charges and countercharges were made at this time in the court case that followed involving Washington Water Power and its officials. I was not directly involved although I had, if the charges were correct, been subjected to a lot of the political pressure which came from the past political financing action cited in the case.

I knew there was a Sammy Lee in Hong Kong, having had dinner with him and his wife as arranged by Perry in 1969 after we had made a private/public power declaration of peace. I do recall the night when I was sitting in a local restaurant with Jerry Buckley, lobbyist of Washington Water Power. We watched a number of the personalities involved in the West Seattle Bridge issue, including Perry, enter a small, private dining room off to the side, and Buckley remarked to me, "I wonder what's going on behind that door tonight."

The next time I heard from Perry was in June 1980 when I received a letter from him from the penitentiary in Pensacola, Florida. He wanted to know whether I could assist him in locating some type of job in the Northwest, preferably on a state or local government payroll, which would allow him to qualify for a State retirement pension. In the letter he asked me not to contact anyone about this except former Speaker of the House Bob Schaeffer, the only other person to whom he was writing. He stated that his release date would be July 30. After considerable thought, I wrote back and said that it was my feeling that perhaps it would be better for all concerned, including him, to go elsewhere and start a new life. I stated that while I would be willing to help if I could, I did not feel that I should try to prevail upon the Supply System or one of the PUDs to make a job for him. He later did return here and, I understand, worked for the State Ferry System under the Department of Transportation for a while. He never contacted me again. I would still help him if I could because once a person who makes a mistake pays his debt to society, he should be allowed to continue living his life without further penalty.

In November 1979, the 68th Amendment to the State Constitution was approved by the voters, establishing a regular session of the Legislature in each year. During the odd-numbered years, the regular session would be limited to 105 consecutive days; and in each even-numbered year, the regular session would be limited to not more than 60 consecutive days. Special legislative sessions were allowed but limited to no more than 30 consecutive days when called by the Governor or by a two-thirds vote in each house. However, special sessions would be limited to the purposes cited in the Governor's proclamation or the legislative resolution calling them into session unless, again, a two-thirds vote in each of the houses should approve the broadening of the scope.

To a long-time lobbyist like me, this appeared to be a big step forward for maintaining a lay citizen Legislature. It was becoming very difficult for ordinary people to serve when they had to give up nearly six months of their time in the odd-numbered years and sometimes up to 60 days in the even-numbered years from their jobs or professions to serve, even though action had been taken to increase the salary and per diem of legislative members. However, this change would not eliminate the many special meetings which were to be held by particular legislative committees. Looking back on some of the sessions I had to cover, I was reminded of the old cartoon with the caption: "Born Thirty Years Too Soon."

On the federal legislative scene, things speeded up on the Regional Power Act. Following the December 20 meeting with Senator Jackson, in which proposed amendments agreed on by the Public Power Council had been presented, he introduced the same legislation in the new 96th Congress as S-885, accompanied by our proposed amendments. Public power was once again united on the regional legislation. S-885 was marked up in early July, reported on July 30, and passed by the Senate on August 3, 1979, incorporating all the Public Power Council amendments with the exception of those pertaining to Plants No. 4 and No. 5 of the Supply System.

I was in Washington, D.C., attending to the Senate markup meetings for the amendments in July when I was informed that the members of the House of Representatives from the State of Washington were going to have a retreat at Camp Hoover. Arrangements had been made through Congressman Norm Dicks. Camp Hoover was located south and west of Washington, D.C., in the mountains. It had been constructed for the use of President Herbert Hoover back in the late 1920s. Each State of Washington congressional member was to go there on Friday night accompanied by only one aide. I was informed that Sterling Munro, Bonneville Administrator, accompanied by Earl Gjelde, his assistant, and Larry Hittle, their attorney, would be there for study and discussion of the Regional Power Act. Congressman Don Bonker told me that he did not want the members of Congress to be overrun by the Bonneville viewpoint and asked whether I might be available to attend. I stated that I would have to be in town over the weekend anyway, so I would be glad to participate if asked to do so.

He arranged for me to go, which caused some controversy when a private power lobbyist who was also in Washington found out that I was to go there. It even ended up with a phone call from Congressman McCormack to my wife in Seattle demanding to know whom I was representing. Of course, her proper answer was simply "local public power." The private power lobbyist did not gain admission, but John Gibson from Mayor Royer's staff of Seattle did show up. We had a lively evening and one day discussing the Regional Power Act. I tried to get Plants No. 4 and No. 5 included in the Regional Power Act so that they could be financed under the Act. I lost, because it was the considered opinion of those present that to include those two plants under the Regional Power Act would cause the bill to be defeated. But I did secure agreement that if the plants could not be locked in under the Act they would not be excluded from its provisions for transmission and backup reserves for plants then under construction.

Further study of S-885 as enacted by the Senate showed that while Public Power Council amendments had been adopted with the exception of those to include Plants No. 4 and No. 5, certain questions were raised by other amendments. The Public Power Council had to take a stand that S-885 as enacted was not acceptable and, in a meeting with Senator Jackson on August 31, I outlined this and told him we intended to pursue the legislation in the House and to seek needed amendments. House hearings then commenced in September. During that same month, Bonneville came out with a draft outline on an administrative allocation policy and procedure which posed a new problem for the consumer-owned utilities. We needed time to analyze this outline of administrative allocation policies based on current laws, and compare it with the allocation policy being sought under the new proposed legislation to see whether the new bill would benefit us. We asked that hearings on the bill scheduled for September 19 be postponed, and when this request was denied, we requested that any further action be delayed until our comparison could be finished. This in effect meant no action would be taken on the legislation until the Second Session of the 96th Congress.

From then on, I became busily engrossed in negotiations and redrafting of the legislation in the House of Representatives. This legislation contained new concepts for a Regional Planning Council, and Congressman Dingall insisted that the Act also contain language to provide substantial protection for fisheries and wildlife resources. The method for computing different rates for the direct service industries and the publicly owned utilities to offset the cost of exchange power to the investor-owned utilities was very intricate. There was open and direct opposition to the bill, especially from Oregon Congressman Jim Weaver, and even active public power opposition from segments of local public power such as public utilities in northern California, Douglas County PUD, and the Midwest Electric Consumers Association. However, on September 24, 1980, HR-8157 was passed by the House of Representatives and then, after going to conference with the Senate, came back in a conference report under the number S-885. Between November 12 and 14, 1980, it was passed by the House, with the Senate concurring in the report on November 19, 1980. Thus was passed the Pacific Northwest's Electric Power Planning and Conservation Act, Public Law 96-501.

Two events occurred in October 1980 which would set the stage for the 1981 legislative session, the last one for me as a consultant to the Public Utility Districts. On October 10, Bob Ferguson, new Managing Director of the Supply System, appeared before the State Senate Energy and Utilities Committee. After giving a report on the situation and current status of the Supply System and its construction problems, he proposed statutory changes, including (1) the right to finance plants by the negotiated sale of bonds instead of the currently required competitive bidding procedure; (2) a law to allow the Supply System to establish a security force; and (3) corrections in the competitive public bidding process which would give the Supply System the right to negotiate a cost-plus contract with the contractor under set restrictions to complete construction of a plant at the direction of the Supply System rather than the discretion of the contractor. This, incidentally, was the amendment which should have been sought back in 1977 when we got the change-order law which permitted a contractor, once he got the public bid, to add extra charges by means of change orders.

The second event, which occurred on October 21, I later characterized as "jousting with the Light Brigade." It was on this date that the Light Brigade staged a press conference at the State legislative offices in the Sea-Tac

Office Building to unveil proposed legislation to "place a cap on the unlimited spending of the Washington Public Power Supply System."

Attending the conference were a number of State senators and representatives – all of them acquaintances and good friends of mine. Orchestrating the affair was the Brigade's usual spokesman for such occasions, Dwight Pelz. Dwight is the son of an old-time friend of mine, Dick Pelz, who became my friend when he served as Administrative Assistant to Congressman Don Magnuson in the 1950s. Evidently, the two Pelz children, Dwight and Kathy, came out of that stormy era of anti-Vietnam protest as young adults, moved to Seattle, and became engrossed in anti-nuke/anti-establishment activities. On his dad's advice, Dwight came to my home to meet me. He unabashedly indicated that he was "extreme" in his views about the way the Supply System did things – politically and as a business. I told him that this did not shock me, since I got involved as a young political activist back in the 1930s as a local public power firebrand. I told him that as long as he was sincere in his thoughts and gave other persons the right to their opinions and worked within the system to promote his beliefs, I would not criticize him.

Dwight had organized the Light Brigade and he served as a paid coordinator to stage its events. The Brigade was made up of lower income persons, older persons, and, with due respect, some I would label as being the kind who do not do their own thinking but are easily led or misled. They staged protest meetings and attended hearings to give their views on electric rates and the actions of public officials. They were against nuclear power. On one previous occasion, at a Supply System Board meeting in Richland, I had seen how Dwight would orchestrate the actions of his followers. The group was there to protest a certain action. During and after it presented its position, which the Board always allowed, Dwight, standing in a corner, would signal to the group to mutter, applaud, or boo. It was quite a show, and the news media loved it.

Anyway, here we were at the staged press conference on October 21 at the Sea-Tac Office Building with a good turnout of local news media – print, radio, and television. The senators and representatives were seated around a horseshoe-shaped table at the front of the room. Just before kicking off the news conference, Dwight waltzed up to the front and placed a child on the table in front of one of the senators. I learned that it was his new three-month-old daughter. Around the baby's neck was a sign reading "I can't afford the cost of nukes," or something to that effect. Well, the press took their pictures and the conference commenced. It opened with statements by the chairman of the Light Brigade castigating the "cost overruns of Whoops," followed by caustic remarks from another about the "villain aluminum plants getting all the low-cost power." Then several legislators made brief remarks, but none of these were too pointed.

The scenario, which Dwight had developed, was to have all the speeches made and then to have those present sign a scroll which enumerated the basic points of the proposed legislation. The scroll would then be delivered to the Supply System office next door. I was merely sitting in the audience as an interested spectator, but State Senator King Lysen spoke up and said it was not necessary to carry the scroll over to the other building because "one of the Supply System's representatives is here—Mr. Ken Billington." This of course set off the crowd because I was fair game for the news media.

Frankly, I was not there representing anyone. I was there because I was curious, as a long-time public power lobbyist, to see what was going to be proposed. At any rate, I was asked to come forward. As I rose, I thought to myself, "How do I handle this?" Arriving at the front, I said, "I have no authority to represent the Washington Public Power Supply System. But if you wish to accept me as a free American citizen, voter, taxpayer, and electric ratepayer who has been serving local public power for over 40 years and who supports the continued construction of needed generating plants to keep the lights on in the Pacific Northwest—then I will be happy to oblige." I continued, "I must apologize to my many good senator and representative friends present for not having my six-month-old new granddaughter Kendra with me. I am sure she would join me in accepting her rightful societal obligation and duty to help pay for a needed power supply." "Hiss! Boo!" went the crowd.

I then concluded, "After witnessing this news conference and hearing the misstatements being made, I do believe the Light Brigade should change its name to the No Lights Brigade." Needless to say, there was considerable chatter at that point and the conference broke up. Bryan Johnson of KOMO shoved his mike at me and said, "Ken, say that again." So I did and elaborated on the issues a little. Senator Ray Moore dashed up to me and said, "That's telling 'em, Ken."

I am not so sure. Looking back on the event, I become saddened when I see how the young political activists of today—Dwight Pelz, George Duvall, Mike Beaudoin, each a very bright young person—are using older and less well informed persons to promote their own personal views. I have and have had faults—but never that kind. But, also, looking back on that day, it was fun to "joust with the Light Brigade." You know, thinking back now, I do not believe they ever delivered their scroll.

The years 1979 and 1980 were, indeed, interesting, turbulent, and tiring.

1981 – Retirement

The 47th Session, with its first odd-year session limited to 105 days, convened on January 12, 1981. It would be my last session in service to the public utility districts as their lobbyist. Jim Boldt, coming on as the new Executive Director in mid-1978, had taken hold of the job with a strong hand and I had enjoyed working under this young man's direction as he learned the ropes. Jim had tremendous ego, as well as ability. Earlier, he had forthrightly told me that while he appreciated my support for him, as long as I was present, he felt that he was standing in my shadow. I stated that certainly it was not my intention to stand behind his chair and still try to run the Association as its Executive Director, but after 30-plus years in the Association, I was regarded as an elder statesman in local public power service, so it was natural if unfortunate that not only did a lot of the Commissioners and Managers bypass Jim to seek me out, but the news media and others involved in electric power supply matters did too. I told him that I intended to finish out my contract with the Board of Directors to remain until July 1, 1981, and at that point to stop any consultant work for the Association or others in the power field.

To begin with, this session saw the start of a new ballgame in the legislative arena. The 1980 elections saw the defeat of Governor Ray in the primary by State Senator Jim McDermott, who was then opposed and defeated by King County Executive John Spellman, making Spellman the new Republican Governor. Republicans took control of the Senate by a 25 to 24 majority, resulting in a complete change of committee chairmanships after many, many years of Democratic control. This happened under severe tension, Senator Peter von Reichbauer, elected as a Democrat, having changed his party affiliation to Republican, and in that way giving the Republicans their one-vote control. Over on the House side, the Republicans were in control by a 56 to 42 majority. Undoubtedly, the so-called GABSCAM federal indictments which had been issued against former Democrat House Speaker John Bagnariol, a lobbyist friend of his named Patrick Gallagher and Democrat Senate Majority Leader Gordon Walgren, had been reflected in the November elections.

Conflict and controversy over the Washington Public Power Supply System had reached a fever pitch. New Managing Director Bob Ferguson had not only served notice in November of the need for new added legislation but had also started a "from-the-ground-up" re-evaluation of the estimated cost to complete the five nuclear plants then under construction.

The Light Brigade was to sponsor legislation putting a cap on Supply System financing, and challenges were being raised over the need for Plants No. 4 and No. 5, with legislative requests for a separate, outside study to be funded by electric ratepayers. When Senator Ted Bottiger's move in the 1980 Session to change the Executive Committee composed of representatives of local utilities to a three-person, state-appointed commission was defeated, he had started a State Senate investigation of the Supply System.

Our contact and relationships with legislators during this time were very turbulent. I had used the word "weird" to describe the 1979 and 1980 sessions under dual House Speakers, but after the inquiry report was issued early in the 1981 Session, I would end up labeling that session as "the damndest session I've ever seen." It really was not as bad as that sounds, since Jim and I were quite successful under the circumstances. But it was a fitting climax to my 30 years of lobbying experience.

Our legislative agenda was twofold, affirmative and defensive. We needed legislation, as previously outlined by Managing Director Ferguson, which would include the right of the Supply System to negotiate a construction contract instead of putting it up for public bids in the final construction stages of any given nuclear plant, during its completion and start-up. Using numerous contractors at this stage would make such work more costly and very complex. Next, we had to obtain legislative authority for a security force in order to get final license approval from the Nuclear Regulatory Commission. The anti-nuclear power forces had seized upon this requirement as a means to block licensing and operation of the plant. On top of this, we ran head-on into the strong political position of some local law enforcement officers who did not want a separate or independent security force in their areas. Finally, legislation was needed to allow the negotiated sale of revenue bonds. Bond houses had already started the practice of submitting only one bid whenever the Supply System went to the money market under a public bid law.

The need for a negotiated construction contract put us squarely up against the tremendous political strength of the contractors and their associations. Getting authorization for a security force was not going to be easy, and while negotiated bond sales could be demonstrated to be a proper and cost-saving business practice, the controversy over the Supply System was so intense that emotion overran reason.

The second part of our agenda was naturally to stop any punitive legislation that would strip the local utility members of their authority to appoint the Board or the Executive Committee. Certainly, any legislation proposed by the anti-nuclear people would take that authority away, while leaving us with the responsibility. Finally, we wanted to retain the right of the local utilities to decide whether a plant would be terminated or completed since they had the direct responsibility of providing a power supply.

One of the most turbulent public hearings in which I ever participated took place on February 20, 1981, in the State Senate chamber before a joint meeting of the House and Senate Energy and Utilities Committees. It centered on SB-3510 and its House companion bills, HB-325 and HB-445, which were sponsored by the Light Brigade. If passed, they would have brought construction then under way by the Supply System to a grinding halt. They were being presented as "let the people vote" issues. The Light Brigade had done an excellent job of turning out an anti-Supply System crowd, and the halls and galleries were packed. Members of the Committees were seated on the floor with testimony being given from the podium. Jim and I waded in and, frankly, in order for both of us to get a chance to speak, he spoke on behalf of the Washington PUD Association and I represented the Pierce County Cooperative Power Association, a long-standing group of mutuals and small city systems on the border of Tacoma Light's service area. Earlier, they had asked me to act as their legislative consultant, and with Jim's approval I agreed to do so.

The argument was hot and heavy, and the part of my statement which created the sharpest reaction was my personal criticism of a pamphlet which State Senator King Lysen had previously circulated, which included the direct statement, "Utilities across the State are committed to WPPSS in amounts in excess of $30,000 per family. You might look at the nuclear construction program as a $35,000 mortgage on your house." This was indeed a false statement. Financing was by revenue bonds, not mortgage bonds, and the Supply System did not have the right of levying taxes. By no stretch of the imagination could future electric rates be seen as being a "mortgage on your house." My testimony said, "The kindest comment one can make on that type of misleading and false statement is 'liars can figure and figures can lie.' " Senator Al Williams, Democrat of Seattle, jumped to his feet and said, "I have admired you for years, but this is a sad day to see you come here and not speak to the issue but castigate people who support this bill and castigate a member of this body." That hurt, since I had spent most of my life as a liberal and a pro-public power spokesman, and I had developed a respect for Senator Williams, who had chaired the Energy and Utilities Committee until the week before, when the Republicans took control of the Senate. However, the incident did demonstrate how the situation was. The bills did not pass during that legislative session.

During the session, we pounded out a compromise with the contractors concerning the right of the Supply System to use a negotiated contract in the last stages of construction on a nuclear plant then under construction; a bill to allow negotiated bond sales; and a bill to allow establishment of a security force tied to the local law enforcement agencies. Coming against us was a bill to restructure the Executive Committee and Board of the Supply System, plus a second bill to establish an outside, independent study on the need for Plants No. 4 and No. 5.

The legislative action went as follows. HB-339, the Supply System financing bill, was passed and sent to the Senate, where the independent study bill was attached to it. The House was opposed to a study bill and, thus, to protect the needed financing bill, the House took SB-3797, the previously passed Senate Board-restructuring bill, and attached the financing bill to it. This meant that there were two financing bills, each of which had a section we didn't like: HB-339, the original bill with the study bill attached; and SB-3797, the Board-restructuring bill with the financing bill attached. Over on the Senate side, HB-304, the Supply System security force measure, was amended on the Senate floor and then passed to the House by a 33 to 15 vote. The Senate simultaneously passed HB-339, the original financing bill with the study bill attached to it, and sent it to the House by a 38 to 10 vote.

The House countered by sending SB-3797, the Board-restructuring bill with the finance bill attached, to the Senate by an 89 to 8 vote. However, when HB-304, the Supply System security force bill, came back to the House for a vote on concurrence to the Senate amendments, the House voted not to concur and sent the bill back to the Senate, requesting that the Senate recede from its amendments. When SB-3797 came to the Senate for a vote on concurrence with the House amendments, which included the negotiated financing amendment, supporters of the study bill recognized that an approval vote here would mean that HB-339 would no longer be necessary and, thus, the study would die. The Senate thus voted not to concur with the House amendments and sent the bill back to the House.

On Saturday morning, April 25, one day before the mandatory adjournment time, HB-339, the negotiated financing bill with the study bill amendment came over to the House for a vote on concurrence with the study bill amendment. The House voted 56 to 42 not to concur with the study bill amendment. At this stage, the House now held SB-3797, Senator Gould's Board-restructuring bill, and the Senate held HB-304, the security force bill, and HB-339, the negotiated financing bill. The center of controversy was the independent study ("study bill") issue. The Senate supported the study and the House did not.

The rest of Saturday and most of Sunday passed with no further action on Supply System legislation. The midnight deadline for the end of the regular session approached, and all interested parties were into negotiations. Throughout the Capitol Building, legislators, the Governor's staff, industry representatives, private utility and Association lobbyists (Jim and I) conducted discussions aimed at a compromise to break the deadlock. At 11 p.m., the Senate decided to set one hostage free, HB-304, the security force bill. The Senate voted to recede from its amendment and passed the bill with a 33 to 15 vote. At 11:50 p.m., a final effort was made. The House brought SB-3797, the Board-restructuring bill with the financing bill attached, onto the floor. Within two minutes the House voted to adhere to its vote for passage of the bill with the financing bill attached. The bill was then immediately transmitted to the Senate for concurrence. Unfortunately, the Senate had become entangled in a budget measure that had the members quite confused and, therefore, the Board-restructuring bill was never "read in." At midnight, the gavel fell and the session ended.

For the next three hours, legislators, their staff members and lobbyists milled about in confusion. It became obvious that something had to be done. Party leaders met behind closed doors to discuss their options. However, negotiations broke up without reaching a compromise. At 3 a.m. Monday morning, Representative Bill Polk, Speaker of the House, announced that the Governor was calling a Special Session to convene at 9 a.m. the following day, Tuesday. Throughout the rest of Monday and well into the evening, negotiations took place in an effort to reach some form of compromise on the "study bill" issue. When the Special Session convened on Tuesday, an agreement had been reached.

The "study bill" that eventually passed was substantially different from the one originally proposed. It mandated a $1.5 million study to be conducted by the joint Washington Energy Research Center of the University of Washington and Washington State University. The director of the study would consult with representatives of the Supply System, the Pacific Northwest Utilities Conference Committee, the publicly owned and investor-owned utilities participating in Plants No. 4 and No. 5, and the direct service industries served by Bonneville. The study itself would be conducted under the supervision of a nine-member steering committee with one member from the Supply System, one member from the participating publicly owned utilities, and one member from the participating investor-owned utilities. The other six members would be appointed by the Chairs of the

Senate and House Energy and Utilities Committees. The steering committee would approve the selection of consultants by the study director; review the study plan; meet regularly with the director; suggest actions to preserve the time schedule; provide technical advice when appropriate; review and comment on study drafts; and, finally, evaluate the completed study. In the final evaluation, the steering committee could submit dissenting views and challenge the study's underlying assumptions.

In addition to the steering committee, a legislative subcommittee of eight members would be appointed by the President of the Senate and the Speaker of the House. This subcommittee would also review study progress, advise the director, and serve as a clearinghouse for concerns expressed by the director or the steering committee. The final study would be completed by March 15, 1982, following submission of a preliminary draft to the Legislature by January 31, 1982. All of this was incorporated in SB-3972, and the one-day Special Session was adjourned following passage of the financing bill, the Board-restructuring bill, and the "study bill."

The Board-restructuring bill did require that outside directors be placed on an executive board, now to be composed of eleven people. But selection was to be made by the established Board of Directors of the Supply System. While this meant outside persons would serve on the Board, the local utilities retained the authority to select them.

Some consternation over the proposed study of the need for Plants No. 4 and No. 5 occurred in late May 1981 when Bob Ferguson recommended to his Board of Directors that construction of the plants be slowed down. The review of cost estimates was indicating a substantial increase in final completion costs of Plants No. 1 and No. 3 which meant that these plants would need more cash available to keep their construction on schedule. It was indicated that the revenue bond market might not support needed financing for all four plants.

The worst was yet to come for the Supply System. As I sat in the Senate gallery on Tuesday, April 28, 1981, the first and last day of the First Extraordinary Session, I wrote the following:

This is the last day of the First Extraordinary Session of the 47th Legislature and when the President of the Senate and Speaker of the House rap their gavel for "sine die" adjournment, it, too, will be my "sine die." The regular and special sessions have been very rough and hard, but as usual it has been fun, enjoyable, exhilarating. My 30 years plus in the legislative arena have let me work and associate with some of the world's more intelligent and nice people including this year's 147 legislators, plus "Cowboy" Cherberg. And thus it comes to a halt with the phrase used by the Speaker of the House and the President of the Senate when either side sends a bill to the other side—"Message Received"!!

On June 30, 1981, my work for local public power came to an end except for a small consultant job I performed in late July and early August 1981 as a personal favor to the Commissioners and Manager of Benton County PUD.

In early 1960, the PUD had proposed to the City of Richland that it merge the two utilities and permit the PUD to take over the operation of the City system. At that time, the City system had rejected the proposal outright, which caused some actual embarrassment of the PUD from a public relations standpoint. However, in 1981, the City Council approached the PUD Commission to discuss a possible sellout of the City system to the PUD. On the recommendation of Commissioner Bob Graves of Benton County PUD, the City asked me to make an initial study about the feasibility of the proposal. I explained that it was not my intention to continue to do consulting work, but I accepted that assignment.

The City of Richland's electric system had been deeded, free of charge, to the City by General Electric when Richland took over what had been a General Electric-sponsored city established as part of the defense effort of the 1940s. Since the system had been constructed to meet a temporary need under government control, substantial renovation and improvement of the system had been necessary after the city takeover. It became apparent to me after brief study that, while the City had been forbidden to use electric revenues directly to pay for other City projects under its contract with Bonneville and oversight of the State Auditor's office, it had been following the practice of many municipally operated city light systems and using indirect methods of subsidizing the City. For example, a City Council could establish a low charge for streetlight service by its own utility without any oversight from the State. When I compared the charges for streetlighting in Richland with charges for that service in other cities served by investor-owned utilities and public utility districts, I found substantial subsidizing of the City by its electric system.

I found also that a substantial number of revenue bonds to finance electric system improvements and repairs had been issued at a 6 percent to 7 percent interest rate, but with a bond covenant saying that should the City dispose of any or all of its electric utility properties, all such bonds would have to be recalled. Even if the Benton County PUD were to pay the City an amount of money that covered only the cost of the system, the necessary financing would have a 10 percent to 12 percent rate of interest. It took only a brief period of study to reach my conclusions. At a meeting with the City

Council and the City Manager, I stated that it would not be wise to hire additional consultants or bond attorneys, or go into any substantial financial analysis and study to determine the costs of running the electric department by separating them from the costs of running the other departments, since all City departments used joint bookkeeping, customer services, and computers. I told them I would recommend to the PUD that the two systems not be merged at this time. To do so would penalize the electric ratepayers of both systems. Thus, my consultant work was terminated.

There was to be one more "PUD political activist" involvement for me, a PUD formation election held in Asotin County in November 1984. In this instance it centered on water utility service.

Electric service in the area is still furnished by The Washington Water Power Company. Washington Water Power also owned the water utility serving the City of Clarkston and some of the nearby fruit orchards. Previously, in the 1960s, local people tried to form a PUD to take over both the electric and water utility services. The effort was crushed by Washington Water Power's all-out political action and strength.

Then Washington Water Power sold its water utility to another private corporation. There was talk that this had been done because the water utility was no longer an asset, having been totally depreciated and being in need of repair. The new private company was a subsidiary of a nationwide holding company owning several private water utilities. To some, this takeover smacked of the old holding company hierarchy arrangement.

As a new owner, the new company applied for and received a 25 percent rate increase – undoubtedly based on the purchase price paid to Washington Water Power – and then immediately applied for an additional 69 percent rate hike.

Local people responded by circulating petitions and proposing an election to form a PUD. Washington Water Power opposed the move, even though it no longer owned the water utility. The company realized that a PUD, once formed, would have the needed authority not only to take over the water utility but also to move to take over the electric service should that also become the desire of the local people. Washington Water Power sent in its political troops, having its employees knock on doors to ask people to vote against the PUD formation.

I received a call from Oliver Rosseau, long-time Granger and friend who had been a leader in the earlier PUD formation effort, who said the local Chamber of Commerce had asked the PUD proponents to furnish a speaker for a debate and discussion forum. I was happy to accept his invitation to present the PUD side, and I agreed to stay overnight to attend a rally of the PUD supporters.

My opponent was Tom Savage, Washington Water Power district manager at Davenport and former local Washington Water Power manager in Asotin County. Also appearing was the general manager of the Clarkston General Water Company. It was a lively occasion.

I would have no way of knowing whether my presence helped, but it was a joy to receive a call from Oliver the day after the election and hear that PUD formation had been approved by the voters.

Voter approval of the Asotin County PUD demonstrated that our State still had an effective law which can be used by local people to fight private monopoly abuse. We could still practice progress under democracy.

Summary

The 1975-1981 power supply era was perhaps the most turbulent of my years of service. Much of the controversy centered on the use of nuclear energy for power purposes. Besides the emotional political fights such as the statewide initiative in 1976 to block all nuclear plants and similar efforts in the Legislature, there were many factors beyond the control of the local utility officials which had a tremendous bearing on what happened.

The nation's failure to standardize and stabilize nuclear plant designs and the needed safety regulations on the construction and operation of nuclear plants resulted in catastrophic construction delays and rebuilding when a regulation was changed with severe cost increases.

Soaring inflation increased interest rates and made building a nuclear steam plant, with a large initial plant investment and low fuel costs, more costly in the long run than a coal-fired or oil-fired steam plant having a smaller capital investment but higher fuel costs. This was particularly bad for the Pacific Northwest where the major decision had been made to go nuclear.

For a region where abundant low-cost electricity had been a major tool for economic development, the sudden sharp electric rate increases which were predicted to go even higher in the future would become one factor contributing to a power surplus.

Heavily armed with hindsight, the anti-nuclear forces criticized the decisions to invest in nuclear power which were made when nuclear power looked like the best way to serve the public interests. However, progress was made in this period.

The necessary statutes were passed for the Supply System to finish and place in operation its first, and to this date only, complete nuclear powered generating plant, Washington Nuclear Power - 2, located on the Hanford Reservation near Richland, Washington. Construction was completed under the liberal change order law which was used legally, but whose use went beyond what I consider to have been the original intent of the law. Other laws provided the right to negotiate sale of revenue bonds, which any proper proprietary business operated entity should be entitled to do; the right to hire a needed security force in order to abide by nuclear licensing requirements; and the right to sign a "negotiated" contract for start-up completion of a nuclear generating plant.

"Outside appointees" were mandated to serve on the Executive group of a joint operating agency such as the Washington Public Power Supply System, and an ongoing administrative auditing procedure was established so that line management activity could be reviewed by the governing board of a joint operating agency, who would be provided with published reports of such activity, which would be filed with the Legislature.

Perhaps the greatest progress was passage of the Pacific Northwest's Electric Power Planning and Conservation Act by Congress, which established the joint regional Pacific Northwest power supply program.

While the Act was drafted for the purpose of answering an anticipated power shortage for the 1980s, which turned into a power surplus, a strong part of it established a regional program for the conservation of electric energy to balance with any needed new power generation. The program is administered under recommendations of a State-appointed Pacific Northwest Power Planning Council in partnership and cooperation with a stronger federal power agency, the Bonneville Power Administration. While early years under the Act have been turbulent, it does permit coordinating a regional river system with regionally integrated hydroelectric and steam power served electric distribution systems and a solid cost-effective regional electric conservation program. While the rightful self-interest of separate and individually owned utilities will continue to be present, all utilities in the region are "in bed together" on electric power supply and usage whether or not they recognize it.

A unified approach to this Pacific Northwest power supply program by the State of Washington public utility districts joined by the other consumer-owned municipal and cooperative utilities can provide a continuing strong voice and participation to place not-for-profit electric rates and service ahead of private power monopoly profits.

Will this unified "voice" be present? I believe so, because the past is prologue to the future.

8

WPPSS
Victim or Culprit?

THIS CHRONICLE on public power events would not be complete with-out a special section on the Washington Public Power Supply System. I was directly involved in its organization in 1956 and 1957. I was directly in-volved in the selection of its first Managing Director, the selection of its first projects, and the securing of its Hanford Generating Plant. I was present in most of the Public Power Council meetings when the Supply System was asked to start construction on the five nuclear plants it attempted to build as public power's portion of the proposed Hydro-Thermal Accord. At no time did I have a direct vote on Supply System actions, but I did have con-siderable influence with many of those persons who did. I was concerned in the 1970s when I saw a tendency for the Supply System staff to get too big for its britches and emphasize that the Supply System was a "corporate" entity. I felt used by that staff in 1977 when I helped put on the law books the very liberal change order statute which, in my opinion, they then used to the detriment of regional ratepayers. Thus, I have been closely associated with the Supply System from the beginning to today's myriad of legal argu-ments and court rulings and decisions.

I personally did not understand or agree with the decision of the Wash-ington State Supreme Court that the power sales contracts on Plants No. 4

and No. 5 were invalid. But I am not an attorney, and the Court has the final decision, which was perhaps technically accurate under a literal reading of the law. A municipal corporation such as a PUD or joint power agency has only those powers specifically written by the Legislature, but no one can buy "electricity" without buying the two elements of electricity, namely, capacity and energy. You can't get either without getting both, and you can't get electricity without getting both. The law does specifically provide for the purchase of "electricity" — and to make sure the consumer can get energy, a utility must provide capacity. The only way one can finance capacity is on a "take or pay" contract basis. No one knows if a dam will hold water or a generator will spin until the project is completed. Utilities must pledge the credit and earnings of the utility to raise the needed capital by which to construct any future power supply project, and some of the decisions the utility makes about construction are good and some are bad. But the Supreme Court has spoken — and that is that.

It is beyond my imagination and my understanding of logic to see how the present lawsuit in the federal court can be based on charges of fraud. I know that only a court can determine if such a charge is true or false, but how anyone in an organizational structure like that of the Supply System could have acted fraudulently or even conspired to act fraudulently is beyond me. This would be especially unlikely for the men and women who at all times were striving conscientiously for the lowest possible cost power supply for their neighbors and friends. No self-interest, financial or of self-esteem, could have prompted them to act as they did. Mistakes might have been made but they were honest ones.

Thus, my section on the Washington Public Power Supply System is going to take a different approach from many of today's current writings on the subject. It will pull together some of the events previously written about in this chronicle, and it might give the reader a different insight into what happened following the very successful efforts of the Supply System to construct and operate the Hanford Generating Plant by 1966. What has happened since that time has traceable causes.

It is now 1987, ten years after the utilities signed contracts to proceed with Plants No. 4 and No. 5, ten years after the statewide anti-nuclear plant initiative political fight, and ten years after the first load forecasts indicated a dropoff in electric load growth. What a view one can get by using 20/20 hindsight. Even those of us who stubbornly defended the Supply System and fought for construction of Plants No. 4 and No. 5 up until they were abandoned in January 1982 can see things now which we couldn't see then. Perhaps we were too close to the forest to see the trees.

By 1976, the Supply System was, as D. Victor Anderson in his book *Illusions of Power* labeled it, a "Juggernaut careening with increasing momentum towards disaster." Don Pugnetti, longtime editor of the *Tri-City Herald* and then editor of the *Tacoma News-Tribune*, recently wrote, "One of the managers of the WPPSS compared work on the Hanford No. 2 plant to 'going down the highway at 70 miles an hour in a defective truck while making repairs to the engine.'" One now can readily see the problems and failures from a financial standpoint in the *Bond Buyer* newsletter articles, titled "WPPSS: From Dream to Default," written by Howard Gleckman. Ironically, the articles end with the statement, "Asked what went wrong with WPPSS, one investment banker replied, after being promised anonymity, 'Nothing went wrong. We all made money, didn't we?'"

Victim or culprit? Was the Supply System a victim which looked like a culprit in the minds of many people? There were factors and events which, if evaluated fairly and fully, shed a different light on WPPSS—or "Whoops." Frankly, after reviewing these in later years, I strongly commend the men and women—policy people, management, and plant employees—who stuck with the Supply System and fought all the way to put Plant No. 2 on line in December 1984. Yes, seven years late at a cost seven times the original estimates. But, it's a wonder, under the adversities they faced, they got even one plant on line.

Factor. In 1966, severe legislative and administrative political fights between private power and public power were still raging and would continue until 1969.

At the request of the National Hells Canyon Association, the Northwest Public Power Association, and the Washington PUD Association, the Supply System had directly challenged private power on the middle Snake River dam sites. The fight, starting in 1960, went through the Federal Power Commission procedures to the U.S. Supreme Court. In June 1967, the Supply System won for public power not only on the basic issue of preference but also for construction of the best dam. Yes, when the Federal Power Commission awarded the license to the private power combine, which license the court vacated, it had awarded a license for a dam designed and proposed by the Supply System. I mention this to show that the Supply System was an entity through which consumer-owned utilities could act jointly before it became involved with Hanford or nuclear power.

Factor. In November 1966, responding to Bonneville Administrator David Black who established the Joint Power Planning Council, public and cooperative power utilities formed the Public Power Council to offset a direct move by the private power companies to form a new utility organiza-

WNP2 Nuclear Plant on the Hanford Reservation was put into service by the Washington Public Power Supply System in 1984.

Courtesy WPPSS

tion for coordinating construction of privately or local publicly owned thermal plants in the Pacific Northwest. The proposed organization was to include only the private power companies, the generating public power utilities, and the larger public utility districts of Washington. Public power rejected private power's divide and conquer method, stating that, in negotiating the new hydro-thermal program under the Joint Power Planning Council, it would be united in the Public Power Council and speak with "one voice."

Thus, when Phase I of the Hydro-Thermal Accord was announced in October 1968 and formalized in April 1969, seven plants were proposed: the Centralia coal-fired plant, private power sponsored but with 28 percent public power participation; Portland General Electric's Trojan nuclear plant, with a 70/30 private/public participation; Eugene Water and Electric Board's nuclear plant, with a 70/30 public/private participation; a Supply System nuclear plant at Roosevelt Beach, with 100 percent public power participation; Jim Bridger Unit 1, coal-fired in Wyoming with 100 percent private power participation; and two nuclear plants to be constructed on the rim of Puget Sound – sponsors and participants to be determined later. Walter Hickel, Secretary of the Interior in the Nixon Administration, approved the Accord on October 27, 1969, and action moved forward.

Factor. The decisions about what public power plant would be built, or what the public power portions of any plant would be, or even when and where plants were to be located, were made through the Public Power Council. In 1967, the Supply System approached the Public Power Council to get permission to build a nuclear plant, but because of the political disputes, the decision was that first public power participation in the Hydro-Thermal Accord would be to pick up a 30 percent portion of the Trojan nuclear plant, which the Eugene Water and Electric Board had already unilaterally agreed to do. The Public Power Council then put the Eugene Water and Electric Board 70/30 plant two years ahead of a Supply System plant in the regional schedule.

Further, the Supply System did not make load and resource forecasts. These were made by the utilities. History shows that major responsibility for this was deeded to the private power companies in 1946 under the so-called Tacoma Agreement which resulted in establishing the Pacific Northwest Utilities Conference Committee in 1950 with its Blue Book on regional power needs and resources. While some of the large public power utilities did their own forecasting, most of the utilities which relied on Bonneville for the bulk or all of their power relied very heavily on Bonneville assistance and guidance for load and resource forecasting. Certainly, Bonneville consolidated these public power needs and actually made the public power portion of the regional forecasts. Since Bonneville had ongoing requirement contracts with the public and cooperative utilities, specific contracts with its direct service industry customers, and rolling contracts with the private power companies, it had to make forecasts in order to determine its ability to meet these contracts.

Factor. Why did the Supply System get involved with nuclear power? In the period 1964 to 1976, many responsible engineering studies showed that nuclear plants were more cost effective than coal-fired plants. Most certainly, this was true in the states of Washington and Oregon, which were far removed from the large-quantity-producing coal mines on the other side of the Rocky Mountains. Cost-effectiveness was the reason so many utilities elsewhere in the nation, even those with coal supplies, turned to nuclear plants. The Tennessee Valley Authority is a good example.

Factor. In a private corporation, a board can and does delegate full authority to its management to make major decisions on when, where, why, and how generating plants are to be constructed. Of course, private management keeps its board advised of its work, but management can move with full authority. Conversely, in a public corporation—the Supply System—by law, delegation of authority by a board to its management is limited. The Supply System had some very intelligent, honest, and hard-working members on its Board and Executive Committee, but they were also persons who had responsibilities to their own local utilities or their own businesses. They faced complex engineering and construction decisions which were difficult to comprehend. Decision making and resulting action could become time consuming and arduous for policy people and management. The law required a two-layer decision-making process – a decision by management must have a second or final approval by the Board.

Factor. Under the federal nuclear regulatory process, there was ongoing confusion with no standardization of plant design or construction. Specific safety criteria and standards were set forth and then altered or changed. In the meantime, the utility and its architect-engineer would have proceeded under the old rules. Also, every architect-engineer would try to design a "new Cadillac" instead of copying an already built "Ford." Designs jumped from the plant size of 400 to 600 megawatts, proven efficient in the 1950s and 1960s, to over 1,000 megawatts. Design played leapfrog with science, aiming for increased capacity. Plants were constructed as they were designed because nuclear plant construction was a "developing art." The Supply System had to balance that against a constantly changing regulatory safety and quality assurance program that was being carried out by the Nuclear Regulatory Commission. A plant could be approved only after it was completed, unlike a dam.

Factor. Since the Supply System was a public entity, any material or work exceeding $10,000 had to be obtained through a contract let under the public bidding process. In 1970, when the Plant No. 2 site was moved from Roosevelt Beach to Hanford, Russ Richmond, Bonneville Administrator, emphasized that under the new equal opportunity policy of the federal government, he hoped smaller contracts could be used to encourage the participation of more contractors. I recall assuring him that this would be automatic under the public bid law. Little did I realize that public bids would become an albatross around the neck of the Supply System.

This good public policy bid law, when matched up with a fast track design engineering and construction process, an unstable regulatory climate, and a public corporation two-layer decision and approval process resulted in the Supply System having 440 general contractors to oversee and supervise on the five plants.

This multiplicity of contractors not only resulted in severe union jurisdictional disputes, but the interaction of contractors caused the sites to become a quagmire of conflict. The result was what I have termed "contractor on-the-job blackmail" – bid low, work high, bail me out or suffer a falling domino effect of slowdown or shutdown of the whole project and a delay in the construction schedule. Construction efficiency suffered greatly.

Factor. The open meetings law. This is a law I strongly support. The only political financial contribution made by the PUD Association while I was its Executive was in 1972 to the Coalition for Open Government which sponsored the open meetings initiative. They were in financial trouble and we gave them $500 for their campaign.

It's a good law, but starting in the late 1970s, after the emotional anti-nuke initiative in 1976, it turned the Supply System's Board and Executive Committee meetings into three-ring news media circuses during some very stressful times. It placed those whose job it was to find and correct mistakes, and to make changes and improvements, in a position of defending or excusing the methods they used to try to improve things. This wasn't conducive to orderly but frank, tough, direct discussion and decision-making when it might have been essential. It destroyed customary internal board/management discussion confrontations which were needed.

Please understand, I am not criticizing this public law. But the "right of the public to know" led to chaos in the controversial arena of nuclear energy, and it was, in my opinion, more destructive than constructive at this critical time.

Factor. Inflation. Who could foresee the inflation which hit this country in the 1970s, after every one of the plants had been placed under construction? It was especially severe in the construction industry. Public power financing of any major generating facility always included the capitalization of interest during construction. Interest rates more than doubled during the time the plants were under construction. The rising cost of money was a major factor in escalating the total estimated costs of these plants.

Factor. What happened to the Supply System is not unique. The entire nation's nuclear power plant program, including its regulatory process, has been a debacle. Unlike other nations which have had moderate success in the use of nuclear energy for power purposes, we have failed here in the United States. And that story can be found at Seabrook, Long Island Lighting's Shoreham, the TVA, and, yes, in private power board rooms here in the Pacific Northwest — behind closed doors. Most people forget the mid-1970 to 1982 plans of private power to build nuclear plants. Pacific Power and Light had plans for six plants about 60 miles from Hanford. Portland General Electric's Pebble Spring and Puget Power's Skagit 1 and 2 were abandoned — and the ratepayers will feel the results.

Now with those factors in mind, here are some historical dates and happenings.

May 1970. Six months after the Hydro-Thermal Accord got under way, the voters of Eugene brought the Eugene Water and Electric Board's and the Public Power Council's first choice public power nuclear plant to a screeching halt. In June, the Public Power Council turned to the Supply System to move its plant ahead two years in the schedule and to get the Hanford Generating Plant converted to a power-only facility. The Supply System responded. However, studies showed that conversion of the Hanford Generating Plant was not feasible, so planning for construction of Plant No. 1 went forward, with 100 percent public participation – net billing the power to Bonneville.

August 1970. To gear up administratively, the Supply System reorganized its Board authority. A five-person "strong" Executive Committee of the Board was established with a provision that it could be enlarged to seven should Seattle City Light and Tacoma Light join the Supply System.' The Executive Committee was assigned definite Board powers, including the authority to hire and fire the Managing Director. Executive Committee positions were allocated to individual or groups of member utilities, which reflected near equal number of customers, kilowatt-hour sales, and gross revenues. This balanced the interests of the larger utilities which could go it alone or join other power supply efforts, with the smaller utilities which needed the Supply System as a power supply "umbrella." Seattle City Light joined in March 1971 and Tacoma Light in October 1972.

January 1971. The threat to shut down the Hanford Generating Plant by the Nixon Administration intensified the need for an additional or replacement plant. Almost simultaneously with the start of Plant No. 1 at Hanford, Plant No. 3 with a 70/30 public/private participation was started at Satsop. Both were started at the request of the Public Power Council, Bonneville, and the private power utilities.

August 1972. The new Internal Revenue Code redefined the federal government so that it was no longer an "exempt person" in the rules governing sale of goods and services from a facility financed by tax-exempt municipal revenue bonds. When this happened net billing sale of power to Bonneville with regional underwriting of the plants could no longer be used unless taxable bonds were used to finance the plants. Direct individual utility contracts or "participants' agreements" were used to finance plants started after this date to retain the lower-cost tax-exempt funding.

October 1973. Does history tell us of an Arab oil embargo? Here in the Pacific Northwest we already had a solid energy base in electricity. Utility people and many others said, "Let's go all electric as fast as we can and avoid further dependence on oil." The Supply System and the other utilities, had to move fast because there was a growing waiting list for the nuclear plant reactors being manufactured, and even qualified architect-engineering firms were becoming hard to find.

December 1973. Phase II of the Hydro-Thermal Accord opened with the so-called Seattle Treaty, an agreement on how many and what kind of plants would be needed to meet anticipated load growth from 1982 through 1987. Public power would furnish two plants. It appeared that substantial cost savings could be made and site certification could be more easily obtained by building a "twin," or identical, plant alongside a plant then in the planning or early construction stage. Thus, it was logical to "twin" Plant No. 1 with Plant No. 4 at Hanford, and Plant No. 3 with Plant No. 5 at Satsop. Again, with the blessing of everyone involved.

1975–1976. When Seattle City Light made its Energy 1990 Study, the utility decided not to participate in Plants No. 4 and No. 5. A new concept in load forecasting called econometrics was used for this study. The Pacific Northwest Utilities Conference Committee was at the same time having its load forecasts reviewed using an econometrics method. Both studies predicted lower load growth, but, while load growth estimates were dropping, complications in nuclear plant construction, labor strikes, and contractor disputes were forcing substantial delay in completing the plants. While loads were growing more slowly, resources to meet the loads were also to come on line more slowly.

June 1976. Bonneville Administrator Don Hodel issued a notice of insufficiency to all public and cooperative utilities, stating that Bonneville would not guarantee their power needs after June 1983. Direct service industries were told their Bonneville power contracts would not be renewed. Of those industries, 85 percent were in the service areas of the public and cooperative utilities. Eighty-eight utilities responded to solicitation for Plants No. 4 and No. 5 power contracts with a 133 percent subscription sign-up by July 1976.

November 1976. The anti-nuclear power initiative was defeated by the State of Washington voters, but anti-nuclear public awareness and opposition was heightened.

February 1977. Special legislation was obtained for the Supply System which allowed very liberal change orders in existing contracts. Instead of facing up to the problem of contracting under the public bid law, which we might have worked out in the then existing favorable legislative climate, they sponsored a law which only made the problem worse. I was personally involved in this and feel that the management of the Supply System made a severe misjudgment. The Supply System management did not level with its Board or with me. It passed the House 90 to 0 and the Senate 48 to 0, with one senator not voting, having left the floor to abstain out of friendship and trust for me. I had testified, along with Supply System personnel, that contract changes ranging up to several hundred thousand dollars might be involved. Imagine my chagrin when one of the first work order changes under the new law cost over $700,000, and my outright anger a short period thereafter when a change order restructured a major contract to the tune of $96.7 million.

July 1978. Theodore Berry & Associates, a nationally renowned management consultant firm, was hired by Bonneville to study the Supply System and its relationship with Bonneville. At issue was Bonneville's oversight of the Supply System. The firm's report, issued in early 1979, while complimentary in some ways, contained strong criticism and suggestions for change. The report was not too well accepted by some Supply System people.

1979 Legislative Session. Mandatory management performance audits of the Supply System management were passed by the Legislature. These were to be made by a Board-appointed administrative auditor, but the law required that the audits be relayed to the Legislative Council.

February 1980. The Managing Director of the Supply System was terminated. A State Senate investigation of the Supply System commenced in May. The report was issued to the next legislative session.

1981 Legislative Session. The legislative response to the investigation report was a law mandating that four "outside non-utility directors" be appointed to the Executive Committee and calling for an independent study of the need for Plants No. 4 and No. 5.

May 1981. The new Managing Director of the Supply System, who had been hired the previous June, reported to the Board of Directors that a "from-the-bottom-up" review of the budget indicated that the total cost for all five plants would exceed $24 billion. He recommended a moratorium on Plants No. 4 and No. 5 construction due to financing difficulties.

November 1981. Initiative 394 forbidding sale of future bonds without voter approval was passed overwhelmingly. It was declared unconstitutional by the State Supreme Court in April 1982, but it had a further dampening effect on Supply System financing.

January 1982. Participants failed to agree on how to finance any necessary costs during a construction halt on Plants No. 4 and No. 5, and the Managing Director of the Supply System recommended cancellation of the plants. The Board of Directors voted to terminate the plants. The 1982 Legislative Session mandated a new Executive Board, giving it specific powers over the construction and operation of nuclear plants. It would be composed of eleven persons, five selected by and from the full Board of Directors, three "outside" Directors selected by the full Board of Directors, and three appointed by the Governor and confirmed by the Senate. Various lawsuits were filed with all and various parties attempting to protect what they viewed as their particular interests and rights.

May 1983. Construction on Plants No. 1 and No. 3 was stopped and the plants were placed on hold for future completion to serve regional power supply needs.

June 1983. The Washington State Supreme Court ruled that the participation agreements signed by the Washington public power utilities on Plants No. 4 and No. 5 were invalid and thus the stage was set for the largest default on municipal revenue bonds in the nation's history. It came on August 18, 1983. Many more lawsuits clouded the issues, the largest one being filed by Chemical Bank, as bond trustee, alleging fraud by almost every person or utility or firm involved in Plants No. 4 and No. 5. The case is in the federal courts today.

In spite of all its troubles, the Supply Sytem is still a going concern. Little Packwood Dam is still churning out kilowatt-hours; the Hanford Generating Plant which, on several occasions, has kept the lights on in the Pacific Northwest, has been churning out kilowatt-hours; and even Plant No. 2, with a temporary problem that required it to operate below full capacity, has done a commendable job of churning out kilowatt-hours, having ended its first full year of commercial operation December 20, 1985.

Is the Supply System a victim or a culprit? Only time—the future, and then history—can tell. To me it was a victim of outside events and other factors beyond the recognition, understanding, or control of those who had to make decisions for the Washington Public Power Supply System.

9

Public Power Pioneers and Personalities

WE HAVE low-cost electricity here in the Pacific Northwest primarily because of the local public power program. First, Seattle City Light, Tacoma Light, and other municipal (city owned) utilities, built their hydro plants; then the strong PUD and rural electric cooperative movement joined to promote the construction of the many federal dams and the federal transmission system; and finally the individual PUDs built the publicly financed major mainstream and other dams. These low-cost resources, which will be here for years to come, were secured for us all by dedicated men and women who placed the public interest ahead of private monopoly profit.

Much has been written and spoken about great public power leaders in the Pacific Northwest. There is the saga of J. D. Ross, "Father of Seattle City Light." There is the "Hail Columbia" story of Jim O'Sullivan who fought for the great Grand Coulee Dam. There are references to the stalwart promoter, Republican, and editor/publisher, Rufus Woods of the *Wenatchee Daily World*. Dr. Paul J. Raver, as long-time Administrator of the Bonneville Power Administration and later as Superintendent of Seattle City Light, had a great deal to do with the advancement of public power in the Pacific Northwest. U.S. Senator from Washington (later Judge) Homer T. Bone,

Oregon Senators Charles McNary and Wayne Morse, Washington Senators Warren G. Magnuson and Henry M. Jackson, and many others made impressive contributions to the public power program. Albert Goss, Henry Carstenson, Lars Nelson—all State of Washington Grange Masters— would be named on any roster of important contributors to the movement, and they would be joined by long-time State Grange Master of Oregon, Elmer McClure. From organized labor ranks, E. M. "Ed" Weston and Joe Davis, as Presidents of the Washington State Labor Council, and James Marr, head of the Oregon State Federation of Labor, were strong supporters.

Most of these names are recognized as leaders in promoting the public power program in the Pacific Northwest. But along with them were many others, some of whom I have mentioned in previous chapters but who should receive special attention.

The first is Kirby Billingsley. If you were to ask me who I would rank as number one, the person who in my opinion has done the most to promote low-cost public power in the State of Washington and the Pacific Northwest, he is the person who would come to mind.

➤Kirby Billingsley

Kirby Billingsley, long-time Commissioner and Manager of Chelan County PUD in Wenatchee, Washington, is the person who sold me on the idea of writing this history of the public power movement.

I can't remember just when I met Kirby. It was some time in the 1940s when he was a Commissioner of Chelan County PUD and up to his elbows in the Columbia Basin Commission involved in the reclamation project next to Grand Coulee Dam. He was one of the leaders in the State PUD Association when the Association kicked out of that office certain personnel who had socialistic tendencies. I worked alongside him on that when I was a volunteer layman in public power work, helping form the Public Power League to offset the socialistic Public Ownership League. I served as President of the Power League in 1947, when we brought Frank Stewart from Vancouver to Seattle as Executive Secretary of the State PUD Association.

Little did I realize in those days that I would eventually be working as an Executive of the State PUD Association in which Kirby played a prominent role.

Kirby's history in power and reclamation development goes back to the time in the 1920s when he worked as a reporter and then as Managing Editor at the *Wenatchee World* under publisher Rufus Woods. Kirby was dis-

KIRBY BILLINGSLEY
Courtesy Chelan County PUD #1

patched many times to Washington, D.C., or Olympia, or elsewhere, to keep pushing for such development. He is well-known in government office circles, of course, and I always enjoy remembering that after I went to work as Executive Secretary in 1951, time and again when I entered an office in Washington, D.C., after sending in the name Ken Billington, I would get clear inside the door and the person I had come to see would look up and say, "You are not the person I expected." I would say, "That is correct. You were expecting Kirby Billingsley." It wasn't until about 1956 or 1957 that Kirby came back from a trip to Washington, D.C., and said, "Ken, you have finally arrived. The other day I sent my name into an office and when I was shown in, the man looked up and said, 'You are not the person I expected.'"

Kirby's first official job for Chelan County PUD started in May 1945 when he was appointed as PUD Commissioner. In December 1953, he resigned and was appointed Chelan County PUD Manager.

It would be impossible to enumerate all the things Kirby did in behalf of low-cost public power, but a few come to mind at the moment. It was he who promoted the formation in 1952 of the Electric Consumer Information Committee in Washington, D.C., to provide an organization whereby farm, labor, business, and public power people could coordinate their plans and actions on projects of mutual interest.

In 1953, Kirby was selected to be the PUD representative on the Washington State Power Commission, but he stepped aside so that I could maneuver the appointment of Tom Quast of Snohomish County PUD for that job. The Quast appointment was essential in creating a closer bond among the public utility districts in the State of Washington. It was Kirby who led the fight against the merger of The Washington Water Power Company and Puget Sound Power and Light Company when that was imminent in our State in the early 1950s. It was Kirby who early recognized that unless the local PUDs stepped forward to replace the faltering federal government development of the Columbia River, the dam sites at Priest Rapids, Wanapum, Rocky Reach, and Wells would go by default to the private power companies. At his insistence, Chelan County PUD filed for a preliminary permit on the Rocky Reach site in November 1953.

During the period that public utility districts were being activated in the State of Washington, two distinct viewpoints developed. One group, which in those days centered in the law firm of Houghton, Coughlin, Cluck and Henry, believed that the only way to acquire private company properties for a PUD was by exercise of eminent domain, or condemnation. This law firm had obtained some good condemnation awards under which certain PUDs acquired such properties at low prices. On the other side were the "negotiators" who believed that the best way for a PUD to acquire properties was by negotiated sale through the efforts of a fiscal agent who would make a behind-the-scenes deal with the private power companies for the disposal of certain of their properties.

Kirby believed in negotiated sales, but at the same time, he recognized that in order to maintain a good bargaining position against a well-financed entrenched monopoly, the public needed the right of eminent domain and condemnation. Chelan County PUD, under his leadership as a Commissioner, was well-known for using this kind of maneuvering. For example, to head off a merger between Pacific Power and Light Company and Washington Water Power, Chelan County PUD filed condemnation proceedings against Pacific Power and Light's southwest Washington power dam at Merwin.

Chelan County PUD led a group of three PUDs which were seeking to acquire properties of Washington Water Power from Howard Aller, President of the parent holding company, American Power and Light Company, and Chelan County PUD was very active in negotiations for the Puget Power properties. When it appeared that the City of Seattle was going to condemn the Rock Island Dam project, Chelan County PUD moved ahead with its own condemnation procedure against the Puget Power plant. The PUD also condemned the Washington Water Power Chelan Falls Generating Plant and the nearby distribution properties. While some of these efforts were not totally successful, they did result in strengthening local public power. At times, the best defense is a good offense.

This tendency of Kirby's to always move ahead caused some conflict with his own neighboring public power people, such as the disagreement between Douglas County PUD and Chelan County PUD over the reservoir level between the Rocky Reach Dam and the proposed Wells Dam.

In 1951, when the federal government restricted the issuance of revenue bonds to acquire private power property, it was Kirby who dispatched Frank Stewart clear to Miami, Florida, to meet with President Harry Truman and obtain a reversal of the ruling. It was Kirby who prevailed upon Governor Rosellini to go to Washington, D.C., in 1962 and fight for the Hanford Generating Plant.

Kirby always carries with him a little note pad, and time and again, in the middle of conversations, whether at luncheon tables or in negotiating meetings, you would witness him making little notes on that pad. You knew very well that his mind, as well as being on the current conversation or topic, was also flitting around to touch on moves he must make and calls he must make to keep going ahead. It was a common joke among our people that if you missed Kirby, you should look for the nearest telephone booth. Boxers get cauliflower ears from the ring, but if you want to know a man who has a callous on his ear from the telephone, meet Kirby Billingsley. The telephone was not only an instrument of convenience and speed, it was a weapon in his hands.

Another facet of his character was that while he worked practically 20 hours a day on behalf of public power, he always seemed to have time to turn aside from work to help people. For example, in the late 1960s, Kirby heard that a lady who had worked for the State PUD Association over 25 years before was dying of cancer in a Portland, Oregon, hospital. He took time from a busy schedule to go see her, and he even urged me to write her a word of cheer—which I did.

I have been in his office when a telephone call would come in on a matter completely unrelated to any of his personal, business, or public power efforts, and I would observe him making moves to help people for no apparent reason. When I asked him why he expended his energy on this type of activity when I knew how much he was working on the public power program, his only comment was, "Someone has to do something."

I know that not everyone admires Kirby as much as I do. There are those who have accused him of feathering his own nest during his years of public service. I don't know anything about that, but even if he did, the millions of dollars that have been saved for the people of our State as the result of his efforts, his imagination, his ideas, his manipulation, yes, and even his deviousness, would entitle him to be well-compensated for his work.

I use the word "deviousness" not as a criticism, but rather as a description of the way the man sometimes did things through other people instead of directly. This, incidentally, is probably the reason many people will not recognize his essential role in public power development, thinking that the people he worked through were the people who originated ideas that in reality were Kirby's.

I have had some terrific knock-down-and-drag-outs with Kirby. We have had very great differences of opinion because his outlook was provincial—his purpose was to keep the benefits of public power development of the resources of his area in the north central Washington counties—and my role was to see that all of the public resources of the State were shared in a statewide, or even a region-wide, program for the Pacific Northwest.

Several times we crossed swords. The first time was in 1953, after I had come to work in 1951 as an Executive of the State PUD Association. Kirby was a man who pushed things along, and thought of their financing and administration as secondary. When I came to work for the State PUD Association, I found a bank account of just over $300, a secretary whose salary was due, a $2,250 bill for a dead horse merger fight from an attorney hired at Kirby's insistence, a $500 printing bill from an abortive effort to start a PUD magazine, very few solid members in the Association, and not much anticipated income. I had cut my ties from Vancouver, Washington, and Clark County PUD as personnel director, so the first year, 1951, had been rather trying, including waiting on my own paycheck several times.

In 1953, to block the sale of Puget Power to a group of PUDs, Kinsey Robinson, President of Washington Water Power, maneuvered a proposed merger of the two private companies. Kirby bounced into my office in the Jones Building late one evening with fire in his eyes and plans on his mind. Looking at me he said, "We have got to hire attorneys, we've got to have newspaper publicity, we've got to get going on this thing right now." I rolled back in my chair and said, "Just who in the hell is going to pay for it? We are not going to have any dead horses to bury in the PUD Association as long as I am Executive Secretary." While I would honor an individual PUD Commissioner's right to order me around if he was a strong leader in the movement, I felt it was necessary to stand my ground, even though it might mean the loss of my job. I had to make sure that one Commissioner was not going to control the State PUD Association. Things got a little tense but all of a sudden Kirby smiled and said, "You're right, we've got to put first things first." We had no trouble in the merger fight, although the bulk of the expense did fall on Chelan County PUD, which was ever willing and always ready to move ahead.

A second disagreement between Kirby and me occurred in 1957 over whether the Wells Dam should be turned over for construction and operation to the Washington Public Power Supply System, the joint operating agency of sixteen public utility districts. The conflict boiled up on an evening when Kirby was taking me to the bus station in Wenatchee so that I could return to Seattle. Owen Hurd, Managing Director of the Supply System, was coming to the Wenatchee area to make a speech at Bridgeport at the Chamber of Commerce in which he would propose that the Supply System take over construction and operation of the Wells Dam.

The Douglas County PUD Commissioners had served notice on me that they would insist on a specific allocation of a sizable portion of the output of the dam in perpetuity for the benefit of the people of Douglas County. I had relayed this to Owen Hurd, who did not recognize that Douglas County needed this specific allocation. He, therefore, was moving ahead with his plans to make the speech prior to getting agreement with the Douglas County PUD Board on a specific power commitment to that County.

Meanwhile, Kirby told me that Guy Myers had put together a deal between Douglas County PUD and Puget Power in which Puget Power agreed to furnish all the engineering expenses for the dam in exchange for the right to buy any power from the Wells Dam in excess of Douglas County PUD's needs. He also told me that at the meeting the next day, as soon as Owen had made his proposal, Ross Heminger, who was a respected man of the community, was going to propose that while this joint operating agency construction sounded fine, he thought it would be better for Douglas County PUD to go it alone on its own project.

I got in touch with Owen as soon as I could and tried to alert him to this maneuver, telling him to pledge 200,000 kilowatts of capacity from the Wells Project to Douglas County PUD if the Supply System took over construction and operation, to head the PUD off from the deal with Puget Power. I argued with Owen that this amount would only be a drop in the bucket of the power which the Supply System would have fifty years later when Wells Dam would be paid off, and I told him that I had the verbal agreement of two Douglas County PUD Commissioners that 200,000 kilowatts would be enough to persuade them to deal with the Supply System. Owen again stated that he did not see the necessity of that. He made the speech, heard the words of Ross Heminger which turned the tide toward a local ownership project, and found that the show was on the road for local ownership of Wells Dam – and the deal with Puget Power.

A third time that I disagreed with Kirby was over the retention of Guy Myers as fiscal agent in the construction of the Rocky Reach Dam.

Riding over to Wenatchee one evening on the Empire Builder with Kirby and Jack Richardson, Commissioner of Chelan County PUD, I expressed myself rather vociferously against the need for a fiscal agent on Rocky Reach Dam. My arguments did not convince them, and in fact they did more harm than good since they got back to Guy Myers, and he did not have a very good opinion of me thereafter for the few years remaining prior to his death. I will concede that later on in the contract negotiations, Guy Myers did play an essential role. Yet, I had seen similar financial transactions take place in the Grant County PUD construction of Priest Rapids Dam without the help of a fiscal agent.

Perhaps the easiest way for anyone to verify my view of the value of Kirby Billingsley to public power is to visit Rocky Reach Dam and see one example of the way he used local public power resources to bring non-electric benefits to the people of his area. He built the Rocky Reach facilities at the insistence of his wife, Ella, who was not only a strong supporter of Kirby's public power activities but who was a tireless promoter of the many non-power benefits he left behind when he retired.

Rocky Reach Dam, in my opinion *his* dam, is one of the most interesting dams on the Columbia River system: its Visitors' Center, its "Look a Salmon in the Eye" room, its "Wild Horses to the Sea" artistry, its cultural exhibit displays and picnic areas, and its outstanding Museum of Electricity in the dam itself may not flow through a light socket – but they are there to be enjoyed by all future visitors because a strong public power person saw that the consumer needed more than just electricity from a PUD. I opposed spending money on this display because it increased the cost of power, but one visit proved how wrong I was.

A little-known change in federal laws in 1963 required that in order to get a federal license, a builder of a dam had to provide something more than just a concrete edifice for the local people. Now, all the Chelan County PUD dams at that time were being operated under licenses granted previously. But as relicensing or amended licenses for new additions were secured, Kirby Billingsley insisted that provision be made for new parks, swimming beaches, boat launch ramps, parking areas, view areas, nature trails, and other water-related recreational or environmental improvements. It took a lawsuit against Puget Power – the principal purchaser of Chelan County PUD excess power – to settle the matter, but Ella and Kirby had their way, and although those benefits were built for local people, they are there to be enjoyed by all who visit.

Kirby retired from his PUD Manager position in December 1968, but he ran for and was again elected to his PUD Board in 1970. He remained on that Board until 1976 when he was finally retired for good after a re-election defeat.

∾Clarence C. Dill

C. C. Dill of Spokane, Washington, was a classic example of the old-time senator portrayed by Senator Claghorn on the Fred Allen show, but underneath the stereotype he was a qualified attorney who fought for his client's legal rights, and at all times he was a champion of public power.

When he was a young attorney in the Spokane area, he decided that his life would be spent in the political arena, and he ran for Congress first in 1914. He served two terms as a Representative, but was defeated in his re-election try in 1918. Then in 1922, he ran for and won a seat in that august body, the United States Senate, and he was re-elected in 1928.

It was in the Senate that his role in the Pacific Northwest came to be very important, when his behind-the-scenes activity helped get the construction of Grand Coulee Dam started. On July 14, 1967, in conjunction with the Public Power Powwow held at Grand Coulee Dam, we scheduled a meeting of the Association's Board of Directors. I thought it would be well to invite Senator Dill and have him once again recount the story of how the dam was started. I regret that I did not have a tape recorder to get the details

SENATOR C. C. DILL
Courtesy BPA

428 �֍ *People, Politics & Public Power*

of the fight for the dam in his own words, but here is a paraphrase of the story as he told it.

Senator Dill and Rufus Woods, Billy Clapp, Jim O'Sullivan, and all the high dam pushers had been very busy. It was around 1930 or 1931 when Senator Dill made a trip to Albany, New York, to meet with the Governor of that state, Franklin Delano Roosevelt.

He spoke to the Governor about the proposed dam at Grand Coulee and promised to go out and start capturing delegates to the Democratic Convention for Governor Roosevelt to offset the drive to nominate Al Smith in return for a commitment by Roosevelt that he would get behind the construction of the dam. Between that time and the Convention in 1932, Dill made several trips to Albany, and each time he was able to report to Roosevelt that he had a new batch of delegates for him. The Senator recalled that when he delivered the Maine delegation to the Roosevelt camp, Roosevelt remarked, "As Maine goes, so goes the Nation." Everyone knows, of course, that Roosevelt was nominated and elected; but some may have forgotten that he campaigned in the Pacific Northwest on the public power issue.

After the election, Senator Dill was called down to the White House to meet with Roosevelt about the construction of what Dill always referred to as "my dam." Roosevelt, driving ahead as usual, made a definite pledge that he would build the dam, but he wanted several days in which to study it.

At first Roosevelt proposed that they borrow the money from the Reconstruction Finance Corporation (RFC). Senator Dill countered this by reminding the President that RFC money was available to the states only on a matching fund basis, and, most certainly, he could not anticipate any large appropriations for this type of construction from the State of Washington at a time when the nation was at the bottom of the Depression.

Roosevelt then suggested using some money out of the Public Works Administration (PWA), but Dill had to point out to the President that there was no provision in the PWA law for the development of water power. The President said, "Dill, that's your problem up on the Hill, so you go up and get that bill amended whereby I can get the money for your dam."

Senator Dill went back to the Hill and with Senator Carl Hayden of Arizona worked out a simple amendment. By adding the words "development of water power" to the PWA bill, they slipped the provision through Congress. Dill always enjoyed telling how Hayden merely "penciled the words in" the bill before his Committee. (Hayden verified the penciling-in story when I found myself reminiscing with him and Senator Magnuson about Pacific Northwest projects after a congressional committee hearing I attended in Washington, D.C.)

It should be realized that there was tremendous opposition from the Midwestern congressmen and senators against any reclamation projects in the Pacific Northwest or even in the other Western states. There were farm surpluses. Farmers were burying their pigs, dumping their wheat, and not harvesting their corn because of the Depression. Therefore, any suggestion that the federal government bring more land under farm production met with resounding opposition from the Farm Belt.

However, this amendment went through unnoticed. After the bill was signed, Dill went back to the White House and asked the President to get construction started on "my dam."

By this time Roosevelt was a little squeamish because a lot of money was being spent and he wasn't sure that he could spend the amount needed for Grand Coulee Dam in the Pacific Northwest. It was then that he sent Dill to meet with a number of the bureau heads in Washington, D.C., in an effort to dissuade him, but he did not reckon with the Senator's tenacity.

Finally, the President said, "All right, I will grant $60,000,000 for a low dam." However, about this time, Secretary of the Interior Ickes entered the picture and stated that his engineers had studied the project and that the cost would be exorbitant. Next came a meeting of Dill, the President, and Secretary Ickes. Ickes argued long and hard against spending all that money, but Dill again prevailed. The President turned to Ickes and said, "Mr. Secretary, I want you to issue that order immediately granting this money and getting that project under construction."

At that time, Congress was in a terrible panic, drafting and preparing bills and passing them as fast as it possibly could, and many of these bills did nothing but extend executive authority. Many of the orders for projects being issued at that time carried the signatory, "By Order of the President." As Ickes reached the end of the room, he turned and said, "Well, this order will be 'By Order of the President.'" And the President, with that long yellow cigarette holder of his and his jaw jutting out, said, "Yes, this will be 'By Order of the President.'" It was thus that the dam at Grand Coulee, even though a low dam, got under way.

About that time, however, the project hit a roadblock. Before the dam could be built, some core drilling and investigative engineering were needed, and this work could not be paid for by the federal funds. The President called Dill in and said, "You're going to have to get $375,000 out of the State of Washington for this work." Dill said that would be nigh impossible.

Nevertheless, he leapt on the train and didn't even stop in Spokane, but went directly to Olympia.

In the Governor's chair at that time was Clarence D. Martin, an old-time political friend of Dill's who came from Cheney, a small town south of Spokane. That night at the Governor's mansion, Dill spent several hours arguing with the Governor that he would have to appropriate this money. The Governor said, "I just don't see how it can be done." The next day, however, Dill discovered that the Legislature had just appropriated bonds for some emergency construction funds, whereupon he and the Governor called in Attorney General Hamilton, who called in two of his top legal aides to see what their opinion would be on the legality of applying $375,000 of the State's funds to the federal Grand Coulee project.

One aide's opinion was that it was unconstitutional; the other's opinion was that it was all right. Dill argued with the Attorney General that it had to be done, so they asked the Assistant Attorney General who had approved it to write up the opinion with the help of Senator Dill.

Once again Grand Coulee Dam was on the road.

Copies of telegrams to Rufus Woods from Jim O'Sullivan in 1933 during the fight to get the dam under construction and then a letter to Woods in 1942 from Albert S. Goss, National Grange Master, state that Senator Dill had to be "pushed" to get the dam and that the real driving force in Congress for Grand Coulee was Congressman Samuel D. Hill. I would not question O'Sullivan's or Goss' statements, but history shows that once he was "pushed," Dill had a great deal to do with getting the dam started.

When Senator Dill did not run for re-election in 1934, there were strong rumors that he was involved in certain land development projects which were to come from the Grand Coulee Dam. His administrative assistant was Frank Bell, who in later years was indicted by the Grand Jury in the investigation of the Grant County PUD over the construction of the Priest Rapids Dam by Merritt, Chapman & Scott Construction Co. At any rate, Dill re-opened his law practice in Spokane.

He ran for Governor of the State of Washington in 1940 but was defeated. He then appeared on my scene as an attorney for the Pend Oreille County PUD, a small PUD located in the farthest northeast county in the State of Washington. This PUD was managed until May of 1967 by a controversial local figure named Perc Campbell. Campbell had been very active in Pend Oreille as a County Commissioner, a PUD Commissioner, and a promoter of an electric cooperative which was formed to bring rural electric service to the area when the PUD could not get financing as fast as a co-op could get a loan from the Rural Electrification Administration. He became Manager of the cooperative and then Manager of the Pend Oreille County PUD when it went into business in the late 1940s by taking over the cooperative.

As I watched from the sidelines, it appeared to me that the PUD fell victim to a clash of personalities among the local people, stirred up by outside private power interests, the self-centered management of a large electric cooperative headquartered in Spokane but serving a part of Pend Oreille County, and the overriding power of the large Seattle City Light system. However, the severe attitude of the Pend Oreille County PUD management under Perc Campbell, and its refusal to compromise when good business sense would have dictated a compromise, led the PUD down the path of controversy. This controversy was stirred up a great part of the time by the engineer, Harold Sewell, and Dill, the attorney, who reaped substantial fees from the various court cases the disagreements led to. Senator Dill told me about the controversy over the Boundary Dam built by Seattle City Light versus the Z Canyon Dam the Pend Oreille County PUD proposed.

Pend Oreille County PUD had gone ahead with its own project at Box Canyon in the early 1950s, but they had trouble when a contractor could not meet a time schedule and a second contractor had to take over. The PUD had attempted to finance the dam through the RFC, but when that agency was closed down, they had to issue revenue bonds at a time when the market was not too good.

The PUD then was able to purchase and acquire outright, in simple fee, the holdings of Hugh Cooper when they were sold by his estate. Cooper had been an engineer very active in the development of potential hydroelectric sites in the northeastern part of the State. He had been involved in the studies around Grand Coulee and had carved out for himself the Z Canyon site, a very narrow gorge where the entire Pend Oreille River turns itself on its side, so to speak, to get through. It was a natural dam site.

When Seattle City Light came in and filed for a preliminary permit and later a license to build the Boundary Dam downstream from the Hugh Cooper site at Z Canyon, which would flood Z Canyon out, the fight was joined. First, prolonged Federal Power Commission hearings were held, from which Seattle City Light emerged the victor with a license to build Boundary Dam.

Next came the fight over acquisition of the Pend Oreille County PUD property by Seattle City Light, which needed the land for reservoir flooding to build the Boundary Dam. Next, after Seattle won this fight, came the fight over establishing the value of the property.

The Pend Oreille County PUD, of course, was claiming that its property was a very valuable hydroelectric site worth millions of dollars, but, of course, Seattle City Light's viewpoint was that without a federal license the land was worth only what land would be worth for ordinary reservoir usage.

Seattle kept winning at every point. In the meantime, the legal procedures were quite drawn out with substantial fees for the attorney involved, Senator Dill.

A fourth fight erupted between Pend Oreille County PUD and Seattle City Light because Seattle had entered into a contract with the Pend Oreille County PUD for the Box Canyon power output. The contract had been negotiated by Dr. Paul Raver to keep the dam from sliding into the hands of The Washington Water Power Company. An argument arose over the fact that the PUD was taking power out of the Box Canyon power project at a rate lower than that at which it was selling power to Seattle. Seattle arbitrarily lowered its rates by deducting certain amounts from its monthly payments to the PUD for the power, and again there was litigation.

Now, I would like to state specifically that when I was maneuvering behind the scenes, trying to get the parties together for compromise, I was on the side of the PUD. I felt as strongly as Perc Campbell did that the local people should have the right to their God-given resource of falling water on the Pend Oreille River, just as the people of Seattle had the right to use its God-given natural port of Elliott Bay. Natural resources belong first to local people. I tried repeatedly to get Dr. Raver and Perc Campbell to sit down and negotiate a compromise. In defense of Perc Campbell, I would have to say that Paul Raver, as Superintendent of Seattle City Light, had agreed with the PUD to seek a joint ownership project on this stretch of the river; but he could not sell his proposal to the Seattle City Council and the Corporation Counsel of Seattle, who as an individual was anti-PUD. Even so, there would have been ways and means of compromise.

At one time Seattle would have been willing to award the PUD substantially more output from the Boundary Project than the amount which was finally awarded in the Federal Power Commission license to be pulled back for use in Pend Oreille County at cost.

I kept trying to convince Perc Campbell that as long as he got the milk from the cow he should not worry about who owned the cow. He kept insisting that the Pend Oreille County PUD had to own part of the project. I feel that his insistence on this point was what caused the PUD to lose the battle.

Nevertheless, I think his attitude was hardened by the attorneys and engineers, who always seem to make out very well in these controversial cases.

So it was that as we approached another battle over the dams, namely, the value of the PUD property, I was amazed one day to have Senator Dill walk into my office and casually propose that, since they had been beaten three times in a row after prolonged legal fights, possibly I could go to Dr. Raver and make a back door deal and get the PUD a million to three million dollars for the site, which as he put it, "wouldn't be missed in a big project such as Boundary," and which "would reimburse the District for all of its out-of-pocket expense," which, my mind added, the PUD had been put to by the attorneys and engineers in the long legal fight over the dams.

It took all my willpower to keep from rolling back in my chair and saying: "Yes, you can say that now, after you have sucked them dry for your purposes." I didn't, and I have often wondered afterwards why I didn't.

Possibly it was because I recognized that there are very few things that take place in our American economy which are not prompted by the desire of individuals to make money for themselves. There are people who willingly serve long and hard hours motivated primarily by a belief or a principle. I am quite sure that in some instances, men who have made money in the public power field also share this basic belief. And while I regard Senator Dill as the type of person who used public office and service to public agencies for his personal benefit, I would have to point out that during the many years when it was not too popular to be known as a public power man—when such men had epithets such as "Socialist" flung at them—he had the courage to stand up and be counted on the side of public power.

Of Senator Dill's later life, I have two stories to tell. The first happened at a Bonneville Regional Advisory Committee meeting in February of 1973 in Seattle. We were all at the Olympic Hotel and Senator Dill came in too late to hear the announcement that those desiring to go to a luncheon where Senator Magnuson would speak should purchase their tickets, because seating was limited and there was a substantial crowd. I had purchased my ticket as I came in.

When we recessed at noon, I found Senator Magnuson talking to a number of people. Just as I finished shaking hands and saying hello, Senator Dill appeared and said to Magnuson, "Senator, I am going to go out and get a bite to eat and then I am going to come back and listen to your talk." Maggie said, "What do you mean, Clarence? You aren't going to join us for lunch?" Dill said, "My plane was fog-bound and I got here too late to get a ticket." Maggie turned to me and said, "Ken, you can get him a ticket; he certainly should be at this lunch. In fact, he should be at the head table." I extended my ticket to Senator Dill, but he said, "No, Billington, I am not going to take your ticket." Maggie insisted that I find one for him somewhere, so I scurried around and got hold of Ferris Gilkey, Seattle Area Manager for Bonneville, and told him I was in desperate need of a luncheon ticket. He immediately got me one, probably by taking it away from one of his staff members. But by this time Maggie was determined that Clarence Dill should be at the head table. Well, at fifteen minutes before everyone is to sit down, that's a pretty difficult assignment, especially when the head table has been booked up by prior designation. I took Senator Dill to the Williamsburg Room where lunch was to be held, sized up the situation, and noticed that the seating was at circular tables of eight, one of which was directly to the right and in front of the podium, very much in view of the television cameras. I led the Senator to the table and got him to sit down. I said, "Would you like a drink?" He said, "Yes, I would." So I went to get a scotch and water. On my way to the bar, I saw Maggie and went over to him and said, "Look, I couldn't get Senator Dill at the head table, but I put him directly to your right at the first table facing you, and if you want to make some appropriate remarks, by all means do so."

When Magnuson was introduced and came to the podium, his opening words were these: "A number of years ago, a President of the United States came to this very hotel and made some very complimentary remarks about me, one of them being that sometimes I come into the Senate and make a little speech and before anyone knows it another Grand Coulee Dam is constructed." (Magnuson was referring to the time when President John F. Kennedy came to Seattle during the 1962 senatorial races.) He continued, "I want you to know that the credit for building Grand Coulee Dam does not belong to me. It belongs to a man, Clarence C. Dill, sitting right over here." He pointed toward Senator Dill, and the entire assemblage rose to its feet with loud applause. The old Senator remained seated and sincerely accepted the plaudits. Tears formed in his eyes and I, too, had to blow my nose.

During the lunch Senator Dill said to me, "Billington, I pray each day that tomorrow I will not awaken. My wife is gone; my brother is taken care of; any other living relative is of no avail; I would like to proceed with that public-speaking trust fund that you and I discussed some time ago."

My second story is about the trust fund.

It was either in October or November of 1972 that I had a phone call at home on a Sunday afternoon. I immediately recognized the voice when he said, "Billington?" I responded, "Yes, Senator." He said, "How many PUD Associations do we have now? Aren't there four of them?" I said, "No, at one time there were four area Associations in the State, but we now have consolidated them and only have one called the Southwest PUD Association and one which we call the Eastern Washington PUD Commissioners' Association. And then, of course, there is the State PUD Association." He said, "I thought at one time we had several more." I said, "Yes, that is right, there used to be a Puget Sound PUD Commissioners' Association. And at one time there was a beginning Southeast PUD Commissioners' Association." He said, "Well, I would like to set up a trust fund to provide some prizes for public speaking or oratorical contests, or possibly debates, to be participated in by high school students in PUD counties on the topic of public power."

I asked what he was thinking about. He said that since he was all alone, and had some mortgage bond investments that returned around 8 percent per year, by setting up a fund of around $15,000 or $16,000, he could see an income which could be used for the purpose of these contests. He said he would write a codicil to his will to provide for this trust fund and that he would send it over for my consideration. I told him that I would be very willing to work with him on the project, but I frankly dismissed it in my mind as an older man's Sunday conversation.

Sure enough, in January 1973, while I was at the legislative session, a letter from C. C. Dill came to the Olympia office in which he outlined a proposal to set up a public power speaking contest from a trust fund, and he included the draft of a codicil for his will to establish the fund. I edited the codicil to show the proper name of the State PUD Association and sent it back to him.

During the next few months we corresponded on the subject. One day in early 1974, he called to say that he did not want to wait until his death to start this contest, and that since some of his bonds were maturing in October of 1974 he wanted to take those funds and use them for prizes.

Since he had these bonds in the Metropolitan Mortgage Co. of Spokane, he directed me to get in touch with Loren Howe, the attorney for that mortgage company. He also asked if I would sit down and write a preliminary outline on the program and project. I agreed to do this.

I had previously talked him into broadening the topics so that they would cover other public services as well as power. I had argued that while he had been a leading public power person, his service in the Congress and Senate also encompassed other matters. He agreed to this, and so we proceeded.

By September of 1974 we had finalized the arrangements, and I invited him to come to our Board of Directors' meeting on Friday, September 20, 1974, at the Benton County PUD office in Kennewick. George Kennett, the Manager of Pend Oreille County PUD, which Senator Dill had served

The C. C. Dill Public Speaking Trust Fund was signed at the Benton
County PUD #1 office in Kennewick, Washington, September 20, 1974. *Left
to right:* Ken Billington, Executive Director, Washington PUD Association;
Ted R. Teitzel, Commissioner, Lewis County PUD #1, and Association
President; Senator C. C. Dill; and R. O. "Bob" Archer, Commissioner,
Clark County PUD #1, and Association Secretary-Treasurer.

for many years, arranged for long-time former Commissioners Fred Schwab and Major Fountain to bring the Senator to Kennewick.

Well, he came to the Board meeting and made one of the best speeches I
have ever heard him make. This time I had a tape recorder, although I
would have to say it was a little bit noisy and the tape is not of the best
quality. Nevertheless, it does give one the sense of his speech, which was
dedicated to benefiting the younger persons of our society and dwelt on the
need to promote the ability to speak publicly. He kept saying that when you
get up to speak you are "head and shoulders above the crowd, so why not
be head and shoulders above the crowd in your ability to speak?"

According to the rules the Senator laid down, the speakers would be
judged 50 percent on the basis of their eloquence and delivery and 50 percent on their topic and its content.

Following his speech, we had the signing ceremonies, in which President Ted Teitzel and Secretary-Treasurer Bob Archer signed on behalf of
the PUD Association. We closed this portion of our Board meeting by presenting Senator Dill with a birthday cake on which Grand Coulee Dam
was carved in frosting. You see, on the next day, Saturday, September 21,
1974, the Senator would celebrate his 90th birthday.

The PUD Association received a $16,000 mortgage bond paying 8 per-
cent, with interest earnings of approximately $2,600 every two years.

Junior and senior students in all high schools located in PUD counties operating electric utilities are eligible to participate in the contests. An Eastside contest awards four prizes and a Westside contest awards four. First prize is $100; second prize, $75; third prize, $50; and fourth prize, $25. Teachers and outside persons are the judges.

Following the October or early November public speaking contest on the Eastside and Westside, the first and second place winners of those two contests are brought to Seattle in the early part of December. Here again, we have outside judges. And once again, the speeches are evaluated for eloquence and delivery and topic and content. The winner of the statewide contest receives $800 and the second place winner, $400.

As Senator Dill said, "I want the prizes to be substantial enough to create an interest and also be of help." He closed his speech before my Board by saying that if fortune was good to him and he could depart this life, then the trust fund would be increased, as he had provided in his will for certain additional funds, unless they were needed to maintain his body and soul on earth.

The first C. C. Dill public speaking contests were held in 1976. The Eastside contest was held at Ephrata High School, and the Westside contest was held at a Chehalis high school. Contestants from a number of the high schools from throughout PUD counties participated.

The two top winners from the Eastside were from Ephrata and Kennewick and the two top winners from the Westside came from the same high school at Mountlake Terrace. Vera Claussen, my Assistant Executive Director, organized and conducted the contests with the statewide final in conjunction with our 1976 Annual Conference in December. We taped the proceedings with the four speakers, and as a highlight I played a brief telephone message from Senator Dill which I had recorded.

Following the Conference, I made a special trip to Spokane where I played the entire proceedings for the Senator, letting him hear the four youngsters give their presentations. When I asked him to be a judge and select the one he thought was the top one, without telling him who had won, he picked the winner our judges had picked. The Senator and I had lunch together that day, and as usual I was impressed by his alertness and mental awareness although his physical abilities seemed to be on the decline at 92 years of age.

By letter dated January 10, 1978, from Janet Wallace, Secretary to Senator Dill, I learned of his illness and hospitalization. On Sunday, January 15, before I had a chance to drop the Senator a line, I read of his death. His will increased the trust fund for student orators to $25,000.

Senator Dill could be called a political opportunist, but I realize that he made his opportunities in politics. He established a record in his fight for Grand Coulee Dam which in later years he was to capitalize on to become, for example, our government's representative at a World Power Conference in Melbourne, Australia. He was not really a power expert, but he had a big voice and a gift of gab which permitted him to pass for one. On the other hand, he was an asset to the United States delegation in Australia and elsewhere because he had that friendly politician's smile, warm handshake, and outgoing personality. On these occasions he would expertly play the part of Senator Claghorn.

Most importantly, Senator Dill served an essential role in the development of public power in the Pacific Northwest. The personal wealth which he obtained by such service was indeed minute compared to the millions or even billions of dollars of benefits which came to the Pacific Northwest as the result of his efforts, whether his work was prompted by an altruistic belief or by outright political opportunism. I was disappointed in him for some of his activities during the conflict between Pend Oreille County PUD and Seattle City Light, and, most certainly, I thought it was wrong for him to ask me outright to use my personal friendship with Dr. Raver, Superintendent of Seattle City Light, to recoup some of the cost to the PUD in its long legal opposition and challenges. But for all his faults, here was a man who came to Spokane as a newspaper reporter and teacher; who studied law at night; who developed a brilliant talent for public speaking at a time when you sought congressional office by driving into the middle of a town in a horse-drawn buggy and standing up on the street corner to deliver your views; who used political savvy to get a pledge from a presidential aspirant on great Grand Coulee Dam; who followed through to get that pledge honored; who worked hard for a very small PUD under severe attack by a large investor-owned utility, at meager wages in the early years; and who has now left a trust fund to help future young Washingtonians develop the art of oratory and public speaking.

➤Nat W. Washington

While writing this book, dedicated to the many men and women who served in the ranks of local public power, I find that one person stands out in my mind as deserving of great credit. That is Nat W. Washington who served in the Washington Legislature from 1949 to 1979 from the 13th Legislative District, composed primarily of Grant and Kittitas counties and later a portion of Yakima. Nat was local public power's strongest supporter in the Legislature, and the one who served there the longest. He was elected

SENATOR NAT WASHINGTON
Courtesy BPA

to the House of Representatives in 1948, spent the 31st Session there, and then was elected to the State Senate in 1950, where he served from 1951 through 1978, when he did not run for re-election.

I first met Nat when I helped draft some PUD legislation in 1949. I got to know and appreciate him as a strong fighter for public power in the Legislature from 1951 through 1969, when peace was made between private power and public power there.

After that, Nat traded in the "white hat" he wore for local public power to wear a "white hat" for ecology. The need to protect our environment from pollution demanded legislative attention during the early 1970s, and when the first Committee on Ecology was established in 1973 in the State Senate, guess who was named Chairman. His entire legislative record shows dedication to the public interest.

Nat and his law partner, James Wickwire, were retained by the Grant County PUD as counsel in 1948, following his return from service with the U.S. Army during World War II. Prior to his military service he had worked on the legal staff of the Bonneville Power Administration and thus he knew about and became involved in the private versus public power political fights early on.

In fact, Nat's father, as Grant County's Prosecuting Attorney, had been an early supporter in the fight for Grand Coulee Dam, but had tragically drowned in 1926 in the Columbia River near the place where the great dam is located.

My close legislative relationship with Nat started in 1953 when the local public power utilities sought legislation to permit them to act jointly to build large generating plants. Grant County PUD was moving toward construction of the Priest Rapids Dam project and was seeking the support and involvement of other local public power utilities.

Actually, it had been Nat who had urged the Grant County PUD Commission to move ahead on the project by filing a condemnation suit against the holdings of a private power company at the site to counter possible moves by Seattle City Light or Tacoma Light to acquire those properties if, as was anticipated, deauthorization legislation was forthcoming from Congress, which had locked up the site for a federal dam in 1950.

It was Nat who was a leader in passage by the State Senate in 1953 of the joint operating agency law. He stood with me when we were called down to Governor Langlie's office in 1955 following Nat's win in the State Supreme Court which permitted Grant County PUD to move ahead and prevented Langlie's State Power Commission from taking over the Priest Rapids Dam project. He moved quickly in 1957 to make certain that public power authority that had been legislatively tied to the State Power Commission was retained when that Commission was abolished.

It was Nat who "blew the whistle" on questionable management practices in Grant County PUD in 1958 leading to a Grand Jury investigation to clean up corrupt administration in that District.

Yes, he did do legal work for the Grant County PUD, and, yes, he received payment of legal fees for such work. I know that because I got directly involved in the matter, over his strenuous objections, in 1956, just as the contractual arrangements on the sale of Priest Rapids power were completed and bond resolutions had been prepared for financing the project. Nat was the counsel for the PUD, but a leading national bond counsel law firm had been retained to help with the work. Negotiations with the top lawyers of the power purchasers, including all the large private power companies in the Pacific Northwest, had been tough. Grant County PUD was trying to retain as much of the power as it could for its own use — and yet it needed the contracts to underwrite the project financing. I received a call from John Dawson, lead attorney of the New York bond counsel firm, asking if I was aware of the amount Washington and Wickwire were charging as local attorneys for the PUD. For a moment I thought he meant the fees were exorbitant, but he didn't. He said that Nat's ability and persuasiveness were terrific and had resulted in tremendous benefits for the District, but that he was astounded to learn what Nat was charging for his legal work.

I called Nat, and when he told me what he planned on billing the PUD, I, too, was astounded, having learned of the usual legal fees of bond counsels, private power attorneys, and, yes, public power attorneys by that time. I told him to double the fee, and some hot words between us followed. I couldn't win — with him. But he overlooked the fact that I also knew every one of his PUD Commissioners very well. The fees were still below what I felt they should be when it was finally settled — and looking back on the contracts, they were the best that any of the PUDs negotiated as the years progressed and as other dams were constructed on the Columbia with sale of power to other utilities.

Many benefits and improvements in the PUD law came from Nat's legislative leadership. He was always seeking laws to permit or provide greater efficiency in the operating districts. Probably the greatest tribute I could give him would be to quote the words a top private power lobbyist used to describe him and his legislative actions after public power won a hard legislative fight — but I can't quote them here because they are unprintable.

In 1978, at the annual meeting of the Washington PUD Association, State Senator Nat W. Washington was awarded our Earl Coe Award. The inscription on his award reads: "Legislative service is a basic foundation of our free American democracy. Long service given in the consumer or public interest is even a higher honor to be recognized and to be praised. Such recognition and praise is here given."

Those words were truly appropriate for Nat.

➤R. W. Beck

Probably the most important formative years for R. W. "Bob" Beck, head of R. W. Beck and Associates, engineers, were spent under the guidance of J. D. Ross, "the Father of Seattle City Light." I recall being told that Beck started as a pole locator for Seattle City Light and then was picked up as a chauffeur for J. D. Ross and from there progressed to his top engineering position as a public utility analyst. I don't actually know if Beck had a formal degree in electrical engineering, but he had a native ingenuity developed over years of practical experience with which he could outshine even

R. W. "BOB" BECK
Courtesy R. W. Beck and Associates

the most brilliant electrical utility engineer. Coupled with this was his ability to put two and two together and come up with good policy. When these talents were sprinkled with a basic sincerity and honesty and ability to communicate with people, you had quite a man.

In the mid-1930s, he took a leave of absence from Seattle City Light to go to Nebraska and there, working with Guy Myers who was the fiscal agent for purchasing privately owned utility operations in that state, Beck helped to acquire all the private power lines in that state. His ability to establish fair market values gained him quite a reputation in banking circles, and he was able to outline for bankers the technical aspects which were essential in proving that a utility purchase was financially sound.

When J. D. Ross was appointed the first Bonneville Administrator, he hired Beck to be his chief engineer. However, when Grays Harbor County PUD became the first PUD in the State of Washington to make a negotiated purchase of private power property under Guy Myers' guidance, Beck left Bonneville, did his usual good job of establishing a fair value on the property, and then accepted the job as the first manager of that PUD because the success of public power in the State depended to a great extent on the success of that purchase. Once he had that PUD working well, he returned to engineering full-time and established his own firm. Much of the work of his firm dealt in analyzing the financial and management operation of electric utilities. He worked with Myers and other financial groups to purchase and establish public power utilities, and then broadened the scope of his firm by establishing a second division of design engineering. While the firm could efficiently design a hydroelectric dam, it could also make the necessary financial analysis to determine the value of the project. The firm also broadened its engineering capabilities to do water and sewer utility work.

I recall being present in 1952 when Beck met Myers head-on over increasing the purchase price the PUDs were offering to Puget Power. Myers was a strong public power supporter but was in the movement primarily to make money. Beck was a public power supporter because he believed in the concept of public ownership of electric utilities.

Myers wanted to sweeten the price to Puget Power, and proposed doing so at a meeting in his Olympic Hotel suite with the PUD representatives, which I had been invited to attend. Beck was astonished, rose out of his chair, went across the room where Myers was seated, hit his fist on the card table in front of Myers, and said, "You can't do it!" While the financing might work out, Beck said it wasn't fair to the PUDs. Beck could have lost a substantial amount of work for himself and his firm — and thus a lot of money—if Myers had taken exception to his outburst, but Myers backed down.

The Beck firm developed a reputation as sound, reliable, and qualified engineers-analysts for public power operations. They were regarded this way not only in local utility circles but also in investment banking circles, where a good reputation was essential to raising needed capital. The firm did give quality service, but in a very austere atmosphere. I guess most of us who were "rural" in nature were not impressed by fancy offices and classy surroundings. But one of the attacks then being made on the PUD people by private power was that we were inefficient rubes, or farmers trying to run power systems.

I had been attending the meeting and negotiating sessions of the PUD representatives on the Puget Power purchase where various PUD Commissioners and management representatives would gather each week at the Beck firm's office in an old building across the street from the Olympic Hotel. To seat the group, six old green war surplus desks would be pushed together, around which the assemblage would gather. Myers would come over from his suite in the Olympic Hotel (he also maintained a suite at the Ambassador Hotel in Los Angeles and his actual "home" in a suite in New York's Gotham Hotel), and the meeting would be on.

One day I invited Bob Beck down to lunch at Green's cigar store on 3rd Avenue where I told him how much I appreciated his support for public power and how impressed I was by the quality of his firm's services. But I went on to give him some advice: "Bob, a lot of the people with whom we have to deal relate efficiency to personal and office appearances, and frankly when a bunch of people working on a hundred million dollar deal meet in an old office around war surplus desks, even the news reporters covering the event get a negative impression." A short time later, I got the word that the Beck firm was moving to the Tower Building, and it gave me great pleasure when Bob showed me his new corner office on the fifteenth floor. The firm has never been pretentious compared to some other professional and legal groups I have known, but it made a change in which I had a small part, and its looks started to match its efficiencies.

During the 1950s when many PUDs started to build new or permanent office buildings, I kept encouraging them to go all out to offset the attempts of private power to imply that we were inefficient. Some very beautiful but also very efficient buildings were built in local PUD areas, and the positive image they conveyed made my job as a PUD representative a little easier, and it gave people a feeling of pride in their local PUD. When Klickitat County PUD dedicated its new White Salmon office, Bernard Pollard, editor/publisher of the Mt. Adams *Sun*, a local weekly, prepared a dedication issue in which he coined the phrase "Progress Under Democracy" in an advertisement. Needless to say, I was fast in getting his permission to use the phrase statewide, and it became the Association's slogan for all printed matter thereafter. The private/public war was fought on a lot of fronts using a lot of methods.

When I became closely acquainted with Bob Beck, I met his wife Marge. I had heard that Bob had been married previously, but I never did get the story on the first Mrs. Beck. I understand that Marge arrived on the scene during Bob's work on the Nebraska power purchases. While we males always pride ourselves on being rough and ready and the leaders and the dominant sex, most times when you look behind any successful man, you will usually discern a top-flight female. She is either a natural leader (or at least an originator of ideas), or she is the understanding type who will give him the support he needs when the going gets rough. Marge was a combination of both. I know she gave Bob a great amount of comfort, but she was also just as much a driving force as Bob was, and, in fact, she may have been bit more of a manipulator of people than Bob was. She was blunt and lovable. I was glad that I could count her as a friend and not a foe. One of the tragedies in Bob's life was her death. They were just getting to the stage of life where they could relax and enjoy some of their success. He had a pretty rough time in the period following her death, but then again good things come to good people and another fine lady entered his life. I was rather amazed to receive word that Bob Beck had remarried. His selection was a very pretty but quiet girl whom I had met when she was the cashier at the Vance Hotel coffee shop. I think both his choice and its timing surprised a lot of his friends, but I know that Roberta, his new wife, gave him a lot of comfort and support.

Bob's sound judgment of character was not only reflected in his wives. Perhaps the greatest attribute of this man was his dedication and firmness in developing brilliant young engineers. He sought out and brought to his firm only those of the highest caliber and ability. To name one without naming them all might be a disservice, but certainly Herb Westfall, Bob Gallup, Gordon Jorgensen, Kit Carson, and Bill Trommershausen (or "Trommy" as we called him), were the proof of the pudding of Bob Beck's ability to choose outstanding people. Bob constantly demonstrated a basic belief, support, and untiring effort in behalf of the consumer interest in utility service. Fortunately, in later years, this brought him not only a high level of respect and admiration for his abilities and qualities, but also substantial personal financial success in the consulting and design engineering firm he had established.

Being personally and closely acquainted with and working with Bob Beck until his death in 1968 was one of the highest privileges of my public power life.

➤Guy C. Myers

I first became acquainted with fiscal agent Guy Myers in the 1940s before I went to work for public power. Later, I learned that he originally worked with the Montana Power Company and became involved in the financing of publicly owned utilities which were issuing revenue bonds for an irrigation district in that state. In the early 1930s, he met J. D. Ross, Superintendent of Seattle City Light, when Ross was trying to raise some money through Wall Street in New York, and after helping Ross he became involved in negotiated purchasing of private power properties for newly formed PUDs to help activate them. Myers also helped with activation of the TVA and financing of local public power systems in that region of the country, and helped the Nebraska public power districts buy out the private power companies in that state.

I regarded Myers as an honest man. He admired honesty and told stories about instances of it he found in his work. He always chuckled about the fact that when he would go out to lunch with J. D. Ross during the Great Depression to discuss a business deal in which Myers would be commissioned to raise some much needed cash for Seattle City Light, Ross was so scrupulous about not accepting kickbacks that he would never even let Myers pay for the lunch. Another Myers story concerned the purchase of the Seattle Transit System by the City of Seattle. One day when the deal was about to be closed, the Mayor of the city appeared and suggested that since a political campaign was coming up, the manufacturer of the new buses might possibly want to make a $10,000 donation to it. The manufacturer was more than willing to put up the contribution, but Myers, who was handling the negotiated sale, refused to go along and was fired, losing thousands of dollars in a commission he had done much to earn.

Besides hearing his stories, I witnessed two incidents that demonstrated this man's honesty. The first happened in 1948 in the office of Doug Caples, attorney for the Clark County PUD, after the District bought the properties of Northwestern Electric in that county. The District acquired the property by condemnation, but while the condemnation suit was pending, it still had a contract with Myers to pursue a negotiated purchase. The contract gave Myers his usual 1 percent of the purchase price and stated that this amount would be paid to him "upon acquisition," without specifying the method of acquisition. The award jury set the price at $4,837,500. I was

GUY MYERS
Courtesy BPA

448 ✳ *People, Politics & Public Power*

present in Caples' office the day Myers met with the PUD Commissioners. Caples informed him that the contract was valid and that while the PUD intended to accept the award, Myers as its fiscal agent was entitled to his fee. Myers responded that if the District was going to accept the condemnation award rather than use his services as a negotiator, he would not accept the fee. He reached over on Caples' desk, picked up his contract, and tore it in two. It isn't often that a young person gets to watch a businessman throw $48,375 in the wastebasket.

The second event occurred in 1952 when Myers was busily engaged in negotiating the sale of Puget Power to six public utility districts. His commission, 1 percent of the purchase price, would be in the neighborhood of $1 million. In early October, I received an early morning call from Myers. He said, "Ken, I am in a jam. Tom Ross and Jack Jones," the two PUD Commissioners from Kitsap County, "called me this morning and said they want a political contribution for a Republican by the name of Hump Kean, former mayor of Bremerton, who is running against State Senator Jack Rogers." Rogers was said to be in the private power camp. I said, "Guy, I am quite new in this field, but I assume this is an accepted practice and certainly in view of the sizable commission which you are going to get from the Puget Power sale, this should not bother you." He responded by saying, "Ken, if I ever give one penny to anyone for political purposes or make any type of a payoff, my effectiveness as a negotiator is gone." He said that Jones and Ross had threatened to "pull out of a deal" unless he paid up. At first I thought either Myers or the Commissioners were kidding, but neither of them was. Here was a man about to make a $1 million commission who did not see his way clear to make a $500 political contribution.

I did not know what to do, but then an idea for another place to get that $500 contribution occurred to me. At the time that the joint utility system which was providing a joint insurance program for a number of the PUDs had been established, several Commissioners had suggested that if the PUD Association carried the insurance, this might be a method of raising funds to finance the Association. They were thinking of Electric Bond and Share, which, following disbursement of the common stock of various private utilities, missed enjoying the profits coming from the holding company stock ownership hierarchy, and thus used EBASCO Services, a service organization, to bring in money by providing various services to the formerly held subsidiary companies. Among these services were engineering work and consultant work on insurance coverage for Pacific Power and Light and Washington Water Power.

I had objected to financing the State PUD Association through a service organization, insisting that it stand on its own, separate and apart from any business transaction between the districts and any of its consultants or service groups, but we did serve as coordinator and record-keeper for the joint utility system which provided the insurance, and it was agreed that a district must be a member of the State PUD Association to participate in the joint insurance program. Commissioner Chauncey Price of Skamania County PUD, who was the lead organizer in the joint insurance program, and R. C. "Rod" Rodruck, Sr., head of Pacific Underwriters Corporation which provided the insurance, put the program together, and out of their discussion came a voluntary offer to put up to 50 percent of any commission Rodruck made on the sales of liability insurance into public power promotion. There never was nor would there ever be any established amount of his contributions, and they would always be to causes he believed would support public power. I thus called Rodruck and told him the situation. He didn't ask any questions, and at 7:30 that night he and I went to the Fauntleroy ferry dock. When Commissioner Tom Ross walked off the ferry, Rodruck gave him an envelope containing a $600 contribution for the State senatorial political race.

I tell this story to demonstrate that Myers was above reproach. At that time, the man was wealthy. He maintained a full-time suite at the Olympic Hotel in Seattle, a full-time suite at the Ambassador Hotel in Los Angeles, a full-time suite at the Gotham Hotel in New York City, and a New York office on Wall Street. In the previous four years he had negotiated sales of PUD properties involving approximately $30 million which alone would bring him around $300,000 in commissions. But when pressured for $500 with the threat of losing a $1 million commission if he refused, he stood on principle.

In 1953, my wife and I were invited to his suite at the Olympic Hotel where he told me that while he always operated more or less as a lone wolf, he wondered whether I might be interested in becoming his associate as a fiscal agent, which he felt offered me considerable opportunity. I thanked him for his offer but declined stating that while such a job would certainly mean more money for us, we felt there was more to living than making money and that our decision would be for me to remain in my public power position with the PUD Association. I enjoyed very much being in the company of this man because he was quite learned and I always felt that while he had to be a maneuverer in his work, he was never dishonest.

He had one idiosyncrasy, namely, that when he went from Seattle to New York, which he did practically every other week, he always went by way of Los Angeles. This always puzzled me, and it was many years later, after his death, that Bob Beck told me Guy Myers had another business.

He was a bookstore owner. I did recall that he always seemed to have a lot of new books at his hotel suite here in Seattle each time he returned from New York.

In the early 1950s, when Myers was working on the Puget Power purchase, a number of bitter editorials against the purchase and also in support of the proposed merger of Washington Water Power and Puget Power appeared in the *Seattle P-I*. I wondered about this until Myers told me that earlier in New York he had sought the services of a professional writer to do a history of local public power here in the Pacific Northwest. He was on the verge of hiring the writer when he found out that the man enjoyed alcohol a little too much. Myers, who was a teetotaler, dropped the man, who later turned up as chief editorial writer here in Seattle for the *P-I*. Some of the editorials, then and later, were very bitter against public power and "mystery man" Myers, who used to chuckle over the writer's evident attempts to get even.

In 1956, I lost my friendship with Myers. I was riding over to Wenatchee on the train one evening with Manager Kirby Billingsley and Commissioner Jack Richardson of Chelan County PUD when they told me they had just arranged for Myers to be fiscal agent on the financing of Rocky Reach Dam. I knew that he had been involved in the extension of the Rock Island Dam and then the ultimate purchase of that project by Chelan County PUD, and that he undoubtedly had something to do with the arrangement of Puget Power to advance the initial financing on the Rocky Reach Dam construction. However, I didn't think a fiscal agent was needed in the construction of a new dam such as Rocky Reach. I took the position that a fiscal agent was very desirable in negotiating the purchase of private power properties but was not needed for construction of a project financed on its own proven feasibility. Word of my opposition got back to Myers and from that point on he never contacted me or invited me to his hotel suite. Later, of course, I became aware that he undoubtedly had a part in urging Douglas County PUD to go forward with the Wells Dam partnership with Puget Power, and he became fiscal agent on that project also. Had I been successful in my efforts to have the Supply System take the project over from Douglas County PUD, there would have been no need for a fiscal agent because under the joint operating agency law, issuance of revenue bonds was by competitive bid rather than by negotiated purchase. Myers was one of those opposed to my efforts to get John Dawson's amendments to the PUD revenue bond section through the 1957 Legislature, and when I heard this, in truth, it became an added stimulant to me to put the law through in the 1959 Session. His death in 1960 meant that he never had the opportunity to make use of the new and better law on revenue bond financing. I was sorry to hear of his death because he was a potent force in getting public utility districts in the State of Washington activated and getting needed public power dams financed, and he was always honest in his dealings with me.

～Jack Cluck

Jack Cluck was probably the highest qualified and most knowledgeable attorney practicing municipal or PUD power law in the Pacific Northwest. He was certainly one of the most interesting public power personalities who lived and served here until his death in January 1983.

He was a Democrat by political persuasion and would be classed as very liberal. He had been on the side of the consumer in utility service since graduating from the University of Washington law school in the early 1930s. He began practicing law for the Washington State Grange when the Grange was pushing to form public utility districts and get them activiated in our State. He was one of those present in December 1936 on the day the Washington PUD Commissioners' Association was organized at Grange headquarters. He did well financially as a partner in one of the leading law firms handling PUD condemnation cases to acquire private power properties. About one-half of the PUDs in business today got there via the condemnation route, and his law firm—Houghton, Cluck, Coughlin and, originally Henry, then Riley—handled every PUD condemnation case, as far as I know. I was present when agreement was reached on the purchase of the Snohomish County PUD properties from Puget Power. Guy Myers, the fiscal agent who headed up the efforts to acquire PUD properties by means of negotiated sale, could not get Snohomish County PUD Commissioner John Erlandson's approval of the purchase until legal fees for Jack Cluck, who was pursuing a condemnation case for the Snohomish County PUD, were paid in full. They were paid, but some people called it "legal blackmail." In my opinion, those legal fees were insignificant compared to the total savings brought to the Snohomish County PUD ratepayers as the result of Jack's legal skills and tenacity, and the fees were related to this sale because Puget Power would not have negotiated the sale without the pressure of an active condemnation case. Myers knew it, Erlandson knew it, and I knew it the evening that payment was agreed upon.

Jack's other love in life besides public power was the Group Health Cooperative of Puget Sound, which he helped to organize. He carried one of the top legal medical cases through the State Supreme Court when local medical bureaus refused to recognize the professional status and rights of practicing physicians working for the Cooperative.

Jack was definitely of a "cooperative" mind. He helped form a cooperative to purchase certain properties on Hood Canal where he and his associates carved out a good summer and weekend recreational and living area.

Jack was a physical fitness person, but not to the extent of being a faddist. However, as regular as the sunrise, he would insist on enjoying a fast-paced walk of some duration. He had a long stride and should you be foolish enough to accompany him, a pair of short legs (which is my heritage) would not suffice too well. He was an ardent swimmer who lived on the east shore of Lake Washington facing Mercer Island. One day, while I was enjoying my son's very fast fun boat, I came upon this swimmer clear in the middle of the lake a good two miles from a dock. I slowed down and came to a stop so as not to endanger the swimmer, and who should greet me from the water but Jack Cluck? I offered him a ride as if he were a hitchhiker because it seemed to me a long distance back for him. He declined and I took off—slowly, at first.

Jack and his law firm always held a Christmas open house, a merry mixture of bourbon highballs and Christmas carols. He and another of his partners had good voices, and while I was not as good as they were, I could carry a tune. We would always look forward to a rousing good songfest at those parties.

I depended on Jack Cluck's legal ability to work out the various changes and improvements in the PUD law during my time at the Legislature. Time and again, I would come up with some idea which sounded good, and by the time I got the return call from Jack, he had looked up all the legal ramifications. By that word "all," I mean *all*. Sometimes what I was proposing was not too workable, but after twenty years of being coached by him on legal matters, I felt highly complimented one day to hear him say, "Ken, you are a good lawyer." We had been discussing and actually arguing over certain wording in a proposed law. I, of course, had no law degree, but in drafting, studying, amending, and working on laws being considered and passed by the Legislature, I did gain legal knowledge under his tutoring. From that day, I always referred to him as my "law professor," not my lawyer.

By 1970, Jack had tried to retire, or at least slow down, but just then the Washington Public Power Supply System became very active in the hydrothermal program. Since Jack had been the leading legal advisor for the Supply System in its beginning years, and some very complex contracts and legal issues were at stake, his services were once again required full-time. I attended many conferences of attorneys and policy level people, and I can hear at this moment the booming voice of Jack saying, "Now, now, just a

JACK CLUCK

moment, just a moment, let's look at that again, let me check it out, just a moment." He always had to analyze each word, phrase, and mark of punctuation. Sometimes his meticulousness and thoroughness would frustrate me a little, especially when I was trying to meet a legislative deadline or strategy requirement. I know that I put pressure on him unmercifully, and his favorite trick to get back at me would always be to say, "Ken, how've you been, how've you been? Don't you think it's time for you to take it a little easier and slow down a bit?" This was just his kind way of saying, "Get out of my hair and give me time to get you a correct answer."

Jack was married to a lovely lady named Sylvia during all the years I knew him. I heard that they met while they both were instructors for aircraft pilots during World War II. Sylvia was always a delight, as a hostess at their home whenever I was an occasional guest, and at the annual Christmas open house and songfest where she wore a cute little Scandinavian outfit. They had no children, but adopted "all God's children" into their lives, and especially those persons who were not quite as fortunate as some of the rest of us.

Being liberal, social-minded Democrats, Jack and Sylvia were always found in the front ranks of those who were opposed to the war in Vietnam; were for women's rights; were seeking better medical services at reasonable rates; or were just seeking a better way of life for whoever needed help. They have contributed, and they fit my definition of "beautiful people."

It was a privilege to be a friend and working compatriot of Jack Cluck in local public power efforts.

➤Five Old-time PUD Commissioners

No chapter on the people I encountered in the public utility district movement in the State of Washington would be complete without vignettes of Gus Jaspers, Gus Peters, Preston Royer, Billy McKenzie, and Chauncey Price, old-time Commissioners who served in the 1930s, 1940s, and early 1950s.

These old-time PUD Commissioners were dedicated to serving the public interest by serving public power. Our affluent urban society might look upon them as being rather corny or rural. Most of them were without formal education. However, I found them to be well-read, fast thinking, sometimes slow to move, but always very determined. They were honest men. The ones I have named are representative of a lot more, and it is my hope that covering these few will not be a disservice to those not named, but will demonstrate the type of public servants the people in the PUD counties had working and fighting for low-cost public power.

Gus Jaspers

Gus Jaspers of Wahkiakum County PUD was a very small man physically and he walked with a zip-zip-zip type of prance. He would remind you, and certainly no disrespect is intended, of a banty rooster – and well he might, because he had great courage. He came from a relatively small District, but he was a leader among the Commissioners. I remember him best for his actions during the 1951 Legislature, the year of the Spokane Power Bill fight. Gus was on the scene and I treasure his report of crossing swords with Clif Erdahl, Commissioner of Utilities of Tacoma. Erdahl had sided with the private power companies on the Spokane Power Bill, and Gus really told him off, calling him a "private power stooge."

Gus was a great man to hold meetings, and truly this was essential at this time in PUD history because so many things were happening so fast and so much opposition was being thrown at the individual districts that, if the Commissioners had not got together and supported each other, they could have become disheartened. Gus was a strong leader in the Southwest Washington PUD Commissioners' Association, as it was known in those days. Nothing would delight him more than to hold a meeting all day Friday, appoint a special committee for work Friday night, spend until one or two o'clock that night drafting resolutions or statements or plans for action, and then to have everybody meet again on Saturday morning to act on the resolutions and statements and plans.

In the many years that I attended these meetings, first as a layman, then as an employee of a PUD, and finally as Executive Secretary of the PUD Association, I never witnessed a glass or a bottle of liquor in the committee meeting room. Unlike so many so-called committee meetings, these were serious deliberations on everything from the federal power program to the latest PUD acquisition or labor contract negotiation or any other essential matter concerning public power.

Gus Jaspers passed away in the early 1950s, but he had left his mark as a little man with a big mind and strong determination – and the courage of a lion.

Gus Peters

Gus Peters of the Lewis County PUD was a huge man. His hand was the size of three of mine, and when you shook it you knew your hand was being shaken. Yet he had a gentle nature toward life and the other fellow. He served until 1964, but in his later years he suffered a stroke which impaired him somewhat and slowed him down. The period I like to recall him in is the 1940s. This was the time when there was a showdown on socialism in the State PUD Association, and big Gus, who served as President for two years, was right in the middle of it. In those days, it took courage to stand up for public power because it had not gained the respectability which it enjoys today. Gus had no fear and he was honest. He was a religious man and I can recall visiting his home where Mrs. Peters would read to him out of the Bible as their entertainment.

Prior to Gus' death, I visited him at the hospital in Chehalis to deliver to him a plaque acknowledging his Presidency of the State Association. That was indeed a privilege, but a greater one was that he asked me to read to him out of the Bible.

Preston Royer

Preston Royer came from the Benton County PUD. He was truly an interesting person. I didn't get too close to him at first, probably because I was wearing bow ties about the time I met him. He worked in a cooperative dairy creamery and didn't like city slickers. He was not a formally educated man and yet he was well-read. I was amazed when I visited his home to see his collection of fine books. He also had a fabulous collection of Indian relics, being a great student of Indian lore.

Preston never drank anything but milk, and it must indeed have given him energy, because many times he would get up in the middle of a meeting and take off with a rafter-shaking tirade in furtherance of a particular viewpoint.

Another thing about him which interested me when as Executive Secretary I would sit at the front of the meeting with the President, facing the audience, was that I would glance over and note that Preston was asleep. At least I thought he was asleep. But now it dawns on me that this man had the ability to relax and listen at the same time. Many a time I have seen him come wide awake and come right to the point of the discussion even though in the previous minutes I had expected to hear a snore from him. He was very opinionated and if he didn't like someone it would be hard to change him. Probably the most interesting time I ever had with him was when we were returning from a Southwest Washington PUD meeting in Shelton by way of Bremerton. We just missed one ferry and had to wait an hour for the next one. We walked uptown and he disappeared into a small novelty store. When we were again seated in the car waiting for the ferry, out of his pocket came a harmonica. Being a kind of left-handed musician myself during the 1930s, I enjoyed music, and Preston really had a gift for playing that harmonica. Most of the tunes were old-timers, but they were done with perfection. This was a side of this man which I would never have suspected. Getting to his funeral involved some personal difficulty, but I would have made it at any cost. He was basic, honest, forthright, and determined.

Billy McKenzie

One of the finest persons I ever enjoyed meeting was a Scotsman from the Chelan County PUD area named Billy McKenzie. He had a great sense of humor and a Scottish brogue to go with it.

Left to right: Commissioner Chauncey Price, Skamania County PUD #1; Clyde D. Linville, Skamania County Prosecutor and attorney for the PUD; and Skamania PUD Commissioner Harry A. Card on the steps of the Skamania County Courthouse in January 1940 just after the successful condemnation action that permitted the PUD to acquire the properties of the West Coast Power Company in Skamania County.

Riding down the Columbia River Highway south from a meeting at Okanogan County PUD, Billy recounted to me his first experience in bringing service to a rural customer as a PUD Commissioner.

Before purchasing the Puget Power properties, the District had embarked upon a program to expand electric service to some of the more rural areas. He told about arriving at this farmhouse north of Lake Chelan just as the linemen cut the new service in. As he said in his Scottish brogue, "Kennie, the grreatest moment in my life came as this farm wife turned on an electric light bulb. She actually had tears in her eyes. She had spent many years at that location without the benefit of electric service. Her thanks to me made every bit of the worries, the arguments, and the troubles we had in securing our electric utility worthwhile." In that statement, Billy McKenzie was reflecting what most of the old-timers had: a feeling in their hearts for the consumer. Their only interest was in bringing the benefits of public power to their neighbors.

Chauncey Price

Chauncey Price of Carson, Washington, Commissioner of the Skamania County PUD, was a friend of my father. He was the Scattergood Baines of that county. He had a sawmill; he ran a grocery store; he had an insurance business; he graduated from the University of Washington with a degree in law many years ago; he had served in the Legislature; he was always buying and selling real estate; and he in truth was a fine example of the free enterprising capitalistic American. Yet, here he was, one of the most ardent champions of public power which was being labeled "socialistic" by its opponents. He was quite liberal in his political views, but he never let this enter into his PUD services. Chauncey served on the Committee of Commissioners which selected the new Executive Secretary at the time that I was hired. He actually favored another man who was older and had somewhat more experience, and I believe the reason was that I had been raised with Chauncey's sons and he just could not see a young man filling the job. Nevertheless, after I was hired, he was a bulwark of strength in making my job an easier one.

I treasure my file of the letters he used to write, most of the time on stationery that he had pilfered from hotels, which always contained the soundest of advice and recommendations.

Since Chauncey was an insurance man, he recognized the benefits which could come to the PUDs through a joint insurance program. It was he, therefore, who led the way for the formation of the Washington Public Utilities Power and Water Distribution System which was later changed to the Washington Public Utility Districts' Utilities System, a joint entity established under the 1949 joint action law, which Chauncey set up with another old-time public power supporter, Robert C. Rodruck, Sr., of Pacific Underwriters Corporation. Chauncey spent many days of his life traveling to and from member districts promoting this joint insurance program. Finally, in 1952, three districts agreed to join and this placed the program in effect. The program grew to include many of the PUDs. It would be impossible to compute the thousands of dollars saved on premiums by this joint insurance program enjoyed by these districts as provided and promoted by Chauncey.

But Chauncey, because he was a strong personality, had a great many political opponents in his local county. When an industrial promoter approached the Commission with a proposal to condemn the properties of Pacific Power and Light located in the northern part of the county, he stood firm against the arrangement because he realized the promoter was thinking only of his large consultant commission. This opposition was used to imply that he was against industrial development, and criticism of him for this resulted in a recall election in 1958, a terrible event in the small county. In the end Chauncey was retained in office with a nine-vote margin. There is no question in my mind that the strain of the event and the unhappiness which it brought to him, when good friends turned on him, contributed to the heart attack which later took his life.

Chauncey Price was short in stature, but he stood very tall in public power ranks in initiative, determination, and service.

The local public power program these men served — coming from the grassroots to stop abuses of the consumer by the private power monopolies — led to the greatest low-cost public power hydroelectric development systems in the nation. While these individual utility systems provide the main elements to prevent monopoly abuse — i.e., local control and not-for-profit electric service — they operate as region-wide totally integrated electric systems. Public power has been used as an economic tool to promote farming and industry and business in the Pacific Northwest. Most importantly, the "electric servant" has made personal living easier for all of our families.

People, using politics, made public power available and made it work.

Index

Dubro, Morgan: 115
Durgan, Ken: 32, 34
Durkan, Martin: 175-76, 243, 273, 337, 351, 363
Durning, Marvin: 360, 363
Durocher, Hector: 269
Duvall, George: 397
Dyar, Ken: 324, 326, 379

Earl Coe Award: 204, 208-9, 263-64, 349, 442
Eastvold, Don: 84
Edison Electric Institute: 183-84
Eisenhower, Dwight D., 73-75, 104, 128, 163, 228; opposition to federal power, 109, 124-25, 136
Eisenhower Administration: 73-74, 90-91, 100, 102, 109, 115, 163
Eldridge, Don: 240, 307
Electric Bond and Share: 4-5, 449
Electric Light Association: 45
Electric Power Consumers Information Committee: 68, 422
electric service, rural access to, 4-5, 11, 13, 16-17, 20, 28, 68; see also rural electric cooperatives
Ellis, John, 242, 244, 283, 287-88, 290
Elmgren, Bill: 294
Elmhurst Mutual: 379
Elmore, Howard: 127, 323-24, 340
emergency clause: 86, 92, 345
eminent domain: See condemnation of utility property
environmental protection: 295-98, 305, 332, 365, 368, 377, 395, 441
Erdahl, C. A. "Clif": 43, 50, 64, 71, 73, 75, 78-79, 84, 86-87, 92ff, 127, 141, 160, 238-39, 259, 283, 304, 309, 329, 456
Erlandson, John: 452
Eugene Water and Electric Board: 97, 230, 238, 302, 313, 348, 379, 411-12, 415
Evans, Daniel J.: 179, 181, 195, 207, 209ff, 220-21, 240ff, 249, 252-54, 278-80, 292, 295-98, 311-13, 315ff, 326, 337ff, 351, 356, 358-60, 366, 368, 391
Evans, Ed: 207, 238

Faler, George: 188
Farrington, Clayton: 178
Federal Power Commission: 5, 22, 27, 63, 69, 71, 74, 89-91, 102, 104-6, 108, 114, 116-17, 123-26, 128, 138, 140, 142, 156, 161-62, 164, 168, 173, 183, 191, 205, 226-27, 260, 263, 269-70, 366, 410, 432-33
Ferguson, Robert L.: 391, 395, 398-99, 403
Ferry County PUD: 41, 164
Finley, States Rights: 109-10
Fischer, Ed: 283-85, 290-92, 356, 369, 382, 391
Flanagan, Ed: 81-82, 114
Foleen, Ray: 315
Foley, Tom: 221
Folsom, Morrill F.: 180-81
Ford, Dick: 331
Fountain, Major: 437
Francis, Vic: 189
Franklin County PUD: 41, 304
Frayn, Mort: 53, 81, 87, 335
Freeman, David: 372
French, Bob: 77
Frisbee, Don: 27, 272, 281-84, 353
Fussel, Ed: 95

Gallagher, Patrick: 398
Gallup, Bob: 314, 318ff, 327, 446
Ganders, Stanton: 81
Garretson, Harry: 321
Garrett, Avery: 176, 180-81, 223
Garton, Art: 76
General Electric Company: 6, 160-61, 404
Gibson, John: 394
Gilkey, Ferris: 256, 269, 435
Gillette, Bob: 237-38, 271
Gilman, W. C.: 95
Gissberg, Bill: 241, 250-51, 255
Gjelde, Earl: 394
Gleckman, Howard: 410
Goldhammer, Bernie: 206, 267, 310, 314-17, 327
Goldmark, John: 178
Goldsbury, John: 382
Gordon, Walter: 92-93, 105
Gorton, Slade: 154-55, 179-80, 305
Goss, Albert: 10, 13, 17, 420, 431
Gould, Susan: 390, 401
Graham, Bob: 101
Graham, Robert V.: 387
Grand Coulee Dam, 5, 11-13, 18, 39, 92, 148, 161, 419-20, 427, 429ff; Third Powerhouse legislation, 217ff
Grant, Cary: 194
Grant County PUD, 41, 69-70, 85, 102-5, 107, 109ff, 121, 124, 127, 140, 142ff, 156, 161, 168-69, 202,